Virginia Woolf

A *Modern Fiction Studies* Book

Virginia Woolf

AN *MFS* READER

Edited by Maren Linett

The Johns Hopkins University Press

Baltimore

© 2009 The Johns Hopkins University Press
All rights reserved. Published 2009
Printed in the United States of America on acid-free paper
9 8 7 6 5 4 3 2 1

The Johns Hopkins University Press
2715 North Charles Street
Baltimore, Maryland 21218-4363
www.press.jhu.edu

ISBN 10: 0-8018-9117-5 (hardcover)
ISBN 10: 0-8018-9118-3 (paperback)
ISBN 13: 978-0-8018-9117-5 (hardcover)
ISBN 13: 978-0-8018-9118-2 (paperback)

Previously published essays © Purdue Research Foundation, 1956, 1963–64, 1968, 1972, 1981, 1988, 1992, 1996, 1998, 2002, 2004

Library of Congress Control Number: 2008942666

A catalog record for this book is available from the British Library.

Special discounts are available for bulk purchases of this book. For more information, please contact Special Sales at 410-516-6936 or specialsales@press.jhu.edu.

The Johns Hopkins University Press uses environmentally friendly book materials, including recycled text paper that is composed of at least 30 percent post-consumer waste, whenever possible. All of our book papers are acid-free, and our jackets and covers are printed on paper with recycled content.

In memory of Rachel Levin Troxell

CONTENTS

Preface   ix

Acknowledgments   xv

What's Woolf Got to Do with It? Or, the Perils of Popularity   1
  Brenda R. Silver

GRANITE, RAINBOW, AND THE LURE OF LANGUAGE

The Word Split Its Husk: Woolf's Double Vision of Modernist Language   43
  Bonnie Kime Scott

Virginia Woolf's Pedagogical Scenes of Reading: *The Voyage Out,*
  The Common Reader, and Her "Common Readers"   60
  Susan Stanford Friedman

Night and Day: Virginia Woolf's Visionary Synthesis of Reality   87
  Melinda Feldt Cumings

From Short Story to Novel: The Manuscript Revisions of
  Virginia Woolf's *Mrs. Dalloway*   98
  Charles G. Hoffmann

On One of Virginia Woolf's Short Stories   116
  James Hafley

The Meaning of Elvedon in *The Waves:* A Key to Bernard's Experience
  and Woolf's Vision   122
  Joseph Allen Boone

SUBJECTIVITY, TRAUMA, AND COMMUNITY

The Subject in *Jacob's Room*   137
  Edward L. Bishop

Consolation Refused: Virginia Woolf, the Great War, and
  Modernist Mourning   171
  Tammy Clewell

Trauma and Recovery in Virginia Woolf's *Mrs. Dalloway*   198
    Karen DeMeester

"The Central Shadow": Characterization in *The Waves*   220
    Susan Rubinow Gorsky

Society, Morality, Analogy: Virginia Woolf's World between the Acts   238
    Don Summerhayes

The Pageant in *Between the Acts*   247
    Marilyn Zorn

THE ETHICS OF REPRESENTATION

Ethical Folds: Ethics, Aesthetics, Woolf   257
    Jessica Berman

"Robbed of Meaning": The Work at the Center of *To the Lighthouse*   280
    Mary Lou Emery

Orienting Virginia Woolf: Race, Aesthetics, and Politics in
    To the Lighthouse   300
    Urmila Seshagiri

Orlando's Voyage Out   327
    Karen R. Lawrence

Sublime Barbarians in the Narrative of Empire; or, Longinus at Sea
    in *The Waves*   355
    Laura Doyle

The Politics of Modernist Form; or, Who Rules *The Waves*   378
    Patrick McGee

The Jew in the Bath: Imperiled Imagination in Woolf's *The Years*   400
    Maren Linett

Afterword   419
    Mark Hussey

Appendix: Fiction Analyzed in Particular Chapters   423
Bibliography   425
List of Contributors   433
Index   439

Virginia Woolf has achieved a palpably canonical status as a novelist, theorist of modernism, feminist, and social analyst. She is unquestionably the woman writer most likely to be taught in courses on modern British fiction, Anglo-American modernism, twentieth-century British literature, and twentieth-century women's literature, and usually the only early twentieth-century woman writer to be the subject of single-author courses.

Her canonicity is visible in the history of *Modern Fiction Studies*. To commemorate the fiftieth anniversary of its founding in 1955, *MFS* commissioned its fourth special issue on Woolf. There were issues of the journal devoted to Woolf in 1956 (edited by Maurice Beebe, the journal's first editor), 1972 (edited by William Stafford and Margaret Church), and 1992 (edited by Ellen Carol Jones), and the anniversary issue (edited by Laura Doyle) appeared in 2004. The regularity of these special issues demonstrates both Woolf's stature and the close relationship between the journal and Woolf criticism: until the *Woolf Studies Annual* was founded in 1995, *MFS* was the principal place to publish on Woolf, and it remains a leading venue for Woolf scholarship. Indeed, *MFS* has not only reflected Woolf's prominence but, with its consistent attention to her work, has also significantly nurtured it.

This anthology of essays collects the most provocative, the most thorough, the most intriguing articles on Woolf published in this premier journal over the course of its half century of publication history. The essays cover all of Woolf's major novels—*The Voyage Out, Night and Day, Jacob's Room, Mrs. Dalloway, To the Lighthouse, Orlando, The Waves, The Years,* and *Between the Acts*—with significant mention of her long essays *A Room of One's Own* and *Three Guineas* and additional articles on the short story "Moments of Being" and on her reputation. Extensive references to her diaries and letters round out the volume's coverage of Woolf.

Although Woolf was often attacked as an ivory-tower aesthete from the 1940s to the 1960s and sometimes much later (see Brenda Silver's chapter in this volume for a history of Woolf's popular image), she nevertheless has always drawn serious critical attention. Her literary stature has, in fact, only grown, in part because her work has been amenable to various, competing approaches to literary criticism. With its detachment, irony, and ambiguous symbolism, it provided rich material for New Critical interpretations. And the formal innovations of Woolf's work have easily led critics to structuralist readings. On the other hand, Woolf's intense concern with identity and mental processes has guided critics to illuminating psychological readings, while her scrutiny of social interaction and community has prompted social and political interpretations. The essays included here from the 1950s through the early 1980s, for example (those by Hafley, Zorn, Summerhayes, Hoffmann, Cumings, Gorsky, and Boone), draw on New Critical strategies for a close reading of Woolf's imagery and symbolism, while also stressing issues of subjectivity. The 1960s articles use these methods to bolster a tendency toward social analysis (even in the context of textual editing), while the 1970s articles focus on philosophical and technical aspects of the texts.

In the 1980s and 1990s, Woolf's implicit and explicit feminist critiques were foregrounded as feminist literary criticism became a powerful academic force. Bonnie Kime Scott's 1988 chapter demonstrates this newly potent feminist critical approach. And in the 1990s and beyond, Woolf's exploration of otherness of various kinds (race, nation, and class, as well as the opacity of interpersonal relationships) has lent itself to multicultural, postcolonial, and ethical interrogations, often with feminist slants. This set of approaches is visible especially in the final section of the collection.

Although recent essays may in many cases mesh more easily with current scholarly expectations, I want to stress the value of the earlier arguments: they often find unity and artistic transcendence where more contemporary readings see disunity and fragmentation. Reading the earlier essays reminds us that there is another side to what we now choose to see. Woolf did indeed live and participate in an age of deep skepticism, but she also believed, as she says in "A Sketch of the Past," that there is a pattern behind the cotton wool of everyday life, even if it is up to us to envision or extract that pattern. Like her contemporaries T. S. Eliot and James Joyce, she viewed art as a possible means of discovering the unity and transcendence that had previously been the province of religion. To hear only "dispersity" (as the gramophone in *Between the Acts* has it) and not its accompanying "unity" is to hear only part of the music.

The first chapter in the collection, by Brenda Silver, serves as an introduction to Woolf criticism by surveying the ways Woolf has been enlisted by popular culture. The rest of the essays are divided into three thematic sections, each arranged chronologically according to the novels it considers. The first main section, "Granite, Rainbow, and the Lure of Language," emphasizes Woolf's techniques for exploring the ways fact, vision, and language interact. Through the intermingling of fact (which Woolf sometimes called "granite") and vision (which Woolf sometimes called "rainbow") arise individual imagination, perceived reality, and the art of fiction. This section focuses on Woolf's *words* and her acute analyses of literary envisioning.

Bonnie Kime Scott's chapter in this section contrasts Woolfian metaphors for masculine creativity such as towers and sandcastles with feminine images such as the sea, seeds, and natural growth, and analyzes the stakes of this division in Woolf's writing. Susan Stanford Friedman's chapter on *The Voyage Out* and *The Common Reader* focuses on their representations of reading, drawing connections to our own readings and showing how Woolf experiments on the borders between tradition and innovation. Melinda Feldt Cumings analyzes *Night and Day*, discussing the processes through which the characters work to synthesize fact and vision to live within a heightened reality. Charles Hoffmann's article discusses the short stories that relate to *Mrs. Dalloway* alongside the manuscript versions, arguing that the early emphasis on social and political conflict is muted in the published novel. James Hafley describes Woolf's short story "Moments of Being: Slater's Pins Have No Points," tracing the subtle interplay between knowledge and imagination in Fanny Wilmot's perceptions of Julia Craye. And Joseph Boone discusses the meaning of the Elvedon estate Bernard sees or imagines in *The Waves*, arguing that it comes to represent, among other things, the "insubstantial territory" created by the intimacy of the characters.

The second thematic section, "Subjectivity, Trauma, and Community," treats subjectivity in itself and as it is implied in the process of characterization, as well as the perils to subjectivity caused by war's traumatic shredding of the social fabric. Its focus on Woolf's psychosocial vision allows this section both to consider the ways social groups respond to and mourn traumatic events and to treat the hazards and comforts of community.

Edward Bishop's chapter in this section uses ideas from Louis Althusser and Bertolt Brecht to analyze subjectivity as it plays out in and is questioned by *Jacob's Room*. Tammy Clewell's chapter argues that in *Jacob's Room* and *To the Lighthouse*, Woolf refuses the accepted forms of mourning in order to resist false closure and empty consolation. Karen DeMeester reads *Mrs. Dalloway* through the lens of trauma studies, arguing against accounts of Septimus as schizophrenic and suggesting that both the form and content of the novel are influenced by representations of trauma. Susan Gorsky explores the complex representation of character in *The Waves* on two levels: the technical means by which Woolf represents people who are both separate and mystically connected and the personal means by which the characters can conceive of themselves as individuals who are simultaneously formed by and in each other. Don Summerhayes links the thematic elements of *Between the Acts* (its evocation of fruitlessness and "psychic insularity") to its style (its repetition and detachment) finding regenerative power only in Lucy Swithin whose religion blinds her to much of reality. And Marilyn Zorn focuses on the pageant in *Between the Acts*, suggesting that it reveals to its audience and to Woolf's readers that recognition of the individual behind the roles she plays is crucial to the formation of community.

The third section, "The Ethics of Representation," brings together some of the most interesting accounts of Woolf's ethical and political imagination. These chapters consider the ways Woolf represents other minds in general and in particular the minds of those who differ from her according to early twentieth-century notions of class and race. They also, necessarily, consider the place of the Empire in Woolf's imaginative work. The chapters in this section, all published after 1990, together compose a nuanced view of Woolf's attempts to represent otherness.

The first chapter, by Jessica Berman, opens with a summary of feminist critiques of French philosopher Emmanuel Levinas, moving into a consideration of the relationship between ethics and aesthetics especially as evidenced in Roger Fry's artistic theories; Berman then turns to *Orlando* and *To the Lighthouse* to consider the confluence of ethics and aesthetics in Woolf's practice. Mary Lou Emery's chapter focuses on the representation of Mrs. McNab in *To the Lighthouse* in terms of class and gender—suggesting that she is both dehumanized and multiply gendered—and analyzes representations of the "natural" and the "mechanical" in the novel. Urmila Seshagiri explores the racial politics of *To the Lighthouse*, stressing the ambivalent power of Lily Briscoe's "Chinese eyes" by contextualizing that label within the Orientalist discourses of avant-garde art.

Karen Lawrence moves on to study the politics of *Orlando* by focusing on the voyage to Turkey: she reads tropes of masculine adventure in the East alongside tropes of erotic freedom, then considers the meaning of Orlando's repatriation as a woman in England. Laura Doyle traces a "racial and imperial substructure" within the history of ideas of the sublime and then turns to *The Waves* to argue that Woolf works against such a substructure while retaining an investment in the sublime. Patrick McGee responds to Jane Marcus's influential article "Britannia Rules *The Waves*," arguing that Woolf does not transcend imperialist ideology but does expose the limits of European culture; to this end, he focuses on processes of individuation represented in the novel and considers the politics of modernist form. My own contribution focuses on an antisemitic scene in *The Years*, resisting the assumption that Woolf's antifascism entails philosemitism; on the contrary, this chapter traces the links among Woolf's antipathy toward Jews, her worries about intellectual and imaginative freedom, and her antifascist commitments. An afterword by Mark Hussey speculates about the future of Woolf studies as we approach the centennial of her novels' publications.

For the convenience of teachers using the anthology in courses, there is a bibliography that lists all of the articles on Woolf published in *MFS* arranged by date and by author's name. There is also an appendix that charts which Woolf novels are discussed in which chapters in this volume. A professor who wishes to quickly find essays on a particular novel may look to this appendix; there she will find in boldface type those authors who treat the novel as their main topic, and in roman type those that discuss it more briefly but still make significant claims.

The essays collected here represent various styles, various degrees of theoretical engagement, various time periods and points of view. Four of them—by DeMeester, Clewell, Seshagiri, and Berman—are among the seventy-five articles on any topic most commonly accessed through Project Muse during the past three years; indeed, DeMeester's is the article accessed most often.

A note on preparing these essays for publication in this anthology: The articles that make up this collection span fifty years of scholarship and have been left mostly as they were written. Occasionally, they have been edited to remove errors in spelling or grammar or to standardize word usage. As much as possible, Woolf's punctuation reflects the original manuscripts and publications. Strikethroughs in the original manuscripts have been retained to show Woolf's creative process.

These twenty articles provide an excellent cross-section of the history of Woolf criticism. Such a cross-section will, I hope, be useful to Woolf scholars generally, to teachers and students in courses on Woolf, and to the wide range of literary scholars whose interests coincide with any of Woolf's multiple intellectual, political, and artistic facets.

ACKNOWLEDGMENTS

This anthology was conceived first in conversations between John Duvall, the editor of *Modern Fiction Studies*, and Claire McCabe Tamberino, at the Johns Hopkins University Press. I am grateful for their embrace of the idea and for their willingness to entrust its development to me. John Duvall has also been very helpful along the way as questions came up, and *MFS* editorial assistants Rebecca Nicholson-Weir, Michael Mauritzen, and Martin Whitehead have unearthed pertinent files. I also appreciate Leslie Batty's valuable help securing permissions.

At the Johns Hopkins University Press, a series of editors have skillfully guided the book through production: I would like to thank Trevor Lipscombe, Bronwyn Madeo, Suzanne Flinchbaugh, Alex Handley, and Michele Callaghan. I am grateful to all of the contributors to *MFS* over the past fifty-plus years whose excellent work on Woolf meant dizzying decisions as I was selecting the essays to reprint. Many thanks, too, to Mark Hussey for agreeing to write the afterword for this volume.

As I worked on the collection, John Paul Riquelme, Bonnie Kime Scott, and John Whittier-Ferguson provided helpful guidance. My faculty reading/support group at Purdue fulfilled its support role beautifully, and I want to thank Jennifer William, Tansel Yilmazer, Elizabeth Kiss, Jennifer Sharkey, and Ann Kirchmaier. I also want to thank my family—Deena Linett, David and Penny Linett, Peter Linett, and Cheryl Slover-Linett—for their enthusiasm about my work and my spouse Dominic Naughton for his consistent encouragement. Our children Ruth and Lev did not exactly help me get work done, but they provide a wonderful counterbalance to academic life.

My dear friend Rachel Levin Troxell died, after an inspiringly spirited battle with cancer, while this book was in production. I dedicate it to her memory.

Figure 1.
Calvin and Hobbes © 1990 Universal Press Syndicate. Reprinted with permission. All rights reserved

WHAT'S WOOLF GOT

TO DO WITH IT?

OR, THE PERILS OF POPULARITY

Brenda R. Silver

In the fall of 1990, the irrepressible Calvin (of *Calvin and Hobbes*) transformed himself into a public figure by holding a frame before his face. "Now that I'm on television," he tells Hobbes, "I'm different from everybody else! I'm famous! Important! Since everyone knows me, everything I do now is newsworthy. I'm a cultural icon." For Calvin, the implications of this status are clear: "Watch," he continues, "I'll use my prestige to endorse a product!" (figure 1). In this age of spectacle and commodification, to be a cultural icon is, we know, to sell, and in Calvin's case, as in that of "stars" such as Mary Lou Retton, what they sell is often less important in defining their status than the appearance of the face and name in support of it.[1] Ironically, though, the very pervasiveness of the image can come to undercut its "meaning" and ultimately its "prestige"; signifier and signified cease to have any necessary connection, and the multiplication of the image becomes the subject of sarcasm and derision, not power.

What happens, then, when the icon is not Calvin or Mary Lou Retton but Virginia Woolf, whose prestige over the past twenty years has risen not only in the academic and intellectual worlds, the worlds, we could say, of high culture but in the popular realm as well? In February 1991 the *New York Times Magazine* put her at the top of the list of "What's In" in the Modern Language Association (Matthews 57); at the same time, she has been used to market products ranging

Originally published in *Modern Fiction Studies*, Spring 1992.

from throw pillows, to fashion clothing, to the city of New Orleans, to a glossy, coffee table collection of portraits from the National Portrait Gallery in London, to *The New York Review of Books*. Woolf, it is clear, sells, and not just to one audience. Even more striking is the breadth of her name and face recognition, suggested by her appearance as a cultural marker in texts as divergent as *Los Angeles Times* editorials, George Will columns, ACTUP anticensorship marches, Michael Innis mysteries, the hard rock group Virginia Wolf, Sesame Street, and Hanif Kureishi's 1987 film *Sammy and Rosie Get Laid*. One aspect of my subtitle, then, "the perils of popularity," leads back to the question, implicit in the first part of the title, that motivates this essay: what representations of Woolf have emerged from the proliferation of her image and her name, and what do these representations tell us about the sites of cultural contestation in which they appear?

The other perils that concern me here have to do with the critic rather than the subject of criticism: the seductions and dangers confronting the critic who enters the world of popular culture and reputation studies and finds herself in the position that feminist critics, as Meaghan Morris pithily notes (14–15), seem inevitably to find themselves in: that of complaining yet again about the exclusion of women, gender, and/or feminism from the discourse. Yet the more I tracked the trajectory of Woolf's image, the more I tried to locate it within the debates about high and low culture, the more convinced I became that battles about "culture" and cultural authority are not only gender encoded but also reveal startlingly contradictory impulses. This was certainly true of the debates occurring in the United States during the 1950s and 1960s, when Woolf, as Diana Trilling snidely remarked, presented a "special case." For one thing, she was clearly representative of "high art," but as a woman she was also subject to the discourses that have consistently gendered mass culture as feminine. Again, she was clearly on the side of an "intellectual aristocracy" or "elite," with a distinctive set of tastes similar to those tastes that cultural critics such as Dwight MacDonald seemed to be advocating for the United States.[2] But her own works, both during her lifetime and for twenty-five years after her death, were denounced or dismissed by this same group of critics, first, for being classbound and then, for exhibiting a sensibility that was not only feminine but morbid: a sensibility that demoralizes and detracts from real intellectual thought and real public values. There are, it appears, elites and elites, and what constitutes their authority or desirability depends not only on who has the power to draw the boundaries and designate what goes where but also on gender.

Keenly aware of the politics of tastemaking, American feminists in the 1970s subversively laid claim to Woolf's image—to her face and her name and her writings—to articulate a new social and cultural text. In many ways they were wildly successful: witness her current visibility and status and their continued association with a feminist agenda. But as so often happens, success can transform subversive- ness into respectability or invite iconoclasm. In the United States, for example, *The New York Review of Books* has elevated Woolf to an icon of western civilization on a par with Shakespeare, the other figure simultaneously featured in their "special offer to . . . readers" for David Levine t-shirts,[3] even as it has persistently ignored the majority of (feminist) critical studies that made her a major cultural figure or found a "respectable," that is nonfeminist, critic to review them negatively. Their own political and cultural agenda we could say, their claim to speak for "legitimate" culture, manifests itself graphi- cally every time the advertisement appears. Meanwhile, in Britain, where Woolf's reputation has always faced a different conjunction of local restrictions, Woolf's status led to her role as protagonist/target in the 1991 television series *J'Accuse*, where cultural icons were brought to trial and found wanting. In this case the goal was not to legitimize Woolf but to dethrone her.

Rather than being delighted, then, by Woolf's current popular- ity, I have grown increasingly uneasy, an uneasiness generated by my research into the construction of Woolf as cultural icon in the popular realm—the realm of journalism, film, television, theater, and advertising—over the past thirty years.[4] This process has of- ten occurred without reference to her writings, illustrating that the "popularity" of a literary figure does not necessarily depend on or lead to an increased knowledge of her works. In order to explore why I find her popularity and her "prestige" problematic, I want to outline a series of moments that mark turning points in the public awareness of "Virginia Woolf" and that illustrate the battles waged over or through her image. In particular, I want to chart the recur- rence, almost from the moment of her death, of a configuration of tropes that more than any other has dominated the representation of "Virginia Woolf": that associated with fear. What, I want to know, might this reiteration mean? What exactly is at stake?

I

On 12 April 1937, just before *The Years* made its way to the best seller list in the United States, Virginia Woolf made her way to the cover of *Time* magazine. Man Ray provided the photograph (fig- ure 2). Inside the magazine the cover article begins:

> Last year Margaret Mitchell of Atlanta, Ga. wrote her first novel, *Gone With The Wind*. Last week Virginia Woolf of London, England published her seventh, *The Years*. Margaret Mitchell's book has sold more copies (1,300,000) than all Virginia Woolf's put together. But literary brokers who take a long view of the market are stocking up with Woolfs, unloading Mitchells. Their opinion is that Margaret Mitchell was a grand wildcat stock but Virginia Woolf a sound investment. (93)

Ironically, in justifying this prediction of Woolf's value to *Time*'s middlebrow audience, the anonymous writer proclaims Woolf "not just a highbrow writer but perhaps a great one," whose audience is "the Intelligent Common Reader" and who "writes about the common gist of things." This defense was necessary, the article tells us, because by 1937 Woolf had become the target of "jealous juniors" who "derisively style her 'The Queen of Bloomsbury'" and want to dismiss her works. The irony of the defense is twofold. First, Woolf herself had in an essay called "Middlebrow," written in 1932 but unpublished until after her death, vehemently denounced this breed and proudly accepted the title "highbrow." Second, in delineating why, for this reader at least, Woolf presented nothing to fear, the author sketches a portrait of Woolf as potentially very scary indeed. For one thing, "Nervous readers will find *The Years* not nearly such heavy going as their knowledge or hearsay of Virginia Woolf might lead them to expect"; the novel is "straight," not experimental. In addition, although she comes from a "thoroughbred" English literary background, where she knew and read everyone significant, her own criticism is tolerant and appreciative, like "Sam Johnson's." Again, although she "had done her bit for the feminist cause," setting forth "the now-classic requisite of modern women who want independence: '500 [pounds] a year and a room of one's own,'" she still believes that what the writer needs is an androgynous mind and "that it is fatal to be a man or women pure and simple; one must be woman-manly or man-womanly" when one writes. Finally, when young, she may have been "in appearance a pure pre-Raphaelite, [but] she was actually more like an emancipated Bryn Mawr girl," participating in a hoax on the English navy; now, at 55, she is "the picture of a sensitive, cloistered literary woman," but instead of being an "invalid's retreat" (like Proust's) or a "chamber of nightmares" (like Joyce's), her workroom is "a room with a view" (*Time* 93–96).

Despite *Time*'s attempt to claim Virginia Woolf for its version of the common reader, the underlying portrait, the one being contested in the *Time* essay, became after her death in 1941 the prevailing intellectual and popular view. Highbrow, mandarin, elite: any way

Figure 2.
Virginia Woolf. Photograph by Man Ray. © 1992 Man Ray Trust—ARS

you look at it, her face evoked images of "sensibility," class privilege, experimental prose, distinction. *The Years*, the book that established her "popularity," fell into an abyss of critical and pedagogic silence; even her feminism, like the woman's movement in general, faded from view.

     The first significant moment, or event, that marks Woolf's reentry into public consciousness was the publication of *A Writer's Diary* by her husband, Leonard Woolf, in 1953. The book was fairly widely reviewed on both sides of the Atlantic, and, despite Leonard's decision to exclude almost everything that did not pertain to her "intentions, objects, and methods as a writer" (ix), it generated as much interest in knowing more about her personal life as it did about her work. (In part, the reviewers wanted to know what Woolf had said about her friends and acquaintances that was so damning that Leonard chose not to publish any of it, "to protect the feelings or reputations of the living" [vii].)

But the major event that precipitated Woolf into public awareness was, of course, Edward Albee's play *Who's Afraid of Virginia Woolf?*, which opened in New York in 1962 and London in 1964 before becoming a film, starring Richard Burton and Elizabeth Taylor, in 1966. From 1966 on, "Virginia Woolf" became a "household word" even among people who had no idea that there was an actual woman behind the name or what she was known for.[5] Liz Taylor appeared on the cover of both *Look* and *Life*; *Vogue* had a review by Arthur Schlesinger Jr.; the film received fourteen nominations for Academy Awards. But in 1973 one review of Quentin Bell's biography of Woolf began with the anecdote of a woman nudging an editor carrying the book and asking, "Was there a real person called Virginia Woolf? I saw the play but not the movie" (Duffy 93); while another recounted an exchange in which Gordon Haight tells us he used the name "Virginia Woolf" to recall to the wife of a retired British major what Bloomsbury was. "Her face lighted up at once. 'Oh yes, she was the one in that dirty movie!'" (Haight 426).

Albee's play, then, or more accurately its reception, is crucial to the construction of Woolf's public image, raising fascinating questions about who reviewed it, where, in what terms, the differences between the reception of the play and the film and what they tell us about the two media. Here I will concentrate on the ramifications of the title, taking its question, its riddle, with its emphasis on fear, very seriously indeed. For whatever else people may have taken away from the play or film, and however they interpreted the term "Virginia Woolf," her name became synonymous with the power to elicit fear and wreak psychological death or destruction.

From the moment the play opened, the title provoked talk and controversy; Lewis Funke, writing in the *New York Times* column "News of the Rialto," claimed to have received "letters of protest [about the title] to this department's mailbag": "How, indeed, did Mr. Albee dare poke fun at the late English novelist, who, to many on both sides of the Atlantic, was one of the greats of this century?" (21 Oct. 1962). I am reminded here of Woolf's description of certain of Jane Austen's admirers, who, she wrote, would "resent any slight upon her genius as if it were an insult offered to the chastity of their Aunts" ("Jane Austen at Sixty" 433). Funke's sarcasm signals one aspect of Woolf's iconicity at the time the play appeared, a form of protectionism that needs to be distinguished from her reconstruction by feminists during the 1970s; an example of this attitude occurs in the review of the film that began, "No one would be particularly surprised if that fine and sensitive English novelist Virginia Woolf were turning over in her grave at every mention of the most talked-about movie these days": not because of the title (she liked a joke) or the treatment of illusion and reality, "but because of the foul language and profanity" (Hartung 474). Albee himself showed a certain amount of compunction about the title: he wrote to Leonard Woolf for permission to use Woolf's name, apparently worried, in Malcolm Muggeridge's telling of the story, that "in view of Virginia's tragic end, it might be distasteful to her relict" (38). The title was also linked, again according to "News of the Rialto," to the appearance of Virginia Woolf paperbacks in bookstores (Gardner, 2 Sept. 1962); whether readers began asking for them or the publisher saw a good thing and anticipated sales is unclear.

Albee himself explained publicly only that he had seen the phrase written on a blackboard in a bar in the Village (Funke, 18 Nov. 1962); what he did not say was that it was a gay bar. This latter fact is crucial to one aspect of the title that runs as a subtext through the discourse surrounding the play and, even more, the film: that associated with homosexuality, homophobia, and misogyny. This subtext had emerged into the light by 1964 when Tom Driver accused Albee of being fundamentally dishonest: of presenting what had to be homosexual liaisons in the guise of heterosexual marriage. The homophobia motivating this charge resides in his explanation: that heterosexual couples would never exhibit the kind of sustained sadomasochistic psychology or behavior apparent in the play ("I do not deny that heterosexual couples engage in *some* of the same behavior and show *some* of the same psychology" [39]). By the time the film was reviewed, this response had become more common. *Newsweek*'s reviewer was explicit: "[Albee] has not really written about men and women, with a potential for love and sex, however withered the potential may be. He has written about saber-toothed humans who cannot reproduce, and who need to draw buckets of blood before they can feel compassion for each other" ("Who's Afraid . . ." 84). John Coleman, writing in the *New Statesman*, is more oblique: "there's a sense that the line of attack relies too much on something stranger and more splenetic than the humdrum bitcheries of marriage. I think, as others have said, that some special bleeding is before us" (103).

What do these reviewers fear? The feminizing effect of male homosexuality? Or women themselves, like Martha perhaps, the female protagonist, whose role as castrating bitch—and childless woman—is commented on by almost every reviewer of both the play and the film? ("Is it some acquired sexual frigidity which causes her to seek gratification in a constant emasculative assault on her husband?" [Hewes 29]) Why should Albee's study of impotence and sterility, personal and cultural, evoke this particular homophobic and/or misogynistic response? And, perhaps most important here, what did Woolf have to do with it? How did it shape her image?

The simplest answer points directly toward Bloomsbury and anticipates the appearance of memoirs and biographies at the end of the 1960s that would make the homosexuality and bisexuality of its members public knowledge. While the initial performance of the play in New York (1962) preceded the emergence of an openly gay culture and press, there was enough underground knowledge in the gay community and in the theater community to link not only Albee but also Virginia Woolf to a homosexual subplot and alarm its straight reviewers. By 1966 the cultural terrain had shifted, and the film soon acquired the status of camp. Liz Taylor had a lot to do with this, in particular her imitation of Bette Davis, a camp idol, in the opening segment; Susan Sontag's essay on camp, published in 1964, provided one context for reading the film in this way. The rise of an openly gay sensibility and discourse during this period, then, might well account for the more openly homophobic attacks on Albee's play in its cinematic version.[6]

To the extent that the play was perceived as reflecting a gay sensibility, the misogyny directed at Martha and associated with "Virginia Woolf" raises the vexed issue of gay male misogyny. But the impact of the play's misogynistic message, the fear of bitchiness and impotence conveyed to the public through the press, was far more extensive. Cynthia Grenier, one of the few women who reviewed the play, saw the Paris production and had no trouble detecting that "the 'Virginia Woolf' [the characters] are afraid of, of course—there is no way around this, a hundred details in the play point to it—is the specter of the dominant female."

But more than a Strindbergian battle between the sexes and wills—a frequent comparison in the reviews—is at work here, for the "specter of the dominant female" troped as "Virginia Woolf" belongs to another set of responses to the title as well: those that point directly to the debates about high and mass culture that dominated much of the cultural discourse in the United States during the Cold War. Although the British reviews were generally more explicit, and more ironic, about the play's contribution to these battles-of-the-brows than the American reviews (one said it had "a low brows-will-be-persecuted title" [Pryce-Jones 213]), the most extensive critique of the play from the perspective of its claims to cultural class came from America, from Diana Trilling.

At first glance, a reading of "Virginia Woolf" from this perspective would appear self-evident; as noted above, the image of her that dominated the intellectual world in the States was the upper-middle class, snobbish, intellectual aristocrat with impeccable literary and social credentials, definitely a lady and definitely a highbrow. At this level, the title becomes an academic or intellectual joke, made possible by the happy conjunction of her name with the animal in the fairy tale and the Disney song.[7] Here again Lewis Funke provides an insight into the way the title was initially read. Three weeks after his sarcasm about the angry letters he'd received, he passed on to his *Times* readers the information that in the mid-thirties Professor John Hawley Roberts of Williams College used to give an extracurricular lecture on Woolf with the title "Who's Afraid of Virginia Woolf?," a title that rather than being "a sneer at the writer" was meant to encourage readers who might at first glance find her too difficult (18 Nov. 1962). In contrast, the "sneer" perceived in Albee's use of the phrase and in his play would be equivalent to thumbing one's nose at a figure associated with (European) standards of taste and authority, of order, civilization, and manners—an act of defiance. This reading is supported by Janet Flanner's report on the Paris production in *The New Yorker*, where she records that the French saw the "American academic couple . . . as true and informative natives of our land and . . . the complete opposites of any professional couple imaginable connected with the Sorbonne" (68).[8]

Trilling's essay, published originally in *Esquire* as "Who's Afraid of the Culture Elite?," and in a slightly different version in her *Claremont Essays* as "The Riddle of Albee's *Who's Afraid of Virginia Woolf?*," while accepting the association of Virginia Woolf with high culture, reads the title not as an act of defiance but of appropriation: a dangerous blurring of distinctions between the cultural classes.[9] For Trilling, the riddle is why this play, which she intensely disliked and which she describes as a "canvas of hopelessness and desperation," whose message is "life is nothing, and we must have the courage to face our emptiness without fear," should be so extraordinarily popular among "the American theatregoing public . . . decent respectable middle-class people" ("Riddle" 211, 214, 211). Her answer is that its popularity has less to do with its explicit message than with its concealed purpose and appeal: its seduction of its audience by granting them a sense of privilege, of being "in," in "an exclusive club," a cultural club or "closed circuit" (a phrase she borrows from Mary McCarthy), located within the play in the academic, intellectual community, in which "virtue . . . is defined by taste" (218–219, 217, 221). In this light, the intellectual joke inscribed in the title is directed to the audience, which receives a "gift of cultural status" (221) by having shared in its humor. People go to the play, as they read advertisements, to learn "the signals by which we advance in prestige and leave the indiscriminate democratic masses behind us" (224).

But however much Trilling deplores the culture club, she is *not* making an argument for middlebrow or mass culture, which she calls variously a "fabrication" or a "monolithic culture," dictated by the "officers of the cultural club" (226). Mass art's borrowing from high art, she concludes, its narrowing of the divide between the two, might be perceived as a victory for democracy, but for her it represents something different and dangerous: an attitude of conformity, linked to the "complacency of the radical intellectual" in the postwar period, that needs to be exposed and fought (226–227). "The cultural radical has become a popular Broadway success—and this alone should be enough to alert us to reassess his premises" (227).

What Trilling feared was not "Virginia Woolf" as aristocratic arbiter of taste but the homogenization of culture, associated in part with a democratization of education and changes in the media, and the particular ideological stance inscribed by this process.[10] Here, the contradictory status accorded Woolf in the high/low discourse constructed by intellectuals in the postwar period becomes significant. Fourteen years earlier Trilling had dismissed Woolf as a culturally insignificant icon, arguing that she represented a form of elitism that was not only gender and class specific but divorced from the broader social community ("Virginia Woolf's Special Realm"). Now, however, as she turned away from a community perceived to be more and more influenced by the cultural manipulation exemplified by Albee's play, she is forced to recognize Woolf as a sign whose cultural significance was greater than she, Trilling, had been willing to admit: to see her as an emblem of the true cultural elite under attack by Albee and the "mass *non*-thinking" (227) he and his play represent:

> *Who's Afraid of Virginia Woolf?* Mr. Albee calls his play, and even this title which has no perceivable relation to the story Mr. Albee is telling, suddenly reveals its no doubt unconscious meaning. Who indeed need be afraid of the lady-writer of Bloomsbury, that quintessential literary aristocrat whose cultural fortress could once be thought so impregnable to the assaults of a vulgar democracy? Certainly not Mr. Albee, or George or Martha, or Nick and Honey. And certainly not a public let in on Mr. Albee's cultural secret, that distinction, whether of birth or achievement, is merely a joke, that the values which once supported our society no

longer prevail, and that modern man is on his desperate, ugly, and meaningless own. ("Riddle" 222)[11]

Trilling's ambivalence about Woolf's cultural status points to yet another discourse evoked by Albee's title and illustrated by the responses to the play: the strong tradition among intellectuals that troped high culture, high art, including modernism, as male and mass culture as female. The figure of Virginia Woolf, as I noted earlier, inscribes the faultlines revealed in this tradition when an actual female, not "Woman" or "the feminine," is involved; and the play, both in terms of its title and its reception, makes them visible. The title, that is, leads in two different directions. One puts "Virginia Woolf" and the fear she evokes on the side of high culture, a high culture that is either cheekily defied or dangerously appropriated, depending on your point of view. The other associates the fear elicited by "Virginia Woolf" with fear of the feminine or feminized masses, and hence with fear of consumption (or of being consumed), of excess, of the potential destruction or feminization of the cultural (not to mention the political) powers that be.[12] This projection ties "Virginia Woolf" once again to the image of the dominant woman and aligns it with the figures of the Sphinx and Medusa.

To illustrate the powerful role of gender in the discourses surrounding mass culture we need only ask, why not *Who's Afraid of Thomas Wolfe?* The pun would still work, the hint of high culture and its defiance would still be there, but we would lose the fear of the feminization of culture that is also inscribed in the title of another work from this period that relies on puns and gender to make a similar point: *From Beowulf to Virginia Woolf* (Myers). Mass or popular culture may well use figures from high culture to legitimize itself,[13] but when that figure is a woman, she brings with her as well the threat of annihilation. Men can never be that scary.

Albee's title generates this fearsome figuration of "Virginia Woolf" both by its status as a riddle and its place in the discourse that equates the masses with the "mob" or "crowd" and genders them all as feminine. As Andreas Huyssen describes this discourse at the end of the nineteenth century, a time when culture was facing not only feminization but feminism, fears of the mob and of revolution were inseparable from "a fear of women, a fear of nature out of control, a fear of the unconscious, of sexuality, of the loss of identity and stable ego boundaries in the mass" (196). For Gustave le Bon, writing during this turbulent period, the danger of the crowd was best understood through the figure of the Sphinx. "Crowds," he wrote, "are somewhat like the sphinx of ancient fable: it is necessary to arrive at a solution of the problems offered by their psychology or to resign ourselves to being devoured by them" (cited in Huyssen 196). Albee's title may be only one of a number of riddles within the play, but it has the first and the last word: it is tauntingly introduced by Martha at the beginning; George, in his victory over her, appropriates it for the penultimate line. As a result, that which we must understand or risk being devoured by is "Virginia Woolf."[14]

The other figure central to this particular discourse was suggested by Robert Brustein in his review of the play when he identified whatever it is out there that Albee and we fear but cannot yet face directly—that is, "Virginia Woolf"—with the Medusa head (29–30).

The conjunction of images—Medusa, Sphinx, and Virginia Woolf—radiates outward in a number of critical directions. One, rooted in Sigmund Freud's equation of Medusa and castration, points to the associations made between Medusa's head and male hysteria (Hertz); another to studies of Medusa and the evil eye (Siebers); and still a third to readings of the Medusa story as a ritual sacrifice for the sake of the community (Joplin). But any approach to Medusa and the Sphinx must confront the dominant affect at work, fear and perhaps envy: a fear of powerful female figures that, among other things, locates the violence perpetrated against women in the women themselves. (Medusa, you may recall, in some versions of the story once a beautiful woman, was punished by Athena either for having attracted the attentions of Poseidon or for having been raped.) From this perspective, women too have much to fear in this construction of Virginia Woolf; they have certainly understood the stakes. Patricia Joplin, for example, exploring the intersection of violence and the repression of women's voices, writes that "Behind the victim's head that turns men to stone may lie the victim stoned to death by men" (52). And Teresa de Lauretis prefaces an analysis of the silencing of women's desire in narrative and culture with the rhetorical question, "What became of the Sphinx after the encounter with Oedipus on his way to Thebes? Or, how did Medusa feel seeing herself in Perseus' mirror just before being slain?" (109).

II

De Lauretis' response to her revisionary riddles foregrounds yet another aspect of the conjunction of Medusa, Sphinx, and Virginia Woolf at work in the gendered construction of cultural icons. Although the answers are known, she replies, at least to the question about the Sphinx, we don't know them offhand because "Medusa and the Sphinx, like other ancient monsters, have survived in hero narratives, in someone else's story, not their own" (109). For the most part, that is, although there are exceptions, women have not been represented in our culture as either heroes or creators of culture.[15] It is against this tradition that Hélène Cixous, exhorting women to reclaim their bodies, to write their own stories—to reconfigure culture and its obsession with heroes—restores Medusa to life and pictures her laughing.[16] But does this make her a heroic figure, the kind on which legends and public reputations are based?

This question becomes more than academic when read against John Rodden's study of the "making and claiming of 'St. George' Orwell" as cultural icon. The discourse of the hero and the heroic, Rodden argues, "hovers at the border" of any study of the "making of a literary figure" (10). Throughout his detailed projection of a model for exploring reputation and his extensive reading of its application to Orwell, Rodden continually refers to the literary figure as "he" and adduces male examples. Only when he confronts the feminist critique of Orwell, a critique that for all his attempted even-handedness and stated understanding of the historical moment in which it appeared (the 1980s) he finds totally misguided, does he acknowledge that gender might play a role in the construction and perception of iconic figures: "the gender gap is there. Many women cannot 'read themselves into' Orwell very easily. . . . Their feelings of letdown, which their high expectations deepen and sharpen, points to the large problem of heroic identification across gender. . . . The range of Orwell's fractured reception within the radical/liberal feminist audience reflects variously the urge for a heroism that transcends gender modeling, [and] the longing for intellectual heroes who are heroines too . . ." (225). What Rodden doesn't confront, in addition to the fact that heroes and heroines do not occupy the same or even parallel positions in our culture, is what happens when the literary figure, the cultural icon, is a woman. How would the discourse work—or *not* work?

Judging by the reception of Quentin Bell's biography of his aunt, Virginia Woolf, in 1972—the next moment I want to highlight—Woolf was neither heroic nor the hero of her own story; if anyone was, it was Leonard, described by almost every reviewer as a "saint." This response is crucial to the public image of Woolf, because by the time the biography was published, her currency, her name value, had increased dramatically. The book received an enormous amount of coverage in the popular press, where the various reviewers staked out well-demarcated ideological positions, including their response to the emerging women's movement. For the purposes of my argument here, three aspects of the biography's reception demand note. First, the reasons offered in the reviews for the increased interest in Woolf did not point to her stature as a writer but to Albee's play, the women's movement, and, and, most of all, the outpouring of books by and about Bloomsbury that preceded and accompanied the biography's publication. (Significantly, Bloomsbury appears in this discourse not only as a camp taste but as a precursor to the radical subcultures of the 1960s and early 1970s.) When reviewers did mention her literary reputation, it was often to complain that enough was enough, that we didn't need any more critical works about Virginia Woolf's novels.

Second, Bell's decision *not* to make the work a literary biography, *not* to explore her writing, focused popular attention almost totally on Woolf's personality and her personal life, in particular her "madness," her suicide, and her sexuality, including her sexual molestation by her half-brothers and her relationships with women.

Finally, almost without exception—and the exceptions were women—no one questioned what it meant that her biographer was her nephew, presumably with a vested interest in the family portrait of Virginia, a portrait premised on the assumption that yes, she was a precocious "genius" (and the deployment of the word "genius" both in the biography and the reviews serves to empty it of any substantial meaning) and extremely good company, but that she was also difficult, delicate, asexual, apolitical, and often out of touch with reality.[17] (Families, it should go without saying, have a way of labelling or assigning places to their members that often bear little relationship to the individual's social relations and image in the rest of the world.) But instead of questioning Bell's position vis-à-vis his subject, the vast majority of reviewers credited his insider's view as revealing "the truth," a stance that he has capitalized on ever since. This "truth" helped create an image of Woolf as twentieth-century madwoman with a bedroom of her own—witty and malicious, yes, and productive, but again, all of the above: delicate, ethereal, asexual, apolitical, and so on—and this image still has a great deal of currency, at least in the nonacademic world, today. Edward Gorey's cartoon, drawn for the cover of the revised edition of *From Beowulf to Virginia Woolf* in 1984, provides one example (figure 3); Alistair Cooke's introduction to the 1990 Masterpiece Theatre presentation of *A Room of One's Own*, performed by Eileen Atkins, another. In Cooke's representation, "Mrs. Woolf," the "saint of the Bloomsbury set," was characterized at the time of the original talks at Cambridge by her "tremulous voice" and her total lack of financial reality. And while most (American) reviewers of Atkins' rendition have praised her embodiment of Woolf's intellectual strength and humor, critics such as John Simon cannot resist adding that "Miss Atkins, sturdier by far, could have blown Mrs. Woolf with one breath from Bloomsbury to Billingsgate."

In the year following the Bell biography, 1973, an event occurred

Figure 3.
Beowulf and Virginia Woolf. Drawing by Edward Gorey. © 1984 by Edward Gorey. Reprinted by permission of Donadio & Ashworth Inc.

that, while equally representative of the cultural moment, signaled a strong counter current: the founding of a company called Historical Products Inc., which undertook to bring history alive by making its actors, including its women actors, literally visible—in this case on t-shirts. Woolf's image was one of the first printed and sold; soon, it seemed, her face was everywhere in the women's movement as it then constituted itself, signifying a sense of political excitement, activism, and comraderie. The image and the circulation of Virginia Woolf produced by the t-shirt phenomenon created an alternative discourse to that evoked by the Bell biography, and from this moment on, "Virginia Woolf" became a primary site for the waging of a large number of cultural battles, not least among them those about feminism itself.

III

At this point I want to skip from 1973 to 1987 and *Sammy and Rosie Get Laid*, bypassing both the publication of Nigel Nicolson's *Portrait of a Marriage* (1973), which elevated Woolf's sexual life—that is, her relationship with Vita Sackville-West—to best-sellerdom, and the outpouring of articles on the "Woolf cult" elicited by her centenary in 1982, one of which observed, not without irony, "She has become the Marilyn Monroe of American academia, genius transformed into icon and industry through the special circumstances of her life and work" (Dudar 32).[18] Significantly, all sides in the debate about her reputation at the time shared the perception that Virginia Woolf existed as an icon only in the United States, not in Britain. This distinction marks very real differences between the two cultures, not the least of which is the powerful role that social as well as cultural class still plays in Britain. Nevertheless, the trope of fear, manifested disparately perhaps but nonetheless there and often to the same end, seems to transcend national boundaries. In 1978, for example, the English writer Alan Bennett transformed Albee's title and drama into a television play called *Me, I'm Afraid of Virginia Woolf*, where the Man Ray photograph of Virginia Woolf (figure 2), defaced first by having "a large pair of tits" drawn on it (49) and then by having its nose erased, is integrally linked to the English professor Hopkins' acceptance of his homosexuality, his falling in love. Class is involved: Hopkins' students are adults in the Mechanics Institute; Bloomsbury is involved: Hopkins finds it ironic that struggling so hard in her writing to escape time and circumstances Woolf is now remembered almost primarily as the center of a group; lesbianism is involved: first in a conversation between Hopkins and his mother, later in relation to "Virginia's . . . very intimate relationship" with Vita Sackville-West (58). But most of all, "Life" and sex are involved, set against art, and here Virginia Woolf is most found wanting. At the end of the scene in the classroom, Hopkins' about-to-be-lover addresses the photograph of Woolf directly, asking, "Well, love. Was it worth it?" and introducing Woolf to "Posterity" before depositing the poster in the wastebasket (61–62); earlier he had argued, "If Virginia Woolf had been born in Brighouse she'd never have got off the ground" (59). Finally, the blood from Hopkins' nose, hit by a young man angry at the protagonist's gaze while he kisses his girl, stains the novel by Woolf he's been reading all day and becomes the symbol of his newfound homosexual love. Whatever else "Virginia Woolf" may be in this play, her "meaning" never escapes her first representation: an exchange in which a female bus conductor asks whether Virginia Woolf is funny and Hopkins replies, "Killing" (38).

But it is *Sammy and Rosie Get Laid*, written by Hanif Kureishi and directed by Stephen Frears (who also directed Bennett's play for television), that offers the most ambiguous variations on the themes so powerfully evoked by Albee twenty-five years earlier, telling us a great deal about the location and representation of cultural anxieties in moments of social change and crisis. For if Albee's play appeared at a time when the phenomenon of mass education and the demographics of who was being educated raised the threat of the homogenization of culture, the feminization of culture, and the intellectual or dominant woman, Kureishi's film conveys the fractures and contradictions in postmodern, postcolonial, Thatcherite Britain, contradictions embedded in the multifaceted and indeterminant image of Virginia Woolf presented within the film.

How does Woolf perform this role? As in Bennett's play, through the presence of a poster-size reproduction of one of her best-known photographs, silently looking out at the actors and toward the viewers in many of the central scenes of the film. When I first wrote about the representation of Woolf in this film, I posed the question of its "meaning" as follows: What is Virginia Woolf doing in Hanif Kureishi's self-consciously postmodern depiction of London in the late 1980s, and why is she presiding over a race riot and the burning of the inner city? The poster of Woolf hangs in the study of Rosie, social worker, feminist, sometime political activist; Woolf's writings, in their distinctive Hogarth Press covers, figure prominently in the center of her bookshelves. Rafi, Rosie's father-in-law, the Pakistani politician returned to the "Home Country" to escape death threats occasioned by his brutal persecution of his enemies, sees the flames from the riot superimposed on Woolf's image and experiences her gaze with horror. In a film where the text of T. S. Eliot's *Waste Land* covers the outside of a trailer parked on a waste ground reclaimed by a countercultural, multiracial community, the status of "high" modernism in the world of postmodern, postcolonial, metropolitan London is very much at stake, and Virginia Woolf seems to have become an icon representative of modernism itself. Yet has she? And if so, what do she and her gaze represent? Aloofness? A life and a writing style out of touch with the political realities of her own day let alone those of

Figure 4.
Sammy and Rosie Get Laid © 1987 Cinecom Entertainment Group.

the present? Or is her presence more contemporary, and perhaps more sympathetic? Does it evoke her feminism, including her insistence on the interconnections of the public and private spheres, and her elevation by modern-day feminists such as Rosie (whose political commitments within the film are highly ambiguous) to the position of "matron saint" (Zwerdling 33)? Given the history of the British perception of Woolf as the elite, snobbish Queen of Bloomsbury and, oh yes, minor experimental writer, what does her centrality in this distinctly political film suggest? Does she preside over it as modernist, as feminist, as pacifist, as highbrow, as sapphist, as suicide, as failed liberal anti-imperialist? And how do we begin to decipher the film's construction of her enigmatic, silent, Mona Lisa–like stare?[19]

In the process of exploring these issues, I found myself inexorably drawn to the fact that the one reaction to the photograph explicitly specified in the script was horror. Whose horror is it, I began to ask, and is the film really as undecidable, at least in relation to fear, as I had originally thought? While I still believe that the "meaning" of the sign "Virginia Woolf" in the film is multiple and will shift,

Figure 5.
Sammy and Rosie Get Laid © 1987 Cinecom Entertainment Group.

in a distinctly postmodern fashion, in accordance with the discourse in which it is located (that is, feminism, modernism, suicide, and so on), the reiteration of tropes generated by the Albee play, particularly that associated with fear, constitutes a pervasive subtext that crosses discursive boundaries and constructs Virginia Woolf in surprisingly familiar ways.

The key scene occurs in Rosie's study, where the newly arrived Rafi has been put to bed under the eyes of Virginia Woolf. As described in the script:

> RAFI *lies in bed in the half-lit room. He's asleep, having a nightmare. He cries out, then awakes. He lies there being stared at by Virginia Woolf, which becomes more horrible the more she looks at him. The noise from outside rises around him. It could be in his head or for real: he doesn't know. He sits up. On the edge of the bed he pulls cotton-wool out of his ears. He covers his face with his hands.* (Kureishi 12–13)

In the film, the camera shifts back and forth from Rafi's startled stare to the photograph of Woolf, moving closer and closer until Woolf's

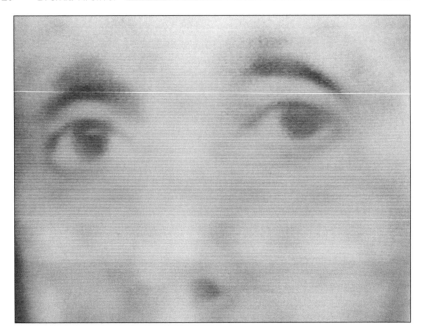

Figure 6.
Sammy and Rosie Get Laid © 1987 Cinecom Entertainment Group.

eyes fill the screen (figures 4–6). What looks like lace curtains cover the portrait; flames burn at the bottom of the frame. Woolf might be presiding over sacrificial rites, or she might be the sacrifice. At any rate, Rafi's reaction is terror; still wearing his nightclothes, he runs from the room and the house.

Ironically, the two references I have found to Woolf's appearance in this scene portray its meaning as self-evident and overdetermined. One commentator, for example, writes that the "shot of Rosie's photograph of Virginia Woolf seemingly enveloped in flames (caused by the street fire reflected in the window) is too obvious a bit of underlining" (Quart 41), while another notes that "the *content* of Frears's images, for which Kureishi himself may be responsible, is occasionally redundant or excessive: see the shot that frames Virginia Woolf's photograph in flames" (Cardullo 356). But underlining what? redundant of what? Virginia Woolf, the priestess of Bloomsbury and high culture may be "burning," but does the film—do we—cheer or regret this? Again, the recurring motifs I have been tracking provide some insights.

To begin with Bloomsbury, introduced into the discourse about the film by Gayatri Spivak, who reads Rosie not only as representing "the British ideological subject of radicalism," but as confronting the failure of the position that Raymond Williams describes in his essay on "The Bloomsbury Fraction": "The early confidence of the position [in the civilized individual], in the period before 1914 has, in its long encounter with all these other and actual social forces, gone, in Leonard Woolf's title, downhill all the way" (cited in Spivak 81). In his essay, Williams grants the Bloomsbury Group a significant role in the development of British culture. Although it remained a fraction of the ruling class, he notes, it was distinguished from it by its awareness of the contradictions in its class position and by its social and political critique, including its social conscience, its anti-imperial and antimilitaristic stance, and its desire for the equality of women. The limits of Bloomsbury's position, he continues, are contained in their basic premise, that of the "civilized *individual*" (Williams 165), which ultimately split the public from the private sphere and left class formations in place: "The social conscience, in the end, is to protect the private consciousness" (167). Yet Williams does not diminish what the group stood for or the genuineness of its critique; its position, he argues, must be understood historically and distinguished from its naturalization as the far less politically radical construct—a "social conscience" or the "civilized" norm—in more recent stages of British culture.

In her reading of the film, Spivak notes that there is "in a very unemphatic way the real representative of the old Bloomsbury fraction" (81): Alice, the character played by Claire Bloom, whose family had been in India for generations, who loved Rafi, and who, as the film progresses, ultimately rejects him. What Spivak doesn't mention is the portrait of Woolf, which not only brings Bloomsbury visibly into the film's political discourse but also provides a visual counterpart to Alice, who is made to look like her. Yet it is Woolf who not only stares down at Rafi after his nightmare but who witnesses the exchange where Rosie defends Rafi ("I don't hate him") against the Black women, Rani and Vivia, who want to confront him for his political crimes; Rani replies, "This is liberalism gone mad!" (Kureishi 38).

But if the Woolf/Bloomsbury configuration connotes politics, it also, as in the past, simultaneously connotes sexuality: bisexuality, homosexuality. As Spivak notes, Rosie is herself heterosexual, but her friends are lesbians. I would add that Alice, again standing in for Woolf, finds immediate acceptance among the lesbians, even as she defends her own sexual choices in terms of the social mores of her time.

Read against this background, the fear located in Virginia Woolf occurs in the necessarily intertwined realms of the political and the sexual. In terms of Rafi's politics, for example, there appears to be no way to decide whether his horror of "Virginia Woolf" is justified or not. We are not, I think, meant to reject Rafi out of hand, despite his politics, just as we are not meant to reject Rosie or Alice. Given this undecidability, "Bloomsbury" and "Virginia Woolf" can be articulated either as moral outrage, in which case we have no empathy with Rafi when he runs in terror from her gaze (or when he commits suicide), or as the failure of the British, represented by Woolf, to understand the complexity of both the colonial and the postcolonial situation ("liberalism gone mad"). In the latter case, Rafi's fear of "Virginia Woolf" is justified and we share it. But there is also more. "Virginia Woolf" may well mirror or reflect Rafi's worst nightmares, but his nightmares, as the film progresses, have as much to do with the breakdown of his expectations of "the family" and "home" as they do with his political past. And within this latter discourse the Woolf/Bloomsbury configuration is troped once again as a threat to manhood, heterosexuality, marriage, and the patriarchy: a threat to the family that Rafi had, ironically, abandoned earlier but wants Sammy and Rosie to reproduce, in part by having children. He is, in fact, quite explicit on this point in a scene with Rosie where he associates her feminism with lesbianism—and childlessness. Not only Woolf but Albee's Martha, both of them childless women, stand behind Rosie here.

Within the context of a (patriarchal) sexual discourse, then, Rafi has clearly defined fears of Virginia Woolf; Sammy, I suspect, shares at least some of them, although he would never admit it. Where Kureishi and the film stand on this configuration is even more problematic, and I want to illustrate why by returning to the figure of Medusa, introduced into the film's discourse through the photograph Kureishi blows up to poster size and displays so prominently in Rosie's room.

My entry here is through an exchange when Rosie asks Sammy, "If you had to choose between sleeping with George Eliot or Virginia Woolf, who would you choose?" and he replies, "On looks alone, I'd go for Virginia" (Kureishi 52). Leaving aside the implications of the comparison of Woolf to Eliot, which has its own history in the materials I've been examining, I want to focus on her reduction to her "looks alone." Woolf, as everyone knows, was an extraordinary looking woman, and we know this to a great extent from the many photographs of her that have made their way into the public domain. Probably the most famous is the photograph of Virginia Stephen by G. C. Beresford, taken in 1902, when she was twenty (figure 7).[20] Here we see the young Virginia, in profile, looking off into the distance. This is the photograph that appeared on the front cover of Bell's biography and in many of the reviews; it appears now on the

Figure 7.
Virginia Stephen at age twenty. Photograph by George Charles Beresford.
(National Portrait Gallery, London)

cover of the book of portraits from the National Portrait Gallery, London, as well as providing the model for the images of Woolf seen on t-shirts and mugs. This is the beautiful daughter of the beautiful Julia Jackson Duckworth Stephen, who was herself the model for her aunt, the famous Victorian photographer Julia Margaret Cameron, as well as for the painter Edward Burne-Jones. (Again, photographs of both Woolf's mother and sisters often display the family profile: see figures 8–9.) Woolf wrote an introduction to a collection of Mrs. Cameron's photographs and clearly had an interest in the field, allowing herself, however grudgingly, to be photographed by some of

Figure 8.
Julia Duckworth Stephen, Virginia Woolf's mother. Photograph by Woolf's
great-aunt Julia Margaret Cameron. (National Portrait Gallery, London)

the most famous artists of her time. Photographs of Woolf come with
a family and cultural history attached to them.

Woolf's interest in photography, albeit conflicted, resulted in the
numerous photographs of her that are nearly as well known as the
Beresford: the portraits by Man Ray taken in 1934 when Woolf was
fifty-two (figures 2, 10) and the portraits by Gisèle Freund taken in
1939 when Woolf was fifty-seven (figures 11–12). Then, there is the
photograph Kureishi chose for his film, one of three studio portraits

Figure 9.
Left: Vanessa Stephen (Woolf's sister), *center:* Stella Duckworth (Woolf's half-sister), and Virginia Stephen. Photograph by H. & R. Stiles.

taken by Lenare at Vita Sackville-West's request in 1929 (figure 13; see also 14).[21] Significantly, this is almost the only photograph where Woolf looks more or less directly into the camera and hence at the viewer. Woolf is portrayed neither in the pose associated with female (for example, Mary's) receptivity, the profile, or staring into the distance. Staring in our direction, the portrait poses a series of questions associated with the female gaze: about what happens when women, traditionally troped as the object of the gaze, look back.

One answer, of course, is that she becomes Medusa. Here, Woolf, who herself had written, "What does one fear?—the human eye," becomes the woman who looks, and in Stephen Heath's formula, "If the woman looks, the spectacle provokes, castration is in the air, the Medusa's head is not far off" (92). But other renderings besides Freud's are also important here. As one commentator on Medusa's stare explains its power, it is always in front of you, reflecting back to you, as in the mirror, your own image and your own impending death:

> Like the image of yourself reflected by the mirror that always sends back your own gaze, the head of the Gorgo—contrary to the artistic conventions or archaic art where characters are always painted in profile—is always

_____

Figure 10.
Virginia Woolf. Photograph by Man Ray. © 1992 Man Ray Trust—ARS

represented frontally. The glimmer of its staring eyes beams down on its spectators, sending them its fascinating frontal gaze. Whoever sees the head of Medusa is changed in the mirror of its pupils . . . into a face of horror: the phantom-like figure of a being who, in passing through the mirror and leaping over the boundary that separates light from darkness, has immediately sunk down into formlessness and is now a nothing, a nonperson. (Vernant 144)

No wonder Rafi, shadowed in the film by the victims of his torture and his rejection by Rosie and Alice, fears Woolf's stare.

Figure 11.
Virginia Woolf. Photograph © Gisèle Freund / Photo Researchers.

But Woolf's photographs in general, not just the Lenare photograph, prove frightening to their viewers. The history of Woolf's public
image provides us with a history of reviewers/critics reading Woolf's
character from her photographs, a history in which the photograph
that accompanies a review, including its caption, becomes almost as
important as the review itself. Listen, for example to Diana Trilling,
reviewing, nastily, the reissue of *The Common Reader* and a new
collection of Woolf's essays in 1948; the photograph referred to is
by Man Ray (figure 2).

Figure 12.
Virginia Woolf. Photograph © Gisèle Freund/Photo Researchers. Fresco in background was painted by Vanessa Stephen Bell.

Probably anyone acquainted with the name Virginia Woolf is familiar with the remarkable photograph of her which has so regularly appeared along with her work—the long tense face at once so suffering and so impervious, the large, too-precisely socketed eyes and the full, too-precisely outlined mouth rimmed with humor but also with conscious vanity, the aristocratic nose and the surely troublesome hair dressed in such defiance of whatever fashion. Unmistak-

Figure 13.
Virginia Woolf. Photograph by Lenare.

ably it is the portrait of an extreme feminine sensibility, of a spirit so finely drawn that we can scarcely bear to follow its tracings. But just as unmistakably it is the portrait of a pride of mind a thousand times more imposing than an army of suffragettes with banners. Here without question—we decide merely on appearances—is someone who conforms to the rules of neither the feminine nor the feministic game, someone who demands that we recognize her as a quite special instance of her sex. ("Virginia Woolf's Special Realm" 1)

Trilling then provides an answer to the question of why critics have treated Woolf so specially: that artists, like most people, pretty much get the response they ask for. Her own response to Woolf's photographic image illustrates beautifully the process that naturalizes the photographic message as purely denotative: as inherent in the image and not in the cultural codes of the producer and/or consumer. Trilling, we are supposed to believe, contributes nothing to the process; we might wonder how much this is a mirror image.

Trilling is not alone: the reviewers of both *A Writer's Diary* and of Bell's biography consistently make unexamined, unself-conscious extrapolations from the photograph to the woman to the works. Mark Schorer, reviewing the *Diary* in the *New Republic*, writes: "Fear. This is what a stranger, who knew her face only from the many august and sometimes admonitory photographs, would least have expected to find in her. But fear, by which one means uncertainty about her own worth, was apparently among her first qualities" (19). The photograph here is one by Lenare (figure 14). The fear Schorer is writing about is Woolf's fear of reviews; what I hear is the reviewer's fear.

By the time I had absorbed the dismissive review of the *Diary* by Joseph Wood Krutch, accompanied by a Freund photograph (figure 11) that bears the caption "Virginia Woolf: 'morbidly affected,'" and the far more positive review by Elizabeth Bowen that uses another Freund photo (figure 12), captioned "Virginia Woolf: 'Praise and fame must be faced'"—not to mention the review of Bell's biography where Beresford's profile (figure 7) is captioned "Virginia Woolf: Gothic Madonna" (Oberbeck)—I had become convinced that any study of Woolf's iconicity is inseparable from her photographic images. An example from a writer with a very different perspective underlines the point: Jill Johnston reviewing the Bell biography in *The Village Voice*. Johnston is explaining why the revelations about Woolf's sexual history, including the incest, gave her a shock:

> Growing older and studying photos of her it might occur to me fleetingly that here was a woman who couldn't possibly have enjoyed sex. I suppose I would try to imagine her in bed and I couldn't even see her in a nightgown much less in bed. If she ever did anything besides pose for the portrait I was looking at it would be sitting at calculated ease in a slightly stuffy victorian drawing room serving tea. (27)

But then Johnston turns this traditional reading of Woolf's image around: with the knowledge of Woolf's sexual history provided by Bell, Johnston, author of *The Lesbian Nation* and an outspoken advocate of radical feminism, not only criticizes Bell's argument that the incest prevented her from "normal" sexuality—heterosexuality—but makes an argument that Woolf would almost certainly have been sexually attracted to women anyway.

Johnston's subversive move emphasizes how firmly battles around Woolf's status as icon are linked to battles about her image in the most literal or visual sense of the term.[22] John Rodden, locating the etymology of "reputation" or repute in the process of re-thinking ("L. re-putare, to think again"), in the image created through the Other's perception (55), defines that image as a "visual representation—'a picture made out of words'"; his study of Orwell is framed as a tour through a portrait gallery (5). Later he argues that without a "face . . . the clear image of the literary (and sometimes private) personality," a writer will neither move beyond literary circles and into the mass media nor cross the "inter-generational divide" (91). For Rodden, the discourse of image, face, and portrait remains metaphoric, operating through verbal portraits of the man. In Woolf's case, we have to take Rodden literally: to see the photographs and the uses to which they are put as central, not peripheral, to the conflicts inscribed in her construction as cultural icon. David Levine, for example, chose the Beresford profile as the model for the famous drawing that first appeared with Elizabeth Hardwick's sarcastic review of Woolf, Strachey, and Bloomsbury in 1973; he chose, that is, to caricature the familial face. In contrast, the publicists for the Women's Center at the University of Massachusetts in the early 1970s chose a Lenare photograph (figure 14) as the model for a poster that also includes a defiant passage from *Three Guineas*: "And let the daughters of uneducated women . . . sing, 'We have done with war! We have done with tyranny!' And their mothers will laugh from their graves, 'It was for this we suffered obloquy and contempt! Light up the windows of the new house, daughters! Let them blaze!'" Rather than being afraid of Woolf or her gaze, these women, reclaiming Medusa's power as their own, used her as a talisman. Like the mothers in Woolf's passage, like Cixous's Medusa—but unlike the figures in Albee's play or Rafi in *Sammy and Rosie*—they were laughing.[23]

I want to conclude by returning to what earlier I referred to as the t-shirt phenomenon and link it both to the use of Woolf's image on the UMass poster and to the concept of the gift; for my first Woolf t-shirt, like the UMass poster and almost all of my Woolf objects were gifts: from colleagues, from students, from friends. While the semiotics of t-shirts, their role as conveyers of messages, have been read in numerous ways by cultural critics, and while one could read the Woolf t-shirt in particular, with its reproduction of Woolf's photographic image, as an example of kitsch or commodification or

Figure 14.
Virginia Woolf. Photograph by Lenare.

subcultural resistance, the significance of the t-shirt in its original
manifestation in the 1970s is located elsewhere. To the extent, that
is, that Virginia Woolf was already associated with fear, wearing her
image on one's chest, like Perseus' or Athena's or the Greek warriors'
wearing of Medusa's head on their aegis or shield, became an act of
both defiance and self-protection: a claiming of her powers, including
her powers of agency, anger, and feminism. Equally important, the
role of the t-shirt in the 1970s was performative, rooted in the realm
of doing or initiating. Functioning as a form of "symbolic exchange,"
the circulation of the t-shirt and its status as gift served to counter
the image of Woolf constructed by the Bell biography, including her
artistic and psychological privatization.[24] Bell's biography, that is,

pushed the writings and the writer into the realm of a "high culture" where the genius/artist was divorced from politics and the public realm; it also divorced the woman from her art by depicting her not as a writer but as a case study. In contrast, the exchange of t-shirts by women in the 1970s broke the boundaries between high culture and popular culture, private and public, elite and mass; the result was not only to rewrite Woolf's relationship to the public realm but also to transform her into a sign or token of the possibility of community itself.

IV

It is now, of course, 1992 and things have changed. Last year critics across the United States outdid themselves in praising the theatrical production of A Room of One's Own as a sign of high art, culture, and civilization, even while dissociating it from contemporary feminism. To cite just one example, Howard Kissel writes, "This concern with literature as something beyond special pleading is what raises Woolf above most of her feminist successors. Some of the ideas she articulates are now commonplace. Her lofty, scathingly witty tone, however, is no longer part of feminism. For that, you have to read the anti-feminist Camille Paglia" (see also Simon). Meanwhile, in Britain, Channel 4 refused to broadcast the Masterpiece Theatre version of the play nationally, in part because of its iconoclastic program on Woolf in J'Accuse. For Tom Paulin, the Ulster poet who organized the J'Accuse program, as well as Terry Eagleton, John Lucas, A. S. Byatt, and Angela Carter, the other accusers, Woolf's elevation to the status of cultural icon is comprehensible only in terms of her tragic life, the "fragile beauty of her more flattering portraits," and the misperception that her writings and politics— including her feminism—were a rebellion against Victorian values.[25] This misperception would disappear, they argue, if people actually read her novels, diaries, and letters and were willing to admit how reactionary (in terms of class, imperialism, and anti-semitism) she actually was. Images of Virginia Woolf, we could say, abound, and, "according to the channel under consideration, in a certain sense the meaning of the message changes, and perhaps also its ideological weight" (Eco 149). Although power is involved in this dissemination of "meaning" through the mass media, Umberto Eco argues, its location is multiple and elusive. But given the examples of the play's reception in the press and the TV program, I am less convinced that we have achieved a state of egalitarian blurring.

What is clear from this proliferation of messages is that the performative role played by "Virginia Woolf" as sign and image, the battles waged over her circulation and meaning, are still powerful makers and markers of our culture today. Radically disparate speakers, spread out across the current ideological terrain, claim or disclaim her name and authority in battles about politics, sexuality, cultural values, taste, feminism, anger, and "political correctness" that shape public perceptions and sometimes public policy. Reputation studies may teach us that the perils of popularity always involve appropriation—the remaking of the figure in one's own image—but that shouldn't blind us to the fact that images have a decidedly material impact on discourses and behavior alike. And to the extent that representations of Woolf still bring with them not only fear but a fear that is linked to gender, to high and low culture, to institutional and social struggles for power, authority, and voice, it is important to continue to ask, Who *is* afraid of Virginia Woolf and what exactly is at stake?

Acknowledgments

This chapter originated as a talk presented to the Department of English, University of California at Santa Barbara, and the Humanities Forum at Dartmouth College; I wish to thank both audiences for their lively interventions. I am also grateful to Michael Cadden, E. Mason Cooley, Richard Corum, Helene Foley, Lynn Higgins, Marianne Hirsch, Richard Kay, Harvey Teres, and, especially, Louise Fradenburg, for talking through the ideas and reading drafts of the chapter. Numerous people have provided me with the references to Woolf that made this work possible; Mark Hussey and Nancy K. Miller, in particular, deserve note and thanks.

Notes

1. After the 1984 Summer Olympics in Los Angeles, where she won the Gold Medal for all around gymnastics, sixteen-year-old Mary Lou Retton's multiple endorsements made her a highly—some would say annoyingly—visible public presence.

2. See, for example, Andrew Ross (42–64) and Harvey Teres. With the recent exception of Janice Radway (708), no one exploring the battles about highbrow, lowbrow, and middlebrow culture refers to Woolf's essay "Middlebrow," a strongly worded defense not only of being a

highbrow but also of the alliance she perceived between high- and lowbrow against middlebrow.

3. The first ad selling David Levine's caricatures of both Woolf and Shakespeare appeared 21 July 1983 (*New York Review of Books* 36); both were pictured in the ad. For a number of years the ad began, "here is your chance to sport your literary preferences" (for example, 18 Jan. 1990: 43). From 29 March 1990 on, however, Woolf is pictured by herself, with the comment: "*The New York Review of Books* is offering David Levine t-shirts to our readers, featuring either Virginia Woolf or William Shakespeare" (44).

4. I am making a distinction here between the academic battles over Woolf's writing, which is not the topic of this essay, and the construction and deconstruction of her public image.

5. I have problematized "household word" to indicate that we are still talking about households with enough access to the media to have seen the film or read/heard about it.

6. Philip Roth's 1965 review of Albee's *Tiny Alice*, "The Play that Dare Not Speak Its Name," which asks, "How long before a play is produced on Broadway in which the homosexual hero is presented as a homosexual, and not disguised as an *angst*-ridden priest . . . ," also deserves note. There was at this time an ongoing debate about the role of homosexuality in the American theater; see also Richard Schechner (9).

7. As reported in the media, the costs of using the Disney tune forced Albee to substitute *Here We Go 'Round the Mulberry Bush* instead ("A Woolf in the Bush").

8. I am grateful to E. Mason Cooley for pointing me to the Flanner article and discussing its contexts.

9. The citations are to the revised version, indicated as "Riddle."

10. Trilling explicitly comments that the new cultural establishment and the new academicism have appropriated what *appears* to be "our most radical impulse in the theatre," and that this phenomenon is not limited to cosmopolitan New York: "Tomorrow it will be everyone in the United States who will have the requisite sophistication for Mr. Albee's play, having been prepared for it, if not by their novels, then by their television programs, and if not by their television programs, by their mass-circulation magazines" ("Riddle" 225–226). Tellingly, Trilling's source is the editor of a "slick women's magazine" (226). See Jonathan Freedman for a reading of the role of the spread of education in the debates about high and popular culture during the 1950s and 1960s.

11. In the *Esquire* version, Albee's use of the title was not unconscious but had a "purpose" (83).

12. See, in particular, Andreas Huyssen, Tania Modleski, "Femininity as Mas(s)querade" and "The Terror of Pleasure," and Patrice Petro. For an example of the fear of the feminization of the academy, see Walter Ong 119–148.

13. For a recent study of the legitimating process, see Jonathan Freedman. All his examples of both high culture figures and popular appropriators are male; women and gender are excluded from the discussion.

14. The last line is Martha's reply: "I . . . am . . . George . . . I . . . am . . ." (242).

15. Exceptions in the classical world include goddesses and the Amazons, a rich source for contemporary feminist writers and critics.

16. See also Muriel Rukeyser's resurrection of the Sphinx in her poem "Myth."

17. The exceptions were Cynthia Ozick, Ellen Hawkes Rogat, and Jill Johnston. Ozick's essay on the biography, published originally in *Commentary* as "Mrs. Virginia Woolf" and reprinted in *Art and Ardor* as "Mrs. Virginia Woolf: A Madwoman and Her Nurse," graphically illustrates this point.

18. Peter Watson, writing about the "cult" for a British audience, reads the comparison to Monroe as "apparently without irony or any trace of humour." More recently, Angela Carter repeated the comparison, this time in conjunction with Woolf's iconicity and her tragic life and death (*J'Accuse*).

19. See Silver, "Textual Criticism as Feminist Practice" 193–194.

20. The dates for this and the following photographs are those provided by Elizabeth P. Richardson in *A Bloomsbury Iconography.*

21. Richardson 295. The Man Ray photos seem to have been commissioned by *Harper's Bazaar* (Richardson 299); the Freund photographs are the result of Victoria Ocampo's intervention. See Freund 131; for Woolf's version, see *L* 6:342–343, 351.

22. See Helen Wussow for an exploration of the use of photographs in biographies of Woolf.

23. See Joan Coldwell and Susan R. Bowers for readings of the feminist reclamation of Medusa. In Coldwell's words, "Under the impact of feminism, a negative horror image of woman as a literally petrifying monster has been triumphantly embraced as an emblem not of abasement but of exaltation" (423). See as well Linda Williams' reading of the woman's look, particularly when directed toward the monster, as "at least a potentially subversive recognition of the power and potency of a non-phallic sexuality" (90).

24. A model for this reading is provided by Modleski's discussion of feminist criticism in "Some Functions of Feminist Criticism; Or, the Scandal of the Mute Body."

25. Gillian Beer, and to some extent Terry Eagleton, are the only witnesses for the defense.

Works Cited

Albee, Edward. *Who's Afraid of Virginia Woolf?* New York: Pocket, 1963.

Bell, Quentin. *Virginia Woolf: A Biography*. New York: Harcourt, 1972.

Bennett, Alan. *Me, I'm Afraid of Virginia Woolf. The Writer in Disguise*.
London: Faber, 1985. 29–72.

Bowen, Elizabeth. "The Principle of Her Art Was Joy." Rev. of *A Writer's
Diary*, by Virginia Woolf. *The New York Times Book Review* 21 Feb.
1954: 1, 26.

Bowers, Susan R. "Medusa and the Female Gaze." *NWSA Journal* 2 (Spring
1990): 217–235.

Brustein, Robert. "Albee and the Medusa-Head." Rev. of *Who's Afraid
of Virginia Woolf?*, dir. Alan Schneider. *The New Republic* 3 Nov.
1962: 29–30.

Cardullo, Bert. Rev. of *Sammy and Rosie Get Laid*, dir. Stephen Frears.
The Hudson Review 41 (Summer 1988): 353–356.

Cixous, Hélène. "The Laugh of the Medusa." In *New French Feminisms*,
ed. Elaine Marks and Isabelle de Courtivron. Amherst: U of Massachusetts P, 1980. 245–264.

Coldwell, Joan. "The Beauty of Medusa." *English Studies in Canada* 11
(Dec. 1985): 422–437.

Coleman, John. Rev. of *Who's Afraid of Virginia Woolf?*, dir. Mike Nichols.
New Statesman 15 July 1966: 103.

Cooke, Alistair. Intro. *A Room to One's Own*, dir. Patrick Garland. *Masterpiece Theatre*. Boston: WGBH. Jan. 1991.

De Lauretis, Teresa. *Alice Doesn't: Feminism Semiotics Cinema*. Bloomington: Indiana UP, 1984.

Driver, Tom F. "What's the Matter with Edward Albee?" *The Reporter* 2
Jan. 1964: 38–39.

Dudar, Helen. "The Virginia Woolf Cult." *Saturday Review* Feb. 1982:
32–34.

Duffy, Martha. "V." Rev. of *Virginia Woolf: A Biography*, by Quentin Bell.
Time 20 Nov. 1972: 93–94

Eco, Umberto. *Travels in Hyper Reality*. New York: Harcourt, 1986.

Flanner, Janet (Gênet). "Letter from Paris." *The New Yorker* 26 Dec.
1964: 67–68.

Freedman, Jonathan. "Autocanonization: Tropes of Self-Legitimation
in 'Popular Culture.'" *Yale Journal of Criticism* 1 (Fall 1987):
203–217.

Freund, Gisèle. *The World in My Camera*, trans. June Guicharnaud. New
York: Dial, 1974.

Funke, Lewis. "News of the Rialto." *New York Times* 21 Oct. 1962: sec.
2: 1; 18 Nov. 1962: sec. 2: 1.

Gardner, Paul. "News of the Rialto." *New York Times* 2 Sept. 1962: sec.
2: 1.

Grenier, Cynthia. "'Virginia Woolf' Claws Way to Compassion in Paris." Rev. of *Qui A Peur de Virginia Woolf?*, dir. Franco Zeffirelli. *New York Herald Tribune* (Paris Edition) 2 Dec. 1964: n.p.

Haight, Gordon S. "Virginia Woolf." Rev. of *Virginia Woolf: A Biography*, by Quentin Bell and *Recollections of Virginia Woolf*, ed. Joan Russell Noble. *The Yale Review* 62 (Spring 1973): 426–431.

Hardwick, Elizabeth. "Bloomsbury and Virginia Woolf." *New York Review of Books* 8 Feb. 1973: 15–18.

Hartung, Philip T. Rev. of *Who's Afraid of Virginia Woolf?*, dir. Mike Nichols. *Commonweal* 22 July 1966: 474–475.

Heath, Stephen. "Difference." *Screen* 19.3 (Autumn 1978): 51–112.

Hertz, Neil. "Medusa's Head: Male Hysteria under Political Pressure." *The End of the Line: Essays on Psychoanalysis and the Sublime.* New York: Columbia UP, 1985. 161–216.

Hewes, Henry. "Who's Afraid of Big Bad Broadway?" Rev. of *Who's Afraid of Virginia Woolf?*, dir. Alan Schneider. *Saturday Review* 27 Oct. 1962: 29.

Huyssen, Andreas. "Mass Culture as Woman: Modernism's Other." Modleski, *Studies in Entertainment.* 187–207

J'Accuse: Virginia Woolf, writ. Tom Paulin and dir. and prod. Jeff Morgan. Fulmar Productions for Channel Four, London. 29 Jan. 1991.

Johnston, Jill. "The Virgins of the Stacks." *The Village Voice* 16 Nov. 1972: 27–28.

Joplin, Patricia Klindienst. "The Voice of the Shuttle is Ours." In *Rape and Representation*, ed. Lynn A. Higgins and Brenda R. Silver. New York: Columbia UP, 1991. 35–66.

Kissel, Howard. "A 'Room' of Great Dimensions." Rev. of *A Room of One's Own*, dir. Patrick Garland. *Daily News* 5 Mar. 1991: 33.

Krutch, Joseph Wood. "Bloomsbury Mistress." Rev. of *A Writer's Diary*, by Virginia Woolf. *Saturday Review* 13 Mar. 1954: 17.

Kureishi, Hanif. *Sammy and Rosie Get Laid: The Script and the Diary.* London: Faber, 1988.

Life. Cover photograph of Elizabeth Taylor. 10 June 1966.

Look. Cover photograph of Elizabeth Taylor. 8 Feb. 1966.

Matthews, Anne. "Deciphering Victorian Underwear and Other Seminars." *New York Times Magazine* 10 Feb. 1991: 42–43, 57–59, 69.

Modleski, Tania. "Femininity as Mas(s)querade." *Feminism Without Women: Culture and Criticism in a "Postfeminist" Age.* New York: Routledge, 1991. 23–34.

———. "Some Functions of Feminist Criticism; Or, the Scandal of the Mute Body." *Feminism Without Women.* 35–58.

———. "The Terror of Pleasure: The Contemporary Horror Film and Postmodern Theory." *Studies in Entertainment.* 155–166.

———, ed. *Studies in Entertainment: Critical Approaches to Mass Culture.* Bloomington: Indiana UP, 1986.

Morris, Meaghan. *The Pirate's Fiancée: Feminism Reading Postmodernism.* London: Verso, 1988.

Muggeridge, Malcolm. Rev. of *Virginia Woolf: A Biography*, by Quentin Bell. *Esquire* Mar. 1973: 38, 42.

Myers, Robert Manson. *From Beowulf to Virginia Woolf.* New York: Bobbs-Merrill, 1952.

————, *From Beowulf to Virginia Woolf*. Rev. ed. with cover by Edward Gorey. Urbana: U of Illinois P, 1984.

New York Review of Books. Advertisement for David Levine T-Shirts. 21 July 1983: 36; 18 Jan. 1990: 43; 29 Mar. 1990: 44.

Nicolson, Nigel. *Portrait of a Marriage*. New York: Atheneum, 1973.

Oberbeck, S. K. "Fragile Genius." Rev. of *Virginia Woolf: A Biography*, by Quentin Bell. *Newsweek* 20 Nov. 1972: 126, 128.

Ong, Walter. *Fighting for Life*. Ithaca: Cornell UP, 1981.

Ozick, Cynthia. "Mrs. Virginia Woolf." *Commentary* Aug. 1973: 33–44. Rep. as "Mrs. Virginia Woolf: A Madwoman and Her Nurse." *Art and Ardor*. New York: Knopf, 1983. 27–54.

Petro, Patrice. "Mass Culture and the Feminine: The 'Place' of Television in Film Studies." *Cinema Journal* 25.3 (Spring 1986): 5–21.

Pryce-Jones, David. "The Rules of the Game." Rev. of *Who's Afraid of Virginia Woolf?*, dir. Alan Schneider (London). *Spectator* 14 Feb. 1964: 213–214.

Quart, Leonard. Rev. of *Sammy and Rosie Get Laid*, dir. Stephen Frears. *Cineaste* 3 (1988): 40–41.

Radway, Janice. "The Scandal of the Middlebrow: The Book-of-the-Month Club, Class Fracture, and Cultural Authority." *South Atlantic Quarterly* 89 (Fall 1990): 703–736.

Richardson, Elizabeth P. *A Bloomsbury Iconography*. Winchester: St. Paul's Bibliographies, 1989.

Rodden, John. *The Politics of Literary Reputation: The Making and Claiming of 'St. George' Orwell*. New York: Oxford UP, 1989.

Rogat, Ellen Hawkes. "The Virgin in the Bell Biography." *Twentieth Century Literature* 20 (Apr. 1974): 96–113.

Ross, Andrew. *No Respect: Intellectuals and Popular Culture*. New York: Routledge, 1989.

Roth, Philip. "The Play that Dare Not Speak Its Name." *New York Review of Books* 25 Feb. 1965: 4.

Rukeyser, Muriel. "Myth." *The Collected Poems*. New York: McGraw-Hill, 1978. 498.

Sammy and Rosie Get Laid, writ. Hanif Kureishi and dir. Stephen Frears. London: Cinecom, 1987.

Schechner, Richard. "Who's Afraid of Edward Albee?" *Tulane Drama Review* 7.3 (Spring 1963): 7–10.

Schlesinger, Arthur Jr. "Who's Not Afraid of Virginia Woolf?" Rev. of *Who's Afraid of Virginia Woolf?*, dir. Mike Nichols. *Vogue* 1 Aug. 1966: 59.

Schorer, Mark. "A Writer's Mirror." Rev. of *A Writer's Diary*, by Virginia Woolf. *New Republic* 1 Mar. 1954: 18–19.

Siebers, Tobin. *The Mirror of Medusa*. Berkeley: U of California P, 1983.

Silver, Brenda R. "Textual Criticism as Feminist Practice; or, Who's Afraid of Virginia Woolf Part II." In *Representing Modernist Texts: Editing as Interpretation*, ed. George Bornstein. Ann Arbor: U of Michigan P, 1991. 193–222.

Simon, John. "Two from the Heart, Two from Hunger." Rev. of *A Room of One's Own*, dir. Patrick Garland. *New York* 18 Mar. 1991: 76.

Sontag, Susan. "Notes on 'Camp.'" *Partisan Review* 31 (Fall 1964): 515–530.

Spivak, Gayatri Chakravorty. "In Praise of *Sammy and Rosie Get Laid.*" *Critical Quarterly* 31 (Summer 1989): 80–88.

Teres, Harvey. *Renewing the Left: Politics, Imagination, and the New York Intellectual.* Oxford: Oxford UP, 1996.

Time. Cover photograph of Virginia Woolf and "How Time Passes." Rev. of *The Years,* by Virginia Woolf. 12 Apr. 1937: 93–96.

Trilling, Diana. "The Riddle of Albee's *Who's Afraid of Virginia Woolf?*" *Claremont Essays.* New York: Harcourt, 1964. 203–227.

———. "Virginia Woolf's Special Realm." Rev. of *The Moment and Other Essays* and *The Common Reader,* by Virginia Woolf. *New York Times Book Review* 21 Mar. 1948: 1, 28–29. Rep. as "Virginia Woolf: A Special Instance." *Claremont Essays.* New York: Harcourt, 1964. 87–94.

———. "Who's Afraid of the Culture Elite?" *Esquire* (Dec. 1963): 69–92.

Vernant, Jean-Pierre. "In the Mirror of Medusa." *Mortals and Immortals: Collected Essays,* ed. Froma I. Zeitlin. Princeton: Princeton UP, 1991. 141–150.

Watson, Peter. "Virginia Woolf Follows in Monroe's Footsteps." *Times* (London) 22 Feb. 1982: 22.

Watterson, Bill. *Calvin and Hobbes.* Cartoon. *The Valley News.* White River Junction, VT. 2 Oct. 1990.

"Who's Afraid . . . ." Rev. of *Who's Afraid of Virginia Woolf?,* dir. Mike Nichols. *Newsweek* 4 July 1966: 84.

Williams, Linda. "When the Woman Looks." In *Re-Vision: Essays in Feminist Film Criticism,* ed. Mary Ann Doanne, Patricia Mellencamp, and Linda Williams. Los Angeles: University Publications of America, 1984. 83–99.

Williams, Raymond. "The Bloomsbury Fraction." *Problems in Materialism and Culture.* London: Verso, 1980. 148–169.

"A Woolf in the Bush." *Theatre Arts* Dec. 1962: 8–9.

Woolf, Leonard. "Preface." *A Writer's Diary,* by Virginia Woolf. New York: Harcourt, 1953, vii–x.

Woolf, Virginia. "Jane Austen at Sixty." *Nation and Athenaeum* 15 Dec. 1923: 433–434.

———. "Julia Margaret Cameron." *Victorian Photographs of Famous Men & Fair Women,* by Julia Margaret Cameron. Intro. by Virginia Woolf and Roger Fry. London: Hogarth, 1926. 1–8.

———. *The Letters of Virginia Woolf.* Vol. 6. Ed. Nigel Nicholson and Joanne Trautmann. 6 vols. New York: Harcourt, 1980.

———. "Middlebrow." 1942. Rep. in *Collected Essays.* Vol. 2. New York: Harcourt, 1967. 196–203.

Wussow, Helen. "Virginia Woolf and the Problematic Nature of the Photographic Image." *Twentieth Century Literature* (Spring 1994): 1–14.

Zwerdling, Alex. *Virginia Woolf and the Real World.* Berkeley: U of California P, 1986.

Granite, Rainbow, and the Lure of Language

THE WORD SPLIT ITS HUSK

WOOLF'S DOUBLE VISION OF

MODERNIST LANGUAGE

Bonnie Kime Scott

These queer little sand castles, I was thinking. . . . Little boys making sand castles. . . . Each is weathertight, & gives shelter to the occupant. . . . But I am the sea which demolishes these castles. . . . What is the value of a philosophy which has no power over life? I have the double vision. I mean, as I am not engrossed in the labour of making this intricate word structure. I also see the man who makes it. I should say it is only word proof not weather proof. We all have to discover the natural law & live by it. . . . I am carrying on, while I read, the idea of women discovering, like the 19th century rationalists, agnostics, that man is no longer God.

Virginia Woolf, *Diary* 18 November 1940

In private fantasies, like this late diary entry, as in formal essays like "Modern Fiction" and "The Narrow Bridge of Art," Virginia Woolf initiated a continuing feminist challenge to the high temples, reconstructed labyrinths, and reinforcing scaffoldings erected by the Godlike men of literary modernism. She goes on to list T. S. Eliot as one of the "little boys" building castles for her engulfment. Her assessment of men of the next generation, "The Leaning Tower," detected a privileged architecture already tilting from new, outside social and political forces (*Collected Essays* 2:

Originally published in *Modern Fiction Studies*, Autumn 1988.

170–172). Through a series of architectural and natural metaphors, Woolf found the structure and power to declare that, as a woman, she had a different, more varied relation to language than many of her male contemporaries. Her female critical persona may assume the position and strength of a natural demolishing agent, the sea. Or she may visit the leaning tower, but unlike its inhabitants, she need not remain. She has her own philosophy that valorizes life, and she is able to read the word-builder as well as the word; her "natural law" enveloping "watertight" or inescapable constructions becomes, not simply an opposed alternative, but a new process, a "double vision" of modernist language.[1]

Woolf's frequent discussions of words articulate a quest or desire for new effects, serving new subjects, as is typical of modernists. Woolf repeatedly seeks "transparency" in words (for example, "A Sketch" 93). This is not wishing them away, or aspiring to simple representation; I do see it as connected to her struggle against the materialism of the Edwardians and the egotistical display of the moderns. She shows a double focus in saying that she wants to write "from deep feeling and not just love of words" (*Diary* 2: 248). Her comment in "Modern Fiction" that "it is a mistake to stand outside examining 'methods'" (*Collected Essays* 2: 108) is related to this attitude. In the notebook she kept while first reading *Ulysses*, she shows competence in keeping track of "method," as the text seemed to dictate. But the author's ability to get "thinking" into language interested her more than his "machinery" ("Modern Novels" notebook).

There is much in Woolf's sea fantasy to resonate with and still to direct contemporary feminist theory on both sides of the Atlantic. In a manner that suggests the French feminism of Julia Kristeva, Woolf questions the static, retentive qualities of phallogocentrism and disrupts the "phallic position" in cultures where "speaking subjects are conceived of as masters of their speech" (Kristeva 165). The adequacy of Kristeva's depiction of woman's relation to language is more problematic. Woman's creation of "an imaginary story through which she constitutes an identity" could serve to describe Woolf's repeated creation of fantasies, both in her diary and her essays, but it need not be taken as a negative symptom. Kristeva's statement that in women's writing, "language seems to be seen from a foreign land . . . from an asymbolic, spastic body," has several interesting points, including its "asymbolic" term and its focus on the body at a primal level and interval of action (166). Woolf could not altogether object to it, having reported that she read *Ulysses* "with spasms of wonder, of discovery" (*Diary* 5: 353). But in its suggestion of abnormality and limitation of Woolf to a remote asymbolic position, Kristeva's statement misses the mobility and power of the metaphors and

fantasy-making processes that we shall be examining.[2] Still developing the fantasy of the epigraph, Woolf had to remind herself that it
was "essential to remain outside" (*Diary* 5: 340), implying choice,
or perhaps the temptation to linger on the shore after demolishing
castles. In sharing with her readers a concern about egotism and
isolation from life and history, she wrote as one capable of such things
("Modern Fiction").

Kristeva's paradigms for women writers come out of Jacques
Lacan's theories of origination of language, which associate the symbolic order of the word with the law of the father, signified by the
stiffened phallus, suggested in the erected sand castles of Woolf's
fantasy exposition. This phallic model applies to men's provision of
the word to women in Woolf's novels, as we shall see. For numerous female-associated word origins and preverbal expressions, it is
useful to turn to Kristeva's definition of the semiotic, prelanguage,
associated with a "pre-Oedipal" mother who precedes gender differentiation. Characterized by "basic pulsations" (the "spastic body"
of "Oscillation"), neither sign nor position, the semiotic is a mobile,
"provisional articulation," admitting analogy only to "vocal or kinetic
rhythm."[3] It resembles Woolf's tidal sea, and we will see it again in
mud and water imagery and syllabic utterances frequently associated with elderly women in Woolf. In the texts we shall examine, the
preverbal is not the narrow, mad, withdrawn assignment resisted in
experientially based Anglo-American feminist criticism.[4] It pressures
conscious, verbal areas, entering the social world of doubly visioned
word-workers. These are Woolf's adult characters, living out the
historical and social crises of the early twentieth century, subject to
decaying patriarchal laws of gender in life, language, and art.

The outsider position Woolf's persona occupies as the sea is
suggestive of the sociological "wild zone" of women's shared experiences and discourses hypothesized by the American "gynocritic" Elaine
Showalter ("Wilderness" 184–187), and of Woolf's own conception
of the "outsider's society," developed in her most obviously political
work, *Three Guineas* (106–121), and in much recent "lupine" Woolf
criticism.[5] It is worth noting, however, that in the diary entry and
in fictional metaphors we shall be considering, Woolf uses the first
person, in a contemplative strain that she often takes when expressing her position toward words. I take this to be the groundwork for
collective visions. She does partake of a previous, ongoing tradition
of "women discovering" in the opening fantasy. Sandra Gilbert and
Susan Gubar have used the oppositional model of a battle of the
sexes as the central paradigm of their reading of twentieth-century
literature, *No Man's Land*. In one aspect, Woolf does storm the male
castle. But her contemplative maneuver of becoming the sea in order

to do so moves this conflict to a more cosmic and spiritual level, and depends on metaphorical expression—action in figurative or literary use of words.

The tradition of assigning male creativity to architectural metaphors—the construction of castles and towers—is classical; modernist men embraced it and the practice is ongoing in feminist criticism. Wyndham Lewis, one of the harshest critics of the feminine in Woolf (*Men without Art* 170), advertised an architectural, mechanical, urban age in *Blast* and his manifestoes of vorticism. It was T. S. Eliot who first erected a classical scaffolding for Joyce's *Ulysses* ("*Ulysses*, Order and Myth"), a work that opens in a tower (although interestingly one from which an impoverished Irish would-be artist will be locked out).[6] More recently, Maria DiBattista finds that Woolf adopted the ordered, sequential "narrative scaffolding" of *Ulysses* for *Mrs. Dalloway* but found it unsuited to her essentially different mind, which contrasted "feminine reticence" to "garrulous virility and its generative improvidences" ("Joyce, Woolf" 100, 112). Recalling Joyce's interest in the creations of Daedalus, Carolyn Heilbrun charges that "in concentrating on the labyrinth, he lost Ariadne's thread." In *Woman and Nature,* Susan Griffin reformulates the previous male architectural design of the "labyrinth" to accommodate fully realized women and men (159–161).

A second (but not necessarily oppositional) set of metaphors locates the origin of language in feminine-associated nature. This too has a tradition, one that feminists must entertain with caution. Hélène Cixous has critiqued the Western, hierarchical binaries of Culture/ Nature, Man/Woman, as "always the same metaphor . . . beneath all its figures, wherever discourse is organized" (63). The natural and contemplative modes detected in Woolf suggest an affinity to Romantic tradition, an aspect of modernism suppressed in much of the canonical criticism from Eliot to Hugh Kenner.[7]

As a natural metaphor, in addition to the seascape of the epigraph, I want to introduce the seed-scape of "the word split its husk," a phrase taken from *Mrs. Dalloway*. Woolf frequently uses figures of words as seeds, usually sown by female or androgynous planters;[8] the process suggests a compos[t]ing of the word in mud or water and encompasses the swelling and exploding into life of the germinating seed. To humans experiencing it as fantasy, it evokes or may even promote sexual orgasm and is not insistent or dependent upon heterosexual activity. It also provides a strategy for writing about the body, a resistance discussed in "Professions for Women," where a fantasized young woman writer sends her imagination fishing, only to have it dashed against "*to speak without figure* . . . something about the body, about the passions which it was unfitting for her as a woman to say" (*Collected Essays* 2: 287–288, emphasis mine). The seed metaphor relates in a limited way to Derrida's linguistic concept of "dissemination" with its figure of sowing.[9] It also evokes the mythic traditions of Demeter, the goddess of the corn and Persephone, visitor to darkness and consumer of seeds. Woolf's friend Jane Harrison, as a feminist classicist and an expert on rare languages, was certainly a resource for metaphors attached to ancient myth, religion, and ritual.[10] Woolf's water imagery has, understandably, been associated with a death wish—most notably by James Naremore. I am suggesting a more positive process. The sea at high tide rises to the castle, representing an advance, not a retreat into death. While the seed's germination process requires falling into dark and treacherous territory, it offers the prospect of renewal. Elaine Showalter's controversial reading of Woolf's room as "both sanctuary and prison" (*A Literature* 264) can also be revised once we are aware of germination of language in apparent retreat. Even Woolf's sense of modernist fragmentation has a positive association, as the husk splits and drops away from the emerging germ. These figures of water, mud, and seed envelop the signifier in the signified. The process must be carried on with painstaking observation, receptivity, silence, and patience, qualities Woolf assigned to women in their conventional social roles (*A Room* 69–71).

The physical qualities of engulfing sea and seed have affinities to the description of the "psychological sentence" of the "feminine" gender that Woolf identified in Dorothy Richardson's writing—an experimental sentence "of a more elastic fibre than the old, capable of stretching to the extreme, of suspending the frailest particles, of enveloping the vaguest shapes." In the spirit of her epigraph, Woolf considers the double vision of the woman (Richardson) as well as the words. She admires the fact that Richardson's sentence is undertaken with an attitude of neither pride nor fear "of anything she may discover in the psychology of her own sex" ("Dorothy Richardson" 191).[11]

Rapture and self-empowering consciousness are aspects of Woolf's primordial experience of words, recorded in "A Sketch of the Past." This essay on her earliest childhood memories evokes both seaside and garden settings appropriate to the natural metaphors of sea and seed. She records three "moments of being." The first and third show initial helplessness at male violence—a pummeling by her brother Thoby and a man's suicide. The only satisfactory one emotionally comes from contemplation of a simple, natural system: "I was looking at the flower bed by the front door; 'That is the whole,' I said. I was looking at a plant with a spread of leaves; and it seemed suddenly plain that the flower itself was a part of the earth; that a ring enclosed what was the flower; and that was the real flower; part earth; part flower." She has words for it, "This is the whole." With maturity came the linguistically aided ability to respond to shocks of violent male events. "I make it real by putting it into words. . . . The wholeness means that it has lost its power to hurt me. . . . It is the rapture I get when in writing I seem to be discovering what belongs to what." Perhaps she sees what the man belongs to. Her ultimate sense of awareness comes when she merges personally with word and life, quite apart from any male predecessor (she mentions Shakespeare and Beethoven), and with no recourse to a divine model: "There is no God; we are the words; we are the music; we are the thing itself" (71–72).

Mrs. Dalloway provides a series of encounters with the word by characters of both sexes. Authority figures, particularly men, are an important source of words, and only men engage in actual writing. Mrs. Dalloway's first and most persistent memories of her former suitor, Peter Walsh, are his word performances, "It was his sayings one remembered" (4). In their early failed relationship, Peter tried to supply Clarissa with her critical vocabulary, and—more subtly— with the aesthetic and world vision attached: "She owed him words: 'sentimental,' 'civilised'; they started up every day of her life as if he guarded her" (53–54). They also confined her and defined her, to some extent, for life, despite the fact that she resisted a permanent alliance with him.[12] An interesting irony about Peter's supposedly memorable sayings is that Clarissa readily alters his words. A comment, "Musing among the vegetables?" shifts in her memory to "I prefer men to cauliflowers," and by the end of the paragraph the cauliflowers have become cabbages (4)—a plentitude of plant life, at least. Clarissa's looseness with words includes an amusing, momentary difficulty re- calling Peter's name. Peter's words were not always constructive and amusing; they could work horrors, as they did when his word "star- gazing?" interrupted Clarissa's overpowering feeling of love for Sally at Bourton. In her yielding to "the charm of women," we encounter for the first time a muted figure, both of female sexual anatomy and germinating seed. She had felt "the world come closer, swollen with some astonishing significance, some pressure of rapture, which split its thin skin and gushed and poured with an extraordinary alleviation over the cracks and sores!" (46–47). This unarticulated, sexually sug- gestive, semiotic, lesbian event offers immediacy of the world without words, "inner meaning almost expressed" (47). Inspired by another woman and self-alleviating, it is preferable to anything Peter offered in words. It remains as a pressure on her consciousness.

An older, dryer Mrs. Dalloway has a routine encounter with words of authority on her morning walk—an errand notably in quest of flowers. "A disc, inscribed with a name" extended to a police officer by a chauffeur is "magical" to this Clarissa. It "burnt its way through . . . to blaze among candelabras, glittering stars, breasts stiff with oak leaves, Hugh Whitbread and all his colleagues, the gentlemen of England, that night in Buckingham Palace." Penetration and façade are attributes of this fantasy, and Clarissa identifies it with the party she plans. "She stiffened a little; so she would stand at the top of her stairs." We might suspect that the word effect of officialdom is just as inhibiting as Peter's words. Clarissa's stiffness atop the architecture of stairs has a phallic, monumental, artificial quality, suggesting artificial support. She has lost the liquid rapture of preverbal emotion.[13]

The most remarkable word display in *Mrs. Dalloway* is the much-commented upon skywriting—an event which escapes Mrs. Dalloway's recording.[14] The very process of writing words, as reported by the narrator, is alarming. It "bored ominously into the ears of the crowd" and depends upon a futuristic machine, an instrument of the recent war, the airplane, "dropping dead down." Among the observers are a "stiff white baby" and a woman who seems to be sleep-walking, suggesting stultification by the word. Efforts at decipherment produce ugly words—trade names.[15] The narrator ambiguously reports, "The clouds to which the letters E, G, or L had attached themselves moved freely, as if destined to cross from West to East on a mission of the greatest importance which would never be revealed, and yet certainly so it was—a mission of the greatest importance" (29). In a political dimension, the narrative suggests an all too typical pattern of the Western imposition upon the East. As in Woolf's *Diary* entry, nature dissipates the word. Only in this dissipation is there "exquisite beauty," and this is perceived by Septimus Smith, a man marginalized by his war-scrambled brain. Septimus' process with the sky words borders on madness. He sees "signals" and relates them to his own "mission" but at this point does not know the words and language that will elaborate this role. The sounds of letters read from the sky bring a second natural element into play; trees come to life. For the moment, he controls these hallucinations (31).

Like Clarissa Dalloway, Septimus receives words of authority. The word "time" is uttered by his wife Rezia to remind Septimus of his appointment with mental authority, Dr. Bradshaw. This man will later sentence Septimus to an institution (in effect, to death) with the authority of his word, "proportion," and the threat of enforcement by law. Bradshaw is notably uncomfortable with Septimus' "educated" use of words—particularly the punning "Holmes' homes" (147). For one thing, Septimus' phrase is inaccurate about ownership, and Bradshaw corrects this, "One of *my* homes, Mr. Smith." The original pun has the additional dimension of metonymy, where Holmes becomes the architecture those of his profession have constructed to confine and convert mental and verbal disorder. Woolf's choice of a male outsider as punster may indicate a connection of word play with male expression. Woolf was capable of such punning in her letters, most notably in reaction to Wyndham Lewis' attack on her feminine version of modernism.[16]

When Rezia utters the word "time" in the park, Septimus associates it with an apocalyptic event—the return of his slain soldier love, Evans, and his own mission. His apprehension of "time" presents an obvious seed figure. There is an explosion: "The word 'time' split its husk; poured its riches over him; and from his lips fell like shells, like shavings from a plane, without his making them, hard, white, imperishable words, and flew to attach themselves to their places in an ode to Time, an immortal Ode to Time." It is then that Evans emerges: "But no mud was on him; no wounds; he was not changed" (105). The spontaneous flowing and splitting resemble Mrs. Dalloway's unverbalized expression of lesbian love, cited earlier, a feeling comparable to Septimus' unacknowledged longing for Evans (Lilienfeld 3). The unuttered, emerging word articulates desire. The split husk issues forth beautiful materials, shells, and shavings. Despite the recurrent figure of shells as protective, secreted forms, molded to life (for instance, Bernard, *The Waves* 255), Septimus' shells and shavings are not living things; they are not planted and cannot grow as a living seed would. They attach to an established literary form, the ode, and have the hard, monumental immortality imagined in Keats's "Ode on a Grecian Urn." They lead Septimus to the delusion of becoming a Godlike man with a divine mission, a heroic pose satirized by Woolf. That Septimus hears Greek from sparrows (a symptom taken from Woolf's own illness [Bell 1: 90]) also suggests nature's music confined in a classical form. In Septimus' hallucination, Evans comes forth "unchanged," untouched by regenerative mud; the results will be disastrous to Septimus. He has only partial access to an alternate process of word generation.

Additional encounters with words are experienced by Peter Walsh and Rezia Smith. Peter encounters "a frail quivering sound, a voice bubbling up without direction, vigour, beginning or end, running weakly and shrilly and with an absence of all human meaning into

> ee um fah um so
> foo swee too eem oo—

the voice of no age or sex, the voice of an ancient spring spouting from the earth." It is a lost song of love.[17] Although initially ungendered, its singer is identified as a battered, primeval woman (122–123). Schlack associates her with Ceres (152–153). There is a form of eternity, not static permanence, but a natural cycle of compos[t]ing here, as the figure witnesses "the passing generations—the pavement was crowded with bustling middle-class people—vanished, like leaves, to be trodden under, to be soaked and steeped and made mould of by that eternal spring—

> ee um fah um so
> foo swee too eem oo" (124).

Rezia Smith, whom Schlack connects to Ceres and strewn flowers (53), also plays briefly with words. Separated from Septimus briefly in the park, Rezia's words express longing; they fall unheard. "Her words faded. So a rocket fades. Its sparks, having grazed their way into the night, surrender into it, dark descends, pours over the outlines of houses and towers; bleak hillsides soften and fall in." She cries to no one "by the fountain in Regent's park," and her darkness resembles the ancient England that preceded the advent of the Romans (34–35). Outcast women's words tend back to earth burial and the primordial. Septimus' deadly, ugly resting place on area railings is transformed by Rezia's imagination into "cornfields," a "hill, somewhere near the sea . . . stirrings among dry corn, the caress of the sea, as it seemed to her, hollowing them in its arched shell and murmuring to her laid on the shore, strewn she felt, like flying flowers over some tomb" (228). His final gesture, and even his last words, "I'll give it you," are communicated, lodged in Clarissa, who understands why he has "thrown it away" (280–284). The man is completed in women's perceptions of him.

The Waves and *Between the Acts* both feature natural garden settings and reinforce the metaphors and fantasies of word generation of *Mrs. Dalloway*. Susan, the maternal, rural, and earth-bound "character" of *The Waves*, is the most obvious sower of literal seeds in *The Waves*. She deals in "silence" or a one-word answer to her lover (98–100). Bernard, the personage who comes closest to narrator, spokesperson, and author in the work, has great facility with words. Like James Joyce and his persona, Stephen Dedalus, Bernard keeps an alphabetical notebook to assert control over words. He glibly provides the phrases needed for public occasions and much of the narrative that summarizes the five other characters. But by midlife he is dissatisfied with his derivative, "meretricious," soon to be forgotten phrases and wants finally to speak "in a child's words of one syllable; without shelter from phrases" (287). He drops his "book, stuffed with phrases" for a charwoman to collect and anticipates a time of earth burial "when the storm crosses the marsh and sweeps over me where I lie in the ditch unregarded. I need no words" (295). Rhoda, the least successful character in social situations, is inarticulate; she cannot make ideas cohere. As frustrated word-workers, both Rhoda and Bernard try the planting figure we have seen previously: she "flung words in fans like those the sower throws over the ploughed fields" (205). Bernard throws "his mind out as a man sows seeds" (217). The bare ground is unpromising for both planting efforts, although I think the characters of *The Waves* function better with the alternate process of word generation than did those of *Mrs. Dalloway*. Escaping his daily existence to mourn Percival in an art gallery, Bernard becomes a patient sower, aware of the differences between writer and artist:

> Something lies deeply buried. For one moment I thought to grasp it. But bury it, bury it: let it breed, hidden in the depths of my mind some day to fructify. After a long lifetime, loosely, in a moment of revelation, I may lay hands on it, but now the idea breaks in my hand. Ideas break a thousand times for once that they globe themselves entire. They break; they fall over me "Line and colours they survive. . . ." (157–158)

Rhoda has an internal language that silently creates primitive landscapes and basic geometric shapes; she reconceptualizes the dead young man, as had Rezia and Mrs. Dalloway in the case of Septimus Smith:

> Percival by his death, has made me this gift, let me see the thing. There is a square; there is an oblong. The players take the square and place it upon the oblong. They place it very accurately; they made a perfect dwelling place. Very little is left outside. (163)[18]

But Rhoda is outside and her gestures are more fluid and explosive: "The sweetness of this content overflowing runs down the walls of my mind" (163). She lets loose, "into the wave that dashes upon the shore, into the wave that flings its white foam to the uttermost corners of the earth I throw my violets, my offering to Percival" (164). She also envisions dark pools (164) and gazes into ponds with minnows (136).[19] Her images of the desert (164) and her journey to look from a hill in Spain into Africa display a gravitation toward the primitive. Rhoda, like Woolf in the opening quotation, identifies with the sea: "I am like the foam that races over the beach . . ." (130). In her last fantasy of the novel, she plants herself with a "sheaf" or "garland" in the waves, welcoming her own "dissolving" (206).[20]

The visual, the inarticulate, and the word of one syllable planted in dirt or water find their ultimate expression with Miss La Trobe, the lesbian playwright of *Between the Acts*, a self-proclaimed "outcast" who scribbles on the margins of the manuscripts she writes for community performance (211). In the course of her drama, she uses pageantry, dancing, and mirrors that deconstruct, not mere words, but worlds, ages, and people's images of themselves. She is assisted by ludicrous, low elements—the "primeval voice" of a cow expressing "dumb yearning for a lost calf when the wind rose, and in the rustle of the leaves even the great words became inaudible" (140), and raucous starlings, as we shall see. In her sensitivity to the primeval, she is doubled throughout the work by old Lucy Swithin, who follows primeval history despite the authoritative scorn of her brother Bart, the family patriarch. Like Rhoda, Lucy is an observer of fishponds. She "gazed at the lily pool, 'All gone,' she murmured, 'under the leaves'" (204), an interpretation of nature and time reminiscent of the old woman's spring of song in *Mrs. Dalloway*. Lucy cannot directly articulate her tribute, but she does communicate it:

> "You've given me . . ." She skipped, then alighted—"Ever since I was a child I've felt . . ."
> She gazed at Miss La Trobe with a cloudless old-aged stare. Their eyes met in a common effort to bring a common meaning to birth. They failed; and Mrs. Swithin, laying hold desperately of a fraction of her meaning, said: "What a small part I've had to play! But you've made me feel I could have played . . . Cleopatra!" (152–153)

B. H. Fussell has noted the improbability of the Cleopatra identification (272). But Miss La Trobe senses meaning: "You've stirred in me my unacted part," she meant (153). This ill-expressed thanks, the attention to the unarticulated act, and the stirring of feeling in one woman by another reverberates the love Mrs. Dalloway feels for Sally and adds another dimension of desire to the complex relations of characters in Woolf's last novel.[21] "Dispersed are we" is a refrain for La Trobe's pageant, and her self-dispersal has found receptive ground, unpremeditatedly, unpredictably in Lucy.

The process of word generation and communication by Miss La Trobe contrasts to the violent, warring, uncommunicative sexual "perversion," competition, and generation practiced by Giles, Isa, William, Mrs. Manresa, and others of their generation in patriarchal plots that go back to the Greeks. Bound up in the family, Isa is an even more dubious artist than Miss La Trobe. Isa has no audience; her verses are hidden away in account books (15), volumes Woolf learned to dread as a patriarchal weapon while living with her widowed father.

Despite the fact that Miss La Trobe has just completed one play and communicated with Lucy Swithin, she feels no mastery of words. She has a vision of rock and figures but no words: "It would be midnight; there would be two figures, half concealed by a rock. The curtain would rise. What would the first words be? The words escaped her" (210). The rock is as puzzling as Rhoda's monuments. It would take patient contemplation to envision what was obscured by its static mass. The "two figures" have suggested a new creation myth to some; it is not impossible that they hold promise that Giles and Isa may start anew, a view encouraged by their injection into the final sentence of the novel. Yet, since word generation is at stake, the "figures" could even be figures of language, akin to the metaphorical seeds and seas we have been discussing. When words come, they are preceded by Miss La Trobe's drinking or watering them; they spring from the place where they were planted, the primordial mud, and are associated with dumb animals:

> She raised her glass to her lips. And drank. And listened. Words of one syllable sank down into the mud. She drowsed; she nodded. The mud became fertile. Words rose above the intolerably laden dumb oxen plodding through the mud. Words without meaning—wonderful words. (212)[22]

A final fertilizing moment comes in a typical distraction (or inspiration) from nature. The tree outside is suddenly "pelted with starlings," a motif that had first appeared when La Trobe departed her pageant, declaring it a "failure." The birds then "pelted" the tree "like so many winged stones," a description that echoes the cast seed metaphor and commences their devouring of seeds. They also have a semiotic language; they made the tree "a rhapsody, a quivering cacophany, a whizz and vibrant rapture, branches, leaves, birds syllabing discordantly life, life, life, without measure, without stop devouring the tree. Then up! Then off!" (209). They reappear in the final scene, setting off Miss La Trobe's final vision in words: "She set down her glass. She heard the first words" (212).[23] There is no show of words. Readers must collaborate by imagining them.[24]

The eccentric outsider, Miss La Trobe, has gathered and clothed her village performers, wound her gramophone, and mounted an invasion of the patriarchal enclave of Pointz Hall. At the end of the drama, written at the close of Woolf's life, she retreats to mental solitude in the unlikely setting of the village pub. She sinks into the abstract, contemplative phase of her work with words, setting the conditions for a new cycle of creativity. Perhaps, having deconstructed England's past, she focuses more narrowly on her final "orts and scraps and fragments" of the present, upon the privileged but embittered Giles and Isa figures of modern Britain. Her simple, humble composting of writer and word allows a troubled earth to bring forth new words and silently challenges us, Woolf's ultimate collaborators, to discover and read them.

Notes

1. Norman Friedman uses "double vision" to mean a state of balanced subjective and objective perceptions in *To the Lighthouse*, a more passive, stable paradigm than I am suggesting. His discussion of the feminine aspects of water imagery is relevant to my treatment of this metaphor, however. For a more deconstructive model of "conditions of seeing" in Woolf, see Thomas G. Matro, who offers a list of earlier Woolf criticism that, like Friedman's, offers paradigms of aesthetic order and androgynous balance (212–213).

2. Sandra Gilbert and Susan Gubar also resist the "foreign land" positioning of Woolf in relation to language and offer their own set of productive Woolfian fantasy types. In one, a "voyeuristic" role is directed toward interpreting her "affiliation" to earlier women writers. A second fantasy relates more closely to language and male modernists like Joyce—a "fantasy about a utopian linguistic structure—a 'woman's sentence' . . ." used to overthrow "the sentence-as-definitive-judgment, the sentence-as-decree-or-interdiction" (196–205, 228–231). I find more variety in Joycean sentencing than they do and more use for French feminist paradigms of writing the female body, although both of these may reflect the greater emphasis upon metaphors (as opposed to characters and plots) in my analysis.

3. This definition of the semiotic is derived from Toril Moi's translation (161) of Julia Kristeva's *La Revolution du Langage Poétique* (24).

4. For example, Mary Jacobus resists a feminine linguistic domain of "marginal madness or nonsense," where the woman writer encounters "oppression and confinement" (12). See also the Introduction to the special number of *Yale French Studies*, "Feminist Readings: French Texts/American Contexts" (Gaudin et al.) and the cautious essay by Ann Rosalind Jones, "Writing the Body: Toward an Understanding of *l'écriture féminine*" in Elaine Showalter, *The New Feminist Criticism*.

5. See Jane Marcus, Preface, *Virginia Woolf: A Feminist Slant* and her "Still Practice, A/Wrested Alphabet" for application of this term to female literary and artistic communities in Woolf's life. She discusses the history of "lupine" criticism in *Virginia Woolf and the Languages of Patriarchy* (xi). Woolf's admiration of anonymous collective visions is treated sensitively by Maria DiBattista and Brenda Silver.

6. My arguments that Joyce could work from a feminine perspective on language are contained in my *James Joyce* (109–129), a work that repeatedly compares Joyce's literary strategies and metaphors with those of Woolf.

7. Hugh Kenner's neoclassical interpretation of modernism is most evident in his *Dublin's Joyce*. He assigns Woolf a set of "treacly minds"
   in *The Pound Era* (553) and continues the assault on Woolf in *The
   Sinking Island*. For discussions of Woolf's affinities to the Romantics,
   see DiBattista and Beverly A. Schlack.

8. It is an item of interest that Leonard Woolf titled the first volume of
   his autobiography *Sowing*, and although Virginia certainly enjoyed
   their garden, sharing it with women writers like Katherine Mansfield
   and Elizabeth Bowen, and composing *Between the Acts* there, Leonard
   was the more active gardener. The female or androgynous sower is
   a departure from the biblical sense of sowing one's seed, where the
   act usually refers to male procreation.

9. For an analysis of "dissemination" as "a feminist gesture" see Gayatri
   Chakravorty Spivak. Derrida's concept also evades the necessity of
   male insemination. Mud in the scheme of this article may bear some
   function comparable to "hymen" in his paradigm.

10. Woolf's participation in the feminist revision of classical mythology
    impinges upon this essay, particularly in *Between the Acts*. See
    Sandra D. Shattuck on Woolf's resonances with Harrison in her final
    work. Shattuck's discussion of the violence of language in the paral-
    lels with Greek mythology centered in Giles and Isa constitutes one
    vision; Miss La Trobe, on whom I concentrate, suggests a second.

11. See Rachel Blau DuPlessis' discussion of Woolf's feminine psycho-
    logical sentence as a way of "breaking the sentence; breaking the
    sequence" (31–33).

12. Schlack places Peter in the tradition of eighteenth-century critics of
    female foibles (55–56).

13. See Elizabeth Abel for a discussion of a double (male versus female)
    narrative structure in *Mrs. Dalloway*. Abel associates a subordinated
    pre-Oedipal, feminine plot with Bourton, "a pastoral female world
    spatially and temporally disjunct from marriage and the sociopolitical
    world of (Richard's) London" (166).

14. See, for example, DiBattista, "Joyce, Woolf and the Modern Mind"
    (107–109).

15. The opening of *The Voyage Out* offers a comparable scene in which
    Helen Ambrose contends internally with her grief over leaving her
    children while walking through a commercial district of London
    (12).

16. Marcus discusses the importance of Woolf's revision of Lewis' "taking
    the cow by the horns" to "taking the bull by the udders," and her
    coy attribution of the phrase to Vanessa Bell in *Virginia Woolf and
    the Languages of Patriarchy* (136–139). See Lewis (164–167).

17. J. Hillis Miller identifies her song of vanished love as "Allerseelen"
    by Richard Strauss (190). The lyrics feature flowers, heather, and
    "last red asters." Miller's interpretation emphasizes a return from the

dead, a regaining of lost loved ones. Although Miller offers a cyclical paradigm, he argues for a more retentive form than the one that is offered in this essay.

18. Naremore sees the "triumph" and "consolation" of this containment as "fragile and pathetic," as I think Woolf intended (183).

19. Underwater life, down with fish and egglike vegetation, is attractive to the persona of Woolf's "The Mark on the Wall" as well. This is the metaphorical essence of feminine modernism repudiated by Wyndham Lewis.

20. Jinny's own throat becomes a dark breeding place for words: "Words crowd and cluster and push forth one on top of another. . . . The single and the solitary mate, tumble and become many" (*Waves* 104).

21. When her brother tells Lucy she mustn't "thank the author," he is already too late; Lucy has earlier followed her impulse to do so, although she seems not to remember (*Between the Acts* 203, 206–207).

22. Marilyn Brownstein has pointed out to me that the Latinate word "copulated" is used for the fertilizing process in the earlier typescript. See *Pointz Hall*, ed. Mitchell Leaska (117). The later typescript is much like the final version. An interesting detail dropped in the final version is the observation that "wonderful words; attached to nothing" (*Pointz Hall* 433). In contrast, one might recall that the words detected by Septimus Smith in *Mrs. Dalloway* attached themselves to the traditional form of the ode.

23. Trees figure in the reassuring cycle of immortality imagined by Mrs. Dalloway: "somehow in the streets of London, on the ebb and flow of things, here, there, she survived, Peter survived, lived in each other, she being part, she was positive, of the trees at home . . . being laid out like a mist between the people she knew best, who lifted her on their branches as she had seen the trees lift the mist, but it spread ever so far, her life, herself" (12).

24. DiBattista sees this final creative act as an act without an audience (*Virginia Woolf's Novels* 234). I feel that it demands a reader's collaborative turning inward. On words in *Between the Acts* see also Nora Eisenberg and Sallie Sears.

Works Cited

Abel, Elizabeth. "Narrative Structure(s) and Female Development." *The Voyage In: Fictions of Female Development*. Eds. Elizabeth Abel, Marianne Hirsch, and Elizabeth Langland. Hanover: UP of New England, 1983. 161–185.

Bell, Quentin. *Virginia Woolf: A Biography*. 2 vols. London: Hogarth, 1972.

Cixous, Hélène. *The Newly Born Woman*. Trans. Betsy Wing. Minneapolis: U of Minnesota P, 1986.

DiBattista, Maria. "Joyce, Woolf and the Modern Mind." *Virginia Woolf: New Critical Essays*. Eds. Patricia Clements and Isobel Grundy. New York: Barnes, 1983. 96–114.

———. *Virginia Woolf's Novels: The Fables of Anon.* New Haven: Yale UP, 1980.

DuPlessis, Rachel Blau. *Writing beyond the Ending.* Bloomington: Indiana UP, 1985.

Eisenberg, Nora. "Virginia Woolf's Last Words of Words: *Between the Acts* and 'Anon.'" *New Feminist Essays on Virginia Woolf.* Ed. Jane Marcus. Lincoln: U of Nebraska P, 1981. 253–266.

Eliot, T. S. "*Ulysses*, Order and Myth." *Dial* 75 (1923): 480–483.

Friedman, Norman. "The Waters of Annihilation: Symbols and Double Vision in *To the Lighthouse*." *Form and Meaning in Fiction.* Ed. Norman Friedman. Athens: U of Georgia P, 1975. 240–258.

Fussell, B. H. "Woolf's Peculiar Comic World: *Between the Acts*." *Virginia Woolf: Revaluation and Continuity.* Ed. Ralph Freedman. Berkeley: U of California P, 1980. 263–283.

Gaudin, Colette, et al. "Introduction." *Yale French Studies* 62 (1981): 2–18.

Gilbert, Sandra, and Susan Gubar. *No Man's Land: Volume One: The War of the Words.* New Haven: Yale UP, 1988.

Griffin, Susan. *Woman and Nature: The Roaring Inside Her.* New York: Harper, 1978.

Heilbrun, Carolyn. Unpublished paper, Modern Language Association Convention, 1984.

Jacobus, Mary. "The Difference of View." *Women Writing and Writing about Women.* London: Croom Helm, 1974. 10–21.

Kenner, Hugh. *Dublin's Joyce.* Bloomington: Indiana UP, 1956.

———. *The Pound Era.* Berkeley: U of California P, 1971.

———. *The Sinking Island.* New York: Knopf, 1988.

Kristeva, Julia. "From 'Oscillation between Power and Denial.'" Trans. Marilyn A. August. *New French Feminisms: An Anthology.* Eds. Elaine Marks and Isabelle de Courtivron. New York: Schocken, 1986. 165–167.

Lewis, Wyndham. *Men without Art.* London: Cassell, 1934.

Lilienfeld, Jane. "The Genderization of Genre: The Lesbian Subtext of Virginia Woolf's *Mrs. Dalloway*." Unpublished paper, Modern Language Association Convention, 1984.

Marcus, Jane. "Still Practice, A/Wrested Alphabet: Toward a Feminist Aesthetic." *Tulsa Studies in Women's Literature* 3.1/2 (1984): 79–97.

———, ed. *Virginia Woolf: A Feminist Slant.* Lincoln: U of Nebraska P, 1983.

———. *Virginia Woolf and the Languages of Patriarchy.* Bloomington: Indiana UP, 1987.

Matro, Thomas G. "Only Relations: Vision and Achievement in *To the Lighthouse*." *PMLA* 99.2 (1984): 212–224.

Miller, J. Hillis. *Fiction and Repetition.* Cambridge: Harvard UP, 1982.

Moi, Toril. *Sexual/Textual Politics: Feminist Literary Theory.* New York: Methuen, 1985.

Naremore, James. *The World without a Self: Virginia Woolf and the Novel.* New Haven: Yale UP, 1973.

Schlack, Beverly Ann. *Continuing Presences: Virginia Woolf's Use of Literary Allusion.* University Park: Pennsylvania State UP, 1979.

Scott, Bonnie Kime. *James Joyce.* Feminist Readings Series. Brighton: Harvester, 1987.

Sears, Sallie. "Theatre of War: Virginia Woolf's *Between the Acts.*" *Virginia Woolf: A Feminist Slant.* Ed. Jane Marcus. Lincoln: U of Nebraska P, 1983. 212–235.

Shattuck, Sandra D. "The Stage of Scholarship: Crossing the Bridge from Harrison to Woolf." *Virginia Woolf and Bloomsbury: A Centenary Celebration.* Bloomington: Indiana UP, 1987. 278–298.

Showalter, Elaine. "Feminist Criticism in the Wilderness." *Critical Inquiry* 8 (1981): 179–205.

——. *A Literature of Their Own: British Women Novelists from Brontë to Lessing.* Princeton: Princeton UP, 1977.

——, ed. *The New Feminist Criticism: Essays on Women, Literature and Theory.* New York: Pantheon, 1985.

Silver, Brenda. *Virginia Woolf's Reading Notebooks.* Princeton: Princeton UP, 1983.

Spivak, Gayatri Chakravorty. Translator's Preface. *Of Grammatology.* By Jacques Derrida. Baltimore: Johns Hopkins UP, 1976. ix–lxxxvii.

Woolf, Virginia. *Between the Acts.* 1941. New York: Harcourt, 1970.

——. *Collected Essays of Virginia Woolf.* 4 vols. Ed. Leonard Woolf. London: Hogarth, 1966.

——. *The Diary of Virginia Woolf.* 5 vols. Ed. Anne Olivier Bell. San Diego: Harcourt, 1977–1984.

——. "Dorothy Richardson." *Virginia Woolf: Women and Writing.* Ed. Michèle Barrett. London: Women's Press, 1979. 191–192.

——. "The Mark on the Wall." *A Haunted House and Other Stories.* New York: Harcourt, 1970. 37–46.

——. "Modern Novels." Unpublished notebook in Berg Collection, New York Public Library.

——. *Mrs. Dalloway.* 1925. New York: Harcourt, 1953.

——. *Pointz Hall: The Earlier and Later Typescripts of "Between the Acts."* Ed. Mitchell Leaska. New York: University Publications, 1981.

——. *A Room of One's Own.* 1929. San Diego: Harcourt, 1957.

——. "A Sketch of the Past." *Moments of Being.* Ed. Jeanne Shulkind. New York: Harcourt, 1976. 64–107.

——. *Three Guineas.* 1938. New York: Harcourt, 1966.

——. *To the Lighthouse.* 1927. New York: Harcourt, 1964.

——. *The Voyage Out.* 1915. New York: Harcourt, 1948.

——. *The Waves.* 1931. San Diego: Harcourt, 1959.

VIRGINIA WOOLF'S

PEDAGOGICAL SCENES

OF READING

THE VOYAGE OUT, THE COMMON READER,

AND HER "COMMON READERS"

Susan Stanford Friedman

I read—then I lay down the book—& say—what right have
I, a woman to read all these things that men have done?
They would laugh if they saw me.
>   —Virginia Woolf, 1903 Diary (quoted in Alice Fox,
>   "What Right Have I, A Woman?" 249)

[The common reader] is guided by an instinct to create
for himself, out of whatever odds and ends he can come
by, some kind of whole—a portrait of a man, a sketch of
an age, a theory of the art of writing.
>   —Virginia Woolf, The Common Reader (1)

You know the scene, the scene of your students
reading Woolf. If you are not (yet) teachers, you can imagine it; you
can recreate the scene of your own first reading of Woolf. At least for
those of us far from the scenes of elite education, there is (at first)
the confusion, bewilderment in their (our) eyes, the sense of reading on quicksand, the fear of speaking uncertainty, the resistance to
uncovering bafflement—the resistance, period. Think back on To the

Originally published in *Modern Fiction Studies*, Spring 1992.

Lighthouse, you, your students, virginal readers. What is happening? Where are we? Who is thinking? Who is speaking? What time is it? Where (oh *where*) is *the* voice that will make sense of these shifting and sliding voices, moving sometimes even within a single sentence from one center of consciousness to another? The whirl dizzies, the vertigo of reading Woolf for the first time.

We might think that in this postmodern media age—with the multiple, split narratives of a *Northern Exposure* or *L.A. Law*, with the visual montage of startling juxtapositions on MTV, with fragmentation of unitary authority in the competing voices of media anchors whose personalities are more news than the news—that our students would feel right at home with the disruptions of a Woolf text. That most of them do not is a sign of the normative power for the printed page of traditional conventions of representation established by the novel, especially the nineteenth-century realist novel.

We all have our strategies for teaching Woolf, for breaking down this initial resistance, for calming students down, for urging them to take up the challenge. We may contextualize: by setting the scene of Edwardian and postwar England; narrating tales of Bloomsbury, the Stephen household, the marriage to Leonard, the love for Vita, the incidents of incest, the bouts of illness; by staging the grand entrance of modernism; by theorizing the feminist and the feminine. We may show slides of impressionist, postimpressionist, and cubist art or present parallels in filmic technique. We may begin with some short stories—"A Mark on the Wall," "Kew Gardens," "The New Dress"—to build up a careful craft of reading that can be adapted for the longer texts. We may introduce Woolf's textual practice through the voice of the theorist in "Modern Fiction," "Mr. Bennett and Mrs. Brown," and *A Room of One's Own.* We may exhort the students to climb the mountain of textural challenge; the view at the top is worth it, the effort ultimately exhilarating (you can do it; you, the little engine that could). We may lecture or split the class into small groups, each with a task to perform and report. We may "brilliantly" synthesize or sit in the silence until students begin to speak. We may encourage impressionistic responses to what they think they did not understand. We may lead them to unravel a passage, piece by piece. We may dramatize; pound the desk to mark the heartbeat and the tick-tock of the lighthouse beam.

Our strategies, of course, differ by the context in which we teach (where is our classroom? who are our students? how large is the class?); by the kind of course in which Woolf appears (a course in modernism? on women's writing? on the novel? on the short story? the essay? on British literature? on feminist theory? on just Woolf herself?); by our pedagogical principles along the spectrum of authority; and by the various critical methodologies we and our students use (we can all cite the prism of perspectives). We and our students read the Woolf we read through the lens of juxtaposition, through what and who surrounds the presence of the text. Our strategies, of course, must reflect and address those juxtapositions; they are various, historically specific, and individual. This seems obvious. And no different from the pedagogical issues we face in teaching other writers.[1]

But there is a difference worth examining in teaching Woolf—the difference her differences make. Her texts seem to invite, indeed to compel, pedagogical self-reflexivity. In part, this need results from the confusion and resistance of our students, especially in their first reading of a "major" Woolf text. But equally significant, I believe, is the way her texts signal the need for a self-conscious examination of our related reading and teaching practices. The fragmentation and communalization of narrative authority in *To the Lighthouse*, *A Room of One's Own*, or *The Waves*, for example, implicitly call into question a unitary reading experience, as well as a pedagogical model based on the teacher's transmission of what she or he knows into the students' receptively waiting minds. Each textual disruption of convention invites a matching reading strategy that has pedagogical implications. For *how* we read affects *how* we teach our students to read. The text's pedagogical efforts in teaching us *how* to read it imply a related pedagogy for our teaching of it.[2]

Woolf's probing, relentless, often fantastical experimentalism compels self-reflexivity about how we read.[3] Her texts violate the boundaries of expectation as these have been erected by literary tradition and orthodoxy—which may be why so many of our students feel so violated, even betrayed in their initial confusions. No writer writes outside convention; no reader can read without it. Woolf's experimentalism lies not in some imaginary wild zone, to echo Elaine Showalter in "Feminist Criticism in the Wilderness," but rather in her interrogation of the borders between tradition and innovation. The impact of her collective and female "we" in *A Room of One's Own* ("call me Mary Beton, Mary Seton, Mary Carmichael or by any name you please—it is not a matter of any importance," 5) depends for its effect on our association of the essay with the authoritative and masculine "I."[4] The wild wit of *Orlando* goes unheard unless we read the mock heroics, evolving stylistics, and shifting voices of the fictional biographer against the grain of the conventions of biography to which Woolf's own father had so ably contributed in his *Dictionary of National Biography*. The refractions of space and time in *To the Lighthouse* require, like cubism, the reader's broken expectation of "ordinary" representation. The refraction is itself the point, established only if we experience disorientation. Like the writing, the reading locates itself at the borders, caught between the already written and its textual violation. In this sense, Woolf's work anticipates Luce Irigaray's concept of women's linguistic "parody," a mimicry that burrows inside the dominant discourse to overthrow it ("Power and Discourse," *This Sex* 74–78).

However, Woolf's persistent and exuberant experimentalism should not be reduced to the qualities of "feminine" writing identified by poststructuralist theorists as inscriptions of phallogocentrism's Otherness. Woolf's writing did indeed anticipate recent theories of "feminine" poetics, concepts which can in turn usefully inform our readings of her work.[5] But the familiar list of poststructuralist disruptions threatens to become a new orthodoxy at odds with Woolf's insistent and perpetual innovations at the borders of the heterodox. Like the male avant-garde, Woolf's writing performed what Alice Jardine has termed "gynesis": "the putting into discourse of 'woman' as that *process* diagnosed in France as intrinsic to the condition of modernity; indeed, the valorization of the feminine, woman . . . as somehow intrinsic to new and necessary modes of thinking, writing, speaking" (25). But Mary Carmichael's broken sequences are not the same as Joyce's gynesis. Although the deconstruction of phallogo-centric forms of "identity," "subjectivity," and "authority" are surely part of the feminist project of Woolf's writing, her experimentalism does not eliminate these concepts as much as it forges new forms of them suited to women. There is too much assertive agency in Woolf's experimentalism for it to be confined to the position of a poststructuralist feminine Otherness or a Lacanian Imaginary.

This self-conscious, deliberative agency has direct bearing on the pedagogical function of her narratives. The readers these texts teach us—and by extension, our students—to become are not dutiful daughters of the masculine Word, not passive recipients of High Art (or High Modernism) but rather active, engaged readers positioned at the borders of convention and innovation, encouraged to interrogate prevailing orthodoxies of representation. Our active agency and flexibility as readers are built into the very nature of her experimentalism. For Woolf is perpetually undoing what we readers long to take for granted as we settle into the warm couch of a good read. Little in *To the Lighthouse*, for example, prepares us for the highjinks of *Orlando*, just as *Orlando*'s disruptions do little to help us read *The Waves*. Each text sets the ground for its own experiments, which it teaches its readers to interpret. The appeal each text makes, therefore, is to a thoroughly active reader who becomes its second author through the act of reading.[6]

Published in 1915 as Woolf's first voyage into and out of

literary convention, *The Voyage Out* is a parable about reading, one that reproduces the story of our resisting students and suggests an alternative pedagogy for us as readers and teachers. Like all *Bildungsromane*, the narrative of *The Voyage Out* is fundamentally pedagogical, motivated by the protagonist's education into the ways of the adult world. But at a metalevel, *The Voyage Out* examines the place of reading in the narrative of development: specifically, Rachel Vinrace's double reading of life and of the world of letters. As the privileged reader whose development ends in death, Rachel serves as both positive and negative model for reading. Against the foil of all the other characters who read, Rachel's mode of reading is generally favored, but because her reading leads toward her death— whether causally or not matters little—her method remains suspect, a dire warning about the dangers of reading to one's psychological and physical health.

As Christine Froula observes, everyone is always reading a book in *The Voyage Out*, a trope that underlines the role that books play in cultural initiation. Along complementary lines, Beverly Ann Schlack argues that the books people read function as a major device for characterization, serving to undermine and comment upon an array of different personalities. But as Froula also notes, Rachel's education involves initiation into "the book of the world" as well as books off a shelf.[7] Reading in *The Voyage Out* is presented in binary terms that oppose the reading of people with the reading of books. Both are interpretive acts, but the locus of one is the social arena, supremely the tea table, whereas the locus of the other is the printed page for which the universities and libraries are guardians. Women, on the whole, excel in reading the book of life; men, on the other hand, control the production and interpretation of the printed word.

Helen and Ridley Ambrose—Rachel's aunt, uncle, and surrogate parents in the novel—are presented as archetypal readers of each type.[8] Ridley is a recluse, shut off from the life of the hotel, incapable of living except through his books. He devotes himself entirely to translations and editions of Greek, first Aristotle and then Pindar, that difficult lyric celebrant of the state and military victory. Functioning as synecdoche for all books, Greek occupies for Ridley the privileged position in the hierarchy of the written word. He tells Rachel: "But what's the use of reading if you don't read Greek?"[9] Helen, on the other hand, is the one who "knew how to read the people who were passing" by interpreting the complex cultural codes of class and gender (*Voyage Out* 11). She, like the others, often carries a book and discusses literature, but she is more often shown in conversation while she works steadily on her embroidery of a tropical scene, synecdochically representing the scene that is to unfold before our eyes when Rachel and Terence declare their love in the steamy forest. For Helen "the great commonplace book" of life "lies open beside us as we talk" (46). Helen's reading anticipates Robert Scholes's formulation in *Protocols of Reading:* "We read life as well as books, and the activity of reading is really a matter of working through signs and text in order to comprehend more fully and powerfully not only whatever may be presented therein but also our own situations, both in their particularity and historicity and in their more durable and inevitable dimensions" (18).

Both Ridley and Helen—and the types of reading they embody— are undermined through a satiric irony reminiscent of Jane Austen, the writer both revered and disparaged in the novel.[10] Ridley remains illiterate before the "book" of life, thereby representing the sterility of a life lived entirely on the page of a dead language. Helen, a more positive reader, is nonetheless often shown to misread the people she interprets. Her initial reading of Rachel as a tiresome young woman who would seek endless intimacies turns out to have been completely wrong. Her misreading of Rachel's illness contributes to the death of her charge. Her selection of Hirst, a young Ridley-in-the-making who consistently misreads people as the one to help her "complete" the sheltered Rachel's "education" is laughable. "D'you know," Helen tells Hirst just after he has infuriated Rachel with his arrogance about books, "I believe you're just the person I want . . . to help me to complete her education? . . . Why shouldn't you talk to her—explain things to her— . . . ?" It is not primarily books Helen wants Hirst to explain, but life: "It's the facts of life, I think. . . . What really goes on, what people feel, although they generally try to hide it?" (163–164). Not only Hirst's misogyny, but also his complete illiteracy in reading the "commonplace book" of life, entirely unsuit him to the task that Helen sets for him. Neither she nor he is aware of what the reader "reads" him to be as the scenes of his own innocence and arrogance unfold before our eyes.

Like Helen and Ridley, Hirst is treated with considerable irony, symptomatically evident in his iconoclastic reading of Sappho during the church service. While the clergyman drones on in a sermon that inspires Rachel, in an ephiphanic flash, to lose her faith, Hirst enjoys reading Sappho's steamy Ode to Aphrodite, an act which in the larger narrative signals the disruptive power of a female discourse of desire against the master discourse of religion (230). The double irony, however, is that the female desire Hirst can read in a book (mediated by Swinburne's translation) is one that he cannot read in the "book of life." He repeatedly misreads Rachel's response to him, missing completely her mixture of rage and awe. And his pleasure in Sappho is undermined by his earlier gynophobic and prudish explosion to

Hewet: "What I abhor most of all . . . is the female breast. Imagine being Venning and having to get into bed with Susan! But the really repulsive thing is that they feel nothing at all—about what I do when I have a hot bath. They're gross, they're absurd, they're utterly intolerable!" (184). Hirst uses Sappho to rebel against the church, but he remains unaware of the way in which the book he reads undermines his hegemonic position as a masculinist reader.

Anticipating the pattern of deconstruction so evident in later works, Woolf establishes the binary of reading in *The Voyage Out* only to deconstruct it. As the scenes of reading proliferate and as characters are shown to gravitate toward one pole or the other, we come to see reading as a multidimensional act in which cultural texts and "the great commonplace book" of life are not only distinct but also interpenetrating. Given the intertextuality of any language of interpretation, reading books and reading life are ultimately interrelated activities. The lives people lead play out the scripts of various cultural texts, which in turn inscribe in various displaced forms the lives of those who produce them and of those whom they represent. Language itself, Julia Kristeva reminds us in her adaptation of M. M. Bakhtin, is intertextual. Each "word (text)," she writes in "Word, Dialogue, and Novel," "is an intersection of word (texts) where at least one other word (text) can be read. . . . [A]ny text is constructed as a mosaic of quotations; any text is the absorption and transformation of another" (*Desire* 66). Reading the book of life is an activity shaped by books already read. The "already written" is present in how we read both books and life. Conversely, the life we lead shapes how we read, absorbs what we read into the textuality of our lives. About the intertextual process of reading both books and lives, Scholes writes in *Protocols of Reading*: "reading is: writing the text of the work within the text of our lives" on the one hand (10); and on the other hand, "When we become aware of ourselves, we are already thoroughly developed as textual creatures. What we are and what we may become are already shaped by powerful cultural texts" (27).

The intertextuality of reading life and books is the focus of many scenes of reading in *The Voyage Out*. Clarissa and Richard Dalloway, for example, give Rachel as a parting present Jane Austen's *Persuasion* with their name and address inscribed on the flyleaf. This gift replicates the persuasive effect the Dalloways have had on the bedazzled Rachel in inducting her into the social order of British family and empire. As Austen's final novel, *Persuasion* both reifies and questions the marriage plot that dominates all her novels. The text of the Dalloways' address insures Rachel an entrée into the upper class milieu where she can live out Austen's persuasive plot to make an excellent marriage. *Persuasion* mimetically mirrors the ideological imperative

Rachel must learn to read. Conversely, the social script for a young woman of Rachel's class plays out in the plot of the novel. Exposed to Austen's textual plot, which she says she does not like because Austen is "so—so—well, so like a tight plait" (62), Rachel reads the similar script acted out before her eyes by Arthur and Susan, whose roll in the grass binds them together in an engagement that disgusts Rachel as much as their lovemaking (140).

Rachel's reading of this scene, upon which she unexpectedly stumbles with Terence, instructs us in the reading of her own courtship plot. The repetition of reading scenes invites us to read the woven strands of her engagement, made up intertextually of social and textual scripts. The scene in the forest where Rachel and Terence become persuaded to marry, for example, recapitulates the Ur-plot of Austen's novels and fulfills the ideological imperative for romance and marriage.[11] Educated by earlier scenes of reading, we readers are also attuned to the larger cultural and textual grid within which this forest scene exists. The biblical Garden of Eden, the ardent forests of Shakespeare's comedies, the garden maze of sexual seduction in Fanny Burney's *Camilla*, the forest scene in Nathaniel Hawthorne's *The Scarlet Letter*, the jungle scene of Joseph Conrad's *Heart of Darkness*—all resonate to produce a vibration that is at once sensual and foreboding, pregnant with the sense of romance, transgression, and potential doom. In case we miss our cues, Woolf's imagery is directly allusive, gesturing at specific literary texts as well as cultural symbols. The journey up the seething river into "the great darkness" of the South American jungle is described as a "driving into the heart of the night," with unmistakable echoes of Conrad's *Heart of Darkness* (264–265). Hirst's warning to "Beware of snakes," the lush and scented foliage, and the "red fruit" that Terence picks up to throw all evoke the cultural and textual iconography of Genesis as it has been endlessly (re)read in Western culture.

It is within this network of readings—and the meanings of reading—that Rachel's story of development is narrated. Reading functions in the novel as a trope for education, itself a figure for initiation into the adult world of the social order. The marriage plot that dominates the story of Rachel's initiation is, we learn, both a formal structure, a property of narrative, and also a thematic structure operating with the force of normative cultural values.[12] Rachel's *Bildung* is charted, in part, by the development of her ability to read the intertextually constructed "commonplace book" of life and the elite book of the printed page. In learning to read, she instructs us in how to read her story. Consequently, it is worth our while to understand just what kind of a reader she is.

As we might expect from the triangulated family romance of

protagonist-daughter and surrogate parents, Rachel as a reader combines aspects of both Helen and Ridley. She reads books with the intensity of Ridley, and she reads people with the acumen of Helen. However, her reading of life colors her reading of books, and conversely, her reading of books shapes her reading of life. Moreover, her fluid combination of reading books and life is not undermined through irony, but is rather privileged in the novel. Like Ridley, she withdraws to the isolation of her room, first on the ship and then in the villa. A prototype of a room of one's own, Rachel's space is "large, private—a room in which she could play, read, think, defy the world, a fortress as well as a sanctuary. Rooms, she knew, became more like worlds than rooms at the age of twenty-four" (123). Scattered carelessly everywhere in her room, books offer a world which she enters with intensity and concentration to ask the cosmic questions: "'What I want to know,' she said aloud, 'is this: What is the truth? What's the truth of it all?'" (123).[13] Rather than re-editing an already much edited Greek text as Ridley does, Rachel loves "the moderns" and "books in shiny yellow covers," like Ibsen and Meredith, who offer her heroines whom she becomes in the act of reading: "Ibsen's plays always left her in that condition. She acted them for days at a time, greatly to Helen's amusement; and then it would be Meredith's turn and she became Diana of the Crossways. But Helen was aware that it was not all acting, and that some sort of change was taking place in the human being" (123–124). Reading what she likes involves for Rachel an identification in which the text becomes life and her life becomes the text.

Anticipating Woolf's later modernism as well as poststructuralist linguistic theory, Rachel's reading also involves her recognition of the materiality of language. She reads with great attention to each word: "Rachel read what she chose, reading with the curious literalness of one to whom written sentences are unfamiliar, and handling words as though they were made of wood, separately of great importance, and possessed of shapes like tables or chairs" (124). The text she creates in her reading is like a postimpressionist Cézanne still life, its "tables" and "chairs" (re)arranged through her literal and material relation to words.[14] "In this way," we learn, "she came to conclusions, which had to be remodelled according to the adventures of the day, and were indeed recast as liberally as any one could desire" (124). Rachel is an active reader who shapes and is shaped by the texts she reads. The "adventures of the day" from the "commonplace book" of life influence Rachel's reconstruction of the text. And the materiality of the words she picks up and handles helps structure the parts she plays in living.

Woolf's emphasis on Rachel's *choice* of what she reads is also significant. "Rachel chose modern books," we learn, and "Rachel read what she chose" (124). Rachel is quick to reject what she does not like, what she cannot identify with, like Jane Austen. As Schlack points out, what Rachel likes and does not like to read is an important device of characterization. Her preference for Emily Brontë's *Wuthering Heights* over Austen signals the wild spirit beneath her vague exterior and sheltered existence, one that would climb the heaths with Catherine and Heathcliff in an imaginative landscape seemingly beyond the social order and its prescriptions of gender difference (*Continuing Presences* 57–58). Rachel's eclectic reading, based on her own desire rather than on a work's status in the canon, emphasizes the dialogic nature of her engagement with the printed word.

Yet, as a young woman educated informally at home, in contrast to the university-educated Hewet and Hirst, Rachel is also vulnerable to assertions of her ignorance. Men repeatedly set themselves the task of educating Rachel by selecting what she should read (unlike the learned Miss Allan, for example, who discusses various authors with Rachel but does not impose a reading list on her). Mr. Dalloway insists not only on Austen but also on Edmund Burke. Hirst infuriates Rachel at the dance by assuming that she has read nothing but Shakespeare and the Bible and by then insisting that she "begin" her education with Gibbon's *Decline and Fall of the Roman Empire*. But she is flattered the next day by his note attached to volume one of Gibbon's massive history and his recommendation that she not bother with "the moderns," except for a book by Wedekind that he will give her. Rachel never reveals to Hirst what she has actually read or that the "moderns" are her favorites. Her silence sustains his arrogance, and her awe for his knowledge of books leads her to attempt to read what he tells her to read. With Gibbon and a Balzac recommended by Ridley under her arm, she dutifully sets out for an afternoon of reading in the garden. What happens is instructive for the contradictions in Rachel's reading of books. Setting aside the French novel, the less prestigious genre that was associated with the seduction of young women (both heroines and readers), Rachel attempts the Gibbon and is at first swept away by the grandeur of his description of imperial conquest and the resistance of exotic Africans and hardy northern barbarians. Thoughts of the "book of the world turned back to the very first page" merge seamlessly into a sense of wonder about Hirst and Hewet: "From them all life seemed to radiate; the very words of books were steeped in radiance" (175). Their "radiance" and the "radiance" of books become one as Rachel wonders if she is in love, and if so, with whom. The text of history becomes the script of Rachel's life, foreshadowing her conquest in love and her ultimate resistance.

Rachel reads people and events with the same idiosyncratic intensity that she reads books. Her initiation into the social realm from which she has been largely sheltered by her reclusive aunts in suburban Richmond is presented as a series of exposures that she must learn to read as if she were interpreting a book. The introduction of the worldly Dalloways into the narrative signals the onset of Rachel's education in the "great commonplace book" of life. Ignoring Helen's disdain for the aristocratic couple, Rachel is infatuated with their "radiance," a glow based on their class, their style, their gender-inflicted positions in the world as former Member of Parliament and lady. In psychodynamic terms, Rachel's "love" for Richard and Clarissa becomes a transferential scene in which she projects onto them unresolved complexes about her dead mother and often absent father. In particular, she invests in Richard a kind of exalted authority. "I know nothing!" she tells him. "You ought to make me understand" (65). His response—a heavily ironized defense of British nationalism and imperialism—impresses Rachel mightily. Not until his sudden assault—the passionate kiss he imposes when the lurching ship throws them together in the midst of a storm—does Rachel become aware that she must read beneath the surface of his authority, his stance as the perfect husband and fatherly advisor. His kiss, her initial pleasure, then disgust and subsequent nightmare become the "book" of life she must read. Helen tries to brush off the incident with a cynical allusion to male desire: "It's the most natural thing in the world. Men will want to kiss you, just as they'll want to marry you. The pity is to get things out of proportion. It's like noticing the noises people make when they eat, or men spitting" (81). But Rachel exhibits an oedipal desire to know, fueled in part by the incestuous overtones of her initiation into sexuality. "No . . . I shan't do that," she tells Helen. "I shall think about it all day and all night until I find out exactly what it does mean" (80). She does not deny her own pleasure ("I liked him, and I liked being kissed"), but she reads this episode as evidence of her own confinement in the masculine economy of desire.

"So that's why I can't walk alone!"
By this new light she saw her life for the first time a creeping hedged-in thing, driven cautiously between high walls, here turned aside, there plunged in darkness, made dull and crippled for ever—her life that was the only chance she had—the short season between two silences.
"Because men are brutes! I hate men!" she exclaimed. (82)

How she reads this scene foreshadows how she reads subsequent scenes of desire—first that of Arthur and Susan, which she also finds disgusting, and then her own, whose meaning she can never quite articulate. She certainly does not "hate" Terence, nor does she think he is a "brute." Certainly she desires him, as the two scenes in the forest suggest, as well as their erotic horseplay that leaves her "thrown to the floor, where she lay gasping, and crying for mercy" (298). Not terrified, however, Rachel cries ecstatically and mysteriously, "I'm a mermaid! I can swim" (298). However, Rachel's earlier readings of Dalloway's kiss and the courtship of Arthur and Susan have schooled us to read beneath the surface of her "happiness" and the difference of their courtship. As readers of Rachel, we take over for her when she remains largely inarticulate about her own engagement. We note the foreboding signs that her marriage will make her life a "hedged-in thing, driven cautiously between high walls." Once engaged, Terence begins, in spite of himself, to act out the ideological and narrative script of conventional romance, in which he, as the man, instructs and guides the woman. He sharply criticizes her reading of worthless moderns, like Ibsen; he tells her she must answer all the congratulations of their engagement while he works on his novel; he announces that they should have one boy and one girl. Rachel resists these assertions—first by claiming superiority for wordless music over books, and then by her silence and withdrawal.

Rachel's ultimate resistance, of course, is her illness, which we must read for her as a symptomatic effect of her unarticulated reading of the meaning of her impending marriage. Her headache begins, significantly, as many have noted, on a hot day when Terence is reading her Milton's *Comus*, which in a figurative sense is the immediate cause and sign of her illness. Her own reading of this scene as well as the scene of her engagement is displaced onto the fever and subsequent hallucinations. Her cryptic dreams, if we only knew how to read them, contain in the distorted speech of the dream-work her reading of her life. Reading the scene of her engagement has, in short, made Rachel sick; but we have access to her interpretation only through reading its effect.

It is not my purpose here to unravel the web of meanings we have been schooled to read in Rachel's symptomatic resistance to the marriage plot. Rather, I want to explore what it means for us as readers that the novel's privileged reader sickens, withers, and dies before our very eyes—at least in a figurative sense because of what and how she reads. She is initially set up as a model reader who integrates and balances better than any other character the intertextual task of reading both books and life. Her death is a shock, in part because it undermines what the narrative has encouraged: our identification with Rachel as a reader, our attempt to read the book of her life inscribed in the novel we are reading with the same methods she has taught us. By example, she shows us how to read, then warns us with her death that this way of reading is dangerous.

What, then, does Woolf's first voyage into and out of literary convention tell us about reading Woolf? Her experimentation with the marriage plot breaks the conventional woman's *Bildung* but does so at the price of her heroine's life. Her scenes of reading perversely teach us how to read the intertextuality of books and life, only to suggest that if we follow Rachel's example, we too might "sicken" in some figurative if not literal, sense. How, then, would Woolf have us read, and by extension, teach our students to read?

This pedagogical question takes on even greater urgency in the context of the changes Woolf made in the numerous drafts of *The Voyage Out* from approximately 1908 until 1913, changes painstakingly reconstructed by Louise DeSalvo and evident especially in the difference between the 1910 text she called *Melymbrosia* and the new text she wrote from 1911 through 1913 with its new and final title, *The Voyage Out.*[15] As many have noted, Rachel changes significantly in the process of revision—in general from what Elizabeth Heine calls "an intelligent, outspoken, critical young feminist" to "a vague and innocently naïve dreamer" (298). In particular, Schlack argues in "The Novelist's Voyage from Manuscripts to Text," Woolf makes Rachel "increasingly naïve and innocent of book learning." She is "progressively less well-read," and "the cumulative effect of Woolf's deletions is a Rachel Vinrace shorn of any wisdom or knowledge derived from reading Browne, Keats, Nietzsche" (326). "Any strong spark of wit or sophistication from Rachel had to be smothered," Heine writes; "many of the scenes had to be reimagined from a naïve point of view" (305). Woolf mutes Rachel's critical intelligence, silences many of the sharp opinions Rachel initially articulated, and opens a wider gap between the men as guardians of the book and Rachel as the sheltered and uneducated young lady. Why does Woolf withdraw from her portrait of Rachel as an articulate, well-read young woman who shares so much with the young Virginia Stephen who presided with her sister Vanessa over the early Bloomsbury evenings? What does Woolf's construction of a less knowledgeable and independent reader mean in connection with the text's paradoxical parable about reading itself? Less assertive as a reader in *The Voyage Out* than she was in *Melymbrosia*, Rachel is the text's privileged reader whose mode of reading is undermined by the failure of her *Bildung*. Again, why? And what does this mean for how Woolf would have us read?

Louise DeSalvo reads these changes in Rachel—and the novel

in general—as an instance of self-censorship. The completion of *Me-lymbrosia* in 1910, with its blunt social criticism and overt feminism, contributed, DeSalvo believes, to Woolf's illness in the summer of 1910. The subsequent drafts of *The Voyage Out*, whose critique was more muted and indirect than *Melymbrosia*, were produced during the development of her relationship with Leonard Woolf and reflected her withdrawal from the earlier version's radicalism. "The writing of the novel," DeSalvo concludes, "was becoming a voyage out—a voyage *away from* the bluntness, the candor, the openness, and even the subtlety—with which Woolf had handled her material in this version" (Introduction xlvi).[16] I think there is considerable evidence to support her interpretation of self-censorship, not only in *The Voyage Out* but also in the composition of Woolf's later novels (such as *The Years*) and in the production of women's modernism in general. For a number of women writers in the modernist period, revisions of these texts reflected a sometimes conscious, sometimes unconscious negotia-tion between the desire to speak and the need to repress what was forbidden in their narratives of modernity. Often revisions, in making their texts more artfully modernist, also disguised the inscribed desire through mechanisms of condensation, displacement, and representa-tion akin to the grammar of the dream-work described by Sigmund Freud in *The Interpretation of Dreams*.[17]

However, self-censorship does not fully explain the changes in Rachel *as reader* from *Melymbrosia* to *The Voyage Out*. And as a reading of Woolf's life in relation to the production of autobiographical fiction, self-censorship does not fully address how Woolf's constant return to the scene of writing the novel functioned within her con-struction, through writing, of a self—how, in other words, the story of Rachel's failed *Bildung* related to Woolf's efforts to make her own development a success. I have argued elsewhere that writers who repeatedly revise autobiographical material or produce a series of closely related autobiographical texts engage in a scene of writing that is analogous to the scene of analysis.[18] The split subject of auto-biographical writing—what Woolf calls the "I now" and the "I then" in "A Sketch of the Past"—reproduces the pedagogical scene of analysis in which the analyst and analysand work through the analysand's transferential repetition of repressed desire. Writing autobiographical fiction can be seen as a "writing cure" in which the "I now" and the "I then" collaborate in the (re)construction of a narrative that undoes the work of repression. The writer's constant return to the scene of autobiographical composition—through endless revision—reproduces the psychodynamic of transference and working through, what Freud called the attempt to move from repetition to recollection.[19]

Within this context, Woolf's difficulty in completing *The Voyage*

Out signals the transferential return of the repressed. The change in Rachel from a sharply critical reader into a relatively more passive one suggests that in the later version, Woolf was able to confront what she had repressed in the earlier drafts—namely, that part of herself which she considered "dangerous" to her health. The later Rachel is more like the Woolf who had a breakdown after she completed *Melymbrosia* in 1910. The Rachel of *The Voyage Out* whose resistance to the marriage plot speaks increasingly only through somatic symptom has more in common than the bolder Rachel of *Melymbrosia* with the Woolf who experienced delirium in 1910, ambivalence and anxiety during her courtship and engagement, and intermittent signs of illness in 1911 through 1913. In *The Voyage Out*, Woolf may have been exploring more directly than she could yet do in *Melymbrosia* the roots and dimensions of her illness by examining the psychodynamics of a less critical, more passive Rachel.

Woolf may also have been engaged, in the final months before her descent into two years of severe illness (1913–1915), in an attempt to "kill off" that part of herself whose resistance to patriarchy takes the symptomatic form of madness. Many critics have noted that the death of Rachel "kills off" the conventional marriage plot in *The Voyage Out* and functions to free Woolf to construct different kinds of narratives in later novels. I would add that *The Voyage Out* may have been additionally "killing off" the kind of female reader of books and people who is most likely to be victimized. Woolf's subsequent formation of a resilient, resisting, and dialogic reader she calls "the common reader" supports this interpretation of *The Voyage Out* as a parable about reading. The "common reader" is a persona whose portrait Woolf draws in the opening essay of *The Common Reader* (1925), but whose independent stance she had herself been forging through years of anonymous reviewing for the *Times Literary Supplement*. As Woolf began to recover from the lengthy illness of 1913–1915, her main intellectual activity was her reviews for the *Times Literary Supplement*, for which she produced a staggering number on books they selected. Gradually, work on her short stories and *Night and Day* began to take precedence; by 1920, when she was working on *Jacob's Room*, she started refusing requests for reviews and selecting the books she would review on her own schedule.[20] I want to suggest that the formation of herself as a "common reader" through this period of intense, largely anonymous reviewing not only contributed significantly to her recovery but also emerged dialectically out of the death of Rachel in *The Voyage Out*. This "common reader," who prefigures characters like Lily Briscoe and Miss La Trobe, rises phoenix-like out of the ashes of Rachel's failed *Bildung*. Retaining some aspects of Rachel's mode of reading, the "common reader" abandons what contributed to her destruction. The death of Rachel allowed Woolf to "kill off" in a textual sense those aspects of her own reading that threatened her "health." In "life" Woolf may not have been able to sustain this "murder," but in her subsequent texts, she constructed a reader of life, books, and their intertextuality who was not defeated by what she read.

In "The Common Reader," the brief essay that opens her first volume of criticism, Woolf constructs the reading persona that makes the collection of disparate essays cohere around a "common" stance toward the tradition of letters. Woolf borrows the term "common reader" from the dean of British criticism, Dr. Johnson, who rejoiced in the "common reader" and "the common sense of readers, uncorrupted by literary prejudices" (*Common Reader* I 1). Paradoxically gaining authority by identifying with Johnson's dissociation from it, Woolf distinguishes the "common reader" from "the critic and the scholar." "He is worse educated," she notes, and "He reads for his own pleasure rather than to impart knowledge or correct the opinions of others" (1). The "common reader" is no expert, and, like Woolf herself, the "common reader" has little formal education and no scholarly credentials. "He" (or she) has, in other words, none of the public trappings of authority. Rather, the "common reader's" authority is self-created, founded in pleasure and intellectual independence. "Above all," Woolf states in the passage I have used as an epigraph, "he is guided by an instinct to create for himself, out of whatever odds and ends he can come by, some kind of whole—a portrait of a man, a sketch of an age, a theory of the art of writing" (1). For the "common reader," reading is a creative act, an expression of agency freed from the need to measure up to accuracy. "He never ceases, as he reads," Woolf continues, "to run up some rickety and ramshackle fabric"; his reading is "[h]asty, inaccurate, and superficial. . . . [H]is deficiencies as a critic are too obvious to be pointed out" (1–2). But what may be negative qualities within the university become positive acts of creativity outside its walls. The common reader's "ramshackle fabric" is the patchwork of ideas and pleasure that Woolf's "The Common Reader" celebrates and justifies.

Woolf's heavy use of the generic "he" for her "common reader" screens the gendered dimension of her persona and the critique of reading it embodies. The position of the uneducated reader was one occupied very frequently by women of Woolf's class—those she later calls in *Three Guineas* "the daughters of educated men" whose families poured all their money into "Arthur's Education Fund" and did not send their daughters to school (*Three Guineas* 4). This woman-as-common-reader reads outside the system of expertise constructed within Oxbridge, positioned outside in a material sense because of the denial of access to higher education, but positioned outside in an ideological sense as well because the "fact" of "Arthur's Education Fund" has meant "that though we [women] look at the same things, we see them differently" (*Three Guineas* 5). Woolf's woman reader in *Three Guineas* inherits the position of "the common reader" and anticipates the definition of women proposed recently by Linda Alcoff as a "positionality" whereby "women use their positional perspective as a place from which values are interpreted and constructed" (434). Woolf's "common reader" occupies the position of "ignorance" only from the perspective of the "insiders"—the sons of educated men who exert power in the public sphere from which women are largely excluded. As she reflects in *A Room of One's Own*, after narrating her afternoon at plushy Oxbridge and evening at impoverished Fernham, "I thought how unpleasant it is to be locked out; and I thought how it is worse perhaps to be locked in" (24). The defining element of the "common reader" is his or her *positionality* as outsider—or to be more precise, since no one can exist "outside" culture, as one who occupies and interrogates the borders between canonical and marginalized traditions.

While Woolf's "common reader" paved the way for the explicitly feminist female personae of *A Room of One's Own* and *Three Guineas*, Rachel was the "common reader's" predecessor. She, like "he," is badly educated and reads for her own pleasure. Outside the system of reading represented by the classics and embodied by the university men—Ridley, Hirst, and Hewet—Rachel's reading is a scrapbag of disparate fabrics most consistently represented by "the moderns." Her intensity, her tendency to ask cosmic questions, her recognition of the interpenetration of books and life, her independence of judgment, her love for the materiality of words are all qualities that Woolf's "common reader" persona exhibits in the various essays of the volume.

But the "common reader" also differs *as a reader* from Rachel in ways that help us understand what her death warns us against *as readers*. Where the "common reader" refuses to accept the authority of the scholar and critic, Rachel invests tremendous authority in her male mentors—Richard, Ridley, Hirst, and Hewet. She is initially swept away by their "radiance," which shines particularly in their authority as masters of the word. Inwardly, she also resists their various authorities, but increasingly this resistance takes only silent forms. The wordless realm of music becomes her basic defense, and she becomes more and more silent as Terence talks ever more volubly about their impending marriage. Ultimately, the silent world of her hallucinations and illness encases her resistance, which she can express only symptomatically. Woolf's "common reader," on the other hand, establishes an authority outside the university, one that reflects, assesses, prods, probes, pushes, and judges what s/he reads.

Unlike Rachel, the "common reader" can even take on the classics and the canonical literature of England without being over-whelmed either by them or by ignorance of them. The essays that Woolf selected or wrote for *The Common Reader* assert her right and ability to discuss the great masters from the position of one who was not educated at Oxbridge, who was not elected to the Cambridge Apostles, as so many of her male Bloomsbury friends had been. In "The Pastons and Chaucer," the first substantive essay in the volume, Woolf invades the house of Chaucer through the back door by reading the collection of family documents of an upper middle class family, the Pastons, and imagining how they would read Chaucer. The next essay tackles the Greeks by making a virtue of seeming ignorance. "On Not Knowing Greek" opens with a bold assertion of her own and all readers' lack of knowledge of the Greeks: "For it is vain and foolish to talk of knowing Greek, since in our ignorance we should be at the bottom of any class of schoolboys, since we do not know how the words sounded . . . and between this foreign people and ourselves there is not only difference of race and tongue but a tremendous breach of tradition" (24). "Ignorance" becomes the privileged base from which the "common reader" constructs "a portrait of a man, a sketch of an age, a theory of the art of writing" (1). The "common reader," in other words, is able, unlike Rachel, to negotiate *in words* the difficult border between established tradition and the position of the outsider.[21]

In her reading practice, Rachel constructs her own literary tra-dition in which "the moderns" play a particularly central role. But in contrast to the "common reader," she is unable to articulate a defense of her creation-as-reader. When Terence exclaims in reference to Ib-sen, "God, Rachel, you do read trash!" she responds only indirectly with a question: "Does it ever seem to you, Terence, that the world is composed entirely of vast blocks of matter, and that we're nothing but patches of light . . . ?" (292–293). And she makes no attempt to defend her dislike for Hirst when Terence exclaims in his defense, "But you'll never see it! . . . because with all your virtues you don't and you never will, care with every fibre of your being for the pur-suit of truth! You've no respect for facts, Rachel; you're essentially feminine" (295). The "common reader," on the other hand, moves gradually away from engagement with the masters into explorations of noncanonical genres (such as letters, diaries, and biographies of "the Obscure"), women writers, and "the moderns." Rachel's cryptic defense of her reading reappears more directly stated in "Modern Fiction," where the "common reader" rejects the "materialists," who pile on "facts," and privileges the modern "spiritualists," who repre-sent how the "ordinary mind . . . receives a myriad impressions . . . an incessant shower of innumerable atoms" that form "a luminous halo, a semi-transparent envelope surrounding us from the beginning of consciousness to the end" (*Common Reader* I 152, 154). "The Patron and the Crocus," a brief essay near the end of the collection, defends the creative power of the reader whose impending judgment influences the writer: "For a book is always written for somebody to read . . . [someone who is] in a very subtle and insidious way the instigator and inspirer of what is written. . . . To know whom to write for is to know how to write" (211, 214). The volume concludes with the "common reader's" defense of the exhilarating, if dizzying "chaos of contemporary literature," cut off by the war from its precursors. In "How It Strikes a Contemporary," the "common reader" urges other readers to "respect one's own instincts, to follow them fearlessly and, rather than submit them to the control of any critic or reviewer alive, to check them by reading and reading again the masterpieces of the past" (237–238).

Rachel could not publicly sustain such an independent stance, however much her "instincts" as a reader moved her in that direction. Similarly, she could not maintain a critical distance in negotiating the intertextual association between books and life. Even though she could reject the tyranny of the marriage plot in Austen's novels, she was unable to prevent herself from living out that tyranny in her own engagement—except through the absolute withdrawal of death. The "common reader" overthrows "the tyrant" of "plot" in "Modern Fic-tion," but Rachel is gradually silenced in its "thrall" (*Common Reader* I 153–154). As we contrast the reading practices of Rachel and the "common reader," we may find that it is not only the power of ideol-ogy that engulfs Rachel but also her habit of complete identification with what she reads. She *becomes*, it should be recalled, Ibsen's heroines for "days at a time," living out the script of what she reads in a grand romantic gesture. In reading the "great commonplace book" of life, Rachel similarly becomes the feminine Other of the courtship plot even as she resists it. In terms of Shoshana Felman's concept of reading as transference, Rachel is captured by what she reads—from books, from life, and from their intertextuality. Swallowed up in the complex of cultural texts, Rachel cannot negotiate a pathway of her own, a *Bildung* that can balance desire and a separate identity.[22]

Woolf's "common reader," in contrast, always maintains a cer-tain distance from what is read. Woolf prevents total identification—a fusion or merger of reader and character—by always sustaining a critical voice, a stance or positionality that fosters flexibility, fluidity, a wary independence. The "common reader" is not like Mrs. Ramsay, whose gaze becomes one with what she sees (*To the Lighthouse* 97). Instead the "common reader," in intricate maneuvers of rhetorical play, guards against complete identification, protects her separate identity with a critical stance that is never fixed. Rachel's engulfment in the interpenetrating books of words and life is a negative model for Woolf, a mode of reading that she "kills off" with Rachel's death and replaces with her persona of the "common reader." In so doing, Woolf anticipates Rachel Brownstein's *Becoming a Heroine*, in which she warns against illusionary effects on women readers who throw themselves "headlong and hopeful" into the lives of heroines whose model lives they necessarily fail to realize in the real world (xviii).[23] Woolf's formulation of the critical "common reader" also anticipates Judith Fetterley's notion of the "resisting reader," who refuses the "immasculation" and "schizophrenia" imposed by reading canonical texts. But where for Fetterley the resisting reader is engaged in "exorcising the male mind that has been implanted in us" (xxii), Woolf's "common reader" resists all texts—at the same time she engages with them—not just male texts, nor even male-identified texts by women, but all texts. She has much in common with the "feminist dialogic reader" characterized by Patricia Lorimer Lundberg, one who experiences "the 'heteroglossic' multiplicity of perspectives in a text" and refuses to "be controlled by the surface meaning in a text" (12). Woolf's reader is positioned perpetually at the border, guarding her separate stance, refusing to be engulfed by any text, dialogically engaging with the orthodox and the heterodox alike. Woolf's reader is like her writer—always experimenting at the border.

What does the "death" of Rachel as reader and the birth of the "common reader" mean for us as readers, as teachers of readers? What do Woolf's pedagogical narratives and personae have to teach us about the pedagogical scene of teaching in our various classrooms? At first glance, our "common students" appear to have little in common with Woolf's "common reader." For her persona of the reader-as-outsider in no sense suggests an unread reader. Many of our "common students" may be extremely adroit in reading the "book of life," but few are aware of the intertextuality of "books" and "life." And which one of us, let alone our students, can claim to be as well-read in English literature as Woolf's "common reader"? Woolf's self-education in her father's library, her work with private tutors, and her years of disciplined reading and reviewing can scarcely be reproduced in our classrooms. Her education was the product of her time, her class, her gender, and her drive; it appears to have little to do with the attempt on the American educational scene to provide a higher education to vast numbers of students who are increasingly less familiar with the tradition of letters as Western culture becomes more visually oriented.

But if we probe more deeply at the parable of reading implicit in *The Voyage Out* and the formation of the "common reader," we can find much to enrich our pedagogical questions. In particular, we can respond to Woolf's invitation to foster the critical stance and authority of our student readers. Rather than project Woolf's modernist experimentalism as an esoteric discourse for the educated or avant-garde elite, I think we need to encourage our students to become like Woolf's "common reader"—flexible in their expectations, fluid in their ability to follow innovations, independent in their critical judgments, aware of the intertextuality of life and books. We should not encourage them to find one character with whom they can totally identify; nor should we suggest that Woolf's texts contain a blueprint for their lives. We should urge them to read with intensity, with pleasure, with all their "big" questions, with attention to the feel of words, the fabric of form. Above all, we can attempt to create a classroom—the room—for reading in which they, from their position as "common student-readers," can create for themselves their own readings. More easily said than done.

Notes

An earlier version of this chapter was presented at a session of the 1989 Modern Language Association convention on "Teaching Virginia Woolf." I am indebted to Pamela Caughie for her superb work in organizing the panel and for her criticism of my original paper.

1. See Margo Culley and Catherine Portuges, *Gendered Subjects*, for discussions of feminist pedagogy.

2. For other examinations of the relation between reading practices and pedagogy, see for example Shoshana Felman (*Jacques Lacan*) and Marcel Cornis-Pope. Felman suggests that the central significance of psychoanalysis for teaching is its performative "theory of practice" that proposes a dialogic, not monologic, "process of reading" and learning (23, 69–98). Cornis-Pope shows how his students' self-conscious engagement with a text by Henry James represents a narrative that rewrites the text.

3. For recent discussions of Woolf within an experimentalist tradition, see for example Rachel Blau DuPlessis, "Woolfenstein" and *Writing beyond the Ending* (31–46, 162–177); Toril Moi (1–17); Makiko Minow-Pinkney (especially 1–23, 187–196); and Rachel Bowlby. Moi's argument that American feminist critics (prototypically repre-

sented by Elaine Showalter in her critique of Woolf) rejected Woolf's experimentalism is inaccurate and does not take into account the evolution of Woolf criticism in the United States. In the 1950s and 1960s, Woolf was valued primarily, if at all, for her formalist innovations, which were read as entirely separate from the politics of her feminist "tracts," considered to be irrelevant to her art and scarcely worth mention. Herbert Marder's pathbreaking *Feminism and Art: A Study of Virginia Woolf* (1968) asserted the centrality of feminism for Woolf; and much American Woolf criticism of the 1970s sought to assert the importance of her feminist critique and vision to her achievement, including her formalist innovations. The honoring of Woolf as a founding "mother" of twentieth-century feminist criticism and theory was so widespread that the extent and virulence of Showalter's attack on Woolf in *A Literature of Their Own* was profoundly shocking, as I suspect it was intended to be, a dynamic that Moi completely misses in using Showalter as her exemplary American feminist reader of Woolf. The emphasis on Woolf's political vision in American Woolf criticism of the 1970s needs to be understood in the context of its precursor: the New Critical emphasis on formalism and suppression of political and material questions. By the late 1970s and 1980s, Woolf criticism in the United States began to examine the connection between Woolf's politics and form; in the 1980s, many Woolf critics have used poststructuralist theory.

4. For discussions of this communal "I," see for example DuPlessis, *Writing* (162–177) and Jane Marcus, *Virginia Woolf and the Languages of Patriarchy* (163–188).

5. See for example Minow-Pinkney's reading of Woolf in relation to the Lacanian Imaginary and Kristevan semiotic in *Virginia Woolf and the Problem of the Subject* and Gayatri Chakravorty Spivak's deconstructive reading in "Unmaking and Making in *To the Lighthouse*," *In Other Worlds* (30–45).

6. The pedagogical aspect of Woolf's texts in the creation of active readers anticipates a key debate in reader-response criticism—namely, the issue of whether the text through its promptings or the readers dominate the reading process. See Patrocinio P. Schweickart's discussion of this debate and her advocacy of a feminist reader-response criticism in "Reading Ourselves: Toward a Feminist Theory of Reading" (Flynn and Schweickart 36–37). For an overview of different reader-response approaches, see Susan R. Suleiman and Inge Crossman, especially Suleiman's "Introduction: Varieties of Audience-Oriented Criticism" (3–45).

7. See also Patricia Klindienst Joplin, who writes that *The Voyage Out* is a "book about books, a book about education and the ways fiction shapes life" (2).

8. As Jane Marcus argues in "Other People's I's (Eyes)," Mr. and Mrs. Ramsay in *To the Lighthouse* also represent prototypical "masculine" and "feminine" modes of reading; but she focuses on their binary

reading of books, the one aligned with the symbolic register of language, the other with the semiotic.

9. On the significance of Greek for Woolf, see, for example, her "On Not Knowing Greek" (*Common Reader* 24–40); William Herman, who points out that Woolf worked very hard at Greek and read widely in the original; and Marcus, "Other People's I's (Eyes)," in which she argues that the binary "Greek" and "barbarian" underlies Woolf's general deconstruction of patriarchal reading practices.

10. Ridley is often associated by critics with Woolf's father, Leslie Stephen, while the younger, iconoclastic Helen is connected, along with her companion in the novel, Hirst, with the early days of Bloomsbury, when the Apostles from Cambridge [a secret society of intellectuals founded at Cambridge University in 1820] would come to Gordon Square [in the Bloomsbury area of London] for talk and companionship at the salon of the beautiful Stephen sisters. Woolf's irony expresses considerable hostility for the often lionized culture of Bloomsbury books and talk. For discussions of irony in *The Voyage Out*, see, for example, Schlack, *Continuing Presences* (1–28); Virginia Blain; and John Bayley, who argues that the novel's irony is strongly "parodic" and more "combative" than her later fiction (74–76).

11. The scene is not, as many have noticed, a traditional courtship scene. There is enormous stress on silence, which can be read as a liberating or ominous break from convention. There is their odd repetition—"'We love each other,' Terence said. 'We love each other,' she repeated" (271)—which can be read as mimicry or as a mark of equality (as DuPlessis argues in *Writing*). Especially in light of the previous scenes of courtship, I think the scene presents itself to us ambiguously, with the significance of its difference ultimately indeterminate.

12. For some discussions of the marriage plot in relation to the women's *Bildungsroman*, see for example DuPlessis, *Writing*; Joseph Allen Boone; and Nancy K. Miller. For an analysis of Rachel's *Bildung* in relation to patterns of initiation, see Froula and (more briefly) De-Salvo, Introduction (xxxix–xl).

13. Rachel's questions anticipate those of Lily Briscoe and of the anonymous narrator in "Time Passes" in *To the Lighthouse*.

14. Rachel's relationship to words parallels Stephen Dedalus' fascination with words in James Joyce's *A Portrait of the Artist as a Young Man*, published in serial form in the same year that *The Voyage Out* appeared. Joyce, however, stresses the precocity of Stephen's fascination, while Woolf emphasizes Rachel's awkwardness. Stephen's birthright is the Word, whereas Rachel is fundamentally alien to it. The materiality of language evident in both texts is gender-inflected.

15. See DeSalvo, "Sorting" and Introduction. As DeSalvo has reconstructed the story of the novel's tortuous composition, Woolf produced an essentially complete version of *Melymbrosia* (Extant Draft B) from March 1909 until March 1910. From about March until September

1910, Woolf was very ill and was sent to a nursing home. In 1911 she began a different version called *The Voyage Out*, whose composition overlapped the period of Leonard's courtship, their engagement (May 1912), and marriage (August 1912). After their wedding trip in the fall of 1912, she revised this version and gave it to Gerald Duckworth in March of 1913, after which she became severely ill through 1915. She corrected the proofs in the spring and summer of 1913 (before her suicide attempt in September 1913), but the novel was not published until after her recovery in 1915. DeSalvo has reconstructed the 1910 version and published it under the title *Melymbrosia*.

16. For critiques of DeSalvo's reading of self-censorship, see Joplin and Blain, both of whom argue that the final version is a "better novel" (and for Blain, more "political" because its style decenters the more conventional narrative authority of *Melymbrosia*). DeSalvo, however, does not claim that *Melymbrosia* is a "better" novel than *The Voyage Out*; rather, she says that *Melymbrosia* is a "finished" text Woolf chose not to publish because of its less disguised feminism.

17. I make this argument more fully, with H.D. as example, in "Return of the Repressed in Women's Narratives." Self-censorship is also evident, differently gendered, in the production of Joyce's modernism, as I have argued in "The Return of the Repressed in Joyce." For the story of Woolf's changes in *The Years*, see Marcus, *Languages* (57–74) and the special issue of the *Bulletin of Research in the Humanities* on *The Years*.

18. See my "Return of the Repressed in Women's Narratives," "The Return of the Repressed in Joyce," "The Writing Cure," and *Penelope's Web*.

19. See Sigmund Freud, "Further Recommendations in the Technique of Psychoanalysis: Recollection, Repetition and Working Through" (*Therapy* 157–167). For discussion of collaborative narrative construction, see Freud, *Dora* (30–32) and Roy Schafer, "Narration in the Psychoanalytic Dialogue." For a connection between analysis, transference, and pedagogy, see Felman, "Psychoanalysis and Education: Teaching Terminable and Interminable" in *Lacan* (69–98).

20. See Woolf's Diary, vols. 1 and 2 (especially 65–66).

21. Space prevents a thorough analysis of *The Common Reader* as a volume, with essays selected, organized, and deployed in such a way as to comment on the task and nature of literary criticism and history. But a cursory comparison of Woolf's table of contents with T. S. Eliot's in *The Sacred Wood: Essay on Poetry and Criticism*, published to acclaim in 1920, is instructive. Where Eliot engages with the masters, Woolf moves from the masters to a polyvocal tradition including such frequently ignored genres as letters, essays, and biography, as well as women writers. Woolf reviewed *The Sacred Wood* in the *Athenaeum*; see vol. 2 of *Diary* for her ambivalent feelings of admiration, anger, and rivalry about Eliot (64–77).

22. This is the very issue that troubles Clarissa in *Mrs. Dalloway*; it is resolved textually by splitting off her potential for madness and projecting it onto the figure of Septimus. For a discussion of reading as transference, see Felman, "Turning the Screw of Interpretation."

23. In support of her basic thesis, Brownstein quotes Woolf's essay on George Eliot: "The heroine figure in literature is traditionally a metaphor for 'something that is perhaps incompatible with the facts of human existence,' an ideal or a romantic or a literary value" (xxvi).

Works Cited

Alcoff, Linda. "Cultural Feminism versus Post-Structuralism: The Identity Crisis in Feminist Theory." *Signs* 13 (Spring 1988): 405–436.

Bayley, John. "Diminishment of Consciousness: A Paradox in the Art of Virginia Woolf." *Virginia Woolf: A Centenary Perspective*. Ed. Eric Warner. New York: St. Martin's, 1984. 69–82.

Blain, Virginia. "Narrative Voice and the Female Perspective in Virginia Woolf's Early Novels." *Virginia Woolf: Critical Essays*. Ed. Patricia Clements and Isobel Grundy. London: Vision, 1983. 115–136.

Boone, Joseph Allen. *Tradition Counter Tradition: Love and the Forms of Fiction*. Chicago: U of Chicago P, 1987.

Bowlby, Rachel. *Virginia Woolf: Feminist Destinations*. Oxford: Basil Blackwell, 1988.

Brownstein, Rachel M. *Becoming a Heroine: Reading about Women in Novels*. New York: Viking, 1982.

Bulletin of Research in the Humanities. Special Issue on *The Years* 80 (Winter 1977).

Cornis-Pope, Marcel. "Poststructuralist Narratology and Critical Writing: *A Figure in the Carpet* Textshop." *Journal of Narrative Technique* 20 (Spring 1990): 245–265.

Culley, Margo, and Catherine Portuges, eds. *Gendered Subjects: The Dynamics of Feminist Teaching*. London: Routledge, 1985.

DeSalvo, Louise A. Introduction. *Melymbrosia*, by Virginia Woolf. xiii–xliv.

———. "Sorting, Sequencing, and Dating the Drafts of Virginia Woolf's *The Voyage Out*." *Bulletin of Research in the Humanities* 82 (Autumn 1979): 271–293.

———. *Virginia Woolf's First Voyage: A Novel in the Making*. Totowa: Rowman, 1980.

———. "Virginia Woolf's Revisions for the 1920 American and English Editions of *The Voyage Out*." *Bulletin of Research in the Humanities* 82 (Autumn 1979): 338–366.

DuPlessis, Rachel Blau. "Woolfenstein." *Breaking the Sequence: Women's Experimental Fiction*. Ed. Ellen G. Friedman and Miriam Fuchs. Princeton: Princeton UP, 1989. 99–114.

———. *Writing beyond the Ending: Narrative Strategies in Twentieth-Century Women Writers*. Bloomington: Indiana UP, 1985.

Felman, Shoshana. *Jacques Lacan and the Adventure of Insight*: *Psychoanalysis in Contemporary Culture.* Cambridge, MA: Harvard UP, 1987.

——. "Turning the Screw of Interpretation." *Literature and Psychoanalysis: The Question of Reading Otherwise.* Ed. Shoshana Felman. Baltimore: Johns Hopkins UP, 1980. 94–207.

Fetterley, Judith. *The Resisting Reader: A Feminist Approach to American Fiction.* Bloomington: Indiana UP, 1978.

Flynn, Elizabeth A., and Patrocinio P. Schweickart, eds. *Gender and Reading: Essays on Readers, Texts, and Contexts.* Baltimore: Johns Hopkins UP, 1986.

Fox, Alice. "Virginia Woolf at Work: The Elizabethan *Voyage Out.*" *Bulletin of Research in the Humanities* 84 (Spring 1981): 65–84.

——. "'What Right Have I, A Woman?': Virginia Woolf's Reading Notes on Sidney and Spenser." *Virginia Woolf: Centennial Essays.* Ed. Elaine K. Ginsberg and Laura Moss Gottlieb. Troy: Whitson, 1983. 249–256.

Freud, Sigmund. "Fragment of an Analysis of a Case of Hysteria." 1905. *Dora: An Analysis of a Case of Hysteria.* Ed. Philip Rieff. New York: Macmillan, 1963.

——. "Further Recommendations in the Technique of Psychoanalysis: Recollection, Repetition and Working Through." 1914. *Therapy and Technique.* Ed. Philip Rieff. New York: Collier, 1963.

Friedman, Susan Stanford. *Penelope's Web: Gender, Modernity, H.D.'s Fiction.* New York: Cambridge UP, 1990.

——. "The Return of the Repressed in Joyce: (Self)Censorship and the Making of a Modernist." *The Languages of Joyce.* Ed. Rosa Maria Bosinelli, Christine van Boheeman, and Carla Marengo. Philadelphia: John Benjamins, 1992.

——. "Return of the Repressed in Women's Narratives." *Journal of Narrative Technique* 19 (Winter 1989): 141–156.

——. "The Writing Cure: Transference and Resistance in a Dialogic Analysis." *H.D. Newsletter 2* (Winter 1988): 25–35.

Froula, Christine. "Out of the Chrysalis: Female Initiation and Female Authority in Virginia Woolf's *The Voyage Out.*" *Tulsa Studies in Women's Literature* 5 (Spring 1986): 63–90.

Heine, Elizabeth. "The Earlier *Voyage Out:* Virginia Woolf's First Novel." *Bulletin of Research in the Humanities* 82 (Autumn 1979): 294–316.

Herman, William. "Virginia Woolf and the Classics: Every Englishman's Prerogative Transmuted into Fictional Art." *Virginia Woolf: Centennial Essays.* Ed. Elaine K. Ginsberg and Laura Moss Gottlieb. New York: Whitson, 1983. 257–268.

Irigaray, Luce. *This Sex Which Is Not One.* Trans. Catherine Porter. Ithaca: Cornell UP, 1985.

Jardine, Alice A. *Gynesis: Configurations of Woman and Modernity.* Ithaca: Cornell UP, 1985.

Joplin, Patricia Klindienst. Rev. of *Virginia Woolf's First Voyage Out*, by Louise DeSalvo. *Virginia Woolf Miscellany* 16 (Spring 1981): 2–3.

Kristeva, Julia. *Desire in Language: A Semiotic Approach to Literature and Art.* Trans. Leon S. Roudiez. New York: Columbia UP, 1980.

Lundberg, Patricia Lorimer. "Dialogically Feminized Reading: A Critique of Reader-Response Criticism." *Reader* 22 (Fall 1989): 9–37.

Marcus, Jane. "Other People's I's (Eyes): The Reader, Gender, and Recursive Reading in *To the Lighthouse* and *The Waves*." *Reader* 22 (Fall 1989): 53–67.

——. *Virginia Woolf and the Languages of Patriarchy*. Bloomington: Indiana UP, 1987.

Marder, Herbert. *Feminism and Art: A Study of Virginia Woolf*. Chicago: U of Chicago P, 1968.

Miller, Nancy K. "Emphasis Added: Plots and Plausibilities in Women's Fiction." *Subject to Change*. New York: Columbia UP, 1989. 25–46.

Minow-Pinkney, Makiko. *Virginia Woolf and the Problem of the Subject: Feminine Writing in the Major Novels*. New Brunswick: Rutgers UP, 1987.

Moi, Toril. *Sexual/Textual Politics: Feminist Literary Theory*. London: Methuen, 1985.

Schafer Roy. "Narration in the Psychoanalytic Dialogue." *On Narrative*. Ed. W. J. T. Mitchell. Chicago: U of Chicago P, 1981. 25–50.

Schlack, Beverly Ann. *Continuing Presences: Virginia Woolf's Use of Literary Allusion*. University Park: Pennsylvania State UP, 1979.

——. "The Novelist's Voyage from Manuscripts to Text: Revisions of Literary Allusions in *The Voyage Out*." *Bulletin of Research in the Humanities* 82 (Autumn 1979): 317–327.

Scholes, Robert. *Protocols of Reading*. New Haven: Yale UP, 1989.

Showalter, Elaine. "Feminist Criticism in the Wilderness." *The New Feminist Criticism*. Ed. Elaine Showalter. New York: Pantheon, 1985. 243–270.

——. *A Literature of Their Own: British Women Novelists from Brontë to Lessing*. Princeton: Princeton UP, 1977.

Spivak, Gayatri Chakravorty. *In Other Worlds: Essays in Cultural Politics*. New York: Methuen, 1987.

Suleiman, Susan R., and Inge Crossman, eds. *The Reader in the Text: Essays on Audience and Interpretation*. Princeton: Princeton UP, 1980.

Woolf, Virginia. *The Common Reader: First Series*. 1925. New York: Harcourt, 1953.

——. *The Diary of Virginia Woolf*. Ed. Anne Oliver Bell. 5 vols. New York: Harcourt, 1977–1984.

——. *Melymbrosia*. Ed. Louise DeSalvo. New York: New York Public Library, 1982.

——. *A Room of One's Own*. 1929. New York: Harcourt, 1957.

——. "A Sketch of the Past." *Moments of Being: Unpublished Autobiographical Writings of Virginia Woolf*. Ed. Jeanne Schulkind. New York: Harcourt, 1985.

——. *Three Guineas*. 1938. New York: Harcourt, 1963.

——. *To the Lighthouse*. 1927. New York: Harcourt, 1955.

——. *The Voyage Out*. 1915. New York: Harcourt, 1948.

NIGHT AND DAY

VIRGINIA WOOLF'S VISIONARY

SYNTHESIS OF REALITY

Melinda Feldt Cumings

The title of Virginia Woolf's second novel *Night and Day* suggests the tension present in all her fiction between the moonlit world of vision and the sunlit world of facts. Her protagonists must continuously and creatively synthesize these poles, symbolically transforming the mundane reality of the day according to the visionary ideals of the night. In *Night and Day* dream is a metaphor for the process common to all of Woolf's novels in which the rational, separative logic of ordinary reality—what she sometimes calls the facts of existence—can be dissolved by the emotional, unifying illumination of an extraordinary insight—the vision. In such a timeless moment the private boundaries of the self expand to encompass a larger cosmic truth. This trancelike egoless state of the night sphere of Virginia Woolf's second novel is a manifestation of the same visionary consciousness experienced by all her protagonists from Clarissa Dalloway hypnotized by the rhythmic motion of her needle sewing, to Mrs. Ramsay lulled into selflessness by the beams of the lighthouse, to Eleanor Pargiter dreaming of a "New World" at the conclusion of *The Years*.[1] Only through such a vision can Katharine Hilbery and Ralph Denham ultimately reconcile their paradoxical desire for individuality and union in *Night and Day*.[2]

Like the mismatched lovers in Shakespearean comedy, Katharine and Ralph must extricate themselves from their false involvements with William Rodney and Mary Datchet while discovering each other.[3]

Originally published in *Modern Fiction Studies*, Summer 1972.

The resulting conventional paraphernalia of misunderstandings, accidental meetings, and self-deceptions create the plot for the day world. But because of the counterpoise of the night sphere, the tone is entirely different from that of most romantic comedy. Woolf transforms the traditional plight of the unsuited lovers by a metaphysical emphasis on the vision over the fact. The facts of the shifting pairs of characters in this romantic game of musical chairs become the moral reality of men and women whose relationships either foster or deny the individual's ability to express his inner vision.

Katharine Hilbery, for instance, is portrayed from the first scene as living an iceberg existence in which most of her creative consciousness is submerged. As she sits pouring tea, the symbol of the exterior social reality of her daily life, only "a fifth part of her mind" is occupied.[4] The remaining four-fifths devoted to her hidden nighttime love of the abstract beauty of mathematics is unawakened in her relationship with William Rodney. Though Katharine walks through the London streets like Clarissa Dalloway thriving on the vitality of "the great and eternally moving pattern of human life" (79), the girl searches for something fixed behind the flux. Katharine seeks in the perfection of numbers the harmony behind "all this petty intercourse . . . the dense crossings and entanglements of men and women" (106). She finds her ideal only in the night world where the multiplicity of day dissolves into unity.[5]

Katharine's dream state is a kind of platonic universe in which:

> there dwelt the realities of the appearances which figure in our world; so direct, powerful and unimpeded were her sensations there, compared with those called forth in actual life. There dwelt the things one might have felt, had there been cause; the perfect happiness of which here we taste the fragment; the beauty seen here in flying glimpses only. . . . It was a place where feelings were liberated from the constraint which the real world puts upon them; and the process of awakenment was always marked by resignation and a kind of stoical acceptance of facts. (145)

Although Katharine describes her vision as a dream, it embodies a superior reality. It is here that she encounters the "magnanimous hero" who is able to understand her need to come to terms with an absolute vision of existence. This need is embodied for Katharine in the Pythagorean abstraction of numbers as "something that hasn't got to do with human beings" (203). She glimpses the wholeness she searches for appropriately while stargazing. Just as the candles in Mrs. Ramsay's dining room will later create a focus for hypnotic unification in *To the Lighthouse*, here the flickering light of the stars is the catalyst to vision:

> Somehow, it seemed to her that they were even now beholding the procession of kings and wise men upon some road on the distant part of the earth. And yet, after gazing another second, the stars did their usual work upon the mind, froze to cinders the whole of our short human history, and reduced the human body to an ape-like, furry form, crouching amid the brushwood of a barbarous clod of mud. This stage was soon succeeded by another, in which there was nothing in the universe save stars and the light of stars; as she looked up the pupils of her eyes so dilated with starlight that the whole of her seemed dissolved in silver and split over the ledges of the stars for ever and ever indefinitely through space. (205)

In the dialectic common to Woolf's moments of vision, opposition becomes synthesized through a cosmic negation of polarities. The positive image of the pageant or procession, a dominant symbol of the continuity of life in Woolf's canon, is replaced by the negative primordial ape, but both must dissolve in the void of illuminated unity. Katharine's ego, symbolized by the pupil of her eye, dilates with the inner light of her experience until "the whole of her seemed dissolved."

Even in her relations with others, Katharine Hilbery attempts to come to terms with the unifying dream that stands behind mundane expressions of emotion. Katharine is at least half-serious when she offers to Mary Patchet a platonic explanation for human emotional motivation: "It's not love; it's not reason; I think it must be some idea. Perhaps, Mary, our affections are the shadow of an idea. Perhaps, there isn't any such thing as affection in itself" (287). The coldness of Katharine's analysis of love results mainly from her lack of experience with feelings and from her need to make contact with an ultimate reality beyond the individual. Like her preoccupation with the cool light of the stars and the abstract principles of mathematics, this attitude toward emotion represents her strivings for a higher, almost mystical ideal of unity: "a consciousness of a *beyond*, of something, which though it is interwoven with it, is not of the eternal world of material phenomena, of an *unseen* over and above the seen."[6]

Katharine expresses her vision of such a momentary, egoless illumination within the individual as she thinks of her friends as symbolic "lantern bearers":

> She thought of three different scenes; she thought of Mary
> sitting upright and saying, "I'm in love—I'm in love"; she
> thought of Rodney losing his self consciousness among
> the dead leaves, and speaking with the abandonment of
> a child; she thought of Denham leaning upon the stone
> parapet and talking to the distant sky, so that she thought
> him mad. Her mind . . . seemed to be tracing out the lines
> of some symmetrical pattern, some arrangement of life,
> which invested, if not herself, at least the others, not only
> with interest, but with a kind of tragic beauty. . . . They
> were the lantern bearers, whose lights, scattered among
> the crowd, wove a pattern, dissolving, joining, meeting
> again in combination. (331–332)

Through their loss of "self consciousness," these characters provide
the glow of their enlightenment for the human procession. They suggest a thread of unity, "some symmetrical pattern," underlying the
apparent chaos of existence.

Katharine herself is one of these "lantern bearers." Despite
her analysis of "this perpetual disparity between the thought and
the action, between the life of solitude and the life of society, this
astonishing precipice on one side of which the soul was active and
in broad daylight, on the other side of which it was contemplative
and dark as night," Katharine cannot make the transition between
night and day (358). Even though, while gazing at the night sky,
she affirms the "dream nature of our life . . . beyond which lay . . .
nothing more than darkness" while declaring her intention "to forget
herself, to forget individual lives" by stepping "beyond the region
where the light of illusion still makes it desirable to possess, to love,
to struggle," Katharine discovers that Mary Datchet's renunciation of
the particular for the universal remains an unattainable ideal (373).
Only when she accepts the "friendship" of Ralph Denham is Katharine
able to bridge the gap between these worlds.

For Ralph Denham a dream world also exists that he endeavors
to keep sharply distinct from daytime reality. The cool starlight that
illumines Katharine's vision of truth is complemented by another
symbol of light in Ralph's spirit of flame:

> It seemed to him that this spirit was the most valuable pos-
> session he had; he thought that by means of it he could set
> flowering waste tracts of the earth, cure many ills, or raise
> up beauty where none now existed; it was, too, a fierce
> and potent spirit which would devour the dusty books and
> parchments on the office wall with one lick of its tongue,

and leave him in a minute standing in nakedness, if he gave way to it. (129)

His love for Katharine, the product of a "mystic temper which identified a living woman with much that no human beings long possess in the eyes of each other," is contrasted with the girl's aversion to human entanglements (408). While Katharine keeps her eyes turned to the stars, Ralph finds through her a merger of the night world of dreams and daytime reality: "She had filled the shell of the old dream with the flesh of life" (150). Like many other male characters in Virginia Woolf's novels, Ralph Denham experiences moments of heightened reality through a woman.

This interdependence of the male and female principles can be demonstrated by comparing two scenes, one in which Ralph feels at one with Katharine and another in which he feels alienated. The respective rapture and annihilation experienced are presented not as a conventional lover's reactions, but are rendered in nearly cosmic terms. Like Katharine's visually induced trance created by the luminescent pulsation of the stars, Ralph enters a nearly hypnotic state by the rhythmic repetition of his lover's name:

> He lost his sense of all that surrounded him; all substantial things—the hour of the day, what we have done and are about to do, the presence of other people and the support we derive from seeing their belief in a common reality—all this slipped from him. So he might have felt if the earth had dropped from his feet, and the empty blue had hung all round him, and the air had been steeped in the presence of one woman. (235)

This experience follows the pattern of the visionary ritual common to all Woolf's novels. By concentrating on a rhythmic sight, sound, or motion and by repressing the logical faculties, the character loses the sense of his or her self as a separate entity. In fact, the spirit often seems to expand beyond the bonds of the body feeling itself floating in space above the earth. When Ralph tells Mary whom he has seen, the mere articulation of Katharine's name recreates the attitude of ecstasy: "The lips just parted, the fingers loosely clenched, the whole attitude of rapt contemplation, which fell like a veil between them" (243). Ralph's posture is echoed in a scene immediately following by Katharine "as she sat rapt in thought upon the ground . . . there was something improper to him in her self-forgetfulness . . . seeming unconscious of everything" (259).[7]

In contrast to the bliss Ralph feels when he is united to the cosmos through his love of Katharine, he undergoes the inverse of this transcendent experience when he feels he has lost her. As he walks along the river he is unable to enter a positive trancelike state through the rhythmic movement of the waters. Although the prerequisite suppression of the rational faculty occurs—Ralph's brain was "alert, but without understanding"—he feels no timeless unity with the cosmos; instead, the "world had him at his mercy" (161). Nor is there a harmonious emotional synthesis of the unity and multiplicity of existence: "He made no pattern out of the sights he saw" (162). Here, Woolf's recurrent stream of life metaphor illustrating the paradox of continuity and flux becomes upset. Ralph is adrift in the stream, and instead of moving in harmony with the current, he feels his ego threatened by the loss of control of his own destiny. Another common metaphor, that of illumination, which is the usual culmination of vision, is also reversed in this scene. The fog obscures the lights, which seem "suspended upon a blank surface" and temporarily "all bright points in his life were blotted out; all prominences levelled" (162).

In a development of this scene, Ralph at the conclusion of *Night and Day* once more wanders the night streets of London in a surrealistic odyssey in search of Katharine. At this point the dominant image in Ralph's mind is of "a lighthouse besieged by the flying bodies of lost birds, who were dashed senseless, by the gale, against the glass" (417). In a dualistic vision common to Woolf's characters, he sees himself as both the lighthouse, "steadfast and brilliant," and the birds, "whirled . . . senseless against the glass" (418). Ralph's exhaustion transforms the evening into the symbolic expression of his own inner landscape: "In his state of physical fatigue, details merged themselves into the vaster prospect, of which the flying gloom and the intermittent lights of lamp-posts and private houses were the outward token" (418). Katharine's house, the object of his weary quest, is the emblematic center of his moment of illumination:

> Lights burnt in the three long windows of the drawing room. The space of the room behind became, in Ralph's vision, the center of the dark, flying wilderness of the world; the justification for the welter of confusion surrounding it; the steady light which cast its beams, like those of a lighthouse, with searching composure over the trackless waste. In this little sanctuary were gathered together several different people, but their identity was dissolved in a general glory of something that might, perhaps, be called civilization. . . . Physically, he saw them bathed in the steady flow of yellow light which filled the long oblongs of the windows; in their movements they were beautiful; and in their speech he

figured a reserve of meaning, unspoken, but understood. (418–419)

Katharine's previous brief vision of the radiating spirits of her friends as "lantern-bearers" for the human race is summed up in Ralph's perception of man's creations—civilization expressed in the domesticity of a lit-up house glowing like a lighthouse in the darkness. The ultimate illumination for Ralph seems to issue from Katharine herself: "He did not see her in the body; he seemed curiously to see her as a shape of light, the light itself" (419).

Ralph's moment of vision, represented by the alternating identifications of the lovers as lighthouse and lost animals, is echoed by Katharine's final search for Ralph through the London streets. The noises of traffic and pedestrians composing the vital rhythm of the city prepare Katharine to lose herself in the flow of life and to surrender to love:

> The deep roar filled her ears; the changing tumult had the inexpressible fascination of varied life pouring ceaselessly with a purpose which, as she looked, seemed to her, somehow, the normal purpose for which life was framed; its complete indifference to the individuals, whom it swallowed up and rolled onwards, filled her with at least temporary exaltation. The blend of daylight and of lamplight made her an invisible spectator, just as it gave the people who passed her a semitransparent quality. . . . They tended the enormous rush of the current—the great flow, the deep stream, the unquenchable tide. She stood unobserved and absorbed, glorying openly in the rapture that had run subterraneously all day. (465–466)

The illumination Ralph associates with his beloved is symbolically transformed from the light of Mary's lamp to Katharine herself: "The steady radiance seemed for a second to have its counterpart within her; she shut her eyes; she opened them and looked at the lamp again; another love burnt in the place of the old one" (474). When she finally reaches Ralph after her wanderings of self-discovery, Katharine's vision is intensified: "An extraordinary clearness of sight seemed to possess her on beholding him" (479).

Ralph's expression of affection terminates Katharine's isolation. By idealistically affirming Katharine as "the only reality in the world," while practically outlining his financial relationship to his family, Ralph combines the worlds of night and day and inspires an exultation in Katharine that she has never felt before (313). The objects associated with previous transcendent moments, mathematical symbols and the stars, blend in Katharine's mind with the flowing river until "she had no consciousness at all":

> books of algebraic symbols, pages all speckled with dots and dashes and twisted bars, came before her eyes . . . and all the time she was in fancy looking up through a telescope at white shadow-cleft disks which were other worlds, until she felt herself possessed of two bodies, one walking by the river with Denham, the other concentrated to a silver globe aloft in the fine blue space above the scum of vapours that was covering the visible world. (317)

The sense of dissociation from reality, a kind of spiritual dualism, which Woolf's characters often express in their moments of "almost supernatural exultation," approaches traditional descriptions of the split personality of the schizophrenic (319). Here, the spirit is metamorphosed to "a silver globe" floating high above "the visible world." Nor is this split limited to the character experiencing transcendence; it occasionally extends to the object of perception. Thus, Ralph wonders whether the Katharine he loves is the same as the real Katharine. Though he is "strangly transfigured" with "a keenness of sensation," "a mastery of his faculties," and vistas before him of "no perceptible end," Ralph, like Katharine, is unable to sustain the ecstatic moment.

This clarity of vision with its simultaneous ecstasy creates frustrations in the relationship of the lovers. When the visionary moment fades because of its ephemeral nature, they find their love difficult to sustain. In the face of cosmic unity, the human being can be reduced to comic proportions as when Katharine thinks of Ralph: "So little, so single, so separate from all else he appeared, who had been the cause of these extreme agitations and aspirations" (479). The tension between solitude and sharing becomes the concluding focus of *Night and Day*. Ralph's angry response to Katharine's stargazing self-absorption, her "lapses," is countered by Katharine's description of the alternation of unity and individuality, merging and separating, which she feels in herself: "It's not boredom . . . Reality—reality . . . I cease to be real to you. It's the faces in a storm again—the vision in a hurricane. We come together for a moment and we part" (501).

The struggle to achieve the reconciliation of the vision with the fact through partnership represented in the relation of Katharine Hilbery and Ralph Denham or even William Rodney and Cassandra Otway is not Virginia Woolf's only alternative. In her portrayal of Mary Datchet, Woolf offers the possibility of visionary consciousness in the single life.[8] Mary's motto, "To know the truth—to accept without bitterness" (274), is a complement to Katharine's theory, "It's life that matters, nothing but life—the process of discovering, the everlasting and perpetual process" (138). For Mary, the vision of reality entails "a transformation from the universal to the particular" (275). Unlike Katharine's earlier, unawakened and abstract reaction to the vitality of the London streets, Mary's transcendent moments are generated by contact with mankind as individual human beings: "In the eyes of every single person she detected a flame; as if a spark in the brain ignited spontaneously at contact with the things they met and drove them on" (272). This metaphor of the flame, the persistent symbol of illumination in Woolf's art, appears also when Katharine thinks of Ralph and in Ralph's letter to her as a symbol of human potentiality.[9] It is by one of these sparks that Mary enjoys a moment of being:

> From an acute consciousness of herself as an individual, Mary passed to a conception of the scheme of things in which, as a human being, she must have her share. She half held a vision; the vision shaped and dwindled. . . . But if she talked to anyone, the conception might escape her. Her vision seemed to lay out the lines of her life until death in a way which satisfied her sense of harmony. It only needed a persistent effort of thought, stimulated in this strange way by the crowd and the noise, to climb the crest of existence and see it all laid out once and forever. Already her suffering as an individual was left behind her . . . as she shaped her conception of life in this world, only two articulate words escaped her, muttered beneath her breath—"Not happiness—not happiness." (273)

Her vision culminates in a paradox just as Ralph's did: "She was at once the sufferer and the pitiful spectator of suffering; she was happier than she had ever been; she was more bereft; she was rejected, and she was immensely beloved" (293). In contrast to Mary who moves away from ego-centered individualism and the possessiveness of love to an embracing of humanity in general, Katharine and Ralph must grow from emotional isolation to visionary awareness through personal involvement on a one to one level.

Night and Day concludes with an affirmation of this rhythm of blending and opposition in the sunburst drawing made by Ralph as a wordless pledge of love: "It represented by its circumference of smudges surrounding a central blot all that encircling glow which for him surrounded, inexplicably, so many of the objects of life, softening their sharp outline, so that he could see certain streets, books, and situations wearing a halo almost perceptible to the physical eye" (522). Like the symbol of the lantern or the lighthouse, Ralph's drawing suggests the radiance of human beings when the bonds of the ego are dissolved "softening their sharp outline" and their transparency when the aura of the inner illumination becomes visible as a "halo" for others to see by in the dark. When Katharine acknowledges the similarity of her and Ralph's views of life, this symbol, a dot surrounded by flamelike rays, becomes the expression of their unity. Katharine's inarticulate revelation of love continues this fire imagery:

> But he persuaded her into a broken statement, beautiful to him, charged with extreme excitement as she spoke of the dark red fire, and the smoke twined round it, making him feel that he had stepped over the threshold into the faintly lit vastness of another mind, stirring with shapes, so large, so dim, unveiling themselves only in flashes, and moving away again into the darkness, engulfed by it. (534–535)

The symbol of the light glowing in darkness, the day within night, is the dominant and concluding symbol of the novel.

In their attempt "to piece together in a laborious and elementary fashion fragments of belief, unsoldered and separate, lacking the unity of phrases fashioned by the old believers," Katharine and Ralph strive to fashion unity out of multiplicity, to awaken the dream in reality, and ultimately to create the transcendent moment in time (537). Appropriately, their "vision of an orderly world" swims "miraculously in the golden light of a large steady lamp" (537). The symbols of illumination—starlight, flame, lamplight, fire, lighthouse—join with Woolf's other important symbol, water, as the lovers enter "the enchanted region" in the final visionary moment of *Night and Day.*

> What woman did he see? And where was she walking, and who was her companion? Moments, fragments, a second of vision, and then the flying waters, the winds dissipating and dissolving; then, too, the recollection from chaos, the return of security, the earth firm, superb and brilliant in the sun. . . . Pausing, they looked into the river which bore its dark tide of waters, endlessly moving, beneath them. (537–538)

Through love Katharine and Ralph momentarily dissolve the barriers of individual consciousness to become one with the flow of existence.

Night and Day, then, deserves study in any account of Virginia Woolf's fiction that considers the primary tension in her art between the visionary moment and the matrix of material reality out of which it is generated. Because of its less condensed and polished form, Woolf's second novel reveals the ritual of achieving ecstatic awareness better concealed by the organic integration of her mature works. However, a careful examination of *Night and Day* reveals not the great differences in the vision between Woolf's early and late novels but the consistency with which she pursued her quest for a synthesis of dream with reality.

Notes

1. For a complete description of this pattern see Melinda Cumings, "Visionary Ritual in the Novels of Virginia Woolf," Diss. Univ. of Wisconsin 1972, where I argue that a common process occurs in Woolf's art by which her characters achieve vision and outline the stages prerequisite to its attainment. Many steps in the ritual parallel the stages of mystical encounters.

2. Critics have tended to deal with _Night and Day_ too harshly. Though Woolf evaluated it in her diary as "a much more mature and finished and satisfactory book than _The Voyage Out_," James Hafly in _The Glass Roof: Virginia Woolf as Novelist_ (London: Russell & Russell, 1963), 27, sums up the general scholarly view of _Night and Day_ as "perhaps the least satisfying of Virginia Woolf's novels."

3. Josephine O'Brien Schaefer, in _The Three-fold Nature of Reality in the Novels of Virginia Woolf_ (The Hague: Mouton and Co., 1965), 51–52, analyzes the novel in terms of its parallels with Shakespeare's _Twelfth Night_.

4. Virginia Woolf, _Night and Day_ (London: The Hogarth Press, 1930),1. Further references to this edition follow quotations.

5. Harvena Richter, in _Virginia Woolf: The Inward Voyage_ (Princeton: Princeton University Press, 1970), 122, observes: "Night with its mysteries, intuitions, and dreams, is related to woman; daylight with its rationality and logic, to man." However, Richter simplifies the complex texture of dream and reality in _Night and Day_ when she applies this opposition too strictly. Ralph Denham, whom she classifies in the daylight sphere, is also obsessed with a dream world, like Katharine Hilbery.

6. F. C. Happold, _Mysticism: A Study and an Anthology_ (London: Penguin Books, 1963), 18–19.

7. Katharine Hilbery's posture foreshadows Mrs. Ramsay's attitude of contemplation in _To the Lighthouse_.

8. Woolf often uses single women as foils to married women in her novels. They include visionary artists like Lily Briscoe and Miss La Trobe.

9. Herbert Marder, in _Feminism and Art: A Study of Virginia Woolf_ (Chicago: University of Chicago Press, 1968), 141, notes that the flame image is "closely related, if not exactly equivalent to the lighthouse." He also traces its appearance in other of Woolf's works.

FROM SHORT STORY TO NOVEL

THE MANUSCRIPT REVISIONS OF

VIRGINIA WOOLF'S *MRS. DALLOWAY*

Charles G. Hoffmann

I

The manuscript version of *Mrs. Dalloway* consists of four notebooks and a typescript of an early chapter, "The Prime Minister," all in the Berg Collection of the New York Public Library, and three volumes of notebooks in the British Museum, which are the main manuscript of *Mrs. Dalloway*. Jacqueline Latham in her article, "The Origin of *Mrs. Dalloway*,"[1] quite correctly shows that A. J. Lewis[2] and Wallace Hildick[3] were mistaken in their assumption that the opening passage in the British Museum manuscript (the scene involving Peter Walsh in Westminster, corresponding to pp. 72 ff. of the novel)[4] constitutes the beginning of a new version of the novel, Since Miss Latham goes into detailed evidence showing the origin of the novel in the short story, "Mrs. Dalloway in Bond Street," and the Berg Collection notebooks, it will be unnecessary for me to repeat that account. There is further evidence in the story itself to reinforce Miss Latham's thesis. In both the short story and the manuscript version of the "Prime Minister" chapter (corresponding to the motor car scene in the novel, pp. 19 ff.) Mrs. Dalloway is buying gloves (not flowers as in the novel) for her party that night when she and Miss Anstruther (not Miss Pym as in the novel) hear the backfiring of the car.

Furthermore, the "Prime Minister" chapter begins exactly at the point where "Mrs. Dalloway in Bond Street" leaves off. The lat-

Originally published in *Modern Fiction Studies*, Summer 1968.

ter ends: "There was a violent explosion in the street outside. The shop-women cowered behind the counters. But Clarissa, sitting very upright, smiled at the other lady. 'Miss Anstruther!' she exclaimed."[5] The "Prime Minister" begins: "The violent explosion which made the women who were selling gloves cower behind the counter, & Mrs. Dalloway & Miss Anstruther, who were buying gloves, sit very upright, came from a motor car."[6] The connection between the two "chapters" is direct and obvious, linking them together as a unified, continuous narrative.

More importantly, the same holograph notebook that contains the "Prime Minister" chapter continues with an early although shorter version of the meeting between Clarissa Dalloway and Peter Walsh (corresponding to pp. 59 ff. of the novel). The manuscript version of the scene ends with Peter Walsh leaving as Clarissa's daughter Elizabeth enters the room (corresponding to page 71 of the novel). The British Museum notebooks begin at that point with the next scene, Peter Walsh in Westminster, continuing the narrative as on page 72 of the novel. Thus the Berg Collection notebooks and the British Museum notebooks form a continuous version of the novel from its origin in the short story to a complete novel.

However, what is of greater significance than the continuity of the manuscript notebooks is that the early notebooks of the manuscript show an important shift in thematic focus and narrative design through the introduction of Septimus Smith in the novel. In the Introduction to the Modern Library edition of *Mrs. Dalloway*, Virginia Woolf wrote that "in the first version Septimus, who later is intended to be her [Mrs. Dalloway's] double had no existence; and . . . Mrs. Dalloway was originally to kill herself, or perhaps merely to die at the end of the party" (vi). Having decided on October 6, 1922, to write a novel tentatively to be titled "At Home " or "The Party," Virginia Woolf planned (and on the same day began writing) the "Prime Minister" chapter as a continuation of "Mrs. Dalloway in Bond Street," using the already completed story as the first chapter of the novel and the "Prime Minister" as the second. Septimus Smith does not appear as a character in either the "Bond Street" story or in the first version of the "Prime Minister" chapter. Instead, a Mr. H. Z. Prentice, who is later discarded as a character altogether, is given prominence as a foil to Mrs. Dalloway and a political antagonist of the prime minister.

The manuscript notes for this chapter explicitly state the main theme of the novel as originally conceived: "To give 2 points of view at once: authority vs irresponsibility." The Prime Minister in his motor car is "authority passing through the streets" whereas the "Scullywags," free but irresponsible, are to be represented by "a man of the thoughtful class. ugly. not deformed,"[7] Mr. H. Z. Prentice, a middle-class radical. Although not explicitly stated in the notes, it is implicit in the chapter itself that Mrs. Dalloway represents the conservative upper middle class, which accepts tradition and authority. Thus the thematic focus of this early version of the chapter is quite different not only from the final published version, but also from the second version of the chapter when Septimus Smith is first introduced. The main theme is emphatically and explicitly one of political and social conflict with decided overtones of class consciousness, whereas in the novel this theme became subsidiary and is muted in the personal conflict between Clarissa Dalloway and Doris Kilman.

The political and social conflict is dramatized in the manuscript version when H. Z. Prentice overhears Edgar J. Watkiss, a working-class man, identify the car as the Prime Minister's in humorous yet "respectful accents": "This information convinced H. Z. Prentice & at the same moment fired him with bitterness. For if the workers can talk like that about the Prime Minister, what hope is there thought H. Z. Prentice, giving one look at the motor car, & shoving his way through & cutting down a back street—for human progress?"[8] Prentice's antitraditionalism and antiauthoritarianism is in direct contrast to Mrs. Dalloway's acceptance and familiarity with the world of royalty and prime ministers:

> She, too, looked; but not quite in the way the rest did. After all, her husband Richard Dalloway, had lunched in the Queen's presence. There is a bodyguard surrounding those immortal faces; a ray of light falls upon them. . . .
>   This light rested for a second upon Clarissa's face, making it different from the other faces, quicker, less inquisitive; yet it had a reverence. For the Queen, thought Clarissa, goes to hospitals, opens bazaars.[9]

Prentice wastes no thought on the upper classes represented by the Dalloways, but he is incensed that the lower classes represented by Watkiss should show reverence and respect for the privileged classes represented by the Prime Minister: "'What I can't tolerate,' he tells his companions at lunch, 'is the attitude of the working classes.'"[10]

It is through the character Prentice that the emphasis of this early version of the chapter is political and social rather than introspective and personal. It is in the revision of this chapter that Virginia Woolf shifts the focus and emphasis of her novel by introducing Septimus Smith. The notes for a revision of the novel reveal the shift in focus from external political and social concerns to internal perspectives.

In the same notebook but dated October 16, 1922, and headed "a possible revision of this book" she wrote:

> Suppose it to be connected in this way:
> Sanity & insanity.
> Mrs. D. seeing the truth. S. S. seeing the insane truth. . . .
> The pace is to be given by the gradual increase of S's insanity on the one side; by the approach of the party on the other. . . .
> The Question is whether the inside of the mind in both Mrs. D's & S. S. can be made luminous—that is to say the stuff of the book—lights on it coming from external sources.[11]

In revising the "Prime Minister" chapter Virginia Woolf retained the first half, which is the progress of the Prime Minister's car through the streets of London and which is quite similar in narrative details to the final, published version. The revision is a reworking of the luncheon scene immediately after Prentice makes his remark about the lower classes. The political theme is retained but a new theme and focus is added through the introduction of Septimus Smith as a friend of Prentice, who is also present in the restaurant:

> Suddenly as he [stopped], the agitation suddenly died down. There was nothing more to be said. An extraordinary flatness fell upon the company, who were for the most part drinking coffee. There was complete silence. And then Septimus Smith laughed. Nobody had spoken to him, & therefore he must have been laughing at something he thought, or saw. H. Z. Prentice, feeling very uncomfortable, said something quite irrelevant. Septimus quick looked at the table cloth, which seemed to him of astonishing whiteness. The silver vase, with the leopard's head holding a ring in its mouth, had, too, an extreme significance, [for the leopard had opened its mouth, Septimus thought; & winked, & that had made him laugh][12] which had excited him profoundly, seemed connected with the brilliant cloth & the flashing silver & the sense which possessed him of his own astonishing insight & importance. (He was a man of about twenty seven, with eyes rather far apart, a pale face, & very white teeth.) His heart was beating very fast. Everything had momentarily become very splendid & very simple. Yet physically he felt as if, unless something cool & firm restrained his heart it would fly into pieces.[13]

The portrayal of Septimus's insanity is rather self-consciously and crudely directed toward showing his eccentricity of behavior in a normal situation to emphasize his "madness" so that the unintended effect is that of an "outsider" attempting to imagine what the world must look like to a "mad" man. Virginia Woolf, although she had already conceived of the basic connection between Clarissa Dalloway and Septimus Smith in their separate but equally illuminating perspectives on truth, had not yet achieved a sympathetic and poetic approach to Septimus's "insane truth." This weakness in character portrayal is even more evident in the following passage in which Septimus, having left the restaurant, has an hallucination:

> As he stood by the hat shop, he saw the sky full of birds, purple & red, descending. They fell through his body, giving him actually the sensation of gliding, swooping, alighting to the admiration of multitudes, who beheld him with terror (but he knew he was safe) & received him, as he bestowed upon them his extraordinary gift with a rapturous clamour of love. He was some sort of Christ, probably. And the news must be communicated at once—at once!—there was no time to lose—to the Prime Minister.[14]

The Messianic hallucination is too abrupt. The reader instead of being sympathetic with Septimus's tragic condition, or illuminated by his vision, finds his ravings ludicrous. Even his resolve to kill himself arises not out of a sense of personal guilt and tragedy, but out of an hallucinatory desire to be a "martyr": "as I am going to die I will kill the Prime Minister & some one who has everything I want like Ellis Robertson. (he had been named for the editorship of the new daily paper) I shall be immortal, he thought, my name will be in all the placards."[15]

These passages are the earliest attempts by Virginia Woolf to render Septimus's madness and are therefore understandably rough in details. But the perspective of Septimus's "insane truth," however crudely portrayed at this stage in the novel's development, is implicit in the situation of his breakdown. What was needed at this point, as she wrote in her diary on October 29, 1922, was time "to think out *Mrs. Dalloway* . . . to foresee this book better than the others and get the utmost out of it."[16] She broke off the writing of the novel until she discovered the method by which she could illuminate the two contrasting perspectives of Clarissa and Septimus, what she calls in her diary her "tunnelling process" by which she can "dig out beautiful caves" behind her characters. Peter Walsh provides that "tunnel" to Clarissa Dalloway and the introduction of Lucretia as Septimus's wife provides it for Septimus Smith, as is evident in the British Museum notebooks.

II

The latest notebook in the Berg Collection on *Mrs. Dalloway*, dated variously from November 9, 1922, to August 2, 1923, bridges the gap in time between the Berg Collection and the British Museum manuscripts and indeed overlaps the date of the beginning of the latter. More importantly, this notebook is a kind of writer's diary containing a running commentary on the work in progress. These unpublished notebook entries, when combined with the entries in the earlier notebooks and with the published *A Writer's Diary*, form a complete record of the genesis and development of design, theme, and character portrayal in *Mrs. Dalloway.*

The design of the novel is planned in detail in these notes. From the beginning, as indicated in the March 12, 1922, notebook, Virginia Woolf saw the design of the novel as the converging of everything in the party at the end. This basic design is reinforced and expanded upon in the November 9 notes to include the theme of life and death: "All must bear finally upon the party at the end; which expresses life, in every variety & full of antic[ipa]tion; while S. dies." But in the November 19 notes for the first time she thinks in terms of no chapter breaks. Eliminating chapter breaks would reinforce the effect she desired "of being incessant," of keeping the "texture unbroken" except that one must break into the texture "to give the surrounding—time & space—as well as the individuals." To achieve this "tunneling process," she considers first the possibility of using a chorus or "an observer in the Street—at each critical point who acts the part of chorus." But the main function of the "chorus" would be structural rather than thematic, that of providing a link between scenes, and on February 26 she considers instead the possibility of dividing the novel "like acts of a play into five, say or six" scenes. Ultimately, Virginia Woolf used a combination of several methods to link the separate parts of the novel—the motor car and the airplane, the observer, and although there is no formal division into "acts" the novel is divided into a half dozen or so major scenes—but the main method, the progress of the hours, is inherent in the structure of the novel with its events taking place in one day. Indeed, the "dance" of the hours so dominated the pattern of the novel that Virginia Woolf considered *The Hours* as an alternate title.[17]

The entry for November 9, 1922, indicates an important

development in theme, as important as the original shift from a political and social theme to the idea of truth being seen from the perspectives of sanity and insanity: "Suppose the idea of the book is the
contrast between life & death. All inner feelings to be lit up. The two
minds. Mrs. D. & Septimus."[18] Here the theme of life and death, the
meaning of life and the fear of death, is seen as the ultimate focus of
the novel; but as can be seen in the manuscript version that evolved
out of these notes, the sanity-insanity theme becomes an integral
part of the theme of life and death, and even the original political
and social theme, although drastically changed and subordinated, is
utilized as a corollary to the main theme.

It is possible to trace the development of the theme in relation
to character portrayal in some detail. For example, the opening passages of the British Museum notebooks (corresponding to pp. 72 ff.
of the novel) exist in three versions, each with a different thematic
emphasis.[19] In the first version, Peter Walsh, upon hearing the toll-
ing of St. Margaret's, is reminded of the futility of his past in general
and of his failure to marry Clarissa in particular. He then sums up
his youth: "He had been sent down from Oxford. He had drunk too
much. He had been a socialist. But the future of civilization lies, in the
hands of such young men. of such young men as himself he meant."[20]
Although the above passage is largely retained in the novel (75) and
even expanded, the second version of the scene shifts the thematic
focus to Clarissa and her recent illness: "She has been ill, he thought,
& the sound [of St. Margaret's] expressed languor & suffering. It was
her heart, he remembered, & the bell tolled for death that surprised
in the midst of life."[21] The theme of life and death is expanded and
sharpened in the third version so that, as in the novel, it becomes
dominantly dramatic, thereby subordinating the political and social
theme of the first version:

> She has been ill, & the sound expressed languor & suf-
> fering. It was her heart, he remembered: & the sudden
> loudness of the final stroke tolled for death that surprised
> in the midst of life. Clarissa falling where she stood, in her
> drawing-room. No! No! he cried. She is not dead. I am not
> old. He was glaring almost ferociously at the statue of the
> Duke of Cambridge.[22]

Septimus's vision in his madness (corresponding to pages
104–105 of the novel) provides an ironic contrast to Peter Walsh's
fear of growing old and approaching death. The August 2, 1923, entry in the notebook states the general theme of Septimus's desire to
accept life that is confounded by people and their demands of him:
"Sense of falling through into discoveries—like a trap door opening.

. . . The shd. be a fairly logical transition in S's mind. beauty of natural things. This disappears on seeing people. His sense of their demands upon him: What is his relation to them? Inability to identify himself with them."[23] These notes become transformed in the manuscript to the following passage of Septimus's ecstatic joy at the beauty of natural things:

> He had only to open his eyes. Some weight was on them. A door was shut. He pushed through; he woke; he saw into life. Long streamers of the sun caressed him, the trees waved welcome. Everything was alive, was conscious of his coming. . . . Each movement was timed. And the trees, then the grass, & the sun; & to look was only to gladden Septimus. We welcome, the world seemed to say, we accept; we laugh. Its beautiful, said Septimus. Nothing was ugly. As his eyes fell, beauty sprang up—a movement, a colour, a [break in ms.] Merely to watch a leaf quivering filled him with exquisite joy.[24]

But then Death in the form of Evans (it is actually Peter Walsh approaching) appears to Septimus and the mood of ecstasy is destroyed and fear of death takes its place.

Septimus's suicide is not a negation of life; it is instead paradoxically an affirmation of life, for "he did not want to die. He did not want to kill himself. Life itself was admirable."[25] Like Clarissa's parties, his suicide is intended as an offering of his self to humanity: "'An offering' he murmured, with some idea of prayer in his mind— the window sill was an altar; & so in the belief that he was giving up to humanity what it asked of him he sprang vigorously, of his own free will, on to Mrs. Filmers area railings."[26]

Although Virginia Woolf found it difficult to write Septimus's "mad" scenes, as she notes in her *Diary*, particularly the scene leading to his suicide that is considerably revised in its details in the manuscript, she nonetheless solved the main problem of connecting the real world with Septimus's insane truth. The original version of Septimus's insanity in the "Prime Minister" chapter lacked this necessary connection, but in thinking through her approach to Septimus, she discovers the means by which his externality can be presented without sacrificing the perspective of his insanity. On November 9, 1922, she writes:

> Septimus (?) must be seen by someone. His wife? She to be bounded in S? Simple, instinctive, childless. . . .
> She is to be a *real* character.
> He only real in so far as she sees him. Otherwise to

exist in his view of things: which is always to be contrasting with Mrs. Dalloway[']s.[27]

The portrayal of Septimus is much surer, much closer to the published version once Lucrezia is introduced in the manuscript in the Regent's Park scene.

Lucrezia, therefore, is intended to be more than a mere observer helplessly witnessing her husband's breakdown: Septimus's tenuous hold on reality is through her, and *her* reality frees Virginia Woolf from the awkward expository explanations of Septimus's strange behavior in the earlier manuscript chapter. The fact that she is his wife intensifies the tragedy of his breakdown; her being an alien in London, alone, not knowing where or to whom to turn for help, reinforces Septimus's internal alienation. And as a reflector, she provides the needed external perspective on Septimus; through her "passionateness," her "Southerness," her "instinctiveness," she is to see him "as a woman sees him. feels him alternately far & near."[28] In a passage corresponding to pages 99–100 of the novel, Lucrezia is the means by which the past is told without resorting to Septimus's distorted perspective:

> There Septimus sat, in his overcoat, staring at the sky. His lips were moving. He was talking to himself, or talking to Evans, a dead man. She had never even known him [Evans]. He was a nice quiet man not handsome, not big, not clever like Septimus [,] who had been killed. Such things happen to everyone. Everyone gives up something when they marry. She had to give up her home. She had come to live here, in this awful city. But Septimus had grown stranger—stranger. He had let himself think about horrible things, so could anyone. He had begun to forget things. He frightened her. He said people were talking behind the wall of the bed room. Mrs. Filmer thought it odd. He had seen an old woman in the leaves of a plant. And then he was as happy as he could be for hours together. They went to Hampton Court where all the flowers were out. Suddenly he had said "Now we will both kill ourselves."[29]

With this background the reader is well prepared when, a few moments later, Septimus, seeing that Lucrezia is not wearing her wedding ring, views it as a symbolic portent: "So our marriage is over, he thought with extreme relief. I am now free."[30] And again, a few moments later, the reader is willing to accept without further need of explanation Septimus's vision of Evans, corresponding to pp. 105 ff. of the novel.

It is to Septimus, however, rather than Lucrezia, that Virginia

Woolf devotes more of her concern in these preparatory notes. For example, on November 19, 1922, she writes, "That Septimus should face through all extremes of feeling—happiness & unhappiness—intensify. [He] should always remain inside human affairs."[31] This rapid alternation between the extremes of feeling is evident in the continuation of Septimus's thoughts after he has noticed that his wife is no longer wearing her wedding ring:

> Trees are alive. Everything is alive. There is no crime. (And this all can be proved; Darwin; said the voice[)] A Skye terrier trotted past. Septimus trembled. Its turning into a man! he cried. The head seemed to him to be wrinkling up like a man's. he thought, shutting his eyes, with a sense of divine relief, I can now see the truth of everything.[32]

At the same time Septimus's breakdown is intended as the tragedy of any young man of his social background who had gone through the war unscathed physically but who was deeply affected mentally by the experience. In the same notebook entry Virginia Woolf writes: "[Septimus] might be left vague—as a mad person is—not so much character as an idea—This is what is painful to her [Rezia]—becomes generalised—universalised. So can be partly R; partly me."[33] In a manuscript passage corresponding closely to pages 127–128 of the novel, the following generalized portrait of Septimus occurs:

> London had swallowed up in her time many armies of young men called Smith, has thought nothing of fantastic Christian names like Septimus, with which their parents have sought to distinguish them. Lodging in Islington or off the Euston Road, the great experience which changes a face in two years from a pink, perfectly innocent oval to a face contracted, horrible, suspicious, suffering, took place, day by day, night by night, without record. . . . Sensitive, vain, callous, aspiring; a nervous man; mastered by impulses, & fears; proud of his temperament, affectionate; conscious of low birth & gentle birth; at once a snob & a socialist; uneasy in manner; with more surface than usual exposed naked to the heats & colds of life—such were the seeds in him, which, all muddled up, lived, as live they might, in a lodging off the Euston Road.[34]

Partly through the personal and subjective reflections of Rezia and partly through the general and objective commentary of the author-narrator, Septimus Smith is at once character and idea, individualized as a character and universalized as an idea, as he must be to be Clarissa Dalloway's foil.

If Septimus is "real" only in so far as Lucrezia sees him except that "he must be logical enough," Virginia Woolf further notes, "to make the comparison between the two worlds," Clarissa also "must be seen by other people," as a later entry, dated February 26, 1923, in the same notebook suggests.[35] It is mainly through Peter Walsh that we view Clarissa Dalloway outside of herself.

Apparently, at some point between May 7 and June 18, 1923, Virginia Woolf again began working on the novel, writing the scene between Clarissa and Peter Walsh found in the original notebook after the completion of the "Prime Minister" chapter but separated from it by an essay on Dorothy Richardson. Although this scene is undated, it is apparent from the later notebook that the use of Peter Walsh as a character in the novel first occurred to her on May 7, 1923, perhaps suggested, however, by one of the men referred to in Mrs. Dalloway's memory in "Mrs. Dalloway in Bond Street": "There shd. now be a long talk between Mrs. D. & some old buck. Hurry over. His view of her. Her substratums of feeling about dead youth the past: with her anxiety about Dick threading it together. Story to be provided by Elizabeth. Must all be kept in upstir; in extreme of feeling."[36] And the next entry is dated merely the 18th [May?]: "The talk between Mrs D & P. W. might now go on to a confession by him:"[37] This in brief is an outline of the early scene between Clarissa Dalloway and Peter Walsh, corresponding to pages 59–72 of the novel. There are many differences between the manuscript version and the novel, and the long, important monologue of Clarissa that precedes it is not found in the early version; but the main pattern of alternation between polite, surface conversation and substrata of thoughts and feelings is established and sustained in the manuscript version.

> A strange meeting!
> For it was a question what each had done in the past year, a summing up made necessary by the fact that she had refused him: For she had refused to marry him twenty years ago.
> He has failed, thought Clarissa, & they met, now & then, like this. He came to her. He wanted her. And if they had married, what would have happened.
> It[']s an abominable hour to talk, said Peter Walsh, sitting down. She has grown older he thought. I shan't go into the whole matter, he thought, for poor dear, she's grown older.[38]

As in the novel, Peter confesses to Clarissa that he has fallen in love with a married woman, but unlike the novel he asks her directly at the end of the scene, "Why didn't you marry me?" But Clarissa is saved the embarrassment of an answer by the entrance of her daughter, Elizabeth, as in the novel.

On June 18, 1923, Virginia Woolf recorded in the diary-like notebook:

> Too thin & unreal somehow. Must now go on to make Peter walk away through the Green Park with the sound of the hour in his ears. The merit of this book so far lies in its design, wh. is original—very difficult.
>
> P. W. should now walk in a great state of excitement in Green Park, as if on the waves of the sound: which should die out & leave him somewhere in the Green Park. He should dislike the thought of Clarissa; yet be excited by her: should all the time be on the defensive against people who think him old. That was why he ran away from Elizabeth. But he must *think*; not merely see.[39]

Self-critical of the scene between Clarissa and Peter she has just written, she nonetheless goes on to plan the next scene, Peter Walsh in Westminster. Nine days later, on June 27, she began writing the scene which begins the British Museum manuscript, transforming the notes into the reality of the actual scene. Despite the difficulty with the beginning, Virginia Woolf seems to have hit her stride, and the manuscript version progresses smoothly and rapidly, and more closely to the final text. "Thinking out" the novel over the months covered by the diary notebook resulted in a clarification of its theme, in a greater depth in its character portrayal, and in a tightening of its structural design.

It is largely by means of the long scene with Peter Walsh in Westminster and Regent's Park (and the later one leading to the party) that we come to "know" Clarissa Dalloway from the "outside." The "facts" about her personality are presented by Peter Walsh: "Clarissa had grown hard, he thought, & a trifle sentimental. . . . There was something cold about Clarissa, he thought. She had always, even when I first knew her, a sort of timidity which in middle age, becomes conventionality, & then it[']s all up, he thought."[40] This highly critical view of Clarissa—Peter is still unwilling to admit he has grown old too—is tempered later by a more judicious analysis of her personality: "There was so little of the instinctive in her—She was so unmaterial; & yet in some profound way, so exquisitely feminine."[41] Similarly, he mixes criticism and admiration of her personality: "Her emotions were all on the surface. Beneath, she was very shrewd—a far better judge of character than Sally, for instance, and with it all—possessing that woman's gift, that essential one: of making life wherever she happened to be."[42] And later, on his way to her party, he pays tribute to Clarissa: "She had influenced him more than any other person. And always in this way, coming before him, appearing so damned cool, lady like [,] critical; or ravishing, romantic, recalling some field, some English harvest. She brought back the country, more than in London."[43] So that at the end he feels an empathy with her: "But what is it, he asked himself, What is beginning to form in me, & What is about to happen? By what name can I call it? This terror, this ecstasy? It is Clarissa."[44]

"For there she was." These final words of the novel were written October 9, 1924,[45] and the "real" Mrs. Dalloway is known to the reader at the end, for as Virginia Woolf wrote in her diary notebook on June 19, 1923, "every scene would build up the idea of C's character. That will give unity, as well as add to the final effect."[46] The final effect is that the reappearance of Clarissa Dalloway at her party is the culmination of the revelation of her whole personality. It is revealed through a combination of externality and internality, thought and action, past and present (and even future in the sense that Septimus's death becomes the metaphor of her own death), her own reflections and the thoughts of others like Peter Walsh and Sally Seton who reflect upon her, and finally through time and space by which she becomes part of all that surrounds her.

Ultimately, however, the "whole" Mrs. Dalloway is known because the reader has shared her most private thoughts, and her most private thoughts are about life (her past and present) and death (her future that is linked metaphorically with Septimus's suicide). Although we have learned much about Clarissa from Peter Walsh and others, it is only through her own thoughts that her portrait is complete, for Peter's egotism, Sally's change of status and Doris Kilman's prejudice do not present a true portrait of Clarissa's personality.

In the middle of the final scene of the novel, the party, as Clarissa makes her way through the various groups, Virginia Woolf wrote the following notes:

> A general view of the world.
> The different groups:
> All sketched in.
> She makes her way gradually to the Bradshaw group.
> This was about Septimus. The visualness [of] what happened.
> Goes into the little room. The clock striking her whole life.
> Sees the old lady put her light out.
> Transition to Richard & Elizabeth. . . .
> Then to Peter & Sally on the stairs.[47]

These notes become transformed into the following passage as Clarissa leaves the Bradshaws to go into the little room where she is alone: "The party's splendour fell to the floor, so strange it seemed to her alone in all her finery [,] lips still tingling, words, emotions, shaping, about to break: all of a sudden congealed in a figure of formidable & loathsome significance: the Bradshaws: speak. He had killed himself."[48] And, as in the novel, she feels her own body experiencing a violent death, but then she wonders why Septimus has committed suicide: "Why pluck your flower like that? In this dumb colloquy he was the youth she had dreamt of; he was the argument, this & the dawn; the fair hill top with Peter chattering; home & the evening, & this he was, & he had done what they had none of them dared—thrown it, out of the window."[49]

The answer comes to her:

> He [Septimus] had determined that there should be at least a testimony—was that it? An attempt to communicate—feeling. The impossibility, as things are, of reaching the centre which, mystically yet indubitably, all sorts of people feel evading them; the [unsatisfactoriness] of life; the distance; how always, always, closeness draws apart; rapture flew; one is alone. That he may have meant. There was an embrace in death.[50]

It is the giving of his life of his own free will as an offering, just as she gives her parties as an offering of herself, that Clarissa comes to understand intuitively after experiencing his death in her mind. It is through the "embrace" of death that Septimus becomes Clarissa's double so that she is able to come to terms with her own past. As she sees the old lady in the room opposite turn out the light, Big Ben chimes, "striking her whole life":

> One, Two, Three; & she was extraordinarily happy; she felt no pity for the young man who had killed himself; none for his wife; none for herself; nothing but pride, nothing but joy; for to hear Big Ben strike Three, Four, five, six, seven, was profound & tremendous. . . . She must go back: breast her enemy; she must take her rose; Never would she submit—never, never!
> Eight, Big Ben struck, nine, ten, eleven; &
> But Clarissa was gone.[51]

She has gone back to the party (Life), for she has life yet to live, and the last stroke of Big Ben is not yet for her. She will not give in to the enemy (Death), for Septimus's death has reconciled her to life and destroyed her fear of death.

III

We come full circle to the short story. After Virginia Woolf completed the ending of the novel, she returned to the beginning and on October 20, 1924, revised the short story, "Mrs. Dalloway in Bond Street," as the opening of the novel. The revision is a complete rewriting of the story so that the manuscript version of the beginning is very close to the final, published version. And yet the main elements of character, theme, technique and style are already extant in the original story—Mrs. Dalloway herself, the theme of life and death (including the refrain "Fear no more the heat o' the sun"), the alternating movement between externality and internality, the stream-of-consciousness technique, and the lyrical style. What was needed was to fill in the past of Mrs. Dalloway, only hinted at in the story. For example, the clause "fresh as if issued to children on a beach," which appears in the second paragraph of the story, is sufficient to suggest to Virginia Woolf the whole of Mrs. Dalloway's reverie about the past when she was a girl of eighteen and "burst open the French windows and plunged at Bourton into the open air." Her being observed and silently complimented by Scrope Purvis, and the striking of Big Ben, both of which appear in the story, are expanded upon, as is the meeting with Hugh Whitbread, with past and present merging in her mind.

The merging of the past and the present "to give the moment whole"—Mrs. Dalloway's love of London and sense of being part of its history both past and present, her progress through the streets of London on an errand as the external frame of the scene, her thoughts about her husband Richard and daughter Elizabeth and about the war and death, her party that night, and finally the short scene in the shop in Bond Street ending with the "violent explosion" in the street outside—all are integral elements of the original story which although thoroughly revised in details testify to the close relationship between the story and the opening scene of the novel. The only truly major element of the first scene in the novel not found in the story is Peter Walsh and his relationship to Clarissa's past, for Peter Walsh, like Septimus Smith, had no "existence" in the original manuscript beginning of the novel.

Thus, Peter Walsh, who becomes the major "chorus" illuminating Clarissa Dalloway but who was not conceived of as a character until May 7, 1923, is introduced at the very beginning in Clarissa Dalloway's first reverie. Septimus Smith, who becomes Mrs. Dalloway's "double" but who was not conceived of as a character until October 16, 1922, after the first version of the "Prime Minister" chapter was written, is introduced early in the final manuscript revision of the scene, replacing H. Z. Prentice, who is entirely written out of the novel, as the one who overhears Edgar J. Watkiss say, "The Proime Minister's kyar." Virginia Woolf made a final revision of the whole novel in typescript,[52] the same method she used in revising her first novel, *The Voyage Out*. But this final revision was largely a matter of refining details and style. The holograph version is complete in all its major elements.

Acknowledgments

I gratefully acknowledge the following permissions: from the Henry W. and Albert A. Berg Collection, New York Public Library, Astor, Lenox, and Tilden Foundations to examine and quote from the five manuscript items of *Mrs. Dalloway*; from the Trustees of the British Museum to examine and quote from the manuscript notebooks; from Leonard Woolf, Mrs. Woolf's literary executor, to quote from the various notebooks; from Harcourt, Brace and World Co. to quote from *Mrs. Dalloway*. Also I wish to acknowledge the Research Grant-in-Aid I received from the American Council of Learned Societies that made this research possible.

Notes

1. Jacqueline Latham, "The Origin of 'Mrs. Dalloway,'" *Notes and Queries* 211 (March 1966), 98–99.

2. A. J. Lewis, "From 'The Hours' to *Mrs. Dalloway*," *The British Museum Quarterly* 27, nos. 1–2 (Summer 1964), 15–18.

3. Wallace Hildick, "In That Solitary Room," *Kenyon Review* 27 (March 1965), 302–317; *Word for Word* (London, 1965), 177–187.

4. Virginia Woolf, *Mrs. Dalloway* (New York, 1925). Subsequent references are to this edition.

5. Virginia Woolf, "Mrs. Dalloway in Bond Street," *Dial* LXXV (July, 1923), 27.

6. Berg Collection, holograph notebook dated March 12, 1922, 133. These notes are included in the same notebook as #3 of *Jacob's Room*.

7. Ibid., 132.

8. Ibid., 135.

9. Ibid., 145–147. Alternate pages are paginated from page 133 in the MS.

10. Ibid., 143.

11. Ibid., 153.

12. The passage in brackets is cancelled in the manuscript.

13. Berg Collection, holograph notebook dated March 12, 1922, 155.

14. Ibid., 155–157.

15. Ibid., 159. A typescript version of the "Prime Minister" chapter is also to be found in the Berg Collection. Although undated, on the basis of the evidence of revisions, it postdates the holograph version. However, although it contains numerous minor revisions of style and detail, it is essentially the same as the holograph version and therefore a revised copy rather than a rewriting of the chapter. The most significant difference is that the typescript version ends with a brief, one-sentence transition from Septimus Smith to Mrs. Dalloway at home as she notices people looking up to see the skywriting airplane.

16. Virginia Woolf, *A Writer's Diary* (New York, 1954), 53.

17. Berg Collection holograph notebook dated variously from November 9, 1922, to August 2, 1923. Since this notebook is unpaginated, quotations from it are noted in the text according to the date of entry.

18. Ibid.

19. Wallace Hildick refers to four separate versions of the opening of the Peter Walsh scene, but since the third attempt he refers to is merely a corrected version of the first two sentences and part of the third sentence of the previous version, I prefer to refer to three rather than four versions. Cf. Hildick, *Word for Word*, 180.

20. British Museum, Add. MS. 51044, 5–6.

21. Ibid., 8.

22. Ibid., 12.

23. Berg Collection, holograph notebook dated variously from November 9, 1922, to August 2, 1923.

24. British Museum, Add. MS. 51044, 62.

25. Ibid., Add. MS. 51046, 21.

26. Ibid.

27. Berg Collection, holograph notebook dated variously from November 9, 1922, to August 2, 1923. The question mark after Septimus indicates Mrs. Woolf had not definitely settled on Septimus as the name, and indeed in the British Museum notebooks the name Bernard Warren Smith is used at one point.

28. Ibid.

29. British Museum, Add. MS. 51044, 55–56.

30. Ibid., 58.

31. Berg Collection, holograph notebook dated variously from November 9, 1922, to August 2, 1923.

32. British Museum, Add. MS. 51044, 58.

33. Berg Collection, holograph notebook dated variously from November 9, 1922, to August 2, 1923. The reference in the last statement is to the method of viewing Septimus from the "outside"—partly from Rezia's point of view, partly from the author's in her role as author-narrator.

34. British Museum, Add. MS. 51044, 103.

35. Berg Collection, holograph notebook dated variously from November 9, 1922, to August 2, 1923.

36. Ibid.

37. Ibid.

38. Ibid., holograph notebook dated March 12, 1922, 185–187.

39. Ibid., holograph notebook dated variously from November 9, 1922, to August 2, 1923.

40. British Museum, Add. MS. 51044, 11.

41. Ibid., 89.

42. Ibid., 91. See page 114 of the novel.

43. Ibid., Add. MS. 51046, 32. See pages 232–233 of the novel.

44. Ibid., Add. MS. 51045, 113. See page 296 of the novel.

45. Ibid.

46. Berg Collection, holograph notebook dated variously from November 9, 1922, to August 2, 1923.

47. British Museum, Add. MS. 51046, reversed side, 70.

48. Ibid., 86.

49. Ibid.

50. Ibid., 88. The bracketed word, unsatisfactoriness, is included but cancelled in the MS.

51. Ibid., 98.

52. The typescript itself is unavailable.

ON ONE OF VIRGINIA WOOLF'S

SHORT STORIES

James Hafley

I do not suppose that very many people have read Virginia Woolf's short stories with anything like the attention that is given to her novels. "Kew Gardens" and "The Mark on the Wall," which are called short stories mainly because we now conceive of the essay merely as a form for the objective communication of verifiable truths, are familiar at least in part, since they have been quoted from to illustrate things about the novels; "The New Dress," among the short stories proper, seems to be the anthologists' favorite, and is therefore perhaps the best-known of them. The point is that you can still surprise people by telling them to read "The Duchess and the Jeweller" or "Lappin and Lapinova": the fact that Virginia Woolf, of all people, wrote something with a "plot" comes rather as a shock. And however well you may know the stories you can constantly surprise yourself by rereadings of, say, "The Shooting Party" or "Solid Objects" or "Moments of Being": it is in this instance the shock that always attends the contemplation of perfection or near perfection.

I should like to hold up for brief consideration here the story called "Moments of Being." It is primarily worth looking at simply for itself, as a beautifully accomplished artwork; but it is also valuable in so far as it offers a microcosmic illustration of some of Virginia Woolf's technique in the novels, as well as the other short stories. It was first published in *Échanges*, for December 1929, under its original title, now its sub-title, "Slater's Pins Have No Points"; and subsequently included in *A Haunted House* (1943). And I have chosen to write about it rather than one of the other stories for no better reason than that it happens to be my favorite among them.

Originally published in *Modern Fiction Studies*, Winter 1956.

The situation in "Moments of Being" is, or seems at first, quite simple: Fanny Wilmot, a young music student, has been listening to her teacher, Julia Craye, perform a Bach fugue; Fanny's corsage has fallen from her dress, and as she looks about on the floor for the pin with which it has been fastened, she creates for herself the story of Miss Craye's life, having been started upon this imaginative performance by Miss Craye's sympathetic remark that "Slater's pins have no points—don't you always find that?" The "action" of the short story—what it imitates—is not at all the past life of Julia Craye, but the mind of Fanny Wilmot engaged in the composition of that life; and so the story is about Fanny, who in a matter of seconds brings together all the wisps of information and pseudo-information that she has ever heard about her teacher and synthesizes them, in the light of the remark about pins, into what is for her a pattern just as complete and revelatory as the Bach fugue to which she has been listening; and the form of her composition takes, quite appropriately, the form of a fugue, as the theme—"Slater's pins have no points"—is stated and developed by one voice after another, the entrance of each new voice being indicated by a shift in time sequence, and is then given its comprehensive resolution. The story begins with the theme, stated by Julia; when Fanny Wilmot has partially developed this theme, she states it herself, but assumes Julia's voice to do so—that is, she puts inverted commas around the phrase. After some additional development, the theme is again stated, this time in Fanny's own voice; and she goes on to complete the development. The theme appears a fourth time at the end of the story, after Fanny has realized all of the possibilities that it suggested to her and has resolved it. But it is stated here by Julia again: the end of Fanny's fugue becomes the opening measure of any other person's—of the reader's, for example—just as the last chord of the Bach fugue played by Julia had coincided with the first measure of Fanny's, spoken by her.

Fanny's mind works largely with images; it is to her amazing that a woman like Julia Craye—poised, serene, self-contained with her art—should know anything about pins: about the world in which pins are bought and used and judged. For Miss Craye lives in the "cool glassy world of Bach fugues," just as her twin brother Julius, now dead, had lived as an archaeologist in a world of "Roman glasses." Surely Miss Craye must be conscious of "the pane of glass" which separates her world from *the* world, separates herself as it separated Julius from ordinary people; all that she really has is a "glassy surface" to see. Her favorite flowers are crocuses, those "glossy bright flowers," and she can be pictured counting out some of her meager supply of money to purchase not pins but "an old mirror."

Miss Craye has never married, and it is natural that to a young girl like Fanny Wilmot this would be the most persistent fact, the one responsible for whatever directions her story will take. (Ironically, Julia's remark about the pins has actually "transfixed" Fanny, who nevertheless thinks, "What need had [Julia] of pins? For she was not so much dressed as cased, like a beetle compactly in its sheath, blue in winter, green in summer.") Fanny does not think of Julia directly as a spinster, but, more kindly, as living in a world apart from the *real* one, having on her face a look that seems to say

> "Stars, sun, moon . . . the daisy in the grass, fires, frost on the window pane, my heart goes out to you. But," it always seemed to add, "you break, you pass, you go." And simultaneously it covered both these states of mind with "I can't reach you—I can't get at you."

And Fanny reasons that it is to break such a spell that Julia has attempted familiarity with the everyday world of Slater's pins. Fanny seems torn between a regret that Julia should so lower herself and a fear that perhaps the real world, which *is* mutable and transitory, may not withstand the sudden entrance of this woman whose own life seems to embody a permanence and certainty that "life itself" cannot manage. She must at once defend Miss Craye and defend the world; she does so, of course, and quite without realizing it, by melding the two in the fluid permanence of her meditation.

On another level, then, the short story itself achieves the same synthesis of opposites as an artwork. This paradoxical unity is most succinctly imaged by the description of Julia at the end of the story: "Out of the night she burnt like a dead white star." The ingenious ambiguity there—whether "dead" is to be taken as qualifying "white" or "star," that is to say—offers a syntactical equivalent of the overall ambiguity. For if Julia has finally gone beyond the pane of glass that separated her from the stars, has finally become the star she looked at through a glass darkly, there is also the meaning that by reaching out for life itself, in the very act of breaking down the barrier and entering the real world, she has lost her own life. Again, "out of the night" may be read either as "in the otherwise dark world" or as "from the night in which the other stars still shone"; for there is a sugges- tion that if Julia has lost her own life she has also destroyed the "real world" which—as Fanny would have it, and we must remember that it is Fanny's consciousness rather than Julia's which these ambigui- ties define—she had been so eager to possess. (The fact that I am not trying to "do an Empson" here will I think become clear if it is noticed that the problem and techniques involved in this story are present in every one of Virginia Woolf's novels as well.)

But this situation is given its final dimension by another word in the short story: when Fanny has completed her story of Julia Craye's past life, and has found the pin, she looks up and discovers Julia seated before the window "in a moment of ecstasy," holding a flower in her hands; but now, Fanny thinks, she really *sees* Julia—now that she has evidently realized the other woman's life. She knows now that Julia remained unmarried through fear of entering into the uncertainties, the flux, of "reality," preferring to remain in the secure world that was defined, stabilized, and immobilized for her by her music and her brother's archaeological specimens; preferring to remember vividly how lovely Kensington had been in the days when "it was like a village," and to criticize the modern life, "to denounce acridly the draughts in the Tubes." And as for men, naturally Julia preferred to believe that their only use was, surely, to protect women. It is a moment of triumph for Fanny, then, the moment in which suddenly she "understands" Julia Craye, believes her to be happy in her own way, after all, and can divorce herself from the music teacher without compunction or rancor. And there follows this remarkable passage:

> All seemed transparent, for a moment, to the gaze of Fanny Wilmot, as if looking through Miss Craye, she saw the very fountain of her being spurting its pure silver drops. She saw back and back into the past behind her. . . . She saw Julia—

The key word, the *real* revelation—by which I mean that which is given to the reader of the story, as distinct from the revelation apparently given to Fanny—is of course that one innocent adjective, *transparent*. Fanny is now "looking through" Julia, and all *seems* transparent for her, whereas all *is* transparent for the reader: by developing this fugue on the theme of Slater's pins, Fanny has put herself, though she does not realize it during the course of the story, precisely into Julia Craye's situation as she had first imagined it. It is now *she* who observes a glassy surface, who has entered a cool glassy world of her own making and stands behind a pane of glass that separates her from reality.

Julia Craye is seated before the window, just as her brother's Roman vase had stood in the window and been jealously guarded from possible danger when a child entered the house; Julia now stands in the same relation to Fanny as the vase did to Julius, and as the music does to Julia herself. For Fanny, too, this is a "moment of ecstasy," and the story concludes as she "pinned the flower to her breast with trembling fingers," transfixing it as she had been transfixed. Julia, so Fanny imagines, can think after one of her rare trips alone to Hampton Court to see the flowers that it was a victory. It was something that lasted; something that mattered for ever. She strung the afternoon on the necklace of memorable days, which was not too long for her to be able to recall this one or that one; this view, that city; to finger it, to feel it, to savour, sighing, the quality that made it unique.

Yet, Fanny goes on to think, "one pitied her for always doing everything alone." But so it is with this moment, the moment of this short story while Fanny searches for the pointless pin of reality and at the same time creates, herself, what she believes to be the "real" meaning of Julia Craye. That meaning depends for its life upon its isolation, its separation from life itself by the pane of glass upon whose surface it is seen—or, for either way will do, the mirror in which it is a reflection of Fanny herself. Thus, when "Julia opened her arms. Julia kissed her on the lips," Fanny can believe that "Julia possessed it"—reality. She has imagined Julia as grasping, clutching at life as she clutched at the flower in her hands; "but she did not possess it, enjoy it, not entirely and altogether." And again, following the abortive love scene on the Serpentine—one that exists, of course, only in Fanny's consciousness—she has imagined Julia's thinking, "I can't have it, I can't possess it." But now Fanny's apparent realization of Julia seems also to be Julia's realization of the goal that Fanny has created for her; so, "Julia opened her arms" recalls the love scene; and, from Fanny's isolated point of view, "Julia possessed it." The nature of Julia's ecstatic moment we do not know; the nature of Fanny's we do; they are both of them, in Hardy's phrase which gives the story its title, "moments of being." And the final question, of course, is the meaning of this "being" which exists so precariously, so privately, so preposterously in its false truth. But that is a question which the author need not, should not, answer; and the reader, if he tries to answer it, can only follow along exactly the same path that Fanny Wilmot started down when she lost her pin and bent to look for it.

What you have got to do, Virginia Woolf says with her short stories and her novels, is settle for the ambiguity, the pin and the rose, reality and the pane of glass; for it is, finally, only the ambiguity which is clear-cut and only the paradox which allows the moment of being. Fanny Wilmot's truth is pointedly false; it has led her perhaps away from reality and certainly to a moment of complete self-deception; but, on the other hand, Slater's pins have no points.

■   The idea has come to me that what I want now to do is to saturate every atom. I mean to eliminate all waste, deadness, superfluity: to give the moment whole; whatever it includes. Say that the moment is a combination of thought; sensation; the voice of the sea. Waste, deadness, come from the inclusion of things that don't belong to the moment; this appalling narrative business of the realist: getting on from lunch to dinner: it is false, unreal, merely conventional. Why admit anything to literature that is not poetry—by which I mean saturated.

—Virginia Woolf, *A Writer's Diary* (1954)

THE MEANING OF ELVEDON

IN *THE WAVES*

A KEY TO BERNARD'S EXPERIENCE

AND WOOLF'S VISION

Joseph Allen Boone

Near the beginning of *The Waves*, the child Bernard creates a story to rescue Susan from her "knotted-up" sorrow. By conjuring words from the "depths" of his mind, he imaginatively carries her to the mythical kingdom of Elvedon. What Bernard sees—or imagines—when he and Susan peer over its wall holds a lifelong significance for him. The images of the lady writing between the long windows and the gardeners sweeping aside the leaves with great brooms become symbols whose significance continually expands, a fact to which Bernard's mature recollections of Elvedon attest. But what, exactly, is Elvedon a symbol of, and how is its meaning generated? In one of the earlier drafts of the novel,[1] Bernard makes specific reference to the Elvedon experience as a moment of "vision," and it deserves to be examined as such. However, the mysteriously rich psychic territory of Elvedon has remained all but unexplored by critics. This study attempts to demonstrate how very evocative the Elvedon memory is of the evolution of Bernard's identity—for the impression made by the woman and sweepers reflects the progressive stages of his development from unborn child to adult maker of phrases. And in the end result, Elvedon becomes not only Bernard's final "language" of defiance, but Woolf's own attempt to articulate a meaning beyond words.

Originally published in *Modern Fiction Studies*, Winter 1981–1982.

Woolf's desire to find a language for vision is shared in the text by Bernard, the would-be writer whose quest for a mode of expression commences in his initial account of Elvedon. Echoing all the other characters (except the silent Percival) in his need to question the meaning of life, Bernard finds himself haunted by mystic moments that seem pregnant with untold meaning. His lifelong desire is to find "the phrase I want . . . to enclose once and for all some notion haunting me";[2] the visionary flashes come and go, such as the sighting of the fin rising about the gray waste of waters, "that we shall in time to come uncover and coax into words" (307). As such he seems to verbalize Woolf's intent in the very act of conceiving the novel to "come to terms with these mystical feelings"—feelings for which her mind evolved the concept of an "abstract mystical eyeless book: a play-poem."[3] For Bernard, the near impossibility of articulating his thoughts also brings out his desire for a *new* language, "some little language, such as lovers use, broken words, inarticulate words, like the shuffling of feet on the pavement" (342). Yet at this very moment, facing death, Bernard realizes the inadequacy of all language, of his special gift, to uncover the hidden meaning of visionary moments: "I need a howl, a cry" (381). Woolf's experimental use of language and image in *The Waves* exists as a response to this need. Images and symbols suggest cumulative meaning intuited by the reader through their repeated occurrence and context; references like Elvedon participate in the evershifting, nonverbalized flux that runs beneath the surface of life and of the novel. Woolf's sense of having attained a new "freedom and boldness" through such use of imagery is apparent in the exultant diary entry written the day that *The Waves* was finished: "I am sure this is the right way of using them—not in set pieces, as I had tried at first, coherently, but simply as images, never making them work out; only suggest."[4] By turning to the first appearance of Elvedon in the text of *The Waves*, we will begin to see the ways in which Elvedon "suggests" the shape of Bernard's life and Woolf's vision of existence.

The original "journey" to Elvedon unfolds as Bernard's response to Susan's anguish; he uses his talent of storytelling to dissolve the barrier between their separate selves: "when we sit together, close . . . we melt into each other with phrases. We are edged with mist. We make an insubstantial territory." Figuratively, this "insubstantial territory" where Bernard's imagination touches Susan's mind becomes that of Elvedon. In contrast to an early draft, where the children's adventure is presented as an actuality,[5] the literalness of the event is much less clear in the published version: whether or not the children physically venture into the beechwood has become unimportant compared to the adventure of the mind that unfurls as Bernard verbally takes Susan "ever so far beneath us." For the child Bernard continually presents storytelling as the process of traveling *beneath* the surface of daily life, into the "secret territory" or "underworld" that is his special "universe" (189). As an adult he will describe the world of inner time in very similar language: "my dreaming, my tentative advance like one carried beneath the surface of a stream . . . I wish to go under: to visit the profound depths" (253).[6]

Woolf strengthens the sense of descent into a timeless world through Bernard's description of entering the woods as sinking to the bottom of the sea: "We shall sink like swimmers just touching the ground with the tips of their toes. We shall sink through the green air of the leaves, Susan. We sink as we run. The waves close over us, the beech leaves meet above our heads." By immersing the children in this world of fluid consciousness, Woolf links the unfolding experience to the novel's dominant metaphor of water, the origin and end of all life. The order in which the elements in Bernard's story appear (the white house, the stable clock, the rooftops, the stable boy) furthers the feeling of approach from above, sinking to the bottom. The appearance of the clock and then the "flats and heights of the roofs" are described as if Bernard and Susan are falling past them to the sea-floor: "We touch earth, we tread ground," Bernard says.

The suggestion of a mythic world being summoned into existence also characterizes this "sinking" passage. For the manner in which objects appear, one by one, gradually filling the scene, creates an effect like that of the opening prologue, where the neutral landscape gradually takes on color, form, and dimension. The sense of entering a mythical realm increases when Bernard bestows upon it a name vaguely resonant of fairy lore and medieval romance: "This is Elvedon. I have seen signposts at the crossroads with one arm pointing 'To Elvedon.'" As the two words hidden in the name reveal, "Elvedon" is an "elf-eden," a diminutive fairies' paradise perfectly fitted to the children's size. Three times Bernard asserts that they are the first humans to enter this primeval landscape, and his words lend an incantatory effect to this reminder of the mythic Eden. Similarly, the set pieces in the description—ringed wood, walled-in house, and gardens—invoke a timeless, enclosed realm. Yet, as in Milton's representation of Eden, there are also signs of continual process: rotten oak apples, funguses, "the patter of some primeval fircone falling to rot among the ferns." As such, this netherworld foreshadows the "unlit world where the leaf rots and the flower has fallen" of the third prologue (226). In detailing the effects of process within a timeless setting, the Elvedon passage also echoes the double sense of time achieved by the novel as a whole: couched between the one great cosmic day of the prologues, there exist entire lifetimes; conversely, deeper within the finite life of the individual, marked by the daily sequence that moves toward death, there exists an inner realm that is timeless. Thus Woolf conjectures in her diary,

> Now is life very solid or very shifting? I am haunted by the two contradictions. This has gone on forever; will last forever . . . this moment I stand on. Also it is transitory, flying, diaphanous. I shall pass like a cloud on the waves. Perhaps it may be that though we change, one flying after another, so quick, so quick, yet we are somehow successive and continuous, we human beings, and show the light through.[7]

In the Elvedon passage the light shows through, unveiling the goal underlying this quest, at that moment when the children spy over the opaque wall hitherto obstructing their vision and see for the first time the woman writer and sweepers.[8] The movement of the brooms seems to fuse with that of writing into a continuous yet fixed motion, another image of the dual sense of time that Woolf describes above. In the later references we learn that the gardeners are sweeping aside leaves—emblematic of reaching under, of going beneath, just as Bernard and Susan have sunk below the waves/treetops. The fact that the motion of the brooms corresponds with the woman writing implies that writing is also a kind of mystical delving beneath the surface: "As usual I feel that if I sink further I shall reach the truth," Woolf states in her diary as she prepares to begin writing *The Waves*.[9] These analogies strengthen the reader's conviction that Bernard is not merely taking Susan into the woods but narrating a world into existence as he creates it in his mind.

Significantly, as Bernard looks over the wall into the heart of his creation, Woolf chooses to enter the mind of Susan, who corroborates the boy's vision: "I see the lady writing. I see the gardeners sweeping." Under the spell of his imagination, she no longer sees only the beetle in the grass, nor is she "tied down with single words" for this moment. Instead, she makes her contribution as she says, "If we died here, nobody would bury us," a statement which reinforces the sense of mortality already implicit in the natural decay of the landscape. Again, Woolf uses the scene to convey the larger theme of mutability, an inevitable part of the natural cycle symbolized in the rising and falling action of the waves.

This reminder of death combines with the thrill of danger characteristic of fairy tales when Bernard warns Susan not to move: "if the gardeners saw us, they would shoot us. We should be nailed like stoats to the stable door. . . . We shall be shot like jays and pinned to the wall!" The adventure reaches a climax when Bernard commands Susan to run; they have been spotted, will be shot. The language shifts tone: they must "escape," "hide," follow the "secret path" away form the "hostile country." Having stolen secret knowledge from the nether side of existence, Bernard's "underworld," they must return to the surface of life "without looking back"—Orpheus leading Eurydice out of Hades, Persephone returning to her mother, Lot and his family leaving Gomorrah: the mythic parallels abound. The reader is left with the conviction that upon the children's return some kind of quest has been completed, some nonverbal knowledge gained. Yet the meaning of the quest has not been consciously assimilated, a fact which seems linked to the reality that, like all of Bernard's stories, the verbal adventure tapers off inconclusively. Although he begins a poem to describe the ascent of a wood-pigeon "breaking cover in the tops of the beech trees" (we later learn this phrase is part of a poem honoring Susan), his words, soaring out of reach like the bird, escape Susan's comprehension, bringing the adventure of Elvedon to an end. Yet as a metaphoric signal to the reader, the description of the wood-pigeon "breaking cover" gives the quest motif its perfect conclusion. For the spiraling double moment—first sinking into the depths of green water, then soaring higher and higher with the wood-pigeon—reproduces the paradigmatic descent/return lines of the archetypal journey into the psyche.

In the first reference to Elvedon after this two-page account, that scenario merges its meaning with a different experience as Mrs. Constable gives Bernard his bath. As if figuratively reexperiencing his original creation, Bernard says, "I am covered with warm flesh" as the sponge is squeezed above him: "Water descends and sheets me like an eel" (192). Immediately he connects this sensation, the formation of an individual personality that is Bernard exclusively, with the previous scene: "Rich and heavy sensations form on the roof of my mind; down showers the day—the woods; and Elvedon; Susan and the pigeon. Pouring down the walls of my mind, running together, the day falls copious, resplendent" (192). Thus, as actual water coats the surface of his physical being, Elvedon-as-water gathers within Bernard to form one of these droplets of experience that crystallize the moment into something complete, full: in this instance, his identity. This recognition of self has also surfaced in the prior action of seeking out Susan under the tree: "It was Susan who cried, that day when I was in the tool-house with Neville; and I felt my indifference melt. Neville did not melt. 'Therefore,' I said, 'I am myself, not Neville,' a wonderful discovery" (343).

Thus, on one level, Elvedon is tied to Bernard's recognition that

"I am myself"; the memory represents a basic stage in his formation of identity. But Elvedon signifies more, even to Bernard as a child. If it is indeed a child's fantasy, imaginatively evoked, one wonders what in Bernard's mind inspired the connected images that remain with him his entire life—the woman writing, the gardeners sweeping. In fact, Woolf suggests that Bernard's story records a vestigial memory, part of his preconscious history *preceding* identity; his telling of it thus becomes a process of recovering an original status buried beneath layers of memory. The key to this truth lies in the London party scene in the fourth section. The six adults recall their earliest memories in short, childlike phrases reminiscent of the first pages of the text. Bernard's contributions link three significant memories. First is the sponge bath that "creates" him: "Old Mrs. Constable lifted her sponge and warmth poured over us. . . . We became clothed in this changing, this feeling garment of flesh" (261). Then he adds a second memory—"At Elvedon the gardeners swept and swept with their great brooms, and the woman sat at the table writing"—which we have already seen Bernard associate with the bath experience. The third memory, a new element, is that of leaving for school, which concludes, "A second severance from the body of our mother" (261). Literally, of course, his birth is the first severance, but figuratively, the bath establishing his consciousness of separateness as a created being ("We became clothed. . . .") is the initial severance. All of a sudden, it dawns on the reader that what Bernard sees welling from his imagination as he tells of Elvedon is an illustration, a pictorial representation, of this primary shock of recognition. He sees a woman who is not-him in an unpeopled landscape; the very action of *seeing* her records the separation from her that he remembers the first time as Mrs. Constable bathes him. Sitting at the core of his subconscious in a primeval setting is his mother; sweeping away the obscuring leaves of ordinary experiences, the gardeners prepare the way for this visionary glimpse of the deep truth residing at the core of Bernard's being. Because he regains this truth by visiting the underlying depths of consciousness preceding individual awareness, Bernard at this point also becomes representative of a collective consciousness greater than himself. In this light the woman becomes not only Bernard's mother, but the *magna mater* of matriarchal creation myths.[10]

But the lady at Elvedon also writes, creating from words as she created Bernard from flesh, as he in turn creates this vision for Susan. The analogy between the maternal principle and creativity is valid in the sense that Woolf, after all, is also Bernard's creator, birthing him along with all the other characters of *The Waves*.[11] These interlocked metaphors are much more explicit in the first manuscript draft, where the "solitary narrator" of that document is telling herself "the story of the world from the beginning." "She" looks at the folds of a crumpled gray napkin in the shadowy darkness of a room not unlike that of the nursery in the interludes or that of the house at Elvedon. The wrinkled folds then become the waves of an immense ocean, Woolf's symbol of the unconscious; these waves in turn became mothers bearing children who, cast upon the shore, become the characters of the novel, the children inhabiting the garden:

> Here the folds of the napkin, much crumpled, seemed to display . . . waves succeeding waves; endlessly sinking & falling; . . . waves that were . . . of . . . many mothers, & again of many mothers, & behind them many more, endlessly sinking and falling, & lying prostrate, & each holding up . . . as the wave pass[ed] its crest. . . . a child. . . . For every wave cast a child from it; before it sank into the obscure body of the sea; . . . She had had her child.[12]

In this passage we see how closely linked are the themes of creation as a mythic account of human origin and as a creative process captured in writing. In the published edition of *The Waves*, the meanings contained in the above passage are collapsed into the background of the Elvedon memory, where the woman writing at the core of Bernard's mind is also an image of his mother.

Thus, the Edenic presentation of Elvedon first of all records a vestigial memory—the perfect existence Bernard experienced in the womblike security of his preconscious youth. As an incident narrated into existence for Susan, the scenario becomes a representation of his initial recognition of severance from the mother, hence, a recognition of individual identity. The visionary quality surrounding the memory of Elvedon thus derives from its importance as an epoch in Bernard's dawning consciousness. Furthermore, Elvedon functions as one of Woolf's "suggestive images" by which her own vision of existence is imparted; consequently, the image becomes part of the new "language" created by the text of *The Waves*. And as an example of Bernard's creativity, dipping into the depths of the imagination where invention reveals truths, Elvedon will finally become the equivalent of Bernard's own private language—the "howl" or "cry" he seeks when phrases fail, when he hurls his final defiance at Death on the last page of the novel.

Like Woolf in the persistency of his attempt to define the nature of reality, the adult Bernard begins to view the Elvedon experience from a perspective that reverses its initial associations. Previously a mirror of his subjective inner world and ancestral past, Bernard's new understanding of Elvedon looks to the future and renders the memory into a symbol of the forces of externality: irrevocability, fixity, death. At first glance Woolf seems to promulgate the classic existential stance when she has Bernard speak of the "stupidity of nature," effort, and defiance. However, Bernard's final perspective and last voice demonstrate how different Woolf's vision of life actually is. The affirming aspect of her philosophy, dependent on a vision of the circular nature of time and reality that circumvents the linear progression toward death as the only end, makes itself felt in the Elvedon references that surface while Bernard summarizes his life in the final soliloquy of *The Waves.*

Bernard's doctrine begins to emerge when, recalling Elvedon, he identifies Susan's sorrow as his "enemy": thus his cry, "let us explore," originally a summons to the imagination, becomes an act of defiance in the face of passivity.

> 'This is not to be borne,' I said as I sat beside her. . . . I then first became aware of the presence of those enemies who change, but are always there; the forces we fight against. To let oneself be carried on passively is unthinkable. 'That's your course, world,' one says, 'mine is this.' 'So let's explore,' I cried. . . . (343)

In this context Elvedon becomes a creative response to the antagonistic forces of life. As Bernard says in one manuscript draft, "We fight . . . . Every breath is an act of hostility. I create." Bringing Elvedon into creation, making a world come alive out of words, indeed demonstrates the occasional ability of language, rightly used, to overcome suffering and separateness: "A phrase . . . What is a phrase? It is victory; it is triumph; it gives one dominion."[13] Thus, Bernard's lifelong goal of bringing people together, of making the effort to articulate one's needs, is seen as originating in that moment under the beechwood when he first creates Elvedon. In the novel's final passages, Bernard turns again and again to Elvedon as symbol of the effort necessary to counter the enemies of life.[14]

However, in what at first seems a contradiction, the vision over the wall at Elvedon *also* becomes "the enemy." For as a symbol of the future rather than the past, the memory of the gardeners and the lady brings Bernard to a recognition of the irrevocability of life: "Transfixed, stopped dead, I thought, 'I cannot interfere with a single stroke of those brooms. They sweep and they sweep. Nor with the fixity of that woman writing.' It is strange that one cannot stop the gardeners sweeping nor dislodge a woman" (343). This interpretation actually repeats, from a different angle of perception, the childhood awareness Bernard experienced in the bath. That was a moment of *self*-awareness; this is a recognition of the *other*, the unchangeable forces outside the self. They are unchangeable precisely because they are external: "Outside the undifferentiated forces roar," Bernard will say (353). Thus, Bernard identifies as his personal enemy the fixity that the woman and sweepers represent as part of the unmovable powers of the natural world, powers mythically ever-present: "There they have remained all my life. It is as if one had woken in Stonehenge surrounded by a circle of great stones, these enemies" (343). Fixity, of course, is another name for death, the true enemy against which Bernard wages battle. On the last page of the novel Bernard will ask, "What enemy do we now perceive advancing against us?" and provide his own answer, "It is death. Death is the enemy" (383). Foreshadowing the defiant charge he will then make against death, Bernard links the Elvedon memory with *the end*, rather than the beginning, of life: "The gardeners swept; the lady at the table sat writing. But I now made the contribution of maturity to childhood's intuitions—satiety and doom; the sense of what is inescapable in our lot; death" (363). For Bernard the symbolic meanings of Elvedon have come full circle, encompassing the whole life-cycle, from birth to death, of the individual.

With these insights into his childhood vision surfacing in his mind, Bernard in effect proceeds to invent his own metaphoric "language" for vision by consciously rendering the event "symbolic," this being one way of coming to grips with the forces it now signifies. By transmuting experience (real or imagined) into the symbolic (recognizing its externality as such), Woolf implies that we may gain the only permanence possible in life—the eternal permanence of symbolism countering the deathly grip of fixity. Bernard again revisits the past as this understanding amplifies his perception of Elvedon yet one more degree:

> On the outskirts of every agony sits some observant fellow who points. . . . 'The gardeners sweep . . . the lady sits writing.' Thus he directed me to that which is beyond and outside our own predicament; to that which is symbolic, and thus perhaps permanent, if there is any permanence in our sleeping, eating, breathing, so animal, so spiritual and tumultuous lives. (349)

The search for permanence, as always, is matched by the mutability implicit in the adjectives modifying the word "lives." But by transforming Elvedon into his personal myth ("In the beginning," he commences as he sums up his life in the final section of the novel), Bernard, near death himself, is able to approach an acceptance of this contradiction of life ("Now is life very solid or shifting?") that Woolf recorded in her diary. Elvedon, like life, has become something "solid" in its permanence and omnipresence in Bernard's mind, yet something constantly "shifting" in its suggestive meanings: it thus functions as a total unit of meaning in the symbolic language by which Woolf gives voice to what she sees as life's inexpressible truths.

Bernard's acceptance of the paradoxes of permanence and change depends on his growing recognition—which he has intuitively sensed from boyhood—of the reality of the underlying world of circular time. In the final soliloquy he recalls Elvedon at the instant that he identifies the surface order of life as "a convenience, a lie. There is always deep below it . . . a rushing stream of broken dreams . . . elm trees, willow trees, gardeners sweeping, women writing . . . it is alive too and deep, this stream" (353–354). Whereas the surface of life, regulated by linear time, guides us irrevocably to death, the stream of memory and association beneath this surface reverberates with a nonending life common to all humanity. In letting himself fluctuate between these realms of time, Bernard expresses his acceptance of this paradox of existence in a penultimate moment of inspiration:

> With a shock of emotion one feels, "There are figures without features robed in beauty, doomed yet eternal." . . . Time has given the arrangement another shake. Out we creep from the arch of the current leaves, out into a wider world. The true order of things—this is our perpetual illusion—is now apparent. Thus, in a moment, in a drawing-room, our life adjusts itself to the majestic march of day across the sky. (365)

In the "wider world" ungoverned by linear time, the "true order" exists in the dual nature of our "doomed yet eternal" lives. The last sentence illustrates the way in which the text as a whole defines this philosophy, for its juxtaposition of the lives of the characters ("our life") with the mythic day of the interludes ("the majestic march of day") achieves an equivalent sense of ceaseless progression amidst the fixed eternal moment.

Bernard finally learns to speak this truth, although the last moments of his life (we assume, without knowing for sure, that the crash of the wave in the last sentence signifies his death) reflect a vacillating attitude toward this knowledge. His lowest moments of depression occur when the external wasteland, "the stupidity of nature" (363), most tauntingly confronts him—appropriately, after perceiving Susan's compromise to life (363); then, when the sun goes into eclipse and life becomes a "dust dance" in which "those fabulous presences, men with brooms, women writing" become as "mutable, vain" (375) as he feels his own existence to be. But the sun returns, the earth becomes a pendant drop of experience, and the language of what is now a life-affirming battle cry is renewed: "Always it begins again; always there is the enemy . . . the effort waiting" (380).

But the enemy, death, is now seen as only one turn in the cycle, the opposing movement out of which the forces of creation are born. Likewise, the eternal cycling of Elvedon's shifting connotations—from vestigial memory to symbol of fixity—recreates *within* Bernard the "doomed yet eternal" message of the external natural cycle, such that he can rightly say at the text's end, "And in me too the wave rises" (383). Thus, by becoming one with the "true order of things," Bernard learns to speak the eternal "language" of renewal and to sound his battle cry against the enemies of life. Consequently, the nonverbal meanings of "the old image" (363), Elvedon, collapsing together the many stages of Bernard's life, coalesce in the "howl" or "cry" that Bernard gives voice to in the last moments of his life as he flings himself defiantly (still "unvanquished and unyielding") against "you . . . O Death!" A defiant yet exultant participant in what he knows now to be "the incessant rise and fall and fall and rise again" (383) of the waves and of life, Bernard makes of his death a visionary moment that eloquently suggests Woolf's own attempt in *The Waves* to articulate a vision of reality beyond words.

Notes

1. My sources for the manuscript versions are: (a) *The Waves: The Two Holograph Drafts*, transcribed and edited by J. W. Graham (Toronto: University of Toronto Press, 1976). What Graham calls "Draft I" actually consists of two versions and several "false starts." "Draft II" is much closer to the novel as it stands in print and (b) Jean Tobin, "Virginia Woolf's *The Waves* and *The Years* as Novel of Vision and Novel of Fact," Diss. University of Wisconsin 1973. Tobin researched all of the manuscripts in the Berg Collection at the New York Public Library and quotes from six versions, which she refers to by Woolf's working title, "The Moths," i–vi.

2. Virginia Woolf, *Jacob's Room and The Waves* (New York: Harcourt, Brace and World, 1959 [*Waves*, original date, 1931]), 354. All quotations are from this edition. Hereafter, page citations will be included in the text of this paper *except* in the analysis of the *original* Elvedon passage, to be found on pages 185 and 186 here; I have omitted the page numbers to avoid undue repetition.

3. Woolf, *A Writer's Diary*, ed. Leonard Woolf (New York: Harcourt, Brace and World, 1953), 7 November 1928 entry, 134.

4. *Diary*, 7 February 1931, 162.

5. "He said, 'Let's explore' for There was a clearing in the beechwood . . . & beneath, at the bottom of the steep slope, lay an old white country house . . . They went to Elvedon and saw . . . ." *Holograph*, Draft I, 78–79.

6. Another clue to the fact that a mental rather than physical journey follows is that the call to Susan "let us explore," utilizes the subjunctive formula ("let's") that typically precedes Bernard's stories in the first section.

7. *Diary*, 4 January 1929, 137.

8. In Graham's "Draft I" it is interesting to note that the highly-charged images of the woman and sweepers are at first deemphasized—obviously, Woolf evolved their symbolic significance. At first the narrator states, "But the point of this story is ~~of course~~ not that they saw a lady writing at a table in the drawing room. . ." (*Holograph*, 15). The setting is named on the next page: "And they went to Elvedon, & saw a lady writing . . . but this was not the memorable part of the . . . expedition" (16). Then, we finally get a new view, for "~~the mind~~ is haunted with the figure of a lady, writing, between two windows" and now the adventure is "seen through the soul" (17). The rest of the passage is revelatory in connecting this inception of Elvedon's symbolic significance with the necessity of articulation: "And the solitary [Woolf's designation of the narrator herself] is no longer solitary: & the mind, like a vine. . . . has forever now to find an ~~interpretation~~ a phrase to ~~encircle~~ . . . net things in: for otherwise they must perish. And then when the phrase has been found, it must be spoken aloud, to somebody, ~~who But~~ else" (17).

9. *Diary*, 23 June 1929, 140.

10. The watery world through which Bernard has floated can thus be seen as a reexperiencing of his preexistence in his mother's womb. Significantly, the other human figures associated with this landscape are mother-figures: Mrs. Constable and Susan.

11. Woolf herself makes the analogy clear in her diary on various occasions. Speaking of the "insatiable desire to write something before I die," she also says, "And yet oddly enough, I scarcely want children of my own now," because her writing fulfills that need, having become "my one anchor" (*Diary*, 20 December 1927, 119). While working on the conclusion to *The Waves*, Woolf states in a similar vein: "I had a day of intoxication when I said, 'Children are nothing to this'" (28 March 1930, 151).

12. *Holograph*, Draft I, 9–10.

13. "The Moths VI," quoted in Tobin, pages 211 and 209, respectively.

14. For instance, Bernard remembers, "Then when I was a child, the presence of an enemy had asserted itself; the need for opposition had stung me. I jumped up and cried, 'Let's explore'" (363); "I will not consent," he again interprets this incident (374); "It is the effort and the struggle, it is the perpetual warfare, it is the shattering and piecing together—this is the daily battle, defeat or victory, the absorbing pursuit" (364).

Subjectivity, Trauma, and Community

THE SUBJECT IN *JACOB'S ROOM*

Edward L. Bishop

"Hey, you there!" comes the call in Louis Althusser's famous anecdote of interpellation, and the individual thus hailed turns around and becomes a subject, becomes a subject because he recognizes that the call is for him, because "*individuals are always-already subjects*" (Althusser, "Ideology" 176). Ideology "recruits" subjects, and what I want to suggest here is that Jacob is "recruited" by ideology, from that first shout by his brother, "Ja—cob! Ja—cob!" (*Jacob's Room* 5), which recruits him for the family, to the point where he answers offstage the pointing finger and "I Want You!" of Lord Kitchener's famous recruiting poster and is enlisted in the war that kills him.

Jacob has been much misunderstood, repeatedly maligned for not being the character readers have expected him to be. Some have accepted this as a good thing, on the grounds that Virginia Woolf could not create character anyway and at least *Jacob's Room* makes no claim to creating character; others have grumbled that she *does* manage to show the other characters in the book, and thus her claims that we can never really know another person are disingenuous.[1] What all the negative criticism underscores is that, in the figure of Jacob, Woolf is not representing *character*; what she is exploring is the construction, and representation of, the subject.

I. Character

In *Reading People, Reading Plots* James Phelan argues that we can approach character through three main categories: the thematic (character as idea), the synthetic (character as artificial construct),

Originally published in *Modern Fiction Studies*, Spring 1992.

and the mimetic (character as person).[2] These categories are never mutually exclusive, and we can see that Jacob falls under all three. The thematic aspect is obvious, Jacob represents the young men who died in the war; the synthetic is foregrounded by the narrator herself who wonders about the possibility of knowing another human being (119–121) and about the legitimacy of drawing character (262). It is when we get to the mimetic that things become troublesome. Whether we figure Jacob inhabiting an actual world or merely a *possible* world, readers have been persistently concerned with his lapses as a mimetic character, apparently unwilling to regard him solely or principally as a thematic element or a synthetic construct.

In *Jacob's Room* Woolf seems to be giving us a "type-like individual," a character who, while representing a class, is nevertheless an individual.[3] We see him interacting with a wide variety of characters; we see him engaging in various activities; and we are given information about his appearance, background, and attitudes not only through the narrator but also through other characters. Woolf seems determined to make him represent but at the same time transcend his category of the educated young man in the early twentieth century.

Yet she stops short and leaves us on the verge of identification. Readers agree that this is the case, but little has been said about how this is achieved, and less still about why.

To address the "how" first: in an article on literary character from the point of view of cognitive psychology, Richard J. Gerrig and David W. Allbritton argue that one way readers become immersed in literary worlds is through causality. Readers tend, as in real life, to attribute the cause of events to characters rather than to other circumstances in the situation. In reading a novel we accumulate information to generate expectations about what is to come, and we regard the characters as the determinants of the action to such a degree that even with highly formulaic works (such as James Bond novels) or works that are well known and have been read before (such as *Hamlet*) we fail to notice the formula, and we *do* experience suspense even if the work is familiar to us:

> Readers are so solidly predisposed to find the causes of events in the characters rather than in the circumstances that reflection upon the "formula" plays no role in their immediate experience of the novel. (383)

Authors can exploit this tendency on the part of the reader, and at the very least are unlikely to undermine it. However, the slight sense of dislocation we feel with Jacob derives from the fact that he seems continually impinged upon. Whether in romance or politics, it is difficult to conceive of a motivation for Jacob.

The first James Bond novel begins "James Bond suddenly knew that he was tired. He always knew when his body or his mind had had enough, and he always acted on the knowledge," giving us, Gerrig and Allbritton point out, information that from the first will allow us to predict how Bond will react (380). The same is true of course of nonformulaic characters; one of Jacob's most famous contemporaries is introduced as one who eats "with relish the inner organs of beasts and fowls," and, we are told, "He liked thick giblet soup, nutty gizzards, a stuffed roast heart, liverslices fried with crustcrumbs, fried hencods' roes. Most of all he liked grilled mutton kidneys . . ." (Joyce 45). Jacob, on the other hand, is first denominated as an absence—"Well, if Jacob doesn't want to play. . . . Where is that tiresome little boy?" (*Jacob's Room* 3)—and first encountered, after a long modifying phrase, climbing a rock: "Rough with crinkled limpet shells and sparsely strewn with locks of dry seaweed, a small boy has to stretch his legs far apart, and indeed to feel rather heroic, before he gets to the top" (7). The syntactic blurring is deliberate. Jacob emerges from the rock, is made as if he were part of it, and (as several critics have remarked) he never fully becomes separate from his environment. Further, he is already interpellated as a member of the family, already hedged about by rules, the right way to play, the permitted space.

If we consult the manuscript of *Jacob's Room* we cannot doubt that this embeddedness is deliberate. There, Woolf begins not with Betty Flanders but with Jacob on the beach, in the instant that he realizes that he is lost. Here is the opening paragraph of text:

> Beyond the rock lay ~~a pool shiny green~~ something shiny on the sand. A few small fish, left by the tide, beat ~~with~~ up & down with their tails. On the edge of the wave, paddling their feet, stood a single line of gulls; &, Jacob was trotting towards them when the light came across the waves. ~~At that moment he felt that he was lost. He knew then that he was lost.~~ . . . He then saw that the beach went on & on; he saw that there was a new line of hills above it—in short he was lost.

The light is the lighthouse: "Pointing at him across the sea came the light from the lighthouse." It is menacing: "The light ~~was the worst most frightening,~~ . . . This was the worst:" And the time is not mid-afternoon, it is midnight: ". . . all bright ~~& hostile.~~ & hostile. This was what happened at midnight; but quite alone he was running lost on the beach."[4] *This* is the sort of scene we recognize: the hero coming to consciousness of his separateness, embarking on the voyage of life; all the trappings are there—the "waves creaming up to him" (*Jacob's Room* MS I 2), the lighthouse singling him out, the magic hour of midnight. Here surely is a character to whom we would attribute causality. But Woolf chose to suppress all this.

In the published text Jacob emerges from a welter of characters: Betty, the Mr. Connor who owns the yacht, Archer, Captain Barfoot, the landlady, Seabrook, Mrs. Jarvis, and Charles Steele, who populate the page before Jacob appears. Further, where it is usual for a central character to be surrounded by minor characters less complex and dynamic,[5] the minor characters in *Jacob's Room* often have more interior life than Jacob. Charles Steele we never see again, but the narrator can tell us with authority that he

> was pleased by the effect of the black—it was just *that* note which brought the rest together. "Ah, one may learn to paint at fifty! There's Titian . . ." and so, having found the right tint, up he looked and saw to his horror a cloud over the bay. (6)

With Jacob we rarely get such a sense of motive or reaction. In the next section, in which Jacob discovers the crab and then the "enormous" couple on the shore, only by inference do we get a sense of his horror. And we are denied a sense of how he might react in future situations.[6] In the manuscript draft we see his determination: "And here was a jawbone with teeth in it. That must be taken home.—If he could escape with it—But the light again—'Nanny, Nanny!' he cried" (*Jacob's Room* MS I 4). Yet in the final version, Jacob discovers the skull, and the section ends with the curious sentence, "Sobbing, but absent-mindedly, he ran farther and farther away until he held the skull in his arms" (*Jacob's Room* 9).

So what is happening here? Introductions are crucial, yet Woolf, far from creating character, seems to be going out of her way to *un*-create character. I am sympathetic to the arguments of John Knapp and others who argue for the mimetic element in character—not that it necessarily *should* be there but simply that it is radically unavoidable.[7] The writer is going to have to work overtime to avoid it, and critics from Arnold Bennett on who have complained about Woolf's characters are ignoring the fact that Woolf is working against the familiar paradigms. Her statement about *The Waves* is well known ("Odd, that they [*The Times*] shd. praise my characters when I meant to have none" [*Diary* IV 47]), but nine years earlier, on 20 October 1922, thanking David Garnett for his praise of *Jacob's Room*, she wonders "how far can one convey character without realism?" (*Letters* II 571). To Lytton Strachey on 10 October 1922 she speaks of "the effort of breaking with complete representation" (*Letters* II 569). Her move was deliberate.[8]

Woolf returns at the end of the chapter to the crab Jacob has captured in his first scene; the chapter closes with the crab "trying with its weakly legs to climb the steep side; trying again and falling back, and trying again and again" (*Jacob's Room* 16). The incident is more of a motif than a method of characterization. It tells us what will happen to Jacob, but it is the *text* associating Jacob with entrapment and death rather than anything in his character deciding his fate—quite unlike, for instance, the baby tuckoo passage in *Portrait* that prefigures much of Stephen's character even as it sketches his circumstances.

Robert Wilson, working from Bakhtin in a recent article, argues that "self-consciousness is the 'artistic dominant' that governs the construction of character"; without it a character would be "merely the collocation of its traits" (83). Voice, says Wilson, manifests the characterhood of a character (82), and a "character possessing full characterhood, is typically confessional" (84). The only confessional figure in *Jacob's Room* is the narrator (of whom I will say more later); in Jacob there are certainly not the "two contending voices" that Bakhtin found in Dostoevsky's characters; his character is not "internally dialogic" and neither is it "interactively dialogic." Woolf favors reported dialogue over direct discourse in all her novels, but in *Jacob's Room* she eliminates internal dialogue and much dialogue between characters. The manuscript scene with Clara in the garden, and the climactic scene with Sandra on the Acropolis, dramatize Jacob's anxieties much more extensively than in the published text.[9]

So the novel is not confessional and is not a psychobiography. It has been observed that the history of narrative in Western literature is distinguished by an inward turn, an increasing emphasis on rendering mental states, yet Woolf seems to be veering away not only from rendering mental states (there are no "moments of being" in *Jacob's Room*) and from giving us the kind of information we could use to infer them but also seems bent on frustrating those automatic processes which cause a reader to identify with a character.

II. The Postmodern Subject

Early reactions to a book are often blind hits but uncannily on the mark, and those who did not like what Woolf was doing were often clearer about what was actually going on in the novel than those who praised it. The *Times Literary Supplement* noted that Jacob is "lovable since his friends and several women love him"; he is "the mutest of all heroes" and "Mrs Woolf's method increases his silence." Further, "[w]e do not know Jacob as an individual, though we promptly seize his type" and "it might still be questioned whether her beings, while they intersect, really act upon each other." Noting that there seems to be no good reason for all the minor characters, the reviewer concludes that the book "is not Jacob's history simply, nor anyone else's, but the queer simultaneousness of life" (Majumdar and McLaurin 96–97). There is no mention of the fact that Jacob dies in the war, not a single mention of the ideological.

Perhaps this absence is because the armistice was still two weeks short of being four years old and one had only to mention the name Flanders; the point was still too obvious and too painful to need comment. Yet other reviewers also passed over the issue in silence, and the *Yorkshire Post* was unsure exactly what happens at the end: "Jacob (we gather) has been killed in the war" (Majumdar and McLaurin 107). But in questioning whether or not Woolf's method does not "condemn" the characters "to be external," the *Times Literary Supplement* reviewer has put his finger on the issue: these characters are "condemned," they do "intersect" rather than interact; they are as W. L. Courtney said in the *Daily Telegraph* "puppets" (Majumdar and McLaurin 104), but they are not as he felt *Woolf's* puppets. They are subjects, puppets of ideology—the church for Mr. Floyd, patriarchy for Betty Flanders—and, as Mrs. Jarvis finds in breaking away from the church, they can break away but they cannot break out. You may, like Julia Hedge, choose the discourse of feminism, but you are interpellated nonetheless.

Woolf is showing the action of ideology in constructing human character, revealing the process and effect of subjectivity. Arnold Bennett felt that characters need to "clash" with one another and complained that the younger generation is "so busy with states of society as to half forget that any society consists of individuals" (Majumdar and McLaurin 113). Rebecca West concurred: "it is not about individuals at all" (Majumdar and McLaurin 101). Again, turning this around, we see that Bennett *has* seen what is there, he just does not want to; the book is about society and the individual's relationship to it, about ideology, in Althusser's sense of the word.[10]

Thomas Docherty addresses the issue of holding the mirror up to nature and quotes Northrop Frye's reminder that the poem is not itself the mirror image of nature but that which causes nature to be reflected. Thus the images Hamlet shows his mother of Claudius and Old Hamlet are to make Gertrude see *herself*. This, says Docherty, is what happens in some twentieth-century fiction:

> an author describes a character to a reader; but the pur-
> pose, far from being an attempt to "make the reader see"
> the supposed object of the description, is rather an attempt
> to make the reader see him or herself and to perform an
> act of self-evaluation in terms of the position which the
> text has made the reader occupy. The means adopted for
> this are precisely those adopted by Hamlet: the emotional
> manipulation of the reader, placing him or her in a position
> where, through seeing a character described in relation to
> that position, indirectly the reader will see him or herself
> described, or posited. (42)

This is precisely what Woolf is doing in *Jacob's Room*: the reader
finds him/herself "posited," but most have not liked it, and resisted
it, taken refuge in the discourse of mimetic characterization and said
Jacob is a failure.

Some recent studies of character address the problem of literary
character from the point of view of the subject, and it is tempting
to use these in an analysis of *Jacob's Room*. In dealing with Woolf's
novel, however, one can only go so far with them. In the postmodern
novel, writes Docherty,

> The stability of "character" is replaced with the more mo-
> bile "subject" (and often the novels are narrated by an
> anonymous first-personal subject); in some cases, instead
> of characters we seem to have fragmentary "instants of
> subjectivity" none of which seem to be related to each other,
> and none of which seem ever to develop into a more stable
> Self. The reader is involved in this fragmentation, for he or
> she has to make piecemeal sense of these "subjects" in a
> disjointed and sometimes self-contradictory way. (xv)

In a writer such as Samuel Beckett the individual is no longer
equated with the mind, nor even with the body; character becomes
a "word-mass" (the term is actually E. M. Forster's), it is "that which
mediates between the author and reader through words," it is "the
implied voice" (Docherty 34). But Jacob, although presented in a
fragmentary way, is not fragmentary in the way of the postmodern
subject, and he is not reduced to a voice; indeed, as we have seen,
he is prevented from having a voice.

However, it is not the scattering of the self that Woolf is examining but rather the process of interpellation, and here Docherty's
remarks on proper names are useful. In what he calls "essentialist"
conceptions of character the proper name is a way of summing up,
containing the existence and significance of a character. Further,

> if the name, replete with all its potential significances, comes first (anterior in temporal occurrence as well as noumenally primary), then we may say that the character, in metaphysical senses, is "dead." In this case the character is merely a function in a plot, labelled before the enactment of that function and with a totally limited potential for change or development. (49)

Docherty is of course talking about the kind of naming that takes place so prominently in Woolf's other novels; the cries of "Rachel, Rachel!" in *The Voyage Out* or "Mrs. Ramsay, Mrs. Ramsay!" in *To the Lighthouse*, or here the cries of Archer and of Bonamy that bracket the fiction, "Ja—cob! Ja—cob!" But in *Jacob's Room*, undercutting these namings is the naming by the author. Just as "Oedipus" means "swollen-foot" in a work where recognizability is central to the plot (see Docherty 49), so "Flanders" tells the reader that Jacob is fore-doomed. He may think he is choosing—"'I am what I am, and intend to be it,' for which there will be no form in the world unless Jacob makes one for himself. The Plumers will try to prevent him from making it" (*Jacob's Room* 55)—but the plot happens to him, and unlike a Greek tragedy we know this from the start even on a first reading. He is dead before he is born into the text, his patronymic already a citation from the text of the First World War.

C. L. Barber's (*Shakespeare's Festive Comedy*) conception of names as either "ceremonial" or "historical" can bring this further into focus. In the former view names are fixed, they have a place in a ritual; in the latter they have their own authority and are capable of change (cited in Docherty 51). Jacob is trying to be the latter but is doomed to be the former; he is the crab in the interpellative bucket. He has been placed in that bucket by the Plumers but also by Woolf.

The name is the locus around which characterization takes place, and it also gives the reader a position to inhabit and from which to view the world of the fiction. Formerly, writes Docherty, novels elicited "sympathy" for characters, which asked us to see from their point of view but did not require us to give up our own. In postmodern works we are "made to have empathy . . . quite literally involved and positioned within an other's subjectivity" (Docherty 83). Again we can see that *Jacob's Room* does not fit the realist mode, but neither does it fall into the postmodernist.[11] We are denied sympathy, but neither, to use the term in Docherty's way, do we achieve empathy. Yet we are thrown back upon ourselves; Jacob does make us see the ways in which we are "posited."

III. The Brechtian Subject

In January 1920, the same month that she conceived her "new form for a new novel" (*Diary* II 13), Woolf was reading her husband's new book, *Empire and Commerce in Africa: A Study in Economic Imperialism*;[12] in April, just after drafting the opening scene of *Jacob's Room* she read Maynard Keynes's *Economic Consequences of the Peace*—"a book that influences the world without being in the least a work of art" (*Diary* II 33). I suggest that Woolf wanted to write a book that would influence the world while being indeed a work of art and that would go much deeper than merely swaying government policy. More than exposing the "Presbyterian" temperament of President Wilson (Keynes 26) and/or the subtle cynicism of Clemenceau (Keynes, 20, 26) Woolf would lay bare, with the slow inevitability of a Greek tragedy, the web of ideology that entrapped them, us, all. Keynes's book leaves us feeling "if only . . ." President Wilson had been different; Leonard Woolf's book suggests "if only we would recognize that 'there is no logic of events . . . only a logic of men's beliefs and ideals'" (8). Virginia Woolf's book undercuts the ground from which we might wish, "if only. . . ."[13]

Virginia Woolf's brother-in-law Clive Bell, writing on her "painterly vision" in the *Dial* says "she does not intend us to share [the emotion of the scene]: she intends us to appreciate, to admire" (Majumdar and McLaurin 144). Bell is arguing that what Woolf wants us to respond to is the form. I think he is right in that she is keeping us aloof from the emotion of the scene, but not so that we will appreciate the significant form.

As Woolf was correcting the proofs of *Jacob's Room*, Bertolt Brecht, sixteen years younger than Woolf, was just getting his first plays published, and it would be more than a decade before he articulated his ideas of *Verfremdungseffekt*, the alienation effect. Nonetheless, his distinctions between traditional Dramatic Theater and Epic Theater are useful for coming to terms with what goes on in *Jacob's Room*.[14] I have highlighted certain key elements in his list:

Dramatic Theater	**Epic Theater**
plot	narrative
implicates the spectator in a stage situation	**turns the spectator into an observer, but**
wears down his capacity for action	**arouses his capacity for action**
provides him with sensations	forces him to take decisions

experience	picture of the world
spectator is involved in something	he is made to face something
suggestion	argument
instinctive feelings are preserved	brought to the point of recognition
in the thick of it, shares experience	**stands outside, studies**
human being taken for granted	**human being the object of inquiry**
he is unalterable	alterable and able to alter
eyes on the finish	eyes on the course
one scene makes another	**each scene for itself**
growth	**montage**
linear development	in curves
evolutionary determinism	**jumps**
man as a fixed point	man as a process
thought determines being	**social being determines thought**
feeling	reason

(Willett, *Brecht on Theatre* 37)

Clive Bell had noted that the hero is "built up out of other people's reactions to him. . . . Jacob is not merely affecting, he is being
affected" (Majumdar and McLaurin 146–147), never considering that
Woolf might have had a social purpose behind her work. Yet if we look
over the chart we can see that in making the reader an observer, forcing him or her to a recognition, treating the human being as a subject
of inquiry, moving in jumps, and employing montage as a means of
making the point that the social being determines thought, *Jacob's
Room* is more profitably to be examined in terms of social drama than
impressionist painting—or any purely formalist approach.

The methods of the new theater were to break the spell; to
make the spectator use his or her critical sense. Lights, musicians,
even state hands must be visible: the process of showing must itself
be shown. Even the actor's duty was to show attitudes, not express
feeling. The aim was not to alienate the spectator in the sense of
making him or her hostile (although this certainly happened and did
with *Jacob's Room* as well); the aim is "detachment" and "reorien-

tation" (Willett, *Theatre of Bertolt Brecht* 170–177). The *Pall Mall Gazette* complained that *Jacob's Room* had no story, "no perceptible development of any kind" (Majumdar and McLaurin 99). The *Daily Telegraph* concluded with the positive, "In its tense, syncopated movements, its staccato impulsiveness, do you not discern the influence of Jazz?" (Majumdar and McLaurin 105); but perhaps the most insightful remark was made by the petulant reviewer in the *Saturday Review*: "the dot-and-dash method leaves much to be desired. . . . [T]o leave the simple-minded reader guessing at connexions which might just as well be made clear for him, is a positive injury to art. It distracts from the solid object of the imagination. It destroys concentration" (Majumdar and McLaurin 106). Exactly. Jazz and impressionism engage aesthetic concentration, albeit of a different sort from representational art, but concentration all the same. Woolf wants concentration (and what the reviewer is here talking about is really absorption in the story and characters) but of a different sort. And she does not simply want absorption in the design, in the significant form; what Walter Benjamin said of Brecht is true of Woolf, she is less interested in the "development of actions" than in the "representation of conditions" ("Epic Theater" 150).

Jacob is like a Brechtian actor: he demonstrates an attitude much more than he expresses a feeling; he grows but does not change. As in Brecht these things cannot be kept completely separate, but if we start with the assumption that feeling will be a by-product, peripheral and incidental rather than central and essential, we find the figure of Jacob (figure rather than character) unusually effective, rather than surprisingly defective. If the readers identify with the psychological experience of the characters, then they will be "concerned with issues of individual morality rather than with larger social structures" (Bennett 24).

The interpenetration of ideology and form manifests itself in several aspects. In *Jacob's Room* readers have been struck by how Woolf violates the chronology of a book that bears at least a superficial resemblance to a *Bildungsroman*,[15] mentioning in the second chapter (*Jacob's Room* 30) Jacob's meeting with the Rev. Floyd that occurs near the end of the book (*Jacob's Room* 297). Althusser, in "'The Piccolo Teatro': Bertolazzi and Brecht," observes that in classical theater the "hero's temporality was the sole temporality, all the rest was subordinate to it. . . . And quite naturally, the spectator seemed to 'live' the play by 'identifying' himself with the hero, that is, with his time, with his consciousness, the only time and the only consciousness offered him" (147). The "dissociated structure" of Brecht makes this impossible, as does the cavalier chronology of the narrator in *Jacob's Room*.

Walter Benjamin notes in "What is Epic Theater?" that in Brecht's theater "hardly any appeal is made to the empathy of the spectators" (150); instead of empathy, astonishment is produced. This is often done through the interruption of events so as to produce the feeling of alienation. In *Jacob's Room* this interruption happens throughout, and perhaps most dramatically at the end, where the expected conclusion simply is not provided (many first-time readers are not even certain initially that Jacob has died). Further, "Like the pictures in a film, epic theater moves in spurts. Its basic form is that of the shock. . . . This brings about intervals that, if anything, impair the illusion of the audience and paralyze its readiness for empathy" (153). Brecht's stated aim was to foreground the ideological, and many of the techniques or qualities of his drama are techniques we find, obviously with some modification, in *Jacob's Room* as well. The form of the novel with its space breaks is part of an ideological, rather than epistemological, reorientation.

Susan Bennett reminds us that Brecht's *verfremdung* is not simply, although the term was coined after his 1935 trip to Moscow, a translation of *ostranenie*, the "defamiliarization" of Shklovsky. It is political as well as aesthetic, and, to quote Fredric Jameson, "The purpose of the Brechtian estrangement-effect is . . . to make you aware that the objects and institutions you thought to be natural were really only historical: the result of change, they themselves henceforth become in their turn changeable" (58). This is what Woolf was doing: exposing the unnaturalness of these institutions that seem so natural (and so naturally lead to war) that the causes seem to lie elsewhere.[16] And as Brecht said, these new works "are not going to satisfy the old aesthetics" (Willett, *Brecht on Theatre* 21–22).

Thus it is that the aesthetic and the ideological intersect. Readers have remarked on the elegiac qualities of Woolf's fictions and of *Jacob's Room* in particular. There is sadness when Jacob dies, but how then can we reconcile that with the fact that readers feel they are held aloof from Jacob? Woolf allows us to know Jacob well enough that we credit his charm, and he is young, and thus there is regret when he dies. But there is another sadness, the sadness of recognition, recognition that he has become a subject, and this is tied to the recognition (which many readers have wanted to resist) through him of our own subjectivity. Thus there is the sadness of identification (rather than sympathy or empathy) with Jacob's plight. The prototypical modernist hero is the alienated individual, and in *Heart of Darkness* Conrad has Marlow say "We live, as we dream, alone" (57); but Woolf is investigating the flip side of Marlow's quest—how we are dreamed by ideology. The name "Jacob" means "usurper" but in fact he usurps nothing. The loss of Jacob is the loss of *our* self, and thus we mourn even though we do not know him.

Makiko Minow-Pinkney concludes her fine chapter on *Jacob's Room* with the qualification, "If the novel in these various marginal ways calls into question the phallogocentric ideology, it none the less faces the embarrassing problem that its own hero is a man" (52). But it is not embarrassing that the hero is a man; it is inevitable. Jacob is not an allegorical figure or type, a *bearer* of a theme. The theme is in his characterological being. If we see him as *representative* of patriarchy then the force of the critique is naturally undercut by the celebratory aspect of his presentation. However, if we see him as *constituted* by patriarchy, as character in the ceremonial sense indicated by Barber above, and thus as a figure in a ritual sacrifice, then the celebratory only makes the horror greater.

Jacob is raised entirely by women. Minow-Pinkney points out that an extraordinary number of the men in the book are maimed, and the one serious would-be step-father for Jacob is mentally castrated by Betty Flanders (*Jacob's Room* 31). Why does Woolf go to such lengths to ensure that Jacob does not have a father? Again one reason is because it would reduce the situation to individual psychology. A father or father figure would incarnate the values of patriarchy.[17] He too is interpellated—"'Merchant of this city,' the tombstone said; though . . . he had only sat behind an office window for three months . . . well, she had to call him something. An example for the boys" (*Jacob's Room* 18)—an interpellation that has nothing to do with his character and everything to do with his subject position within the ideology of the family. In the book he is never called by his last name; "Flanders" is reserved for Jacob, passed on by his mother who, unlike Mrs. Jarvis, rather admires male leadership.[18] The family preserves and purveys the dominant political ideology; effectively as well as metaphorically, Jacob's father is the State. Where Keynes was showing how personalities shape the economic consequences of the peace, Woolf was showing how personality is shaped by the economic configuration of the peace, a peace that she like Keynes saw as leading inevitably to war.

Thus far I have been talking mainly about the characterization of Jacob, but the links between ideology and form extend to his milieu as well. To return to Benjamin's observations on the film and the "shock" value of the new art in "The Work of Art in the Age of Mechanical Reproduction," comparing the art of the painter and that of the cameraman, he speaks of the deliberate fragmentation that militates against the "total picture." What distinguishes film, according to Benjamin, is its "tactile" quality:

> [the art of the Dadaists] hit the spectator like a bullet, it happened to him, thus acquiring a tactile quality. It promoted a demand for the film, the distracting element of which is also primarily tactile, being based on changes of place and focus which periodically assail the spectator. (238)

So it is in *Jacob's Room* where the space breaks jolt us from one scene to the next. And this technique is related to the prevailing ideology. Benjamin's image of a "bullet" is apt, and he develops this theme in a note:

> The film is the art form that is in keeping with the increased threat to his life which modern man has to face. Man's need to expose himself to shock effects is his adjustment to the dangers threatening him. The film corresponds to profound changes in the apperceptive apparatus—changes that are experienced on an individual scale by the man in the street in big-city traffic, on a historical scale by every present-day citizen. (250 n. 19)

Thus it is not simply a question of optics, the multiple perspectives of cubism, but a felt rhythm, the beat of modernization within modernism. For all that its settings include Cornwall and Greece, *Jacob's Room* is more a city novel than is *Mrs. Dalloway*.

Seymour Chatman agrees with David Daiches' early analysis that argues that the technique shows the flux of experience, but Chatman goes on to explore the ideological implications, arguing that the sudden shifts support

> a picture of modern life filled with empty busyness, distraction, and lack of commitment. This impression is confirmed by the contents of the novel: the meaningless roar of motor traffic outside Jacob's room in London, the idleness of interminable party-conversation, the breeziness of Sandra's infidelity and her husband's calm acceptance of it, and so on. (53–54)

Jacob's occupation is deliberately anonymous, and Woolf stresses the herd quality of it all:

> About half-past nine Jacob left the house, his door slamming, other doors slamming, buying his paper, mounting his omnibus or, weather permitting, walking his road as other people do. Head bent down, a desk, a telephone, books bound in green leather, electric light. . . . "Fresh coals, sir?" . . . "Your tea, sir." . . . Talk about football [. . .]

> while letters accumulate in a basket, Jacob signs them. . . .
> (*Jacob's Room* 150)

Chatman notes also Woolf's "unprecedented decision to give proper names to even the veriest bystanders" (54). This naming of everybody mocks the notion of naming as a way of knowing the person, stresses the notion of interpellation, of naming as a way of calling the individual into being as a subject. Here the naming is part of the ethos of the city; it is a bit frantic, the text is naming everybody in sight, and all it does is confuse us. Rather than augmenting the mimetic, rather than constructing a background for the central character, this random naming has a leveling effect; we do not know who is important.[19] It is this feature of the book that exasperates first-time readers more than anything else, and yet the thing is done advisedly; it alienates the reader and reminds him or her of the alienation that takes place in mass culture; it establishes from the outset Jacob's status as a cog in the machine. The lambent cry "Ja—cob! Ja—cob!" is lost in the bureaucratic naming of faceless subjects of the state.

IV. The Narrator

Chatman also briefly touches on the ideological implications of the narrative perspective, noting that in the episode of the argument at Cambridge (*Jacob's Room* 71), the narrator is

> outside, prowling in the courtyard, straining but unable to hear what is being said. . . . Why is she outside in the cold if not because she is a woman? The whole effect argues the cultural starvation felt by intellectual women in early twentieth-century England. . . . (55)

This is true, and the famous passage about dogs in church (*Jacob's Room* 49) reinforces the narrator's exclusion. But she also goes anywhere and does anything she wants at other times in the text. She can be out in the cold watching the lights of Cambridge but also soaring over Europe watching the lights of Paris, Constantinople, London (273). She can watch the *Phaedrus* invading Jacob's mind (184), and she herself can invade his room.

Woolf is (through the narrator) exploring the subject position of women, and it is a very different position from that of young men. She is excluded but by that very fact is accorded a kind of power. Being denied access to the archives of Cambridge, she is able to see the Cambridge archive, in Foucault's sense of the word.[20] Alex Zwerdling (74) draws our attention to this reflection on the career of Woolf's cousin H. A. L. Fisher (historian, Fellow of New College, Oxford, Cabinet Minister) in *Moments of Being*:

> What, I asked myself the other day, would Herbert Fisher have been without Winchester, New College and the Cabinet? What would have been his shape had he not been stamped and moulded by the patriarchal machinery? Every one of our male relations was shot into that machine and came out at the other end, at the age of sixty or so, a Headmaster, an Admiral, a Cabinet Minister, a Judge. (*Moments of Being* 1976, 132)[21]

Teresa de Lauretis, in "Strategies of Coherence: The Poetics of Film Narrative," writes: "feminism understands the female subject as one that (unlike Althusser's or Jameson's or Eco's) is not either 'in ideology' or outside ideology (e.g., in science) but rather is at once inside and outside the ideology of gender . . . at once 'woman' and 'women'" (192). The narrator is able to describe Jacob's room, to produce the text *Jacob's Room*, precisely because she is not in that room; she is of course in a room of her own, but she maintains a consciousness of the interpellated nature of that space ("wherever I seat myself I die in exile" [*Jacob's Room* 114]) that Jacob and those educated like him at Cambridge lack.

The narrator is in fact flaunting her power, flaunting her status not as a mimetic character but as a textual construct, so that the book is less about the possibility of knowing another person (for all her commentary on the subject) than it is about the making of a person in art. *Jacob's Room* is self-conscious not just in its construction of Jacob but also in its construction of the narrator; her comments on art have a different status from those of Lily Briscoe in *To the Lighthouse*, for we are meant to believe in Lily as a character. Here the narrator is both character and device, and we are meant to watch as well as to identify with her search for Jacob, to feel her desire and yet to appreciate the moral and political dimensions of her project.

Teresa de Lauretis speaks of the contradiction of women wanting "authority and authorship when those notions are admittedly outmoded, patriarchal, and ethically compromised" (192), and the narrator here is deconstructing the whole notion of authoritative character construction. She *could* tell us about Jacob, but she *will not*. As I have said, Woolf tells us more in the manuscript; but she does not simply eliminate Jacob's interior monologue, she gives us a narrator who reminds us what she is doing and what she could have done:

"I say, Bonamy, what about Beethoven?"

("Bonamy is an amazing fellow. He knows practically everything—not more about English literature than I do—but then he's read all those Frenchmen.")

"I rather suspect you're talking rot, Bonamy. In spite of what you say, poor old Tennyson. . ."

("The truth is one ought to have been taught French. Now, I suppose, old Barfoot is talking to my mother. That's an odd affair to be sure. But I can't see Bonamy down there. Damn London!") for the market carts were lumbering down the street. (119)

Here are Jacob's thoughts running in rather obvious counterpoint to his utterances—in short, Woolf could do it if she wanted to, and win Arnold Bennett's approval, but she does not. De Lauretis speaks of contemporary filmmakers developing "the means, conceptual and formal . . . to tell stories resisting the drift of narrativization" (193), the "ideological coercion" of linear narrative (Silverman 215), and Woolf is doing precisely that in *Jacob's Room*, refusing authority, dealing with the problem of showing the march of progress without herself reproducing that march in her narrative.

Kaja Silverman's remarks on cinematic suture are helpful here. In viewing a film, the viewer will experience the first shot as "an imaginary plenitude" but then almost immediately become aware of an absent field, of a limiting frame on what he or she sees. This sense of lack inspires the desire to see more, and the "cut" that divides one shot from the next discloses what has been absent in the first shot (203–205). It is in part this process, this creation of a signifying chain in which one shot becomes a signifier of the next, and the signified of the previous one, which drives the narrative forward (205, 213). So it is with *Jacob's Room*. The space breaks on the page fragment the narrative into "shots," short takes which emphasize their incomplete status, inscribing a lack which we desire to fill, a gap or wound which we desire to suture over.

In classic cinema this is a subtle, almost seamless process, but in some films (Silverman uses *Psycho* as an example) the cuts, the negations of each shot, are deliberately exposed. Further, in *Psycho* we are obliged to make "abrupt shifts in identification":

> These identifications are often in binary opposition to each other; thus the viewing subject finds itself inscribed into the cinematic discourse at one juncture as victim, and at the next juncture as victimizer. These abrupt shifts would seem to thwart the process of identification. . . . However, quite the reverse holds true. The more intense the threat

of castration and loss [Silverman is relating suture to the
Lacanian entry into the symbolic order], the more intense
the viewing subject's desire for narrative closure. (Silverman 206)

In *Jacob's Room* we too (like the viewers of *Psycho*) are made to
oscillate between different subject positions, between that of Jacob
and that of the narrator.

The basic structural unit for this oscillation is, in the cinema, the
shot/reverse shot formation, "a cinematic set in which the second shot
shows the field from which the first shot is assumed to have been
taken" (Silverman 201); the following passage from *Jacob's Room*,
which leads into one of the most often quoted asides by the narrator, is similar to a shot/reverse shot sequence, in which both shots
are from the point of view of characters in the narrative. It exposes
both how the desire for suture works in the reader and how we are
inscribed in two different subject positions:

> Great men are truthful, and these little prostitutes, star-
> ing in the fire, taking out a powder-puff, decorating lips
> at an inch of looking-glass, have (so Jacob thought) an
> inviolable fidelity.
>
> Then he saw her turning up Greek Street upon an-
> other man's arm.
>
> The light from the arc lamp drenched him from head
> to toe. He stood for a minute motionless beneath it. . . .
>
> It was as if a stone were ground to dust; as if white
> sparks flew from a livid whetstone, which was his spine; as
> if the switchback railway, having swooped to the depths,
> fell, fell, fell. This was in his face.
>
> Whether we know what was in his mind is another
> question. Granted ten years' seniority and a difference of
> sex, fear of him comes first. . . . Even while you speak and
> look over your shoulder towards Shaftesbury Avenue, des-
> tiny is chipping a dent in him. He has turned to go. As for
> following him back to his rooms, no—that we won't do.
>
> Yet, that of course, is precisely what one does. (*Ja-
> cob's Room* 158–159)

A startling passage. We are first inscribed as Jacob, feeling the
sudden sick horror of seeing a woman for whom he cares (the precise nature of the affection is not an issue here) with another man.
Then, over the space break, the shot is reversed. We do not shift 180
degrees, but perhaps 90. We see him, not from Florinda's viewpoint
but from that of the narrator; nevertheless it is the narrator-in-the-

scene, the narrator who is ten years older, who feels "fear," then "a desire to help," and who follows him home and stands outside in the street beneath his window.

At the same time the hailing by the narrator ("Even while you speak and look over your shoulder . . .") interpellates us as reading subjects and as voyeurs. Benjamin says we identify with the camera, with the cinematic apparatus ("The audience's identification with the actor is really an identification with the camera. Consequently the audience takes the position of the camera . . ."), or, more properly, with its fictional representation (Benjamin, "Work of Art" 228; Silverman 216). But what this deliberate hailing does, like the deliberate foregrounding of the cuts for each "shot" of the narrative, is to make us aware of the process. We in fact have already been interpellated as voyeurs; this call induces a self-consciousness, an alienation in Brechtian terms, that makes us recognize our role.[22] So, we are prevented from fully identifying with Jacob because of the nature of his characterization (limited access to his consciousness, and so on), and this identification is further disrupted by our forced oscillation between his subject position and that of the narrator.[23]

If we "hang vibrating" over anyone it is the narrator herself, who, paradoxically, is characterized more fully as a mimetic character, as an autonomous self, than the ostensible focus of the text. It is her impulses we know, her voice we hear, where with Jacob all is denied. And yet we are continually jolted back from her as character to her as narrative device. The boundaries between her and the narrative are shifting and fluid. To what extent is she *in* the narrative created by a pseudo-author? To what extent are we to conceive of her as *producing* this narrative? As in a Brechtian drama, in which an actor will engage us in a scene and then put up a placard and remove a prop in preparation for the next scene, the narrator continually violates the frame.

Barry Morgenstern argued twenty years ago in *Modern Fiction Studies* that the narrator must not be identified with Woolf, that she, the narrator, creates a portrait of herself. But *why* would Woolf want to create such a portrait? I would suggest that the function of the narrator is not to engage us in her search for Jacob but rather, as with Jacob himself, to engage but disengage us, so that we participate in her search but watch it at the same time. And watching, what we begin to suspect is that, as with Peter Walsh's dream of the "Solitary Traveller" in *Mrs. Dalloway* or the "restless searcher" in *To the Lighthouse*, the narrator here is searching for the wrong thing.

The solitary traveller is tempted by visions that "proffer great cornucopias" (*Mrs. Dalloway* 86); the searcher in *To the Lighthouse* wants to find "some absolute good, some crystal of intensity . . .

which would render the possessor secure" (*To the Lighthouse* 199); and the narrator of *Jacob's Room* feels "One word is sufficient" if only one could find it (*Jacob's Room* 116). But as Lily realizes, all we are granted are brief moments of illumination, "matches struck in the dark" (*To the Lighthouse* 240). The "one word" will never be found; a decade later Bernard in *The Waves* will declare, "I need a howl; a cry" (*The Waves* 295), but of course he cannot get it. As with Peter, Bernard, and the searcher of *To the Lighthouse*, we are engaged in this quest but at the same time made to realize that it is misdirected. It is not just that one can never know another person, it is that we can scarcely be sure what it is to be known. There is not a solid core of selfhood that can be captured, a situation the narrator directs us to when, after saying "there remains over something which can never be conveyed to a second person save by Jacob himself" (which argues a degree of self-consciousness and a unified and coherent self), she adds: "Moreover, part of this is not Jacob but Richard Bonamy—the room; the market carts; the hour; the very moment of history" (*Jacob's Room* 120). She goes on to ask us to "consider the effect of sex" and to lament that "[e]ven the exact words get the wrong accent on them" (120), which suggests that the narrator herself imperfectly realizes the quixotic nature of her quest. She concludes that "something is always impelling one to hum vibrating, like the hawk moth, at the mouth of the cavern of mystery. . . . [W]hat remains is mostly a matter of guess work. Yet over him we hang vibrating" (121). The pronoun shift from "one" to "we" marks the split between the narrator and the reader: we grant that "one" does do this sort of thing, but at the same time "we" do not hover over Jacob. For the text has already made us realize the importance of "the room; the market carts; the hour; the very moment of history."

V. History

So we are to watch the narrator writing, or trying to write, Jacob's history. But what is history? "All history backs our pane of glass. To escape is vain," the narrator says, wondering if this is what accounts for Jacob's sorrow (78). This suggests an unproblematic view of history. Yet other comments challenge such a view. Taking the statement by Louis Montrose that a prominent concern of the new historicists is with "the processes by which [work] incorporated into English Culture and the British educational system has helped to forge and perpetuate a dominant ideology" (27), we might be tempted to label Woolf's narrator a new historicist.

At Cambridge, Sopwith talks in "silver disks" that only later prove all to have the same impress, "a Greek boy's head" (64); and, more telling, the light of Cambridge is associated with Julian the Apostate (72), the emperor trained in Christianity but attracted to the blend of paganism and philosophy presented by his tutors, which he then tried to restore—although it had never in fact existed. In her comment on "the Greek myth" late in the book, the narrator articulates what we have already felt watching Jacob and Timmy tramp down Haverstock Hill, sure that they are "the only people in the world who know what the Greeks meant," sure that Florinda by sitting upon his knee is doing as "did all good women in the days of the Greeks" (127): that this has less to do with Aeschylus than with Bacchus and undergraduate hubris.

Jacob reads the *Phaedrus*, "becoming (so it seems) momentarily part of this rolling, imperturbable energy, which has driven darkness before it since Plato walked the Acropolis," admirable, surely. But it does not drive back the darkness on his own acropolis:

> Meanwhile, Plato continues his dialogue; in spite of the rain; in spite of the cab whistles; in spite of the woman in the mews behind Great Ormond Street who has come home drunk and cries all night long, "Let me in! Let me in!"
>
> In the street below Jacob's room voices were raised.
>
> But he read on. For after all Plato continues imperturbably. . . . Jacob, who was reading the *Phaedrus*, heard people vociferating round the lamp-post, and the woman battering at the door and crying, "Let me in!" as if a coal had dropped from the fire, or a fly, falling from the ceiling, had lain on its back, too weak to turn over. (184–185)

Woolf herself loved Greek, but like Stephen's aesthetic theory in *Portrait* that is punctuated by Lynch's irreverent comments and passing traffic, the context of Jacob's reading of the *Phaedrus*, a dialogue on rhetoric and love, shows what needs to be "Let in" to his philosophy. His mind may combine with the "enormous mind" (183) of the British Museum, but in acquiring the ability to do so, it has lost the facility to register what is happening outside his window (again, as Chatman reminds us, the place of the female narrator). That the only Aristotle he finds in Greece is a dirty waiter is comic (234), but the elitism is not. The "Greek myth" is not just a fond illusion, it is a dangerous delusion.

Jacob is statuesque (132, 246, 291) in more ways than one. His ability to merge his mind with Plato's, and in so doing to pay no more attention to a woman crying in the street than to a dying fly, is not the antidote to but the shaping impulse behind the reified nonchalance of the "young men in the prime of life" on the battleship who "descend with composed faces into the depths of the sea" (265). Even earlier, when we see Jacob in Greece wondering if in fact Home Rule is the thing for Ireland (235), we realize that the charming undergraduate enthusiasm of feeling one is the only one who understands what the Greeks meant, leads to a more sinister identification of civilization with oneself. Thus Greek literature is placed in the service of an imperialist ideology. It is not innocent, Woolf's sending Jacob to Greece, the founding culture of Western civilization.

As I said, Woolf is going deeper than Keynes or Leonard Woolf in examining the forces that shaped the present state. In *Empire and Commerce* Leonard argues:

> politicians, statesmen, and historians represent the horrible story of man's political development which they call history, as almost entirely determined by the "logic of events" or the "logic of facts." But in history there is no logic of events and no logic of facts, there is only a logic of men's beliefs and ideals. (8)

Virginia Woolf would agree with this assessment of the "logic of events": the narrator's aside on the "unseizable force," that "the men in clubs and Cabinets" say drives our lives and rips through the nets of novelists, is this historical inevitability (*Jacob's Room* 264–266). And she would agree with her husband that politicians who assume that political evils are inevitable, and therefore counsel resignation, are producing a climate which leads to "commercial rivalry between nations, the struggle to markets, tariffs, armaments, and war" (Leonard Woolf 8). But where Leonard sees this resulting from a blind confusion between "beliefs" and "facts" and wants us to attend to the logic of men's beliefs in understanding and shaping policy,[24] Virginia Woolf is showing in *Jacob's Room* that the notion of there being a "logic" to men's beliefs is extremely problematical.[25] Leonard Woolf declares on the first page of his study that "Man is infinitely above the beasts because he is self-conscious, because he reasons and acts on reason, because through his reason he is able to control his destiny" (3). The parallelism is beautiful and the confidence engaging; the whole appeal of the book, through an array of facts and details that even he acknowledges may be bewildering, is to reason.[26] *Jacob's Room* argues not that man is irrational; indeed, one of Jacob's distinguishing characteristics is his rationality. The problem is an uncritical faith (to pick up Leonard's metaphor) in that reason; *Jacob's Room* dramatizes how we exercise that reason within an envelope of ideology, how having been produced as subjects all that we (the pronoun includes not just men but women like Betty Flanders who have absorbed or at least are impressed by these values) will do is reproduce the prevailing system, go on producing trade rivalries, tariffs, and war. Electing new leaders, changing political parties, creating a League of Nations will do little as long as the underlying ideology goes unrecognized, as long as the mirror, as Althusser puts it, remains unbroken.[27]

Jacob's Room with its fragmented form breaks up the master narrative for which Leonard Woolf searches:

> I have often probably mistaken the trail. All kinds of preconceived ideas and prejudices . . . have caused me to stray from the right path, to confuse beliefs, to mistake one desire for another, to impute wrong motives, to misrepresent acts and facts. . . . But I do not think that we have ever lost our sense either of purpose or of direction: we have never wandered from the trail to follow any other quarry than certain beliefs and desires shaping human policy and determining human action in Africa. (315)

That it is the "right" path, and that he has "never" wandered from it, except to bag the elusive quarry of human desire and, presumably, bring it back to the trail, suggests both in its combination of the metaphors of salvation and hunting, and in its absolutism, the dangerous certainty that Virginia Woolf was trying to dismantle in *Jacob's Room*, showing that the very idea of "rational argument" is one imbibed through an ideological state apparatus, the university—in part through the idiosyncratic teaching of the dialogues of Plato, whose *Republic* Leonard Woolf invokes at the beginning of his study.

VI. The Press

In May of 1917, Woolf published three reviews in the *Times Literary Supplement*: (1) "A Cambridge V.A.D" on May 10, on the memoirs of a member of the Voluntary Aid Detachment, a "nursing service auxiliary to the armed forces" (*Essays* II 114 n. 1); (2) "Mr. Sassoon's Poems" on May 31, on his *The Old Huntsman and Other Poems*—Sassoon had been injured in April and was recovering in England protesting vigorously against the war and would soon be declared to be suffering from shell shock; and (3) "The Perfect Language," published between the other two on May 24, a review of *The Greek Anthology* in the Loeb Classical Library.

In the first paragraph of "The Perfect Language" she talks of how the Loeb library, with its facing translations, at last recognizes "the existence of the amateur" (*Essays* II 114). This is significant because

> [t]o our thinking the difficulty of Greek is not sufficiently dwelt upon, chiefly perhaps because the sirens who lure us to these perilous waters are generally scholars of European reputation. They have forgotten, or never knew, or for reasons of their own choose to belittle, what those difficulties are. (*Essays* II 115)

The appropriation of culture for ideological ends is thus quietly but firmly indicated. The publishing of the Loeb library is a politically enabling, a revolutionary, act. "We shall never be independent of our Loeb" she says, and to turn it around, it is the Loeb that makes those like her independent of the Professor Sopwiths of the world. Greek itself

> will not agree to be a respectable branch of learning which we are well content to admire in the possession of others. A branch of learning suggests a withered stick with a few dead leaves attached to it. But Greek is the golden bough; it crowns its lovers with garlands of fresh and sparkling leaves. (*Essays* II 116)

Her enthusiasm for the language is extreme—"Greek literature is not so much literature as the type of literature, the supreme example of what can be done with words" (*Essays* II 118)—and we can see in it the source of Jacob's enthusiasm ("when all's said and done, when one's rinsed one's mouth with every literature in the world . . . it's the flavour of Greek that remains" [*Jacob's Room* 125]). But she is aware of the exclusivity of reading Greek ("the few who read Sophocles perfectly are about as singular as acrobats flying through space from bar to bar" [*Essays* II 115]), and her sense of its incomparable beauty, its status as "the perfect form of human utterance" purged of any "irrelevant vulgarity" betrays an almost desperate quality. The attraction of this perfect language is made clearer when contrasted with what she was reading in her own language at the same time— the memoirs of a V.A.D. nurse who attests to the horror of trench life and the vulgarity of the common soldier, and the poetry of an officer who she wishes would write more of such lines as

> Where have you been, South Wind, this May-day
>   morning,
> With larks aloft, or skimming with the swallow
>   (*Essays* II 121)

but is constrained by circumstance to use his talent to make us feel "the most sordid and horrible experiences in the world" in such lines as these from "The Hero":

> He thought how 'Jack', cold-footed, useless swine
> . . . . how he'd tried
> To get sent home; and how at last he died,
> Blown to small bits. And no one seemed to care
> Except that lonely woman with white hair.
>   (*Essays* II 120)

There is the desire to avoid such experience, the knowledge that she cannot, and the recognition that even the study of Greek can never be a politically disinterested act.

Readers observe that *Jacob's Room* is a war book without much war in it, that in *Mrs. Dalloway* and *To the Lighthouse* as well the war is crucial but marginalized. In all these novels it is important not as a cause but as a symptom. Not only does Woolf want to avoid the inevitably compromising situation of trying to denounce war while celebrating individual heroics, she wants to show that war is merely the logical outcome of a system in which, as Leonard said, the progression is "markets, tariffs, armaments, and war" (8).[28] It happens to be in Europe; it could be in Ireland; it could be, as the drunken woman crying in the street reminds us, in the home.

The system that produced Jacob also produced George and Gerald Duckworth, the two halfbrothers who sexually molested her. The issue has been explored in detail by Louise DeSalvo; what I want to address briefly here is the importance of *Jacob's Room*, the physical commodity, as an act of resistance. Readers have long noted that Woolf's first experimental novel is *Jacob's Room*; her first experimental work is her sketches. The notion seems to be that the sketches were a warm-up to an aesthetic shift that manifested itself in the movement from the traditional *Night and Day* to the iconoclastic *Jacob's Room*. But what changed more radically than her aesthetics were the conditions of production: in 1917 she acquired a printing press. Thus it is that she can write "Kew Gardens" and print Mansfield's "Prelude" while producing the novel that so disappointed Mansfield ("we had never thought to look upon its like again" [Majumdar and McLaurin 82]). Woolf's first two novels were published by Gerald Duckworth, subjected to the scrutiny of Edward Garnett, their reader, and then approved by the man who had held such power over her in her youth. *Night and Day* (published 1919) was written for Gerald Duckworth and Company, "The Mark on the Wall" (1917) and "Kew Gardens" (1919) for the Hogarth Press. On 22 May 1917 she writes to Vanessa, "We have just started printing Leonards story; I haven't produced mine yet . . ." (*Letters* II 155–156). It is clear from this and the surrounding letters that "The Mark on the Wall" was written for, called into being by, the Hogarth Press.

The extent to which Modernism was in fact a function of small presses and little magazines, in a new economic climate created by factors as diverse as the Net Book Agreement of 1899 and the invention of the linotype machine, is something that is just beginning to be recognized, and Woolf's own development is part of a larger shift that I cannot go into here.[29] But in terms of her own career it is clear that while Jacob is swallowed up by the "men in clubs and cabinets," the book that contains him, *Jacob's Room*, escapes the "clubman's" view of literature that she attributed to Gerald.

Further, although the Hogarth Press was very much within the capitalist system (Leonard was proud that it never lost money), it contests it to the extent that the control over the product is in Virginia Woolf's case transferred from the publisher to the writer. One must be cautious in claiming too much for this. Her position with regard to the prevailing power structure was ambivalent. She was Leslie Stephen's daughter, a cabinet minister's cousin, a regular reviewer for the major newspaper in the country. She could publish a pamphlet like "Kew Gardens" in a print run of 150, from a press no one had heard of, and be guaranteed reviews in periodicals such as *TLS* and the *Daily News* (by E. M. Forster, who made a point of telling readers where they could acquire the book), and perhaps even an affectionate parody (like that in the *Athenaeum* by Roger Fry).

Nevertheless, the publication of *Jacob's Room* represents a subversion of what she called the "patriarchal machinery." Aware of her own privilege, Woolf contests the interpellations of parent, parliament, and the publishing industry, using her power to show how that system creates subjects who march so dutifully, so inevitably, into war. The book was not, as David Daiches hazarded in his early study, written "for the sake of the style" (61). In all its aspects, from its subject Flanders (at once character and ghost), to the material conditions of its production, it was involved in breaking the mirror, making readers aware of the ideology that interpellated not just the hero of the book but the readers themselves.

Notes

1. See Jean Guiguet, 224, and James Hafley, 52. Writing thirty years after Hafley, Baruch Hochman begins his discussion of Woolf by noting, "Many things did not interest Woolf, and character in its classical sense was one of them" (*Test of Character* 157).

2. Phelan's article on *The Waves* provides a useful summary of his model for analyzing character developed in *Reading People, Reading Plots* ("Character and Judgment" 409).

3. The term is David Fishelov's, who combines E. M. Forster's "flat" and "round" distinction with a distinction between the "textual" and "constructed" (for example, that which involves the reader's experience of the world) levels of the literary work to produce a fourfold typology of characters: the "Pure Type," the "Pure Individual," the "Individual-like Type," and the "Type-like Individual" (426).

4. *Jacob's Room* (holograph) MS I 3, 5. The holograph draft of the novel is contained in three volumes, housed in the Berg Collection of the New York Public Library. I am grateful to Professor Quentin Bell and to the Henry W. and Albert A. Berg collection, New York Public Library, Astor, Lenox and Tilden Foundations, for permission to quote from the manuscripts. I also wish to acknowledge the grant from the Social Sciences and Humanities Research Council of Canada that enabled me to study the manuscript.

5. See Hochman. Writing of *Pride and Prejudice*, he says, "Characters who stand at the centre of a work . . . are ordinarily flanked by lesser characters, of lesser complexity, dynamism, and wholeness. Such flanking characters generally serve compositional as well as thematic purposes. . . . The progressive diminution of centrality, repleteness, complexity, and interest creates the space within which the central character can be experienced in all her vividness, complexity, and coherence" (*Character in Literature* 68).

6. Gerald Mead notes that a common narrative device used in film is to place the character "in a situation that is quite detached from subsequent plot events. . . . The next time we see that character, we know who she or he is in the sense that we know how he or she will react; in fact, we anticipate his or her reaction. It is this kind of device that gives a filmic character an air of consistency . . ." (448). Dealing with the way character interacts with plot, Phelan notes that one of the disconcerting features of *The Waves* is the way in which the "potential" of an action "to set in motion a chain of events is never actualized." He cites the "primal kiss" that Jinny gives Louis in episode one, a kiss that evokes responses from Louis and all the other characters, but which is forgotten in Louis' next speech, signaling a movement into a "new lyric moment" but undercutting conventional narrative development ("Character and Judgment" 414–415).

7. "Readers of literature have always had to base their understandings of fictional characters on that preexisting world those readers inhabit or could inhabit or could create" (Knapp 350).

8. Virginia Blain argues that "Woolf's technique deconstructs the whole notion of an integrated self as a unifying principle either for characterization or narration" (133).

9. In the goodbye scene with Clara, for instance, Woolf moves inside Jacob's mind: "I haven't said it Jacob thought to himself. I want to say it. I can't say it. Clara! Clara! Clara!" (*Jacob's Room* MS I 123), where in the published text he is mute. See Edward L. Bishop 123–126.

10. Terry Eagleton maps out a continuum for the term, giving six definitions ranging from (1) the most general, which identifies "ideology" loosely with "culture," to (2) "ideas and beliefs . . . which symbolize the conditions and life-experiences" of a particular group, all the way to (6) "deceptive" beliefs which arise not simply "from the interests of a dominant class but from the material structure of society as a whole" (29–30). Most of the time I use the term in the more general sense used by Althusser, meanings (1) and (2), wanting to stay away from the issue of the extent to which the discursive fields Jacob is embedded in involve *deliberate* distortion; nevertheless a study of the different orders of ideology, not just different kinds, at play in *Jacob's Room* would be extremely useful.

11. In any case, the debate over literary character rages on. Robert Rawdon Wilson says "old troglodytes never die, they just dissolve into their caves" (80 n. 7), but in fact in a recent issue of *Style* devoted to character the troglodytes are out there fighting. The articles by Hochman and Wachs, and by Knapp vigorously oppose postmodernist subjectivity: "The discourse in question has, by our lights, failed on two fronts. On the one hand, it has failed to intimate alternative modes of self-organization. . . . On the other, it has deflected attention from the dramatic struggle, within texts and characters, for selfhood, or personhood, or identity" (Hochman and Wachs 392); "The next reason for questioning the poststructuralist mandate, therefore, concerns the lack of heuristic potential found in the critical reliance on Freudian, neo-Freudian, and Lacanian models of human personality" (Knapp 350).

12. "Reading Empire & Commerce to my genuine satisfaction, with an impartial delight in the closeness, passion, & logic of it; indeed its a good thing now & then to read one's husbands work attentively" (7 January 1920, *Diary* II 5). In a letter to Margaret Llewelyn Davies on 3 January 1920 she writes, "I'm reading it for the 2nd time—to me it seems superb (*Letters* II 413).

13. She was at this time also organizing speakers for the Women's Co-operative Guild (*Diary* II 22), writing on the "Plumage Bill" (*Diary* II 53), publishing Gorky's *Reminiscences of Tolstoi*, reviewing Chekhov's *Cherry Orchard*, composing a "counterblast" to Arnold Bennett (The Intellectual Status of Women," a letter to the *New Statesman*), and lunching with socialists Sidney and Beatrice Webb. While starting Jacob's travels on the continent, Woolf herself was traveling with Leonard to Manchester where he was to be adopted as a candidate for the Labour party. As Jacob was heading down Italy in a train, Woolf was putting off a trip to Rodmell because of a threat of a General Strike and discussing Ireland, disarmament, and other topics with H. A. L. Fisher. And so on. She told the women at Manchester that

she was not a politician, incurring their disapproval, and she writes on 16 November 1921 that some "politics are beginning to interest me, as I suppose they interest City men—like a football match" (*Diary* II 143). The point is that on the streets, in her home, in the drawing rooms of others, in the theater, and down in the basement with the Press, Virginia Woolf was involved with social issues, but searching for a way of dealing with them that would not be like a football match—where the teams change but the game remains the same.

14. Jane Marcus compares Virginia Woolf to Brecht and Walter Benjamin in "Thinking Back through Our Mothers": "The reason for the 'plotlessness' of Woolf's novels is that they reverberate to the rhythm of the common life, not of the individual life" (11). The connection with Brecht is mentioned by Toril Moi, who notes how for Brecht a "noncontradictory perception of the world" is a reactionary one (11), and by Pamela Caughie (4, 19), but on the whole it has been ignored.

15. Judy Little argues that *Jacob's Room* is an "attack" on the form, that "It seems almost as though Virginia Woolf deliberately chose the traditions of the *Bildungsroman* in order to play havoc with them" (109).

16. As Sara Ruddick puts it, "Unlike Thoby's, Jacob's death is the avoidable outcome of institutionalized violence. When the 'overpowering sorrow,' the atmosphere of *Jacob's Room*, is named, the name is history" (193).

17. Woolf would explore these tensions later in *To the Lighthouse*. The *Jacob's Room* manuscript includes details that were cut and developed in the later novel (such as having Mr. Clutterbuck take opium [*Jacob's Room* MS I 115]), but even in the motif of the skull and the independence of Jacob we can see prefigurations of James Ramsay.

18. "Women would have felt, 'Here is law. Here is order. Therefore we must cherish this man. He is on the Bridge at night'. . . . 'Yet I have a soul,' Mrs. Jarvis would bethink her, as Captain Barfoot suddenly blew his nose in a great red bandanna handkerchief, 'and it's the man's stupidity that's the cause of this, and the storm's my storm as well as his'. . . . But Betty Flanders thought nothing of the kind" (*Jacob's Room* 41). The associations with the ship of state are obvious.

19. Isobel Grundy takes a different view, arguing that the names, which are often very similar, "accurately reflect the shared history of the race that lies behind individual difference" (213).

20. "By this term I do not mean the sum of all the texts that a culture has kept upon its person as documents attesting to its own past, or as evidence of a continuing identity; nor do I mean the institutions, which, in a given society, make it possible to record and preserve those discourses that one wishes to remember and keep in circulation. . . . The archive is first the law of what can be said, the system that

governs the appearance of statements as unique events. . . . [I]t is that which differentiates discourses in their multiple existence and specifies them in their own duration. . . . It is the *general system of the formation and transformation of statements*. . . . [I]t is not possible for us to describe our own archive, since it is from within these rules that we speak. . ." (Foucault 128–131). The use of archive in *Jacob's Room* is explored in "Archive and Ruin in *Jacob's Room*" by John Mitchell.

21. See also her long account of lunching with him 18 April 1921 while she was at work on chapter 12, "Jacob in Italy" (*Diary* II 112–114).

22. The narrator's moves are like the "trick shots" of Hitchcock—such as the opening of *Psycho* where the camera moves from an urban skyline to penetrate a venetian blind and enter a hotel window (see Silverman 206); the narrator's entry into Jacob's room strikes us as a violation, makes us voyeurs: "Jacob's rooms, however, were in Neville's Court; at the top; so that reaching his door one went in a little out of breath; but he wasn't there" (*Jacob's Room* 59). The sudden physicality granted the narrator with "a little out of breath" and her surprise that he isn't there ("Dining in Hall, presumably") makes the subsequent detailing of the room—cards from societies, books, a Greek dictionary with petals pressed between pages, his shabby slippers—an invasive act; we are like private investigators, quietly turning over the physical clues to a life, alert for the subject's possible return. One might ask, does part of the unease we feel with *Jacob's Room* derive from the fact that it is a *female* gaze directed at probing a *male* subject? It does feel different when the narrator goes into Angela's room in "A Woman's College from Outside" (*Complete Shorter Fiction* 139–142), a story that began life as part of *Jacob's Room*. But there Angela is present, and thus we are observers rather than interlopers.

23. I have elsewhere briefly related the space breaks to the cinematic device of "freeze-frame" (Bishop 128–130), and other writers have called the technique of *Jacob's Room* "cinematic," but no one has yet made a study of the novel from the point of view of film technique and theory.

24. Leonard Woolf wrote to Keynes, "I expect your psychological analysis of Wilson is absolutely correct. It explains everything" (quoted in Skidelsky 380).

25. Laura Moss Gottlieb's insightful comparison of Leonard's *The Intelligent Man's Way to Prevent War* (1933) and Virginia's *Three Guineas* (1938) documents a split in their political attitudes, and a reluctance to acknowledge these attitudes even to each other, that is in place at least a decade earlier.

26. "The reader was warned in the earlier chapters of this book that I proposed to plunge him into a maze of facts and details. . . . He may perhaps feel now . . . that we have often lost our sense of purpose

and direction in the forest of facts through which we have wandered" (Leonard Woolf 315).

27. Althusser writes that classical theater presents themes that are ideological but which it does not acknowledge as ideological, and asks, "But what, concretely, is this uncriticized ideology if not simply the 'familiar,' 'well-known,' transparent myths in which a society or an age can recognize itself (but not know itself), the mirror it looks into for self-recognition, precisely the mirror it must break if it is to know itself?" ("The Piccolo Teatro" 144).

28. In *A War Imagined* Samuel Hynes writes, "War is not the subject of the novel, but it is the termination of it, the event after which no story remains to tell." He goes on to link *Jacob's Room* with Clive Bell's essay "Before the War" and Maynard Keynes's *Economic Consequences of the Peace* in evoking a lost Eden; but although the novel "treats that time with gentle nostalgia . . . at the same time it dismantles it, breaking it into narrative fragments without a centre" (344). Zwerdling notes how Woolf's attitude toward the time before the war, and Cambridge in particular, is very different from that of someone like Lytton Strachey (75).

29. See Shari Benstock and Bernard Benstock and Norman Feltes' chapter on "Net books and *Howard's End*," especially 86–87 on the movement from "commodity-books" to "commodity-texts," marketing certain books with a "reputation-value" as a way of interpellating an unknown reader, as opposed to selling to a known market.

Works Cited

Althusser, Louis. "Ideology and Ideological State Apparatuses." *Lenin and Philosophy*. Trans. Ben Brewster. London: NLB, 1971. 127–186.

———. "'The Piccolo Teatro': Bertolazzi and Brecht." *For Marx*. Trans. Ben Brewster. New York: Vintage, 1970. 129–151.

Benjamin, Walter. "What is Epic Theater?" *Illuminations: Essays and Reflections*. Ed. Hannah Arendt. New York: Schocken, 1968. 147–154.

———. "The Work of Art in the Age of Mechanical Reproduction." *Illuminations*. 217–251.

Bennett, Susan. *Theatre Audiences: A Theory of Production and Reception*. London: Routledge, 1990.

Benstock, Shari, and Bernard Benstock. "The Role of Little Magazines in the Emergence of Modernism." *The Library Chronicle* 20.4 (1991): 69–87.

Bishop, Edward L. "The Shaping of *Jacob's Room*: Woolf's Manuscript Revisions." *Twentieth Century Literature* 32 (1986): 115–135.

Blain, Virginia. "Narrative Voice and the Female Perspective in Virginia Woolf's Early Novels." Clements and Grundy 115–136.

Caughie, Pamela L. *Virginia Woolf and Postmodernism: Literature in Quest and Question of Itself*. Urbana: U of Illinois P, 1991.

Chatman, Seymour. "The 'Rhetoric' 'of' 'Fiction.'" Phelan, *Reading Narrative* 40–56.

Clements, Patricia, and Isobel Grundy, eds. *Virginia Woolf: New Critical Essays*. London: Vision, 1983.

Conrad, Joseph. *Heart of Darkness*. 1899. Harmondsworth: Penguin, 1989.

Daiches, David. *Virginia Woolf*. Norfolk: New Directions, 1942.

de Lauretis, Teresa. "Strategies of Coherence: The Poetics of Film Narrative." Phelan, *Reading Narrative* 186–206.

DeSalvo, Louise. *Virginia Woolf: The Impact of Childhood Sexual Abuse on Her Life and Work*. Boston: Beacon, 1989.

Docherty, Thomas. *Reading (Absent) Character: Towards a Theory of Characterization in Fiction*. Oxford: Clarendon, 1983.

Eagleton, Terry. *Ideology: An Introduction*. London: Verso, 1991.

Feltes, Norman. *Modes of Production of Victorian Novels*. Chicago: U of Chicago P, 1986.

Fishelov, David. "Types of Character, Characteristics of Types." *Style* 24 (1990): 422–439.

Foucault, Michel. *The Archaeology of Knowledge*. Trans. A. M. Sheridan Smith. New York: Pantheon, 1972.

Gerrig, Richard J., and David W. Allbritton. "The Construction of Literary Character: A View from Cognitive Psychology." *Style* 24 (1990): 380–391.

Gottlieb, Laura Moss. "The War between the Woolfs." *Virginia Woolf and Bloomsbury: A Centenary Celebration*. Ed. Jane Marcus. London: Macmillan, 1987. 242–252.

Grundy, Isobel. "'Words without Meaning—Wonderful Words': Virginia Woolf's Choice of Names." Clements and Grundy 200–220.

Guiguet, Jean. *Virginia Woolf and Her Works*. Trans. Jean Stewart. London: Hogarth, 1965.

Hafley, James. *The Glass Roof: Virginia Woolf as Novelist*. Berkeley: U of California P, 1954.

Hochman, Baruch. *Character in Literature*. Ithaca: Cornell UP, 1985.

———. *The Test of Character: From the Victorian Novel to the Modern*. East Brunswick: Associated University Presses, 1983.

———, and Ilja Wachs. "Straw People, Hollow Men, and the Postmodernist Hall of Dissipating Mirrors: The Case of *David Copperfield*." *Style* 24 (1990): 392–407.

Hynes, Samuel. *A War Imagined: The First World War and English Culture*. New York: Atheneum, 1991.

Jameson, Fredric. *The Prison-House of Language: A Critical Account of Structuralism and Russian Formalism*. Princeton: Princeton UP, 1972.

Joyce, James. *Ulysses*. Harmondsworth: Penguin, 1986.

Keynes, John Maynard. *The Economic Consequences of the Peace*. 1919. London: Macmillan, 1971.

Knapp, John V. "Introduction: Self-Preservation and Self-Transformation: Interdisciplinary Approaches to Literary Character." *Style* 24 (1990): 349–364.

Little, Judy. "*Jacob's Room* as Comedy: Virginia Woolf's Parodic *Bildungsroman*." Marcus 105–124.

Majumdar, Robin, and Allen McLaurin, eds. *Virginia Woolf: The Critical Heritage*. London: Routledge, 1975.

Marcus, Jane. "Thinking Back Through Our Mothers." Marcus 1–30.

———. ed. *New Feminist Essays on Virginia Woolf*. London: Macmillan, 1981.

Mead, Gerald. "The Representation of Fictional Character." *Style* 24 (1990): 440–452.

Minow-Pinkney, Makiko. *Virginia Woolf and the Problem of the Subject: Feminine Writing in the Major Novels*. New Brunswick: Rutgers UP, 1987.

Mitchell, John. "Archive and Ruin in *Jacob's Room*." Unpublished essay, 1990.

Moi, Toril. *Sexual/Textual Politics: Feminist Literary Theory*. London: Methuen, 1985.

Montrose, Louis A. "Professing the Renaissance: The Poetics and Politics of Culture." *The New Historicism*. Ed. H. Aram Veeser. London: Routledge, 1989.

Morgenstern, Barry. "The Self-conscious Narrator in *Jacob's Room*." *Modern Fiction Studies* 18 (1972): 351–361.

Phelan, James. "Character and Judgment in Narrative and in Lyric: Toward an Understanding of the Audience's Engagement in *The Waves*." *Style* 24 (1990): 408–421.

———. *Reading People, Reading Plots: Character, Progression, and the Interpretation of Narrative*. Chicago: U of Chicago P, 1989.

———, ed. *Reading Narrative: Form, Ethics, Ideology*. Columbus: Ohio State UP, 1989.

Ruddick, Sara. "Private Brother, Public World." Marcus 185–215.

Silverman, Kaja. *The Subject of Semiotics*. Oxford: Oxford UP, 1983.

Skidelsky, Robert. *John Maynard Keynes: Volume One, Hopes Betrayed 1883–1920*. London: Macmillan, 1983.

Willett, John, trans. *Brecht on Theatre: The Development of an Aesthetic*. New York: Hill, 1964.

———. *The Theatre of Bertolt Brecht: A Study from Eight Aspects*. 3rd ed. London: Methuen, 1967.

Williams, Raymond. "The Bloomsbury Fraction." *Problems in Materialism and Culture*. London: Verso, 1980. 148–169.

Wilson, Robert Rawdon. "Character-Worlds in *Pale Fire*." *Studies in the Literary Imagination* 23 (1990): 77–98.

Woolf, Leonard. *Empire and Commerce in Africa: A Study in Economic Imperialism*. London: Allen and Unwin, 1920.

Woolf, Virginia. *The Complete Shorter Fiction*. Ed. Susan Dick. London: Hogarth, 1985.

———. *The Diary of Virginia Woolf*. Ed. Anne Olivier Bell and Andrew McNeillie. 5 vols. London: Hogarth, 1977–1984.

———. *The Essays of Virginia Woolf*. Ed. Andrew McNeillie. 6 vols. projected. London: Hogarth, 1986–.

———. *Jacob's Room*. 1922. New York: Harcourt, 1923.

———. Jacob's Room Holograph. 3 vols. Berg Collection, New York Public Library.

——. *The Letters of Virginia Woolf*. Ed. Nigel Nicolson and Joanne Traut-
     mann. 6 vols. London: Hogarth, 1975–1980.
——. *Moments of Being: Unpublished Autobiographical Writings*. Ed.
     Jeanne Schulkind. New York: Harcourt, 1976.
——. *Mrs. Dalloway*. New York: Harcourt, 1925.
——. *To the Lighthouse*. New York: Harcourt, 1927.
——. *The Waves*. New York: Harcourt, 1931.
Zwerdling, Alex. *Virginia Woolf and the Real World*. Berkeley: U of Cali-
     fornia P, 1986.

CONSOLATION REFUSED

VIRGINIA WOOLF, THE GREAT WAR,

AND MODERNIST MOURNING

Tammy Clewell

The elegiac dimension of Virginia Woolf's writing was already identified in the first book-length study of her work, when Winifred Holtby called *To the Lighthouse* a "ghost story" aimed at burying the phantom of the dead mother (159). But numerous critics did not take up the challenge of reading her work as a narrative form of mourning until the posthumous publication of Woolf's diary, letters, and memoirs that began in the 1970s. Based on these autobiographical writings, early biographical and critical evaluations reflected a remarkably uniform view, defining Woolf's life and writing as an unfortunate display of pathological grief. Just as biographers attributed Woolf's recurring mental breakdowns and suicide to her failure to mourn the premature deaths of her mother, half-sister, and brother, literary critics claimed that Woolf's unresolved grief marred her fictional achievements.[1] Mark Spilka, in *Virginia Woolf's Quarrel with Grieving*, the only monograph to date focused exclusively on Woolf's textual mourning, suggests that her "lifelong inability to love . . . seems to have been peculiarly intertwined with her lifelong inability to grieve" and argues that her novels suffer "from an emotional vacancy beneath their surface brilliance" (7, 11). Even Elaine Showalter, one of the most widely recognized voices in feminist literary criticism, claims to have found the "real" Woolf not in her fiction but in the story of her disordered bereavement. In Showalter's audacious account, Woolf's concern with "a female tradition" proved to be

Originally published in *Modern Fiction Studies*, Spring 2004.

"stifling to her development" and "a betrayal of her literary genius" because "by the end of her life she had gone back full circle, back to the melancholy, guilt-ridden, suicidal women . . . whom she had studied and pitied" (264).

This project of reading Woolf's fiction as a case history of neurotic grief has now come to an end. In the past decade Thomas Caramagno, Susan Bennett Smith, and John Mepham have produced studies that articulate Woolf's positive reinvention of mourning. Despite diverse textual interests, these critics demonstrate how Woolf defies the orthodox assumption, still reigning in some circles today, that healthy mourning comes to a decisive end when the bereaved have detached emotional bonds and installed consoling substitutes for the loss. Disputing grief as the cause of her mental illness, Caramagno suggests that Woolf suffered from manic-depression, a condition with a physiological source, and goes on to read Woolf's fiction as a "sensitive exploration of certain components of her mood swings that . . . invites us to question how we construct meaning from a text" (3). Smith focuses on Woolf's specifically feminist revision of Victorian mourning. Responding to a social situation in which nineteenth-century grieving was devalued as women's work, Woolf "deviates from tradition," according to Smith, "by not designating women chief mourners and by not feminizing male mourners" (318). Finally, Mepham links the development of Woolf's aesthetics to her critique of traditional mourning and argues that her "insight into the connection between literary form and forms of mourning should be understood not as a symptom but an achievement, an achievement which has cultural and historical rather than purely personal significance" (143).

These critics have convincingly shown how Woolf redefines mourning as an ongoing experience, an endless process where the living separate from the dead without completely severing attachments. What has been less widely appreciated, however, is that Woolf's reinvention of mourning was stimulated by the cataclysmic traumas of the First World War. In her sustained effort to confront the legacy of the war, Woolf repeatedly sought not to heal wartime wounds, but to keep them open. Some of the most disconsolate images in her fiction—the empty pair of shoes that Betty Flanders holds up at the conclusion of *Jacob's Room* to grieve her son's battlefield death and the ravished summer home undone by the passing of the war years in *To the Lighthouse*—testify to Woolf's refusal to engage a process of mourning aimed at "working through" despair and grief. Woolf used her writing to critique her culture's symbolic resources for suturing the private and public ruptures wrought by the war. *Jacob's Room* and *To the Lighthouse*, I will argue, denounce traditional forms of consolation for loss, consolatory paradigms that neutralize grief in antiquated salves and perpetuate gender values counter to Woolf's feminist politics. In waging a gendered form of rebellion against the aim of closure, Woolf's texts define a deliberate refusal to mourn as the only adequate response to death and wartime destruction, to losses that are at once personal and social, emotional and political. The anticonsolatory practice of mourning that Woolf forged in response to the Great War, it should be remarked, has gained widespread currency among contemporary memorial makers, artists, and critics who seek commemorative forms intended to provoke and hurt, rather than console and heal. Anticipating the innovative memorializing acts of Claude Lanzmann's *Shoah*, Maya Lin's Vietnam Veterans Memorial, and the NAMES Project AIDS Memorial Quilt,[2] Woolf's textual practice of endless mourning compels us to refuse consolation, sustain grief, and accept responsibility for the difficult task of remembering the catastrophic losses of the twentieth century.

The Politics and Ethics of Mourning Wartime Loss

Jacob's Room has frequently been read as a modernist critique of wartime idealism, the belief in God, king, and country that led the generation of 1914 to its tragic end. Less attention has been paid, however, to the way Woolf's formal innovations participate in the creation of an anticonsolatory practice of mourning. Consider the way Woolf raises Jacob's death to the level of a complex formal principle. Admittedly, the narrative's complexity is easily overlooked, especially for first-time readers who seem to follow a linear account of Jacob's maturation from youth to manhood. It is not until the novel's close, when Betty Flanders displays her son's shoes, that we definitively discover that he enlisted and died on the battlefield. But Woolf's opening scene already presents Jacob as an absent figure, a boy on the beach whose missing presence forces the painter Charles Steele to complete his landscape with a mournful dab of black paint. Framed between two images of loss, the novel thus unfolds in the very form of an absence. Moreover, the narrative's proleptic structure, its repeated anticipation of Jacob's wartime death in the telling of his life's story, serves as a constant reminder that "the present seems like an elegy for past youth and past summers" (168). In elegizing Jacob as an irrecoverable absence from the start, Woolf refuses to allow even the narrative of his life to compensate for his loss.[3] The shock of his absence, for reasons that will become clear, must be experienced without tempering or cure.

Why did Woolf believe that writing about the war needed to

foster a new consciousness of death, one that stressed its absolute finality? Why did she insist on engaging the reader in an experience of wrenching and unalloyed grief? One reason, the novel suggests, is that nineteenth-century mourning customs no longer adequately expressed the complexities of loss, consoling despair at the cost of a deeper confrontation with mortality. Woolf wrote at a time when mourning rituals had already shed much of their Victorian extrava-gance, but the pages of her novel offer a virtual catalog of traditional modes of celebrating death: tombstones, burial customs, epitaphs, requiems, elegies, and monuments. This cataloging enables Woolf's narrator to parody those vestiges of defensive belief that continued to allow conventional mourning to offer consolation. The narrator, a decidedly skeptical consciousness, includes the religious rebirth of the dead in God and the secular tendency to shroud the dead in bogus praise among the relics of an outworn tradition. If the former fails to register death's finality by promising the transcendence of the soul, the latter serves to legitimate social values that do not honestly reflect the dead, a point the narrator makes when remark-ing that the tombstone for Betty Flanders's husband falsely describes him as a "Merchant of this city" in order to set an "example for the boys" (16).

This critique of graveyard pieties begins with an understanding that mourning occurs not only as a private labor within the psyche but also as a social practice regulated by an array of cultural norms. Woolf undoubtedly recognizes the validity mourning has for analyzing culture and focuses special attention on the way that death rituals operate in the maintenance of class divisions. Her narrator observes Mrs. Lidgett, a working-class woman whose very name suggests her singular wish to "get" a proper "lid" for her coffin.[4] In her brief appear-ance in the novel, Mrs. Lidgett, "[t]ired with scrubbing the steps of the Prudential Society's office," repeatedly visits St. Paul's Cathedral, burial place of royalty and statesmen (65). She frequently admires an ornate tomb where a duke has been buried and "never fails to greet the little angels opposite, as she passes out, wishing the like on her own tomb" (65–66). Mrs. Lidgett's desire for a grave replete with the kind of expensive marble statuary characteristic of traditional burial customs does not escape the narrator's biting sarcasm. And for good reason, since the Victorian working class typically sought in death a level of affluence they had not enjoyed in life. As David Cannadine points out, over one-quarter of the twenty-four million pounds deposited in banks by the working class in 1843 represented savings for funerals (189). The elaborate accoutrements of Victorian mourning, which included everything from lavish funerals, formal garments, black-bordered stationery, special tea sets, and even somberly decorated ear trumpets for the hearing impaired, prompted many late-nineteenth- and early-twentieth-century commentators to argue that mourning rituals served as sources of financial anxiety and commercial exploitation, rather than ritual supports for the dying and their loved ones. It is not surprising, then, that Woolf identifies St. Paul's "ghosts of white marble" as part of the symbolic machinery supporting conventional social "order" and "discipline" (65). The Lidgett scene insists that death, when viewed as a consoling promise of deferred reward, reflects a conservative ideology that perpetuates class division and material hardship in this life by offering compensation in the next.

In promoting a new consciousness of death, *Jacob's Room* does more than criticize the tenacious persistence of consolatory mourning rituals. The novel also responds to what Philippe Ariès has called the "dying of death" in the twentieth century (28). By "dying of death," Ariès means the reduction of death to insignificance, a reduction he attributes to the modern emergence of the secular individual whose values derive solely from earthly satisfactions. The decline in religion decisively downgraded death's uniqueness and impact on life. No longer viewed as a spiritual transition to final judgment, death ceased to occupy a place in the cycle of mortality and immortality. To many observers, this changing attitude about death seemed more and more like an active denial, supporting Sigmund Freud's contention that modern Europeans showed an "unmistakable tendency to put death to one side, to eliminate it from life" (289). Other factors involving the emergence of modernity have also been cited to explain the disappearance of death from the practice of everyday life: the spread of capitalist values, the demands of urban life, and the medicalization of illness and dying.[5] Even the Great War, which temporarily returned an acute awareness of loss to the center of British society, did not ultimately stem the modern dying of death. As Woolf observed just one month after the signing of the Armistice, "the war is already almost forgotten" (*Diary* 1: 227). Writing *Jacob's Room* five years later, Woolf inveighs against this distinctively modern repression. In the same passage where her narrator chastises Mrs. Lidgett's longing for death's "sweet melodies," a London merchant is rebuked for banishing mortality from his thoughts. The old merchant finally visits St. Paul's but sees the cathedral as little more than "a gloomy old place" and hastens away with "no time now" (66). His ongoing lack of interest in meditating among the tombs appears as a willful avoidance, an attitude the narrator finds as reprehensible as Mrs. Lidgett's. Consequently, Woolf navigates through these opposing attitudes about death, through the Scylla of outright repression and the Charybdis of consolatory evasion, in order to move her readers toward a direct confrontation with wartime loss and the social conditions that produced it.

Woolf's uncompromising resistance to consolation and healing in the wake of the Great War stands in stark contrast to widespread mourning practices recently evaluated by Jay Winter. In *Sites of Memory, Sites of Mourning*, Winter suggests that millions of Europeans represented their shared grief and found collective solace in the years following the Armistice through commemorative acts informed by classical, religious, and Romantic traditions (4). In a direct challenge to Paul Fussell's claim that the war ushered in a modern sense of irony in Western cultural expression, Winter argues that "traditional modes of seeing the war" were far more prevalent during the interwar period than "modern" ones (5). In his evaluation, modernist responses might register the anger and disillusionment felt by soldiers and their loved ones, but they could not heal. Only war memorials, literature, and art that adopted resources from tradition and the sacred, Winter concludes, "provided a way of remembering which enabled the bereaved to live with their losses, and perhaps to leave them behind" (5).

In relation to these postwar forms of memorialization, *Jacob's Room* stands out precisely for what it withholds: the text offers no faith in religious immortality, no applause for individual heroism, no celebration of male comradery, no stoical acceptance of fate, no aesthetic smoothing over of the war's human costs of any kind. While it would be ridiculous to think Woolf was against healing as such, she did recognize that the symbolic resources capable of offering consolation, ending mourning, and enabling the bereaved to cut their losses were the very same resources that led to the outbreak and legitimation of the Great War. It was only by renewing and sustaining the pain of wartime loss that Woolf hoped to intervene, changing the social conditions that might allow such a catastrophic event to reappear.[6]

Woolf's was certainly not the only voice protesting the practice of conventional mourning during the period. Siegfried Sassoon similarly railed against didactic memorializing gestures in "On Passing the New Menin Gate," a satirical poem criticizing the war memorial for the inscription, "Their name liveth for ever," placed on the gateway above the names of 54,889 war fatalities (188). For Sassoon, the text carved in "peace-complacent stone" serves to cover over "the world's worst wound" with a consoling promise of heroic immortality, turning the memorial into nothing less than a "sepulchre of crime" (188). Even more analogous to Woolf, Freud also warned against engaging the work of mourning to restore cultural values destroyed by the war. In "Thoughts for the Times on War and Death," a text that Peter Gay has aptly called "an elegy for a civilization destroying itself" (355), Freud focused not on the loss of life but on the loss of "the common possessions of humanity," including many of society's foundational principles: the belief in peaceful relations among nations, the power of human reason to curb violent desire, and the steady march of progress for the individual and state (289). Forced to confront the disappearance of what seemed to be the unassailable ideals of Western culture, Freud cautioned against engaging the mourning process to replace these social ideals with new ones of equal or even greater value. Instead, he deployed grief as a form of cultural critique, exposing idealistic inventions as nothing more than the insubstantial chimeras of a naïve humanism. The overwhelming sense of despair and disillusionment, Freud argued, must be experienced without any defensive shields, for only then can prewar idealism be squarely understood as the untenable and lost products of human endeavor, only then can a "new generation" work to rebuild a "better civilization" on stable ground (285).

Beyond Freud, Woolf places grief in the service of assessing conventional attitudes about gender, displaying a feminist form of bereaved anger toward her male protagonist to show how prewar constructions of masculinity prepared the way for intolerable loss. It is for this reason, in fact, that Woolf insists on a resolutely anti-heroic account of Jacob, repeatedly criticizing him for patriarchal beliefs, relentlessly chastising him for misogynistic behavior. Any effort to understand why Jacob provokes such intense scorn must begin with an account of the novel's narrator. In Woolf's later novels, the narrative perspective often merges with that of her characters, establishing what critics from Erich Auerbach to J. Hillis Miller have addressed as the completely expressive, ubiquitous, and androgynous mind narrating Woolf's fiction (Auerbach 536; Miller 179). In *Jacob's Room*, however, Woolf constructs an intrusive narrator, a narrative persona readers cannot help but confront. We know that "ten years' seniority and a difference of sex" distinguish the narrator from Jacob (94). Woolf defines the narrator, therefore, as older and more experienced, a female character for whom the healing rhetoric of religion, patriotism, or heroism would have flown in the face of her feminist challenge to the masculine status quo. Woolf's narrator refuses, in other words, to idealize the war dead. Such idealizations, she clearly understood, directly or indirectly sustain prewar values, the very values that empowered men and consigned women to the margins of society. By the time Woolf addressed the subject of the Great War in her 1922 novel, the wartime social gains women made in factories, hospitals, and government had all but disappeared with the return of soldiers to the homefront.[7] Woolf would raise the problem of postwar gender inequality sixteen years later in *Three Guineas* (1938) as the threat of the Second World War loomed large, criticizing patriarchal power for directing women "back to their homes" (141). In refusing to lavish unadulterated praise on her protagonist, Woolf's prosaic elegy positions us to see Jacob as her feminist narrator does, as an embodiment of patriarchal attitudes that led to a war many believe to have been fought without real purpose.

Woolf's aggression toward a male protagonist killed on the battlefield, clearly a strategic maneuver of her own to combat pre- and postwar gender constructs, begins early in the novel. The narrator exposes the young Jacob's cruelty by creating sympathy for a crab he carries from the beach and leaves to die. This criticism of male brutality shifts when the narrator follows Jacob to Cambridge, where he commences study in 1906. Jacob may well be an exceptional young man at odds with mainstream society, an intellectual especially sensitive to the nuances of Greek and Elizabethan literature. It should come as no surprise, however, that Woolf's female narrator sees the university he attends as a bastion of paternalism and notices that Jacob's scholarly remarks were often "dull" and "unintelligible" (73). The library Jacob amasses also reflects his belief in male superiority, for he owned the work of only one woman, Jane Austen, and even then "in deference, perhaps, to some one else's standard" (39). Most importantly, the narrator exposes Jacob as a flagrant misogynist. The reproach emerges in an often-cited passage where Jacob criticizes female attendance at a church service in King's College Chapel. He remarks the absurdity of "bringing a dog into church" and draws a comparison between the canine and the feminine. In the same way "a dog destroys the service," Jacob claims, "So do these women," who are "as ugly as sin" (33). In more subtle form, Jacob's misogyny informs the romantic liaisons he makes after college when working as a London lawyer. The narrator sharply criticizes him for taking up with Florinda, a love interest of Jacob's whose willingness to engage in sexual intercourse blinds him to her "horribly brainless" quality (80). Finally, toward the novel's end, the narrator ridicules Jacob for falling in love with Sandra Wentworth Williams, a married woman given over to the kind of romantic musings that led the generation of 1914 to willingly and even enthusiastically sacrifice life for the British cause (141).

By warring on Jacob with aggressive hostility, Woolf rejects the traditional role of submissive and passive mourner, a role historically burdensome to women who carried out the restrictive sartorial codes and social isolation of grieving to a much greater extent than their male counterparts.[8] As part of this passivity, mourners were expected to adhere to the ancient wisdom that counsels *de mortuis nil nisi bonum*, the prohibition against speaking badly of the dead.

In an illuminating passage in "A Sketch of the Past," Woolf challenges this social repression of bereaved anger: "That is one of the aspects of death which is left out when people talk of the message of sorrow: they never mention its unbecoming side: its legacy of bitterness, bad temper, ill adjustment" (123). Rather than glorifying the dead, Woolf's narrator repeatedly vilifies Jacob as a member of an elite masculine world, giving voice to a healthy form of mournful criticism. A similar expression of bereaved anger has recently been analyzed by Jahan Ramazani, whose *Poetry of Mourning*, an impressive study of the anticonsolatory animus in twentieth-century elegies, addresses the importance of contemporary displays of ambivalence and hostility toward the dead. When complaints about the deceased are repressed by self-censorship or the idealizing conventions of the traditional elegy, Ramazani argues, hostility is driven inward, taking an intense and sometimes debilitating form of self-reproach and self-punishment (28). Moreover, Judith Butler has also advocated the externalization of bereaved anger, an issue she relates to the formation of gay and lesbian identity. Butler defines the ego as constituted through identifications partly composed of unresolved grief. When culture prohibits the expression of lost homosexual attachments, Butler rightly claims, "the rage over the loss can redouble by virtue of remaining unavowed," producing types of "gay melancholia" with potentially "suicidal proportions" (148). Butler's commitment to establishing new social institutions for the expression of loss in all its manifestations also motivates Woolf, who succeeds in transforming female grief into feminist grievance. Woolf's central concern, indeed, is to defile the sanctity of the dead for the purposes of living. It is by venting bereaved hostility onto Jacob rather than allowing this anger to foment within the self that the narrator seeks to render the world fit for female habitation.

Woolf advances the work of gender reform through an aggressive mourning discourse by setting up the novel as a bulwark against patriarchal structures of inheritance. Despite his rebellious temperament, Jacob has reaped the benefits of his gender and class, acquiring status in a society he appears to disdain. As the narrator sees him, Jacob appears "satisfied" and "masterly" because "the sound of the clock conveyed to him (it may be) a sense of old buildings and time; and himself the inheritor" (45). To negate this masculine legacy, the narrator begins by raising a familiar elegiac trope, the cataloging of material possessions left by the deceased. Jacob's room contains, among other things, a collection of coats of arms, upper-class calling cards, books of Greek philosophy, and an essay entitled "Does History Consist in the Biographies of Great Men?" (39). These items function as metaphors for Jacob, figurative substitutes that not only seem identical to this elite young man but that also remain after his death. However, Jacob's possessions are not easily passed on, at least from the viewpoint of Woolf's narrator, who sees his things as the lingering artifacts of male privilege. Because the narrator views Jacob's belongings as part of a legacy created by men and for men, she blocks their transmission and contests the motif of elegiac inheritance. No longer guaranteeing an elite young man's enduring presence among the living, Jacob's personal effects become the empty and lifeless signifiers of his absence. Nothing is passed on in Woolf's novel, nothing except for an articulation of the gender constructs that surreptitiously conspired to produce Jacob's death.

Woolf's practice of anticonsolatory mourning, her interest in using grief to foster feminist grievance rather than the social complacency implied by healing in the postwar years, was more than a response to the war in general. It was also intimately connected to the death of her brother, Thoby Stephen, who died of typhoid in 1906 at the age of twenty-five. By all accounts, Woolf remained inconsolable long after Thoby's death and invited readers to hear echoes of him in Jacob when she recorded in her diary the closing line of Catullus's lament for a dead brother, "Ave Atque Vale" ("Hail and Farewell") and wrote "Julian Thoby Stephen 1881–1906" (*Diary* 4: 10). The endurance of Woolf's grief, coupled with what Judith Lee has addressed as her ambivalence toward a beloved brother who nevertheless enjoyed the benefits of masculine privilege (198), could only have reiterated the need for a mourning discourse no longer tied to outworn consolations, false idealizations, and defensive closure. But Woolf may well have gleaned more from filial death than the need for a therapeutic form of ferocious criticism in postwar displays of mourning. Her experience of losing a brother she loved, admired, and elegized in *Jacob's Room* may have motivated and informed Woolf's resolve to forge a new bereaved sincerity, a new language for loss capable of conveying genuine sympathy and profound solemnity for a young man who lived and died during belligerent times.

If the gender politics of Woolf's postwar bereavement entails a rejection of banal and culturally suspect forms of consolation, the feminist ethics of her commemorative practice derives from her representation of the exteriority of the lost other with respect to any signifying system, including the novel in which Jacob figures. Woolf presents Jacob, that is, as a character irreducible to the very narrative that offers his life's story, a refusal to provide an aesthetic or commemorative form that might divest us of the task of remembering. In so doing, her text makes the thought of Jacob's radical otherness possible, an alterity that resists conceptualization by the mourning subject and makes possible our ethical relation to both present and absent others. This is the significance of Woolf's abandonment of conventional characterization, of her narrator's insistence on the inscrutable and unknowable aspects of Jacob's character.

No one has raised the possibility of an ethics of mourning more insightfully than Jacques Derrida. In "By Force of Mourning," Derrida addresses a work of mourning that "would have to fail in order to succeed" and claims that while this failure "is always promised, it will never be assured" (173). His emphasis on the potential for grief work to fail emerges in response to psychoanalytic theories of loss. From Freud to the more recent work of Nicolas Abraham and Maria Torok, mourning has been used to explain the formation of subjectivity, the means by which the infant separates from the mother, acquires language, and accepts linguistic mastery as an adequate compensation for the loss. Derrida argues that psychoanalytic accounts of mourning perpetuate the main assumptions of the philosophy of the subject, reducing the lost other to an object for the mourner. In the conventional sense, mourning allows the lost other to be recovered in the language of the symbolic so that the subject can refuse to admit that something of the self has been lost with the other's departure. Conversely, Derrida shows how failed mourning, an account of endless grief that forgoes recovery and consolation, clarifies a fundamental decentering of self. He defines the "being-in-us" of the lost other as an absolute excess, a kind of exteriority belonging to the other that resides in a space neither properly inside nor strictly outside the psyche. By locating an otherness that resists the subject's attempt to constitute or reconsolidate a sense of strongly bounded identity, failed mourning succeeds in revealing "an essential anachrony in our being exposed to the other" (188). This anachronism indicates an outside that shatters any illusion of strict identity and relates us "to the law of what does not return or come back," that is, to the other's singularity and to our own mortality (192). For Derrida, then, the acknowledgment of another's death entails an acknowledgment of our own death, the mortality we embody as a condition of life. Far from a narcissistic practice, this acknowledgment names the condition for our ethical orientation in the world, the very condition, as Derrida puts it, of "hospitality, love or friendship" (188).

That Woolf's text prefigures Derridean insights should come as no surprise, for poststructuralism has often been understood as a theoretical elaboration of the basic workings of modernist aesthetics. Like Derrida, Woolf insists on the difference between the lost other and the mourner's memory of the lost other, showing how the bereaved narrator refuses to accept her own signifying authority as adequate compensation for Jacob's loss. No fewer than fifteen times does the narrator deflate the interpretations she herself imposes on Jacob, calling attention to the subjective and, indeed, narcissistic quality of her narrative: "Nobody sees any one as he is, let alone an elderly lady sitting opposite a strange young man in a railway carriage. They see a whole—they see all sorts of things—they see themselves" (30–31). And later, "It seems then that men and women are equally at fault. It seems that a profound, impartial, and absolutely just opinion of our fellow-creatures is utterly unknown" (71).

For many of Woolf's contemporaries, the rendering of Jacob's character as an impenetrable entity reflected serious flaws in the novel, indicating the narrator's unreliability and Woolf's own intrusive authorial theorizing. More recent critics, however, understand the narrator's self-defeating remarks as an integral part of Woolf's modernist break with the conventions of Edwardian realism. According to William Handley, Woolf's rejection of omniscience preserves her protagonist's subjecthood and opposes the "war's treatment of human beings as objects" (111). For Alex Zwerdling, Woolf highlights the inscrutable features of Jacob to portray "the sense of someone who remains a permanently unknown quantity," her way of pronouncing the devastating human cost of the war (909). In addition to the political relevance these critics insightfully suggest, Woolf's refusal to pin Jacob down also reveals the ethics of her anticonsolatory mourning. The narrator's willingness to deflate and ultimately abandon her own projections and conceptualizations of Jacob works as a powerful critique of the desire to master loss through the order of representation. Woolf's narrator never forgets, and never allows her readers to forget, the radical heterogeneity of the character she mourns.

What we know with certainty about Jacob amounts to this: he never survived the war to return to his room. To the extent the novel recalls us to irrecoverable loss, it presents Jacob as a character who exists in excess of any individual's memory of him. This ethical recognition of an other who exceeds any constituted sense in the mourner has a strange kind of healing power. It is not the power of consolation or recovery but of acceptance, the healing power that comes from accepting we never heal and that we embody the effects of loss throughout our lives. To grieve such a loss, Woolf suggests, is not simply to embark on a process that can never be complete; it is also to mourn Jacob's death by attending to our own mortality, a way of living in sight of our own inevitable self-loss that Woolf's text offers as a means of dissolving schemes of mastery and destruction linked to forms of death denial. When Mrs. Flanders's question as to what she should do with Jacob's shoes goes unanswered, Woolf's text moves beyond a critique of the consoling and gender-biased rhetoric with which British culture memorialized the war dead. The novel rallies a community of mourners around a mother's inconsolable grief. To mourn Jacob, then, is to acknowledge the absence he has become. And to sustain grief for this absence establishes the possibility for a vigilant relation to a fragile social present, an historical moment, as Woolf rightly recognized, that threatened to repeat the catastrophic violence of a war intended to end war.

The Mourning of Art

In *Virginia Woolf and Postmodernism* Pamela Caughie pursues a productive line of inquiry about the failed artists in Woolf's fiction by evaluating her work in terms of postmodern theories of language. Caughie does not categorize Woolf as a postmodernist, for she "resist[s] generalizing from reading Woolf's work in terms of postmodernism to concluding that she *is* postmodernist" (196). Rather, she uses postmodern concepts to challenge the adequacy of modernist paradigms to explain Woolf's writing. Caughie argues that Woolf's antithetical relation to modernism is particularly evident in her characterization of painters, writers, and dramatists. Woolf's artists not only draw attention to the failure of their own artistic creations; they also reject, in Caughie's analysis, an array of modernist positions, particularly the assumptions "that the artist is a *special* and *self-sufficient* individual, that the artwork is *original* and *autonomous*, and that art is a means of providing *order* or revealing *truth*" (29). The emphasis Caughie places on aesthetic issues that are raised and assessed rather than resolved by Woolf's fictional artists informs my reading of the resistance to formal consolation in *To the Lighthouse*. However, the account of Woolf that Caughie constructs, an account based on her "refusal to choose" any classification for Woolf's work (197), is limited insofar as it treats literary modernism as a set of self-evident assumptions in need of no analysis or explanation. Although in many ways productive, Caughie's study perpetuates the monolithic view of modernist aesthetics as necessarily compromised by an attempt to create "aesthetic harmony or unity out of the flux of experience" (31). Rather than claiming that modernist formulations of language and narrative cannot account for Woolf's writing, I read *To the Lighthouse* as a means of articulating her own practice of literary modernism, a practice that not only engages but also critiques the capacity for formal unity to console a world fragmented by personal and social loss. Having ransacked her culture's healing rhetoric, the religious and patriotic discourses that urged survivors to substitute ennobled memory for wartime loss in *Jacob's Room*, Woolf turns her mourning lens more fully on her own medium, using *To the*

Lighthouse to scrutinize the propensity of literature to serve traditional memorializing aims. Woolf's text dislocates literary and elegiac conventions that historically furnished solace in the wake of painful loss; it also links her specifically modernist disintegration of novelistic unity to the legacy of the Great War. In making the development of Lily Briscoe's painting emblematic of the development of the novel and in interrupting both with the rupturing effects of the Great War, Woolf grounds a practice of anticonsolatory mourning on the very failure of her artist to derive recompense from the work of art. Just as Lily refuses to regard her painting as an aesthetic substitute for the absent Mrs. Ramsay, Woolf's modernist text distances the reader from the consoling and recuperative function of literature itself.

In the "Time Passes" section of the novel, Woolf not only depicts the destructive forces of passing time and of the war years on the Ramsays' summer home; she also puts extreme pressure on one of the central tropes of elegiac poetry: the pathetic fallacy. An integral component of the genre's compensatory machinery, the pathetic fallacy personifies a natural world that mourns along with the bereaved. Whether Spenser's "medows mourne" or Milton's "sanguine flower" is "inscribed with woe," the pathetic fallacy assumes a deep affinity between the human and the natural: it consoles by promising the rebirth of the dead in a natural landscape governed by a cyclical process of growth, maturation, decline, and regeneration. Clearly, the trope undergoes a heightened critique in the commemorative lyrics of the Great War, as soldier-poets came to regard standard elegiac conventions as an ineffectual means of expressing man-made destruction. Nevertheless, the pathetic fallacy and other poetic salves are not wholly annihilated by the experience of mechanized warfare. Consider Ivor Gurney's "To His Love," a poem that takes over conventional funerary practice by advising readers to "forget" the "red wet / Thing" that a soldier has become by covering his body with "violets of pride" and "Masses of memoried flowers" (41). There can be no mistaking the challenge to consolatory closure that Gurney expresses, for the poem ends with the speaker unable to lay his friend to rest. And yet, the poem's predominant theme, the hope for reconciliation, is fully contained within its literary appropriation of conventional social ceremonies for celebrating the dead. Also seeking to magnify and elevate wartime death, Isaac Rosenberg's "Dead Man's Dump" draws on the healing power of the pathetic fallacy. A measure of consolation is found in knowing that the "Earth has waited" for the dead, is "Fretting for their decay," and "Now she has them at last!" (110). While personifying a bereaved landscape, Rosenberg's poem also raises serious doubts about a sustained affinity between natural and human orders, and a plaintive question is posed: "Earth! have they gone into you?" (110). These doubts are never fully resolved and the poem concludes with an image of the inhumane treatment of the deceased body during wartime. Nevertheless, Rosenberg's poem still maintains overt allegiances to the aim of consolation and the "metaphor of resurrection" that Winter finds in even the most realistic, critical, and despairing lyrics of the period (221).

In "Time Passes" Woolf similarly draws on the resources of the pathetic fallacy, the salve that combatant writers used to make death less painful and life more endurable. However, "Time Passes" not only invokes but also repudiates the idea of a natural order mirroring a human one, going so far as to evaluate human projections of grief onto the landscape as a display of the same mastery and violence found on the battlefields of Europe. "Time Passes" opens on one of the last nights of the Ramsays' summer vacation depicted in the novel's initial section. Darkness descends on the house and "certain airs" already "gave off an aimless gust of lamentation" (127), an early anticipation of the deaths of Mrs. Ramsay, Prue, and Andrew Ramsay that occur during the family's ten-year absence from the holiday home. Woolf's narrator begins by recalling the consolations offered by theological and natural archetypes: "divine goodness had parted the curtain and displayed behind it, single, distinct, the hare erect; the wave falling; the boat rocking, which, did we deserve them, should be ours always" (127–28). But in keeping with the critical function of modernism, the narrator confronts the disappearance of both God and the sympathetic responsiveness of the natural world. Indeed, when Mrs. Ramsay dies, the search for meaning and solace yields next to nothing: "no image with semblance of serving and divine promptitude comes readily to hand bringing the night to order and making the world reflect the compass of the soul" (128). While registering both a profound emptiness and at least an ongoing hope for future fulfillment, Woolf's narrator moves on to produce an amazingly insightful account of how the painful extremity of loss gives the pathetic fallacy a powerful and irresistible allure.

Woolf attributes the personification of natural forces to a basic human longing, a longing for kinship with a world capable of overcoming death's finality and providing closure to mourning. The speaker understands, that is, the immense attraction to a conception of nature that grants compensatory meaning to human loss: "it was impossible to resist the strange intimation which every gull, flower, tree, man and woman, and the white earth itself seemed to declare (but if questioned at once to withdraw) that good triumphs, happiness prevails, order rules" (132). When Prue dies from a complicated pregnancy, the narrator remarks the return of pathetic fallacy, a confirmation of nature's sympathy for human bereavement: "the spring with her bees humming and gnats dancing threw her cloak about her, veiled her eyes, averted her head, and among passing shadows and flights of small rain seemed to have taken upon her a knowledge of the sorrows of mankind" (132). In response to the unbearable death of mother and unborn child, the trope buffers the impact of trauma, permitting the consoling illusion that nature participates in human grief and promises the rebirth of the dead with the inevitable coming of Spring. But even here the trope's compensatory power is beleaguered at best, since Woolf's narrator begins to short-circuit an empathetic nature by making Spring, the very season of rebirth, assume the wintry desolation of intense bereavement.

In response to the deaths of Mrs. Ramsay and Prue, the pathetic fallacy lives on, ironically, by virtue of the tentative and questioning attitude with which Woolf's narrator raises it; however, the trope disappears irretrievably as a result of an exploding shell that sends Andrew Ramsay and other soldiers fighting in the First World War to an early grave:

> Did Nature supplement what man advanced? Did she complete what he began? With equal complacence she saw his misery, his meanness, and his torture. That dream, of sharing, completing, of finding in solitude on the beach an answer, was then but a reflection in a mirror, and the mirror itself was but the surface glassiness which forms in quiescence when the nobler powers sleep beneath? Impatient, despairing yet loth to go (for beauty offers her lures, has her consolations), to pace the beach was impossible; contemplation was unendurable; the mirror was broken. (134)

The importance of this key passage resides in the way Woolf links the war's destruction of human life and of the landscape to the shattering of an age-old affinity between the human and the natural. As noncombatants walk the beach and search for meaning in the aftermath of wartime loss, Woolf's narrator insists that "comfortable conclusions" and "sublime reflections" are no longer possible (134), a lost transcendence also echoed in Robert Graves's "Recalling War," which linked the "foundering of sublimities" to the Great War (121). The beauty of the landscape, so long a source of healing in traditional elegiac verse, is now emptied of compensatory potential and suspiciously regarded for its "lures" and "consolations." But Woolf goes even further than tearing apart the seamless fabric that appeared to weave humanity into a natural design. In associating Andrew Ramsay's battlefield death with the complete dissolution of the pathetic fallacy, she foregrounds a correspondence between the practice of personification and the practice of war. The passage identifies the projection of grief with a masculine desire for mastery, the same display of male mastery and sexual aggression that Woolf diagnosed in *Three Guineas* as a primary source of the brutal and protracted fighting of the war (108).

The centrality of Woolf's feminist critique of the patriarchal war machine has long been recognized. Most critics who address this issue, myself included, see the text's critique of masculine attitudes and male dominance as central to her account of the war. Nancy Topping Bazin and Jane Hamovit Lauter observe that Woolf uses war imagery in describing men in the Ramsay circle to connect "domestic and public politics within a patriarchy"; this relationship indicates "how sexism and its concomitant behavior can provide a foundation for either heroism (which can be admirable) or fascism (which is deplorable)" (19). But it is not enough to argue, as Bazin and Lauter do, that "Woolf integrates the concept of nature as destroyer and men as destroyer" (20). To address Woolf's assault on the pathetic fallacy exclusively in terms of her feminist critique of the male ego is not wrong as much as incomplete: such accounts tend to focus on textual themes rather than formal structures, overlooking the impact that the war had on Woolf's literary practice. "Time Passes" undoubtedly reflects Woolf's feminist perspective; however, the section primarily engages what James Haule addresses as Woolf's specifically artistic response to the legacy of the war. In his study of the early holograph and typescript versions of *To the Lighthouse*, Haule demonstrates that Woolf eliminated numerous identifications between the war and masculine aggression and severely qualified Mrs. McNab and Mrs. Bast's ability to rescue the human project from wartime destruction (167). In Haule's provocative thesis, Woolf opted against a direct account of the war's patriarchal source "not because it was unpopular or because she lacked courage but because it was not the 'history' she wanted to write and, however appealing, it was not art" (167). That Woolf labored through extensive textual revisions indicates "her enormous faith in art" as a crucial and distinct expression of the war's impact on character and life (178).

Woolf's dismantling of the pathetic fallacy, it strikes me with some force, evidences her fundamental interest in redefining the conditions of linguistic and artistic practice in light of the war years. If the abiding question raised in *To the Lighthouse* concerns the kind of elegiac art and commemorative practice that is possible after the Great War, Woolf's response could not be more directly demonstrated: art must be stripped of compensatory literary tropes in order to soberly confront the horror and politics of manufactured death. Woolf's practice of anticonsolatory mourning looks ahead to a post-Holocaust vision of art theorized by Theodor Adorno. In addition to his well-known claim about the barbarism involved in writing poetry that aims "at squeezing any kind of sense, however bleached, out of the victim's fate" (361), Adorno redefines the aim of art and philosophy after Auschwitz: "what must come to be known may resemble the down-to-earth more than it resembles the sublime" (364). Equally scornful of elevated sentiment, Woolf uses her writing to discover down-to-earth knowledge, the knowledge that art can no longer responsibly serve the purposes of transcendence, consolation, and redemption. It is for this reason that "Time Passes" details a house ravished by nature, a house where birds nest inside, rain rots the roof, thistles break through floor tiles, and vegetables disrupt flower beds. By highlighting "the insensibility of nature" (138), Woolf strips the pathetic fallacy of all consolatory effects, insisting that when art neutralizes the trauma of private and public loss it obscures the very conditions that produce destructive violence. Woolf's critique of con-solation is reiterated in her treatment of Mrs. McNab and Mrs. Bast, working-class characters who may succeed in salvaging the summer home from destructive forces of nature and time, but who never for-get that the returning Ramsays and friends would "find it changed" (139). Instead of depicting an unchanged place that reassures the mourners of their own temporal continuity, the surviving Ramsay circle returns to a house fundamentally altered by the war years, a house that Woolf poetically represents in order to recall survivors and readers alike to those who can no longer return.

Just as Woolf resists the allure of the pathetic fallacy in "Time Passes," Lily evaluates her own attraction to art's consolatory power. In attempting to complete her painting, a nonrepresentational por-trait of Mrs. Ramsay and her son James begun a decade earlier, Lily still has not experienced the "great revelation" (161), the absence of which had brought her work to a standstill. However, the wartime atrocities that claimed Andrew's life, along with the premature deaths of Mrs. Ramsay and Prue, have made Lily acutely aware that any present solution depends on distancing herself from the compensa-tory imagination of traditional art. Returning to her canvas, Lily both imagines and scrutinizes a consoling image of Mrs. Ramsay, an image of a flower-crowned woman moving across fields with a lover:

> For days after she [Lily] had heard of her [Mrs. Ramsay's] death she had seen her thus, putting her wreath to her forehead and going unquestioningly with her companion, a shade across the fields. The sight, the phrase, had its power to console. . . . But always something—it might be a face, a voice, a paper boy crying *Standard*, *News*—thrust

through, snubbed her, waked her, required and got in the end an effort of attention, so that the vision must be perpetually remade. (181)

The potential for the image to console Woolf's artist is held out even more intensely to the reader, who may hear echoes of the epiphanic revelation experienced by Mrs. Ramsay ten years earlier. Looking up from her knitting and seeing the third stroke from the lighthouse, Mrs. Ramsay seemed to sense "her own eyes meeting her own eyes," an intimation of unmediated selfhood that revealed "a triumph over life when things came together in this peace, this rest, this eternity" (63). This moment of being, as these revelatory flashes typically reserved for Woolf's female characters have come to be called, gives rise to a spectral scene that concludes Mrs. Ramsay's illumination: "There rose . . . from the lake of one's being, a mist, a bride to meet her lover" (64). For Lily, the image of woman and lover, however poignant, cannot be elevated to the level of transcendent truth, much less rendered on her mournful canvas, for she recognizes the intrusion of the outside on the inside, the way the world of others and politics dissolves any artistic claim to apprehending unconditional immediacy. It is by maintaining a resistance to her own desire for healing and closure in the wake of Mrs. Ramsay's loss, a resistance the war years urgently reiterated, that Lily is able to acknowledge that both her mourning and mourning art must be "perpetually remade."

Lily's rejection of aesthetic consolation reveals the profound distance that separates Woolf from the "culture of redemption" isolated by Leo Bersani as a defining characteristic of literary modernism practiced by writers including Marcel Proust and James Joyce (28). In Bersani's account, modernist aesthetics, especially evident in "encyclopedic fiction," imparts meaningful form onto the chaos of experience and compensates for lost transcendence by establishing art as an autonomous sphere in the attainment of truth (178). In contrast, Lily questions the practice of redemptive modernism when she stirs her paints, meditates on loss, and looks to Augustus Carmichael, a friend of the Ramsays whose poetry was well received after the war. She imagines how Mr. Carmichael would respond to the traumatic losses wrought by time and the war: "That would have been his answer, presumably—how 'you' and 'I' and 'she' pass and vanish; nothing stays, all changes, but not words, not paint" (179). Mr. Carmichael, at least as far as Lily surmises, endorses a theory of the aesthetic where the dead endure in the timeless memorials of elegiac art. He invests literature, that is, with a transcendent capacity usually associated with religion, a view of art that becomes a substitute for both the loss of God and the loss of socially performed mourning rituals. Literature, as he sees it, steps in and fills the vacated space of the sacred and of ritual mourning in the postwar years, replacing outworn social ceremonies with the ceremonies of elegiac writing.

Woolf both raises and evaluates this compensatory aesthetic, giving the lie to the assumption that art transcends the determinants of history and politics. Consider her repeated citation of lines from Tennyson's "The Charge of the Light Brigade," a poem where artistic memory serves as an immortal replacement for human life. Tennyson memorializes those who died during the Crimean War battle at Balaclava when an offensive into enemy lines resulted in the death of more than one-third of a cavalry of 637 men. "When can their glory fade?" Tennyson's speaker asks (1036). The answer is implied: their heroic achievement will not be forgotten so long as the poem itself stands as a timeless testament to the noble deed. Woolf's text, in contrast, deflates the ascendancy of poetic memory by identifying the Crimean War leaders who "blundered" in ordering the suicidal charge with Mr. Ramsay, the patriarchal "leader of the doomed expedition" who consistently appeals to female characters closest at hand for consolation and sympathy for having failed to achieve lasting distinction as a philosopher (36). The redemptive aesthetic that Woolf's text challenges, it is interesting to note, is sustained even by a poet as critical of the Great War as Graves. In "When I'm Killed," Graves's speaker imagines achieving immortality not in God or nature but in a literary artifact that outlasts and outshines the very self it mourns. Having rejected religious salvation in counseling the reader not to search for this dead soldier's soul "In Heaven or Hell," the speaker redirects attention to the poetic memorial: "You'll find me buried, living-dead / In these verses that you've read" (29). In line with Carmichael's theory and Tennyson's poem, Graves's self-elegy offers consolation to both writer and reader, the consolation furnished by substituting an immortal literary text for a mortal soldier who may not survive the war. It is this redemptive aesthetic that defines the terms that Lily questions and resists in her effort to complete her "tribute" to Mrs. Ramsay. When she returns to her painting after the decade hiatus, Lily places her easel "not too close to Mr. Carmichael, but close enough for his protection" (147). Woolf's artist seeks, then, to perpetuate the vitality and significance implied by Carmichael's poetics at the same time she determines to disentangle her painting from the notion of commemorative form as a permanent replacement and consoling substitute for human life.

Lily has good reason for rejecting the notion of art as a reflection of aesthetic perfection and timeless endurance. Such a theory overlooks the gender politics involved in canonizing those works that have been designated as the most significant and lasting artifacts of tradition. Like *A Room of One's Own*, which Tillie Olsen insightfully reads as Woolf's elegy for all the women artists absolutely forgotten by history and absolutely lost to tradition (10), *To the Lighthouse* expresses both the desire to recover the lost Mrs. Ramsay and the sheer impossibility of succeeding in the effort. In Lily's case, this awareness of irrecoverable loss, along with an awareness of the social contingency implicit in silencing the lost traditions of women's art, becomes the artistic principle that enables her to complete her painting. Woolf's artist acknowledges that her work might "be hung in attics" or "rolled up and flung under a sofa" (179). Lily thus shifts attention from the "actual picture" to "what it attempted," an attempt to mourn loss through the creation of an artifact (179). In this regard, Woolf focuses on Lily's creative process, a process of bereaved inspiration that begins by recalling Mrs. Ramsay in both loving and aggressive ways. In the course of working on her canvas, Lily not only praises the lost matriarch's power to gather others into a meaningful collective; she also criticizes Mrs. Ramsay's failure to see women beyond their role as wives, a form of mournful aggression Woolf's artist deploys as a means of selecting what she will and will not inherit as part of her maternal inheritance.[9] But for Lily, even this emphasis on the despairing contents of artistic consciousness elicits critical suspicion, for this focus on Lily's own grief "sounded even to herself, too boastful" (179). Woolf moves on, then, to dissolve her artist's narcissistic desire to recover the lost Mrs. Ramsay in the portrait initially intended to immortalize her. This dissolution finally enables Lily to see her painting, as we might see Woolf's novel, through the "tears" and "pain" of mourning, through a perspective clarified by ongoing grief that registers the irrecoverable loss of Mrs. Ramsay and the futility of any aesthetic effort to neutralize the pain that attends it.[10] By sustaining rather than overcoming grief, Lily demonstrates how the very wish to recover the lost object might be placed in the service of creating an anticonsolatory and antiredemptive art.

The final brushstroke down the center of Lily's canvas has often been read as constituting the novel's aesthetic wholeness, as the culmination of Woolf's attempt, in the words of James Naremore, "to attain an absolute unity with the world" (242). Woolf certainly engages this search for an essence beyond appearance. Indeed, the painting's completion suggests both the resolution and fusion of the novel's main thematic concerns: Lily has her vision, Mr. Ramsay completes his quest for self-knowledge, and James and Cam resolve their oedipal struggles. However, there is, as I have sought to demonstrate throughout, a certain irony in Woolf's depiction of art as an aesthetic remedy for the painful experience of loss. In fact, her text does not ultimately reward but critiques nostalgic longing for lost immediacy by employing Lily's canvas to articulate a new relationship between past and present. The issue of relations, it is important to recall, had been fundamental to Lily's painting from the start. In attempting to venerate mother and child in abstract form, Lily questioned "how to connect this mass on the right hand with that on the left" (82–83). When her final "vision" prompts her to draw a line at the painting's center, Lily divides her canvas in two parts, a division that recalls the way "Time Passes" separates the novel's own prewar and postwar sections. At once a thematic and structural feature, this division highlights Lily's awareness that past and present cannot be seamlessly joined together. Put differently, the painting's central line distinguishes a time characterized by Mrs. Ramsay's presence and another by her absence, inviting us to read Lily's final gesture as a sign of the impossibility of fully assimilating the past in the name of a redeemed present. That Lily conveys both absence and presence in the space of a single canvas does not suggest the attainment of a mythic unity typically associated with modernist aesthetics, but rather the fundamental importance she places on a relation to the past that allows the loss of Mrs. Ramsay and prewar cultural values to inform present understanding. Without such an understanding Lily runs the risk, as do we, of endorsing a narcissistic absorption in the self and inviting the cultural amnesia that results from completely digesting the past. In recasting the issue of aesthetic wholeness as a question of relations, Woolf's artist succeeds, then, in granting the present a mournful awareness of losses suffered in the passing of time, losses that cannot be negated through consolatory aesthetic forms but that must be endured and ceaselessly mourned.

It is certainly no secret that Woolf wrote her roman à clef to mourn the death of her own mother, Julia Stephen, who died when Woolf was thirteen. In the extensive scholarship on maternal mourning in *To the Lighthouse*, many critics such as Gillian Beer and Jane Lilienfeld argue that writing the novel enabled Woolf to terminate her protracted grief (Beer 35; Lilienfeld 373). "A Sketch of the Past" is typically cited as evidence for this view, given Woolf acknowledges that writing the novel helped her accomplish "what psycho-analysts do for their patients": "I expressed some very long felt and deeply felt emotion. And in expressing it I explained it and then laid it to rest" (81). The passage clearly draws a connection between finishing the novel and finishing mourning; however, critical commentary typically neglects the way Woolf also dedicates her writing to an exploration of "invisible presences" that the dead leave behind (80). It is this exploration of the enduring trace of the lost other and the historical past that underwrites Woolf's invention of a modernist understanding of mourning and cultural memory.

In her fiction on war and mourning, Woolf dramatizes the endurance of grief to demonstrate that emotional bonds to the lost other have not been severed, that wounds have not healed. In similar fashion, her texts refuse to fully digest and be done with the past. Only by preserving the intractable otherness of the lost other and of the past, only by adapting art to an articulation of "invisible presences," can the possibility for an anticonsolatory practice of mourning be fully realized. Woolf's resistance to healing is important to our understanding of her modernist mourning project, for she asks us to live grief in such a way, to borrow Kathleen Woodward's suggestive formulation, "that one is still *in* mourning but no longer *exclusively* devoted to mourning" (96). With the final brushstroke down the center of her canvas, Woolf's artist shows us why we need to perpetually remake our grief and perpetually remake our memorializing art. Woolf teaches us, finally, that only by refusing consolation and sustaining grief can we accept responsibility for the difficult task of performing private and public memory.

Notes

1. For biographical studies, see Bell and Poole. For critical discussions of unresolved grief in Woolf's fiction, see Love and Rose.

2. For excellent accounts of the resistance to consolation and closure in contemporary memorializing practices, see Homans, especially the essays by Levi Smith and Young.

3. For discussions of Woolf's challenge to elegiac conventions, see Handley, Zwerdling, and Moss.

4. Other critics have linked Woolf's naming of characters to her modernist irony and critique. See Minow-Pinkney and Hermione Lee.

5. Historians and literary scholars agree that mourning practices dramatically declined in the late nineteenth and early twentieth centuries; however, the meaning of this decline is often in dispute. Ariès laments the modern disappearance of traditional death rituals and writes, "This life in which death was removed to a prudent distance seems less loving of things and people than the life in which death was the center" (314–15). Similarly, Gorer links the disappearance of public mourning to "the maladaptive and neurotic behavior" he claims to have observed in Britain and the United States during the 1950s (xiii). In contrast, Cannadine warns against romanticizing conventional ceremonies regarding death and emphasizes that

mourning practices were easily exploited for commercial ends (191). In a manner similar to Cannadine's analysis, Woolf's fiction displays a critical attitude toward traditional mourning.

6. Levenback makes a similar point: "Mourning is itself a key, Woolf will suggest in *Mrs. Dalloway* and in *To the Lighthouse* especially, not only to acknowledging the reality of death but also to gauging what would be called the 'public mood'" (43). But Levenback insists on a progressive narrative of Woolf's developing "war-consciousness" and unconvincingly argues that *Jacob's Room* does not confirm the protagonist's death but "suggests that the implications of the war have not yet been either felt or recognized" (43).

7. For important feminist and historical studies of women's experience during and after the Great War, see Higonnet and Higonnet, Gilbert, Gallagher, and Culleton.

8. For important historical accounts of the Victorian feminization of grief, see Morley and Litten. For a fascinating psychoanalytic study of the devaluing of women's expressions of loss in Western culture from Petrarch to Lacan, see Schiesari.

9. For a good account of Lily's confrontation with maternal loss, see Abel, who suggests that Lily "fashions the mother she now needs, one who, neither engulfing nor diminishing, actively joins in the creation of a shared imaginative space" (79).

10. Joan Lidoff examines the centrality of maternal mourning as a vehicle for Woolf's recreation of the masculine elegy in a female voice. Lidoff insightfully recognizes that mourning for Lily entails a "new assertion of identity" with unfixed boundaries between self and other, but she qualifies Woolf's achievement: "The perception of fluid boundaries in Woolf feels not secure or affirming, but threatening" (56).

Works Cited

Abel, Elizabeth. *Virginia Woolf and the Fictions of Psychoanalysis*. Chicago: U of Chicago P, 1989.

Adorno, Theodor W. *Negative Dialectics*. Trans. E. B. Ashton. New York: Continuum, 1973.

Ariès, Philippe. *The Hour of Our Death*. Trans. Helen Weaver. New York: Knopf, 1981.

Auerbach, Erich. *Mimesis: The Representation of Reality in Western Literature*. Trans. Willard Trask. Princeton: Princeton UP, 1955.

Bazin, Nancy Topping, and Jane Hamovit Lauter. "Virginia Woolf's Keen Sensitivity to War: Its Roots and Its Impact on Her Novels." Hussey 14–39.

Beer, Gillian. "Hume, Stephen, and Elegy in *To the Lighthouse*." *Essays in Criticism* 34.1 (1984): 33–55.

Bell, Quentin. *Virginia Woolf: A Biography*. Vol. 1. New York: Harcourt, 1972.

Bersani, Leo. *The Culture of Redemption*. Cambridge: Harvard UP, 1990.

Butler, Judith. *The Psychic Life of Power: Theories in Subjection*. Stanford: Stanford UP, 1997.

Cannadine, David. "War and Death, Grief and Mourning in Modern Britain." *Mirrors of Mortality: Studies in the Social History of Death*. Ed. Joachim Whaley. New York: St. Martin's, 1981. 187–242.

Caramagno, Thomas. *The Flight of the Mind: Virginia Woolf's Art and Manic-Depressive Illness*. Berkeley: U of California P, 1992.

Caughie, Pamela. *Virginia Woolf and Postmodernism: Literature in Quest and Question of Itself*. Urbana: U of Illinois P, 1991.

Culleton, Claire. *Working-Class Culture, Women, and Britain, 1914–1921*. New York: Palgrave, 1999.

Derrida, Jacques. "By Force of Mourning." Trans. Pascale-Anne Brault and Michael Naas. *Critical Inquiry* 22 (1996): 171–92.

Freud, Sigmund. "Thoughts for the Times on War and Death." *The Standard Edition of the Complete Psychological Works of Sigmund Freud*. Trans. and ed. James Strachey. Vol. 14. London: Hogarth, 1914–16. 275–300.

Fussell, Paul. *The Great War and Modern Memory*. New York: Oxford UP, 1975.

Gallagher, Jean. *World Wars through the Female Gaze*. Carbondale: Southern Illinois UP, 1998.

Gay, Peter. *Freud: A Life for Our Time*. New York: Norton, 1988.

Gilbert, Sandra M. "Soldier's Heart: Literary Men, Literary Women, and the Great War." *No Man's Land*, vol. 2. Eds. Sandra M. Gilbert and Susan Gubar. New Haven: Yale UP, 1987. 197–226.

Gorer, Geoffrey. *Death, Grief, and Mourning*. New York: Arno, 1977.

Graves, Robert. "Recalling War." *Collected Poems, 1959*. London: Cassell, 1959. 120–21.

———. "When I'm Killed." *Fairies and Fusiliers*. New York: Knopf, 1918. 29.

Gurney, Ivor. "To His Love." *Collected Poems of Ivor Gurney*. Ed. P. J. Kavanagh. Oxford: Oxford UP, 1982. 41.

Handley, William R. "War and the Politics of Narration in *Jacob's Room*." Hussey 110–33.

Haule, James. "*To the Lighthouse* and the Great War: The Evidence of Virginia Woolf's Revisions of 'Time Passes.'" Hussey 164–79.

Higonnet, Margaret Randolph, and Patrice Higonnet. "The Double Helix." *Behind the Lines: Gender and the Two World Wars*. Ed. Margaret Higonnet, Jane Jenson, Sonya Michel, and Margaret Collins Weitz. New Haven: Yale UP, 1987. 31–47.

Holtby, Winifred. *Virginia Woolf*. London: Wishart, 1932.

Homans, Peter, ed. *Symbolic Loss: The Ambiguity of Mourning and Memory at Century's End*. Charlottesville: U of Virginia P, 2000.

Hussey, Mark, ed. *Virginia Woolf and War: Fiction, Reality, and Myth*. Syracuse: Syracuse UP, 1991.

Lee, Hermione. *The Novels of Virginia Woolf*. London: Thames, 1975.

Lee, Judith. "'This Hideous Shaping and Moulding': War and *The Waves*." Hussey 180–202.

Levenback, Karen. *Virginia Woolf and the Great War*. Syracuse: Syracuse UP, 1999.

Lidoff, Joan. "Virginia Woolf's Feminine Sentence: The Mother-Daughter World of *To the Lighthouse*." *Literature and Psychology* 32.3 (1986): 43–59.

Lilienfeld, Jane. "'The Deceptiveness of Beauty': Mother Love and Mother Hate in *To the Lighthouse*." *Twentieth Century Literature* 23 (1977): 345–76.

Litten, Julian. *The English Way of Death*. London: Hale, 1991.

Love, Jean O. *Virginia Woolf: Sources of Madness and Art*. Berkeley: U of California P, 1977.

Mepham, John. "Mourning and Modernism." *Virginia Woolf: New Critical Essays*. Ed. Patricia Clements and Isobel Grundy. Totowa: Barnes, 1983. 137–56.

Miller, J. Hillis. *Fiction and Repetition: Seven English Novels*. Cambridge: Harvard UP, 1982.

Minow-Pinkney, Makiko. *Virginia Woolf and the Problem of the Subject*. Brighton: Harvester P, 1987.

Morley, John. *Death, Heaven and the Victorians*. Pittsburgh: U of Pittsburgh P, 1971.

Moss, Roger. "*Jacob's Room* and the Eighteenth Century: From Elegy to Essay." *Critical Quarterly* 23 (1981): 39–54.

Naremore, James. *The World without a Self: Virginia Woolf and the Novel*. New Haven: Yale UP, 1973.

Olsen, Tillie. *Silences*. New York: Lawrence, 1978.

Poole, Roger. *The Unknown Virginia Woolf*. Atlantic Highlands: Humanities PI, 1990.

Ramazani, Jahan. *Poetry of Mourning: The Modern Elegy from Hardy to Heaney*. Chicago: U of Chicago P, 1994.

Rose, Phyllis. *Woman of Letters: A Life of Virginia Woolf*. New York: Oxford UP, 1978.

Rosenberg, Isaac. "Dead Man's Dump." *The Collected Works of Isaac Rosenberg*. Ed. Ian Parsons. New York: Oxford UP, 1979. 109–12.

Sassoon, Siegfried. "On Passing the New Menin Gate." *Collected Poems*. New York: Viking, 1949. 188.

Schiesari, Juliana. *The Gendering of Melancholia: Feminism, Psychoanalysis, and the Symbolics of Loss in Renaissance Literature*. Ithaca: Cornell UP, 1992.

Showalter, Elaine. *A Literature of Their Own: British Women Novelists from Brontë to Lessing*. Princeton: Princeton UP, 1977.

Smith, Levi. "Window or Mirror: The Vietnam Veterans Memorial and the Ambiguity of Remembrance." Homans 105–25.

Smith, Susan Bennett. "Reinventing Grief Work: Virginia Woolf's Feminist Representations of Mourning in *Mrs. Dalloway* and *To the Lighthouse*." *Twentieth Century Literature* 41 (1995): 310–27.

Spilka, Mark. *Virginia Woolf's Quarrel with Grieving*. Lincoln: U of Nebraska P, 1980.

Tennyson, Alfred Lord. "The Charge of the Light Brigade." *Poems of Tennyson*. Ed. Christopher Ricks. London: Longman, 1969. 1034–36.

Winter, Jay. *Sites of Memory, Sites of Mourning: The Great War in European Cultural History*. Cambridge: Cambridge UP, 1995.

Woodward, Kathleen. "Freud and Barthes: Theorizing Mourning, Sustaining Grief." *Discourse* 13.1 (1991): 93–110.

Woolf, Virginia. *The Diary of Virginia Woolf*. Ed. Anne Olivier Bell. 5 vols. New York: Harcourt, 1977–84.

———. *Jacob's Room*. New York: Harcourt, 1950.

———. "A Sketch of the Past." *Moments of Being*. Ed. Jeanne Schulkind. New York: Harcourt, 1976.

———. *Three Guineas*. New York: Harcourt, 1966.

———. *To the Lighthouse*. New York: Harcourt, 1981.

Young, James E. "Against Redemption: The Arts of Countermemory in Germany Today." Homans 126–44.

Zwerdling, Alex. "*Jacob's Room*: Woolf's Satiric Elegy." *ELH* 48.4 (1981): 894–913.

TRAUMA AND RECOVERY

IN VIRGINIA WOOLF'S

MRS. DALLOWAY

Karen DeMeester

Modernist literature is a literature of trauma: in the 1920s, it gave form and representation to a psychological condition that psychiatrists would not understand for another fifty years. Virginia Woolf's characterization of Septimus Smith in *Mrs. Dalloway* illustrates not only the psychological injuries suffered by victims of severe trauma such as war but also the need for them to give meaning to their suffering in order to recover from the trauma. Septimus's death is the result of his inability to communicate his experiences to others and thereby give those experiences meaning and purpose. By bearing witness to his experiences and suffering, Septimus could edify others about not only war but also human nature and the social and political institutions that emerge from and reflect that nature. Septimus's war trauma, however, is perpetuated and its psychological damage aggravated by a culturally prescribed process of postwar reintegration that silences and marginalizes war veterans. To comprehend fully Septimus Smith's tragedy, one must understand the psychological effects of trauma and the process of recovery. Furthermore, critics studying modernist literary forms can enrich their understanding by exploring recent discoveries in the field of trauma psychology, which reveal why modernist forms are so well-suited for depicting the traumatized mind but ill-suited for depicting recovery.

The modernist narrative form of Woolf's novel brilliantly mirrors the mind of a trauma survivor like Septimus. In fact, the modernist

Originally published in *Modern Fiction Studies*, Summer 1998.

literary works written in the decade after World War I constitute a literature of trauma: their forms often replicate the damaged psyche of a trauma survivor and their contents often portray his characteristic disorientation and despair. Imagist poetry and the experimental novels of the postwar decade, for example, reflect the fragmentation of consciousness and the disorder and confusion that a victim experiences in the wake of a traumatic event. Trauma inevitably damages the victim's faith in the assumptions he has held in the past about himself and the world and leaves him struggling to find new, more reliable ideologies to give order and meaning to his post-traumatic life. Like trauma survivors, the modernist writers suffered a similar loss of faith in the ideologies of the past and particularly in the literary forms that emerged from those ideologies. Their works depict in both form and content a modern age severed from the traditions and values of the past first by new discoveries in such fields as psychology, anthropology, physics, and biology, and later by the First World War's unprecedented destruction, the magnitude of which revealed the pernicious potential of technological advancements originally intended to improve and extend life.

In her novels, Virginia Woolf demonstrates the power of the modernist literary form to delineate the psyche of a trauma survivor. Her narrative form preserves the psychological chaos caused by trauma instead of reordering it as more traditional narratives do. Psychiatrist Jonathan Shay describes how traditional narratives restructure the survivor's fragmented consciousness: "Severe trauma explodes the cohesion of consciousness. When a survivor creates [a] fully realized narrative that brings together the shattered knowledge of what happened, the emotions that were aroused by the meanings of the events, and the bodily sensations that the physical events created, the survivor pieces back together the fragmentation of consciousness that trauma has caused" (188). The trauma story, before the survivor has structured it into a "fully realized narrative," is a "prenarrative," which "does not develop or progress in time" (Herman 174). By drawing her narratives from the characters' prespeech levels of consciousness, Woolf created such a prenarrative in her novels and preserved the fragmentation of consciousness that occurs in the aftermath of trauma (Humphrey 2–3). At the prespeech level of consciousness, the character has not yet attempted to order his fragmented thoughts into a sequentially arranged, communicable narrative.

Woolf's stream-of-consciousness narrative form also corresponds to the trauma survivor's perception of time. The survivor's traumatized mind apprehends the traumatic event as ever-present, and his memories of the event often exist in the present consciousness as encapsulated images and fragments of thought that are juxtaposed against other nontraumatic memories but do not meaningfully relate to them sequentially or chronologically. The survivor cannot think of the traumatic event in chronological terms such as "'This was my life before. . . . This is what happened. . . . This is what I became,'" and he struggles to describe his traumatic experience "in a language that insists on 'was' and 'will be' [when] [t]he trauma world knows only *is*" (Shay 191). Consequently, he is unable to integrate the traumatic event into his personal life history and ultimately to reenvision the event as a critical moment in his life but not one that must inevitably define his identity. Woolf similarly contracts time, intermingling the past and future with the present in a continuous flow of narrative time. Woolf's readers, like the survivor contemplating the meaning of the traumatic event, cannot apprehend the text chronologically, because, as Joseph Frank observes, the meaning of the text does not emerge from temporal relationships but rather from spatial ones (10).

One technique Woolf uses to structure her narratives spatially is repetition. She repeats sentences and phrases—for example, in *To the Lighthouse*, using Mr. Ramsey's refrain "Some one had blundered" from Alfred, Lord Tennyson's "The Charge of the Light Brigade," to indicate narrative time, which is easily confused because of the many shifting consciousnesses and their lengthy wanderings away from the story's chronological flow. Woolf also creates set pieces by beginning and ending a section of narrative with the same sentence. These set pieces and refrains suggest a lack of advancement in understanding because the character, despite his intervening speculations, does not revise the original thought but merely reiterates it. The repetition establishes a rhythm of futility in which thoughts fail to lead to new understandings and conclusions. The trauma survivor similarly orders his consciousness by structuring his life around a single traumatic event that he constantly relives and reconsiders in the closed system of his private, subjective consciousness. Consequently, all other events derive meaning from their relationship and association with the traumatic event. The survivor is unable to escape the entropy created by the continuous repetition; caught in his own set piece, he is unable to create forward movement toward recovery.

Although Woolf's form is particularly well suited for depicting trauma and deftly manifests in art a psychological condition that science failed to understand until half a century and several wars later, it is ill suited to depicting recovery. Modernist literature defines the posttraumatic condition, but the task of giving individual and cultural meaning to the suffering falls to later generations of artists. As John Johnston claims, "modern literature defines itself through formalistic, self-reflexive procedures, yet at the same time proves to be essentially transgressive of the inherent limits of the discourse of its time and hence of the categorization of experience the latter articulates" (803). However, "a language wrenched free of its social functions and hence no longer obsequiously obedient to 'discourse' turns out to be intimately close to madness" (803). Meaningful recovery from the "madness" suffered by a trauma survivor requires an escape from the private, self-reflexive view of the traumatic event, because the traumatic event and the debilitating emotions associated with it retain their power when they remain encapsulated and dissociated from the social discourse of the time, the reality of experience, and the social function the suffering may serve. To recover, the survivor must escape the debilitating repetition and the isolation of his own consciousness and reestablish a connection between his pre- and posttraumatic worlds. For recovery to begin, the past must be reclaimed "in order to 'recreate the flow' of . . . life and restore a sense of continuity" (Herman 176). Such an exploration of the past "provides a context within which the particular meaning of the trauma can be understood" (176). He must escape the prespeech chaos of his traumatized psyche and form his fragments of thought into a coherent, communicable narrative.

The ultimate paradigm of the trauma survivor and hence modernist man emerged in the aftermath of the First World War—the shell-shocked war veteran. The severely traumatized war veteran, whom Septimus Smith epitomizes, embodies the essential characteristics of modernist man. The discoveries the veteran made during the war alienated him from his past by undermining his prewar assumptions about himself and the world that had previously given order and meaning to his life. His traumatic war experiences shattered the cohesion of his consciousness and left it fragmented, a stream of incongruous and disconnected images and bits of memory devoid of the connections and relationships necessary to give meaning to those experiences. Septimus Smith's tragedy is inherently related to his identity as a war veteran and trauma survivor; therefore, an understanding of the power of trauma and the psychological injuries it inflicts upon its victims enhances the critic's understanding of the character of Septimus and Woolf's novel in general.

Critics who have previously diagnosed Septimus as schizophrenic and applied a conventional psychoanalytic interpretation to his character have failed to recognize that Septimus suffers not from a psychological pathology but from a psychological injury, one inflicted by his culture through war and made septic by that same culture's postwar treatment of veterans.[1] Septimus's identity as a war veteran makes him a particularly powerful tool with which "to criticise the social system, & show it at work, at its most intense" (Woolf, *Diary* 248), and his testimony is what could give meaning to his suffering. Society, represented in the novel by Septimus's doctors and by Clarissa Dalloway herself, however, silences and marginalizes the war veteran and thereby prevents Septimus from beginning to recover, which results in his suicide, a desperate but futile last attempt to communicate. Septimus's psychological pain does not cause his suicide. It is caused by society's refusal to let him give meaning to that pain: "He did not want to die. Life was good. The sun hot. Only human beings—what did *they* want?" (*Dalloway* 226).

Septimus's neurosis is the direct result of the trauma he sustained during the First World War, and critics applying a strictly psychoanalytic reading to his character not only fail to recognize the destructive power of trauma but also fail to recognize that hysteria, a disorder consistently associated with war neurosis, originates in a traumatic event rather than in sexual repression. The history of the development of psychoanalysis reveals that repression is a consequence of trauma and a symptom of psychological injury rather than its cause. By 1896, Sigmund Freud, in a report entitled *The Aetiology of Hysteria*, claimed that hysteria was caused by "one or more occurrences of premature sexual experience" (203), the trauma experienced as the result of childhood sexual molestation. However, within a year of publishing this report, Freud repudiated this theory because of its disturbing social implications. According to Judith Herman,

> His correspondence makes clear that he was increasingly troubled by the radical social implications of his hypothesis. Hysteria was so common among women that if his patients' stories were true, and if his theory were correct, he would be forced to conclude that what he called "perverted acts against children" were endemic, not only among the proletariat of Paris, . . . but also among the respectable bourgeois families of Vienna, where he had established his practice. (14)

Consequently, "[p]sychoanalysis became a study of the internal vicissitudes of fantasy and desire, dissociated from the reality of experience" (14). Septimus Smith demonstrates, however, that the reality of experience and the trauma suffered as a result of that experience are the causes of his problems as well as the key to his recovery.

Suzette Henke interprets Septimus's character through a Freudian perspective. She misdiagnoses him as schizophrenic and attributes "[h]is loss of cathexis for other human beings . . . to frustrated homosexual desire" for his friend and commanding officer Evans (15).[2] She goes on to cite this repressed desire and guilt as the cause of his megalomaniac fantasies and paranoia (15). In discussing her diagnosis, Henke cites Freud's works of 1914 and 1917, which were written after the study of psychoanalysis had been severed from the reality of experience and focused on fantasy and desire.[3] The reality of Septimus's experience, however, and the trauma he sustained in war are more psychologically damaging than the guilt or humiliation of homosexuality, and witnessing Evans's death is more disturbing than any disgust he may have felt regarding homosexual desires he felt for the dead soldier. Henke goes on to argue that the horrible crime Septimus claims to have committed is homosexuality, but, in light of his combat experiences during the war and what we know of the guilt that veterans often feel as the result of such experiences, it seems more likely that the crime he refers to is the killing and, particularly, killing with indifference that he saw and more than likely participated in. Rezia and Sir William Bradshaw claim that Septimus had done nothing wrong because he had served with great distinction and been promoted, but his success suggests that, although he did nothing beyond the requirements of war, he was probably responsible for destruction and death, whether by his own hands or those of the soldiers he commanded. Although it is often assumed that, because killing is an inevitable part of war, soldiers do it without thought, guilt, or shame, veterans' testimonies often refute this assumption.

Henke astutely describes another symptom of Septimus's neurosis, his idiomatic use of language: "His language degenerates into an idiomatic dialect that is at once the language of the poet and the madman" (17). "Tragically, Septimus Smith is trapped in a private, autistic language that denies him the possibility of direct communication with his fellow men and women" (22). She attributes Septimus's idiosyncratic language to schizophrenia and cites Norman Cameron's conclusion, "The schizophrenic, of course, is not speaking in a foreign language; but he is speaking in an asocial dialect full of idioms that have value only for himself" (Henke 18; see also Cameron 62). Septimus's language, however, is an extreme example of the struggle all trauma survivors experience in trying to create a means of describing their traumatic experiences so that others will fully comprehend them.[4] The limitations of language inevitably frustrate the veteran, and he may, as Septimus does, turn to traditional, socially inscribed modes of expression such as analogy, metaphor, or myth. Much as trauma destabilizes the veteran's ideological assumptions, it also destabilizes his linguistic ones: "Traumatic experience catalyzes a transformation of meaning in the signs individuals use to represent their experiences. Words such as _blood_, _terror_, _agony_, and _madness_ gain new meaning, within the context of the trauma, and survivors emerge from the traumatic environment with a new set of definitions" (Tal, _Worlds_ 16). Communication between a trauma survivor and an untraumatized listener is diminished by a gap in meaning that to an extent exists in all attempts to communicate. Though the listener recognizes the words the traumatized person uses, she cannot comprehend the reality these words represent; there is an irreconcilable gap between the intensity of experience and emotion the veteran wishes to convey and the experience and emotion the listener can imagine and feel. Elie Wiesel, speaking as a trauma survivor, describes the limitations of language as follows: "What can we do to share our visions? Our words can only evoke the incomprehensible. Hunger, thirst, fear, humiliation, waiting, death; for us these words hold different realities. This is the ultimate tragedy of the victim" (Weisel 33).[5] It is important to recognize that Septimus's symptoms—his guilt, numbness, and idiomatic language—are manifestations of a postwar stress disorder, because in recognizing the true nature of his illness, one gains an understanding of the elements necessary for his recovery and hence his failure to recover.

Since the publication of *Mrs. Dalloway*, substantial advances have been made in our understanding of war neurosis and the psychological effects of trauma. For example, it was previously assumed that veterans experiencing symptoms six months after service ended more than likely suffered from the traumatic effects of toilet training rather than combat. Septimus defies conventional notions of shell shock because he suffers from a delayed stress response. He doesn't experience a breakdown until four years after the Armistice and nine months before the novel opens (Knox-Shaw 100). Rezia, remembering Septimus before his breakdown, thinks, "Only last autumn she and Septimus had stood on the Embankment wrapped in the same cloak and, Septimus reading a paper instead of talking" (Woolf, *Dalloway* 22). Contrary to the opinion expressed in the "Report of the War Office Committee of Enquiry into 'Shell-Shock'" published in 1922, the etiology of severe and persistent war neurosis, like that suffered by Septimus, is not a crisis of will or courage as a result of "sudden or prolonged fear" (Thomas 52). Persistent and delayed responses to combat stress occur because traumatic events, especially war, damage the foundations of the victim's identity. According to psychologist Erik Erikson, combat damages the soldier's ego identity, which is "[a] sense of identity [that] produces the ability to experience oneself as something that has continuity and sameness"; and therefore, the soldiers' lives "no longer hung together and never would again" (quoted in Leed 3–4). War neurosis is the result of a shattered sense of identity, the inability to integrate the veteran's identity as a warrior into his pre- and postwar civilian identities.

Woolf's characterization of Septimus illustrates the disillusionment and confusion that result from this postwar identity crisis.

Septimus could no longer be the man he was before the war or have faith in his prewar beliefs and values: "The War had taught him. It was sublime. He had gone through the whole show, friendship, European War, death, had won promotion. . . . He was right there. The last shells missed him. He watched them explode with indifference" (130–31). Septimus "went to France to save an England which consisted almost entirely of Shakespeare's plays and Miss Isabel Pole in a green dress walking in a square" (130). For Septimus, the traditions and conventions of English life and particularly its art lost their meaning, and his disillusionment echoes that of the modernist artist. After the war, he reinterpreted them in light of what he experienced and learned during his time as a soldier:

> he opened Shakespeare once more. That boy's business of the intoxication of language—*Antony and Cleopatra*—had shrivelled utterly. How Shakespeare loathed humanity. . . . This was now revealed to Septimus; the message hidden in the beauty of words. The secret signal which one generation passes, under disguise, to the next is loathing, hatred, despair. Dante the same. Aeschylus (translated) the same. (133–34)

War invalidated the fundamental beliefs that gave Septimus's prewar life meaning.[6] The civilized order of England and its social rubrics, which defined Septimus's assumptions and expectations about himself and his world, could not stand up against the truth that Septimus discovered in war. The war had changed Septimus's understanding of human nature. During the war, he saw humanity stripped of the trappings of civilization and witnessed its primitive nature and its potential for evil and destruction, which is merely constrained—not eradicated—by civilized order. Though Clarissa Dalloway shields herself from the truth with a parasol of social order—"a sacred weapon which a Goddess, having acquitted herself honorably in the field of battle, sheds, and place[s] . . . in the umbrella stand. . . . Fear no more, said Clarissa. Fear no more the heat o' the sun" (43)—the horrible reality of war burned away Septimus's protection, and he attributes his current neurosis to an overexposure to the heat: "It was the heat wave presumably, operating upon a brain made sensitive by eons of evolution. Scientifically speaking, the flesh was melted off the world. His body was macerated until only the nerve fibres were left" (102).[7]

Paradoxically, Septimus claims that despite the raw, exposed nerve fibers, he is unable to feel pain for his own suffering or that of others like Rezia and Evans. Woolf's characterization of Septimus's sensual and emotional paralysis illustrates the numbing effect so characteristic of traumatic injury and the obstruction of grief that contemporary psychologists recognize in their war-veteran clients.[8] During combat, indifference is a survival tool that protects the psyche from being overwhelmed by the horror received through the senses—the sight of mutilated comrades, the smell of their blood and bowels, the incessant sound of their cries and moans heard through the noise of machine guns and exploding shells, and even the taste of death.[9] Though Septimus's inability to feel begins before the end of the war, it is perpetuated and exacerbated by his inability to find meaning in his war experiences and his suffering during and after those experiences. Remarkably, Woolf recognized the shell-shocked veteran's fundamental problem—not the suffering he experienced during the war, but his inability to give meaning to that suffering after the war. As Friedrich Nietzsche claims, it isn't the horror of suffering but rather the realization that the suffering is meaningless and serves no purpose that is so unbearable to the sufferer. As Septimus illustrates, the traumatized veteran suffers in an existential vacuum in which nothing has meaning. Septimus thinks, "his brain was perfect; it must be the fault of the world then—that he could not feel. . . . It might be possible, Septimus thought, looking at England from the train window, as they left Newhaven; it might be possible that the world itself is without meaning" (133).

Psychiatrist and neurologist Viktor Frankl, the founder of what has come to be called the Third Viennese School of Psychotherapy (after Freud's psychoanalysis and Adler's individual psychology)—the school of logotherapy—claims that "man's search for meaning is the primary motivation in his life and not a 'secondary rationalization' of instinctual drives" (Frankl 121).[10] The principles of logotherapy reveal much about how victims of trauma survive and recover from their ordeals because Frankl, a trauma survivor himself, developed his concepts while a prisoner in German concentration camps during World War II.

According to Frankl, the ability to give meaning to suffering is an essential element for survival and recovery. When man's will to meaning is frustrated—what Frankl refers to as "existential frustration"—neurosis occurs. In order to fill the "existential vacuum," the victim must "bring repressed meanings and meaning opportunities to the conscious level of awareness. . . . The awareness and discovery of meaning occur in response to the self-transcendent relationship. Self-transcendence occurs in a relationship with another person, a useful and important cause, or in a relationship with nature" (Lantz 487). Frankl's approach reveals that the pain and suffering of trauma victims, like Septimus, contain meaning and meaning potentials and that "the pain of the trauma experience can be transformed into meaning awareness, as opposed to being repressed and/or acted out" (Lantz 487). Woolf demonstrates her early understanding of what logotherapists would later recognize through her description of Septimus's struggle to "discover and make use of unique personal meaning opportunities for self-transcendent giving to the world which can be found within the memories of trauma and terror" (Lantz 487). Septimus's truths are the result of the meaning he discovered in the war, in his "memories of trauma and terror." Septimus learned in war that "Men must not cut down trees. There is a God. (He notes such revelations on the backs of envelopes.) Change the world. No one kills from hatred. Make it known (he wrote it down)" (*Dalloway* 35). Septimus's testimonies are a means of "self-transcendent giving to the world" because they edify others and thereby have the potential to instigate positive social change.[11] The trauma survivor's testimony has the power to destabilize his culture's social, political, and economic status quo and thereby to bring about change in that status quo. Though critics use Septimus's messianic vision of himself as truth-teller to demonstrate his megalomania and his delusions of grandeur, his view of himself as a prophet, despite the seemingly fantastical presentation, is quite valid.

Only through communication could Septimus begin to heal from his trauma, for as he says, "Communication is health; communication is happiness" (*Dalloway* 141). Only through communication could he validate the deaths of the soldiers who haunt him and fulfill the unique role of prophet that the war so brutally prepared him for. To fulfill this role successfully, he would not only have to tell the truth but also to instigate social change by telling those who have the power to accomplish such change. Septimus thinks,

> he, Septimus, was alone, called forth in advance of the mass of men to hear the truth, to learn the meaning, which now at last, after all the toils of civilisation . . . was to be given whole to. . . . "To whom?" he asked aloud. "To the Prime Minister," the voices which rustled above his head replied. The supreme secret must be told to the Cabinet; first that trees are alive; next there is no crime; next love, universal love, he muttered, gasping, trembling, painfully drawing out these profound truths which needed, so deep were they, so difficult, an immense effort to speak out, but the world was entirely changed by them for ever. (101; ellipses in the original)

Woolf seems to understand innately that, for the trauma survivor, telling the story of his trauma or what he learned from that experience is "a personally reconstitutive act and expresses the hope that it will also be a socially reconstitutive act—changing the order of things as they are and working to prevent the enactment of similar horrors in the future" (Tal, "Speaking" 230). After the Second World War, Lawrence Langer echoes what Woolf seems to realize after the First World War when he claims that "in one sense, all writing about the Holocaust represents a retrospective effort to give meaningless history a context of meaning, to furnish the mind with a framework for insight without diminishing the sorrow of the event itself" (quoted in Tal, "Speaking" 229; see also Langer 185).

Although the principal way Septimus could give meaning and purpose to his war experiences is by communicating—sharing his experiences and knowledge with others for their edification and the salvation of future generations—he encounters resistance from members of the community, because his messages, and most war veterans' testimonies, challenge the community's understanding of war and ultimately its view of itself as a participator in the war. Woolf illustrates the conflict between the veteran and his community in her portrayal of the relationship between Septimus and his doctors, Holmes and Sir William Bradshaw. Because war veterans' testimonies threaten the community's social equilibrium and order by challenging its fundamental cultural and ideological assumptions, the community may avoid and deny the truth of the veterans' testimonies. The testimonies may create a sense of instability and confusion in the community, and consequently cause it to suffer the same feelings of disorientation the veteran himself suffers. The symptoms of traumatic psychological injury, such as "[r]epression, dissociation, and denial are phenomena of social as well as individual consciousness" (Herman 9). In its effort to protect and preserve itself from this secondary trauma, the community jeopardizes the veteran's recovery from his own trauma by forcing him to deny or repress what he learned in war and to attempt to resurrect his prewar identity rather than to establish a new one consistent with his experiences as a warrior. The community wants him to be the man he was before the war— the man who was willing to die to preserve the community's social order, a man who "went to France to save an England which consisted entirely of Shakespeare's plays and Miss Isabel Pole in a green dress walking in a square"—and to affirm its belief in that order or to bear the burden of his knowledge in silence.

A struggle for control over the interpretation of the trauma, in this instance war, may develop between the community and the veteran:

> If survivors retain control over the interpretation of their
> trauma, they can sometimes force a shift in the social and

political structure. If the dominant culture manages to appropriate the trauma and can codify it in its own terms, the status quo will remain unchanged. (Tal, *Worlds* 7)

Dr. Holmes and Sir William Bradshaw illustrate the dominant culture's attempt "to appropriate the trauma and . . . codify it in its own terms."[12] Holmes's advice to Rezia to get Septimus to look at "real things, go to a music hall, play cricket" (*Dalloway* 39), suggests that such conventional activities are more representative of reality and truth than what Septimus experienced and learned in war. Holmes and Bradshaw encourage Septimus to revise and repress the understanding and knowledge obtained during the war. They want him to accept and confirm rather than to call into question the socially prescribed notion of warfare that evokes public-school ideals of sportsmanship, etiquette, and ceremony. But Septimus knows the war was no "little shindy of schoolboys with gunpowder" (145) despite the public's attempt to delude itself and the efforts of those in power to promote such a delusion.

Bradshaw represents the social and political forces of a community that does not want revealed "profound truths which needed . . . an immense effort to speak out, but the world was entirely changed by them for ever" (102).[13] Bradshaw's goal is to protect and perpetuate the world of proportion that his life exemplifies:

> Proportion, divine proportion, Sir William's goddess, was acquired by Sir William walking hospitals, catching salmon, begetting one son in Harley Street by Lady Bradshaw, who caught salmon herself and took photographs scarcely to be distinguished from the work of professionals. Worshipping proportion, Sir William not only prospered himself but made England prosper, secluded her lunatics, forbade childbirth, penalised despair, made it impossible for the unfit to propagate their views until they, too, shared his sense of proportion. (150)

Bradshaw ensures that Septimus and others who threaten the social status quo never share their revelations with others in the community, especially not with the Prime Minister. The rest cure Bradshaw intends for Septimus conveniently secludes England's veterans and hides them away from others that they may taint with their revelations. Moreover, the isolation it imposes encourages conversion by weakening the veteran's resolve so that he will deny what he knows to be true just to be allowed to return to society. Despite its designation as a cure, this conversion therapy prevents recovery, because, although it removes any sources of agitation or stress which might aggravate the patient's symptoms, it fails to address the origin of the disorder—the patient's frustrated search for meaning.

Bradshaw's rest cure only robs Septimus of opportunities to achieve self-transcendence and satisfy his will to meaning by limiting his relationships with others and particularly by rendering him unable to pursue actively an important cause—that of communicating and thereby educating those in power about the war they waged but never experienced firsthand. The result of Bradshaw's effort to silence Septimus is twofold: he destroys Septimus's chance to recover by robbing him of the essential way he can give meaning to his war experiences, and he destroys his own culture's meaningful recovery from the war by perpetuating a social, political, and economic status quo that sacrificed a generation of men to the First World War and enslaved and exploited numerous indigenous cultures and their lands to expand its empire. Septimus's suicide is his final "refusal to bow to outside pressure to revise or to repress experience, a decision to embrace conflict rather than conformity . . ." (Tal, *Worlds* 7). Yet his death ultimately changes nothing, because Clarissa Dalloway, who is a trauma survivor herself and recognizes the truth of Septimus's testimonies, refuses to change. Contemplating Septimus's suicide, she thinks, "A thing there was that mattered; a thing, wreathed about with chatter, defaced, obscured in her own life, let drop every day in corruption, lies, chatter. This he had preserved. Death was defiance. Death was an attempt to communicate" (280–81). Nevertheless, she chooses repression and recommits herself to a life, like Bradshaw's, devoted to perpetuating the status quo. Clarissa silences Septimus and robs his death of meaning by refusing to change in response to his message.[14] In spite of her initial horror that death had violated the sanctuary of her party, she returns to her party secure in the notion that Septimus's death will not dispel its magic or the illusion of harmony and order it creates. One also feels sure that no one will interrupt the Prime Minister's conversation with Lady Bruton about India to talk of Septimus's death, even though his testimonies have much to do with that conversation.

Woolf's characterization of Septimus as a martyr who gives his life in a final effort to communicate and thereby to change a culture that perpetuated war and imperialism challenges an interpretation of Clarissa's return to her party, her recommitment to a life of Proportion and her efforts at Conversion, as a triumph. Though Clarissa's reaffirmation of the meaning of her life is a brilliant moment of artistic order and harmony within the novel, it is undermined by the example set by Septimus. Instead of presenting in Clarissa a positive alternative to Septimus's failure to recover from his war trauma, Woolf presents another inappropriate method of dealing with trauma.

Clarissa's faith in social convention as a means of ordering a posttraumatic world originates in her own attempt to recover from a trauma. For Clarissa is a trauma survivor herself, as Peter Walsh explains: "To see your own sister killed by a falling tree . . . before your very eyes, a girl too on the verge of life, the most gifted of them, Clarissa always said, was enough to turn one bitter" (117–18). After the death of her sister Sylvia, Clarissa struggled to find a way to rebel against the whimsical cruelty of the gods and concluded that

> [t]hose ruffians, the Gods . . . who never lost a chance of hurting, thwarting, and spoiling human lives were seriously put out if, all the same, you behaved like a lady. . . . Later she wasn't so positive perhaps; she thought there were no Gods; no one was to blame; and so she evolved this atheist's religion of doing good for the sake of goodness. (117–18)

Clarissa resigns herself to the belief that the world is chaos with no inherent ordering principle or guiding force, so she devotes herself to creating a façade of order. Though she admirably brings beauty and harmony to the disorder and isolation of modern society, at least to its ruling class, her assembling activities merely repress what she knows to be true about the evil inherent in human nature. Like Septimus, she recognizes its presence because to experience a traumatic event or "[t]o study psychological trauma is to come face to face both with human vulnerability in the natural world and with the capacity for evil in human nature" (Herman 7).[15]

Septimus witnessed the evil inherent in human nature during the war and continues to see it in the people back home in England. He comments on the offensive nature of his species, saying,

> One cannot bring children into a world like this. One cannot perpetuate suffering, or increase the breed of these lustful animals, who have no lasting emotions, but only whims and vanities, eddying them now this way, now that. . . . For the truth is . . . that human beings have neither kindness, nor faith, nor charity beyond what serves to increase the pleasure of the moment. They hunt in packs. Their packs scour the desert and vanish screaming into the wilderness. They desert the fallen. (135)

The war revealed to Septimus the primitive, instinctual nature of man—lustful animals that hunt in packs in the desert and wilderness— and the vulnerable underbelly of a civilized culture created by such animals. Clarissa also recognizes the vulnerability of her world as well as the capacity for evil in human nature and even feels it stirring within herself: "It rasped her, though, to have stirring about in her this brutal monster! to hear twigs cracking and feel hooves planted down in the depths of that leaf-encumbered forest, the soul; never to be content quite, or quite secure, for at any moment the brute would be stirring, this hatred" (17).

Clarissa perpetuates the conflict in herself by continuing to repress her understanding of the evil nature of man.[16] She no longer fears the heat of the sun not because it has lost its power but because she reenforces her protective shield, fortifies her defenses. Clarissa protects herself and her community from the evil by assembling people into harmonious social units that move about against a backdrop of beautiful flowers and dresses, well-appointed tables, and insignificant observations about quite serious topics. Though Clarissa Dalloway condemns Bradshaw's method of conversion, which "feasts on the wills of the weakly, loving to impress, to impose, adoring her own features stamped on the face of the populace" (151), she participates in it when she makes people sacrifice their individuality and assemble into social units. "Conversion has her birth in the desire to connect everything up, to impose similarity and to iron out difference" (Webb 280). Clarissa, like Bradshaw, obstructs meaningful recovery by reaffirming her commitment to a flawed culture instead of encouraging it to change. Conversion is a social as well as an individual pursuit:

> But Proportion has a sister, less smiling, more formidable, a Goddess even now engaged—in the heat and sands of India, the mud and swamp of Africa, the purlieus of London, wherever in short the climate or the devil tempts men to fall from the true belief which is her own—is even now engaged in dashing down shrines, smashing idols, and setting up in their place her own stern countenance. Conversion is her name and she feasts on the wills of the weakly, loving to impress, to impose, adoring her own features stamped on the face of the populace. (151)

Clarissa and the members of her social class do not abolish evil; they merely domesticate it. They veil it with social convention and protocol, but the evil is evident in England's perpetuation of its empire and its sacrifice of a generation to war.

Apparently oblivious to the implications of hypocrisy, Clarissa takes comfort in her assembling activities and in obtaining the favor of others. As she is choosing flowers for her party, she says to herself that her fear of the stirring monster within her is nonsense: "she said to herself, more and more gently, as if this beauty, this scent, this colour, and Miss Pym liking her, trusting her, were a wave which she let flow over her and surmount that hatred, that monster, surmount it all; and it lifted her up and up" (19). She also suggests the negative side-effect of such a superficial existence and the loss of individuality and identity inherent in the repression of knowledge in order to conform to socially prescribed ideologies. She laments that "half the time she did things not simply, not for themselves; but to make people think this or that; perfect idiocy she knew. . . . She had the oddest sense of being herself invisible; unseen; unknown; there being no more marrying, no more having of children now, but only this astonishing and rather solemn progress with the rest of them, up Bond Street" (13–14).

Although Clarissa's reaffirmation of life at the end of the novel seems to be a victory, it becomes less impressive when one realizes that she is recommitting herself to a life in which even her creativity is harnessed for the purpose of preserving the order she finds so oppressive. Throughout the novel Woolf includes references to the meaninglessness of Clarissa's life and her coldness and frigidity. Peter Walsh, thinking of Clarissa, says,

> it was her manner that annoyed him; timid; hard; something arrogant; unimaginative; prudish. The death of the soul. He had said that instinctively, ticketing the moment as he used to do—the death of her soul. (89)

> . . . she frittered her time away, lunching, dining, giving these incessant parties of hers, talking nonsense, saying things she didn't mean, blunting the edge of her mind, losing her discrimination. (118)

She remains on the fringe of life, walking the porch at Bourton, watching the woman from her window, standing at the edge of the Serpentine, and even dying through another. She ultimately is able "to hate Conversion and convert, to be both Septimus and part of the world that sacrifices him, to die and continue her life unchanged" (Guth 22–23). According to Deborah Guth,

> It is this standing at the window, on the edge of the Serpentine of life, that constitutes her major problem: the incapacity to commit herself fully. . . . By the end of the novel, as she watches the old woman opposite closing the blinds, she is poised . . . outside the loop of time. This, it would appear, is the condition of her visionary freedom, and this is what invalidates it. (25)

Ironically, Clarissa's effort to suppress the monster within her is what condemns her to a superficial, unfulfilling life. Although she envisions the monster to be the manifestation of only evil, it is also the site of the instinctual impulses and desires that embody the passion her life lacks.

A lack of commitment to change and a dissociation from the reality of experience plagued the modernist literary movement itself, and, in discussing the work of the writers in the 1930s, Jean-Paul Sartre attributes the change in the new generation to its realization of the gap between "literary myth and historical reality" (Sartre 174). According to Sartre, the eccentricity and idiosyncrasy of the avant-garde artist's works alienated him from contemporary society and, consequently, rendered him powerless to instigate change in that society. He claims that "their revolutionary doctrines remain purely theoretical (since they change nothing by their attitude), do not help them gain a single reader, and find no echo among the workers; they remain parasites of the class they insult. Their revolt remains on the margins of the revolution" (141). Moreover, T. S. Eliot said that the works written in the first half of the postwar decade described the death of an old age, not the beginnings of a new one (Hynes 33).[17] Though writers like Eliot and Woolf defined the postwar age, they seemed to contribute little to its healing. The rain never comes to revitalize the Waste Land, and even though Clarissa recommits herself to life and returns to her party, that life lacks meaning and vitality. However, the modernists brilliantly portrayed the effects of trauma, which psychologists were unable to do until decades later, and, as Woolf's depiction of Septimus Smith shows, revealed the potential for recovery within the very nature of the trauma.

It was the artists of the thirties who attempted to give meaning to the war in cultural terms, and it is no coincidence that many of these artists were war veterans. The narratives by authors such as Ford Madox Ford, Robert Graves, Vera Brittain, and Siegfried Sassoon evidence recovery from—rather than the perpetuation of—trauma. They restore order to the fragmented consciousness of the postwar world and reestablish chronological relationships by presenting the war story in a form of "This was my life. . . . This is what happened. . . . This is what I became." Moreover, these novels evidence the rebuilding of identity so essential for meaningful postwar recovery not only in the author but also in the culture. These novels, like the testimonies of all war veterans, force the reader to integrate World War I into his understanding of his culture's identity and history. Cultural identity must be revised to integrate the experience of war into our understanding of ourselves so we may learn from that experience, change, and thereby prevent future wars. Such integration of World War I into our twentieth-century identity seems to take place finally in the last decade of that century, some seventy years after the war to end all wars, in Pat Barker's trilogy of novels, *Regeneration*, *The Eye in the Door*, and *The Ghost Road*.

Notes

1. Septimus's disorder is often discussed as schizophrenia. See articles by Ban Wang, So Hee Lee, and Suzette Henke. Both schizophrenia and posttraumatic stress disorder involve a loss of ego identity; however, as Victor J. DeFazio claims, men suffering from traumatic war neurosis are often misdiagnosed because "[t]he contraction of ego functioning often resembles schizophrenic deterioration while the phobic elaboration that the world is a hostile enemy-infested place is often mistaken for a psychotic persecutory delusion" (38).

2. Henke cites the following incident as evidence of Septimus's homosexual relationship with Evans: "It was the case of two dogs playing on a hearth-rug; one worrying a paper screw, snarling, snapping, giving a pinch, now and then, at the old dog's ear; the other lying somnolent, blinking at the fire, raising a paw, turning and growling good-temperedly. They had to be together, share with each other, fight with each other, quarrel with each other" (*Dalloway* 130). Henke also claims that Evans's emergence from Thessaly in one of Septimus's visions is indicative of the "Greek love" he had for Evans and that he could not express. However, the relationship between soldiers is uniquely close while not necessarily homosexual. Jonathan Shay claims that "Modern American English makes soldiers' love for special comrades into a problem, because the word *love* evokes sexual and romantic associations . . ." (40). In Homer's *Illiad*, Achilles, referring to the death of Patroklos, laments that he has lost his *philos*, his greatest friend. Martha Nussbaum claims that the "emphasis of *philía* is less on intensely passionate longing than on . . . benefit, sharing, and mutuality. . . ." (354; original ellipses).

3. Henke cites Freud's "On Narcissism: An Introduction" and "The Libido Theory and Narcissism."

4. Herman claims, "The conflict between the will to deny horrible events and the will to proclaim them aloud is the central dialectic of psychological trauma. People who have survived atrocities often tell their stories in a highly emotional, contradictory, and fragmented manner which undermines their credibility and thereby serves the twin imperatives of truth-telling and secrecy" (1).

5. Furthermore, Elaine Scarry reveals that this disparity in meaning is also inherent when a person attempts to describe the physical pain associated with traumatic injury: "Physical pain is not only itself resistant to language but also actively destroys language, deconstructing it into the pre-language of cries and groans. To hear those cries is to witness the shattering of language. . . . [T]he person in pain very

typically moves through a handful of descriptive words to an 'as if' construction" (172). Judith Lee concludes from Scarry's claim that "war's purpose is to injure—to cause bodily pain—and thereby to destroy the verbal, material, and ideological signs that constitute the culture embodied in those individuals who are fighting" (181).

6. Kalí Tal explains this process as follows:

> Psychologist Daniel Goleman suggests that personal myths take the form of schemas—unconscious assumptions about experience and the way the world works. The schemas operating in a particular situation determine the actual information an individual absorbs and interprets. Such operations inevitably skew perceptions of events; in fact, that is their purpose. The misinterpretation of what goes on around us is frequently useful as a coping strategy if a properly interpreted event threatens important, foundational schemas. This process results in the "trade-off of a distorted awareness for a sense of security," and Goleman believes that this is an organizing principle of human existence (21). Grand revision of a personal myth must always spring from a traumatic experience, for the mechanism which maintains those foundational schemas will automatically distort or revise all but the most shattering revelations. (Tal, "Speaking" 225)

See also Daniel Goleman.

7. John Del Vecchio in his novel about the postwar adjustment of Vietnam veterans, *Carry Me Home*, echoes Woolf's reference to the war's stripping away of the soldier's skin. Del Vecchio's veteran Robert Wapinski says, "[S]ometimes I feel like I've been shaved by a razor that was set too high. . . . It's like it's taken off my outer layer of skin. It's like my nerves are exposed. Like everything rubs the raw ends" (80).

8. Herman explains that the trauma victim's "[p]erceptions may be numbed or distorted, with partial anesthesia or the loss of particular sensations. . . . These perceptual changes combine with a feeling of indifference, emotional detachment, and profound passivity in which the person relinquishes all initiative and struggle" (43). In addition, Shay observed in working with Vietnam veterans that the "long-term obstruction of grief and failure to communalize grief can imprison a person in endless swinging between rage and emotional deadness as a permanent way of being in the world" (40).

9. Pat Barker in her novel *Regeneration* describes an incident in which a World War I soldier named Burns tastes death: "He'd been thrown into the air by the explosion of a shell and had landed, head-first, on a German corpse, whose gas-filled belly had ruptured on impact. Before Burns lost consciousness, he'd had time to realize that what filled his nose and mouth was decomposing human flesh" (19).

10. Jim Lantz claims, "In Frankl's system of treatment, the human will to meaning is more powerful than the motivational factors of sex, safety, pleasure, achievement, security, comfort, or power" (486).

11. Communicating the story of one's trauma to other members of the community is a crucial element of successful postwar adjustment. Shay refers to this fundamental need to communicate as "communalization," which is "being able safely to tell the story to someone who is listening and who can be trusted to retell it truthfully to others in the community" (4). Tal, in *Worlds of Hurt*, further explains the power of bearing witness to a traumatic event such as war. She claims:

> Bearing witness is an aggressive act. It is born out of a refusal to bow to outside pressure to revise or to repress experience, a decision to embrace conflict rather than conformity, to endure a lifetime of anger and pain rather than to submit to the seductive pull of revision and repression. Its goal is change. The battle over the meaning of a traumatic experience is fought in the arena of political discourse, popular culture, and scholarly debate. The outcome of this battle shapes the rhetoric of the dominant culture and influences future political action. (7)

12. Ban Wang claims that there is "a network of symbols and representations that functions to sustain the political powers that be, and to define the identity of individuals and produce them as subjects of the state. . . . The novel can be read not so much as a systematic penetration into individual consciousness as an exploration of the ways in which the individual tries or fails to establish his or her identity as the subject of the state" (178–79).

13. Wang claims that characters like Bradshaw, Hugh, and Lady Bruton "are produced by the ideological state apparatus, which [he] take[s] to mean the same as the symbolic order in the more empirical form of institutions, functions—through language, social and educational institutions, church, and the media—to reproduce the appropriate subjects for the perpetuation of the political order of the state" (180).

14. Karen L. Levenback points out that Woolf herself recognized little change after the war. According to Levenback, Woolf said in her diary that there was "nothing different in the atmosphere" after the signing of the Armistice, and that "most people have grasped neither war nor peace" (quoted in Levenback 54).

15. Pat Barker's trilogy of novels, *Regeneration*, *The Eye in the Door*, and *The Ghost Road*, explores the way modern war illustrates not only the duality of human nature but also the necessity to satisfy both sides of that nature. Instead of categorizing the two sides as good and evil, as Woolf seems to in *Mrs. Dalloway*, Barker categorizes them as primitive and civilized, instinctual and rational.

16. Deborah Guth explores the separation between Clarissa's inner world and external reality as a means of limiting her understanding:

> Clarissa justifies the distance she keeps from her external life, encoded in her ceremonial attitude, as protection of her inner life which, through its free-flowing associativeness, is felt to be more "real." If one looks closely, however, this inner world is also largely composed of strangely stylized gestures and romanticized self-images. . . . Just as her social self, she feels, is gathered up for presentation to an external audience, so also her inner world is an ingathering of images and imagined gestures, a self she creates for her own edification, a story she tells herself and lives out in the privacy of the soul. (21)

17. T. S. Eliot claims, "From about that date [1926] one began slowly to realize that the intellectual and artistic output of the previous seven years had been rather the last efforts of an old world, than the struggles of a new" (Eliot 271).

Works Cited

Barker, Pat. *The Eye in the Door*. New York: Plume, 1995.

———. *The Ghost Road*. New York: Plume, 1996.

———. *Regeneration*. New York: Penguin, 1993.

Cameron, Norman. "The Experimental Analysis of Schizophrenic Thinking." *Language and Thought in Schizophrenia*. Ed. J. S. Kasanin. 1944. New York: Norton, 1964. 50–64.

DeFazio, Victor J. "Dynamic Perspectives on the Nature and Effect of Combat Stress." *Stress Disorders Among Vietnam Veterans: Theory, Research and Treatment*. Ed. Charles R. Figley. New York: Brunner, 1978. 23–42.

Del Vecchio, John. *Carry Me Home*. New York: Bantam, 1995.

Eliot, T. S. "Last Words." *Criterion* 18 Jan. 1939: 269–75.

Frank, Joseph. *The Idea of Spatial Form*. New Brunswick: Rutgers UP, 1991.

Frankl, Viktor E. *Man's Search for Meaning*. rev. ed. New York: Pocket, 1984.

Freud, Sigmund. "The Aetiology of Hysteria." 1896. *The Standard Edition of the Complete Psychological Works of Sigmund Freud*. Vol. 3. Trans. J. Strachey. 23 vols. London: Hogarth, 1962. 191–221.

Goleman, Daniel. *Vital Lies, Simple Truths: The Psychology of Self-Deception and Shared Illusions*. New York: Simon, 1985.

Guth, Deborah. "'What a Lark! What a Plunge!': Fiction as Self-Evasion in *Mrs. Dalloway*." *Modern Language Review* 84 (1989): 18–25.

Henke, Suzette A. "Virginia Woolf's Septimus Smith: An Analysis of 'Paraphrenic' and Schizophrenic Use of Language." *Literature and Psychology* 31.4 (1981): 13–23.

Herman, Judith. *Trauma and Recovery: The Aftermath of Violence—From Domestic Abuse to Political Terror*. New York: Basic, 1992.

Humphrey, Robert. *Stream of Consciousness in the Modern Novel*. Berkeley: U of California P, 1954.

Hynes, Samuel. *The Auden Generation: Literature and Politics in England in the 1930s*. New York: Viking, 1977.

Johnston, John. "Discourse as Event: Foucault, Writing, and Literature." *Modern Language Notes* 105 (1990): 800–18.

Knox-Shaw, Peter. "The Otherness of Septimus Warren Smith." *Durham University Journal* 87.1 (1995): 99–110.

Langer, Lawrence L. *Versions of Survival: The Holocaust and the Human Spirit*. Albany: State U of New York P, 1982.

Lantz, Jim. "Using Frankl's Concepts with PTSD Clients." *Journal of Traumatic Stress* 5 (1992): 485–90.

Lee, Judith. "'This Hideous Shaping and Moulding': War and *The Waves*." *Virginia Woolf and War: Fiction, Reality, and Myth*. Ed. Mark Hussey. Syracuse: Syracuse UP, 1991. 180–202.

Lee, So Hee. "Madness, Marginalization, and Power in *Mrs. Dalloway*." *Journal of English Language and Literature* 36.4 (1990): 691–712.

Leed, Eric J. *No Man's Land: Combat and Identity in World War I*. Cambridge: Cambridge UP, 1979.

Levenback, Karen L. "Woolf's 'War in the Village' and 'The War from the Street': An Illusion of Immunity." *Virginia Woolf and War: Fiction, Reality, and Myth*. Ed. Mark Hussey. Syracuse: Syracuse UP, 1991. 40–57.

Nussbaum, Martha C. *The Fragility of Goodness: Luck and Ethics in Greek Tragedy and Philosophy*. Cambridge: Cambridge UP, 1986.

Sartre, Jean-Paul. "Situation of the Writer in 1947." *"What is Literature?" and Other Essays*. Cambridge: Harvard UP, 1988. 141–238.

Scarry, Elaine. *The Body in Pain: The Making and Unmaking of the World*. New York: Oxford UP, 1985.

Shay, Jonathan. *Achilles in Vietnam: Combat Trauma and the Undoing of Character*. New York: Touchstone, 1994.

Tal, Kalí. "Speaking the Language of Pain: Vietnam War Literature in the Context of a Literature of Trauma." *Fourteen Landing Zones: Approaches to Vietnam War Literature*. Ed. Philip K. Jason. Iowa City: U of Iowa P, 1991. 217–50.

———. *Worlds of Hurt: Reading the Literatures of Trauma*. Cambridge: Cambridge UP, 1996.

Thomas, Sue. "Virginia Woolf's Septimus Smith and Contemporary Perceptions of Shell Shock." *English Language Notes* 25.2 (1987): 49–57.

Wang, Ban. "'I' on the Run: Crisis of Identity in *Mrs. Dalloway*." *Modern Fiction Studies* 38 (1992): 177–91.

Webb, Caroline. "Life After Death: The Allegorical Progress of *Mrs. Dalloway*." *Modern Fiction Studies* 40 (1994): 279–98.

Wiesel, Elie. "To Believe or Not to Believe." 1985. *From the Kingdom of Memory*. New York: Summit, 1990. 23–35.

Woolf, Virginia. *The Diary of Virginia Woolf*. Vol. 2. New York: Harcourt, 1978. 5 vols. 1977–84.

———. *Mrs. Dalloway*. New York: Harcourt, 1925.

"THE CENTRAL SHADOW"

CHARACTERIZATION IN *THE WAVES*

Susan Rubinow Gorsky

From her first to her last novel, Virginia Woolf displays a persistent concern with the nature of the human being and
thus with characterization. The problem that she defines is how an
author can best present in fiction the ideas about man that to her
contemporaries seemed so startling and new. Certain themes, tightly
tied to her complex conception of character, dominate Mrs. Woolf's
novels: the individual's sense of identity, the possibility and difficulty
of human communication, the relation of man to his society and to the
natural world surrounding him. Her conception of a human being as
an infinitely complex entity, with roots reaching far into the past and
branches forking and twisting to intermingle almost indistinguishably
with the branches and leaves of its neighbors, raises problems for
both the author and her characters. From the author's perspective
looms a problem of technique: how can one best present such a human being? From the characters' point of view come questions of
thematic concern: what is identity? how can the individual distinguish
himself from his world and from other people? how can one communicate with a person one cannot fully know? In *The Waves* these
questions are explored with an intensity and detail rarely achieved
even in Mrs. Woolf's other writing. And the answers that are given
reflect the ambivalence prevalent in modern literature. The search for
meaning and stability in the modern world is a search that generally
cannot end in a simple affirmation, and in this novel ends in a recognition of "the central shadow"—an acknowledgement of incertitude,
a denial of knowledge, action, and traditional forms of human unity.
Because she could not accept the usual narrative modes of ordering

Originally published in *Modern Fiction Studies*, Summer 1972.

experience, in the *The Waves* Virginia Woolf attempts to redefine the novel as genre, exploring variations or substitutions in plot, hero, verbal style, and characterization. Included in her new presentation of character, a presentation that tries to define adequately and accurately the complex "modern" view of human nature, is a tentative assertion of an alternative means of human relationship: distinctive (and distinctly separate) individuals are replaced by characters who are at once individual, representative, and a unity, and for whom traditional interaction is supplemented by what will here be called cosmic communication—the internalization of another's unexpressed thoughts and experiences.

Mrs. Woolf's well-known arguments against the kinds of characterization achieved by the "materialists"[1] lead her to suggest an alternative method that will more fully suit the new concept of the complex nature of man. She recognizes that in her reorientation of values she must give up some of the more worthwhile (as well as the less useful) aspects of "materialistic" characterization: the greatest loss in her novels, as she foretold, is the "acute sense of the reality of our physical existence."[2] But this loss is well overbalanced by the possibility of presenting what she considers to be the more important internal, psychological, and universal aspects of man. To avoid oversimplification and falsity, three facets of characterization become necessary: the individual, the typical, and (for lack of a better word) the communal. The first is what traditional novels are made of: the existence of each character as a separate and distinguishable human being. The second is again not new, for literature of all time has employed the representative figure. The third, however, is new, and is also the most significant part of Virginia Woolf's answer to the modern problem of communication. In a tongue-in-cheek explanation of why she must discuss Cole's cook's sister in trying to describe Horace Walpole, Mrs. Woolf offers what can be taken as a partial explanation of the communal character and at the same time points to the serious need for the multileveled mode of characterization:

> Horace is partly Cole; Cole is partly Horace; Cole's cook is partly Cole; therefore Horace Walpole is partly Cole's cook's sister. Horace, the whole Horace, is made up of innumerable facts and reflections of facts. Each is infinitely minute; yet each is essential to the other. To elicit them and relate them is out of the question. Let us then, concentrate for a moment upon the two main figures, in outline.[3]

Merely emphasizing the internal aspects of characterization, in opposition to the materialists, is not enough, for man is not simply an individual, even a complex individual. As Neville, echoing the idea presented above, explains in *The Waves*, an essential part of characterization is the recognition of "some group in outline against the sky."[4] The outline emphasizes the links within the group, links that extend backward in time as well as outward through space. It is this notion of the individual as part of a larger whole that enables Mrs. Woolf to round out her characterization of man and leads into an alternative means of communication, a nonverbal sharing of experiences and thoughts, even of events and ideas which could not be shared in any ordinary manner.

The ambivalence of critical response to the characters in *The Waves*—to the six speakers and to Percival, the centrally important seventh whose voice is silent and whose thoughts we never learn—arises in part from a failure to recognize that these characters exist simultaneously on three planes and to consider the implications of this multileveled characterization upon the themes and form of the novel. Readers have said that the novel focuses on seven prominent individuals, that there are six partially developed characters and a seventh figure hidden in shadow, that these are six or seven parts of one human being, perhaps Virginia Woolf or the reader, or even that there are no characters at all.[5] And, in fact, there is some merit in each of these interpretations. Within *The Waves* there is neither a traditional hero nor normally recognizable characters. Instead the putative hero is made mock-hero and destroyed, and the six speakers exist simultaneously as individuals (though not in the usual manner of literary characters) as representative figures and as parts of a communal whole. It is in the interplay among these three levels that the novel achieves its greatest originality and importance: verbal, symbolic, and structural techniques combine to reveal the cosmic communication which provides a counterpoint to the typically modern limitations placed upon more ordinary communication and to the extra barrier added by the form of the dramatic monologues within which each speaker is confined.[6]

Percival, the one character who does not speak, is also the figure through whom the possibility of traditional hero is most directly denied. Through the eyes of his six friends, Percival is seen as a potential hero, a man of action, allied with the classic heroes; but his heroism is undercut and mocked, both through the direct statements of the six speakers and through the formal structure of the novel which denies Percival's putative centrality by making him incapable of meaningful action or of any speech. Even though Percival, whose very name echoes the knights in search of the grail, is repeatedly hailed as a hero, he is also mocked. Bernard provides the first hint of the mock-heroic in the characterization of Percival ("Percival rides a flea-bitten mare, and wears a sun helmet"), but he still regards Percival as a kind of god: "the multitude cluster round him, regarding him as if he were—what indeed he is—a god" (136). Percival is human, needing protection from the sun; he is laughable, a Don Quixote on a mare worthy of Rozinante; and yet he is also at least potentially an ideal, a hero, a god. When Percival dies, it is not a heroic death in battle but a quixotic death through an accident— his horse stumbles, and because the girth is too loose, Percival is killed. Yet at the first dinner party it is Percival who is the necessary center who supplies the catalyst that creates an epiphany, a moment of exalted unity and successful communication for the other six; at the second party, Percival's absence creates a void perhaps most felt by Neville but obvious to all. The six achieve another form of unity through cosmic communication, but at least one source of their potential unity is Percival, and his loss ensures their failure to achieve integration as a whole, single person.

As a representative of the potential hero made the limited mock-hero of the twentieth century, Percival's significance extends beyond the single novel. For the six characters, Percival is a symbol of the heroic—of romance and dream, action and possibility, hope and the future. So, in his failure and death lie not only the loss of an individual human being and a friend but also the destruction of all that this individual stands for. Unlike the Arthurian knight whose name he bears, Percival succeeds in no part of his quest and catches not even a glimpse of the grail. The possibility of knowledge and action, the sense of time and options, and the existence and relevance of heroism die with Percival. For the novel, Percival symbolizes the loss of the traditional hero; and, to borrow a clue from Neville, the "plots" and "reasons" which novel readers may desire are not viable if the hero of the past, capable of physical action, clear knowledge, and meaningful direction in an intelligible world, no longer exists. In this novel, the only possible traditional hero is twice destroyed, first through mockery of form and substance in his inability to speak or to fulfill his potential and then through his absurd death. The destruction of the traditional hero underscores the importance of a new conception of man and a new method of characterization. The six remaining characters have one advantage over their potentially heroic friend: they can speak, and in their speech they reveal and define the three-fold view of human nature.

The six characters are, at the most traditional level, individuals. They may lack the physicality of the creations of the "materialists," but their sense of individuality is as "clear-cut and unequivocal" (167) as the polar sense of human unity, and they walk and sleep, hope and fear, quarrel and love like traditional characters. Although at times they accentuate their differences, so that they are unable to recognize similar needs and responses, their individual reactions to common experiences support their sense of distinctions. For example, when Jinny, as a child, kisses Louis, the experience is animating to Jinny, shattering to Louis, and agonizing to Susan. Rhoda is oblivious of the event, and Bernard is aware only peripherally as he observes and involves himself in Susan's distress (14–18). A series of parallels and oppositions among the characters is established. Bernard and Neville attend college, but Louis must leave school; Jinny and Rhoda remain in the city while Susan returns to her farm. Bernard and Susan each marry and have children while Rhoda and Louis temporarily become lovers. Neville and Jinny are paired in that each chooses a life of varied and at least outwardly ephemeral relationships, yet for Neville, unlike Jinny, all of the partners are somehow one, an idealized reflection of Percival. Louis and Neville desire order and precision while Susan hates both. Jinny and Susan are primarily aware of the physical and real while Rhoda lives in a world of dream and Bernard in one of imagination. Rhoda is silent, nameless, faceless; in contrast, Bernard is a word and phrase maker, multinamed (Byron, Hamlet, Napoleon, and Shelley) and of multiple identity.[7]

A flux between separation and unity is obvious at the two dinner parties, the high points of communion for the six speakers. In periods of separations such as during the arrival of the characters at the first party, their differences and their sense of individuality are sharply delineated. Throughout the party, even as the epiphany, the moment of ecstatic if temporary unity approaches, the characters are sharply aware of their obvious and frequently bruising personality differences. At both this and the second dinner, the contrast of the almost brutal awareness of individualism that precedes and follows the brief moments of unity is striking evidence of the existence of six discrete human beings.

That the characters are individuals is further demonstrated by one of the book's uses of imagery. Each character reveals a pattern of images, a distinct cluster that serves to define the individual human qualities of the speaker, to identify the character to the reader and to his friends, and partly to distinguish his soliloquies from those of the other characters. The speech of each character is made distinct within the mask of the formal monologue by the repetition of key phrases and images. Diction varies from one speaker to the next because of the words repeated in the image patterns: Jinny speaks of the city, its houses and streets, Susan of fields and animals, and Rhoda of water, pillars, mountains, and deserts. While each character's images cover a large scope of reference, the clusters upon examination reveal that individual's outstanding traits: for Neville, order and precision, for Susan, affinities with nature and with elemental passions, and for

Louis, a conflict between frustration in the present and fulfillment in a sense of life's continuity; Jinny is physically oriented, Rhoda is afraid, and Bernard is a prospective novelist. Thus although the characters share essentially the same word patterns and sentence structures, an impression of individual style is achieved because in repeating images the character also repeats phrases, clauses, and whole sentences. However, as Bernard reminds us, these characters are "not one and simple, but complex and many." So, while the identifying tags may be useful in establishing the individuality of the six speakers, they do not, of course, provide a completely satisfactory interpretation of the role of character in the novel.

The images that cluster about each of the six central figures not only serve as a poetic device for identifying the characters to themselves and to the reader but also provide in technique tentative answers to the novel's questions of the relationships among human beings. The characters make use of each other's images to reveal a startling intimacy, shared memories of unshared experiences and ideas, and the magical ability to call each other into being—elements of the cosmic communication to be discussed later. But image-sharing also displays the closest approach to conversation, the more ordinary means of communication desired and attempted by the six friends as individuals. During the first dinner party, semblances of normal conversation appear at the crests of the rising and falling waves of unity. Rhoda's and Jinny's thoughts about the heightening of sense perception lead to Louis's observation of "the roar of London," symbolically imagined as "one turning wheel of single sound." A siren reminds Louis of a ship heading to sea, and Neville, the next speaker, thinks of Percival, who is leaving by ship for India. Next Bernard pictures India, with Percival riding "a flea-bitten mare." In the following soliloquies Rhoda echoes these words, and Louis thinks that "it is Percival . . . who makes us aware that these attempts to say, 'I am this, I am that,' which we make, coming together, like separated parts of one body and soul, are false." It is Percival who allows Louis to state overtly what the pattern of the preceding soliloquies has been demonstrating: while the characters remain separate individuals sitting around the table, there is a moment of unity, of real communication—"there is a chin whirling round, round, in a steel-blue circle beneath" (135–137). Yet this moment of communion is not an ordinary conversation. The characters reflect thoughts from each other's minds; they share images and ideas; but they do not respond in the simple, direct, overt form of a human conversation. The soliloquies seem instead to reflect an experience (which includes conversation) as it sifts down into the characters' minds. Thus the six do not actually speak of Percival "riding alone on a flea-bitten mare" or helping to create their moment of unity, but all share thoughts of him, perhaps brought about by dinner table conversation of his possible future in India or perhaps merely because, having planned this party as a farewell to Percival, all are thinking about his past and current relations with them and his separate future.[8]

Rhoda and Louis, at each dinner party, present the most direct and ordinary attempt at conversation; but these conversations are very brief, are extraordinary in form and content, and at the second party point to the failure of their communication at all levels. During the first dinner, the two are allowed five short speeches separated by parentheses from the remaining soliloquies. Louis calls directly, "Look, Rhoda," to begin this brief conversation, and in the following interchange the two reflect each other's thoughts by echoing words, images, and phrases. The content of the shared soliloquies is not that of an ordinary conversation but instead is relevant for the type of ritual communion that the characters achieve at this party:

> "Like the dance of savages," said Louis, "round the camp fire. They are savage; they are ruthless. They dance in a circle, flapping bladders. The flames leap over their painted faces, over the leopard skins and the bleeding limbs which they have torn from the living body."
>
> "The flames of the festival rise high," said Rhoda. "The great procession passes, flinging green boughs and flowering branches." (140)

At the second dinner, they have two moments of such communication: the first, again segregated from the surrounding soliloquies by parentheses, occurs at the dinner table; the second does not need to be formally separated because it takes place when Rhoda and Louis stand alone having watched the other four "vanish, towards the lake." In each of these "conversations" is revealed the same attempted communication, shown by image, word, and idea exchange, and the same failure to achieve a normal discussion. Rhoda makes overt this final failure and simultaneously reminds us of the destruction of their relationship as lovers: she says that they have lost their possibility of real communication, for they "trust only in solitude and the violence of death and thus are divided." Louis echoes agreement, "for ever . . . divided" (231).

Neville, as he listens to an unreported conversation, provides a partial description of the mode of communication in the novel: "And so (while they talk) let down one's net deeper and deeper and gently draw in and bring to the surface what he said and she said and make poetry" (199). In the most overt forms of conversation in the book, the soliloquies reveal in poetic form what a net dipped into the mind might catch as remnants of shared conversation and experience. In this novel, technique, through image patterns and the form of the dramatic monologue, reveals that at the normal level communication is extremely limited, but an alternative is offered in the cosmic communication possible among closely related individuals, fragments of a potential human whole.

In addition to being individuals, the characters are, in certain ways, representative human beings. They are not merely disembodied voices but have typical physical and emotional responses and grow and develop as natural human beings. When young, they live in the child's world, a blend of fantasy and reality. Slowly the six begin to undergo the process of individualization, first establishing what belongs to each of them, what is a separate natural object, what is another child, and later attempting involvement in personal relationships. They are physical creatures, who bathe, eat, and kiss, walk outside, or sit in a classroom. They are human creatures, who experience the pain of loss or potential loss—the fading of youth, the end of love, the death of a friend. While these six people are also shown by technique and through traits and experiences to be individuals, they nevertheless undergo typical experiences, respond in natural human ways, and thus act as representatives of the "omnipresent, general life" of man. Bernard, who defines himself as "a man of no particular age or calling" (81), underscores the archetypal level of characterization when he comments in his summary that he is unsure of both the date and his present location: it might be "another twentieth of March, January, or September" (296), and he may be in Paris, in London, or in "some southern city" (288), but he does not know—it is either impossible or irrelevant for him to determine these specific details. The universalizing effect of the novel's lack of explicit settings, physical descriptions, costuming, weather, and all the external detail which the ordinary realistic novel includes, is thus reinforced by Bernard's explicit recognition of himself as a potentially archetypal figure. Of course, in a traditional novel characters can also be representative types. In *The Waves*, however, the characters are not only representative but are, in some ways, parts of one whole, of one potentially complete human being; furthermore, this idea is revealed through form, through image-sharing, and through the masks of the dramatic monologues.

To the reader, perhaps the most striking aspect of *The Waves* is the stylistic device of the internalized dramatic soliloquies. In *The Voyage Out*, the hero mentions his desire to write "a novel about Silence, . . . the things people don't say."[9] In two senses, *The Waves* is that novel, both in its obvious silences—the gaps between the monologues—and in the content of the monologues themselves. The characters' words are not speeches, simple soliloquies, or stream-of-consciousness but rather a combination of the nonverbal elements of the human mind with fragments from ordinary discourse, thought, and a form of cosmic communication. The strongly subjective quality of stream-of-consciousness is prevented by the masking medium of the monologue form that restricts verbal style and individualistic organization of thought and idea. The utterances, which are unlike the usual soliloquy in situation and form as well as in intention, are not necessarily delivered in solitude and occasionally provide a vehicle for something approaching dialogue. It is through style, through the interplay between the masklike monologues that deny individual identity by standardized, formal style, and the individualizing aspects of image patterns that the six characters achieve their complex roles; it is through style that the novel defines human and literary character as simultaneously archetype and individual.

To Jinny a word is fire-colored, a bright reminder of a desired dress; to Susan, words are natural objects, like pebbles and sand; to Neville, words are formal and exact and can be a source of ordering; to Bernard, words are alive, creative, and essential. These distinctions, so obvious to the six characters, are totally ignored in the verbal style of the monologues. While each character may be distinguished by his private cluster of images and by his personal responses, interests, and experiences, these differences are presented in a vehicle which serves to blunt and blur the edge of individuality. Each internal soliloquy includes, as the first limitation on distinctions, the tag "said X." While Jinny describes her use of language as careless and Neville and Louis delight in the order and precision of language, the form of all the characters' "speeches" is strikingly similar. Sentence length and structure vary not from individual to individual but from one time period to another. As children, the six speak in brief soliloquies; the sentences are simple and in the opening monologues display an identical syntactical structure and a basic similarity of content. Soon the sentences become increasingly complex, and the number of sentences in each utterance grows. At the first dinner party, as the friends review their life together, they recall their childhood in soliloquies reminiscent in style and structure of those early ones: again, sentences are simple, relatively short, and of minimum number; even the order of the first seven speeches is repeated (124). Although sentence length and complexity change for the group of children as they grow, diction remains largely the same. Even in the opening chapter, children too young to bathe themselves are capable of such words and phrases as "pendant currants like candelabra," "reprieve from conversation," "surmount this unintelligible obstacle," and "unsubstantial territory." The effect of this is both to increase the artificiality of the formal monologue style and to underscore a basic similarity among the six characters.

The idea that the six characters are in some ways a single being is further supported by one of the uses of imagery in the text: the six voices employ each other's identifying image patterns not only to suggest attempted conversation but also to display an inherent unity among themselves and to indicate a type of cosmic or unconscious communication.[10] Thus Bernard tells Susan that "we melt into each other with phrases. . . . We make an unsubstantial territory" (16). From childhood through Bernard's summary, this "unsubstantial territory," the strange unity among the six characters, is displayed by the unconscious sharing of imagery among six parts of one potential, archetypal whole. One image which all six use, with modifications, is a ring or circle: the significance of the sharing of this particular pattern is enlarged because the image itself expresses not only a Jungian concept of personal unity but also the possibility of communication. The encompassing ring can grow outward from the individual so that from each human there can be a "circle cast" to surround others (128–129), or it can be a unity derived from a group of individuals ("Here on this ring of grass we have sat together, bound by the tremendous power of some inner compulsion" [391]). The "steel ring of clear poetry," like a "smoke ring" of words, can connect man to man and man to external objects (128, 167, 169). The image of "a chain whirling round, round in a steel-blue circle beneath" describes the moment of communion at the first dinner party and is echoed to suggest how easily this unity can be broken: "The circle is destroyed. We are thrown asunder" (137, 143, 142). In these instances the characters are not attempting conversation; the image sharing is purely a technical device to suggest a level of cosmic, unconscious communication. In more general terms, all six characters display knowledge of each other's actions, appearances, and thoughts or words by repeating unspoken phrases and images. It is not surprising that their memories contain reflections of their friends' actions which could have been directly observed, but the six share also the phrases and images which their friends use to describe to themselves actions, appearances, emotional responses, and thoughts—words and images that are not exchanged in ordinary, open, vocal discourse.

Besides this, the characters display a magical form of communication by means of which they can, through thinking of each other, virtually bring another into existence or, in a different sense, bring to the surface an additional facet of a unified potential whole created by the conjunction of the six. With Bernard's comment, "Let me then create you. (You have done as much for me)" begins a series of soliloquies in which one character by thinking of another animates the next speaker. Bernard concludes his soliloquy by thinking of Louis, and in the next line Louis speaks, ending his monologue with a description of Susan's simple existence, leading to an introduction of Susan at her farm-home. Her soliloquy concludes with a picture of the evening, first at her farm and then in the city, and with a childhood memory of Jinny; the character who follows is Jinny, at evening, in the city (91–100). The six speakers are participating in a timeless ritual when they make this magical use of each other's names, and Louis, who confirms his sense of self by signing his name repeatedly (167), is not alone in his overt recognition of the potency of a name. Through history, various groups have practiced forms of magic (for good or evil) in which the beneficiary or victim's name is necessary; as a result, some groups feared the exchange of names with potential enemies. At least one contemporary religion still places a taboo upon referring to its deity by name, preferring as one significant alternative, "The Name."[11] In at least one of their variations of mystical communion, the six characters in *The Waves* again underscore their universality.

Neither this magical communication nor the image-sharing is an ordinary or normal form of human intercourse. For these six characters, the human community which is often intellectually posited is a reality, however limited in scope and value: they not only feel but also reveal links with the distant past and with distant friends. The characters themselves, notably Louis and Bernard, overtly comment upon the idea of a vertical and horizontal unity exemplified by the six central figures and existing among all human beings. Through a picture of himself as a stalk whose "roots go down to the depths of the world," Louis presents the vertical relationship: "Up here my eyes are green leaves. . . . Down there my eyes are the lidless eyes of a stone figure in a desert by the Nile" (12). Later he adds that this signifies human community: "I am not a single and passing being" (202). For Bernard, who requires a conscious recognition of human communion, a momentary peace can be found if he allows himself "to sink down, deep, into what passes, this omnipresent, general life" (112). In addition to participating in this form of universal human unity, the six share also a common personal past, an overlapping fund of memories, impressions, and experiences, and the ability to achieve an unusual level of communication, in part through the use of this special fund.[12] The unconscious communication caused by the strange, close unity among the six is a kind of "cosmic" communication because it breaks down the usual barriers of time and space *and* those of the individual mind. However, their mystical communion serves more to suggest their unusual union than to offer a viable alternative to modern man's sense of alienation and isolation (problems which may seem clichés today but which are real to Virginia Woolf and realistically faced by her). Even for these six, the epiphany-like moments of unity are fragile and the attempts at communion limited so that the characters are tossed from the crests of union to the troughs of individual isolation.

The unity among the six is tenuous, and their moments of exaltation, caused by an awareness of their inherent oneness, are quickly destroyed. Yet the need for unity and for the kind of communion which they can achieve is great. The use of the identifying tag, "said X," is significant, especially because the characters are not really "saying" anything. The word "thought," while also inexact, might have been more easily accepted by the reader; still, the concern of the novel with the possibilities and problems of communication provides justification and explanation of the word choice. Although the speakers want and occasionally attempt to communicate through more ordinary conversations, these attempts are necessarily limited by the structure of the characters' utterances. But cosmic communication, accompanied by a recognition of man's essential community with all men and by an awareness of the special unity which these six characters obtain, is shown to be possible. The stylistic formality, which serves to create order and unity, is the prime indication of a direction in the novel beyond the mundane and chaotic to the sense of life as archetypal. Defining the process of achieving stability and meaning by finding something separate from the flux of daily life, Bernard speaks of moving "to that which is beyond and outside our own predicament; to that which is symbolic, and thus perhaps permanent, if there is any permanence" (248–249). Even as he suggests the value of a world beyond flux and chaos, Bernard simultaneously hints that this may be fantasy ("*if* there is any permanence"). Just as the unconscious, cosmic level of communication cannot obviate the need for more direct, personal conversation, so too, existence at the purely archetypal level of characterization, while perhaps providing a way of escaping the ephemeral and chaotic nature of ordinary human life, is, in itself, incomplete. The characters display very close personal and universal relationships and share in the "omnipresent, general life" of man; yet barriers are always maintained so that the six are also individuals, incapable of indulging in traditional or satisfying dialogues and sealed in closely related but finally separate soliloquies.

If the multiple aspects of characterization are to be unified anywhere in the novel, it will be in the final soliloquy because here Bernard speaks alone for the entire group. In his summary, Bernard attempts to review his life for a relative stranger in a restaurant but discovers that in some strange and complex way his life is interwoven with the lives of the other five characters. He can neither speak of himself alone nor think of the six simply as a single unit: he sees them as one and yet separate.

In his summary, Bernard reveals his sense of himself and his friends as individuals. His personal image clusters remain, and he relates the others to their identifying images, providing rapid if thin sketches of the five by defining their individuality in terms of some central facet of character. This method reveals an insufficient concept of human nature both because Bernard is oversimplifying the individuality of each character and because, in defining them only as individuals, he is ignoring the full significance of their roles. They are individuals, but they are also a part of a larger community, a stream from which "there is nothing one can fish up in a spoon" (255–256) without the danger of falsely interpreting the nature of the whole stream by analysis of a teaspoonful of water.

In discussing the process of individualization which the six endured as children, Bernard unconsciously uses one of Rhoda's mental images, suggesting that "we were all different" because "the virginal wax that coats the spine melted in different patches for each of us" (241; cf. 45). By his reflection of an unspoken image in Rhoda's mind, Bernard is ironically revealing their unity even as he discusses their separateness. In his summary, Bernard's constant and unconscious use of the identifying images of the other characters proves his assertion that "there is no division between me and them." Bernard says that he feels himself a part of them all: on his head he feels the bruises that Percival received in falling, in his eyes are Susan's tears, and in his mind is Rhoda's vision of statues. Even more significantly, on his neck is Jinny's kiss to Louis: as a child, Bernard had no knowledge of this event; thus, the cosmic connections among the characters are underscored by his strange perception (289). Bernard assures himself of the reality of the "moment" by reaching out like Rhoda to "touch the hard surface of the table" (267). He muses about his inability to find completeness or perfection in life with words that recall both Louis and Neville, referring to Louis's "women carrying red pitchers to the Nile" and to Neville's problem of "lifting my foot perpetually to climb the stair" (283). This technique reflects two aspects of the unity of characters in this novel—the basic similarities of needs, actions, and responses shared by all members of the human community and symbolized by the six characters as representative types and the special, private unity achieved by these six friends. Bernard recognizes that his life is not his alone but is a strange mingling with the lives of the other five: "I do not altogether know who I am—Jinny, Susan, Neville, Rhoda, or Louis: or how to distinguish my life from theirs" (276); "nor do I always know if I am man or woman, Bernard or Neville, Louis, Susan, Jinny, or Rhoda—so strange is the contact of one with another" (281).

Although these six individuals share a relationship more unified than that of the community at large, even their sense of oneness is limited. Reflecting upon the brief moments of communion enjoyed at the two dinner parties, Bernard recognizes that as close as is their unity, the six have not achieved the integration of a total human being: "We saw for a moment laid out among us the body of the complete human being whom we have failed to be, but at the same time cannot forget. All that we might have been we saw; all that we had missed" (277). In part the particular instance of failure that Bernard describes is a result of Percival's absence from the second dinner party, but it is also a reflection of the fact that these characters, in spite of their deep unity, must remain separate individuals. The unattainable "complete human being" is both Percival and a potential conglomerate archetypal whole. Percival, who was "complete" in an active, potentially heroic way which is admired by (and denied to) the other six, has been proven a failure. His death is reflected in Bernard's words about "the body of the complete human being" who is "laid out among us" as if at a funeral. Mockery reveals his more fundamental failure, the typically twentieth-century inability of the traditional hero to act in full accord with his possibilities. The "complete human being" is also the "whole" man that the six other characters could potentially create but that they fail to achieve fully. The six possess attributes of a single human being but are unable to fulfill their role as archetypal Man both because Percival, the active man or traditional hero, cannot be a part of the whole and because the six firmly and distinctly maintain their individual identities.

In his summary, Bernard comes as close as he can to writing his long-projected novel, a novel that is finally incomplete, suggesting not only his inabilities as an artist but also the limitations of art in the modern world, the inherent impossibility of finishing a story. In the summary, Bernard begins to lose his faith in art as well as in his personal creative talents. Aware of the chaos and flux of life, of the complex depths of the stream from which he tries to fish character sketches of his friends, Bernard begins to feel that the order that art imposes upon reality may be false: he suggests that "life is not susceptible perhaps to the treatment we give it when we try to tell it" (267). Because life is "imperfect, an unfinished phrase" (283), Bernard avoids a perfect, finished conclusion to his summary. Instead, the final pages of the novel underscore the basic ambiguities that cannot be either submerged or resolved. As Bernard walks in some unidentified city on some unspecified night, he sees a light in the sky that he does not dare to associate with the traditional symbol of hope, for "what is dawn in the city to an elderly man standing in the street looking up rather dizzily at the sky?" Yet as the light of the rising sun becomes more noticeable, Bernard is aware of a kind of renewal, a rebirth of individual spirit within him; and so, like Percival whose name he invokes, a potential hero made mock-hero, he attempts to ride against Death, "the enemy." To challenge Death because of a firm sense of individuality is to falsify the complexity of human nature. Bernard is not simply an individual; his life and death are part of a natural cycle in a vast human community. Bernard is well aware that birth and death, joy and sorrow, can be indistinguishable: he did not know whether he should rejoice in his son's birth or mourn Percival's death (two events that significantly occur in close proximity) because both are a part of "the incessant rise and fall and fall and rise again" (297).

At least for Bernard, recognizing the multileveled nature of human existence, while confusing, is essential: "While I hear one or two distinct melodies, such as Louis sings, or Neville, I am also drawn irresistibly to the sound of the chorus" (246). Ultimately, the ambiguity is so complete that it cannot be finally resolved: "And now I ask, 'Who am I?' I have been talking of Bernard, Neville, Jinny, Susan, Rhoda, and Louis. Am I all of them? Am I one and distinct? I do not know" (288). Bernard has "seen clouds cover the stars, then free the stars, then cover the stars again" (294), and he has been conscious of the incessant rise and fall of the waves. So too the characters may seem now separate, now a single entity; once sharply individual, and again fully archetypal. Although one or the other form of characterization may momentarily break the surface most strongly, finally the characters exist not simply at one level, but are one and yet separate, archetype, representative, and individual.

The multilayered nature of characterization in *The Waves* should not be ignored or simply resolved but must be recognized as an essential clue to the intentions and achievements of the book. As Bernard watches the dawn (which may, after all, be lamplight) at the novel's end, he is conscious of the "central shadow": "Light floods the room and drives shadow beyond shadow to where they hang in folds inscrutable. What does the central shadow hold? Something? Nothing? I do not know" (292). Here again the novel reveals that in the modern world there is no grail at the journey's end: potential answers are replaced by an "inscrutable" shadow, and, ultimately, paradox and ambiguity reside at the center of human existence. In a world in which chaos, ambiguity, and doubt are inherent, in which one cannot even know what is in "the central shadow," a novel can neither present the ideas and answers of the past nor be structured around the traditional hero and plot. Traditionally acceptable interpretations of reality, of human identity, of literary character and fictive structure are all examined and largely denied in *The Waves*, a work which widens the boundaries of fiction as it explores new ways of making literature bear new ideas about man and his world.

Notes

1. See "Modern Fiction," *The Common Reader: First Series* (New York: Harcourt, Brace & World, 1953), 150–158, and "Mr. Bennett and Mrs. Brown," *Collected Essays I* (London: Hogarth Press, 1966), 319–337.

2. "Phases of Fiction," *Collected Essays II* (London: Hogarth Press, 1966), 64.

3. "Two Antiquaries: Walpole and Cole," *Collected Essays III* (London: Hogarth Press, 1966), 111.

4. Virginia Woolf, *The Waves* (New York: Harcourt, Brace & World, 1931), 197. All subsequent references are to this edition.

5. The primary tendency in criticism is to see the characters as either sharply differentiated or fully united into a single being. Jean Guiguet, however, approaches a recognition of multileveled characterization suggesting that although the six characters can be distinguished from each other, essentially they represent "a single being." See *Virginia Woolf and Her Works*, trans. Jean Stewart (New York: Harcourt, Brace & World, 1965), 285, 296. Cf. J. K. Johnstone, *The Bloomsbury Group* (New York: Noonday Press, 1954), 362–363. In Mrs. Woolf's diary is revealed her constant sense of a human being as multileveled; for instance, she refers to the "I; and the not-I; and the outer and the inner" as four "dimensions" of "human life." See *A Writer's Diary*, ed. Leonard Woolf (New York: Harcourt, Brace & World, 1953), 250. Therefore, when she says about *The Waves*, "Odd, that they . . . should praise my characters when I meant to have none" (*A Writer's Diary*, 170), she is suggesting not the total absence of characters but the necessity of a redefinition of the concept behind the traditional idea of a character.

6. While it is true that Mrs. Woolf presents characters as simultaneously individual and typical in other novels, it is in *The Waves* that she most fully explores the possibilities of characterization and the meaning of the new modes which she establishes; and the exploration is carried on formally: multileveled characterization is echoed in a double style and divided structure and in the use of clock time, mental time, and cosmic time. Furthermore, in other novels, one element of human nature is emphasized. For instance, Mrs. Ramsay is an archetypal wife and mother, but she is primarily a unique and distinct individual; and, while Orlando is obviously unique and individualized, his central function is to represent a type of man and

woman through all of history. In other novels, too, the boundaries between characters are broken in strange ways: Mrs. Dalloway and Septimus Warren Smith are shown through form to have an odd but important conjunction, and Elizabeth Barrett and Flush recognize their striking similarity extending even to appearance. But the breaking of the traditional boundaries is both more limited in scope and less unusual in presentation in these novels than it is in *The Waves.*

7. For additional orderings into pairs, see James Hafley, *The Glass Roof: Virginia Woolf as Novelist* (London: Russell & Russell, 1963), 107, and Josephine O'Brien Schaefer, *The Three-Fold Nature of Reality in the Novels of Virginia Woolf* (The Hague: Mouton, 1965), 143–144.

8. Ralph Freedman in *The Lyrical Novel* (Princeton: Princeton UP, 1963) agrees that the pattern of image sharing "indicates a semblance of communication among the figures because it is based upon metaphoric inferences from a narrative which is suppressed." Furthermore, the arrangements of "contiguous images" display "Mrs. Woolf's distrust of the possibility of ordinary communication, her belief that states of mind alone can become true points of contact among human beings" (256, 267).

9. Virginia Woolf, *The Voyage Out* (New York: Harcourt, Brace & World, 1948), 216.

10. Cf. Ralph Freedman, 247. Mitchell A. Leaska, in *Virginia Woolf's Lighthouse: A Study in Critical Method* (New York: Columbia UP, 1970), writes that although all the speakers in *The Waves* use their creator's "style," each is distinguishable from the others because each is explicitly identified as the current speaker ("'said Bernard,' 'said Rhoda'") and because each has different "perceptions," which seem from his juxtaposed quotation to be revealed through image-patterns (45). In defining his method of analysis, Mr. Leaska notes that "there is no longer any doubt that an individual's linguistic habits project his personality" and that it is, therefore, possible to determine "what stylistic characteristics" in a given novel serve to "differentiate the narrators" (23). Mr. Leaska's purpose is to discuss *To the Lighthouse,* not *The Waves,* so it implies no criticism of his work to recognize that he has not noted the important point that needs to be made about *The Waves*: since Virginia Woolf manipulates sentence structure, diction, and other elements of verbal style to identify the narrators in *To the Lighthouse,* it is obviously significant that she does not do so in *The Waves.* The primary explanation for this difference in technique is found in the attempt to redefine human nature, specifically, to emphasize the essential unity among the six speakers.

11. In Judaism, God is referred to by such terms as "Adonai" ("Our Lord") or "HaShem" ("The Name"), but never by the tabooed name itself. A contemporary tribe in South America, the Yanomamo, still generally refuses to reveal personal names. See Napoleon A. Chagnon, *Yanomamo: The Fierce People* (New York: Holt, Rinehart and Winston, 1968).

12. This idea bears a striking affinity to Jung's concept of the "collective unconscious," which is defined by Jung as "not individual but universal," the aspect of the mind that is "identical in all men and thus constitutes a common psychic substrate [sic] of a suprapersonal nature which is present in every one of us." See C. G. Jung, The Archetypes and the Collective Unconscious, trans. R. F. C. Hull (New York: Holt, Reinhart and Winston, 1959), 3–4.

SOCIETY, MORALITY, ANALOGY

VIRGINIA WOOLF'S WORLD

BETWEEN THE ACTS

Don Summerhayes

There is a strong temptation to regard *Between the Acts* as Virginia Woolf's last testament, though hardly in the sense that we regard Shakespeare's *Tempest* as his parting message. Whether or not it is safe to give in to the temptation, it seems to me that this novel's complexity and urgency stress the author's concern to provide a key not only to her world—poised above the World War— but also to herself as an artist and a personality and to the nature of her attitude toward the uses of fiction. We are constantly aware, I believe, of what fiction means to Woolf as expression, the "glory" and "agony" her surrogate Miss La Trobe speaks of in this novel, as well as what it means to her as a kind of emanation from the author with a life of its own, and what it may mean to the reader of whom Woolf seems almost obsessively conscious. When we struggle to discover the meaning of *Between the Acts* we find little help in its "ideas" of "plot-structure" or "characterization"; the nature of its style throws us incessantly upon certain poetic devices of diction and rhythm and especially analogy and juxtaposition. Whatever the book is about, or what its "spiritual motive" is (to borrow Francis Fergusson's term) I suspect we cannot come at its meaning better than by paying attention to *how* it seems to say whatever it is saying. Every reader, after all, feels a kind of uneasiness about his relation to the novel: he is in relation to it as the audience gathered on the lawn at Pointz Hall is to the pageant; and if it is possible that the next term in this

Originally published in *Modern Fiction Studies*, Winter 1963–1964.

series is Virginia Woolf in relation to her world, then perhaps we can begin to understand novel, characters, pageant, author, world—*and* reader—by examining their relations. Analogy is not identity, but in the nature of things as they are presented to us in this book, analogy seems the surest way of approaching identification.

The problem of *Between the Acts* that seems to isolate itself as (for me) the crucial one brings to mind three critical comments—by Henry James, T. S. Eliot, and Wallace Stevens—which are widely separated in time and context but which are all applicable to Woolf in general and this novel in particular, and consideration of which might provide a short-cut to defining my approach. In his famous essay on Henry James in 1918 T. S. Eliot remarked in connection with what he called James's "merciless clairvoyance" that "compared with James's, other novelists' characters seem to be only accidentally in the same book." The reason, according to Eliot, is that "the real hero, in any of James's stories, is a social entity of which men and women are constituents."[1] James himself, in the Preface to *The Portrait of a Lady*, remarks that "there is, I think, no more nutritive or suggestive truth . . . than that of the perfect dependence of the 'moral' sense of a work of art on the amount of felt life concerned in producing it."[2] Wallace Stevens, finally, in his essay "Effects of Analogy," suggests that "the corporeal world exists as the common denominator of the incorporeal worlds of its inhabitants."[3] Let me try to show my reasons for finding a relevance for these comments in the novel.

Whatever she may have picked up from later and other writers, Woolf is obviously a good Jamesian, both in her concern with the density of surface action among her characters and in her control of a "hovering consciousness" that broods over her stories outside the experience of any of their characters. She also shares James's clairvoyance and at times can even exercise it mercilessly. One of our common responses to *Between the Acts* is surely surprise and pleasure at the manner in which she manages to combine a delicate, precious, even evasively light touch in her style with a really tough exposure of, say, the urgencies of sexual desire in their almost savage flow under the social patina. No one is likely to suspect Isa Oliver of having no carnality, for example, and in fact her almost crude need for some kind of violent, even masochistic submission to maleness is much more present to us than Mrs. Manresa's more obvious "natural" attractions. (And after all—for another example of merciless clairvoyance—Mrs. Manresa's alliance with William Dodge betrays her lack of seriousness in the sexual play she is constantly rehearsing.) William Dodge's understanding of himself, Giles's understanding of him, Isa's, Lucy's, our own—all face squarely problems of human inadequacy few of us are willing or able to admit.

Sex is not the only area in which Woolf displays this faculty for searching out shy secrets, although it is perhaps the most immediately impressive. She is equally in touch with what I suppose we might call a suppressed or unconscious fear in people of the loss of the self, the disturbed and anxious intuition of everyone in the novel at one time or another that his "existence"—what most concerns his thoughts and emotions—either does not seem to exist for others, or is contemptible to them, or even to himself in moments of clarity. Poor Mrs. Haines in the opening scene, for example, insists "Please, Mrs. Giles Oliver, do me the kindness to recognize my existence."[4] And to suggest, as the pageant seems to do to some witnesses, that there are no personal, unique individuals, but only, as Lucy Swithin complacently puts it, herself and others "dressed differently,"[5] is to suggest a transcendental "unity" that is truly frightening and threatening to anyone who assumes as most of us do that in some inner fastness he is inviolably safe from the intrusion of "otherness." Lucy and Bart may be deeply enough embedded in their remembered pasts not to feel panic at such a threat, but for Isa and Giles—and even more poignantly for Miss La Trobe and William Dodge—it seems to suspend the individual vertiginously over the two "impossibilities" of the Past and the Future: "they felt—how could one put it—a little not quite here or there. As if the play had jerked the ball out of the cup; as if what I call myself was still floating unattached, and didn't settle. Not quite themselves, they felt" (149). What makes Isa and William feel like "conspirators, seekers after hidden faces" in the greenhouse, William says, is the "doom of sudden death" hanging over them—"There's no retreating and advancing" (114).

Clairvoyance is, of course, in a sense the principal manner of communicating in this novel, and the eerie feeling that we have—or might have—when certain scenes are repeated or echoed in later scenes or when images like those of the swallows or starlings recur and vary, accreting some meaning that eludes us, or when the inner monologues of the characters blend into an intermittent unspoken colloquy. Such an eerie feeling comes from a sense that all these subliminal experiences proceed from a common "mediumistic" voice. This is Virginia Woolf's voice, naturally—the mark of her special temperament or genius—but it is also this novel's "world-voice," an idiom in which all separate accents and inflexions are blended into a lingua franca that each character more or less uses. There is an important sense in which such concepts as time, memory, privacy, unity, manipulation, dispersal, and so on, as well as the emotions of "Love. Hate. Peace" (92), as they are defined by the characters who articulate them, represent an imprecise but effectual limitation of consciousness for this world. That is, their definition in the minds of the characters provides a plenum of usable materials for the exercise of conscious (or unconscious) thought or feeling, beyond which no one in the novel can go, and striking the edges of which, as it were, the characters are turned back to repeat and vary what has been done and thought and felt, and especially said, before.

This voice, reverberating through this plenum, seems to me the source of the special aura of gloom pervading the novel. It is more than the gentle sorrow of our apprehension of the approaching deaths of Bart and Lucy—and others too in the war; and more than our pity at what Isa calls her own and what we see to be everyone's "abortive" life, saddled with the burden of "what we must remember: what we would forget" (154); more even than our dismay at the lack of really effective or lastingly effective communication among all these people, except of their shared malaise. It is a gloom that comes, it seems to me, from our sense of the pathetic limitations of this world, its constant flickering reflection of only its own disturbed and perplexed image, and the accompanying suggestion of the fruitlessness of action—of life, itself—in the face of Time's marking of what was or may yet be, but so seldom of what is. More than any fictional world of naturalistic determinism, Woolf's world of baffling multiplicity and psychic insularity seems to suggest the basic existential absurdity or fruitlessness of human life, of itself. That Lucy above all, and after her Miss La Trobe and Isa according to their "gifts," goes on to raise the next curtain and begin the next act in spite of all the discouragement to performance is heartening, but only, I submit, as an illustration of the manner in which humankind can continue to suffer the insufferable. The dignity of the struggle is so fractional and so flimsy.

The struggle and the suffering—*and* the flashes of glory—are the story of history, which perhaps suggest why Woolf has made history such an important motif in this novel. For history is the record of the life of the "social entity," whether it comes to us as the primal vegetable world of Lucy, the solid legacy of Roman Britain that Bart mentions, or the romantic imperial past he dreams of, the local guidebooks and traditions and genealogies, the private or shared memories of individual childhoods or family rituals, or even the newspaper accounts of rape and assassination. Participating in any aspect of this record, an individual must accept the results and implications of the whole process, must be a "last little donkey in the long caravanserai crossing the desert" (155), as Isabel thinks. Or the analogy can be to music, as at the end of the pageant: "The tune began; the first note meant a second; the second a third. Then down beneath a force was born in opposition; then another. On different levels they diverged. On different levels ourselves went forward; flower gathering some on the surface; others descending to wrestle with the meaning; but all comprehending; all enlisted. The whole population of the mind's immeasurable profundity came flocking" (189). Or it can, or course, be to play-acting as the whole pageant demonstrates, and as Woolf stresses when at the end the actors are reluctant to take off their costumes or divest themselves of their assumed identities: "Each still acted the unacted part conferred on them by their clothes" (195). Within time these people are all suspended as in a float or solution, which precipitates historical stereotypes in endless cycles of advance or retreat, but crystallizes only in the unity of death.

We are moving now into the terrain that James's comment on "felt life" reconnoiters, which is the terrain of morality. I should not like to oversimplify James's meaning, which in the context of his description of the artist's function as midwife, architect, and gardener is very complex indeed, but for my purposes here let me remind the reader that James variously describes "felt" life and life felt in terms of "existential" experience, aesthetic appreciation, and moral choice. The felt life concerned in producing a work of art is all of these translated especially through the author's artistic sensibility. Thus, if the amount of felt life concerned in producing *Between the Acts* is substantially what I have said it was above, we might expect to find—as I have argued we do—such existential perceptions as those of psychic insularity, the oppressiveness of time, or the inability to communicate, translated at the aesthetic level—that is, demonstrated in Woolf's style by inner monologue, recurrence of verbal motifs, and ironical detachment from direct statements of meaning. The argument seems tautological at this point only because we have not yet introduced the moral perception; what we ought to expect to find is some moral significance in the existential and aesthetic perceptions, and I believe we do, in the nature of the choices this novel's world allows its human inhabitants.

The gloom I have spoken of, that I believe persistently overrides the "glory," is the gloom of "scraps, orts and fragments" (189) unable except momentarily to impart a "vision" ("A vision imparted was relief from agony," Miss La Trobe thinks, 98) or an "illusion" ("This is death, death, death . . . when illusion fails," she thinks later, 180). It is the gloom of what Melville called "isolatoes," and the recurrent mirror images in the novel intensify our sense of the flat, self-reflecting sides of the cage in which individuals are held. The gloom represents, for Woolf and for Isa, William, and Giles especially, a moral response which is expressed in moral terms by them—as pride, envy, lust, sloth, wrath (and avarice and gluttony are present too in more light-hearted aspects). In this world which seems never to speak of morality except in terms of servant girls or stage-plays or the propriety of manners and appearances, the inescapable introversion and self-sufficiency of every individual makes him constantly sin against charity, a virtue that can be exercised only in company or communion.

Another way of apprehending the gloom of this world, as I mentioned earlier, is as a sense of the fruitlessness of action within Time's treacherous double dealing. Action seems to have no meaning in itself, but rather, as Erich Auerbach notes,[6] seems trivial, commonplace, routine, and important only as it opens up the possibilities of mental and emotional activity of a more or less private nature. Hence the enigmatical punning of the book's title that plays on itself to infinity. Hence also the novel's evasion of action in its usual sense as the concrete manifestation of aspects of the basic conflict or tension of the plot. What we have instead of action, with some notable exceptions to which I shall return, are retrospection of acts in the past—personal, national, primal—and anticipation of acts in the future. Each of the plays within the pageant, even, shows us the present moment as a fulfilment of the past and a promise of the future in a new modulation of a single archetypal plot. The "ten minutes of present time" with which Miss La Trobe wants to "douche" her audience is too strong for them until nature takes her part with the sudden and universal rain that pours down upon them "like all the people in the world weeping" for all people (179–80). Action as a here-now is either abortive and bewildering or evasive and negative. Bart attempts to joke with his grandson and terrifies him. Giles tramples a snake only to bloody his shoes. Isa disguises her poetic journal, William denies altogether that he is an artist, Miss La Trobe refuses to come out from behind her bushes.

The here-now is the locus of choice—the moral imperative—in which the individual must confront his destiny; and except for Lucy and her ironic counterpart, Mrs. Manresa, the characters of this novel seem to find that all "occasions"—manners, conventions, traditions, opportunities—conspire against them. Even art, which ought at least to be "divine" or "demonic," is merely personal, private, hidden, somehow shameful, a nasty secret. In spite of the swift agonies and jubilations like those of Miss La Trobe, the world is made to seem curiously bereft of moral choice, except as morality has slid down the scale to propriety or casual, impressionistic taste. The result, for those characters who are "unhappy," is acedia and the sterile shame it brings.

But Lucy is the exception, old Flimsy whose dreamy allegiance to a vague transcendental unity apparently blinds her to so many realities of suffering and tension. She alone is not locked within a self-reflecting mirror cage but sallies forth, dreamily but in utter good faith, to embrace whatever she can of her whole universe, from before time began to the final harmony that we *"shall"* hear. Her circular tour of the imagination—"one-making"—is not confined to the comforting meditations at which people smile but touches the here and the now which *make* them smile at her own "seraphic" beam. Her regenerative power over William Dodge and Miss La Trobe suggests the moral act that transforms Time's fraudulent transactions into a benign "confidence" game, a moral reality. Disregarding the conventions of age and manners and the patronizing regard of the "sane" for the "flimsy," and above all disregarding the voracious appetite of Time that bankrupts those around her, she strikes quickly into their hearts and renews their lives by doing them the kindness to recognize their existence; for the "honor" is first of all a simple act of kindness, a charity activated by faith and hope. These three abideth, turning Time inside out and making oppression joy. The morality of this novel is not far from that of *The Pilgrim's Progress*, except World War II and the Blitz will have to do for Bunyan's Celestial City.

For Wallace Stevens art communicates by analogy because "the corporeal world exists as the common denominator of the incorporeal worlds of its inhabitants." In other words, using the same materials within the same structure, people reconstruct in their imaginations worlds that satisfy their temperamental requirements or reflect their abilities to "feel" and thus to use the life around them. If we conceive of *Between the Acts* in terms of the whole experience it may contain or embody for all of its inhabitants—that is, a "corporeal world"—we can see the fragmentary experiences and private consciousness of the characters as "incorporeal worlds" built up from the "reality" they share. This perhaps makes clearer my notion of the book's "social entity" or "total consciousness." Woolf's world here—and almost equally in *Mrs. Dalloway* and *To the Lighthouse*—is a world of total analogy, that is, a world in which all actions and thoughts, all manifestations at any rate of human perception and contemplation and choice, are equivalent to each other; and a world furthermore that would be empty without human intercourse and consciousness to inform it—like the dining room "a shell, singing of what was before time was" (36). From the analogical view there can be no villains and equally no heroes, since every character accepts what he needs or can grasp of what is accessible to all and creates the "reality" that for him explains his relation to himself and to what is apparently not himself. Whether the savage, prehistoric, vegetable world is that which Lucy meditates upon, that which Isa's son roots in during his walk, that which Isa and William visit in the greenhouse, or that which Miss La Trobe imagines as the controlling image of her projected play, the reader is constantly invited to recognize a parallel between it (them) and the world in which the cows suddenly begin to cry out or swallows to dart above the artificial lake. All men's thoughts are "primal" thoughts, first thoughts, all actions if they occur are those of prehistoric man rising to his hind feet.

Reality, in other words (one almost writes "in other worlds") is not the content of what is sensed or imagined but rather the form or process of sensing and imagining. (The due course of law in a world of analogy is "procedural" rather than "substantive.") William's rapport with Isa and Lucy is not different in content from the rapport he has "always" (113–4) impotently experienced with women, but the manner of that rapport—Lucy's dreamy and quite un-self-conscious absorption of William into her own unity, Isa's emanation of her hidden misery into his—constitutes what for him approaches a release from a peculiar bondage. Absorbed by Lucy, absorbing Isa, he has become real to himself, has had his self recalled into life; and his thanks to Lucy on departing are essentially the same as hers to Miss La Trobe: thanks for a communion. For Miss La Trobe—and Virginia Woolf—also constantly plays with her humans in terms of absorption and emanation, which are calculated to give them back to themselves, not forfeited by Mr. Streatfield's apologetic message of "opp—pportunity" but able once more, if ever, to see themselves for what they essentially are outside the accident of history or the envelope of convention.

Thus, although I am perhaps laboring the point, it seems to me that, as Virginia Woolf's last "will," *Between the Acts* is an important document. She has faced squarely her understanding of the process by which she knows her world—which, if it is not tautological, is precisely the process of awareness of process—and has offered her understanding in the only terms that make it accessible to her readers. If we come to this novel expecting to find the familiar safeguards against misunderstanding its meaning—whether we look for them in traditional plotting, characterization, or authorial asides, or wherever—we must either adapt ourselves to a situation in which such props have been excised or made to disappear into transparency, or we must end our readings with the disagreeable sense of having been cheated by the novel. If we notice that the process of misunderstanding is one the novel invites us to watch, we have at least the consolation of knowing where to begin: we must begin where Woolf's characters begin, in the realization that there is no unapprehended reality, and that the enigma of misapprehension is the only usable reality we have to begin with. Reality must be no easier for us than it is for them, and as the curtain goes up on the universal love play that is Giles's and Isa's, so as we close the novel a curtain goes up on our own drama.

Notes

1. T. S. Eliot, "Henry James: In Memory," originally printed in *The Little Review*, August, 1918; quoted here from Edmund Wilson, ed., *The Shock of Recognition*, vol. 2 (New York, 1953), 475.

2. Henry James, *The Art of the Novel* (New York, 1934), 45.

3. Wallace Stevens, "Effects of Analogy," in *The Necessary Angel: Essays on Reality and the Imagination* (New York, 1951), 118.

4. *Between the Acts* (New York: Harcourt, Brace, 1941), 6. Subsequent page numbers refer to this edition.

5. *Between the Acts*, 175.

6. Erich Auerbach, *Mimesis: The Representation of Reality in Western Literature* (New York, 1953), 475.

THE PAGEANT IN

BETWEEN THE ACTS

Marilyn Zorn

If the "gifted lady," as the author of *Between the Acts* calls *her* authoress, Miss La Trobe, allows the "intolerable constriction, contradiction, and reduction to simplified absurdity" of Mr. Streatfield and Mr. Streatfield's question, "What . . . Message . . . 'What message' it seemed he was asking, 'was our pagent meant to convey?'"—then, perhaps, the critic may also take his stand before the audience of *Between the Acts* and with simplified, gracelessly moral intentions attempt to answer Mr. Streatfield's question. Perhaps one is condemned and at the same time allowed to make that attempt by Mr. Streatfield himself, who is the representative of the viewers, "their symbol, themselves; a butt, a clod, laughed at by looking glasses; ignored by cows, condemned by the clouds which continued their majestic rearrangement of the celestial landscape, an irrelevant forked stake in the flow and majesty of the summer silent world" (190–191). The reader, like the viewers of the pageant, must inevitably ask the same question that perplexes Mr. Streatfield.

Perhaps also it is indicative of the tone of this last novel that Mr. Streatfield, modest and unassuming as he is, should be given the task of appraising the pageant, which the author reminds us is given this summer for the purpose of relighting the village church—surely a significant piece of information. Let us, therefore, not entirely ignore Mr. Streatfield as he stands in his clerical coat and delivers his version of the pageant:

> . . . were we not given to understand—am I too presumptuous? Am I treading like angels, where as a fool I should

Originally published in *Modern Fiction Studies*, Winter 1956. All citations of *Between the Acts* are from the 1941 Harcourt Brace edition.

> absent myself? To me at least it was indicated that we are
> members one of another. Each is a part of the whole. . . .
> We act different parts; but are the same. (192)

To be sure, these are the words of a country clergyman, written for
him by an author whose clergy often are proponents of a deity who
looks like President Kruger instead of Prince Albert. Yet these words
are not without support. In one of the novel's climactic scenes of
recognition, Lucy says to Miss La Trobe, "you've made me feel I could
have played . . . Cleopatra." There is a suggestion of irony here, for
the only two characters in *Between the Acts* who have an inkling
of the pageant's meaning are religious—in marked contrast to the
agnosticism of the remaining.

The question is posed in moral terms. The author invites us to
look specifically for a "message." Usually Virginia Woolf prefers not
to leave the moral tags hanging so loosely from the web of reality
she weaves. At least she prefers a more articulate and less despised
spokesman. But for a writer of Mrs. Woolf's temperament, matters
of style and structure are a morality in themselves; and moral values, conversely, must be expressed in terms of style and structure.
For was she not, earlier, condemning the Arnolds and Forsythes on
both counts: that the dead wood of structure and convention in the
novel had choked off the essential life to be found there, had put the
counters of value on environment and social and economic position
and not on the individual human soul? Virginia Woolf's famous revolt
was as much a moral revolt as it was a stylistic one.

To interpret the pageant, one must look closely at its function
in the structure of the novel. Many critics, in speculating about the
meaning of *Between the Acts*, have expostulated with Mrs. Woolf for
leaving the real human drama outside the bounds of the book to attend to matters of Elizabethan style and Victorian corpulence in the
sketches that make up the pageant proper. Others, in reading the
novel as an indictment of the human predicament between the two
wars, have emphasized the allegory of the modern skit: "Scraps, orts,
and fragments," a world precipiced about by the chaos that is about
to tumble in upon it and artistically and socially incapable of seeing
beyond the distortions of its own image. The first reading, it seems
to me, is too literal an interpretation of the novel, and the second
gives undue emphasis to the concluding portion of the play. Indeed,
central to the book is the experience of the pageant, as if there, in
that fantastic piece of dish cloths and royal turbans, each has his
essential part and finds his role. The culmination of the pageant in
the theme of Unity, precariously balanced in the midst of Dispersion,
is the central experience of the book. Participation in the pageant is
the true ritual of communion, a taking on of the values implicit in the

act of brotherhood and identification in the individual with a power outside and beyond that of the ego. In Virginia Woolf's own idiom:

> Like quicksilver sliding, filings magnetized, the distracted united. The tune began; the first note meant a second; the second a third. Then down beneath a force was born in opposition; then another. On different levels ourselves went forward; flower gathering some on the surface; others descending to wrestle with the meaning; but all comprehending; all enlisted.

And as the crowd begins to trickle away at the close of the pageant, the gramophone is heard affirming:

> *Dispersed are we; who have come together. But,* the gramophone asserted, *let us retain whatever made that harmony.*
>
> O let us, the audience echoed (stooping, peering, fumbling), keep together. For there is joy, sweet joy, in company.

It is in the light of this transcendent, if momentary, harmony that the pageant must be seen. For the author has inundated the local and particular in this community pageant with the same kind of significance that would attend upon earlier pageants: the religious and communal significance of the mystery pageant. Thus the pageant acts for the novel as a truly ritualistic experience, as a vehicle for releasing the individual from the burden of his aloneness, his absorption in the ego and time, and his subjection to change. For Virginia Woolf, like Marcel Proust, the world of art is the true Arabian Nights: the escape from time, the best means of transcending the flux of time and change.

Of primary concern here is the relationship between the pageant and the audience itself. For Virginia Woolf means us to see the chief characters of her novel—Bart, Lucy, Giles, Isa, Mrs. Manresa, and William Dodge—as the audience of her play; it is to them that we look as a chorus to interpret for us the pageant that unfolds within the center of that human drama. Early in the novel Bart informs Mrs. Manresa that their part in the afternoon's entertainment is an important one—that of being the audience. And it is from their point of view that we watch the central experience unfold.

To illuminate that audience's experience, I have arbitrarily chosen two devices of style that have for Virginia Woolf moral implications. The first concerns the matter of time in the novel, and the second, the dramatic device of recognition. Critics have noted the vast stretches of time conjured up in the chronological space of a single day, which is the time of *Between the Acts.* There is another kind of time involved, however. The time illustrated by the pageant obeys no laws of nature beyond the artist's, and the moments of vision, invoked for us by the pageant, must be read as a transcending of ordinary chronological time and a making of the moment eternal. This is no new doctrine of the author's as her readers know. What is new in *Between the Acts* is the author's affirmation that the artist's vision, shared by the audience through the work of art, is a legitimate vehicle of the moment of being.

First, then, for the matter of time. Chronological time in the novel is strictly contained. The novel takes place in twenty-four hours, observing the unity of *Mrs. Dalloway*. Psychological time, the time of the mind, knows no such bounds, however. Bart remembers his childhood and his youth. Lucy, through her reading of the *Outline of History* stretches time back past the confines of personal memories even of Figgis' *Guide Book*—"The spire of Bolney Minster, Rough Norton woods, and on an eminence rather to the left, Hogben's Folly" (52)—to the edge of human existence and beyond. In Lucy's imagination, time is no longer human, but animal, vegetable—truly prehistoric. But the present is not wholly involved with the past, no matter how ancient; in Giles's mind, so full of the impending war, the future is evoked and shadows the present moment, a summer's afternoon, 1939. Thus the past and the future hang upon the minds of all of the participants in the pageant.

The pageant is, first of all, the world without time. Miss La Trobe is able to designate time as she pleases. And she pleases to evoke the whole of English history in her play. The ages of Elizabeth, Reason, and Victoria whizz by at an alarming rate, to say nothing of the centuries passed over. Moreover, she is licensed to make Eliza Clark, who sells tobacco in the village, appear as Queen Elizabeth and Mrs. Otter of the End House to appear first as an old crone and then as Lady Harriden. Nothing really changes in the pageant world except the costumes. The line of winding figures in the background, the gramophone, all remain the same. That is not to say that significant differences in culture and temperament are glossed over by the author, but they are not the byproducts of chronology so much as of artistic manipulation. Time, which works as a distracting element in the interstices, is at the mercy of the illustration of timelessness which the artist evokes. Moreover, the audience is made to feel the illusion:

> Beauty was on them. Beauty revealed them. Was it the light that did it?—the tender, the fading, the uninquisitive but searching light of evening that reveals depths in water and makes even the red brick bungalow radiant?

> Old Mrs. Lynn Jones, fumbling with her bag, sighed,
> "What a pity—must they change?"
> But it was time to pack up and be off. (195–196)

Thus in the midst of time and change, which work upon nations and continents and human relations, the pageant offers the audience an affirmation of timelessness. "Beauty was on them."

The dramatic, and in this case rhetorical, device of the pageant is recognition. One says rhetorical because the pageant is a spirited and oftentimes gay parody of the contents of a course in "Survey of English Literature." No freshman could mistake the inspiration of Mrs. Otter of End House's speech:

> "Twas a winter's night . . .
> I to whom all's one now, summer or winter . . .
> You say the sun shines? I believe you, Sir . . .
> There's little blood in this arm" (89–90)

or the style of

> "Hail, sweet Carinthia"
> "My love! My lord!" (91)

The whole pageant, indeed the whole novel, is built on this series of echoes and half-echoes from Shakespeare, Shelley, Byron, and Tennyson. Meant to be conveyed is all of English literature from the nursery rhyme to a passage of Isa's that rings clearly of T. S. Eliot: "All's equal there. Unblowing, ungrowing are the roses there. Change is not; nor the mutable and lovable . . . where hand seeks hand and eye seeks shelter from eye" (155). This kind of allusion is the central device of style in the novel. It is as if the author willed that her audience find a traditional body of myth in the evocation of a traditional literature.

For it is not until recognition occurs that communal feeling may spring into being. One need only list the incidents wherein dramatic recognition occurs in the pageant to establish the importance of the device for the pageant and, duplicating the pageant, for its audience as well. Art here simplifies and sharpens the experience of recognition; for Isa and Giles, Bart and Lucy, and the others, life is more complex than it would appear to be when the Prince and Carinthia recognize one another and fall in love. "'It was enough. Enough. Enough,' Isa repeated. All else was verbiage, repetition" (91). Yet certainly we are meant to see the parallelism between that scene and the flash of memory we are given of Giles's meeting with Isa. Time, of course, adds the gentleman in gray and Mrs. Manresa to the lives of the lovers who met fishing for salmon. The eighteenth-century comedy is built on a series of mistaken identities and motives, but the end is accomplished and love finds its way when Flavinda and Valentine confront the two aged intriguers with the realization of their folly and the recognition of true love. About the Victorians, Miss La Trobe is not quite so optimistic. Mr. Budge doesn't recognize the difference between guarding the law and trespassing on the domain of the private soul, between righteousness and self-righteousness. Presumably he cannot see his own hypocrisy. Having hooded their motives from each other, the Victorians have hooded them from themselves.

All of which brings the audience to the essential scene of recognition in the play. The final scene is no pageant. The author merely brings forward a line of mirrors and catches her audience's flatly self-conscious pose of themselves. Nor can the audience ignore the presence of the image. Each must fix his face, affronted by his own reflection, before he can afford recognition of himself or of his neighbor. Thus there can be no meeting, except perhaps a meeting of masks. Few of them dare be even so honest as to make the mirror offered a means toward fixing the outer face, as does Mrs. Manresa.

What Virginia Woolf implies throughout her artificially and deliberately contrived pageant is that no relationship—poetic, rhetorical, or real—between humans is possible without a recognition of the essential soul as distinct from the roles it must play. Recognition and the refusal to recognize the human being for what he is occur throughout the novel as well as the play. Identities are confused and obliterated. Isa's lack of understanding of Giles and his of her are symbolized by Isa's imagining adultery with the gentleman in gray and Giles's actual affair with Manresa (Lust). Giles cannot realize that William Dodge is a human being in need of sympathy because he sees only the mask of William's homosexuality. Bart (aptly named by Mrs. Woolf by the Tereus/Procne relationship with Lucy—"Swallow, my sister, O sister Swallow"), on the other hand, commits a daily rape upon Lucy's sensibilities (his delight in excoriating her religion) and upon little George because he cannot recognize the sanctity of their souls. To Lucy is given the most exquisite and sensitive sympathies of any of them, and even though she cannot remember William Dodge's name, she instinctively knows his difficulty and pities him—does not only pity but can give him love:

> "I'm William," he interrupted.
> At that she smiled a ravishing girl's smile, as if the wind had warmed the wintry blue in her eyes to amber. . . . And he wished to kneel before her, to kiss her hand, and to say . . . but you've healed me. (72–73)

Recognition can lead to reconciliation if it is whole and selfless and honest. This seems to be what Mrs. Woolf is saying. And it is not surprising that this is what the "gifted lady," Miss La Trobe, is saying to her audience as well. After the pageant is ended, the anonymous voice affirms to the audience:

> Before we part, ladies and gentlemen, before we go . . . let's talk in words of one syllable, without larding, stuffing or cant. Let's break the rhythm and forget the rhyme. And calmly consider ourselves. Ourselves. Some bony. Some fat . . . Liars most of us, thieves too . . .
>
> All the same . . . There's something to be said; for our kindness to the cat; note too in today's paper 'Dearly loved by his wife'; and the impulse which leads us—mark you, when no one's looking—to the window at midnight to smell the bean. Or the resolute refusal of some pimpled dirty little scrub in sandals to sell his soul . . . (187–188)

And then begins the "right" piece—"was it Bach, Handel, Beethoven, Mozart or nobody famous, but merely some traditional tune?" (188)—which brings the audience together for the final moment of reconciliation with the scraps, orts and fragments of self and neighbor. A moment of vision, if we are to believe Mrs. Woolf, which justifies the vague longings of the human heart for beauty and serenity, undisturbed by the life of "Monday or Tuesday."

What . . . Message? Only that Mrs. Woolf inundated *Between the Acts* with the rarest and finest thing she knew—her affirmation of the artist's vision, his great gift to the individual and to society: to hold up for one timeless moment the mirror of Reality and catch there the human soul, creating by the radiance of that vision—Harmony.

The Ethics of Representation

ETHICAL FOLDS

ETHICS, AESTHETICS, WOOLF

Jessica Berman

In a recent interview, feminist theorist Drucilla Cornell argues that what we need now is an "'ethical feminism' which
would try to examine the components of feminist theory, and its relationship to a feminist practice, in terms of the relationship between
the aesthetic, the ethical, the political, the moral, and the legal"
(438). Despite her position as a professor of political science whose
training is in law, she places emphasis on the aesthetic aspects of
this ethical feminism, saying that "feminism demands an articulation
of the realm of the aesthetic" in order to understand the relationship
of ethics to material life (439). This article will attempt to begin such
an articulation through the example of Virginia Woolf's work, taking
seriously the notion that the relationship between aesthetics, politics,
and feminist ethics is one that is elaborated in writing and is particularly visible in Woolf. Here I will push toward a feminist model of
ethics that is posed between the radical alterity of Emmanuel Levinas
and its seeming opposite, the ethics of care (or eros), by way of the
figure of "the fold."[1] Ethics, then, will be seen as inhabiting the fold
between beings that brings them into relation, though not necessarily
into a realm of familiarity, normativity, or consensus. In Woolf's work
we can see public ethical and political responsibility arise from the
private moments of eros or care as well as from the call of the radically other stranger, and we can understand her aesthetic inscription
of this ethics as the folding of one over the other in the process of
what Levinas might call the "saying."

Originally published in *Modern Fiction Studies*, Spring 2004.

Intimate Ethics

Levinas's ethical thought rests upon the stark division within the moment of ethical awareness between the self and the face of the other—startling in its otherness, compelling in its demands upon the self. His writing insists upon the other as "infinitely foreign" (*Totality* 194)—the responsibility one feels in the face of the other must arise from beyond the call of the known. Without this otherness one never encounters the ethical or enters into the possibility of ethical existence, which Levinas terms "being otherwise": "being must be understood on the basis of *being's other*" (*Otherwise* 16). This is the radical challenge that Levinas's thought, from its inception, poses to philosophy—the refusal not just of a primary ontology, preceding ethics, but of a philosophy where the other is understood with reference to the same. It inheres in the very definition Levinas gives to ethics: "A calling into question of the same—which cannot occur within the egoist spontaneity of the same—is brought about by the other. We name this calling into question of my spontaneity by the presence of the Other ethics" (*Totality* 43). Even as Levinas's ideas shift over the course of his long writing life, his insistence that ethics not give way to any incorporation or usurpation of the other by the self, even in terms of an attempt to understand its suffering, means that he continually refuses any semblance of relationship between the self and the other. Though Levinas elaborates paternity as the opening up to the experience of ethics and often refers to the other as a neighbor, it is only in his or her radical alterity that the ethical relation is engaged. The intimate scene of a lover's embrace, for example, is explicitly excluded by Levinas from the realm of ethics.

On the other hand, there is a growing body of work that seeks to reconcile Levinasian ethics with the question of intimacy.[2] This problem has been of particular concern to feminist ethicists seeking to move beyond the essentializing aspects of a feminine "ethos of care" without discounting the insight that women's private ethical experience has rarely figured into the ethical scenarios of philosophers (Levinas included). Hegel's reading of Antigone is a case in point here, as Luce Irigaray makes clear, for not only does Antigone serve Hegel as the example of women's lack of ethical consciousness but also, in both her commitment to family and her marginalization, for the incompatibility of family and ethics.[3]

Luce Irigaray and Tina Chanter (in her work based on both Irigaray and Levinas) explicitly critique Levinas for his refusal to consider intimacy as a potentially ethical relation and for his separation of eros from ethics.[4] They argue that the intimacy of the caress—whether between parent and child or between lovers—is indeed an ethical relation, one that serves to bring women to the center of ethics and to bring ethics into the personal sphere—a critique that we can also see nascent in Woolf's writing. Eros then becomes for Irigaray the bodily instantiation of a profound coming together that does not absorb the other: "touching can also place a limit on the reabsorption of the other in the same" (*Ethics* 204). The moment of the caress is the moment of recognition of one's being toward the other as Levinas would put it, but in a more bodily sense, and as such for Irigaray, in a manner cognizant of sexual difference: "Thus a new birth comes about, a new dawn for the beloved. And the lover. The openness of a face which had not yet been sculpted" (*Ethics* 189). Far from raising the disaster of incorporation or usurpation, the caress makes otherness intimate and procreative.

Of course, Levinas rather notoriously raises the question of procreation—or, in *Totality and Infinity*, of filiation or paternity—within his ethics. In the later sections of *Totality and Infinity*, Levinas employs the patriarchal coding of the lover as masculine and the beloved as feminine. This problematic relation with the feminine other is "resolved in paternity" without fully accounting for the participation of the feminine who is always other (*Totality* 271). More specifically, paternity and its converse, filiality, is, for Levinas here, the model for all love that liberates the I from itself by constituting it as also an other (278). The model is revised and extended in *Otherwise than Being*, where the image of the maternal emerges as its bodily supplement, a suffering for the other that is not conscious and thus not equivalent to the demand made on the self in paternity.[5] Thus it is clear that even in this later work Levinas continues to conceive of the paternal-filial continuum as the paradigm for the expansion of self that begins the opening out toward ethics and the only time when an intimate relation can give way to ethical understanding. Still as Vikki Bell puts it, Levinas's "interest in the question of sexual difference was troubling, minimal, and frequently deferred" (163). Further, his writing presumes a model of the feminine as a bodily other defined by the "pre-ontological" situation of maternity (*Otherwise* 78).

But in insisting that we take account of the principle of sexual difference already at the core of discursive systems, always lurking, for example, behind the attempt at the neutral, universal phrase "there is," Irigaray posits the possibility of its limit, of the encounter of subject and other in the embrace—an embrace that does not necessarily end in procreation, nor does it necessarily accede to the neutral universal. In other words, she makes possible an intimate ethics of the caress that avoids Levinas's patriarchal coding. The ethical embrace does not presume the active/passive heterosexual split and corresponding priority on the masculine that lies behind

Levinas's writings on eros, even in the much more subtle later writings, but can arise among women or among men. For Irigaray the
caress always carries within it an insistence on difference, which it
does not in Levinas.

Kelly Oliver approaches this problem from a slightly different
direction, asking the question "why can't the promise of fatherhood
be a promise to/of a daughter?" (196). If the premise for Levinas
is that paternity transforms the ethical subject by drawing him into
the experience of otherness in which he also recognizes himself and
thus into an understanding of the integral connection between his
uniqueness and his encounter with the other, then Oliver wonders,
why should not this experience be all the more poignant when the
father chooses (in Levinas's manner) a daughter? Oliver explains,
"Levinas suggests that paternity opens onto infinity because it is a
relationship with an absolute other in which the I survives. The I
survives because paternity is also a relationship with the same. The
father is his son and yet the son is a stranger to the father and the
paternal relationship makes him a stranger to himself. . . . Wouldn't
the daughter be a stranger child?" (213). In proposing that the
daughter's sexual difference might make the encounter in paternity
all the more significant, Oliver opens Levinasian ethics to another
way of seeing femininity.[6] At the same time, in order to arrive at this
schema she must rework Levinas significantly. For, as she puts it,
in Levinas's writings, "it seems to go without saying that the father
chooses a son rather than a daughter" (213).

Oliver also takes us beyond Levinas's thought by elaborating
a social subject at the core of "family values," thus opening up the
possibility of a realm of ethics within the social domain, which has
traditionally been the realm of women, and which so often figures
at the center of Woolf's work. Rather than accept either what she
terms the "virile subject"—that is, the self-contained punctual self
at the core of most conceptions of individual rights—or even the
Levinasian self, preengaged by the call of the other, Oliver proposes
that at the core of any ethics there exists a social subject that is
the product of love and is "neither opposed to nor identified with
the other" (232). This concept is distinct from Levinas's ethically
inclined self because it never presumes the shock of the absolutely
other as the core experience of being-together. Oliver's concept is
also distinct from Levinas's because it presumes a real role for bodies (both male and female) and bodily love, as well as intimacy, in
the creation of subjectivity. Finally, Oliver's social subjectivity also
pushes beyond the face-to-face of individual ethical encounters into
the realm of community: "If we are social, if our instincts themselves

are social, our bodies are social, then community is not at odds with subjectivity" (232).

In this manner Oliver's feminist philosophy also coincides with the theoretical writings of Jean-Luc Nancy, particularly on the question of community. Through the notion of "being-with" Nancy elaborates what he describes as "between us as first philosophy" (25), which might be seen as a sort of parallel to Levinas's "ethics as first philosophy." Rather than presuppose some sort of original social antagonism, or a responsibility to an other who remains outside the self, Nancy posits plurality as a primary condition of being, or "being singular plural." As he puts it, "'one' or 'it' is never other than 'we.' . . . Being is put into play among us" (27). For Nancy there is no question of a primary being who then responds to the call of an other or who enters into social or family life. Rather, the "essence of Being is only as co-essence" (30). The self coexists with those around it, a primordial being-with that Nancy calls community. The isolated or individual self is a self seen in exile from this community and from the original scene of intimacy. Thus "the co-existent—the other person . . . appears as that which is in itself infinitely withdrawn. It appears inaccessible to 'me' because it is withdrawn from the 'self' in general, and because it is as the self-outside-itself: it is the other in general" (79). Much as do Irigaray, Chanter, and Oliver, Nancy makes clear that intimacy lies at the core of being and is the original site of both ethics and politics. For all these writers, the kind of concerns that arise among women, family, neighbors, and intimates of all sorts— and that often form the primary relationships of Woolf's novels—are also, or even especially, the site of ethics.

Aesthetic Categories

At the same time, however, one can locate this problem of ethics and aesthetics in a different place—that is, in a different division—that which is often described as the conflict between the cognitive (or ontological) and the epistemological. For Kant, morality falls under the category of practical reason because it responds to the possibility of freedom. Kant makes clear that practical reason is nonetheless cognitive: it responds to the a priori concept of freedom. It is thus separate from the kinds of everyday apprehension of precepts that he says correspond to the principle of desire (to fulfill some object) and to cause and effect and thus do not provide us with universal laws (*Critique of Practical* 34). Ethics remains cognitive, while for Kant the question of aesthetics is closer to the technically practical, drawing as it does on feelings of pleasure. The apprehension of the beautiful, which Kant defines as "that which apart from concepts is represented as the object of a universal satisfaction," demands a separate process of reflective judgment, which rests upon the experience of the form of the object and a sensation of the pleasure it affords (*Critique of Judgment* 45).

Yet by the end of the discussion of aesthetics in his *Critique of Judgment*, Kant famously attempts to unite the domain of aesthetics and ethics by claiming that "the beautiful is the symbol of the morally good" (198). He argues for taste or judgment of aesthetic objects as analogous to morality because they "excite sensations which have something analogous to the consciousness of the state of mind brought about by moral judgments" (200). The transition from sensation to "taste" demonstrates the "imagination in its freedom" just as the movement from action to moral judgment demonstrates the "freedom of the will" and its harmony with itself (199). Aesthetic judgments seem to rest on the possibility that the imagination in its freedom will discover some sort of purposiveness even in the nonpurposeful—such as a mountain or a tulip—and thus again create a situation analogous to that accorded a teleological judgment. Yet, despite Kant's appreciation of the bodily sensations of aesthetic pleasure, which he describes in his discussion of the sublime, what is crucial here is the movement beyond sensory experience of the aesthetic object toward the reflective judgment of the aesthetic idea. Thus the possibility that the apprehension of the aesthetic will stand for or symbolize a corresponding moral judgment seems to require it being imagined as separate from our direct experience of it. The connections between ethics and aesthetics here then become predicated on the movement away from experience.

The question of the experience of the aesthetic object, however, becomes the crux of the problem in twentieth-century revisions of Kant especially within the Cambridge/Bloomsbury world that surrounded Woolf. If G. E. Moore announced the "refutation of idealism"[7] around the same time as he published his influential *Principia Ethica*, he began his career as a Kantian and his version of philosophical realism remains indebted to Kant.[8] Paul Levy, in his book on Moore and his Cambridge circle, refers to their language as "neo-Kantian argot" (quoted in McNeillie 10), and in his 1912 article "Kant and Post-Impressionism," Desmond MacCarthy makes clear that there are direct connections between the postimpressionist aesthetics of Clive Bell and Roger Fry and Kant (McNeillie 17). "Significant Form" as an aesthetic principle becomes in many ways synonymous with Kantian conceptions of disinterested beauty. The realist distinction lies not in the conception of the aesthetic object itself—like Kant they focus on form as the immediately apprehensible aspect of aesthetic beauty—but in the process and source of aesthetic judgment. Thus if Kant claims that the pleasure of the form of an object is only produced by the process of reflection and judgment (which is separate from sensation; *Critique of Judgment* 27), the realists argue that the form of a perceived object directly ignites aesthetic emotions. Further, Moore's key claim in the *Principia Ethica* is that what is good cannot be broken down into concepts or properties but is good in and of itself, thus implying that it can be perceived directly through experience of the world. That he uses the experience of color as an example of an unanalyzable concept, like the good, not only brings the aesthetic closer to the empirical but also, as with Kant, ultimately back toward the realm of ethics.[9]

Roger Fry's great theoretical statement "An Essay in Aesthetics" explicitly rejects this connection for postimpressionism. His influential theory is expressionist, defining the graphic arts as nonrepresentational and beyond moral action as well as beyond communication: "Art, then is an expression and a stimulus of this imaginative life, which is separated from actual life by the absence of responsive action. Now this responsive action implies in actual life moral responsibility. In art we have no such moral responsibility—it presents a life freed from the binding necessities of our actual existence" (15). Further, beauty of the kind seen in plastic art, for Fry, is "supersensual, and is concerned with the appropriateness and intensity of the emotions aroused" (22). Thus Fry at once moves beyond *l'art pour l'art* and rejects Ruskinian moralism while still elaborating a formalist aesthetic. The experience of the artwork is the first step toward the arousal of emotion by the formal aspects of its design (and especially its "unity," which allows us to contemplate it as a whole), which, according to Fry, play "upon what one may call the overtones of some of our primary physical needs" (24). Unity, rhythm, mass, space, light and shade, and finally color in the work, all generate imaginative reactions that directly arouse emotions.

I dwell here on Fry's aesthetics because they are so often evoked (along with Clive Bell's less complex concept of "significant form") as the basis for Bloomsbury aesthetics in general and as a major influence on Woolf. As Ann Banfield puts it, "Woolf's aesthetic was not then articulated in theoretical isolation but in Apostolic Bloomsbury, in which Fry's position was so pivotal that Woolf 'wish[ed]' she 'dedicated' *To the Lighthouse* to Fry, recognizing his aesthetic guidance, and came to write a biography of Fry" (247). Fry's aesthetics are also significant in that they demonstrate the degree to which the specific terms of Kantian analysis of aesthetics were still in play in the early years of the twentieth century. This connection can be clearly seen in the relative disdain for color common to both.[10] In paragraph 14 of the *Critique of Judgment* Kant makes clear that aesthetic judgments can be divided into two categories, the empirical and the pure, where beauty as a judgment pertains only to the pure. Empirical satisfactions of the first sort produce only what Kant calls "charm." But what is significant is that "mere color" in either a natural object or a crafted one is considered to produce only charm while form corresponds with the judgment of beauty. The same bias against color appears in Bell's and Fry's writing. The list Fry provides in the "Essay in Aesthetics" concludes only somewhat begrudgingly with color: "colour is the only one of our elements which is not of critical or universal importance to life, and its emotional effect is neither so deep nor so clearly determined as the others" (24). Based in part on a critique of the use of color by the impressionists, Fry privileges the seemingly more complex aspects of form over color. In addition, Fry seems to agree with Kant that plastic art is better at representing aesthetics than is poetry: "The graphic arts arouse emotions in us by playing upon what one may call the overtones of some of our primary physical needs. They have, indeed, this great advantage over poetry, that they can appeal more directly and immediately to the emotional accompaniments of our bare physical existence" (25).[11]

But what does this mean for the questions of ethics and aesthetics in Woolf? If we follow the argument that she was almost completely indebted for her notions of art to Fry, who was her dear friend and an object of her deep admiration, then there seems to be little room for any deep association between aesthetics and ethics or, as per the Kantian tradition, between color, one of the most prominent aesthetic features of her work, and aesthetic significance. Further, the question of writing as a communicative art, or of action as a possible outcome of its work in the world, becomes nearly impossible. On the other hand, Woolf commented in a 1940 letter that her "own point of view [was] entirely different from his" (*Letters* 6: 419). Jane Goldman has also argued persuasively that Fry's influence on Woolf's aesthetics must be seen as more limited. Rather, Goldman argues that Woolf's connection to postimpressionism was more directly through her sister Vanessa Bell, who stands in her own right as an aesthetic thinker, experimenter, and colorist (Goldman 116), and to whom Woolf remarked that her pictures had "changed her view upon aesthetics" (*Letters* 2: 257).[12] Further, Goldman argues that "Vanessa Bell's development as a colourist, and Woolf's response to Post-Impressionism, including, in particular, her understanding of her sister's work, may be at odds with the theories of Fry and Clive Bell" (130). For Goldman, the development of Fry's ideas about aesthetics and their relationship to the world becomes more conservative in the period between the first Post-Impressionist Exhibition in 1910 and the second exhibition in 1912, while Vanessa Bell's and Virginia Woolf's ideas do not. Whatever the progression of Fry's thought, Goldman makes a persuasive claim about the independence of Woolf's own sense of aesthetics and her connection, through her sister, to color as an attribute equal to structural form.

Perhaps even more important, Goldman argues for the relevance of another colorist tradition—that of the women's suffrage movement in Great Britain. Thus the distinction between form and color as aesthetic principles maps onto a distinction between the traditionally male domain of the art gallery and the feminine (and feminist) development of a less purely formal aesthetics at play in the world outside it. Goldman's discussion of the use of color in feminist political movements in Britain makes the case for an alternative tradition, one which we might see at work in the use of purples and greens in Woolf's novels. For our purposes here, however, most salient is the acceptance within those alternate spheres of the possibility of signification, communication, and political or moral implications in postimpressionist art. If Woolf finally prefers writing to painting as an expressive medium, Goldman implies, it is in part because writing is better at bringing those implications to the fore. What the dominance of the concept of "significant form" in the discussion of Bloomsbury aesthetics has done is to obscure the presence of a feminist mode of postimpressionism where color and form are less divorced from experience and where an aesthetics based on this experience may ultimately reconverge with ethics.

The renewed potential for bringing together ethics and epistemology for the problem of aesthetics is crucial for the study of Woolf because so much of her writing takes up the question of ethical reality. As Mark Hussey puts it, "Virginia Woolf's art tells us . . . about our *experience* of the world" (xiii). Banfield's recent work on Woolf and epistemology argues convincingly for the importance of the questions of "reality" in the novels. Andrew's description of Mr. Ramsay's work in *To the Lighthouse*—"think of the kitchen table . . . when you're not there"—begins Lily's ruminations on the table, which land it upside down in her thoughts, lodged in a pear tree (23). In Banfield's view, the table brings together the philosopher and the artist, "the impersonal truth it reveals imparts its austerity to the gazer. . . . [I]t imposes on the observer a discipline that lies in its very unobservability" (50–51). But as Martha Nussbaum observes in her essay on the novel, *To the Lighthouse* is about problems that are "both epistemological and moral" (742). The kitchen table of importance here is neither Mr. Ramsay's unobservable one nor Lily's surrealist vision of a table upside down in a tree. The tables in this novel are made real in being populated and made moral in forcing human connection and obligation into that reality.

To a great degree Woolf's novels revolve around the ways that writing can be the bridge between these realms, bringing the epistemological and moral into conversation with each other, using aesthetics to make an ethical realm—or a fold—between the potentially universal and the personal or to move us back into the Levinasian domain, between the face of the other as stranger and the call of the ethics of intimacy. Woolf offers us a means into the debate that resists the choice between an ontological and a strictly epistemological ethics or one in which ethics and aesthetics carry only an oblique relationship to each other.[13]

Ethical Folds

I want to turn here to Mieke Bal's use of the (Deleuzian) term "fold" as the means of approaching feminist ethics and to the value of the figure of the fold in reading this knot of ethics and aesthetics in Woolf. Bal claims that the figure of the fold can be not only "a powerful tool for overcoming the dichotomy between epistemology and ontology" (324), but, because it highlights questions of representation, the fold can be a means of bringing together subject and object or, as I will claim, subject and subject. As Bal puts it, "the fold stands for a different relation between subject and object, one which bypasses the problem of representation's ambiguity" (327). She speaks of a literal fold as she analyzes the drapery in a Caravaggio painting, but also, following Gilles Deleuze, uses the fold to mean a figurative enfolding of material, whether a gathering of associated ideas or expectations—a folding back of time upon itself—or a bend in the surface of experience that can bring objects into immediate relationship with subjects and subjects into contact with others. "Through the fold," Bal explains, "subject and object become codependent, folded into one another, and this puts the subject at risk" (333). For Bal this putting in risk of the subject obligates us to focus our attention on point of view, whether in a painting by Caravaggio, a sculpture by Louise Bourgeoise (her examples), or, to expand on Bal, a modernist novel by Virginia Woolf. Further, if the putting in risk of the subject that develops from the folding of subject over object or of actions across time makes "the divide between ontology and epistemology untenable" (333), then it also opens it up to a radically new ethical encounter.

True, Deleuze's notion of the fold purports to treat the matter of Gottfried Leibniz and the baroque and not necessarily to offer us a transportable principle of philosophical inquiry. More so than much of his other writing, Deleuze is explicit here about his subject matter and leads us in a very precise and specific analysis of Leibniz's writings, down to mathematical equations and diagrams demonstrating the relationship, for example, between monads and the world or between the virtual and possible world. On the other hand, Deleuze considers Leibniz to be in conversation with the twentieth-century thought of Edmund Husserl and others, making clear that he understands Leibniz's concept of the monad as still suggestive and potentially operative.

In Leibniz's thought, the community of monads and its relationship to bodily possessions, which are always in flux, coming and going, mine and then someone else's, requires what Deleuze calls an "inter-individual" way of being (115). This inter-individuality—or the fabric that forms the temporary and convoluted boundary between bodies even as it creates new ways of perceiving the body's relationship to the world—Deleuze calls "the fold." The fold is in part the monad's turning back on itself and its bodily possessions or the folding between the "levels" separating the soul and the body, as well as between "'species' of monads in the sense of souls." The fold "links the soul that possesses a body to other souls that body possesses" (Deleuze 120). In the baroque it is also the movement of the finite body toward the infinite, made concrete by the representation in baroque painting and sculpture of voluminous folds of material extending past the vanishing point. Consider Bernini (figure 15) whose marble "seizes and bears to infinity folds that cannot be explained by the body," Deleuze suggests (122). Consider Caravaggio (figure 16), whose draped curtains "dictate a cyclical look without outcome," Bal adds (330).

Consider *Orlando*. Think for a minute about one of the pictures of Orlando—"Orlando on her return to England" (figure 17)—draped not only in beads but also in actual drapery (a dress we are meant to presume). Here we see the beads loop around and then disappear, leading our eyes not only off the page but downward toward the edge of Orlando's clothing. Certainly these folds of clothing and loops of beads cannot be fully explained by her body nor contained by the frame of the picture. This is, then, a fold that verges on the baroque, working to take our eye beyond the frame of the possible and toward the infinite cycles "without outcome" that the long history of Orlando's life suggests. It is also a provocative picture in this sense, one that engages with the desires of its viewers to follow those beads out into infinity or inwards toward an engagement with their wearer. We do not read them as a series of atoms strung on a string, the primary building blocks of the perceived world as the early-twentieth-century

Figure 15.
Head of St. Theresa, detail from *Ecstasy of St. Theresa* by Gian Lorenzo
Bernini (1598–1680). Cornaro Chapel, S. Maria della Vittoria, Rome, Italy.
Photo: Alinari / Art Resource, NY

realists described them. The drapery in this picture contributes to
the effect as its folds deepen at the edges; the convoluted surfaces
draw our eyes into their shadows and thus again shatter the surface
of the image, insisting that we enter into connection with this sitter
and her folds. These then are folds like those that Bal analyzes in
a painting by Caravaggio—folds that in our efforts to comprehend
them work to incorporate in the everyday a movement toward the
infinite and to bridge the subject/object rift. As Bal puts it, "through
the fold, subjectivity and the object become co-dependent, folded
into one another" (333).
        Further, we must consider that what we are looking at is "Orlando

Figure 16.
Death of the Virgin, 1605, by Michelango Merisi da Caravaggio (1573–1610)
Louvre, Paris, France. Photo: Erich Lessing/Art Resource.

on her return to England"—in other words Orlando as woman. That the text enfolds us by means of this image even as it broaches the question of Orlando's subjectivity as woman further dismantles our distance from the text, no matter who we are, for the key question here is that of Orlando's woman/manliness—or manly womanness. The page facing the photo, for example, reads, "she was censuring both sexes equally, as if she belonged to neither; and indeed for the time being she seemed to vacillate; she was a man; she was a woman; she knew the secrets, shared the weaknesses of each" (158). Thus the ethical dimension emerges not only in the text proper, the word "censuring" here implying an ethical judgment of each sex, but also in our connection to Orlando as both man and woman, which insists that we not succumb to any of the ethical failings that this passage names. If, by way of the folds in this image, we are brought into an

Figure 17.
"Orlando on her return to England," from *Orlando,* by Virginia Woolf. Photographer unknown. Used by permission of the Hogarth Press and the Random House Group Limited.

intimate encounter with the multisexed being that is Orlando, then we are also forced to acknowledge the demands that this being-together makes upon us. We are placed into an ethical encounter that expands the boundaries of our selves beyond their conventional limits at the same time as it asks us to acknowledge the ethical constraints on both thought and conduct made by that encounter. In other words, the folds of this image bring us face to face, as Levinas might put it, with the demands of otherness, and because this otherness itself is beyond the conventional bounds of sexed beings, we are also here forced to "face" its ethical challenge to our response to sexual difference.

In this way, in this passage of *Orlando*, ontology, in the form of universalizable ethics, and epistemology seem to meet. Orlando censures as though from a priori values, according to which, such behavior as denying "a woman teaching lest she may laugh at you" or being the "slave to the frailest chit in petticoats, and yet to go about as if you were the lords of creation" is seen as immediately and obviously wrong (158). But on the other hand, this censoriousness shifts according to experience and especially here according to gendered experience. The awareness of this "wrong" only emerges in Orlando as woman; the universalizable character of these values becomes clear only when experience makes gendered behavior into an ethical concern.

Further, this ethical dilemma moves beyond the literal level of the text, where moral maxims may be presented as self-evident, to the domain of the relationship between the reader and Orlando, the folding of subject and subject within the textual encounter. Here, ethical feeling is not derived from a universalized maxim as in the realm of morals but rather emerges as a situated response of the imagination, one which looks more like aesthetic judgment. If aesthetic judgment may be seen as a reflective pleasure that begins from sensory experience but also requires a move beyond it to the realm of imagination, then this encounter between reader and Orlando operates in a similar manner. We may take pleasure in our apprehension of Orlando when she is transformed into a woman and becomes able to judge as a woman/man, but it is in our imaginative leap toward that subject position and its possibilities that we understand the ethical demands placed upon us by this moment in the text. The aesthetic demands of this image and of the surrounding text insist on an imaginative leap that is, from its outset, an ethical one.

But the notion of the fold need not remain tied to a portrait appearing as an aesthetic object in the text, ready for our leap into it. There are many other textual images in Woolf's work that approximate the visual fold in Orlando's drapery and make the same ethical/aesthetic demands. In the Window section of *To the Lighthouse*, to take one example among many, we encounter the image of the "crumpled glove" that prompts Lily to ruminate on the question of Mrs. Ramsay's being: "What was the spirit in her, the essential thing, by which, had you found a crumpled glove in the corner of a sofa, you would have known it, from its twisted finger, hers indis-putably?" (49). What follows is a passage of Lily's twisting thoughts about Mrs. Ramsay, ending with her refusal of the moral injunction to marry—"gathering her desperate courage, she would urge her own exemption from the universal law" (50). Thereupon the image of the glove returns: "[Lily] had recovered her sense of her now—this was the glove's twisted finger." And we begin the familiar passage where Lily wonders about the extent of her connection to Mrs. Ramsay: "Could loving . . . make her and Mrs. Ramsay one?" (51). The twisting of the glove throughout this passage marks not only the particular-ity of a singular being—we could know Mrs. Ramsay by her glove's twisted finger—but also the experience of otherness tinged with the desire for intimacy made clear here by Lily's narrating perspective. The twisted fabric conflates terms even as it connects subject (Mrs. Ramsay) and object (the glove) or folds subject (Mrs. Ramsay) onto subject (Lily) onto subject (reader). The twisted glove exists as an object of apprehension for us and for Lily, which makes possible our engagement with the ontological question of singular being as well as with the profound intimacy, seen between Lily and Mrs. Ramsay, that, I have argued, can be the first move toward ethics.

This passage in *To the Lighthouse* thus demands to be read against Levinas's ethics, which would reject the possibility that Lily's embrace of Mrs. Ramsay gives rise to an ethical response to the call of the other—or that the relationship here might be an example of a profoundly ethical experience between intimate subjects. What we understand is that Lily's recognition of Mrs. Ramsay's alterity emerges directly out of Lily's intimacy with, and desire to love, Mrs. Ramsay. This love comes close to what Chanter describes as Irigaray's "insis-tence [on] the alterity of eros" (Chanter, *Ethics* 218). Further, this love demonstrates the demand of being-toward-the-other that arises out of the intimacy of this relationship, one which enters the novel as Lily's constant questioning of her own obligation to Mrs. Ramsay. When Levinas makes clear that being-otherwise inheres in the "say-ing"—the ongoing process of being and articulation—he invokes the kind of shifting, adjusting, and rearticulating that take place in Lily's relationship to Mrs. Ramsay.[14] This intimacy appears through a shift-ing narrative perspective, which works to unsettle any tendency of the text to resolve into a static "said."

Not incidentally, the unsettling tendency also appears in Woolf's use of color in the novel. If for Levinas the aesthetic work of art is problematic in its exhibition of pure essence in the beautiful object or phrase, it is also the place where that essence "recommence[s] being," turning back upon itself in a way that transforms it from a substantive to a verb. Color is crucial in painting, as "red reddens and green greens, forms are produced as contours and vacate with their vacuity as forms." Thus, as he puts it, "the palette of colors, the gamut of sounds, the system of vocables and the meandering of forms are realized as a pure *how*" in which being resounds (*Otherwise* 40).

As many have pointed out, Lily Briscoe is a colorist painter. The famous description of her painting in the first section of the novel shows her as committed to the principle of color in a way that resists the fashion, here presented as masculinist, of black and white: "She would not have considered it honest to tamper with the bright violet and the staring white, since she saw them like that, fashionable though it was since Mr. Paunceforte's visit, to see everything pale. . . . Then beneath the color there was the shape" (18). The shadow of Mrs. Ramsay and James becomes, in Lily's work, a small purple triangle, set off against the white open space and violet of the flowers. That triangle almost vibrates with being through the novel, encapsulating the intensity of Mrs. Ramsay's existence as well as the problem posed by it: "How to connect this mass on the right hand with that on the left" (53). Color then is set to do the work of "being-toward"—deepening—even blurring as in Lily's final version ("it was blurred . . . it was done" [209]) and becoming the impetus for Lily's renewed connection to Mrs. Ramsay in the "Lighthouse" section.

The intervening pages of the "Time Passes" section make even more clear the active force of colorism and the vibrant resonance of imagery in the novel as a whole. We are used to seeing this section as an inscription of time itself, its onward rush of sentences, broken up only occasionally by those declarative statements of human events, showing us the broader forces and rhythms of the natural world. Yet this section is also the place where, as Levinas would put it, the "green greens." That is, the profusion of colors and images—the rusted saucepan, "tortoise-shell butterflies" (137), "black ravens," "pale mushrooms" (140), and of course, "green suffused through leaves" (141), to name only a few—bring the verbal quality of language to the fore. Thus the copula created by this section of the novel is also a copula in another sense, an inscription of the verbal quality of narrative language and its constant push beyond singularity. The folding of the novel at this point, where the "Lighthouse" section presses on top of the "Window," where Lily can be seen to be painting almost on top of her previous canvas, and the trip to the lighthouse beckons again, is thus a folding of ethical significance.

The fold between incarnations of Lily's painting also brings the question of aesthetics and the lived experience that surrounds it into contact with the more conventionally moral realm of Lily's understanding. "The question of relation" is of course what she is trying to paint (148); the remembered pattern in the cloth makes the fold in time that allows Lily to understand not only her aesthetic power but the ethical lesson of benevolence, learned from Mrs. Ramsay as a personal not a public virtue. As Lily puts it in the Lighthouse section, after having resumed her painting and then having been interrupted by Mr. Ramsay, "she would give him [Mr. Ramsay] what she could" (152). This is an ethical statement of a nonuniversalized sort. It is not a maxim Lily will extend to her behavior with all others, or one that might be based in any abstracted position-blind sense of justice. Nonetheless, I argue that it is a viable ethical position—that she ought to give Mr. Ramsay what she could whether he deserved it or not—but it is a position that is made viable by Lily's understanding of her obligation to Mrs. Ramsay, which itself is brought into being by the folds of the text, the memory of tablecloth folded upon cloth, clean canvas folded onto the place where original canvas had been.

But let's return to the twisted glove, as it appears and reappears throughout the passage with which we began. This moment is complex not only in its inscription of the potentially ethical connection between these two women but also as the eruption of Lily's resistance to the universal law of gender and to Mrs. Ramsay's representation of it in marriage. Here we see the series of attributes assigned to Mrs. Ramsay through the vehicle of her glove culminate in the injunction to marry and Lily's rejection of it: "All this [Mrs. Ramsay] would adroitly shape, she would maliciously twist . . . half turn back . . . insist that she must, Minta must, they all must marry" (49). Lily's feeble remonstrance is inconsequential to Mrs. Ramsay but nonetheless provokes her to disrupt the universal claim: "she would urge her own exemption from the universal law; plead for it; she liked to be alone; she liked to be herself; she was not made for that" (50). It can be argued that this resistance is finally what propels Lily's triumph in "The Lighthouse" section of the novel, for her painting reemerges out of her memory of Charles Tansley's comment that women "can't paint can't write" (159) and out of her rumination on Mrs. Ramsay's injunction about marriage: "For a moment Lily, standing there . . . triumphed over Mrs. Ramsay . . . how she stood here painting, had never married. . . . Mrs. Ramsay had planned it. Perhaps, had she lived, would have compelled it" (175). In this sense the twist of the glove, like the fold in Orlando's fabric, brings us to the crux of the relationship between gender, ethics, and aesthetics, asking us again to link our notions of ontology and ethics to reflective judgments of our specific experiences of the world.

Let's turn quickly to another example, one where the fold is not in the form of draped fabric as in *Orlando* or in the form of a crumpled glove as in *To the Lighthouse* but rather, in *Mrs. Dalloway*, appears in the form of window curtains, folded back to allow us to see inside the house across the street. Here the aesthetic dimension of the fold is less as a convoluted surface that invites us to follow it into perpetuity, the way that Bal reads Caravaggio's folds, but more like the fold that Deleuze describes in Leibniz and Bernini, a membrane that exists between bodies, that subsumes collections of monads but is also flexible, fluctuating and "interindividual" (115). This kind of a fold brings relationship into play as a question of movement through the membrane or the opening and closing of the curtain. In *Mrs. Dalloway* we see Clarissa's neighbor, "the old lady opposite," glimpsed only fleetingly through the parted curtains at the window, not in the deep relationship of Lily and Mrs. Ramsay. When this old lady first appears in the novel she stands in Clarissa's mind for resistance to the dogmas of "love and religion" and for a certain laissez-faire: "Did she not wish everybody to be merely themselves? And she watched out of the window the old lady opposite climbing upstairs. Let her climb upstairs if she wanted to; let her stop; then let her, as Clarissa had often seen her, gain her bedroom, part her curtains and disappear into the background" (126). The ethical obligation here in the face of this neighbor (neither an intimate nor a stranger) is to respond directly while resisting the temptation to incorporate her into some normative realm. The possibility is, however, that Clarissa will complacently consider this modest engagement through the curtain enough and never acknowledge the further obligation that this face might imply. By turning away from the mutual connection implied by the membrane and from the obligation imposed by being-with, she would not then attain ethical understanding.

However, when the neighbor next appears, through another one of Woolf's temporal folds in the text, it is at the pivotal moment when Clarissa has been overwhelmed by the news of Septimus's death, which she feels to be her own disgrace (185). This is the moment of ethical awareness in the novel—a moment of response to an other, but also a moment when Woolf's emphasis on the private realm makes clear its constant implications for public morality. Septimus's shell shock is everyone's shell shock; his war death engages us all in the confrontation with death and our responsibility for it. The vision of the old lady is thus transformed: no longer does Clarissa rest content simply to watch and let be, but here she glances out feeling in the view of the night sky "something of her own in it" and is met with the sight of the old woman also there looking out at the sky and straight back at Clarissa (185). "Could she see her?" Clarissa wonders, thus for the first time extending to the woman across the street an agency of her own and a demand to be recognized as a subject with a call for more than laissez-faire. The possibility that she too might find "something of her own" in the sky or in the view from the window back at Clarissa, which might then engage them in a relationship of mutuality, becomes real. That it is this sight which enables Clarissa to make sense of the importance of the death of Septimus and to return to the world of her party further underscores it as a moment of ethical recognition.

Thus if we shift our attention from the often-celebrated final moment of Mrs. Dalloway's party back to the one that slightly pre-cedes it, we see a more direct inscription of ethical obligation and its aesthetics than is usually discussed in this novel. What in *To the Lighthouse* was seen as primarily a moment where intimate ethics confronted the social and moral injunction to marry, here emerges as a matter not only of being-otherwise, but also of the public good. War and its repercussions, class division and the difficulty it poses to Septimus and Rezia, the status of women and its significance for the old lady in the room opposite, for Clarissa, and for the other women in the novel—all enter this moment through the curtain's folds. The parted curtain reveals not only the personal face of Mrs. Dalloway's neighbor, calling forth in Clarissa her recognition of the intersubjectiv-ity of being, but also, and importantly, the public face of social life, marking even these very private moments as politically significant.

We thus return to the question of ethics and its connection to aesthetics and politics. One might argue that the lesson *Mrs. Dalloway* presents us with here is much like Nancy's claim that being-with-the-others is inseparable from being. Thus, our obligation toward subjectivity, or toward an other, always takes part in our obligation toward our community—they are folded into each other. The question of ethics, or of being-otherwise, verges toward the question of politics and cannot be held apart from the demands of public discourse on, for example, war or women's rights. On the other hand, Woolf's work begins with the question of intimacy, of subject to subject relation-ships, which form the basis for ethical understanding. In her work it is clear that intimate relationships open out toward, rather than preclude, response to the other. Further, these relationships are, in Woolf's work, not only mediated by, but occur within, the process of the aesthetic reflection rather than within the realm of the a priori. The connections among ethics/politics/aesthetics cannot be severed.

Rarely pressed to make direct statements about ethics, which she usually considered to be the official domain of her father's work and far too abstract for her own writings, Woolf believed one must "leave the ivory tower of ethics" (*Letters* 6: 414). This is precisely what she accomplishes here in *Mrs. Dalloway* and to a different extent in *Orlando* and *To the Lighthouse.* The ethics of Woolf's writings rest in the folds between ontology and epistemology, between an intimate ethics of eros and a recognition of the public responsibility to respond not only to the face of the singular other but also to the situation of community. What Woolf offers us is an answer to Cornell's call for an articulation of the interconnection of aesthetics, ethics, and politics. Her work points out a way to understand the folds within modernist texts as potentially ethical, bringing the claims of relationship, or the obligation toward being-otherwise into the realm of the aesthetic.

Notes

1. The "fold" is a concept borrowed from Deleuze, but the way in which I use it in this paper is inspired by Mieke Bal's "Enfolding Feminism." The concept also derives from the work of Maurice Merleau-Ponty, especially his notion of the chiasmus (see *The Visible and Invisible*). I am indebted to Laura Doyle for pointing out this link.

2. See for example the special issue of *Feminist Theory* on ethics, edited by Linda Hogan and Sasha Roseneil (vol. 2, no. 2), which is dominated by this question.

3. See Chanter's excellent discussion of Hegel and Irigaray's rereading of Hegel (*Ethics* 89–90).

4. See Irigaray's *An Ethics of Sexual Difference* and *Sexes and Genealogies*; Chanter's own book, *Ethics of Eros*, as well as her edited collection, *Feminist Interpretations of Emmanuel Levinas*.

5. In *Otherwise than Being*, Levinas writes, "In maternity what signifies is a responsibility for others," and it is "one body suffering for another" (75, 79).

6. Oliver's reworking of Levinas has implications for reconceptualizing paternity as well. See the notion of embodied paternity in her chapter "Paternal Eros."

7. This is the title of an essay Moore wrote in 1903.

8. For a systematic treatment of philosophical realism and its connection to postimpressionism and to Woolf, see Banfield. For the connection of Woolf to the continental philosophical tradition see Hussey.

9. See Moore. Although Banfield argues quite persuasively that Russell was more influential than Moore in British postimpressionist aesthetics and in Woolf's work, Moore's *Principia Ethica* remains the only text of its kind that is specifically alluded to in Woolf's work. I am indebted to McNeillie and to Banfield in my understanding of Bloomsbury aesthetics.

10. I am indebted to Jane Goldman for pointing out the issue of color.

11. Kant, though, prefers natural beauty to any crafted object.

12. For a more extensive account of the connection between the work of Vanessa Bell and Virginia Woolf, see Gillespie.

13. Note the vexing problem of the aesthetic, and especially of writing, in Levinas's work, which appears initially as "the said," which is suspect, while "the saying" is privileged.

14. The question of the distinction between the saying and the said is a fraught one in Levinas's writings. While in his earlier writing Levinas seems to denigrate poetry and verbal art as a reduction of an active process into a substantive "said," in his later work he recognizes a deeper connection between the two modes of language: "Through art essence and temporality begin to resound with poetry and song. And the search for new forms, from which all art lives, keep awake everywhere the verbs that are on the verge of lapsing into substantives . . . poetry is productive of song, of resonance and sonority, which are the verbalness of verbs or essence" (*Otherwise* 40).

Works Cited

Bal, Mieke. "Enfolding Feminism." Bronfen and Kavka 321–52.
Banfield, Ann. *The Phantom Table: Woolf, Fry, Russell and the Epistemology of Modernism*. Cambridge: Cambridge UP, 2000.
Bell, Clive. *Art*. London: Chatto, 1914.
Bell, Vikki. "On Ethics and Feminism: Reflecting on Levinas' Ethics of Non-(in)difference." *Feminist Theory* 2 (2001): 159–71.
Bronfen, Elisabeth, and Misha Kavka, eds. *Feminist Consequences: Theory for the New Century*. New York: Columbia UP, 2001.
Chanter, Tina. *Ethics of Eros: Irigaray's Rewriting of the Philosophers*. New York: Routledge, 1995.
———, ed. *Feminist Interpretations of Emmanuel Levinas*. University Park: Pennsylvania State UP, 2001.
Cornell, Drucilla. "Return to the Future: An Interview with Drucilla Cornell." With Elisabeth Bronfen and Misha Kavka. Bronfen and Kavka 435–54.
Deleuze, Gilles. *The Fold: Leibniz and the Baroque.* Trans. Peter Conley. Minneapolis: U of Minnesota P, 1993.
Fry, Roger. "An Essay in Aesthetics." *Vision and Design*. Ed. J. B. Bullen. New York: Oxford UP, 1990. 12–27.
Gillespie, Diane. *The Sisters' Arts: The Writing and Painting of Virginia Woolf and Vanessa Bell*. Syracuse: Syracuse UP, 1988.
Goldman, Jane. *The Feminist Aesthetics of Virginia Woolf*. Cambridge: Cambridge UP, 1998.
Hogan, Linda, and Sasha Roseneil, eds. *Gendering Ethics/The Ethics of Gender*. Spec. issue of *Feminist Theory* 2.2 (2001): 147–244.
Hussey, Mark. *The Singing of the Real World: The Philosophy of Virginia Woolf's Fiction*. Columbus: Ohio State UP, 1986.

Irigaray, Luce. *An Ethics of Sexual Difference*. Trans. Carolyn Burke and Gillian C. Gill. Ithaca: Cornell UP, 1984

——. *Sexes and Genealogies*. Trans. Gillian C. Gill. New York: Columbia UP, 1993.

Kant, Immanuel. *The Critique of Judgment*. Trans. J. H. Bernard. New York: Hafner, 1951.

——. *Critique of Practical Reason*. Trans. T. K. Abbott. Amherst: Prometheus, 1996.

Levinas, Emmanuel. *Otherwise than Being, or, Beyond Essence*. Trans. Alphonso Lingis. Dordrecht, the Netherlands: Kluwer, 1991.

——. *Totality and Infinity*. Trans. Alphonso Lingis. Pittsburgh: Duquesne UP, 1969.

McNeillie, Andrew. "Bloomsbury." *The Cambridge Companion to Virginia Woolf*. Ed. Sue Roe and Susan Sellers. Cambridge: Cambridge UP, 2000. 1–28.

Merleau-Ponty, Maurice. *The Visible and Invisible*. Ed. Claude Lefort. Trans. Alphonso Lingis. Evanston: Northwestern UP, 1968.

Moore, G. E. *Principia Ethica*. Cambridge: Cambridge UP, 1903.

Nancy, Jean-Luc. *Being Singular Plural.* Trans. Robert D. Richardson and Anne E. O'Byrne. Palo Alto: Stanford UP, 2000.

Nussbaum, Martha. "The Window: Knowledge of Other Minds in Virginia Woolf's *To the Lighthouse*." *NLH* 26 (1995): 731–53.

Oliver, Kelly. *Family Values*. New York: Routledge, 1997.

Woolf, Virginia. *The Letters of Virginia Woolf*. Ed. Nigel Nicolson and Joanne Trautmann. 6 vols. New York: Harcourt, 1975–80.

——. *Mrs. Dalloway.* 1925. New York: Harcourt, 1981.

——. *Orlando.* 1928. New York: Harcourt, 1956.

——. *To the Lighthouse.* 1927. New York: Harcourt, 1955.

"ROBBED OF MEANING"

THE WORK AT THE CENTER OF

TO THE LIGHTHOUSE

Mary Lou Emery

I

Critiques of "Western feminism" have demonstrated convincingly that much of feminist discourse constructs its subject through processes of exclusion (see, for example, Minnie Bruce Pratt, Chandra T. Mohanty, Biddy Martin and Chandra T. Mohanty, and Gayatri C. Spivak's "Texts" and "Foreword"). A passage from Virginia Woolf's well-known essay *A Room of One's Own* exemplifies the dynamic: "It is one of the great advantages of being a woman that one can pass even a very fine negress without wishing to make an Englishwoman of her" (52). The sentence constitutes its subject— "woman" and "one"—as exclusively English and white. It excludes black women from the category "woman" and presumes to judge them as "very fine" in the same breath that it criticizes masculine imperialist habits of thought.

Woolf's sentence demonstrates the deconstructive dictum that, in opposing a system of power, "one" nevertheless becomes complicit in the system through the structures of language that oppose, exclude, and appropriate. The sentence also, however, enacts the dialogism Mikhail Bakhtin and Bakhtinian critics claim is inherent in language.[1] It swings between an assumption of one colonialist discourse, to which it replies, and another assumption—"high feminist" and also colonialist—to which it anticipates response.[2] The assumption

Originally published in *Modern Fiction Studies*, Spring 1992.

to which Woolf's sentence responds opposes the English "civilized" subject to the colonized Other and desires simultaneously to claim the Other for England. To that discourse, this sentence replies ironically and critically by inserting the difference of gender in the construction of the English subject. It does so by differentiating between the desires (and their absence) of English male and English female subjects on the occasion of passing an already colonized Other. Thus it lends subjectivity to Englishwomen, who now may have desires of their own different from those of Englishmen, and it criticizes the expropriating actions of male-governed colonialism. But it also repeats the colonialist construction of womanhood as an identity created in the positioning of a "negress" who can be gazed upon and judged by an "Englishwoman." To this second assumption—of womanhood as something characterizing the "one" of the speaker in contrast to the "negress" under the speaker's gaze—the sentence's irony anticipates critical reply. Particularly in the suggestion that something called an "Englishwoman" can be wished for and made by Englishmen resides an invitation to critical response, to the kind of critique that stresses the making of the "free," "civilized," female subject through colonialist discourses.

If we are concerned to criticize and transform the colonialist legacies within "Western feminism," analysis that takes into account the discourses to which a feminist text responds and the ways in which it anticipates reply should help us to do so. If we can identify ideological turning points within especially influential writings by feminist authors in the English canon, for example, we may be able to reflect upon the turnings available to contemporary feminist writers and critics. The canonized status of *To the Lighthouse* as a classic in modernist narrative and the authorizing position of Virginia Woolf in much of contemporary feminist thought make this novel a particularly significant case study. Read dialogically, *To the Lighthouse* sets into motion a critique of English colonialist patriarchy that simultaneously repeats colonialist assumptions about "Englishwomen." It also—by both including and suppressing them—represents the "mumblings" of a counter-discourse.[3]

II

A modernist female *Künstlerroman*, *To the Lighthouse* portrays an unmarried woman who paints and whose single unifying brushstroke at the novel's end announces her long-awaited achievement of artistic vision. Lily Briscoe's "line there, in the centre" represents as well the aesthetic vision of the novel. Her artistic triumph concludes the novel's passage beyond the requirements of hetereosexual romance in Woolf's efforts to "write beyond the endings" of either marriage or death that conventional nineteenth-century novels require. Rachel Blau DuPlessis has argued that *To the Lighthouse* emphasizes brother-sister ties, male-female friendships, and a larger communal vision in which binary oppositions, especially that of masculine/feminine, are undone (96). The undoing of such oppositions, one might add, subverts the local patriarchal power buttressing the colonialist system of England in the beginnings of its twentieth-century decline.

The novel undoes these oppositions, however, not by simply joining them in Lily's painting but by first reversing the values traditionally accorded the binary opposition of masculine/feminine and then displacing them. One way in which Part One of *To the Lighthouse* reverses the hierarchical opposition of masculine/feminine is by removing the masculine "sphere" of activity from the novel. The public world of masculine activity—of business, "high" culture, and academic knowledge—in which Mr. Ramsay makes his living and upon which he founds his identity, is alluded to but absent from the novel. The novel narrows its world to the domestic wherein Mr. Ramsay's professional relationships, as with Charles Tansley, seem more like those of father and son. Within this domestic world, Mrs. Ramsay's creative, sympathetic, and maternal presence reigns supreme, whereas Mr. Ramsay appears at various times and from different points of view as childlike, violently patriarchal, absurdly ridiculous, or comically pathetic. In this way, masculine opposition to Mrs. Ramsay's domestic sovereignty cannot be taken seriously; rather the most significant challenge comes from within the household and from an Englishwoman, one not sufficiently "womanized," however, in Mrs. Ramsay's eyes.

Through the increasing authority of Lily Briscoe's voice, the value and nature of Mrs. Ramsay's powers come under criticism. We see the self-effacement demanded by such middle-class femininity even as characters such as Mr. Bankes and Mr. Ramsay, whom it benefits, continue to idealize it. We sympathize, too, with Lily's inner protests, at the dinner table, for example, when against her wishes she must be nice to Charles Tansley. Mrs. Ramsay may hold court with her Boeuf en Daube, but at great cost to herself and others. We are allowed to see, through Lily's contrary thoughts, that Mrs. Ramsay's insistence upon conscripting Lily to the institution of marriage insists also on the construction of Lily as "civilized," English, and a woman. Lily's marrying will alleviate the strangeness of her Chinese eyes and her eccentricities which make her not beautiful, according to Mrs. Ramsay, not to a man anyway. Within Part One, the question of marriage becomes a question of the making of "woman"; it also signals a novel straining against conventional narrative plotting. However, although it allows for inner dissension, the reversal of sex/gender values and powers afforded by the focus on domestic relations does not suffice to take Lily Briscoe beyond the conventional ending of marriage. For as long as Mrs. Ramsay's "femininity" resides in her loyalty to the institution, she will continue to construct moments of triumph based upon engagements to heterosexual marriage.

In Part Two the inner dialogues generated by Lily Briscoe's protests and the question of who will win in securing the novel's ending result in a narrative break. "Time Passes" breaks the pattern whereby Victorian sex/gender hierarchies are reversed and, in doing so, breaks the ground for Lily's reconfiguration as a Modern Woman. The break is only partially afforded by Mrs. Ramsay's death. Although this section of the novel seems distant from domestic or public or even human affairs, in it, the social violence of war, which Woolf often characterized as masculine, enters the novel and necessarily broadens its scope beyond the house and domestic values. The much larger scale of time and events in Part Two enables the passage from prewar sensibilities to those of the modern postwar period. It allows also the violent and chaotic passage beyond the endings of nineteenth-century fictions.

The passage beyond demands more than the change in Lily's attitude toward Mr. Ramsay that DuPlessis and other critics describe as a turning point (DuPlessis 97, Ruotolo 138, and Zwerdling 199). It demands a theft. For the "we" of Woolf's emerging collective vision is not "all"; the "synthesis of polarities" through the portrayal of a Modern Woman requires, in fact, another "Other," on whom the Otherness of two kinds of middle-class English womanhood is displaced. Although this figure becomes Other, it also, improbably, acts as subject of masculine violence, absorbing its threat and making post-war peace a possibility.

III

At the center of the novel's three-part structure enters a working-class woman named Mrs. McNab who, along with her co-worker Mrs. Bast, is the only literally human presence in the main part of the middle section. However, the "airs" and "darkness" that invade the Ramsays' house in "Time Passes" are personified and militarized forces, "advance guards of destruction." In the midst of trees like "tattered flags," the airs ask, "Were they allies? Were they enemies?" Through figures of winter, night, darkness, and silence,

284 Mary Lou Emery

interspersed with moments of light, summer, and warmth, World War I takes its turns and its toll.

In one of those turns, just at "that moment, that hesitation when dawn trembles and night pauses, when if a feather alight in the scale . . . the house . . . would have turned and pitched downwards to the depths of darkness" (*Lighthouse* 208), Mrs. McNab and Mrs. Bast appear as a "force working":

> But there was a force working; something not highly conscious; something that leered, something that lurched; something not inspired to go about its work with dignified ritual or solemn chanting. Mrs. McNab groaned; Mrs. Bast creaked . . . . they got to work . . . some rusty laborious birth seemed to be taking place. (*Lighthouse* 209–210)

The negatives "not highly conscious" and "not inspired" cast the women as barely human, incapable of giving meaning to their work. Yet they seem about to give birth.

Mrs. McNab and Mrs. Bast labor distinctly as females, but not as fully human females, rather as forces disassociated from Mrs. Ramsay's creative, harmonizing maternity. Because the natural becomes human in this section (the "airs" that ask questions), we might see the dehumanization of Mrs. McNab and Mrs. Bast as the other side of the inversion, a metaphorical naturalization of the cleaning women. The "force working" would then be one associated with nature and its indifference to human meaning. We might also read the metaphorical reversal as a displacement of Mrs. Ramsay's feminine Otherness—her procreative nature—onto the bodies of the colonized women. However, Mrs. McNab and Mrs. Bast are specifically associated, not with nature but with creaking, rusting hardware; furthermore, they pit themselves against, rather than join, "the fertility, the insensibility of nature." No simple inversions or reversals explain their metaphorical connotations. They seem to partake of the female, the inhuman, the natural, and the mechanical simultaneously and indeterminately.

Their indeterminancy is heightened when we consider Mrs. McNab's first appearance in the text at another moment in the downpour of darkness. She enters the Ramsays' house "tearing the veil of silence with hands that had stood in the wash-tub" (196). The image compares her movement to the violent gesture that exposes a hidden, veiled woman. Her washtub hands invade a house coded feminine and veiled by nature, as it were, with a personified silence. In this way, she becomes perhaps human once more, but not as a woman, rather as a violating masculine figure, "grinding [the veil] with boots" (195). Yet the gesture joins her with geological forces which similarly loosen the fold of a shawl "with a roar, with a rupture" (196). Mrs.

McNab invades and occupies the house as did the airs and darkness, natural forces personified and masculinized, and she wins, in the end, a "magnificent conquest over taps and bath" (210).

Why all this metaphorical oscillation? Why does the figure of a cleaning woman inscribe so many contradictions in the coding of colonialist forces, gender, nature, and the human? Most obviously, she seems to embody the incredible chaos of the war, its annihilation of all distinctions previously thought essential to human civilization, including those between self and Other, masculine and feminine, public and private, culture and nature. If Mrs. McNab represents the war's battles and chaos, she also partakes of the violent masculine qualities earlier ascribed to Mr. Ramsay with his plunging brass beak. Her ridiculous lurchings and nonsensical mutterings resemble too his stumbling recitations of Tennyson, embarrassing because meaningless to his children. She labors and gives birth within the house, *and* she assaults it. Thus, in the midst of annihilated ideological distinctions, Mrs. McNab absorbs into her body the opposing gender qualities that shaped the Ramsays' characters and marriage. The old order, with its rigid sex/gender oppositions, is gone.

Yet the Ramsays' house and its objects remain; the human identity, meaning, and value of which they are traces must be recon-structed by fully human voices and wits. It is the task of the female artist to do so. Lily Briscoe cannot achieve her vision, however, unless she escapes the narrative requirements of marriage or death. And she cannot make her escape until "time passes," until Mrs. McNab and Mrs. Bast have forcefully invaded, occupied, and given birth within the house. The ideological dialogue engaged by the novel now no longer concerns marriage but art and the making of "woman" as a creative being and force within the world. The struggle to represent creative womanhood has shifted from Mrs. Ramsay and Lily to Lily and Mrs. McNab. We might best understand the indeterminacy of Mrs. McNab and her coworker as directly related to the modernity of Lily Briscoe. I suggest that Lily's emergence as Modern Woman and artist turns upon the novel's efficacy in responding, not to the Victorian "Angel of the House" ideal of womanhood represented in Mrs. Ramsay, but to the more self-consciously modern discourses of sexology and their descriptions of the "nature" of women.

IV

The writings of the sexologists Havelock Ellis and Edward Carpenter offer a significant context in which to place the gender, colonialist, and class dynamics of the novel. By the 1920s and 1930s,

Ellis' work had become extraordinarily influential and popular. Woolf's library contained volumes by both Ellis and Carpenter; her audience would have been familiar with their ideas, if not their actual writings (Fassler). In defining women's sexual "nature," Ellis described it as inherently heterosexual, masochistic, and ultimately fulfilled in motherhood.[4] The behavior of colonized women and those he called "savages," studied "scientifically" by English anthropologists, served as evidence for his theories, allowing him to universalize some characteristics and prove others by distinction. For example, according to Ellis, because aboriginal women (as do European women) show signs of shocked modesty when an anthropologist comes upon them bathing, all women are, by nature, modest. All women fulfill themselves in motherhood, all women are capable of sexual desire, but only western European women supposedly suffer from frigidity. As part of a theory that glorifies women's sexual and maternal fulfillment, this last point cannot be read as merely descriptive; it labels pejoratively women who remain unmarried or prefer celibacy. Further, it suggests a model of "primitive," "natural" female sexuality somehow desirable yet impossible for "civilized" women to experience fully if at all.

Ellis' writings express an ambivalent primitivism found in other modernist texts. In the paintings of Gauguin, Modigliani, and Picasso, among others, the "primitive" is admired, envied, and appropriated yet insistently differentiated from the "civilized" sensibility for which it provides simultaneously a critique and an Other. Women and "the primitive" are often presented as composite figures in the masklike female faces of these painters' most compelling works.[5] Primitivism and explorations of the feminine conjoin also, although in different ways, in the fictions of Joseph Conrad and D. H. Lawrence. In spite of the differences between Lawrence and Woolf, he too was influenced by the sexologists, especially Carpenter; he devoted much of what he thought of as his primitive (nonlinear, repetitious) narratives to disclosing women's "natural" attractions to the moon and, very much unlike Woolf, to American Indians ("primitives") and to forceful masculinity. As critics of Lawrence have noted, his works are also permeated with misogyny and an associated fear of the masses.[6]

The "Time Passes" section of *To the Lighthouse* refers to the threatening sources of such ambivalent modernist associations: "a purplish stain upon the bland surface of the sea" (201), "death in battle" (192), and the bones that "bleach and burn far away in Indian sands" (192) allude to the war and to the colonies and their increasing rebellions; they prophesy perhaps the postwar events of decolonization, events "difficult blandly to overlook" (201) and sufficient to break the mirror in which Mrs. McNab views herself, recalling songs of her youth. Her mumbling of "an old music hall song" alludes to the mass culture that so many bourgeois intellectuals of the time deplored, even as some of them, like Walter Benjamin, envisioned within it the potential for social democratic change. Not surprisingly, writers of the period often perceived the claims and activities of feminists as an assault by mobs of women, behaving savagely, on the universities, professions, and public streets.[7] The emergence of the Modern Woman devolved upon the same events and ambivalences that, in "Time Passes," break the mirror of the past.

The ambivalences surrounding and associating "the primitive," "the feminine," and "the masses" brought contradictory responses in sexology. For instance, Ellis' diagnosis of frigidity as an unfortunate consequence of civilization and the middle class might have placed in a positive light the view of working-class sexuality as more natural, active, and forceful. Work for women of all classes might have been reimagined along with concepts of their sexuality. Significantly, however, Ellis argued against women working in any occupation outside the home. Clearly, his prescriptions were written for middle-class women only and placed those compelled to work beyond the pale of "civilization." In *Love's Coming of Age*, Carpenter more sympathetically distinguished three types of women: the lady, the "working-wife," and the prostitute, all to be supplanted by labor-saving devices, communally shared housework, and the demands of "free women" for social equality with men. Although sympathetic to the sufferings of the second type whom he also describes as "the household drudge," Carpenter portrays her as lacking "much conscious movement" and "too little illuminated by any knowledge, for her to rise of herself to any other conception of existence" (58). Carpenter sees her much as Woolf presents Mrs. McNab, without inspiration, idea, or imagination. In describing the "Modern Woman," who he believed would change conditions for all women, Carpenter professed beliefs similar to Ellis':

> The women of the new movement are naturally largely drawn from those in whom the maternal instinct is not especially strong; also from those in whom the sexual instinct is not preponderant. Such women do not altogether represent their sex; some are "homogenic," that is, inclined to attachments to their own, rather than to the opposite, sex; some are ultra-rationalizing and brain-cultured; to many, children are more or less a bore; to others, man's sex-passion is a mere impertinence, which they do not understand, and whose place they consequently misjudge. . . . Perhaps the deficiency in maternal instinct would seem the most serious imputation. (Carpenter 66–67)

As Lillian Faderman has pointed out, both Ellis and Carpenter acknowl-edged lesbianism, but Ellis' diagnosis of lesbianism as an "inversion" of the "normal" (Ellis) policed women's sexuality in a newly modern way, while Carpenter could not avoid associating lesbians with "man-nish" women whose maternal instinct he assessed as undeveloped (Faderman). This last alleged characteristic troubled him particularly because, for him, motherhood was "woman's great and incomparable work" (Carpenter 54).

Nevertheless, the sexologists were and still are by some social historians considered progressive. Ellis and Carpenter argued for women's right to sexual pleasure, and Ellis campaigned against the Contagious Diseases Act and for women's suffrage. The writings of Carpenter, in particular, influenced Woolf and other members of Bloomsbury. His relative sympathy for homosexuality and "androgyny" made him less dedicated perhaps to classifying women within the constraints of heterosexuality; his views of ideal heterosexuality, moreover, appear more equitable and balanced than those of Ellis.

Thus, sexology puts Modern Women or even those sympathetic to feminism in a double bind: they might be heralds of a new age, but they were also abnormally nonmaternal and therefore unfulfilled, "victims" of frigidity or lesbianism. Their more "normal" sisters were distinguished by the potential for a "natural" orgasmic heterosexuality, most fulfilled in "innocent" sadomasochism and maternity. We might view sexology as a negotiating discourse. The frequent references in sexological tracts to "savage" colonial natives yoked with diagnoses of European women's sexuality and either disdain for the working class or prognoses for a more socialist future for the masses negoti-ate between admiration for and fear of an overdetermined Other. Its Other is at once savage, female, and multiple. As its name implies, sexology also mediated a perceived gap between popular ideology and science, laying claim to objective methods of observation and clas-sification and giving rise to a plethora of marriage manuals designed for the ordinary middle-class reader. It reinstitutionalized marriage while arguing for changes within marriage relations, and it recolonized women's sexuality while arguing for women's sexual pleasure.

V

Characterizing the "Modern Woman" in Lily Briscoe, Virginia Woolf wrought one compromise with the contradictions sexology presented to feminist thought. By linking Lily Briscoe's vision as a painter with her re-vision of the traditional wife and mother, Mrs. Ramsay, Woolf suggests the infusion of one woman's artistic creativity with that of another woman's more domestic activity. In Part Three Lily cries out, "Mrs. Ramsay!" and conjures the dead woman as she had once sat, "knit[ting] her brown stocking" (300); only after seeing Mrs. Ramsay knitting again and at a distance can Lily complete her painting.

But Lily cannot see Mrs. Ramsay with new eyes until Mrs. McNab has entered the house violently and occupied it in two apparently contradictory ways: as a natural and therefore dehumanized yet feminine force and as a militarized and therefore human, dehumanizing, and masculine force. Following Mrs. McNab's occupation of the house and of these contradictory metaphorical positions, the Modern Woman can have it all (or most of it): androgyny, or the dissolution of masculine/feminine oppositions; female bonding with the domestic, maternal woman; and artistic vision that may grant her public identity. What she still lacks, however, are the "maternal instinct" and "sexual instinct" of the women who "represent their sex" (Carpenter 66–67), and she risks classification as "not a woman, but a peevish, ill-tempered dried-up old maid, presumably" (*Lighthouse* 226), as Lily describes herself. The qualifier "presumably" is important. I think that, textually, Mrs. McNab and Mrs. Bast labor to protect Lily from a sexological diagnosis of "homogenic" or "frigid" and to free her for a revised, more ambiguous modern womanhood. They do so by laboring with their bodies and, momentarily, with their imaginations. The value of their labors—the meaning their labors might have acquired—is, however, stolen from them. As a result of this theft, Lily Briscoe acquires her vision.

When Mrs. McNab's lurching body enters the house, her voice is "robbed of meaning":

> Rubbing the glass of the long looking-glass and leering sideways at her swinging figure a sound issued from her lips— something that had been gay twenty years before on the stage perhaps, had been hummed and danced to, but now, coming from the toothless, bonneted, care-taking woman, was robbed of meaning, was like the voice of witlessness, humour, persistency itself, trodden down but springing up again, so that as she lurched, dusting, wiping, she seemed to say how it was one long sorrow and trouble, how it was getting up and going to bed again, and bringing these things out and putting them away again. (196–197)

The passage raises several questions. If the sound issuing from her lips once had meaning, it was a meaning realized "perhaps" in the realm of popular working-class culture; but how and why has it been robbed of this meaning? How can this witless, meaningless voice yet "seem to say" something about trouble? And, if it is "like the voice of witlessness," how can such witlessness achieve self-reflexivity, as another passage suggests: "she was witless, she knew it" (196).

To answer the first question of how and why Mrs. McNab's voice is robbed of meaning, we must turn to another passage in Part Two. In this passage, Mrs. McNab occupies a more positively human position, as "one woman" or "one person" who, given voice momentarily, remembers Mrs. Ramsay, sees her repeatedly as she had been and hears her voice as she had spoken. She recalls Mrs. Ramsay in the terms of Carpenter's three "types," as a lady:

> Poor lady! . . . She was dead, they said. . . . She could see her, as she came up the drive with the washing, stooping over her flowers . . . she could see her with one of the children by her in that grey cloak . . . Yes, she could see Mrs. Ramsay. (204–205)

The passage gives to Mrs. McNab creative, human memory for the purpose of recalling Mrs. Ramsay. She recalls her former employer as "she" carries a basket of washing; the ambiguity of the pronoun links the two women and their activities. In a structurally similar image, Lily later "sees" Mrs. Ramsay knitting, the act of making and connecting that Lily's final "vision" might be said to achieve in a new way. Thus does Mrs. McNab become human for a moment, connecting the past to the present as her rusty, mechanical labors give birth to something new. She becomes human, it seems, in order to labor with her imagination, and then to have the value of her labor appropriated. For it is precisely the act of seeing Mrs. Ramsay again that allows Lily Briscoe her epiphany:

> "Mrs. Ramsay! Mrs. Ramsay!" she cried. . . . Mrs. Ramsay— it was part of her perfect goodness—sat there quite simply. . . . There she sat. (300)

From this moment of vision, Lily's larger vision unfolds, and she completes her painting.

Admittedly, that both Mrs. McNab and Lily "see" Mrs. Ramsay does not, in itself, imply that the meaning of Mrs. McNab's earlier vision has been stolen in order to facilitate Lily's creativity. The theft becomes more conclusive when we examine the contexts in which both of their voices and visions might (or might not) gain meaning.

Now we can return to the question of how the "voice of witlessness," "robbed of meaning," can yet "seem to say" something. In spite of her meaningless sounds, Mrs. McNab "continued to drink and gossip as before" (198). Evidently, Mrs. Bast understands her gossip; it becomes meaningful to another old cleaning woman, working alongside her, giving birth metaphorically, conquering "taps and bath." The meaning stolen from her voice then must be that which once made her sounds comprehensible ("gay") in some other space— the public spaces of the music hall, the popular stage, or the pubs of her youth. This is a public space different from that occupied by Mr. Ramsay and might offer Lily Briscoe as she progresses in her painting career an alternative to the bourgeois masculine realm that in Part One is implicitly the only world, other than Mrs. Ramsay's domestic one, to which she might aspire. The vulnerability to ridicule of Mr. Ramsay, his academic mind, and his relations with students in Part One make it clear that a place in his world cannot be Lily's aim. So what about the public spaces of Mrs. McNab's youth? Perhaps in ripping the "veil of silence," Mrs. McNab does not violate the house but ends its purdah and makes the appearance of women possible. Can she and Lily Briscoe forge an alliance, labor together, and create an alternative public sphere for women of diverse classes and nationalities?

I think this possibility recurs in Part Three, lingers as a question and possibility, but that finally it is rejected. The modernist female *Künstlerroman* requires instead the theft and the exclusion of Mrs. McNab. The theft is necessary to readers' perceptions of Lily Briscoe's "birth" as an artist and necessary to Woolf's achievement of aesthetic unity.

VI

Haunting the portrayal of women characters as either subsumed by marriage and motherhood or unnaturally independent of them is the "natural" heterosexuality imputed by the dominant masculine discourse to the colonized or working-class woman. It is thus important that Mrs. McNab thinks of her husband and her children. However, the narrative undercuts the "joy there must have been" with her children by inserting parenthetically "(yet two had been base-born and one had deserted her)" (197). If the working-class Scottish woman can appear in the text as natural to the point of witlessness, dehumanized, and dehumanizing, the "rusty," creaking births for which she labors and her previous history of "base-born" children will hardly stand as joyful, fulfilling contrasts to the middle-class female artist, unmarried and without children. Such a contrast, as Mrs. Ramsay provided during her life, would give further evidence of "abnormal" lesbian tendencies or "unnatural" frigidity in the woman artist. With the metaphorically indeterminate representation of Mrs. McNab in Part Two, however, the dichotomy in Ellis' and Carpenter's writings collapses; natural desire and maternal plenitude no longer appear in opposition to overly cultured and therefore repressed and distorted femininity. If we read the image of "tearing the veil" as that of a rescue in which the silence of women is broken, albeit violently, we can find even further indication of the "force" with which Mrs. McNab assaults the house as one that makes possible the emergence of the Modern Woman. But most important, Lily Briscoe as that particular modern woman may now paint and achieve her vision without incurring the charge of unnatural or abnormal womanhood.

Further, Mrs. McNab's appearance as a violent, masculine force *and* as a creature in the act of giving painful birth can inoculate Part Three against Mr. Ramsay's aggressive brass beak and Mrs. Ramsay's self-effacing maternity, in effect curing the Ramsays' marriage of the sadomasochism that Ellis stated was natural in heterosexual relations. Mrs. McNab labors to release Lily from stigma and to free Mr. and Mrs. Ramsay to reform themselves and their marriage.

We see this second result of her labors in the formal narrative structure of Part Three. Just as Lily steps to the edge of the lawn in Part Three to gaze toward the lighthouse, Mr. Ramsay alights upon the shore, springing "lightly like a young man, holding his parcel" (308). The parcel comes from his daughter, Nancy, but was, ten years ago, to be from his wife, and so recalls Mrs. Ramsay and her gift. Immediately before disembarking, "in complete readiness to land he sat looking back at the island," and Cam wonders "What could he see? . . . What was it he sought?" (307). Readers may guess that he seeks his wife, whom Lily's act of imagination, profiting by Mrs. McNab's labors, has brought to life again. The events of these last passages are narrated in a deliberately nonsequential pattern designed to give the effect of simultaneity, "so that one had the sense of reading the two things at the same time" (*D* III 106).[8] The novel's shifting perspective in the final passages creates a discontinuous yet ultimately unified moment in which house and lighthouse, Mrs. and Mr. Ramsay are joined.

Lily's movement to the edge of the garden and the shift of her gaze from Mrs. Ramsay's resurrected presence to Mr. Ramsay's rejuvenated figure create this new order and its re-formed marriage; her brushstroke, "a line there, in the centre," gives it finality and meaning. The resulting meaning for modernist narrative is creation of a formal shape wherein things are separate, even fragmented, yet simultaneously unified or reunified. This new narrative form and the woman artist emerge like twins in the novel's conclusion, and the simultaneity of the passages parallels Lily's assertion of an independence that is at once tied to the past. Moreover, her position as she paints in the garden, between the feminized house and masculinized lighthouse, suggests an androgynous space or perhaps a feminized public sphere. This potential for an alternative public space and the boundaries that ultimately restrict it are the contexts in which Lily's creativity acquires value. In them we also find another clue to the theft upon which that value depends.

The break in the pattern of reversal brought by Part Two with its annihilated dichotomies preempts a more simplistic feminist reversal in which women might occupy a previously masculine public sphere. Lily has moved outside the house and its domesticity but has not moved very far. She paints on the lawn of a summer house far from any urban center of culture and speculates that she will remain anonymous, that her painting will be hung "in the servants' bedrooms" (237). In this trope for anonymity, we find again the possibility of association between Lily and Mrs. McNab.

Will Lily's painting hang in Mrs. McNab's bedroom? What does such a definition of "anonymous" mean? Lily decides that even if her painting were to be flung under a sofa, "One might say, even of this scrawl, not of that actual picture, perhaps, but of what it attempted, that it 'remained for ever'" (267). In this way she modifies Mr. Carmichael's philosophy of art as that which remains forever by ascribing permanence not to the "actual picture" but to "what it attempted." Perhaps this revision opens her mind to the possibility that the staying power of her painting resides in an alliance with another class, of women and of servants, in whose bedrooms it might "invisibly" hang. Confronting the likelihood of her anonymity as an artist, and acting as "one" who can determine the meaning of that anonymity, even if uncertainly, Lily continues to paint and completes her picture.

This response to the hierarchy of values represented by Mr. Carmichael, now become a famous poet dozing in his lawn chair, makes Lily a potential candidate for the Outsiders Society that Woolf describes in her later essay *Three Guineas*. In that essay, anonymity becomes feminine resistance to the overweening pride of the masculine public sphere and its tendencies toward acquisitiveness and war-making. *To the Lighthouse* makes similar associations, although more subtly, and in this light, Lily stands for Outsiders, for peace, and for the prevention of further war. The reference to servants' bedrooms might allude, then, to a possible future in which servants and women painters will form an alternative artistic community.

However, not only does Lily become the "one" who determines artistic value, but also she continues to construct her identity as artist through sharp class distinctions. Although it no longer matters to her that her painting may hang in an attic or be viewed by servants, it no longer matters because the product of her vision, the painting itself, no longer matters; rather the effort and its culminating vision take the place of the object as the thing that will remain forever. Her sensibilities as an artist are defined by contrasting them to those of servants and members of the working class such as Charles Tansley, whose misogyny is coupled in her mind with his cheap tobacco and inability "to know one picture from another" (292). A servant's viewing of Lily's painting attests only to the invisibility of the painting; ironically, this hypothetical anonymity becomes an opportunity for Lily then to redefine artistic value in terms of process, "scrawl," and "attempt." The future of Lily's painting and of Lily as meaning-giver depends on a servant unable to bestow meaning either through her voice or her gaze. Neither Mrs. McNab's bedroom nor the working-class public sphere where her voice once meant something will hold a meaningful audience for Lily's creativity. Rather, Lily makes her triumphant line "there, in the centre," the space analogous to the center of the novel where Mrs. McNab has worked. Thus her "work" of art marks over and supplants the work performed by Mrs. McNab. Much more than Lily's painting, Mrs. McNab, her coworker, and their labors have become invisible, while Lily's "attempt" remains forever, and Lily is the "one" who decides it is so. The servant's central place in the novel has been reoccupied, and her gaze, as well as her voice, has been robbed of meaning.

VII

Although marking the passage beyond heterosexual marriage as a narrative ending, Lily Briscoe's rise as even an alternatively public woman and meaning-giver does not then fully dismantle the ideological dichotomy of public/private that *To the Lighthouse* encodes in Part One as masculine/feminine. A textually as well as more literally overworked figure, Mrs. McNab keys into the complex and contradictory associations of the feminine, the primitive, and, to the extent that she represents the classes of working and colonized people, the masses. She and Mrs. Bast work without "dignified ritual or solemn chanting," as wild, savage, inarticulate forces. Their labor is "uninspired"; they, themselves, cannot give it meaning. They belong to a class of creatures the direct opposite in experience and consciousness to that of the artist; yet they make possible—give birth to—the individual artist's creativity. The metaphorical oscillations through which they are portrayed partake of wartime chaos but also prepare for the emergence of a new order, one in which middle-class English womanhood may connect with its traditional past while moving, exempt from stigma, beyond it.

Creating one kind of feminist vision, the text at its pivotal center preserves the distinction between private and public experience that depends upon a naturalized "Other." The household remains the realm of necessity where labor those who in the classic Greek division of *oikos* and *polis* are unfree, deprived of citizenship and, in this case, virtually deprived of humanity. The novel may undo an opposition of masculine/feminine, but it does so by displacing the hierarchical relation to one of "Modern Woman"/"household drudge." The displacement suggests that, in spite of Carpenter's prophecies, the Modern Woman would not transform the lives of all women with her claims to freedom. The theft from Mrs. McNab that renders her voice and her gaze meaningless is the condition for Lily's completed painting and for the positioning of the middle-class English woman as the arbiter of artistic value and the individual owner of meaningful vision ("I have had my vision").

The case of *To the Lighthouse* and my analysis suggest that modernist feminist women's writing may indeed become complicit in the constitution of a colonized Other at least in part because of its feminist aspirations to write beyond the ending. Such aspirations for public identity and meaning require complicated and creative acts of reenvisioning subjectivity, but they also involve dialogic response to discourses that compromise them.

Modernist European and Anglo-American women writers battled not only the past and its "Angel of the House" ideal of femininity. They also faced the "progressive" doublebinds of sexology's classifications and diagnoses of their sexuality—diagnoses that linked them to "savages" yet deplored their "civilized" repressions; that made "normal" women sexually masochistic yet found "free women" to be pathologically frigid, abnormally "mannish," and nonmaternal; that made sexual passion women's natural right yet one "naturally" governed by husbands. These constraints, in the context of world war and of colonial, working-class, and feminist rebellion, shaped modernists' rejections of conventional realism as much as the desire to be rid of their Victorian past. New characterizations of women and characterizations of Modern Women draw on sexology's types while constructing complex strategies for displacing the Otherness of women's nature as sexology paradoxically defined it.

To the Lighthouse thus reconstructs in Part Three the public/private dichotomy encoded as masculine/feminine in Part One. However, it also reinscribes continually the dialogic qualities of Part One and thus questions its reconstituted dichotomy of Modern Woman/ household drudge. Even as the novel moves toward representing the modern, independent, and creative Englishwoman, it questions the conditions upon which its own closure and "vision" are founded. If Mrs. McNab is "witless, [and] she knew it," by what methods does she know it?

What else does she know? The narrator informs us of the theft she has suffered and thus suggests possible meanings simply unavailable to us, exacted as the price for the meanings we are in the process of discovering. Lily's line at the center draws our attention as readers to other centers and thereby away from the novel's conclusion to its middle where, once again, we encounter the indeterminancy of Mrs. McNab. In this way, the novel's closure invites a return to the chaos it recuperates, and it displaces its own center. Lily's revised aesthetic philosophy values art "work" as creative activity and process, rather than as final result, and thus links the "work" of making art to other labors. In this suggestion of a counter-discourse, *To the Lighthouse* acquires much of its richness and dynamic beauty. If the novel's response to the Victorian marriage plot is the modern female *Künstlerroman*, it is also and simultaneously an anticipation of another question and challenge to the "high feminist" subject it creates.

VIII

It should be clear by now that my point in this chapter is not to question the moral intentions and purposes of Virginia Woolf's writing nor simply to indict "Western feminism" once again. Rather, by reading the modernist narrative strategies of *To the Lighthouse* as responding dialogically to the discourses of sexology, I wish to suggest ways of examining feminist processes of self-representation and exclusion in historically specific ways.

In *To the Lighthouse*, we see a stereotype constructed in the sense defined by Homi K. Bhabha—not a false image or a scapegoat but "an ambivalent text of projection and introjection, metaphoric and metonymic strategies, displacement, overdetermination, guilt, aggressivity" (34). Mrs. McNab as stereotype is not a character but a process of subject-positioning. She "works" structurally at the center of the novel to reposition an ideological dichotomy of private and public so that a new female subject may be negotiated in contest but also in compromise with dominant representations of women's "nature." Those who call themselves feminist critics inherit this model of subject-positioning, but we have acquired also the distance to reenvision it once again. With what dominant representations of womanhood does feminist theory conduct its current negotiations and to the exclusion of whom? What shift or, perhaps, relinquishing of the gaze is called for now to envision a new subjectivity other than that of the reformed middle-class family and its psychologies of "one" individual consciousness? What social relationships, what kind of womanhood, what kind of beauty would Mrs. McNab's knowing "mumblings" disclose were she to tell the story and decide its meaning?

Notes

1. See Mikhail Bakhtin. Graham Pechey's "On the Borders of Bakhtin" has informed my use of Bakhtinian concepts in this chapter.

2. Gayatri Spivak refers to "the language of high feminism within English literature" as that of feminist individualism ("Texts" 273).

3. Helen Tiffin explains and extends the concept of "counter-discourse." According to Tiffin, counter-discursive strategies "invoke an ongoing dialectic between hegemonic centrist systems and peripheral subversion of them; between European or British discourses and their post-colonial dis/mantling" (17). I am not suggesting that *To the Lighthouse* is a postcolonial text, but that, following Graham Pechey's description of "dialogical leakage" in the English novel, it allows for the dialogizing of "at least one side of the imperial relationship"—the colonizer questioning colonization—and thus anticipates its own counter-discourse. See Pechey 54–55.

4. See Ellis. For discussions of Ellis' work in the contexts of feminism and the New Woman, see Margaret Jackson and Carroll Smith-Rosenberg.

5. For a recent exploration of ways in which "the feminine" and "the primitive" conjoin in English modernism, see Marianna Torgovnick.

6. See, for example, Cornelia Nixon.

7. Andreas Huyssen describes a discourse of modernism that associates "the feminine" with the perceived threat of the masses and mass culture. See also Sandra Gilbert and Susan Gubar, vol. 1. In vol. 2, Gilbert and Gubar describe the sexualized language of colonialism and its decline, an association of "the feminine" and "the primitive" that Anne McClintock has explored in her reading of H. Rider Haggard's novels.

8. My interpretation of the concluding passages agrees to a certain extent with that of Alex Zwerdling who describes them as striving "to create the effect of harmony and reconciliation" (208) and acquiring an "apparent poise and decisive finality" (209). However, Zwerdling states that the novel cannot be described as a liberation narrative because Lily clings to the old order and "is not a confident or successful artist." On this last point, I agree with Lucio P. Ruotolo that the kind of liberation suggested in the final scenes of *To the Lighthouse* requires that Lily not achieve what would be for Woolf a questionable public success. But I differ from Ruotolo in my view that, although Lily achieves a certain kind of feminist liberation, she does so through a modernist closure that invokes class and colonialist hierarchies.

Works Cited

Bakhtin, Mikhail. *The Dialogic Imagination*. Ed. Michael Holquist. Trans. Caryl Emerson and Michael Holquist. Austin: U of Texas P, 1981.

Bhabha, Homi K. "The Other Question—The Stereotype and Colonial Discourse." *Screen* 24.6 (1983): 18–36.

Carpenter, Edward. *Love's Coming of Age*. London: Swan Sonnenschein, 1902.

DuPlessis, Rachel Blau. *Writing beyond the Ending: Narrative Strategies of Twentieth-Century Women Writers.* Bloomington: Indiana UP, 1985.

Ellis, Havelock. *Studies in the Psychology of Sex*. 1913. 2 vols. New York: Random House, 1936.

Faderman, Lillian. *Surpassing the Love of Men: Romantic Friendships between Women from the Renaissance to the Present*. New York: Morrow, 1981.

Fassler, Barbara. "Theories of Homosexuality as Sources of Bloomsbury's Androgyny." *Signs* 5.2 (Winter 1979): 237–251.

Gilbert, Sandra, and Susan Gubar. *No Man's Land: The Place of the Woman Writer in the Twentieth Century*. 2 vols. New Haven: Yale UP, 1988–1989.

Huyssen, Andreas. "Mass Culture as Woman: Modernism's Other." *After the Great Divide: Modernism, Mass Culture, Postmodernism.* Bloomington: Indiana UP, 1986.

Jackson, Margaret. "Sexual Liberation or Social Control?" *Women's Studies International Forum* 6.1 (1983): 1–17.

Martin, Biddy, and Chandra Talpade Mohanty. "Feminist Politics: What's Home Got to Do with It?" *Feminist Studies/Critical Studies.* Ed. Teresa de Lauretis. Bloomington: Indiana UP, 1986.

McClintock, Anne. "Maidens, Maps, and Mines: The Reinvention of Patriarchy in Colonial South Africa." *South Atlantic Quarterly* 87 (Winter 1988): 147–192.

Mohanty, Chandra Talpade. "Under Western Eyes: Feminist Scholarship and Colonial Discourses." *Boundary 2* 12/13.3/1 (Spring–Fall 1984): 333–353.

Nixon, Cornelia. *Lawrence's Leadership Politics and the Turn against Women*. Berkeley: U of California P, 1986.

Pechey, Graham. "On the Borders of Bakhtin: Dialogism, Decolonisation." *Bakhtin and Cultural Theory*. Ed. Ken Hirschkop and David Shepherd. Manchester: Manchester UP, 1989. 39–67.

Pratt, Minnie Bruce. "Identity: Skin Blood Heart." *Yours in Struggle*. Eds. Elly Bulkin, Minnie Bruce Pratt, and Barbara Smith. Brooklyn: Long Haul, 1984.

Ruotolo, Lucio P. *The Interrupted Moment: A View of Virginia Woolf's Novels*. Stanford: Stanford UP, 1986.

Smith-Rosenberg, Carroll. "The New Woman as Androgyne: Social Disorder and Gender Crisis, 1870–1936." *Disorderly Conduct: Visions of Gender in Victorian America*. Oxford: Oxford UP, 1985. 245–296.

Spivak, Gayatri Chakravorty. "Three Women's Texts and a Critique of Imperialism." *"Race," Writing and Difference*. Ed. Henry Louis Gates Jr. Chicago: U of Chicago P, 1986. 262–280.

———. "Translator's Foreword" to "Draupadi" by Mahasveta Devi. *In Other Worlds: Essays in Cultural Politics*. London: Methuen, 1987. 179–196.

Tiffin, Helen. "Post-Colonial Literatures and Counter-Discourse." *Kunapipi* 9.3 (1987): 17–35.

Torgovnick, Marianna. *Gone Primitive: Savage Intellects, Modern Lives*. Chicago: U of Chicago P, 1990.

Woolf, Virginia. *The Diary of Virginia Woolf*. Ed. Anne Oliver Bell. 5 vols. New York: Harcourt, 1977–1984.

———. *A Room of One's Own*. New York: Harcourt, 1929.

———. *Three Guineas*. New York: Harcourt, 1938.

———. *To the Lighthouse*. New York: Harcourt, 1927.

Zwerdling, Alex. *Virginia Woolf and the Real World*. Berkeley: U of California P, 1986.

ORIENTING VIRGINIA WOOLF

RACE, AESTHETICS, AND POLITICS IN

TO THE LIGHTHOUSE

Urmila Seshagiri

When twenty-four-year-old Virginia Woolf visited what was then Constantinople in 1906,[1] her daily journal became a vivid travelogue where she recorded her mixed, conflicting impressions of the city and its citizens. Although most of her Constantinople writings bear the trademark spiritedness of her diaries, occasional passages betray a marked uneasiness about the divisions between East and West. Watching the sun set over Constantinople, the young writer muses that

> you realised that life was not lived after the European pattern, that it was not even a debased copy of Paris or Berlin or London, & that, you thought was the ambition of towns which could not be Paris or any of those inner capitals. As the lights came out in clusters all over the land, & the water was busy with lamps, you knew yourself to be the spectator of a vigorous drama, acting itself out with no thought of certain great countries yonder to the west. And in all this opulence there was something ominous, & something ignominious—for an English lady at her bedroom window. (*A Passionate Apprentice* 348)

As the self-sufficient spectacle of Constantinople threatens European cultural sovereignty, Woolf acknowledges the instability of Western identities and influences, despairing that "when we come to

Originally published in *Modern Fiction Studies*, Spring 2004.

consider the question of the West & the East,—then indeed—we lay down the pen, & write no more" (352). Although her pen remained mute on this issue during the balance of her stay in Turkey, it regained its voice in the mature novels she wrote twenty years later. The "question of the West & the East" infiltrates many of Woolf's major works, transforming Englishness and modernity into sites defined by racial difference, imperialism, and Orientalism.

In this chapter, I argue that some of Woolf's most radical literary innovations arise from a material and a formalist politics of race. I begin my argument with Woolf's Constantinople journals because they forge an early link between cultural identities and artistic representation, calling attention to the lines separating self from other. Years after her visit to Constantinople, Woolf's kaleidoscopic representations of selves and others formed the crowning achievement of her experiments with narrative. Her main aesthetic projects—developing a technique of free indirect discourse, rewriting patriarchal literary forms, pioneering new representations of time and space, and creating psychological realism—share a common goal: to draw (and redraw) human relationships by lifting the veils separating individuals. To alter the very idea of literary reality, Woolf devised what Alex Zwerdling has called "the seamless language of fiction," which describes the sometimes fluid, sometimes disjunctive condition of modern English selves and their numerous others (25). I argue that this "seamless language"—its revelations and subversions—is shaped by a rhetoric of race and racial difference.

Certainly, Woolf's interests in racial identity are nowhere as explicit or well-developed as her interests in the politics of gender, war, class, or education. There are no racially focused equivalents of *A Room of One's Own* (1927) or *Three Guineas* (1938), nor are there novels devoted to exploring race and its social construction. And yet, ideas about race shape Woolf's writing across many genres: her letters, essays, and novels allude frequently to racial difference, flirt with cultural crossovers, and draw on images of the racially marked exotic and primitive. Indeed, one of Woolf's foundational theories of the modern novel itself borrows from Turkish culture: in *A Room of One's Own*, Woolf declares that the novel should be "a structure leaving the shape on the mind's eye, built now in squares, now pagoda shaped, now throwing out wings and arcades, now solidly compact and domed like the Cathedral of Saint Sofia at Constantinople" (71). Just as a Muslim mosque perfectly symbolizes Woolf's vision of the English novel's formal versatility, a collection of borrowed racial identities works to depict Englishness in her novels themselves.[2] In Woolf's novels, racial representation locates itself at the nexus of several key modernist discourses, and questions about racial difference accompany Woolf's celebrated challenges to patriarchy, literary tradition, and British imperialism.

My argument concentrates on *To the Lighthouse* (1927), Woolf's elegiac novel about an English family and the brutal end of Victorianism, in which racial alterity offers a provocative source of feminist artistic inspiration. While *To the Lighthouse* critiques the imperialist master-narratives of early-twentieth-century England, it also transforms Oriental perspectives—encoded in Lily Briscoe's Chinese eyes—into arbiters of meaning in a barren postwar world. Subtle tropes of racial difference in *To the Lighthouse* show us that modern subjects cannot maintain faith in an ideal of seamless, unified, globally dominant white Englishness. The well-known feminist politics and formalist aesthetics that answer this novel's questions depend on the often-overlooked narrative position of racial identity: Woolf's remaking of modern English femininity emerges out of complex assumptions about the history, peoples, and art objects of non-Western nations. Recovering the crucial but repressed role of racial politics in *To the Lighthouse* reveals that this novel makes its most radical moves away from literary conventions because of the various aesthetic and political racialisms that inform Woolf's narrative technique.

Reading Woolf, Reading Race

Jane Marcus's 1992 essay "Britannia Rules *The Waves*," which argues that Woolf ironizes the imperial West's culture-making in subject nations, has opened the doors for a host of imperialist readings of Woolf's work. Seizing on the imperialist current running through Woolf's writing, critics have firmly established her place in literary dialogues traditionally dominated by Rudyard Kipling, Joseph Conrad, and E. M. Forster. Imperialist readings, of course, have added a crucial dimension to Woolf criticism. They historicize Woolf's portrayals of imperialist anxiety; they highlight imperialism's seminal role in *A Room of One's Own* and *Three Guineas*, texts traditionally associated with Woolf's gender battles; and they accord significance to previously neglected imperialist encounters and tropes in Woolf's fiction. The body of criticism addressing Woolf's colonialist politics generally casts her as an opponent of the British Empire, a dissenting voice exposing the far-flung consequences of imperialist praxis.[3] However, imperialist readings of Woolf often engender a dangerous critical cohesion between imperial power structures and patriarchal or economic power structures. When Jane Marcus claims that imperialism abroad and class exploitation within England "fused in Woolf's imagination with her own revolt as a feminist" (149), she compresses imperial, class, and gender issues into the same critical model. This compression oversimplifies the cultural dialogues in Woolf's fiction, implying that Woolf's representations of power remain identical across socio-political categories or discourses.[4] In yoking Woolf's feminism to her anti-imperialism, several critics have similarly reduced Woolf's novels to static political tracts and subordinated their aesthetic complexity to a falsely unified ideological stance.[5]

To challenge the idea of Woolf's unwavering opposition to Empire, I interpret cultural and racial difference in Virginia Woolf's novels by reading within *and* without the context of imperialist practice. If critical discourse addresses race solely within the context of imperialism, it narrows the interpretive possibilities of racial and cultural formations in Woolf's literature. While Woolf's objections to British imperialism are widely known, I find that her critique of the Empire is self-reflexive, focused on imperialism's damage to *England* rather than to subject-nations. Woolf always challenges the master narratives of patriarchy and British imperialism, but she does not additionally trouble England's representations of the world outside itself. And because her anti-imperialism does not manifest itself through claims about racial or cultural equality, Woolf's novels often reproduce a wide range of assumptions about nonwhite otherness as well as inscribe tropes of racial difference onto white English identity. In *To the Lighthouse*, Woolf's uses of exoticism, primitivism, and Orientalism are frequently disconnected from material colonialist practice; I propose a critical model for reading this novel that accommodates the full range of Woolf's representations of ethnicity and alterity. My goal here is not to claim that Woolf is racist or that her anti-imperialism is false but rather that the various racially defined threads of her fiction bridge her political interests and aesthetic goals.

Virginia Woolf's fiction reflects the racial diversity that characterizes the aesthetic, political, and social discourses of her lifetime. Whiteness, Englishness, and nonwhite otherness function heterogeneously in Woolf's writing, suggesting an ideological and aesthetic complexity that closed discussions of colonialist politics cannot fully register. Woolf neither reduces racial identities to stereotypes nor self-righteously subverts reductive racism; rather, her constructions of nonwhite peoples and non-Western cultures yield a wide, often contradictory collection of subject- and object-positions. For example, Woolf's motley cast of nonwhite or racially differentiated characters includes polluted, anonymous Indians in *The Waves* (1931), confident Turkish gypsies in *Orlando* (1928), and Peter Walsh's "dark, adorably pretty" Anglo-Indian lover, Daisy, in *Mrs. Dalloway* (1925). Lily Briscoe, although white and English, has "little Chinese eyes"—a crucial point to which I will return—and Elizabeth Dalloway, similarly, is "an

Oriental mystery"; Louis in *The Waves* is also white, but hails from Australia and is therefore branded as the racial and cultural other of the English characters. Geographical spaces outside of Britain are represented as diversely as the characters inhabiting or moving through them: the South America of *The Voyage Out* (1917) and the India of *The Waves* evoke timeless, eternal netherworlds, but Woolf pinpoints specific historic moments with *Orlando*'s seventeenth-century Constantinople and *Mrs. Dalloway*'s colonial India in the 1920s. Finally, these novels burst with the artifacts of colonialism (jewels from India, books on African game hunting, poisoned assegais), as well as the art objects of non-Western cultures (Egyptian pitchers, Turkish hookahs, and Chinese silks).

It is helpful to examine how Woolf's engagement with specific political and artistic discourses contributed to her literary racial poetics, and although her personal relationships have been exhaustively documented and commented on, I mention a few of them here to establish that they encouraged Woolf to interrogate cultural, national, and racial differences. The core of the anti-imperialism that emerges so strongly in Woolf's 1938 polemic, *Three Guineas*, was a reaction against a family legacy of patriarchal nationalism and imperial administration. While Woolf's great-grandfather James Stephen (1758–1832) was an abolitionist in the West Indies, her grandfather Sir James Stephen (1789–1859) was a founding figure of Queen Victoria's empire. Sir James, who served as Counsel to the Colonial Board of Trade, was dubbed "Mister Mother-Country" for his zealous devotion to the ideals and bureaucracy of the burgeoning British Empire at midcentury. His son and Woolf's father, Leslie Stephen (1832–1904), immortalized England's nation-builders in his *Dictionary of National Biography* (first published in 1882). Allegiance to England's colonizing and civilizing mission carried over into Woolf's own generation, most notably in Dorothea Stephen (1871–1965), Woolf's first cousin. Dorothea worked as a Christian missionary in India and published a volume called *Studies in Indian Thought* (1919), and her commitment to conversion drove Woolf to comment that "tampering with beliefs seems to me impertinent, insolent, corrupt beyond measure" (*Letters* 4: 333). The Stephen family's long-standing complicity with colonialism compelled Woolf to resist what she saw as the inevitably oppressive results of overseas conquest.

Leslie Stephen's death in 1904 prompted Woolf and her siblings Vanessa, Thoby, and Adrian to move to 46 Gordon Square in London's then-unfashionable Bloomsbury district, a physical relocation that corresponded to a realignment of Woolf's ideological compass. In Thoby Stephen's famous Thursday night "at-homes" with his Cambridge friends, matters of racial and cultural difference began to shift away from the context of imperialism; Woolf stood at the center of the crossovers and conflicts that characterized the frequently race-focused discussions of Bloomsbury's politics and art. While she kept company with E. M. Forster and John Maynard Keynes, who maintained serious interests in colonialism and national politics, she also brushed up against London's Orientalist fashion craze through her friendship with Lady Ottoline Morrell. In Lady Ottoline's company, Woolf not only attended salons where guests regularly wore East Asian garb, but she herself appeared at a fancy-dress party costumed as Cleopatra. Nonwhite racial identities, freed from their dominant association with colonized subjects, became in Woolf's world—as they were becoming for the English avant-garde—gateways into disruptive or subversive cultural possibilities. Woolf crossed geographical and intellectual boundaries alike in her new life, sojourning to Portugal, Spain, Turkey, and Greece during the same years that she began to assert her presence in London as a literary critic, social activist, and independent thinker; her Constantinople journals, as we have already seen, bear witness to her deepening interests in non-Western cultures.

Woolf's involvement with racial and imperialist concerns was not confined to abstract discussion and comfortable travel. Her roles in two Bloomsbury incidents, the Dreadnought Hoax of 1910 and the Post-Impressionist Ball of 1911, signal an active investment in racial difference and its possibilities for undermining English cultural authority. Woolf's brother Adrian Stephen initiated the Dreadnought Hoax, eager to penetrate Naval security and gain access to the enormous new ship, the H. M. S. *Dreadnought*. Dressed as the Abyssinian emperor and his entourage, Adrian, Virginia, and a group of friends approached Navy officials and demanded a formal tour of the ship. Intended as an insult to governmental authority and institutional bureaucracy, the Dreadnought Hoax was nonetheless rife with cultural distortions that replicated imperialist racial hegemonies. I quote from Hermione Lee's description of the Hoax, which captures these distortions vividly:

> On 7 February 1910, the conspirators got dressed at 46 Fitzroy Square, courtesy of a theatrical costumiers. Adrian was the (bearded) interpreter . . . and the Abyssinians were Duncan Grant, Anthony Buxton (an ex-Harrovian athlete), Guy Ridley (a judge's son), and Virginia, as "Prince Mendax," blacked up, with a moustache, flowing robes and a turban. All the Abyssinians wore what would be described as "the most complete sets of nigger lips." On the train from Paddington to Weymouth, they practised their Swahili, which seemed the nearest thing to Abyssinian,

> from a grammar for the Society for the Propagation of the
> Gospel. . . . Admiral May and the Stephens' cousin, Com-
> mander William Fisher, showed them all round the ship (the
> interpreter improvising in a mixture of broken Virgil, the
> Abyssinians responding with "Bunga-Bunga" and—this was
> Virginia—"Chuck-a-choi, chuck-a-choi"), offered refresh-
> ments which were declined on religious grounds, turned
> down the request for a 21-gun salute, and escorted the
> party back to shore. (278–79)

As Adrian Stephen had planned, juxtaposing incongruous cultural elements fooled the *Dreadnought*'s officials and revealed the
Navy's ignorance of the nations they dominated. But the success of
the caper also came from the participants' willingness to appear in
blackface, to cobble together a "dialect" by substituting one African
language for another, and to pretend allegiance to vague Islamic
dietary practices. The Bloomsburyites' antimilitarism reveals an
ironic complicity with the very imperial violence the hoax intended
to deride, and Woolf's participation in the incident anticipates the
complex, racialized challenges to white British hegemony that crowd
her mature fiction.

In the year following the Dreadnought Hoax, Roger Fry's exhibit "Manet and the Post-Impressionists" enabled Woolf to participate in a second, smaller act of racially charged social subversion.
Traditionally, Woolf's reaction to the 1910 exhibit is read in tandem
with her dictum in "Mr. Bennett and Mrs. Brown" that "on or about
December, 1910, human character changed" (194).[6] But well before
Woolf invoked the 1910 exhibit to catalyze her iconoclastic 1924
discussion of fiction, she used the racial politics of postimpressionism to achieve a minor sexual and social liberation for herself. The
exhibit itself, with its works by Paul Gauguin, Paul Cézanne, Henri
Matisse, Pablo Picasso, Edouard Manet, and Vincent van Gogh,
shocked London's museum-going public; art critics lambasted Fry
for his choice of artists and subject matter.[7] The poster advertising
the exhibit, which Marianna Torgovnick hails as the "English debut
of the primitive in high culture" (85), featured a Gauguin painting of
a nude "native" woman standing next to a Tahitian statue. Both the
form and the content of the exhibit's works scandalized the public:
the nakedness of nonwhite subjects presented through postimpressionism's nonmimetic contours shattered the English art world's assumptions about aesthetic civility. Gleefully aware that the exhibit's
focus on non-Western subjects appalled London audiences, Woolf
and her sister Vanessa Bell attended the Post-Impressionist Ball in
March 1911 dressed as savages "à la Gauguin" (Bishop 22). Vanessa

recalls that "we wore brilliant flowers and beads, we browned our legs and arms and had very little on beneath the draperies" (quoted in Lee 287), and Virginia writes, "Vanessa and I were practically naked" (*Moments* 201). The spectacle of the "bare-shouldered bare-legged" sisters at the ball outraged "indignant ladies who swept out in protest" (Q. Bell 170). Wearing "dresses of the printed cloth that is specially loved by negroes" (*Moments* 200), Virginia and Vanessa's cross-cultural masquerade rejected Victorian modesty in the same way the postimpressionist paintings rejected artistic conventions; like the Dreadnought Hoax, Woolf's challenge to English social norms at the Post-Impressionist Ball reveals an early interest in reordering the boundaries of Englishness through tropes of racial difference.

The 1910 postimpressionist exhibit marked the beginning of Woolf's engagement with the intersection of racial difference and the fine arts in London. The famously expansive circle of artists and writers in Bloomsbury connected Woolf to creative milieux where she encountered modernist aesthetic experimentation based on the forms and tropes of Asian and African arts. Between 1911 and 1918, several members of the Bloomsbury group attended performances by Sergei Diaghilev's fantastically eclectic Ballets Russes, which captivated Covent Garden audiences with performances that merged Western classicism with polyglot global traditions. Spectacles like Nikolai Rimsky-Korsakov's *Schéhérazade*, Alexander Borodin's *Prince Igor*, and Igor Stravinsky's *The Firebird* were lavish in their depictions of Persia, Egypt, and Arabia; under Diaghilev's direction, the Ballets Russes introduced English balletomanes to an exaggeratedly brilliant Orientalist sensibility. Debates about Diaghilev's elaborate aesthetics of otherness propelled the Bloomsbury response to the Ballets Russes, whether intellectual, artistic, or personal.[8] Woolf attended Diaghilev's *Schéhérazade* in 1918, and despite her sense of the piece's foreignness ("we saw our ballet—Sche—[I can't achieve either the spelling or the speaking of it]" [*Diary* 2: 29]), she was a patron of a dance empire built on the merging of non-Western mythologies and narratives with classical Western technique.

In the same years that Diaghilev's ballets were the rage in London, Woolf began her loyal patronage of Roger Fry's many artistic ventures that advocated cross-cultural aesthetic dialogues. As I will discuss in detail later, Fry's formalist doctrines about mixing non-Western art with Western traditions would acquire a feminist dimension in Woolf's racially inflected narrative experimentation in *To the Lighthouse*. Woolf visited the exhibits Fry sponsored, attended his lectures on art history, and, of course, bought art objects from the short-lived Omega Workshops, whose pottery, textiles, furnishings, paintings, and sculptures bore traces of Asian, African, and Native

American influences. In 1920, after the Omega Workshops closed, Woolf attended a show of African carvings that Fry had organized at the Chelsea Book Club. The "obscene" sculptures at the "Niggers' show" (*Diary* 2: 29), as Woolf called it, suggested to her that "something in their style might be written" (*Congenial* 119). At a cultural moment when various factions of the London avant-garde were absorbed with expressing a new kind of English artistry through racial difference, Woolf similarly located stylistic potential in the art objects of non-Western cultures.

Virginia made her most explicit move away from the Stephen family's Victorianism by marrying Leonard Woolf, a Jewish ex-colonial administrator, in 1912. A Jewish man living in England and an Englishman ruling the Ceylonese, Leonard Woolf returned to England after seven years of Civil Service in Ceylon and became a vocal socialist and opponent of the Empire. His acute awareness of the complex vicissitudes of racial and ethnic identity surfaced in his early novel, *The Village in the Jungle* (1913), which illustrates a keen sensitivity to the internal conflicts of a Sri Lankan community, and his better-known anti-imperialist works, like *Imperialism and Civilization* (1928) and *Barbarians at the Gate* (1939), presented polemical arguments against England's economic, political, and religious dominance in other nations. Founding the Hogarth Press in 1917 enabled the Woolfs to publish their own fiction and political writings and, further, to give a voice to many contemporary authors writing on race, imperialism, and civil rights.[9] One of these authors was Vita Sackville-West, whose intimacy with Woolf is usually understood in a lesbian-feminist context. But Woolf's relationship with Sackville-West was also animated by lively debates about cultural relativism and national identity. Vita's marriage to the English diplomat Harold Nicolson took her to Central Asia and the Far East, and her correspondence with Woolf provided a forum for both writers to explore questions of race and nation, belonging and exile.[10] The Hogarth Press published Vita Sackville-West's fiction, poetry, and travel writings; Woolf herself oversaw the publication of works like *Seducers in Ecuador* (1924) and *Passenger to Teheran* (1927), in which Sackville-West created a complex literary geography that simultaneously contested and affirmed imperialist values. We see, therefore, that Virginia Woolf's personal relationships, like her active presence within early-twentieth-century London's artistic and intellectual circles, generated wide-ranging dialogues about Englishness and racial difference. *To the Lighthouse* registers these varied dialogues, and, as the rest of this essay will demonstrate, the novel's representations of race—literal and metaphorical, historical and ahistorical—lie at the heart of its artistic experimentation and its political subversions.

Lily Briscoe's Chinese Eyes

To the Lighthouse is Virginia Woolf's most private and domestic novel, set in a seaside house on the Isle of Skye. Of Woolf's major novels, *To the Lighthouse* is the least explicitly about race or Empire. Whereas characters in *Mrs. Dalloway* travel to and from India, characters in *The Waves* and *Between the Acts* serve as imperial administrators, and characters in *Orlando* witness four centuries of the British Empire's burgeoning overseas conquests, the cast of *To the Lighthouse* moves within the secluded sphere of the Ramsay household. Government, Empire, and war flicker on the novel's peripheries, subordinated to the details and politics of family life. But the marginal imperial and racial paradigms in *To the Lighthouse* emerge as the sites where Woolf remakes the English self: Woolf's deployment of racial alterity in this novel enables her to envision the "life of Monday or Tuesday" in terms other than those dictated by masculine privilege ("Modern Fiction" 287), and her feminist recuperation of narrative development overturns English patriarchy's worldview with discourses and tropes from non-English cultures. The historical, aesthetic, and imperial discourses running through *To the Lighthouse* meet at the site of racial difference, producing an extraordinary balance among three apparently contradictory ideological positions: this novel opposes imperialism, insists on racial hierarchies, *and* valorizes nonwhite otherness.

Each of the novel's three sections questions the stability of English identities rooted in the ideals of a racially exploitative Empire. The first section, "The Window," problematizes the Ramsay family's relationship to the British Empire through equal measures of nostalgia and critique; while the Ramsay house itself metonymically suggests the material and ideological goals of imperial enterprise, the members of the Ramsay family variously comply with and repudiate the Empire's values. In "Time Passes," the apocalyptic devastation that describes the Great War also suggests that imperially dictated identity is fundamentally hollow, prey to the same forces that supposedly protect it. And finally, in "The Lighthouse," Lily Briscoe supplies a new ending to an imperial English life-narrative, committing to an artistry that safeguards her from marriage and the violence of a postwar public sphere. Paradoxically, Woolf secures a new English feminism by attributing non-Western characteristics and perspectives to Lily, whose "little Chinese eyes" exclude her socially *and* elevate her artistically. To articulate a break with nineteenth-century literary mimesis, *To the Lighthouse* incorporates imperializing discourses about race as well as the racialized discourse of English formalism: Woolf's construction of Lily Briscoe as a modern feminist rests on a connection between essentializing, Orientalist attitudes and the visual arts.

Unremarkable events in a single day—taking a walk, going shopping, hosting a dinner party—present competing critical angles on colonialist and racist exploitation in the novel's opening section. Despite continually shifting centers of narrative consciousness, imperialism, like the lighthouse beam, remains a fixed, steady presence throughout the novel's first section, "The Window." On one hand, the Ramsay household, filled with artifacts of imperialist exploitation, emblematizes the transformation of peoples and cultures into commodities for English consumption. These commodities—a book about "the Savage Customs of Polynesia" (27), Mrs. Ramsay's "opal necklace, which Uncle James had brought her from India" (80–81), and the "horrid skull" sent to the family as a hunting trophy (114)—serve as mute reminders of colonized nations whose resources have been plundered. Mr. Ramsay, the patriarch who presides over these commodities, possesses a colonizing, linear intelligence that assimilates the world in terms of power and struggle, hierarchy and history: "Does the progress of civilisation depend upon great men? Is the lot of the average human being better now than in the time of the Pharaohs? . . . Possibly the greatest good requires the existence of a slave class" (43). The Ramsay house and the patriarch at its helm buttress Victorian imperialism, providing the economic and ideological motivation for expanding England's global control. But Empire's solid material presence in the Ramsays' quotidian routine is only applauded by male characters. Woolf's female characters hint at England's progressively fading allegiance to imperialist principles, mocking narratives of colonial life and the Victorian reverence for national institutions. Mrs. Ramsay famously reconstitutes her husband's patriarchal authority as "the fatal sterility of the male" (37); her richly conceived interior life ironizes and subverts the masculine rhetoric of familial hierarchy. The life story and opium-stained beard of the poet Augustus Carmichael invite Mrs. Ramsay's skepticism; his past appears to her an exercise in futility: "an early marriage; poverty; going to India; translating a little poetry 'very beautifully, I believe,' being willing to teach the boys Persian or Hindustanee, but what really was the use of that?" (10). And the daughters of the Ramsay family suggest a resistance to the late Victorian Empire that will increase in future generations ("for there was in all their minds a mute questioning of deference and chivalry, of the Bank of England and the Indian Empire, of ringed fingers and lace" [7]). Thus, "The Window" represents imperialism through sexual polarities: the male characters embrace the imperialist saturation of English private life, while female characters struggle against a totalizing imperial worldview.

The cracks in imperialist and nationalist ideals broaden into chasms in "Time Passes." Using physical and metaphysical violence to represent the horrors of the Great War, Woolf annihilates the family network she has developed so carefully in the novel's opening. By truncating the stories of these characters and describing their deaths between indifferent parentheses, Woolf indicates that the larger life-narratives they represented—Mrs. Ramsay's all-encompassing maternalism, Prue Ramsay's marriage and implicit entry into her mother's role, Andrew Ramsay's dutifully enacted patriotic violence—can have no closure in the postwar modern world. The savage wrecking of these three lives exposes the impermanence of national identities rooted in conquest. By literally killing at-home support for imperialism abroad, Woolf uncovers a deep-rooted cultural need for new narratives of Englishness. Indeed, if the deaths of Mrs. Ramsay, Prue, and Andrew represent the end of Victorianism, the natural chaos assaulting the Ramsay house reaches back to the larger cultural instability of post-Elizabethan imperial Englishness. Although "Time Passes" never mentions a specific historical moment, Woolf's metaphors in this section evoke a historical chronology that begins long before World War I, intimating that English identity has been grounded in asymmetrical, racially exploitative power relations for centuries. Woolf does not illuminate racial inequalities by accommodating the perspectives of nonwhite characters or exploited colonial subjects; rather, she uses the recurring symbols of tea and china to render impossible any belief in the unified, undifferentiated white English subject.

Amid the storms and dust and dampness that beset the Ramsay house, Woolf's images of the family's teacups and china remind us that even the most banal signifiers of English civility stem from centuries of racial exploitation. At the war's inception, the china is "already furred, tarnished, cracked"; then, the "repeated shocks" of the war "cracked the tea-cups"; finally, the dishes silently embody postwar resignation to destruction: "Let the broken glass and the china lie out on the lawn and be tangled over with grass and wild berries" (129, 133, 138). Tea and china, although associated with Englishness for centuries, are nonetheless imported and appropriated from the East with the same violence as Mrs. Ramsay's jewels or the skull that hangs in the children's bedroom. To borrow from Sara Suleri, imperialist history-making is always "an act of cultural transcription so overdetermined as to dissipate the logic of origins, or the rational framework of chronologies" (9). Transforming tea and china into signifiers for Englishness stems from a similarly overdetermined historical process, and Woolf's multiple references to the Ramsays' tea sets and china form a palimpsest of absent colonial spaces and practices.

Porcelain-making and widespread tea-drinking both originally hail from the Tang dynasty in China during the sixth century AD;

their migration to England was enabled by a vast network of British cultural appropriation. When Queen Elizabeth founded the British East India Company in 1600, Britain began its broad-based trade with China, importing silk, tea, and "China ware," as the British called Chinese porcelain dishes. In 1744, when "China ware" had become a commonplace feature of English homes, two porcelain factories opened in England to compete with and eventually undersell the Chinese imports. Although the fast-growing European porcelain industry influenced later designs in English porcelain, the first English manufacturers owed their methods as well as their aesthetics to East Asian traditions; English porcelain was for a long time derived directly from Chinese and Japanese techniques.[11] By the turn of the twentieth century, British porcelain factories ranged from small operations in Ireland and Wales to the great houses of Spode and Wedgwood in England, and the flood of Chinese imports had slowed to an economically insignificant trickle. "China ware," initially valued for its foreign cachet, became assimilated into the English domestic sphere until only the name bespoke its Eastern origins.

Like porcelain, tea's Eastern origins were overwritten by English practices that burgeoned as the Empire grew stronger.[12] The East India Company first introduced tea into England in 1684, when the Company acquired a trading post in the Chinese province of Canton. Even more than porcelain, the history of tea drinking in England supplies a map of colonial brutality: the Opium Wars in 1839 and 1857, arising from Britain's enforced opium-for-tea exchange with China, are but the most extreme consequence.[13] As tea's popularity soared in England over the eighteenth and nineteenth centuries, the colonists worked to cultivate tea in their own territories and become less reliant on Chinese imports. Between 1850 and 1930, the English planted hybrid strains of Chinese tea in Assam, Malawi, and Uganda; Thomas Lipton founded his tea empire in Ceylon; the Brooke Bond Company began cultivating tea in Nairobi; and English colonists introduced the practice of tea drinking to Iran, Morocco, and Turkey.[14] In *To the Lighthouse*, the Ramsays' tea set, found decaying in "all oblivion" by Mrs. McNab, portends the larger destiny of a nation built on what is borrowed or taken by force (139). Tea—imported, transplanted, and imposed as social ritual—signifies the hybrid, culturally divided quality of Englishness.

The minutiae of "Time Passes," like the colonial artifacts that appear in "The Lighthouse," describe an imperial Englishness that has depended historically on the not-English and the not-white. And if the novel's second section begins by exposing the mutually constitutive relationship between racial and cultural violence and English selfhood, its conclusion foreshadows Woolf's final rewriting of white English identity:

> The sigh of all the seas breaking in measure round the isles soothed them; the night wrapped them; nothing broke their sleep, until, the birds beginning and the dawn weaving their thin voices in to its whiteness, a cart grinding, a dog somewhere barking, the sun lifted the curtains, broke the veil on their eyes, and Lily Briscoe stirring in her sleep. She clutched at her blankets as a faller clutches at the turf on the edge of a cliff. Her eyes opened wide. Here she was again, she thought, sitting bolt upright in bed. Awake. (143)

The final emphasis on Lily Briscoe's eyes—which are repeatedly described as "little" and "Chinese" in the novel's opening section—hints that the novel's conflicts will end with a new visual order and that the fundamental act of perception holds the potential to transform English selfhood. Through Lily's "little Chinese eyes," the longstanding imperialist binaries (colonizer/colonized, white/nonwhite, civilized/ primitive) symbolized by tea, china, and the other material evidence of British rule will lose their meaning in the postwar world. However, Woolf replaces these binaries with new racial divisions that make alternative modes of knowledge and perception available to the English subject. Although *To the Lighthouse* renders invisible the colonized subjects whose resources prop up the Ramsays' material existence, it offers a new racial alterity that severs the tie between the English individual and an imperial ideal of collective nationalism.

Reading Lily Briscoe's artistic development in dialogue with the racially derived doctrines of early-twentieth-century English formalism illuminates how *To the Lighthouse* transforms an essentialized understanding of nonwhite racial identity into a template for modern English selfhood. Clive Bell, Woolf's brother-in-law and an influential London art critic, posited one of the most stringent theories of English formalism in his 1914 volume, *Art*. Breaking away from received Western ideas about the symbolic, religious, or ennobling potential of art, Bell's theory of "significant form" privileges abstraction over mimetic representation: "[I]t need only be agreed that forms arranged and combined according to certain unknown and mysterious laws do move us in a particular way, and that it is the business of an artist so to combine and arrange them that they shall move us" (11). Significant form democratizes the aesthetic experience because "we need bring nothing with us from life, no knowledge of its ideas and affairs, no familiarity with its emotions" (25). Because Bell views form as autotelic, rising above "the accidents of time and history" (36), *Art* moves freely through chronologies and geographies and claims formal commonalities among fifth-century Wei figurines, Peruvian pottery, sixth-century Byzantine mosaics, and primitivist drawings by modern European artists like Cézanne and Picasso.

Bell's formalist theories gesture toward but do not probe deeply into the art of non-Western cultures. Roger Fry's formalism, however, centralizes the impact of racial identity on artistic potential, adding specific cultural associations to Bell's rhetoric of formal aesthetic purity. Fry's 1920 collection of essays on formalist aesthetics, *Vision and Design*, spans an eclectic range of artistic traditions, containing essays on paintings by Giotto and Henri Matisse, as well as on artwork by Ottoman and "Mohammedan" artists. The illustrations include a sculpted "Negro" head, a Persian miniature, a "Sassanian" miniature, and drawings by Albrecht Dürer, El Greco, and Georges Rouault. Whereas Bell's *Art* posits an aesthetics of appreciation, Fry's *Vision and Design* employs racial determinism to explain why non-Western cultures create *form* and Western cultures create *concepts*. In its complex cultural dialectic between Eastern, Western, and African arts, *Vision and Design* exalts nonwhite artists whose marvelous creative facilities shame the rational, post-Enlightenment Western artist.

Two essays from *Vision and Design* are particularly relevant to my reading of *To the Lighthouse*: "The Art of the Bushmen," where Fry examines Paleolithic line drawings of animals, and "Negro Sculpture," where Fry discusses the artistic process of "nameless savages" who create exquisitely true sculptures of the human form (100). In these two essays, Fry represents Western (and, specifically, English) art as insufficiently expressive and inherently limited, counterposing instinctual, perceptual African art against rational, conceptual Western art. When a Bushman draws an animal, Fry claims, he strives for and captures the "general character of the silhouette" and not "a sum of its parts" (91–92). The "Negro" sculptor who carves and molds human figures has an extraordinary power "to create expressive plastic form" and "conceive form in three dimensions" (100). Pitting Bushman drawings and "Negro" sculpture against Western drawing and sculpture, Fry continually urges Western artists to achieve the formal perfection common to African artistry. Despite his honest admiration for Bushmen and "Negro" sculptors, however, Fry does not deliver unqualified praise for African arts. He resorts to a colonialist mind/body distinction that lauds African artistry while maintaining the superiority of Western European reason, civilization, and progress. If, historically, white Western artists did not draw forms as well as the Bushmen, Fry argues, "their sensual defects were more than compensated for by increased intellectual power." Indeed, Fry attributes the white artist's deficiencies to his "habit of thinking of things in terms of concepts which deprived him for ages of the power to see what they looked like" (95). Conversely, the "Negro" sculptor has a "logical comprehension of plastic form," but he has not created a great artistic culture because of his "want of a conscious critical sense and the intellectual powers of comparison and classification" (103).[15]

To narrow the aesthetic divide between the "Negro" artist's formal mastery and the English artist's conceptual mastery, Fry points to East Asia and proclaims that Chinese and Japanese line drawings "approach more nearly than those of any other civilized people to the immediacy and rapidity of transcription of Bushman and Paleolithic art." Fry makes the "civilized" Japanese artist a conduit for the Western artist to move from intellectual creation to perceptual creation: "It is partly due to Japanese influence that our own Impressionists have made an attempt to get back to that ultra-primitive directness of vision. Indeed they deliberately sought to deconceptualise art. The artist of today has therefore to some extent a choice before him of whether he will *think* form like the early artists of European races or will merely *see* it like the Bushmen" (97). Commingling centuries and cultures to create new artistic avenues, Fry promises English artists that accessing formal purity is a worthy and attainable goal. The artistic vision of the Negro or Bushman, Fry urges, should be wrested from its culturally paralyzed origins and transported to the sophisticated, civilized, white Western world. If English artists hope to jettison their own moribund artistic legacy, they will have to emulate those nonwhite artists whose perceptions remain unclouded by the trappings of modernity.

The theory that race determines one's relation to formal aesthetics manifested itself concretely in the art objects made by Fry's arts collective, the Omega Workshops. Fry founded the Omega in 1913, hoping to vivify the decorative arts in England by encouraging original and provocative designs for furniture, textiles, and pottery. To this end, he invited twenty-five young artists (including Vanessa Bell, Duncan Grant, Wyndham Lewis, Frederick Etchells, Ethel Sands, and Henri Doucet) to join the Omega Workshops at 33 Fitzroy Street in Bloomsbury. The Omega opened on July 8, 1913, and the artists displayed an astounding array of works that included beads, parasols, carpets, stained glass, tiles, vases, screens, clothing, menu cards, and children's toys. Ironically, what Fry dubbed the Omega's "definitively English tradition" drew its primary inspiration from decidedly non-English cultures (quoted in Spalding 176).[16] From the Workshop's outset, the Omega artists rejected conventional representation and pledged to follow the paths of less "civilized" cultures where art is unspoiled by intellectualism and progress; their efforts to imitate non-Western, premodern perceptual modes supported Fry's view that aesthetic integrity emerged out of an unthinking, sensuous creative spirit. Fry's introduction to the Omega Workshops catalogue reinforces a racialized formulation of artistry consistent with the writings in *Vision and Design*, opening the doors for a more fully global view of decorative art than London had seen:

> If you look at a pot or a woven cloth made by a negro savage of the Congo with the crude instruments at his disposal, you may begin by despising it for its want of finish. . . . But if you will allow the poor savage's handiwork a longer contemplation you will find something in it of greater value and significance than in the Sèvres china or Lyons velvet.
>
> It will become apparent that the negro enjoyed making his pot or cloth, that he pondered delightedly over the possibilities of his craft and that his enjoyment finds expression in many ways; and as these become increasingly apparent to you, you share his joy in creation, and in that forget the roughness of the result. . . . [The Omega Workshops] try to keep the spontaneous freshness of primitive or peasant work while satisfying the needs and expressing the feelings of modern cultivated man. (quoted in Anscombe 32)

The Omega artists capitalized on the ahistorical leanings of formalism, confidently imitating and modifying artistic forms from Africa, the Middle East, and Asia. Accordingly, the artwork produced by the Omega Workshops between 1913 and 1919 demonstrates a dizzying, dazzling cultural hybridity; the Omega artists' varied use of race anticipates Virginia Woolf's own deployment of competing racial discourses in her novels. Some Omega works, for example, focus on the bodies of nonwhite peoples as sites for exploring form, like Grant's painting *The Queen of Sheba*,[17] Etchells's painting *The Chinese Student*, Lewis's painting *Indian Dance*, and Roald Kristian's "African-looking marionettes" (*Omega Workshops* 60). More frequently, the Omega artists borrowed patterns from non-Western art objects and incorporated them into decorative arts. Fry's pottery, for example, shares stylistic affinities with "Mohammedan," North African, and Chinese ceramics. Omega rugs and bedspreads display African motifs, such as "bands of bold patterning and strong black outlines" (Collins 107); a beaded bag by Jessie Etchells appropriates a Native American tribal design; and Henri Gaudier-Brzeska's much-lauded animal sculptures imitate the work of Chinese sculptors of the Zhou dynasty. Omega art embodies the belief that non-Western art is shaped by purer, more direct vision than Western art, and that nonwhite racial otherness floats freely, infinitely interchangeable and adaptable.

Woolf's formalist literary inventions in *To the Lighthouse* reflect the ahistoric, nonmimetic aesthetic philosophy that compelled English formalist painting, sculpture, and decorative arts. In a letter to Fry written shortly after *To the Lighthouse* was published, Woolf famously commits to a narrative formalism that eschews any alliance with symbolism:

> I meant *nothing* by the lighthouse. One has to have a central line down the middle of the book to hold the design together. I saw that all sorts of feelings would accrue to this, but I refused to think them out, and trusted that people would make it the deposit for their own emotions—which they have done, one thinking it means one thing another another. I can't manage Symbolism except in this vague, generalised way. Whether its right or wrong I don't know, but directly I'm told what a thing means, it becomes hateful to me. (*Letters* 3: 385)[18]

Further, Woolf shares Fry's approach to achieving aesthetic purity through racial difference: in *To the Lighthouse*, Woolf's most radical revisions to a nineteenth-century literary legacy stem from the racial alterity she inscribes onto Lily Briscoe. Woolf's Orientalist depiction of Lily Briscoe catalyzes the novel's celebration of formalist aesthetics; race-based formalism in *To the Lighthouse* overturns a narrative economy traditionally structured around marriage and social stability. That Lily Briscoe uses her painting to escape the marriage-plot is, of course, a widely accepted feminist reading of *To the Lighthouse*'s breakthrough modernist ending. Less obvious is the reading that the encrypted foreignness of Lily Briscoe's "little Chinese eyes" first forces Lily's sexual devaluation and subsequently enables her artistic freedom. Racial difference, in other words, provides a meeting ground for social critique and aesthetic innovation in *To the Lighthouse*.

Lily Briscoe's tortured views of patriarchy and marriage shape her reactions to the Ramsay family in the novel's opening section, "The Window," where the narrative flits in and out of her consciousness. In "The Lighthouse," when Lily has rejected marriage and conventional femininity, Woolf makes her the novel's final center of consciousness. Lily's heightened narrative authority is a function of her implicit racial alterity: Woolf uses Lily's "Chinese eyes" to effect the transition between Lily the "skimpy old maid" and Lily the accomplished artist (181). To guarantee Lily's exclusion from marital and sexual economies, Woolf alludes to Lily's Chinese eyes whenever romantic possibilities arise. From Lily's first appearance in the novel, Woolf links her Oriental features to her sexual unavailability: "With her little Chinese eyes and her puckered-up face, she would never marry; one could not take her painting very seriously; she was an independent little creature, and Mrs. Ramsay liked her for it" (17). The "Chinese eyes" invite a host of reductive Orientalist associations; Woolf repeatedly characterizes Lily as inscrutable, diminutive, and unsuited for the married life that awaits the newly engaged Minta Doyle and Paul Rayley: "[Lily] faded, under Minta's glow; became more inconspicuous than ever, in her little grey dress with her little puckered face and her little Chinese eyes. Everything about her was so small. . . . There was in Lily a thread of something; a flare of something; something of her own which Mrs. Ramsay liked very much indeed, but no man would, she feared" (104). While suggestions of Oriental identity impose a mandatory sexual exile on Lily, they also grant acuity to her reactions against social convention. Lily resists sympathizing with Charles Tansley's "burning desire to break into the conversation" during Mrs. Ramsay's dinner-party: "But, she thought, screwing up her Chinese eyes, and remembering how he sneered at women, 'can't paint, can't write,' why should I help him to relieve himself?" (91). Lily perceives marriage as a "degradation" and a "dilution" (102), willingly distancing herself from the paradigms of English femininity trapping Mrs. Ramsay and Prue. The Chinese eyes work to critique as well as to exclude, and Orientalizing Lily's vision helps Woolf to write her out of Victorian patriarchal expectations. As a foreign object of the Victorian gaze *and* as a perceiver in her own right, Lily occupies a textual space bounded and stabilized by racial difference.

The Chinese eyes that look mutinously on gendered social traditions also resist constraining artistic traditions. In concert with Roger Fry's praise for the nonwhite artist's aesthetic sensibility, Woolf constructs Lily's resistance to artistic realism as a function of her Oriental vision. Lily's evolving artistic vision mirrors the novel's critique of a late-nineteenth-century worldview: her first painting is a tortured attempt to express meaning in the Ramsays' world, while the complete self-sufficiency of her final painting rejects prewar social structures. As she recognizes that she has no place in conventionally ordered Victorian society, Lily's paintings become less mimetic and increasingly abstract, pieces of formalist art whose self-referentiality protects the female artist from patriarchy's demands. Lily enters the novel at work on a portrait of Mrs. Ramsay and James, executing this painting in a prewar moment when other artists paint impressionistic "lemon-coloured sailing-boats, and pink women on the beach" (13). Rejecting impressionism's injunction to "see everything pale, elegant, semitransparent," Lily struggles for an art form that breaks completely free of its object (19). And although the "triangular purple shape" she paints to represent Mrs. Ramsay and James seems detached from conventional reverence for a mother and child, Lily subordinates aesthetic achievement to her worry that the painting will "never be seen; never be hung" (52, 48). Because Lily looks beyond the canvas boundaries to determine the painting's worth, this first effort at formal purity fails to achieve what Fry calls "the conviction of a new and definite reality" (239).[19] The broken and devastated material world of the war's aftermath demands the creation of such a reality; it is only then that Lily's Chinese eyes envision a painting that breaks free of the patriarchal and imperialist hierarchies of the Ramsays' world.

Lily awakens to a newly broken civilization at the end of "Time Passes," when, after a stormy night, "tenderly the light fell (it seemed to come through her eyelids)" (142). Eyelids have long been used to differentiate "Oriental" peoples from "Caucasian" peoples; this image not only calls attention to Lily's race-based sexual exile but also anticipates the fruitful connection between Lily's racial identity and her artistic potential. After returning to the Ramsay household and rediscovering her old canvas, Lily hunts for an art form that bears no correspondence to the sexual and racial belief systems of late Victorian English culture. Impressionist paintings adhere too faithfully to the objects they represent, and the material realities of prewar existence have been shattered: ultimately, Lily arrives at a formalist methodology that promises both artistic autonomy and an alternative to the suspended emotional and social expectations that torment the other characters. Anguished by the bleak, incomplete landscape of the Ramsay family, Lily turns to her easel, "screwing up her little Chinese eyes in her small puckered face" (157). Her final, triumphant painting floats free of any signifiers of imperial Victorianism:

> There it was—her picture. Yes, with all its greens and blues, its lines running up and across, its attempt at something. It would be hung up in attics, she thought; it would be destroyed. But what did that matter? She asked herself, taking up her brush again. She looked at the steps; they were empty; she looked at her canvas; it was blurred. With a sudden intensity, as if she saw it clear for a second, she drew a line there, in the centre. It was done; it was finished. Yes, she thought, laying down her brush in extreme fatigue, I have had my vision. (208–9)

Neither the painting's impermanence nor its absence of symbolic meaning hinders Lily from a sense of completion. Her "little

Chinese eyes" attain the "ultra-primitive directness of vision" that Fry attributes to East Asian cultures, and her arrangement of forms is liberating because it is finally autotelic. Privileging the completion of Lily's painting over mending broken familial structures, Woolf creates a racially differentiated model for modern English subjectivity that holds itself separate from patriarchal and imperialist hierarchies. Lily Briscoe's "vision" signals a new English femininity that, paradoxically, employs Orientalist creativity to conceive of itself apart from an Englishness rooted in the colonialist domination of nonwhite races.

Read in the context of Fry's ideas and the Omega Workshops, *To the Lighthouse* resonates with an Orientalism that elevates and emulates the nonwhite, non-Western other's artistry. By scripting Lily's "vision" as the solution to ideologically inadequate or unstable Victorian life-narratives, *To the Lighthouse* answers one set of racialized codes with another. The art that will grant fresh meaning to postwar modernity is as marked by cultural appropriation as the Victorian life-narratives destroyed by the war. The novel's different modes of racial appropriation, which by turn exploit, essentialize, or redeem the resources of non-Western cultures, work together in Woolf's text to create an arc of Englishness that is always racially divided. Despite the novel's wholly private English setting, we see that Woolf carves out abundant textual space for multiple negotiations of racial difference. To read *To the Lighthouse* merely as an opposition to imperialist or nationalist violence is to ignore the rich cultural texture of Woolf's writing: the several discourses operating in the novel's exploration of feminism and aesthetics rewrite Englishness as a confluence of racially differentiated perspectives.

Notes

1. I use Woolf as a surname here although the author was unmarried in 1906 and her name was still Virginia Stephen. For the sake of convenience, I use the name Virginia Woolf for the entire chapter.

2. It is interesting to note that Woolf's cultural musings in her short Constantinople journal suggest the racially or nationally inflected elements of her later writings. Woolf's depiction of the St. Sophia mosque, for example, hints not only at her later description of the modern novel in *A Room of One's Own* but also at the formalism that matures in *To the Lighthouse* and *The Waves*: "St. Sophia, like a treble globe of bubbles frozen solid . . . fashioned in the shape of some fine substance, thin as glass, blown in plump curves; save that it is also as substantial as a Pyramid" (*Passionate* 347). The Islamic custom of walking barefoot in Constantinople amuses Woolf but produces a defiant assertion of English superiority: "we paid our tribute to the

oriental superstition graciously, & shuffled in through the doors with lively satisfaction in our toes; But then I left half my tribute at an early stage, & defiled the carpet with stout English boots" (349); a similar mixture of respect and condescension pervades Woolf's depiction of Turkey and Turkish characters in *Orlando*. A Turkish prayer session creates the awareness, so central to *A Room of One's Own*, of being excluded from practices or places: "The mystery of the sight, & the strangeness of the voice, made you feel yourself like one wrapped in a soft curtain; & the worshippers within are quite determined that you shall remain outside" (*Passionate* 356). These fleeting moments of cultural self-awareness in Constantinople anticipate the lengthy, complex interrogations of English identity in Woolf's later novels and essays.

3. Specifically, see Marcus, Phillips, Lewis, Hovey, Winston, Cliff, Henke, Fox, and Brantlinger.

4. For specific critiques of Marcus's reading of *The Waves*, see McGee, Doyle, and Wollaeger.

5. For notable recent exceptions, see Esty and Sarker.

6. See Pykett 97–98, Schwarz 23–48, Stevenson 58–81, and Zwerdling 145–46.

7. In the "Post-Impressionists" chapter of *Roger Fry: A Biography*, Woolf sympathizes with Fry's desire to introduce non-Western artforms and traditions to England, representing Fry as a misunderstood visionary whose impact was far greater than his critics would acknowledge. A striking passage from the chapter finds Woolf praising Fry for his ability to locate artistry in an otherness until then completely removed from English sensibility: "There were hats, enormous hats, boldly decorated and thickly plaited to withstand a tropical sun and delight the untutored taste of negresses. And what magnificent taste the negresses had! Under [Fry's] influence, his pressure, his excitement, pictures, hats, cotton goods, all were connected" (152–53).

8. The Bloomsbury involvement with the Ballets Russes was grounded in a fascination with the exotic and the Oriental. Clive Bell, Leonard Woolf, and Lytton Strachey frequently wrote about the Ballets Russes in the *Nation* and the *New Statesman*, connecting Diaghilev's cross-cultural innovations with what Lynn Garafola has called "the leftward leaning politics, formalism, and aesthetic concerns that formed Bloomsbury's loosely defined 'ideology'" (316). The painter Duncan Grant designed the sets and costumes for the Ballets Russes production of *Togo, or, The Noble Savage*, which featured a cast of Africans and Mexicans dancing to jazz music and wearing African wigs (Anscombe 111; Garafola 114). At a personal level, Maynard Keynes married the Russian dancer Lydia Lopokova, bringing her into Bloomsbury social circles; Woolf would later call Lopokova her inspiration for the Italian character Lucrezia Warren-Smith in *Mrs. Dalloway*.

9. The Hogarth Press published all of Woolf's work as well as Leonard's early novels, *The Village in the Jungle* and *Three Wise Virgins*. In addition to literature, the Hogarth Press provided a platform for books addressing race and Empire by authors ranging from Members of Parliament to subjects of colonized nations. A sample list of colonial biographies and autobiographies includes *Mrs. Eliza Fay, Original Letters from India*; *Avakkum: The Life of the Archpriest Avakkum by Himself*, trans. J. Harrison and H. Mirrless; *A Woman of India: Being the Life of Saroj Nalini*, by G. S. Dutt; and *An African Speaks for His People*, by Parmena Githendu Mockerie. Books positing political or historical analyses of race relations include *White Capital and Coloured Labour*, by Lord Olivier; *The Race Problem in Africa*, by Charles Buxton, MP; *India in Transition*, by D. Graham Pole; *The Case for West-Indian Self Government*, by C. L. R. James; and *Caste and Democracy*, by K. M. Panikkar.

10. In January 1926 and January 1927, Vita Sackville-West traveled to Persia with her husband Harold Nicolson, who was stationed there as a diplomat with the British Foreign Legation. During her two journeys to Persia, Vita corresponded frequently with Woolf; the letters—alternately meditative, playful, and incisive—formed the basis for much of Woolf's *Orlando*, published a year after Vita's second trip. See DeSalvo and Leaska 77–106 and 143–67.

11. For a detailed history of English porcelain, see Young and Battle.

12. The Chinese had elaborate tea-drinking rituals and practices that were not imported into England as the tea leaves themselves were. Over the eighteenth and nineteenth centuries, the English ritualized tea drinking according to their class divisions, social occasions, and seasons of the year. The evolution of traditions like high tea, low tea, afternoon tea, strawberry tea, summer tea, and the tea party worked to strengthen the associations between tea drinking and Englishness. Like "China ware," tea drinking quickly lost any cultural connection to its Chinese origins.

13. For a historical overview of Britain's tea trade from the late seventeenth century through the twentieth century, see Forrest; Chow and Kramer; and Campbell.

14. See Beauthéae.

15. For further discussion of Fry as an advocate of avant-garde primitivism, see Torgovnick 85–104 and Reed, *Roger Fry* 232–45.

16. For a discussion of the Omega Workshops, imperial ideology, and mass marketing, see Garrity.

17. Duncan Grant's decorative work for the Omega Workshops bore the evidence of his fascination with non-Western art and iconography; the best-known example is his marquetry tray featuring a veiled Oriental woman atop an elephant. However, the paintings and sketches he executed for himself contain a much more overt racial poetics. A

posthumously published collection of works called *Private: The Erotic Art of Duncan Grant* (edited by Douglas Blair Turnbaugh) contains a series of sexual, balletic images of black men coupled with white men. These paintings communicate the same interest in form and movement of Grant's work for the Omega, but they harbor a keen focus on racial otherness and the body. Grant intersected sexuality and racial difference in biblical scenes, like his "Descent from the Cross," where a white Jesus is borne aloft by two nude black men. Similarly, nude paintings of a white Hercules and a black Diomede interpret a classical battle scene as sexualized interracial violence. Created with the "primitive vision" that Fry so admired, Grant's clandestine black-and-white images add a little-known sexual dimension to Fry's doctrines about race and form.

18. Note that, unlike Bell's *Art* and Fry's *Vision and Design*, Woolf's *To the Lighthouse* does not reject art's social or political relevance. Capitalizing on formalism's emphasis on aesthetic autonomy, Woolf justifies her narrative experimentation with the private, domestic, feminized facets of English life. Departing from Bloomsbury's apolitical early formalism, in other words, sharpens the feminist thrust of *To the Lighthouse* and enables Woolf to carry out the literary agenda she sets up in "Mr. Bennett and Mrs. Brown" and "Modern Fiction." For further elaboration of this point, see Reed, "Through Formalism," and Goldman.

19. In the novel's opening section, "The Window," Mrs. Ramsay imagines a domestic formalism that, like Lily's first portrait, is troubled by its impermanence. The fruit bowl she arranges for her dinner party sets up an analogue to Lily's painting:

> Her eyes had been going in and out among the curves and shadows of the fruit, among the rich purples of the lowland grapes, then over the horny ridge of the shell, putting a yellow against a purple, a curved shape against a round shape, without knowing why she did it, or why, every time she did it, she felt more and more serene; until, oh, what a pity that they should do it—a hand reached out, took a pear, and spoilt the whole thing. (108)

Regret that her aesthetic creation cannot remain fixed and permanent signals Mrs. Ramsay's complicity with a broad ideological system that values art's transcendence. Mrs. Ramsay's "formalism" does not carry her through the novel; her death calls for a purer, less materially confined aesthetic sensibility.

Works Cited

Anscombe, Isabelle. *Omega and After: Bloomsbury and the Decorative Arts*. New York: Thames, 1981.
Battle, David, ed. *Sotheby's Concise Encyclopedia of Porcelain*. London: Conran, 1990.
Beauthéae, Nadine. "Tea Barons." *The Book of Tea*. Ed. Ghislaine Bavoillot. Trans. Deke Dusinberre. Paris: Flammarion, 1992. 57–99.
Bell, Clive. *Art*. New York: Stokes, 1914.
Bell, Quentin. *Virginia Woolf: A Biography*. vol. 1. New York: Harvest, 1972.
Bishop, Edward. *A Chronology of Virginia Woolf*. London: Macmillan, 1989.
Brantlinger, Patrick. "The Bloomsbury Faction versus War and Empire." *Seeing Double: Revisioning Edwardian and Modernist Literature*. Ed. Carol M. Kaplan and Anne B. Simpson. New York: St. Martin's, 1996. 149–67.
Campbell, Dawn. *The Tea Book*. Louisiana: Pelican, 1995.
Chow, Kit, and Ione Kramer. *All the Tea in China*. San Francisco: China, 1990.
Cliff, Michelle. "Virginia Woolf and the Imperial Gaze: A Glance Askance." Hussey and Neverow 91–102.
Collins, Judith. *The Omega Workshops*. Chicago: U of Chicago P, 1984.
DeSalvo, Louise, and Mitchell Leaska, eds. *The Letters of Vita Sackville-West to Virginia Woolf*. New York: Morrow, 1985.
Doyle, Laura. "Sublime Barbarians in the Narrative of Empire, or, Longinus at Sea in *The Waves*." *Modern Fiction Studies* 42 (1996): 323–47.
Esty, Jed. "Amnesia in the Fields: Late Modernism, Late Imperialism, and the English Pageant Play." *ELH* 69 (2002): 245–76.
Forrest, Denys. *Tea for the British: The Social and Economic History of a Famous Trade*. London: Chatto, 1973.
Fox, Susan Hudson. "Woolf's Austen/Boston Tea Party: The Revolt against Literary Empire in *Night and Day*." Hussey and Neverow 259–65.
Fry, Roger. *Vision and Design*. New York: Brentano's, 1924.
Garafola, Lynn. *Diaghilev's Ballets Russes*. Oxford: Oxford UP, 1989.
Garrity, Jane. "Selling Culture to the 'Civilized': Bloomsbury, British *Vogue*, and the Marketing of National Identity." *Modernism/Modernity* 6.2 (1999): 29–58.
Goldman, Jane. *The Feminist Aesthetics of Virginia Woolf: Modernism, Post-Impressionism, and the Politics of the Visual*. Cambridge: Cambridge UP, 1998.
Henke, Suzette. "De/Colonizing the Subject in Virginia Woolf's *The Voyage Out*: Rachel Vinrace as *La Mysterique*." Hussey and Neverow 103–08.
Hovey, Jaime. "'Kissing a Negress in the Dark': Englishness as a Masquerade in Woolf's *Orlando*." *PMLA* 112 (1997): 393–404.
Hussey, Mark, and Vara Neverow, eds. *Virginia Woolf: Emerging Perspectives: Selected Papers from the Third Annual Conference on Virginia Woolf*. New York: Pace UP, 1994.
Lee, Hermione. *Virginia Woolf*. New York: Knopf, 1997.

Lewis, Andrea. "The Visual Politics of Gender in Virginia Woolf's *The Voyage Out*." *Woolf Studies Annual* 1 (1995): 106–19.

Marcus, Jane. "Britannia Rules *The Waves*." *Decolonizing Tradition: New Views of Twentieth-Century "British" Literary Canons*. Ed. Karen Lawrence. Urbana: U of Illinois P, 1992. 136–62.

McGee, Patrick. "The Politics of Modernist Form; Or, Who Rules *The Waves*?" *Modern Fiction Studies* 38 (1992): 631–50.

The Omega Workshops 1913–19: Decorative Arts of Bloomsbury. London: Crafts Council, 1984.

Phillips, Kathy. *Virginia Woolf against Empire*. Knoxville: U of Tennessee P, 1994.

Pykett, Lyn. *Engendering Fictions: The English Novel in the Twentieth Century*. London: Arnold, 1995.

Reed, Christopher. *A Roger Fry Reader*. Chicago: U of Chicago P, 1996.

———. "Through Formalism: Feminism and Virginia Woolf's Relation to Bloomsbury Aesthetics." *Twentieth Century Literature* 38 (1992): 20–43.

Sarker, Sonita. "*Three Guineas*, the In-Corporated Intellectual, and Nostalgia for the Human." *Virginia Woolf in the Age of Mechanical Reproduction*. Ed. Pamela Caughie. New York: Garland, 2000. 37–66.

Schwarz, Daniel. *Reconfiguring Modernism: Explorations in the Relationship between Modern Art and Modern Literature*. New York: St. Martin's, 1997.

Spalding, Frances. *Roger Fry: Art and Life*. Berkeley: U of California P, 1980.

Stevenson, Randall. *Modernist Fiction*. Lexington: UP of Kentucky, 1992.

Suleri, Sara. *The Rhetoric of English India*. Chicago: U of Chicago P, 1992.

Torgovnick, Marianna. *Gone Primitive: Savage Intellects, Modern Lives*. Chicago: U of Chicago P, 1990.

Turnbaugh, Douglas Blair, ed. *Private: The Erotic Art of Duncan Grant, 1885–1978*. London: Gay Men's, 1989.

Winston, Janet. "'Something Out of Harmony': *To the Lighthouse* and the Subject(s) of Empire." *Woolf Studies Annual* 2 (1996): 38–70.

Wollaeger, Mark. "Woolf, Postcards, and the Elision of Race: Colonizing Women in *The Voyage Out*." *Modernism/Modernity* 8.1 (2001): 43–75.

Woolf, Virginia. *Congenial Spirits: The Selected Letters of Virginia Woolf*. Ed. Joanne Trautmann Banks. New York: Harcourt, 1989.

———. *The Diary of Virginia Woolf*. Ed. Anne Oliver Bell. 5 vols. New York: Harcourt, 1977–84.

———. *The Letters of Virginia Woolf*. vol. 3. Ed. Nigel Nicolson and Joanne Trautmann. New York: Harcourt, 1977.

———. *The Letters of Virginia Woolf*. vol. 4. Ed. Nigel Nicolson and Joanne Trautmann. New York: Harcourt, 1978.

———. "Modern Fiction." *The Virginia Woolf Reader*. Ed. Mitchell A. Leaska. New York: Harcourt, 1984. 283–91.

———. *Moments of Being*. Ed. Jeanne Schulkind. New York: Harcourt, 1985.

———. "Mr. Bennett and Mrs. Brown." *The Virginia Woolf Reader*. Ed. Mitchell A. Leaska. New York: Harcourt, 1984. 192–212.

———. *Mrs. Dalloway*. New York: Harcourt, 1953.

———. *Orlando*. New York: Harcourt, 1956.

———. *A Passionate Apprentice: The Early Journals 1897–1909*. Ed. Mitchell A. Leaska. New York: Harcourt, 1977.

———. *Roger Fry: A Biography*. New York: Harcourt, 1968.

———. *A Room of One's Own*. New York: Harcourt, 1989.

———. *To the Lighthouse*. New York: Harcourt, 1955.

———. *The Waves*. New York: Harcourt, 1959.

Young, Hilary. *English Porcelain, 1745–95: Its Makers, Design, Marketing and Consumption*. London: Victoria & Albert Museum, 1999.

Zwerdling, Alex. *Virginia Woolf and the Real World*. Berkeley: U of California P, 1986.

ORLANDO'S VOYAGE OUT

Karen R. Lawrence

> The wandering heroes are phallic heroes, in a permanent
> state of erection; pricking o'er the plain. The word coition
> presents genital sexuality as walking; but the converse
> is also true: all walking, or wandering in the labyrinth,
> is genital-sexual. All movement is phallic, all intercourse
> sexual. Hermes, the phallus, is the god of roads, of door-
> ways, of all goings-in and comings-out; all goings-on.
> —Norman O. Brown, *Love's Body*, 50

Virginia Woolf's *Orlando* (1928) stages the mobility
of fantasy and desire; it is a narrative of boundary crossings—of time,
space, gender, sex. A novel that remaps the topography of love's
body, as described by Norman O. Brown above, *Orlando* exchanges
Hermes, the phallic god of the crossroads, with Hermaphroditus, the
child of Hermes and Aphrodite. In this satiric biography of a poet who
begins life as a man in the late 1500s in England and who metamor-
phoses into a woman while on a diplomatic mission to Turkey, desire is
polymorphous, the heterosexual paradigm of adventure destabilized.
The novel's sexual/textual "intercourse" revises the phallic economy
Brown posits, not only in plotting polymorphous sexual possibilities
for its nonphallic picaro. For love's textual body as well is altered in
Woolf's revisionary narrative labyrinth, with its holes "big enough to
put your finger through" (*Orlando* 119).[1]

In the beginning, *Orlando* seems to suggest the adequacy of
the phallic narrative of lunging and plunging. Orlando prepares for
adventure, practicing to be a man's man, engaged in the martial arts
that enable English conquest. We see him "slicing at the head of a

Originally published in *Modern Fiction Studies*, Spring 1992.

Moor" (*Orlando* 13). "[S]ince he was sixteen only, and too young to ride with them [the patriarchs] in Africa or France, he would steal away from his mother and the peacocks in the garden and go to his attic room and there lunge and plunge and slice the air with his blade" (*Orlando* 13). This preliminary flight from the maternal is necessary for Orlando to take his place in the line of male tradition.[2] Yet it soon becomes apparent that the rather androgynous-looking boy finds the Oedipal plots of adventure inadequate. Although he "listened to sailors' stories of hardship and horror and cruelty on the Spanish main" and "their songs of the Azores" (*Orlando* 29), he begins to find their plots limited. The narrator-biographer sums up Orlando's weariness with the plots available to male and female: "But when he had heard a score of times how Jakes had lost his nose and Sukey her honour— and they told the stories admirably, it must be admitted—he began to be a little weary of the repetition, for a nose can only be cut off in one way and maidenhood lost in another—or so it seemed to him" (*Orlando* 31). Castration threats and defloration—these are the plots that elaborate sexual difference, plots that Woolf, along with Orlando, rejects in favor of a more fluid bisexuality.

One could say that *Orlando* wrenches these phallic paradigms of male adventure in a kind of comic, feminist version of the Freudian narrative of bisexuality adumbrated in "The Ego and the Id" (1923) and further developed in "On Femininity" (1933). As Elizabeth Abel demonstrates, although Woolf claimed not to have read Freud thoroughly until 1939, in her novels of the twenties and thirties she engages "the set of terms that generated the debates [unfolding within British psychoanalysis]" (xvi). The Freudian pre-Oedipal child is bisexual; the little girl, a little man until she "falls" into sexual division, a trajectory comically revised in Orlando's protracted psychosexual development.[3] The first hundred pages that explore the development of the male Orlando might be regarded as a prologue to the momentous birth of female subjectivity. Beginning life as a "little man," he suddenly, mysteriously, becomes a woman. In Woolf's version, however, two things happen; first, the polymorphous possibilities of bisexuality continue to circulate. They put into play a new kind of female narcissism/homoeroticism, which is freed from the shadow of Freudian judgment and is represented in a series of mirroring pairs of androgynous lovers. Second, in unveiling the "truth" of Orlando's "castration," Woolf presents a comic deflation of the horrors of the Freudian paradigm: "Orlando looked himself up and down in a long looking-glass, without showing any signs of discomposure, and went, presumably, to his bath" (138). Moreover, the stagy unveiling of Orlando as a woman parodically addresses male fascination, including Freud's, with the enigma of female sexuality. The "erotic life . . . of women," Freud writes in "Three Essays of the Theory of Sexuality" (1905), "partly owing to the stunting effect of civilized conditions and partly owing to their conventional secretiveness and insincerity—is still veiled in an impenetrable obscurity" (248).

Woolf's revisionary gesture of lifting the veil of the "truth" of Orlando's womanhood is deliberately "orientalized." Orlando's sex change is situated in Turkey, where Orlando, the English ambassador, awakens from a seven-day sleep to discover that he is a woman. It is worth asking why, in a fantasy of a transsexual life lived over more than three hundred years, it seemed necessary to plot the text's most radical event *outside* of England, specifically, in the Levant. The inclusion of the topos of travel within the general representation of the mobility of desire suggests that English soil is inimical to the emergence of female subjectivity and sexuality. This centrifugal impulse in the narrative is reminiscent of Rachel Vinrace's voyage out for new models of desire in Woolf's first novel. Even from his first meeting with Sasha, Orlando longs for "another landscape, and another tongue. English was too frank, too candid, too honeyed a speech for Sasha. For in all she said, however open she seemed and voluptuous, there was something hidden; in all she did, however daring, there was something concealed" (*Orlando* 47). Sasha, the Russian princess, introduces the "orientalizing" of sexual mystery early in the text, along with the topos of androgyny (for Sasha's Eastern dress makes her sex ambiguous), but it is during the trip to Turkey that female subjectivity and sexuality emerge, as it were, behind an oriental veil. As in the actual case of James Morris, the British travel writer who went to Casablanca in 1972 for a sex-change operation, Orlando's journey suggests that gender crossing is imagined as a cultural border crossing as well.[4]

In the rest of this essay, I will take up the significance of Orlando's round-trip journey to the East in relation to the mobility of desire I have been sketching. In plotting Orlando's diplomatic journey to Turkey (as male), her sojourn with the gipsies, and return trip to England (as female), Woolf drew on a series of erotic and political projections onto the "East" in British cultural texts of all kinds. Orlando's voyage out from England initially seems designed to fulfill the dictates of male colonial adventure, as Orlando sublimates eros in diplomatic service. (Orlando's "cover story" for leaving England is his desire to flee the temptations of the Archduchess Harriet.) The East quickly serves, however, as a site of erotic freedom and liminality. But this escape is eschewed: Orlando repatriates—as a woman—to England and to English tradition, poetic and otherwise. Exploring an alternative culture with the wandering gipsies, Orlando ultimately decides to face the poetic and cultural legacy she inherits. Unlike

Rachel Vinrace in *The Voyage Out*, Orlando, the woman, makes a round-trip journey. The dual trajectories of the narrative—centrifugal and liberating, and centripetal and domesticating—create a complex "cultural politics" and poetics. In order to extrapolate the fantasy of sexual boundary crossings, the narrative mines the overdetermined figure of Eastern travel, yet ultimately repatriates the erotic, comic possibilities onto English soil.

I begin with the important relationship between travel and female desire, and particularly the orientalizing of this desire, as it is textualized in the letters of Vita Sackville-West (the "model" for Orlando) and Virginia Woolf that were exchanged as Woolf began to conceptualize *Orlando*.[5] The "longest and most charming love letter in literature," as Nigel Nicolson called it (202), might be said to have originated in the letters these two writers exchanged during Vita's Eastern trips in 1926 and again in 1927. From January to May of 1926 and 1927, Vita made two separate trips to the East, settling for a few months in Teheran, where Harold Nicolson had been posted since 1925.[6] During both absences, Virginia and Vita exchanged letter that are love letters, letters of friendship, travel letters, gossip. "But listen; suppose Orlando turns out to be Vita," Virginia writes to her, "and its all about you and the lusts of your flesh and the lure of your mind" (9 Oct. 1927, *Letters* III 428–429). The lusts of Vita's flesh and the lure of her mind were first textualized by Woolf in their correspondence, Vita's physical absence intensifying the desire. The first sketch for the novel that ultimately became *Orlando* was conceived by Virginia as she waited impatiently for Vita's letters from her second trip to Teheran. *Orlando* orginates, along with other "letters of desire," in Vita's absence and figures the other as peripatetic, active, elusive. Like Mary Wollstonecraft's *Letters Written during a Short Residence in Sweden, Norway, and Denmark*—a book of travel letters addressed to an unnamed lover and intended for wide public readership, in which Wollstonecraft duplicated and revised her actual letters sent to her lover, Gilbert Imlay—*Orlando* is both public and private, directed to an audience of one and of many. Moreover, it is part of an erotic exchange in which travel plays a crucial imaginative role. The lover's body is imprinted in the textual "body" of these various texts of desire; sent from great distances, they bring intimacy from afar. This imprint marks as well Vita's travel book, *Passenger to Teheran*, and is traced by Virginia as she reads the proofs of the book that Hogarth Press was about to publish: "The whole book is full of nooks and corners which I enjoy exploring[.] Sometimes one wants a candle in one's hand though—Thats my only criticism—you've left (I daresay in haste) one or two dangling dim places. Its a delicious method, and one that takes the very skin of your shape, this dallying discursive one. . . . [The book] gives this sense of your being away, travelling, not in any particular geographical country: but travelling far away. Now I see . . . what a great affair going to Persia is" (*Letters* III 291). Not only travel, but the travel text, is invested with eros. The spaces of the text offer a delicious invitation to explore.

In *A Lover's Discourse: Fragments* Roland Barthes allegorizes the plot of absence and waiting in gendered terms:

> Historically, the discourse of absence is carried on by the Woman: Woman is sedentary, Man hunts, journeys; Woman is faithful (she waits), man is fickle (he sails away, he cruises). (13)

Even before Vita departs for Teheran, Virginia figures her as the one who travels abroad, while she herself circulates closer to home, but she transforms Barthes's wandering male lover into an image of a maternal voyager. She writes in her diary: "There is her maturity & full breastedness: her being so much in full sail on the high tides, where I am coasting down backwaters" (21 Dec. 1925, *Diary* III 52). (To her husband, Shelmerdine, Orlando's name means "a ship in full sail coming with the sun on it proudly sweeping across the Mediterranean from the South Seas" [*Orlando* 251].) In her letters to Vita during the latter's Eastern travels, Woolf constructs herself sometimes playfully, sometimes anxiously, in writing, as Barthes's "the woman who waits," but now Vita is pictured exotically, as an Eastern Empress: "But Teheran is exciting me too much. I believe, at this moment, more in Teheran than in Tavistock Square. I see you, somehow in long coat and trousers, like an Abyssinian Empress, stalking over those barren hills. . . . And the affectionate letter—whens that coming?" (3 Feb. 1926, *Letters* III 238).[7] Casting herself as the woman who waits and Vita as the traveler allowed them both the room for fantasy, which, like travel, is rooted in distance and absence. The distance allows both Virginia and Vita the pleasure of picturing each other in writing, of dressing each other up exotically for the imagination. (A pleasure that is curiously repeated in the photographs of Orlando and his/her lovers, sumptuously arrayed, drawn from the Sackville-West album, of male and female subjects, that accompany the text of the novel.) The lover's body is eroticized as textual corpus. Virginia wrote to Vita as she worked on *Orlando*: "Orlando will be a little book, with pictures and a map or two. I make it up in bed at night, as I walk the streets, everywhere. I want to see you in the lamplight, in your emeralds" (13 Oct. 1927, *Letters* III 430). What is represented here is not just the erotic setting of the writing (Woolf in bed, composing), but a desire one might call topographic—a desire to plot the geography of the relationship, to graph the lovers precisely in a particular erotic space. For her part, Vita's erotic imagination shades into exoticism; she writes of the desire to abduct Virginia, to place her among other exotic objects. From Luxor, Egypt, she writes: "The wish to steal Virginia overcomes me,—steal her, take her away, and put her in the sun among the objects mentioned alphabetically above. You know you liked Greece. You know you liked Spain. Well, then? If I can get myself to Africa and Asia, why can't you? (But with *me*, please)" (*Letters VSW* 94). Here Woolf is swept away to find a place among the Eastern objects already alphabetized.

It is clear that a very stagy, even literary, Orientalism of abduction, seduction, and disguise fuels these textual fantasies. As Vita travels through the Middle East, documenting her adventures in her letters and travel narrative, she and Virginia draw on a discourse of Orientalism associated with an eroticism of masquerade. The erotic possibilities suggested by the more androgynous Turkish clothes and their associations with the titillation of role-playing fuel these fantasies, as they contribute to fascination, in *Orlando*, with dress-up and cross-dressing. It is the very possibility of shifting roles in these orientalized scenarios and the very staginess of the topos that seem to propel the imagination, as if Shakespeare's Rosalind were crossed with the *Arabian Nights*.[8] The props of Orientalism abet fantasies in which femininity and masculinity are put on and taken off. In one letter, Virginia even pictures herself as a eunuch, divested of the props of sexuality and thus privy to the secrets of the harem: "D'you know its a great thing being a eunuch as I am: that is not knowing what's the right side of a skirt: women confide in one. One pulls a shade over the fury of sex; and then all the veins and marbling, which, between women, are so fascinating, show out. Here in my cave I see lots of things you blazing beauties make invisible by the light of your own glory" (31 Jan. 1927, *Letters* III 320). The phallus becomes a prop to be put on and removed at will, like the skirt, the prop of femininity. Grafting Vita's Eastern travel onto the Western philosophical tradition, Virginia is both the wise platonic philosopher and the eunuch in the harem, out of the game of sexuality.

Disguise, despotism, the harem—these are the familiar elements of the nineteenth-century Orientalism that projected political and erotic fantasies onto the East. The discourse of Orientalism I have been tracing is recognizably one strand in the complex imaginative geography that scholars, from Edward Said on, have documented in European travel narratives and anthropology. This discourse, as recent scholars have shown, is not monolithic but heterogeneous in its mappings of gender and race.[9] As I will show, Woolf's Orientalism in *Orlando* draws on a heterogeneous array of cultural sources, from the arts, literature, and politics. In "Orientalism Reconsidered," Said compares Orientalism and "male gender dominance, or patriarchy, in metropolitan societies: the Orient was routinely described as feminine, its riches as fertile, its main symbols the sensual woman, the harem, and the despotic—but curiously attractive—ruler" (225). But as Peter Wollen points out in a fascinating essay called "Fashion/Orientalism/ The Body," during the twenties Orientalism in the arts, in particular, served a different gender politics that included a redefinition of the "image of the [female] body" (5). Popular versions of Orientalism, in the Russian ballet (like Diaghilev's *Cleopatra* and *Scheherezade*, performances of which Woolf attended at least twice),[10] in opera, and in fashion (in the styles of Paul Poiret, who introduced Oriental fashion to Paris) rewrote the Oedipal scenario in terms of female fantasy. The sexual and political are imbricated in *Scheherezade*, which reflects "both a crisis in the state and a crisis in the family (female desire, homosexuality)" (Wollen 18).

It is this spectacle of Orientalism, so much a part of the European cultural scene of the twenties, that is an important source for the textual fantasies produced in the epistolary exchange between Vita and Virginia and the writing of the "love-letter," *Orlando*. It contributes, as I have said, to the erotics of dressing and cross-dressing that so preoccupy the narrative.[11] *Orlando* is a *put-on*, a comic fantasy in costume that elaborates female desire in various forms of masquerade. Indeed, upon reading the novel, Vita likened Woolf's act of writing to a scene of erotic and exotic dress-up:

> I feel like one of those wax figures in a shop window, on which you have hung a robe stitched with jewels. It is like being alone in a dark room with a treasure chest full of rubies and nuggets and brocades. Darling, I don't know and scarcely even like to write, so overwhelmed am I, how you could have hung so splendid a garment on so poor a peg. Really this isn't false humility; *really* it isn't. . . .
>
> Also, you have invented a new form of Narcissism,—I confess,—I am in love with Orlando—this is a complication I had not foreseen. (*Letters VSW* 288–289)

Woolf's rich imagination produces the textual/sexual embellishment of Vita in *Orlando*, bestowing upon her treasures worthy of the *Arabian Nights*. But if the novel is a loving gesture, expressing homoerotic desire, it is also an invitation to female autoeroticism; Virginia's lavish dress-up of Vita allows the latter to find pleasure in her own jewels, "alone in a dark room" with her treasure.[12]

One can see how homoeroticism was associated with Orientalism in Woolf's earliest conception of *Orlando*, recorded in her diary (and juxtaposed prominently with Vita's absence): "Although annoyed that

I have not heard from Vita by this post nor yet last week, annoyed sentimentally, & partly from vanity—still I must record the conception last night between 12 & one of a new book" (14 March 1927, *Diary* III 130–131). Her first idea is to write a picaresque à la Defoe, about a penniless and unattractive woman who goes to Europe.[13] Suddenly, however, a different fantasy comes to mind, a doubling of women in a book called "The Jessamy Brides":

> Two women, poor, solitary at the top of a house. One can see anything (for this is all fantasy) the Tower Bridge, clouds, aeroplanes. Also old men listening in the room over the way. Everything is to be tumbled in pall mall. It is to be written as I write letters at the top of my speed: on the ladies of Llangollen; on Mrs Fladgate; on people passing. No attempt is to be made to realise the character. Sapphism is to be suggested. Satire is to be the main note— satire & wildness. The Ladies are to have Constantinople in view. Dreams of golden domes. My own lyric vein is to be satirized. Everything mocked. And it is to end with three dots . . . so. For the truth is I feel the need of an escapade after these serious poetic experimental books whose form is always so closely considered. (*Diary* III 131)

Woolf's idea for her novel is a Pisgah sight of Constantinople, a specular and speculative dream of the libidinous East for two English sapphists.[14] In her diary, she alludes to the aristocratic Irish pair, the "ladies of Llangollen," who eloped together at the end of the eighteenth century, capturing the imaginations of the public and of writers like Byron (see Mavor). "Desire is a wonderful telescope and Pisgah the best observatory," Robert Louis Stevenson once wrote (226); Mrs. Fladgate (is floodgate suggested but restrained here?) is only on the threshold of adventure. As Susan Squier points out, the transgressive sexuality of the book that was to become *Orlando* was predicted in the title of Woolf's sketch (and the pair of foppish brides she had envisioned was replaced with the series of androgynous pairs in the novel).[15]

In her revised conception of the novel, however, Woolf literalized the Western fantasy of the libidinous East. In a sense, she plotted a "time out" in the midst of the novel, which resembles the relief she envisioned "The Jessamy Brides" as a whole might provide—"an escapade after these serious poetic experimental books whose form is always so closely considered." The excursus to Turkey, with all its "satire and wildness," must be understood in relation to the sexual and textual problems Orlando experiences in England. For England, the biographer tells us, has become "uninhabitable" for Orlando, as he experiences both poetic and sexual blockages. During the "age of prose," Orlando struggles to produce "The Oak Tree, A Poem." "But as he scratched out as many lines as he wrote in, the sum of them was often, at the end of the year, rather less than at the beginning, and it looked as if in the process of writing the poem would be completely unwritten" (*Orlando* 113). The struggling poet unintentionally, frustratedly, repeats Penelope's strategy of weaving and unweaving, but to no purpose. Having redecorated his home and apostrophized "his house and race in terms of the most moving eloquence" (107), Orlando faces a domestic dead end.

It is at this point that the Archduchess Harriet appears to provide the alibi needed for Orlando's Eastern adventure, and this alibi is lust. Orlando flees the clutches of a woman in love; thus, his request for the ambassadorship seems to confirm adventure's pattern of the flight from women. Yet this flight is a cover story which displaces a more radical kind of "gender trouble," the specter of homoerotic desire that surfaces and is repressed before Orlando's sex change.[16] Harriet's appearance is not the first occasion for this specter, which is introduced with the oriental Sasha, whose sex is indeterminate for Orlando. She/he is seen as "a figure, which, whether boy's or woman's, for the loose tunic and trousers of the Russian fashion served to disguise the sex, filled him with the highest curiosity. . . . But these details were obscured by the extraordinary seductiveness which issued from the whole person" (37). (Here Woolf borrows a Shakespearean model of trans- or supersexual attractiveness.) Orlando feels a homoerotic attraction to this seductive figure and ruefully imagines that he desires one of his own sex: "When the boy, for alas, a boy it must be—no woman could skate with such speed and vigour—swept almost on tiptoe past him, Orlando was ready to tear his hair with vexation that the person was of his own sex, and thus all embraces were out of the question" (38). But what begins as a kind of mirroring between Orlando and his beloved, a same-sex attraction, facilitated by Sasha's clothing, is channeled into a more conventional heterosexual plot in which the androgynous figure is "othered" into the metaphysical tradition of Petrarchan love poetry ("She was a woman. Orlando stared; trembled; turned hot; turned cold . . ." [38]).

This specter of homoeroticism resurfaces with Harriet (whom we learn later is really a man), first in the incestuous impetus behind Harriet's quest for Orlando, for she has seen his picture, which is the image of her dead sister (115). (Thus she seeks in her lover the image of her sister.) But homosexual love is disguised as well in the allegory of Love's anatomy. Love is figured as having "two faces; one white, the other black; two bodies; one smooth, the other hairy. It has two hands, two feet . . . two, indeed, of every member and each one is the exact opposite of the other. Yet, so strictly are they joined together that you cannot separate them." The narrator tells us that love, the "bird of beauty," flies nearer and nearer toward Orlando, yet "[a]ll of a sudden (at the sight of the Archduchess presumably) she [the bird] wheeled about, turned the other way round; showed herself black, hairy, brutish; and it was Lust, the vulture, not Love, the Bird of Paradise . . ." (117–118). This "dung-bedraggled fowl" settles upon Orlando's writing table, making it impossible for him to continue his poetic career. In a book in which figures of rhetoric as well as fashion can obscure the body's parts, this Manichean personification of love comes dangerously close to suggesting anal eroticism (Love shows not the back of the head or the back of the brain, but the "behind"). Because the Archduchess will reveal herself as the Archduke, a man who dresses as a woman to obtain Orlando's love, it is possible that the figures clothe homoerotic passion, a love that dare not yet speak its name in the novel. It is this lust, and its effect on Orlando's writing career, that propels him into the ambassadorship to Turkey. "Thus realising that his home was uninhabitable, and that steps must be taken to end the matter instantly, he did what any other young man would have done in his place, and asked King Charles to send him as Ambassador Extraordinary to Constantinople" (118).[17]

This decision to leave England culminates Orlando's meditation on the vexed relation between sexuality and poetry. For Orlando's preoccupation has been to contemplate the nature of love and how it might be captured metaphorically in poetry. He is continually frustrated by the literary tradition he inherits, which fails to provide the language to represent love: "Every single thing, once he tried to dislodge it from its place in his mind, he found thus cumbered with other matter like the lump of glass which, after a year at the bottom of the sea, is grown about with bones and dragon-flies, and coins and the tresses of drowned women" (101). Even this figure for the workings of the metaphoric tradition is immediately reconsidered by a frustrated Orlando, who (like Penelope) weaves and unweaves his own art: "'A figure like that is manifestly untruthful,' he argued, 'for no dragon-fly, unless under very exceptional circumstances, could live at the bottom of the sea. And if literature is not the Bride and Bedfellow of Truth, what is she? Confound it all,' he cried, 'why say Bedfellow when one's already said Bride?'" (101). But this question itself is disingenuous, for bedfellow and bride, as Orlando soon discovers through his experience with Harriet, are two quite different aspects of love, and, indeed, the confusion of the sex of the partner (bride or bed*fellow*) is displaced onto the semantic debate. To "propitiate" the "austere spirit of poetry," Orlando tries to renounce metaphor—"The sky is blue," "the grass is green,"—but this, too, is ineffectual (101, 102). "Looking up, he saw that, on the contrary, the sky is like the veils which a thousand Madonnas have let fall from their hair; and the grass fleets and darkens like a flight of girls fleeing the embraces of hairy satyrs from enchanted woods." The figures of sexuality return. Orlando's plight leads the biographer to provide a figure for the would-be poet that further complicates this "gender trouble": "when it came to a question of poetry, or his own competence in it, he was as shy as a little girl behind her mother's cottage door" (102). Brides, bedfellows, male poets as little girls— the flight from women that occasions Orlando's trip to Turkey covers over more radical instabilities.

Yet if the impulse behind Orlando's adventures in the Levant is flight from the difficulties of women and poetry, Constantinople quickly becomes a place of "satire and wildness," of political and sexual upheaval. Critics have pointed out the coincidence between the political revolution (the overthrow of the sultan) that disrupts Orlando's tenure as ambassador and his private sexual metamorphosis but have neglected to discuss the way Woolf satirizes the mapping of gender onto the colonial adventure. In her imitation of the fragmented form of Wilkie Collins' *The Moonstone*, a detective story in which officials try to piece together the events surrounding the theft of an Oriental jewel, Woolf represents the "policing of the orient" (as Ronald Thomas has called it) as the policing of sexuality, an effort that is disrupted in the midst of revolution.[18] In depicting Orlando's ambassadorial experience, Woolf complicated the gender politics of her own biographical impulse, representing in Orlando not only Vita but Harold Nicolson as well. (Of course, the sexual politics here is complicated as well by Nicolson's own homosexuality.) Nicolson served as Third Secretary in the British Embassy in Constantinople; the fictional "revolution" against the sultan in *Orlando* draws on the "Young Turks" coup that Nicolson experienced in the Levant in January 1913. Nicolson found himself amidst a frenzy over impending massacres. ("The city was thrown into turmoil. A massacre ensued. The Daoud Pasha barracks were in flames. . . . Fearsome rumours were rife" [Lees-Milne 60].)[19]

Orlando begins his stint in Turkey as a paper-pushing bureaucrat but quickly discovers that the English mission of "policing the orient," protecting white women from the potential abuse of the colonial male, is not wholly congenial to him. Like some of Conrad's characters, Orlando finds himself attracted to the ethos of the other rather than disposed to regulate it. Although Orlando is said to have had "a finger in some of the most delicate negotiations between King Charles and the Turks" (*Orlando* 119), he seems to have had his fingers elsewhere as well. The signs of the relaxation of military male purpose are Orlando's slumming in disguise among the "natives" and are confirmed in his marriage to Rosina Pepita, a Spanish dancer ("a dancer, father unknown, but reputed a gipsy, mother also unknown but reputed a seller of old iron in the marketplace" [132–133]). This match, witnessed by a washerwoman, suggests illegitimacy, a departure from the aristocratic, patriarchal Englishness of Orlando's upbringing.[20]

But Woolf's most direct parody of "official" British Orientalist discourse is found in the papers documenting political revolution. The diary of John Fenner Brigge, an English naval officer, provides one source of the troubling events, a record that classically displays the sexual/political nexus of British imperialism: "when the rockets began to soar into the air, there was considerable uneasiness among us lest the native population . . . fraught with unpleasant consequences to all, . . . English ladies in the company, . . . I own that my hand went to my cutlass" (127, ellipses in text). Brigge continues to describe the "superiority of the British." The "natives" become restless, according to another record, the British bluejackets quell the disturbance, and Orlando begins his seven-day sleep (during which time the duke's secretaries find a marriage certificate to Rosina Pepita, and, on the seventh day, the revolution against the Sultan commences and all foreigners are killed). "A few English managed to escape; but, as might have been expected [the narrator says], the gentlemen of the British Embassy preferred to die in defence of their red boxes, or, in extreme cases, to swallow bunches of keys rather than let them fall into the hands of the Infidel" (133).[21]

Policing the Orient and policing female sexuality are similar, a connection that is most evident in the scene in which Purity, Chastity, and Modesty, the three "graces," uphold the laws of female behavior and decorum. Specifically, they "cast their veils over the mouths of the trumpets" that introduce Orlando's female body (136), but to no avail. The official British veiling of female sexuality, this prophylaxis, is comically undone in the startling transformation of Orlando, which occurs, like the return of the repressed, during his trancelike sleep. The scene of Orlando's unveiling reveals the contradictory impulses behind the male troping of the female "behind" the veil, the impulse at once to hide female sexuality (and with it, according to Freudian paradigm, the knowledge of her castration), and to penetrate its enigma, that is, to lift the veil of the truth of female sexuality. In orientalizing Orlando's sex change, Woolf parodied literary, philo-sophical, and psychoanalytic discourses that represent woman as a veiled mystery which the male imagination seeks to penetrate.[22] This orientalizing of the mystery of the "truth" of female sexuality is evident in Freud's essay "On Femininity," in which he says, "throughout history people have knocked their heads against the riddle of the nature of femininity" and then quotes some lines from a poem by Heine in illustration: "Heads in hieroglyphic bonnets / Heads in turbans and black birettas, / Heads in wigs and thousand other / Wretched, sweating heads of humans" (113). The mystery of female sexuality is linked here, via the lines of the poem, to the riddle of the Sphinx, to the origin of mystery.[23] In placing Orlando's sex change in Turkey—in employing the theatrical "unveiling" of the female body in this oriental surrounding—Woolf burlesques the quest for Isis Unveiled (and perhaps Rider Haggard's *She*, as well as other such narratives, were also on her mind).[24]

Woolf also revises the Freudian narrative of female sexual difference:

> The sound of the trumpets died away and Orlando stood stark naked. No human being, since the world began, has ever looked more ravishing. His form combined in one the strength of a man and a woman's grace. As he stood there, the silver trumpets prolonged their note, as if reluctant to leave the lovely sight which their blast had called forth; and Chastity, Purity, and Modesty, inspired, no doubt, by Curiosity, peeped in at the door and threw a garment like a towel at the naked form which, unfortunately, fell short by several inches. Orlando looked himself up and down in a long looking-glass, without showing any signs of discomposure, and went, presumably, to his bath.
>   . . . Orlando had become a woman—there is no denying it. But in every other respect, Orlando remained precisely as he had been. The change of sex, though it altered their future, did nothing whatever to alter their identity. Their faces remained, as their portraits prove, practically the same. (138)

Orlando comically deflates the symbolic power and horror of the sight of castration upon which psychoanalysis builds its theory of sexual difference. Orlando glances in the mirror "without showing any signs of discomposure." Chastity, Purity, and Modesty, throw "a garment like a towel at the naked form which, unfortunately, fell short by several inches." What is it that falls short by several inches? The referent of the pronoun "which" is ambiguous and suggests that the narrative here parodies the inadequacy of female genitalia in the Oedipal narrative. Orlando's glance is a double rewriting: of Freud's male child confronting the sight of the female genitalia (in Orlando's case, his/her own), of Freud's "bisexual" girl confronting the inadequacy of her own genitalia. Discussing Freud's notion of the bisexuality of the little girl, who begins life as a little boy, Irigaray writes:

> All that remains is to assign her sexual function to this "little boy" with no penis, or at least no penis of any recognized value. Inevitably, the trial of "castration" must be undergone. This "little boy," who was, in all innocence and ignorance of sexual difference, *phallic*, notices how ridiculous "his" sex organ looks. "He" *sees* the disadvantage for which "he" is *anatomically destined*: "he" has only a tiny little sex organ, no sex organ at all, really, an almost invisible sex organ. . . . The humiliation of being so badly equipped, of cutting such a poor figure, in *comparison* with the penis, with *the* sex organ can only lead to a desire to "have something like it too," and Freud claims that this desire will form the basis for "normal womanhood." (48–49)[25]

Yet if Woolf mimes the unveiling of female sexuality, she refuses to replace the "truth" of phallocentric narrative with a corresponding "truth" of female sexuality. Although the narrator, always seeking a clarification that eludes him, announces that "Orlando had become a woman—there is no denying it," the "truth" of female sexuality is anything but plain, as is evident in the strain on the pronominal grammar of the sentences announcing the transformation: "we have no choice left but confess—*he* was a woman . . ." (137); ". . . Orlando remained precisely as *he* had been. The change of sex, though it altered *their* future . . ." (138, my italics). Questions of mixed gender (as evidenced in the grammar) and sexuality remain. Despite the intervention of "Truth," obscurity still functions. Even though the narrator says summarily, "the simple fact" was that "Orlando was a man till the age of thirty; when he became a woman and has remained so ever since" (139), what is figured in the moment of unveiling is a more androgynous fantasy of the elimination of the "truth" of sexual difference. Orlando, like Botticelli's Venus, reveals herself to the viewer's (and reader's) eye, the most "ravishing" and, in a sense, *complete* form in history. "His form combined in one the strength of a man and a woman's grace. As he stood there, the silver trumpets prolonged their note, as if reluctant to leave the lovely sight which their blast had called forth" (138). As Francette Pacteau point out in an excellent essay, "The Impossible Referent: Representations of the Androgyne" (in which she briefly discusses *Orlando*), "Androgyny cannot be circumscribed as belonging to some being; it is more a question of a relation between a look and appearance, in other words *psyche* and *image*. I do not encounter an 'androgyne' in the street; rather I encounter a figure whom I 'see as' androgynous" (62). Orlando is described only in terms of *perceptions* of her (those of the prurient muses, now themselves transformed into peeping Toms; the reader; Orlando, gazing at herself in the mirror).[26] The difference between the hermaphrodite and the androgyne, Pacteau says, it that the former is visible, combining male and female anatomical characteristics, while the latter exists in the realm of the imagination as clothed, masculinity and femininity both operating as masquerade. Woolf takes sexual difference out of the realm of the indicative, despite the narrator's assertions (Orlando is a woman) and into the realm of the subjunctive. Despite the apparent disrobing of the body, Orlando's image displays the instability of sexual difference to the viewer. The remainder of the novel focuses heavily on Orlando's clothes, her dress-up as one sex or the other (or in androgynous clothing, such as the gipsies wear).[27]

Ironically, the narrator appeals to visual representations of Orlando in order to establish that essentially he/she has not changed ("Their faces remained, as their portraits prove, practically the same" [*Orlando* 138]). Attempting to dispel confusion, the biographer "proves" instead that one *cannot* go behind the representation, the iconic image. *Orlando* is Woolf's only novel with photographs; it presents us with portraits of Orlando as male and female, which Virginia painstakingly chose, in consultation with Vita, from the Sackville-West family album of male and female ancestors. Beneath the persistent family resemblance, gender slides from masculine to feminine, creating a kind of androgynous portrait—historically, male and female Sackvilles go into the making of Orlando.[28] (The caption, "Orlando as a boy," suggests this emphasis on his convertible appearance, simulating first one gender, then another.)

Thus the old love-plot of the self and the other must be radically rewritten. The old "plots"—of castration (cutting off the noses) and chastity—are dismissed:

> In normal circumstances a lovely young woman alone would have thought of nothing else [but preserving her chastity]; the whole edifice of female government is based on that foundation stone; chastity is their jewel, their centre piece, which they run mad to protect, and die when ravished of. But if one has been a man for thirty years or so, and an Ambassador into the bargain . . . one does not perhaps give such a very great start about that. (*Orlando* 153–154)

The new "plot" includes polymorphous desire expressed in the attraction of Orlando to androgynous men and to other women, that is, to a set of "mirroring" lovers of both sexes. It is, however, within a female economy that this desire finds its representation.

> And as all Orlando's loves had been women, now, through the culpable laggardry of the human frame to adapt itself to convention, though she herself was a woman, it was still a woman she loved; and if the consciousness of being of the same sex had any effect at all, it was to quicken and deepen those feelings which she had had as a man. (161)

Yet if the very possibility of this polymorphous sexuality burgeons with Orlando's experience in Turkey, first in the sex change and then in the androgynous life of the gipsies, still Orlando returns to England. If the journey to Turkey epitomizes the excursive, fantastic nature of the imagination, what of Orlando's return to England after the change of sex? For I would suggest that as crucial as the centrifugal movement, in the trip to Turkey and in the trope of the fantasy of sexual possibilities, is the centripetal movement staged in Orlando's return home and in the "conserving" of English literary tradition that it signals. It is partly this "rootedness" that lends itself to at least a questioning of textual/sexual subversions at play in the fantasy. As George Van Den Abbeele postulates in his *Travel as Metaphor from Montaigne to Rousseau*:

> In order to be able to have an economy of travel, some fixed point of reference must be posited. The economy of travel requires an *oikos* (the Greek for "home" from which is derived "economy") in relation to which any wandering can be *comprehended* (enclosed as well as understood). In other words, a home(land) must be posited from which one leaves on the journey and to which one hopes to return— whether one actually makes it back home changes nothing, from this perspective. The positing of an *oikos*, or *domus* . . . is what *dom*esticates the voyage by ascribing certain limits to it. (xvii–xviii)

As Van Den Abbeele says, this *oikos* is a feature of all travel, regardless of the literality of the return trip. Yet this suggestion of a conservation, of a bringing back to England of the lessons learned abroad, is crucial to understanding the fulcrum that the Eastern journey provides in *Orlando*. This return, like the departure, involves the exigencies of the poetic imagination (and, ultimately, its troping of love). As in her last novel, *Between the Acts*, Woolf satirized, parodied, revised the English literary tradition but represented the inevitable confrontation between this patriarchal tradition and the woman poet. Orlando's return to England, a return that Rachel Vinrace cannot make for a number of reasons, signals the repatriation of the imagination, a domestication of it. By "domestic," I mean to suggest a particular Romantic ethos (Coleridgean) that figures the mating of the poetical genius and the *genius loci* of English nature. This tradition, as Geoffrey Hartman shows, domesticates the high Miltonic, excursive sublime in an accommodation "of the visionary temperament to an English milieu." In this poetic tradition, we find a "meditation on English landscape as alma mater—where landscape is storied England, its legends, history, and rural-reflective spirit" ("Romantic Poetry and the Genius Loci" 319). If radical freedom seems imaginable at first outside England (where Orlando's sex change occurs) ultimately, there is something too nomadic about the "East," its rootlessness emblematized by the gipsies with whom Orlando cavorts after being liberated from the patriarchal shackles of his diplomatic position. Unlimited freedom of movement has a negative side; Orlando discovers that the lack of attachment is inimical both to poetry and to intimacy of the kind explored in the novel's androgynous pairings.[29]

Specifically, what Orlando discovers is the gipsies' resistance to figuration, a too literal, demystified view of nature that inhibits poetry. For as vexingly cluttered as was the English tradition ("Every single thing . . . he found thus cumbered with other matter like the lump of glass . . ." [*Orlando* 101]), in the world of the gipsies, nothing attaches to anything else; everything is itself and nothing else— simile, metaphor, in short, figuration, is curtailed. It is not merely the particular English disease of the love of nature, as the narrator describes it, that separates Orlando from the gipsies, but the poetic imagination itself: "She [Orlando] likened the hills to ramparts, and the plains to the flanks of kine. . . . Everything, in fact, was something else" (143). Ironically, the trope of the "East," traditionally the site of extravagant mystery, now, in Orlando's sojourn with the gipsies, suggests a nightmare of literalization. Orlando, in contrast, returns to meditating on the nature of the imagination (in Keatsian fashion, she considers whether beauty "resides" in "things themselves or only in herself"). The gipsies, whose freedom from materialism enables a total freedom of physical movement, nevertheless regard Orlando's poeticizing as evidence of a seditious (and anti-utilitarian) restlessness of the spirit. For Orlando, nature is not self-evident but revelatory, mysterious. It is this view of nature (and, hence, the material body) upon which his poetic credo is formed, for the "truth" of poetry, too, is obscure, difficult, not self-evident. Truth, as well as Candor and Honesty, we might remember from Orlando's mock-unveiling, are "austere Gods" for poets as well as biographers. These gods yield their message clothed in figures of thought and speech. (Obscurity, we are told early in the narrative, "wraps about a man like a mist; obscurity is dark, ample and free; obscurity lets the mind take its way unimpeded" [104].) It is not on the open plains of Turkey, but in the peculiarly English weather, with its mists and clouds (one is reminded of the relation between the word "nuance" and the word "nuée," or cloud) that Orlando's poetic spirit is nurtured. The oak tree, although solid and rooted, grows underground as well as above, its sinewy lines of connection hidden from view.

This Romantic repatriation of the imagination I describe seems in many ways like a conservative gesture, a chastening of the imagination in which it runs the risk of being redomesticated in the kinds of familiar patterns that threaten its annihilation.[30] Indeed, the potentially subversive possibilities of fantasy, as described by Rosemary Jackson, for example, would seem to suffer from such a reining in of desire. Does the turn back to English nature, the "alma mater" as Hartman describes it in gendered terms, reinscribe the novel in a poetic tradition and a romantic sexual/textual politics that would cripple, rather than spur, the imagination? Furthermore, the completion of the poem, "The Oak Tree" (a synecdoche, as Maria DiBattista puts it, for Orlando's country estate [113]), might seem to confirm an aristocratic relation between the poetic estate and the country estate, thus capitulating to the most conservative impulses of pastoral rootedness.

Yet Orlando's "homecoming" of the imagination is anything but cosy. She is forced to endure the reading of her new sexual identity, which, indeed, becomes a matter for the English courts. Orlando temporarily loses her estate and hides her manuscript—her sex change not only occasions her loss of property but drastically alters her relation to poetic inheritance. Like Lady Mary Wortley Montagu, returning from Turkey in the early eighteenth century to encounter ridicule from the pen of Pope, Orlando must watch her step in the age of Mr. Pope's rapier wit, flickering tongue ("like a lizard"), and flashing eyes (209).[31] The biographer's treatment of Orlando in the nineteenth century almost skips over the period of Romanticism (presumably more congenial to Orlando's art), and focuses on Victorian domesticity, replete with the Angel in the House that threatens the pen of the "woman" writer.

Orlando's repatriation illustrates more than the hostile climate for a woman writer; it represents a revisionary Romanticism. Woolf tries nothing less than to rewrite the Romantic marriage of *genius loci* and poetic genius, with a woman writer in the latter role, a woman whose ties to the aesthetic traditions are highly problematic. For the generative power of the Romantic imagination, its Coleridgean rootedness in the "genial spirit," is gendered male. Indeed, the Indo-European root of "geniality," "genius," "gender," and "genre" is "gen," which means, "to beget," a male function.[32] Yet Orlando completes and publishes her poem (as well as gives birth to a son).

The final sections end on a note of domestic sublime, in which a kind of grace descends on the language of poetry, as Orlando continues her struggles to express her sense of attachment to the objects of her love. Out of the helter-skelter furnishings of the mind ("What a phantasmagoria the mind is and meeting-place of dissemblables" [176]), Orlando tries to "fabricate" something that mirrors her deepest attachments. Sitting by the oak tree ("She liked to attach herself to something hard" [324]), Orlando redomesticates her imagination, but with a difference.

> Was not writing poetry a secret transaction, a voice answering a voice? . . . What could have been more secret, she thought, more slow, and like the intercourse of lovers, than the stammering answer she had made all these years to the old crooning song of the woods, and the farms and the brown horses standing at the gate, neck to neck, and the smithy and the kitchen and the fields, so laboriously bearing wheat, turnips, grass, and the gardens blowing irises and fritillaries? (325)

Poetry is "a voice answering a voice"—this mirroring voice is both nature's and the "self-same" lover's voices that reflect Orlando to herself. The final ecstatic moment refigures Romantic sublimity ("'Ecstasy!' she cried, 'ecstasy!'" [327]) in which Orlando "produces" the name of her lover:

> "Marmaduke Bonthrop Shelmerdine!" she cried, standing by the oak tree.
>   The beautiful, glittering name fell out of the sky like a steel blue feather. (327)

One might think here of another modernist, Gertrude Stein, who imagined poetry as an embrace in language: "Anybody knows how anybody calls out the name of anybody one loves. And so that is poetry really loving the name of anything and that is not prose" (*Lectures in America* 232). Shelmerdine is for Orlando what she has always already known, and she for him, yet the "otherness" of this self-same lover, figured by travel, suggests that the "self-same" (to return to Irigaray's term) brings something different to the lover from abroad. Orlando's name means to Shel "a ship in full sail coming with the sun on it proudly sweeping across the Mediterranean from the South Seas," and he (a captain) has a name which is a "wild, dark-plumed name—a name which had in her mind, the steel blue gleam of rooks' wings . . . the snake-like twisting descent of their feathers in a silver pool" (*Orlando* 250–251).

At the end of the novel, it is 1928; in these modern times, Shel descends in an airplane to Orlando, ironically, the woman who waits. She remembers the words of the gipsy admonishing her love of her patriarchal inheritance ("What do you need with four hundred bedrooms and silver lids on all the dishes, and housemaids dusting?" [326]). Woolf does not negate the property struggles of her poet-protagonist, the agony of Orlando (female) fighting to retain her relation to her inheritance, as Vita Sackville-West tried to do (indeed, in fiction Woolf reinstates Vita's rightful inheritance). Culture is not escaped in the round-trip journey of the narrative; rather, the voyage out enables a return to the scene of home in which home itself is transformed by the return of Shakespeare's sister, the survivor. For in this representation of a woman writer (unlike that in *A Room of One's Own*), Orlando is a poet with both "world enough and time." As I have tried to show, as excursive and fantastic as is Orlando's imagination, Woolf represents both the necessity of confronting one's "inheritance" and of transforming it with new paradigms of female desire.

Notes

1. Although this phrase of the narrator/biographer refers to the official manuscripts recording Orlando's sojourn in Turkey, I believe it applies generally to the elliptical narrative of the novel. Not only the narrative, with its multiple holes or orifices, but Orlando's writing, too, is suggestively identified with the body of the female despite the dominant patriarchal gendering of literary history: "Stealing away from talk and games, he had hidden himself behind curtains, in priest's holes, or in the cupboard behind his mother's bedroom which had a great hole in the floor and smelt horribly of starling's dung, with an inkhorn in one hand, a pen in another, and on his knee, a roll of paper" (*Orlando* 76). Although the roles of both parents are strangely muted in the narrative, this vignette suggests an associative complex linking Orlando's writing with the smelly hole of nature he spies as he hides near his mother's bedroom.

2. See Paul Zweig's provocative reading of the structure of adventure, which traces the male adventurer's flight from the body of the mother and re-encounter with the body of the female in the terrain of his adventures.

3. In "The Ego and the Id" Freud writes: "For one gets an impression that the simple Oedipus complex is by no means its commonest form, but rather represents a simplification or schematization which, to be sure, is often enough justified for practical purposes. Closer study usually discloses the more complete Oedipus complex, which is twofold, positive and negative, and is due to the bisexuality originally present in children. . . . It may even be that the ambivalence displayed in the relations to the parents should be attributed entirely to bisexuality

and that it is not, as I have represented above, developed out of identification in consequence of rivalry" (641). See Elizabeth Abel's discussion of Woolf's relation to Freud's thought in *Virginia Woolf and the Fictions of Psychoanalysis*.

4. See Marjorie Garber's discussion of Morris's autobiography, *Conundrum*, in *Vested Interests: Cross-Dressing and Cultural Anxiety*: "For Morris, who had journeyed so extensively in Africa, North and South, Casablanca was a special, liminal place, the geographic counterpart of his/her psychological and physiological condition" (336).

5. The publication of the letters between Vita Sackville-West and Virginia Woolf has spawned re-evaluations of *Orlando* as a lesbian text that reflects the two women's intense relationship: to Sherron E. Knopp, the novel "celebrates Virginia's love for Vita" (24) and is "the first positive, and still unsurpassed, sapphic portrait in literature" (33), and Susan Squier views it as "the consummation of her love for Vita" (175).

6. Sackville-West's first voyage out to Teheran was documented in *Passenger to Teheran*, published by Hogarth Press in 1926; her second voyage formed the basis of another travel narrative, *Twelve Days*. Her first trip took her to Egypt, Iraq, Persia, India, and Russia. During this journey to the Middle East, Vita completed her poem, "The Land," upon which Orlando's poem, "The Oak Tree," is based. Although Virginia Woolf herself had traveled to Turkey in 1906, she seems to have drawn on her own experience very little, relying instead on Vita's and Harold's more recent experiences in the East. For her diary entries on her own early trip to Turkey, see *Passionate Apprentice*.

7. Vita, for her part, coaxed this sense of suspense in her correspondent, transforming future destinations into promises of renewed intimacy in writing: "My next letter will be posted at Baghdad and written in the Persian Gulf. It will be all about Virginia. Indeed it may arrive before this one, as it will go part of the way by air" (*Letters VSW* 105).

8. The theatricality of this romantic Orientalism, its conduciveness to elaborate sexual role-playing, was a part of Vita's milieu more than a decade earlier. During the First Balkan War, while Harold was serving in Constantinople (right before their marriage), Vita performed *An Eastern Fantasy* ("a Persian play") in the Great Hall at Knole. She played the part of the Caliph loved by two dancing girls in the production replete with "yashmaks, veils, and flowing drapery" (Lees-Milne 60).

9. In *Critical Terrains: French and British Orientalism*, Lisa Lowe discusses how Said's important work on Orientalism statically presents the gendering of the colonizing discourse and plots the Western observer as invariably male.

10. Virginia records her attendance at a performance of the Diaghilev Ballet Company's *Scheherezade* in October 1918 (*Diary* I 201 n.9)

and again in July 1919 in Leicester Square. At the latter performance, Woolf saw Lydia Lopokova dance. Lopokova, who married Maynard Keynes in 1925, became a "type," in Woolf's words, for Rezia in *Mrs. Dalloway* (*Diary* II 265).

11. The association of Orientalism with an erotics of masquerade is found in the English literary tradition as well. The cross-dressing staged in Turkey in Byron's *Don Juan* provides another strand in the overdetermined context of the Orientalism in *Orlando*. But, as Peter Wollen points out, in the twenties this discourse began to serve a different cultural politics.

12. Luce Irigaray describes this homoeroticism as a form of autoeroticism, a way for a woman to get in touch with herself through the other (the "self-same," she calls the other). As Irigaray points out, in the discourse of psychoanalysis, "nothing of the special nature of desire *between women* has been unveiled or stated. That a woman might desire a woman 'like' herself, someone of the 'same' sex, that she might also have auto- and homo-sexual appetites [*sic*] is simply incomprehensible to Freud, and indeed inadmissible" (101). For an interesting essay on female narcissism in *Orlando*, based on Julia Kristeva's *Tales of Love*, see Ellen Carol Jones, "The Flight of a Word: Narcissism and the Masquerade of Writing in Virginia Woolf's *Orlando*."

13. See Susan Squier's essay on Woolf's revision of Defoe in *Orlando*, in "Tradition and Revision in Woolf's *Orlando*: Defoe and 'The Jessamy Brides.'"

14. Compare Woolf's sketch to Stephen Dedalus' "Parable of the Plums," also titled "A Pisgah Sight of Palestine" in *Ulysses*: "—Two Dublin vestals, Stephen said, elderly and pious, have lived fifty and fifty-three years in Fumbally's lane. . . .—They want to see the views of Dublin from the top of Nelson's pillar. . . .—But they are afraid the pillar will fall, Stephen went on. They see the roofs and argue about where the different churches are" (Joyce 119, 121).

15. "Jessamy," Squier says, is "a man who scents himself with perfume or who wears a sprig of Jessamine in his buttonhole . . . a dandy, a fop" (174). She goes on to say that by the time Woolf planned the novel, the word "Jessamy" suggested as well a parallel term of transgressive sexuality, "Amazon." "In its evocation of the gender line crossings embodied by a foppish male bride, a feminine man, and an 'Amazonian' woman, the initial title for *Orlando* prefigures Woolf's progatonist [*sic*], who in the course of a long life loved both sexes passionately, contracted a marriage to a man whom she jokingly suspected of being a woman (and who entertained the corresponding suspicion that Orlando was a man), and who at the novel's conclusion summons herself ('Orlando?') only to be answered by a multiplicity of selves—of both genders and sexual orientations" (174).

16. I borrow the term from Judith Butler's book on feminism and the subversion of identity.

17. This is a sly rewriting of the flight from women encoded in narratives of adventure, as well as a suggestion of the prevalence of male homoeroticism in the colonial service.

18. See Ronald Thomas' fascinating discussion of the significance of the Indian Mutiny in *The Moonstone* in *Dreams of Authority: Freud and the Fictions of the Unconscious* (203–219).

19. Virginia Woolf's attitude toward ambassadorships, particularly Harold Nicolson's, is captured in a letter from Virginia to Vita: "I am ashamed that any friend of mine should marry a man who may be an ambassador" (quoted in Trautmann 36).

20. Vita Sackville-West's *Pepita* (1937), the story of her maternal grandmother, expresses some of the relish with which she approached this gipsy "detour" in her family history. For Orlando's struggle to recover her legitimate inheritance after her sex change, Woolf might have been drawing on the whole issue of inheritance raised by Pepita's relation with Lionel Sackville-West, who, at the age of twenty, entered the English Foreign Office and met Pepita in Albolote, Spain. Vita writes in the first chapter: "The papers which have provided the material for the first part of this book owe their existence to the fact that in 1896 it became legally expedient for my grandfather's solicitors to take the evidence of a number of people in Spain who, some forty years earlier, had been acquainted with the principal characters involved. The point, in short, was the necessity of proving whether my grandmother, Pepita, had ever been married to my grandfather or not. Several issues were at stake: an English peerage, and an historic inheritance. . . . They dealt with them in their usual dry practical way, little foreseeing that this body of evidence collected in 1896 from voluble Spanish peasants, servants, villagers, dancers and other theatrical folk, would in 1936 be re-read in stacks of dusty typescript by someone closely connected, who saw therein a hotch-potch of discursiveness, frequently irrelevant but always fascinating" (5).

21. In a provocative rereading of *The Waves*, Jane Marcus analyzes the fusion of Woolf's feminism and her critique of British imperialism. This critique is found as well in *Orlando*, particularly in the parody of the official discourses of British Orientalism quoted above. Marcus goes on to argue that *The Waves* is "about the ideology of white British colonialism and the Romantic literature that sustains it. Its parody and irony mock the complicity of the hero and the poet in the creation of a collective national subject through an elegy for imperialism" (145). As I will go on to show, Woolf's relation to Romanticism in *Orlando* is revisionary but not parodic.

22. In "Veiling over Desire: Close-ups of the Woman" Mary Ann Doane offers an excellent overview of the trope of the veil in Western philosophical discourse. The structure of the veil, she says, is "clearly complicit with the tendency to specify the woman's position in relation to knowledge as that of the enigma" (118). The woman as veiled maps onto secular difference the dialectic of truth and appearance; in the discourse of metaphysics, Doane says, "the function of the

veil is to make truth profound, to ensure that there is a depth that lurks behind the surface of things" (118–119). Doane maintains that even in the antimetaphysical discourse of Nietzsche and Derrida, which deconstructs the opposition of truth/appearance, woman still functions tropologically in ways similar to the metaphysical tradition these philosophers are deconstructing. For a fascinating analysis of the function of the veil in a non-Western context, see Malek Alloula's *The Colonial Harem*. Alloula studies postcards picturing veiled Algerian women that were sent by French soldiers during the Algerian war. He analyzes the function of the veil as an extension of "an imaginary harem whose inviolability haunts the photographer-voyeur" (13).

23. Jane Gallop comments on this passage from Freud in *The Daughter's Seduction*: "The enigmatic 'hieroglyphic bonnet' suggests Egypt and in this riddle context reminds us of the riddle of the Sphinx. We think of Oedipus and the way solving riddles leads to blindness. A 'solved' riddle is the reduction of heterogeneous material to logic, to the homogeneity of logical thought, which produces a blind spot, the inability to see the otherness that gets lost in the reduction" (61). See the different signifying pattern of the veil in Arab culture (its resistance to the scopic drive) in Alloula's analysis.

24. See, particularly, the chapter "Ayesha Unveils" in *She*. The burlesque quality of Orlando's unveiling is more reminiscent of the scenes in Joyce's vaudevillian rendition of the Circean world of sex changes in *Ulysses*. "Hide! Hide! Hide!" the three modest sisters shout (*Orlando* 136), like the witches in Macbeth, just as Bloom cheers on Boylan and Molly ("Show! Hide! Show!" [Joyce 462]).

25. Irigaray describes Freud's narrative of the relationship of women to the mirror and to narcissism in the following way: "the flat mirror reflects the greater part of women's sexual organs only as a hole" (89 n.92). Is this the "hole" in the manuscript big enough to put one's finger through? The comparison with Irigaray's mimicking of Freud in *Speculum of the Other Woman* (1974) partly reveals that "postmodernism" is a misnomer because much of its work is an extension of modernist concerns. Lest this comparison seem anachronistic, it is instructive to regard *Orlando* in relation to another satiric "biography," published privately in 1928 by Djuna Barnes, *Ladies Almanack*. Barnes's slim volume, like *Orlando*, was considered a *roman à clef*, of sorts—in Barnes's case, a biography of Natalie Barney and the lesbian circle of writers in Paris in the twenties. *Ladies Almanack* parodied the Freudian phallic economy in satiric tones like those of *Orlando*, but with more explicit address: "'And even at that, what have These Scriveners said of her but that she must have had a Testes of sorts, however wried and awander; that indeed she was called forth a Man, and when answering, by some Mischance, or monstrous Fury of Fate, stumbled over a Womb, and was damned then and forever to drag it about, like a Prisoner his Ball and Chain, whether she would or no'. . . . 'they cannot let her be, or proclaim her just good Distaff Stuff, but will admit her to sense through the masculine Door only'" (53).

26. Drawing on the work of J. B. Pontalis, Francette Pacteau says: "To be assigned to one sex deprives one of the powers of the other and conjures up castration. The androgyne would represent the possession of both 'maternal and paternal phallus'; in disavowing the difference, both sexes regain their 'lost half' and the power that comes with it. Pontalis seems to propose a parallel route to the androgynous resolution for woman and man until he comes to the conclusion that 'The positive androgyne cannot exist outside myth. Incarnated, seen, it is effectively and simultaneously castrated man and woman'" (70). As I have suggested, Woolf narrativizes the myth of androgyny in an alternative "script" from Pontalis' Freud. See also Maria DiBattista's fine discussion of androgyny as comedy in *Virginia Woolf's Major Novels: The Fables of Anon.*

27. See Sandra M. Gilbert and Susan Gubar's discussion of Orlando's sex change as "a shift in fashion" (334).

28. See the letters from Virginia to Vita, 30 October 1927 and 6 November 1927, that describe Virginia's efforts to assemble the pictures from Vita's family album, and to have Vita pose for other pictures taken by Vanessa Bell (*Letters* III 434–435).

29. Contrast this stance with that of Isabelle Eberhardt, the "passionate nomad" of the modern French tradition: "A nomad I was even when I was very small and would stare at the road, that white spellbinding road headed straight for the unknown . . . a nomad I will remain for life, in love with distant and uncharted places" (96). *Orlando* is placed in a decidedly English comic tradition; as Maria DiBattista points out, this return is implied in the pattern of comedy itself.

30. In *The Country and the City* Raymond Williams traces the development of the literary genre of the pastoral, describing the original scene of Theocritus' pastoral as the landscape of the Greek islands and Egypt. As Williams shows, the pastoral was originally concerned with the works and days of the shepherd and goatherd, maintaining a connection with the "working year and with the real social conditions of country life" (16). *Orlando* taps this particular form of working-class pastoral in the vignette of Orlando's sojourn with the gipsies, but the narrative leaves this highly stylized view of "wildness" behind in favor of a more cultivated, English milieu. One of the dangers of such a return is that it lends itself to the charge that despite some alterations, the lay of the land is still rather tame. I want to emphasize that I see the text's Romanticism as revisionary.

31. Indeed, Lady Mary Wortley Montagu might be another source for Woolf's representation of Orlando's ambassadorship because Edward Wortley Montagu held an ambassadorship to Turkey during roughly the period of Orlando's tenure there.

32. Christine Brooke-Rose discusses the representation of genius in the Western tradition: "The really mysterious creative force, however, is genius. . . . Plato called it divine madness, Longinus called it ecstasy

. . . the Romantics Imagination but also Genius. And whatever the name it belongs to man" (255).

Works Cited

Abel, Elizabeth. *Virginia Woolf and the Fictions of Psychoanalysis*. Chicago: U of Chicago P, 1989.

Alloula, Malek. *The Colonial Harem*. Trans. Myrna Godzich and Wlad Godzich. Minneapolis: U of Minnesota P, 1986.

Barnes, Djuna. *Ladies Almanack*. Elmwood Park: Dalkey Archive, 1992.

Barthes, Roland. *A Lover's Discourse: Fragments*. Trans. Richard Howard. New York: Hill, 1978.

Brooke-Rose, Christine. "Illiterations." *Stories, Theories and Things*. Cambridge: Cambridge UP, 1991. 250–264.

Brown, Norman O. *Love's Body*. New York: Random, 1966.

Butler, Judith. *Gender Trouble: Feminism and the Subversion of Identity*. New York: Routledge, 1990.

DiBattista, Maria. *Virginia Woolf's Major Novels: The Fables of Anon*. New Haven: Yale UP, 1980.

Doane, Mary Ann. "Veiling over Desire: Close-ups of the Woman." In *Feminism and Psychoanalysis*. Ed. Richard Feldstein and Judith Roof. Ithaca: Cornell UP, 1989. 105–141.

Eberhardt, Isabelle. *The Passionate Nomad: The Diary of Isabelle Eberhardt*. Trans. Nina de Voogd. London: Virago, 1987.

Freud Sigmund. " The Ego and the Id." *The Freud Reader*. Ed. Peter Gay. New York: Norton, 1989. 628–658.

———. "On Femininity." In *New Introductory Lectures on Psychoanalysis*. Trans. and ed. James Strachey. London: Hogarth, 1974. 112–135.

———. "Three Essays on the Theory of Sexuality." *The Freud Reader*. 239–293.

Gallop, Jane. *The Daughter's Seduction: Feminism and Psychoanalysis*. Ithaca: Cornell UP, 1982.

Garber, Marjorie. *Vested Interests: Cross-Dressing and Cultural Anxiety*. New York: Routledge, 1992.

Gilbert, Sandra M., and Susan Gubar. *Sexchanges*. New Haven: Yale UP, 1989. Vol. 2 of *No Man's Land: The Place of the Woman Writer in the Twentieth Century*. 2 vols. 1988–1989.

Haggard, Rider H. *She*. Oxford: Oxford UP, 1991.

Hartman, Geoffrey, "Romantic Poetry and the Genius Loci." *Beyond Formalism: Literary Essays, 1958–1970*. New Haven: Yale UP, 1970. 311–336.

Irigaray, Luce. *Speculum of the Other Woman*. Trans. Gillian C. Gill. Ithaca: Cornell UP, 1985.

Jackson, Rosemary. *Fantasy: The Literature of Subversion*. London: Methuen, 1981.

Jones, Ellen Carol. "The Flight of a Word: Narcissism and the Masquerade of Writing in Virginia Woolf's *Orlando*." *Women's Studies* 23 (April 1994): 155–174.

Joyce, James. *Ulysses*. Ed. Hans Walter Gabler. New York: Random, 1986.

Knopp, Sherron E. "'If I Saw You Would You Kiss Me?': Sapphism and the Subversiveness of Virginia Woolf's *Orlando*." *PMLA* 103 (January 1988): 24–34.

Lees-Milne, James. *Harold Nicolson: A Biography, 1886–1929*. London: Chatto, 1980.

Lowe, Lisa. *Critical Terrains: French and British Orientalism*. Ithaca: Cornell UP, 1991.

Marcus, Jane. "Britannia Rules *The Waves*." *Decolonizing Tradition: New Views of Twentieth-Century "British" Literary Canons*. Ed. Karen R. Lawrence. Urbana: U of Illinois P, 1992. 136–162.

Mavor, Elizabeth. *The Ladies of Langollen: A Study in Romantic Friendship*. Harmondsworth, UK: Penguin, 1973.

Nicolson, Nigel. *Portrait of a Marriage*. New York: Atheneum, 1973.

Pacteau, Francette. "The Impossible Referent: Representations of the Androgyne." *Formations of Fantasy*. Ed. Victor Burgin, James Donald, and Cora Kaplan. London: Methuen, 1986. 62–84.

Sackville-West, V. *The Letters of Vita Sackville-West to Virginia Woolf*. Ed. Louise DeSalvo and Mitchell A. Leaska. New York: Morrow, 1985.

———. *Passenger to Teheran*. 1926. New York: Moyer Bell, 1990.

———. *Pepita*. New York: Doubleday, 1937.

Said, Edward. "Orientalism Reconsidered." *Literature, Politics and Theory: Papers from the Essex Conference 1976–84*. Ed. Francis Barker et al. London: Methuen, 1986. 210–229.

Squier, Susan M. "Tradition and Revision in Woolf's *Orlando*: Defoe and 'The Jessamy Brides.'" *Women's Studies* 12.2 (1986): 167–177.

Stein, Gertrude. *Lectures in America*. Boston: Beacon, 1935.

Stevenson, Robert Louis. "A Humble Remonstrance." *Memories and Portraits*. New York: Scribner, 1907.

Thomas, Ronald R. *Dreams of Authority: Freud and the Fictions of the Unconscious*. Ithaca: Cornell UP, 1990.

Trautmann, Joanne. *The Jessamy Brides: The Friendship of Virginia Woolf and V. Sackville-West*. University Park: Pennsylvania State UP, 1973.

Van Den Abbeele, George. *Travel as Metaphor from Montaigne to Rousseau*. Minneapolis: U of Minnesota P, 1992.

Williams, Raymond. *The Country and the City*. New York: Oxford UP, 1973.

Wollen, Peter. "Fashion/Orientalism/The Body." *New Formations* 1 (Spring 1987): 5–33.

Wollstonecraft, Mary. *Letters Written during a Short Residence in Sweden, Norway, and Denmark*. Lincoln: U of Nebraska P, 1976.

Woolf, Virginia. *Between the Acts*. New York: Harcourt, 1941.

———. *The Diary of Virginia Woolf*. Ed. Anne Olivier Bell. 5 vols. New York: Harcourt, 1977–1984.

———. *The Letters of Virginia Woolf.* Ed. Nigel Nicolson and Joanne Trautmann. 6 vols. New York: Harcourt, 1975–1980.

———. *Orlando: A Biography.* 1928. New York: Harcourt, 1929.

———. *A Passionate Apprentice: The Early Journals, 1897–1909.* Ed.
Mitchell A. Leaska. New York: Harcourt, 1990.

———. *The Voyage Out.* 1915. New York: Harcourt, 1926.

Zweig, Paul. *The Adventurer: The Fate of Adventure in the Western World.*
Princeton: Princeton UP, 1974.

SUBLIME BARBARIANS IN THE

NARRATIVE OF EMPIRE;

OR, LONGINUS AT SEA IN *THE WAVES*

Laura Doyle

At first glance an idea that transcends history, the sublime, has recently been interpreted historically and revived theoretically.[1] Critics have begun to tease out the political values woven into the sublime as well as to reconfigure it for a postmodern or feminist aesthetic. Working in dialogue with these projects, I trace here a racial and imperial substructure of the sublime discoverable at its inception, in Longinus's treatise *Peri Hypsous* (*On the Sublime*). In the Romantic period the idea of the sublime, while still racially inflected, undergoes a transformation as it becomes a key animating principle for newly racialized narratives of culture: it shapes a story whereby the embrace and subsumption of an ancient racial past propels England toward an imperial future. It is as the British Empire faces the very limits such narratives of sublimity had promised to transcend that Virginia Woolf writes *The Waves*. In this novel Woolf labors to turn the narrative of the sublime inside-out without negating her own narrative's investment in sublimity. *The Waves* thus offers fresh insight not only into the difficulties entailed in any recuperation of the sublime but also into how aesthetics form the inscape, especially the narratival inscape, of the imperial subject.

To signal the direction of my argument, I want to begin by calling attention to the "as if" that generates the entire fictional cosmos of *The Waves*.

Originally published in *Modern Fiction Studies*, Spring 1996.

> The sun had not yet risen. The sea was indistinguishable
> from the sky *as if* a cloth had wrinkles in it. . . . Gradually
> the dark bar on the horizon became clear *as if* the sedi-
> ment in an old wine bottle had sunk. . . . Behind it, too,
> the sky cleared *as if* the white sediment there had sunk,
> or *as if* the arm of a woman couched beneath the horizon
> had raised a lamp. . . . (7; emphasis added)

Immersed in this profusely figured world, the six characters in
The Waves likewise speak perpetually in figures, sinking "down on
the black plumes of sleep" or watching "walls and cupboards whiten
and bend their yellow squares" (27). Woolf foregrounds the liminal
realm occupied by the image, that border zone where subject meets
object, and object all but eludes the grasp of the subject, save by the
sublime mediation of the image, the "as if" of the figure. Woolf thus
apparently adheres to a Romantic poetics of the sublime in which
imagination and image function crucially to ground the human witness
in a scene whose vastness or autonomous existence surpasses his
or her grasp. Furthermore, in rendering her readers' and characters'
encounter with this universe in a rarefied metaphorical language,
Woolf would seem to follow Longinus's principle that "figures are the
natural allies of sublimity" (17.1).

But by calling attention to figure, by flaunting her narrative
dependence on it, Woolf also violates one of Longinus's most honored principles: that in sublime writing the "best figures" are those
which "avoid being seen for what they are" (Longinus 38.3). Woolf
exposes the figure to scrutiny by blithely replacing one "as if" with
another so that a wine bottle might as well be a woman and a sinking movement (sediment sunk) might as well be a rising one (lamp
raised). Heaping her metaphors, she interferes with the sublime flight
by which the writer makes the audience feel, in Longinus's famous
phrase, "as though it had itself produced what it has heard" (7.2).
She denaturalizes the alliance between metaphor and sublimity. She
foregrounds the plastic, utterly fictional nature of the world she is
building even as she describes the most natural or naturalized scene
imaginable—the rising of the sun.

Why? Is Woolf a post-Romantic writer for whom the sublime is, in
Thomas Weiskel's phrase, "a moribund aesthetic" that can be invoked
only ironically (6)? But what if one feels, as I do, that "sublime" in
some unironic sense aptly describes the rhythmic, transporting lyricism of *The Waves*, which Woolf herself referred to as "mystical"?
Perhaps instead *The Waves* is a candidate for Patricia Yaeger's "female
sublime," which emulates the "capacious gestures" of the Romantic
sublime but refuses the appropriative introjection of the sublime
object's radical alterity.[2] We might conclude that Woolf's endlessly

displacive metaphors leave *in* place the objects' imperviousness to figural appropriation.

But then, too, what of the evidence, proffered by Jane Marcus and Patrick McGee, suggesting that the syntax of Woolf's novel is itself a representation and, for McGee, an inevitable repetition of the rhythms of an imperial self? Its insistent naming and renaming belongs, they argue, to the grasping, hegemonic subject epitomized in Bernard (although Marcus argues that Woolf effectively distances herself from this subject while McGee doubts this). If Woolf's novel is a work of the sublime, and if Marcus and McGee are right that its rhythms embody those of a colonizing consciousness, then *The Waves* forces a further scrutiny of the sublime. It suggests that, before we attempt to re-imagine the sublime for a feminist poetics, we need to supplement a gender critique of it with a racial and postcolonial one.

Other evidence also points in this direction. The project of locating a female or feminine sublime is given further pause, and the suspicion of a colonialist, racialized infrastructure given further grounds by the recurrent juxtaposition in Western narratives of a white person's sublime "transport" against a darker person's presence—as if the latter surreptitiously provoked the former. Readers will recall Edmund Burke's theory of the sublime, which associates blackness with terror and tells the story of a mulatto woman who shocks the once-blind child into sublime astonishment as the first object he sees in gaining sight. W. J. T. Mitchell and Sara Suleri have noted this conjunction of race and sublimity in Burke, considering it evidence of the colonial anxiety underlying what they identify as the sublime's specular aesthetic.[3]

More recent stories of the sublime testify to the persistence of this racialization. Consider one of Patricia Yaeger's own examples. In Eudora Welty's story "June Recital," the ecstatic piano playing of Miss Eckhart provokes Cassie's transport which, Yaeger rightly points out, Cassie checks and resists because it signals a transgressive female sexuality. Yet Cassie's resistance to the sexual sublime oddly mingles with race, for this moment calls forth her memory of "a crazy nigger [who] had jumped out of the school hedge and threatened to kill her" (quoted in Yaeger 201). A racial scene intrudes on the sexual one, reinforcing its rhythm of arousal and denial (which is paradigmatic of the traditional Romantic encounter with the sublime). Likewise, in Toni Morrison's exploration of "the way black people ignite critical moments of discovery or change or emphasis in literature not writ-ten by them," she notes how in *The Words to Say It* Marie Cardinal traces the onset of her madness to her experience of listening to Louis Armstrong (implicitly without apparent consciousness of any racial connection). In Cardinal's narrative, she is at first swept away by the music and then experiences what she calls her "first encounter with the Thing" culminating in a sensation of suffocating panic and an apprehension that "I'm going to die!" so that she flees "like someone possessed." Recognizing the dynamics of the "sublime" here, Morrison draws our attention to its racial aspect (vi–viii).

If we place Cardinal's and Welty's stories in the color-threaded tradition of Burke's sublime, we might ask whether a female sublime reweaves or unravels those threads. Is race integral or merely incidental to the sublime, including the female sublime? The question becomes more pressing when we recognize that this intertwining of race and sublimity has a longer, more intricate history than either Suleri or Mitchell recognizes, one which originates with Longinus and takes an important turn in what I will call the early Romantic sublime. This history forms a prelude to Woolf's sublime writing in *The Waves* and in turn draws our attention to the sublime's role in our narratives and our histories.

I.

It is a fact too little noticed that Longinus's *Peri Hypsous* is permeated by his imperial situation—as a Greek writer in imperial Rome. Neil Hertz notes Longinus's "nostalgia" for the golden age of Athens, and he attends to the rhetoric of freedom, slavery, and battle that pervades Longinus's examples (588). But Hertz dwells only on the Greek/Macedonian past and so lets us forget, even as Longinus keeps implicit, the more immediate context in which Rome has repeated the Macedonian subjugation. Michael DeGuy likewise hints in passing that Longinus sought to counter the apparent "decline of the Orient" in celebrating Homer and asks if the sublime is "an aesthetic category motivated by nostalgia?" (7). What these critics understand as an evocation of the past is, however, more accurately understood as a problem of the present.

The immediate political "urgency" (to borrow a favorite Longinian noun) compelling *Peri Hypsous* emerges more clearly when we notice how many of Longinus's examples are structured by an opposition between Greek and Latin writers. This constitutes what we might call the imperialist or racialist principle of the sublime. Not only does sublimity get used as a measure to rank writers by nationality or ancestry, but sublimity of rhetoric is also implicitly staged as a means of resistance to antinational imperialist claims. Longinus's own sublime rhetoric serves this end.

Longinus praises both Latin and Greek writers in his treatise but he implicitly favors the Greek. He singles out Homer, Sappho, Plato,

Thucydides, and Demosthenes as sublime writers or orators; and although he expresses admiration for Cicero and others, he rarely directly refers to them as sublime. In his view, Plato "contended for the chief prize with Homer" (13.30), while "in history Thucydides" emerges the winner (13.40). He sneers at Caecilius, who "[goes so far as] to pronounce Lysias as altogether far superior to Plato" (32.58); but Caecilius, Longinus says casually, "can be dismissed; he is moved by contentiousness" (35.62). The exact source of the contentiousness is left unspecified but it is clear that some sort of polemic is in play here.

How much should we make of this tendency to privilege the Greek? Longinus's closing argument has discouraged critics from reading his treatise politically and paying attention to these contrasts: he concludes by stressing his opinion that freedom is *not* a necessary condition for sublime authorship; it only requires the absence of greed and decadence. While on the surface this seems to mean he has no quarrel with the empire and no interest in politics, a certain cunning may also operate here. For this point leaves open the possibility that the condition of un-freedom might in fact provoke the most sublime speech, a suggestion supported by his citations from Demosthenes and other Greek writers who speak in the face of foreign invasions (38.67, 17.40) and who ask, in sublime prose, "whether we shall be free men or slaves" (22.44). This political subtext comes closest to the surface in chapter 12, where Longinus asks, with tongue in cheek,

> if I, as a Greek, may be allowed an opinion—that Cicero differs from Demosthenes in his grandeur. Demosthenes has a sublimity which for the most part is abrupt and sheer, while Cicero is expansive; and our Greek author might, because with his violence—and furthermore with his rapidity, strength, and vehemence—he as it were both burns and scatters, be compared to a bolt of lightning, while Cicero, like an ample conflagration, spreads and dilates in all directions. (12.27)

Although Longinus appears to compare the sublimity of Demosthenes with that of Cicero, in fact, in referring to Cicero rather than Cicero's sublimity, he never attributes sublimity to Cicero. Moreover, he elsewhere eschews diffusion of feeling (12.27) as counter to sublime energy, which he usually characterizes as "violent" or "vehement." Cicero falls short.

Longinus continues to demur sarcastically ("But you Romans could better judge these matters" [12.27]), while he further hints at the political conditions inspiring his notion of sublimity: "The place for Demosthenic sublimity and surpassing vigor is in appeals to indignation and intense passion, and where, to sum it all up, it is required to shatter the hearer's composure" (12.27). Required by what circumstances? With a vigor surpassing whose? To shatter which hearers' composure? The hearers of Longinus as well as Demosthenes? Repeatedly citing Demosthenes's appeals to freedom, Longinus lets his position be known. Moreover, as critics have noted since the eighteenth century, Longinus allows sublimity's "intense passion" to inflame his own prose, which, when crackled by these occasional sarcasms, in effect enlists sublimity, both formally and thematically, as an instrument of political resistance to an imperialism structured along ethnic lines.

2.

My insistence on the imperialist politics underlying Longinian aesthetics might be impertinent if it did not point toward an important pattern in the subsequent history of the sublime. For when the idea of the sublime experiences its renaissance in the later eighteenth century, a new racialized rhetoric emerges as its twin discourse. Both appear in the immediate wake of the Seven Years War, which consolidated Britain's colonial holdings from the Orient to Canada *and* within the longer historical wake of the English Revolution—itself understood as the reversal of a Norman imperialism. In short a violent conquering history underlies (as I have discussed elsewhere and will briefly review here) the eighteenth-century sublime aesthetic.[4] Its influence is most visible in the *early* Romantic sublime, which sets the stage for Kant and Wordsworth.

In the 1760s sublimity is the value that serves to raise the status of "native" or "barbarian" lyrics—the songs of the warrior-poets Ossian and Regner Lodbrog as well as of the not-yet-canonical texts of Shakespeare and Milton. As in Longinus's argument, a sublime violence or vehemence is discovered in these "barbaric" texts that takes on value within a racialized political discourse and history. To see the parallel we must turn back briefly to the revolutionary period in England when this discourse that eventually informs the Romantic sublime first came to the fore.

In seventeenth-century revolutionary England, dissidents invoked a rhetoric of the "Norman yoke" to defend the claims of the "native" Anglo-Saxons against the Norman monarchy. In mounting their opposition to the papacy and the throne, lawyers, peasants, and religious reformers alike built on the growing scholarship in "Saxonism," that is, in pre-Norman, Saxon words, laws, relics, and customs. Edward Coke drew evidence from the *Archainomia*, a recently available compendium of Anglo-Saxon laws, in making his case for the "common law" interpretation of English government and property rights.[5] The famous Leveller pamphleteer and religious radical Gerard Winstanley was one of those who expanded such materials into a counter-myth of English history: he argued in his "Law of Freedom" letter to Oliver Cromwell that "When the Norman power had conquered our forefathers, he took the free use of our English ground from them" and furthermore that "all Kings from his time to Charles, were successors of that conquest, and all laws were made to confirm that conquest" (22–23). No doubt this myth of Norman against Englishman gave special resonance to Sir Henry Holcroft's 1653 translation of Procupius's *History of the Warres of the Emperour Justinian*, with its proclamation that "No government . . . be conferr'd upon strangers in blood / but such only have the place, to whose race it did belong" (7).

In postrevolutionary generations and certainly by the early eighteenth century, this rhetoric died down as the Parliament, merchants, and professional classes assumed their power. Instead this racialized narrative of English history became calmly codified in the multivolume histories of England written by Hume, Smollett, and others. In these volumes both the earliest Celtic and the later Norman descent stories of England were increasingly eclipsed by the Saxon or Gothic myth of England's origins—of itself as a people humble yet hardy, conquered but rising again.

Against the background of this discursive history, in the 1760s scholars began to collect "native" medieval warrior poetry. I suggest we consider MacPherson's publication in 1762 of the so-called *Poems of Ossian*, as well as that of Bishop Thomas Percy's *Reliques of Ancient English Poetry* in 1764, within this racialized historical discourse. As most critics note, these two works are seminal in the history of Romantic thought (despite the controversy over *Ossian*'s authenticity); what is overlooked by scholars is the way in which these and other volumes articulate a notion of the sublime that yokes it to race—a yoking that crucially determines their seminal role.

Professor Hugh Blair's dissertation on *Ossian*, appended to most eighteenth-century editions, typifies the emergent connection between sublimity and a racialized poetic tradition. He claims that "amidst the rude scenes of nature, amidst rocks and torrents and whirlwinds and battles, dwells the sublime" (172–73). At the same time he particularly celebrates the Celtic ancestry of Ossian and thereby enters a newly controversial debate over which of the original European "races"—Celt, Scot, Briton, or Goth—is most sublime. Blair dissented in fact from the editor MacPherson's claim that Ossian was a highland Scot whose people were utterly distinct from the Celts as well as the Britons who in MacPherson's view were inferior poets (59, 70–74). As they debate the Scottish or Celtic lineage of Ossian, these scholars in the process make racial lineage the foundation of poetic genius and literary paternity. Their literary-genealogical claims are taken up and further debated by others, including Bishop Percy, who are interested in extolling the original talents and pure lineage of the Gothic "skalds" (from whom the Anglo-Saxon poets were said to have descended).

Percy shares the notion of race-specific traditions, but he strongly disputes Blair's privileging and genealogy of the Celtic "bards." While Blair considers the Celts a "Great and mighty people" who are "addicted . . . to poetry" and "altogether distinct from the Goths and Teutones" (96), Percy insists in the prefaces to his extremely popular collections of ancient "Gothic" poetry that the ancient Celts "lack so much as an alphabet of their own" whereas "the institutions of Odin and the [Gothic] Skalds was [sic] the very reverse. No barbarous people were so addicted to writing . . . no barbarous people ever held letters in higher reverence" (Percy, Northern Antiquities 14). For him, the Celts and the Teutonic Goths "were two races of men ab origine distinct" (Percy, Northern Antiquities 16). While they disagree over lineages, however, all of these scholars define sublimity as a racial trait. Imitating those ancestors who had once conquered and reconquered each other in blood, these self-appointed literary-cultural offspring began to do so in a new domestic racial discourse, out of which would ultimately be born the Saxon self-image that would authorize its own violences, sexual and colonial as well as rhetorical.

Most directly, these debates over "true" racial-poetic identities, which pervade the early Romantic discourse of the sublime, began to give shape to new ideas of English literary history. In fact, in the case of Richard Hurd's popular Letters on Chivalry and Romance (1762), these debates began to supplant the well-established debate over the relative virtues of the ancients versus the moderns. The English (and other Europeans) began to claim their own ancient traditions. Hurd thus boldly pits the Gothic against the Greek (preserving Longinus's nationalist principle of the sublime while displacing his classical Greek canon). For Hurd, the "enchanted ground" of England, birthplace of "our forefathers," makes the English "bards . . . more sublime, more terrible, more alarming, than those of the classic fablers" (VI, 54–55). Indeed, inspired by this tradition, Shakespeare's "terrible sublime" ("which not so much the energy of his genius, as the nature of his subject drew from him") is "more poetical for being Gothic" (VI, 55). Hurd finally concludes that "tho' the spirit, passion, rapin, and violence of the two sets of manners were equal, there was yet a dignity, a magnificence, a variety in the feudal, which the [Greek] wanted" (VI, 48). The "Gothic language" itself "helped [them] to work up [their] tempests with such terror" (VI, 50).

Within three decades after the publication of these texts, according to Carl Berkhout, "a 'myth' had developed in the English literary world" (153). Though Berkhout does not say it, this rapidly proliferating myth was racial and implicitly gendered as well as poetical. By the time William Mitford wrote his "Inquiry into the Principles of Harmony in Language and of the Mechanism of Verse, Modern and Antient" (1804), he could speak of the different principles of "Harmony" experienced by "all the races of mankind in their respective languages" as a popular topic: "In our own country, especially of late years, publications, of which it is either the principal or an incidental topic, have been numerous" (1). Mitford builds on Hurd to determine the formal principles of "native" English poetry and to characterize the "energetic language of our early *forefathers*" (132; emphasis added), holding that "the form of the English language has hardly in any degree been derived from the French" (367), for despite the Norman-French invasion (both political and linguistic in his account) "the genius of the [Gothic] Anglo-Saxon pronunciation at length prevailed" (142). These ancient poems were thus figured as the stuff of a racialized native literary paternity.

William Wordsworth internalizes and explictly aims to inherit this "native" and sublime tradition. Wordsworth himself acknowledges that Percy's *Reliques of Ancient English Poetry* was formative of "my taste and nature tendencies" (quoted in Nichol x). Similarly, in noting Robert Burns's influence on him, Wordsworth praises that poet as "energetic, solemn, and sublime in sentiment" exactly because he remains true to "native" influences and resists "the inundation of foreign literature" that might otherwise adulterate his style (quoted in Low 163). In *The Recluse*, even as Wordsworth's poet-persona narrates the influence of native influences on his young self, we can detect the influence of the sublime barbarian poets on Wordsworth. The speaker recalls wistfully that as a child he felt "Motions of savage instinct" among "deep pools, tall trees, black chasms and dizzy crags" and who as an adult is still "pleased / More than a wise man ought to be" by the fantasy of "two Vessels matched in deadly fight": "I wish / Fret, burn, and struggle, and in soul am there." He regrets the passing of his "savage" impulses even as he worries over their intensity, a double movement that prefigures the sublime's pivotal function (717).

In fact, the poem's resolution of this ambivalence toward violent impulses heralds the transition from the early to the late Romantic sublime: "Reason" enters to assure the savage-souled adult not to fear "a want of aspirations" or "foes / To wrestle with, and victory to complete . . . the undaunted quest" for these shall survive "though changed their office." The poet thus bids "farewell to the warrior's schemes." Instead, his "Voice shall speak" "On Man, on Nature, and on Human Life / Musing in Solitude" (717). As in Kant's later work and as is, in effect, dramatized in Burke's change in sensibility from his early writing on the sublime to his later writing on the barbarisms of the French revolutionaries, "Reason" enters the revolutionary discourse of the sublime to contain its violent energies and transgressive scope (an argument I have made more fully elsewhere).[6] In other words, once it serves its function of transporting into the historical present a heroic sublime past, of energizing and *authorizing* the former through the latter, the sublime gets civilized.

Immanuel Kant's writings make particularly manifest this pivotal turning through the sublime. Although not known in English until later, it is remarkable that Kant's *Observations on the Feeling of the Beautiful and Sublime* (1763) appears at nearly the same moment as Percy, Blair, and Hurd's texts and, like them, measures sublimity in relation to national and racial differences. Kant sets out to distinguish among two kinds of "finer feeling," the beautiful and the sublime, both of which include "thought" and "intellectual excellences" and "presuppose a sensitivity of soul" (46). He first associates the beautiful with the feminine and the sublime with the masculine, as several recent critics have analyzed, and then in effect genders nations and races accordingly. Directing our attention to "the mental characters of peoples" (99), he explains that the Italian and the French prefer the beautiful, the German, English, and Spanish the sublime (implicitly masculine and superior).

But most important for my point here, in the second half of chapter 4 Kant initiates the use of the sublime as a pivot for the turn from national to global-imperial race distinctions. He turns his attention from European nation-specific sublime perceptions to the "Oriental" and the "savage races," which distinguish themselves by their relative indifference to the sublime and the beautiful alike (111, 112). While he considers "the Arab" to have a taste for the sublime and therefore to be "the noblest man in the Orient," unfortunately this taste "degenerates very much into the adventurous" (109). Most starkly, the "savage races" of America and Africa "show few traces of a mental character disposed to the finer feelings" (112). The "Negroes of Africa" in particular "have by nature no feeling that rises above trifling" and in fact "[n]ot a single one was ever found who presented anything great in art or science or any other praiseworthy quality" (111).

So here we have the sublime turn that is a racial turn:[7] that dynamical introjection, by reason, of the power of an awesome alien nature reveals itself here as the dynamical reversal of the values of feeling and reason so as to subdue the power of an alien racialized and gendered other. The violence of warring races in European history that inspired the early Romantic sublime gets reconfigured in the aesthetic and philosophical systems of the late Romantic sublime—a coding Kant undertook more precisely, as we know, in *The Critique of Judgement*. In other words, Romantic writers and theorists aligned themselves with the brooding, wild, once-conquered (that is, "Gothic") races of their own lands and then in a subreption itself figured as sublime, refashioned this savage figure into the poetical, reasoning, civilized European, fit to conquer and uplift the savages of other lands. Of course this racial maneuver implicitly maintained the exclusion of women and the feminine from participation in the sublime.

In thus employing aesthetics (and its shading into ethics) as a language for making race and gender claims, Romanticism not only began a discursive braiding that would be formative for modern American and European cultures but also wove a new narrative of the relation between nature and culture: as I will now describe, it shaped a narratival metaphysics—thus establishing the narrative form with which Woolf and others tangle in their revisions of the sublime.

3.

It is a commonplace of criticism that Romanticism takes the theory of the sublime beyond that of a rhetorical mode into the realm of metaphysics. For Longinus, as Samuel Monk and others since have emphasized, *writers* are sublime when they achieve an energy of statement that makes artifice appear natural—so natural it seems generated by the listener rather than the orator.[8] For many late eighteenth-century writers, in contrast, sublimity resides sometimes in things themselves—hanging rocks, rushing torrents—and sometimes in the human poetic response to such things (as in Kant), but it is hardly ever a trick of words. Typically, the male poet or philosopher is considered sublime exactly because he feels the awful transcendence of nature and embraces it enough to contain some part of it in what he writes—thus countering its transcendence of the human.

Yet for both Longinus and the Romantics, sublimity involves an exchange between art and nature, in which one steals from the other to become itself. Longinian and Romantic theories of the sublime stage the encounter of culture with nature, word with object. And this encounter takes place on a highly charged political stage. Longinus repeatedly conflates art and nature as when he refers to figures (though inherently artificial) as "the *natural* allies of sublimity" (17.38) or compares bodies and words (for example, the parts of a discourse) to "the conjunction of limbs with one another" (40.70). Near the conclusion of his treatise he advises that "we should everywhere have recourse to art as an aid to nature; for perhaps the perfect state is that where each of these is in possession of the other" (36.65). I would suggest that art must appear as nature—the rhetoric of the sublime must itself be naturalized—to serve the purposes of Longinus's covertly political project.

In Romanticism, not only do poets and philosphers narrate sublimity as the introjection of a barbarian nature by civilized culture, but the terms of this relation are legibly racialized and implicitly gendered, as we have seen. I want to suggest that this nativist sublime participates in a broad shift in the Western idea of culture—in its new *narrativizing* of culture. That is, the recuperation of racial origins is likely of a piece with the later eighteenth-century shift, traced by Michel Foucault, away from taxonomic or platonic modes of thought toward newly privileged narratival ones. In the early Romantic sublime the most venerable forms of English language and culture get traced not to classical models that invite imitation but rather to preeminently male race ancestors who evolve and bequeath particular practices. The sublime narrates a new story of how nature unfolds into culture, how the cultural subject bespeaks his natural national origin.

The sublime operates here as myth in the Barthesian sense, for, like all forms of myth, the sublime "transforms history into nature" (Barthes 129). Certainly the race, gender, and national narratives which we see in incipient form in the early Romantic sublime unfold as metaphysical narratives of introjection in the late Romantic sublime and then finally by the mid-nineteenth century take on their full force in the form of claims that nature—physical inheritance, kinship ties, proper motherhood—determines a people's culture. Increasingly throughout the nineteenth and early twentieth centuries, both humanists and scientists insist that to take hold of the "race principle," to direct and contain the sexual principle, was to bring about the perfect marriage between body and reason, nature and culture. As finally expressed in Darwinian science, this idea naturalized history by showing it to embody the force of nature's most profound structuring or selective principle—sexual selection for fit races. Thus while by 1850 Robert Knox could claim that "Race is everything: literature, science, art, in a word, civilization depend on it" (3), popularizers such as Caleb Saleeby would soon finish the equation by pointing out that "marriage has become evolved and established as a social institution because of its services to race-culture" (xiii–xiv).[9]

Such naturalizing narratives of cultural history at once recognize, mystify, and sublimate the original "barbaric" violence that gives rise to them. As Barthes points out, "Myth does not deny things, on the contrary, its function is to talk about them; simply, it purifies them, it makes them innocent, it gives them a natural and eternal justification" (143). I would add that narrative as a temporal form fosters this project, allowing the English subject simultaneously to claim access to and create distance from a founding cultural violence by way of a sublimation channeled through racial and sexual lineages. Or again, these new lineage myths enable the English middle class to narrate its sublime turn, via the introjection of barbaric violence, from colonial victim to imperial victor. To say so is also to bring into view the strenuous energies described within the sublime. The modern English ruling subject can presume no labor-free aristocratic access to power and goods. Within the emergent imperial polis, founded on an economy of appropriation, the naturalized Other is willfully, energetically *con*sumed rather than merely *as*sumed as a founding presence. In this sense the sublime functions as a theory of labor, of the labor of an imperialism without divine rights, an imperialism of institutions, incursions, and necessary, difficult internalizations of that which is mastered.

Thus does the sublime form the inscape of an emergent imperial self in willed confrontation with a vast world beyond its immediate perception yet over which it claims dominion. This self is a narrated self, a self in extension and transformation, a self born of violent colonization and then converted into colonizer. Without imperial, racial-patriarchal motive, does the sublime have a story to tell? It is exactly this question that Virginia Woolf takes up in *The Waves*.

4.

If Longinus's *Peri Hypsous* is inflamed by an anti-imperial, nativist "vehemence," and the Romantics transmute this nativist rhetoric of resistance and violence into a remystified imperialist consciousness, with a savage poetic genius at its center, then Woolf, writing as the British Empire exhausts its encounter with a projected savagery, traces the energies of a flagging yet persistent and lyrical discursive economy. Or in other words, if to seize on the poetry of the barbarians is to seize on a narrative by which nature becomes history, Woolf exposes this myth-making logic in both her story and her narrative mode. In grouping her characters around the legendary Percival, Woolf deconstructs the sublimating processes that attend the literary-historical narrative of English culture. And she couples this project with an interrogation of the metaphoricity of language. She practices the Longinian principle of sublime figurativity even while exposing its function in imperial myth-making, including the making of her own narrative.

In *The Waves*, Percival is the embodiment of a mythologized nature around which humans build a history. As suggested by the fact that we never hear his words or thoughts, he is the unspeaking supplement, the recurrent and naturalizing but empty figure in a Barthesian semiotics of myth. In the original legends, Percival seeks the Holy Grail (he is also called Perceval, Parsifal, or Parcival in the tale's various migrations from Ireland to France to Germany to England, a history itself bespeaking the conquering history and interrelated narratives of lineage I have discussed). The metaphysical burden of the sublime finds implicit expression in this quest. The grail is held to be the platter used at the last supper, that last human feast of the divine son of God: to find the grail is to reclaim the pivotal moment in a narrative of transubstantiation, that story converting the awesome transcendental into the human historical. Further, legend has it that when Percival finds the grail, he will save the life of the king, human embodiment of the divine law. So Percival as founding hero of a lineage myth enacts in his story the function which he serves in his culture: the transubstantiation of divinely created but inscrutable nature into readable, reasonable, conquering (or questing) people's history.

Yet Woolf stresses the pagan aspect of Percival, a move consonant with other early twentieth-century recuperations of medieval folk figures, including Wagner's opera *Parsifal*. In fact, this modernist-era interest in folk figures like Percival is a culmination of the nativist and racialist ideologies that we saw emerging in early Romanticism (a trajectory traced by both Leon Poliakov in *The Aryan Myth* and Martin Bernal in *Black Athena*, in different ways). Woolf intervenes in this racialist discourse with her own sly portrait of Percival. As Neville observes, Percival is "'remote from us all in a pagan universe'" (36) and his "'oddly inexpressive eyes, are fixed with pagan indifference upon the pillar opposite'" (36). He is "'heavy,'" "'clumsy'"; "'his magnificence is that of some medieval commander'" (37). And yet "'A wake of light seems to lie on the grass behind him'" (37). Like those sublime medieval barbarians, Percival is blind and dumb yet in his wake comes light, comes consciousness—comes the subject who sublimates and transmutes that barbarity into the nation's imperial racial identity.

Percival serves as organizing principle for the English community figured in the three male and three female characters of the novel. Though he never speaks directly in the text and apparently not much in his fictional life either, that very dumbness or absence of speech

seems an enabling condition for the group formation of the characters: "'Unknown, with or without a secret, it does not matter . . . he
is a stone fallen into a pond round which minnows swarm. Like minnows, we who had been shooting this way, that way, all shot round
him when he came'" (136). Moreover, as the pagan conqueror-figure
who crosses the border into savage lands, he allows the introjection
of that alien Other by his compatriots. As Rhoda envisions it, "'since
Percival, riding alone . . . advances, the outermost parts of the
earth—pale shadows on the utmost horizon, India for instance, rise
into our purview. The world that had been shrivelled, rounds itself;
remote provinces are fetched up out of darkness; we see muddy
roads, twisted jungle, swarms of men . . . as within our scope, part
of our proud and splendid province'" (137). Percival is the figure who
grounds the Eurocentric subject. For the characters, once the world is
made theirs through him in this way, "'comfort steals over us'" and
"'some rapture of benignity'" (137). Thus "'the Oriental problem is
solved'" (136)—in the very figure by whom it is created.

The characters' momentous dinners function as ritual repeti-
tions of this introjection of barbarity for the imperial community. An
imagery of savagery presides as they come together:

> "Horns and trumpets," said Rhoda, "ring out; the stag blares
> in the thicket. There is a dancing and drumming, like the
> dancing and drumming of naked men with assegais."
>   "Like the dance of savages," said Louis, "round the
> camp fire. They are savage; they are ruthless. . . . The
> flames leap over their painted faces, over the leopard skins
> and the bleeding limbs which they have torn from the liv-
> ing body." (140)

Gathered around Percival or, after his departure for India, in honor
of him, they eat flesh—"'we have taken into our mouths the bodies
of dead birds'" (292)—while at the same time noting that "'we have
destroyed something by our presence . . . a world perhaps'" (232).

This destruction of one presence founds another. Bernard traces
their ritual into its next turn, into the imperial project. He celebrates,
just following the passage quoted above, "'the swelling and splendid
moment created *by us from* Percival'" (146; emphasis added) and
leads the movement back "'outside'": "'We, too, as we put on our
hats and push open the door, stride not into chaos, but into a world
that our own force can subjugate and make part of the illumined and
everlasting road . . . . The yellow canopy of our tremendous energy
hangs like a burning cloth above our heads'" (146). The characters
borrow from the savage for the work of civilization. They colonize
savagery in more than the usual sense, inscribing it for their history,

so that they may enter the sequence, and narrate an acculturated temporality: "'We have proved, sitting eating, sitting talking, that we can add to the treasury of moments'" and so show too that "'[w]e are not slaves bound to suffer incessantly unrecorded petty blows on our bent backs. We are not sheep either, following a master. We are creators. We too have made something that will join the innumerable congregations of past time'" (146). They have achieved the transcendence entailed in the British subject's sublimation of barbarity—a barbarity at once their own and projected onto those whom they conquer.

It is this movement from sublimation to transcendence that drives the insistent self-narration noted by Jane Marcus and Patrick McGee, which Bernard describes in imperial terms as "'the incessant rise and fall and fall and rise again'" (297). All of the characters express some form of this grasping, willful subjectivity fed on an imagined savagery. They all fold an imagery of conquering into their breathless, rhythmic, transporting inner speech. An emigré from Australia, Louis brings with him "'relics of myself in the sand that women made thousands of years ago'" (127). He has "'heard songs by the Nile and the chained beast stamping'" (218). He is attuned to "the nightingale who sings among the trampling feet; the conquests and migrations" (218). As colonial subject come to the metropole, he translates the song of the conquered into the speech of commerce. He has "'inherited a desk of solid mahogany in a room hung with maps [and] helped by my assiduity and decision to score those lines on the map there by which the different parts of the world are laced together'" (18). He guides the ship of empire. "'My shoulder is to the wheel; I roll the dark before me, spreading commerce where there was chaos in the four parts of the world'" (168). He performs again the sublime turn, the white man's aesthetic burden: "'The weight of the world is on our shoulders; its vision is through our eyes'" (169).

The women as well as the men express this introjecting, imperial relation to the world, as when Susan boasts that as a mother "'I shall be lifted higher than any of you on the backs of the seasons. I shall possess more than Jinny, more than Rhoda, by the time I die'" (132). She admits even as a young woman that she loves "'with such a ferocity that it kills me when the object of my love shows by a phrase that he can escape'" (132) and so predicts that she "'shall push the fortunes of my children unscrupulously. . . . I shall be debased and hide-bound by the bestial and beautiful passion of maternity'" (132). Rhoda is described as "'eyeless'" like Percival, and like him she is a voyageur, an adventurer, her ship "'sails into icy caverns where the sea-bear barks and stalactites swing green chains'" (19). She dreams herself as the plunderous proud spirit of Britannia ruling the waves: "'The waves rise; their crests curl; look at the lights on the masthead. They have scattered, they have foundered, all except my ship which mounts the wave and sweeps before the gale and reaches the islands where the parrots chatter'" (19).

But much as it reveals Woolf's interest in the politics of the sublime, this thematic material, including the central figure Percival, is only her most apparent engagement with it. To get at the more troubled aspect of Woolf's sublime, we need to recall Longinus's idea that the perceiver or witness of the sublime comes to feel "as if he has himself brought forth what he has only heard" (7.2). The substitutional logic here is the logic of metaphor as well as of myth. It is the logic of the "as if"—and of the interludes of *The Waves*.

5.

> The sun had not yet risen. The sea was indistinguishable from the sky *as if* a cloth had wrinkles in it. . . . Gradually the dark bar on the horizon became clear *as if* the sediment in an old wine bottle had sunk. . . . Behind it, too, the sky cleared *as if* the white sediment there had sunk, or *as if* the arm of a woman couched beneath the horizon had raised a lamp. . . . (7; emphasis added)

The effects of a rising, not-yet-visible sun come into view first through something that is not the sun—not only the sea and the sky but in the text a metaphor. The sun appears in *reflection*, in metaphor, before it emerges as visible fact, which inverts the naturalizing narrative order. Especially as foregrounded in Woolf's syntax of proliferating similes, the very sun's appearance is openly entangled in metaphoric effects. I suggest that, on the one hand, this exposure of metaphor as the fictional transubstantiation of the natural world is of a piece with Woolf's exposure of the racial-patriarchal British subject who introjects a savage origin, itself a fiction, in order to master it for a narrative of the imperial nation. On the other hand, this figural mode is one Woolf does not herself escape and so she remains tied to the aesthetic economy of imperialism which she exposes.

Let me expand on each of these. As I suggested earlier, Woolf makes clear that the character's self-narrating speech is precipitated by the unspeaking and in this sense absent originary mythical presence of Percival. Early in the book, as the boys leave the "cool temple" where perceptions first cluster round Percival, Neville announces: "'And now . . . let Bernard begin. Let him burble on, telling us stories, while we lie recumbent'" (37). With Percival at the center, mute ("'we all feel Percival lying heavy among us'"), Bernard "'goes on talking'" (38). The very fictionality of Percival's presence in the text is represented in the fact that he says nothing and thus opens the space in which discourse and myth proliferate. Moreover, and this is the first point I want particularly to emphasize, the speech that results, Bernard's speech, is and must be utterly figural. In fact, like the interludes that frame the chapters, Bernard's figures are so profuse they become interchangeable: "'up they bubble'" Neville tells us, "'—images. "Like a camel" . . . "a vulture." The camel is a vulture; the vulture a camel; for Bernard is a dangling wire, loose, but seductive. Yes, for when he talks, when he makes foolish comparisons, a lightness comes over one'" (38). Bernard makes buoyant the weight of an indifferent, inscrutable natural world. Most important, he gives it sequentiality, makes it the origin of a communal narrative for the boys. "'Let him describe what we have all seen so that it becomes a sequence'" (37). Grounded by the *figure* of Percival, Bernard makes sight into sentence, visuality into verbality: dumb, savage nature into culture, history, and community. Meanwhile for the reader, Percival's mediated and figured presence marks him as nothing other than a site of projections and productions.

The point is reinforced when Percival dies, and empire dramatically falters: suddenly, as Bernard says, "'The place is empty'" (153). "'About him my feeling was: he sat there in the centre. Now I go to that spot no longer'" (153). When they all gather for the last time at Hampton court, in memory of Percival, Bernard clearly recognizes how the idea of an ancestral past has functioned as a figure, a structure for negotiating with the unknowable yet coveted world beyond: "'But how strange it seems to set against the whirling abysses of infinite space a little figure with a golden teapot on his head. . . . Our English past—one inch of light. The people put teapots on their heads and say, "I am a King!"'" (227).

If we consider that racial-patriarchal mythologies and the sublime both occupy the elusive horizon where culture meets nature, then we can see the importance of the fact that Bernard's speech also occupies this horizon: his storytelling reveals the infinite regression of that horizon—wherein culture endlessly overlays, in order to image forth, nature, even as one artifactual metaphor can intensify while transposing another. In this sense Woolf's engagement with metaphor in this novel is part of her interrogation of the appropriative ontology and aesthetic of the Romantic sublime. She exposes the ancestral figure, and the figural turns, of empire. She makes the sublimating, figurational energy of the imperial self transparent and in this sense she empties its interiority out. She exposes it as a fundamentally figurative self.

Which self, however, for a logocentric culture, and for us as readers, feels brim full—and herein lies the paradox, the difficulty of disentangling Woolf's writing practice and our reading practice from that of her characters. For Woolf's book is itself a matter of meta- phors, beautiful abundant metaphors. Woolf's sublimely figurative world fills our eyes, draws us in like the inhaling waves even as it tells us we are its project, we are the vessels being filled. Woolf herself recreates a spell of myth; she gives us once more the illusion that culture is nature, that her images are the world, that we are in the presence of mimesis, of narrative, of communal history. Though Jane Marcus labors to separate Woolf from Bernard as cultural narrator and metaphor-maker, this task is an impossible one. They share the speech of figures.

Woolf seems to me to point toward this fact near the end of Bernard's closing monologue. We read, ostensibly in Bernard's voice, that something "'lies deep, tideless, immune, now that he is dead, the man I called "Bernard," the man who kept a book in his pocket in which he made notes—phrases for the moon, notes of features'" (291). This strange turn by which Bernard the narrator becomes the narrator of Bernard hints at the presence of Woolf's voice behind Bernard's. Just as Bernard as a child had peeked over the wall at Elvedon and seen a woman writing, so here we as readers peek over that garden wall and see the woman who sits writing this story of the imperial sublime we have been reading. This woman writer behind the male narrator on the one hand sits apart from his world, com- menting on it; but on the other hand she too is a narrator, a figure who creates history anew *through written words*, whose imagery of violence, whose rhythm of vehemence, empowers her text. Without the figure-maker—Woolf, Bernard—the world apparently becomes "immune," "tideless," inaccessible to time, a sublime presence that stands beyond; and yet it seems that the logocentric response is, regardless of gender, always an egocentric response conditioned by an economy of consumption. Woolf thus breeds distrust of the very sublimity her text narrates. As woman writer, Woolf lets us know she speaks a doubled voice, at once inside and outside the circle of an imperialist sublimity; she reveals that her writing moves along, not beyond, its circumference.

Woolf does hint, however, at yet another presence behind her own—and this is her most strenuous attempt to get outside of the sublimating movement she traces. Later in Bernard's closing mono- logue Woolf and Bernard again become conflated when we read that "'My book, stuffed with phrases, has dropped to the floor. It lies under the table to be swept up by the charwoman when she comes wearily at dawn looking for scraps of paper'" (295). The book is at once Woolf's and Bernard's and *ours* (mine lies open on my desk)—

and all will require sweeping up. Bernard and the woman writer and all readers are alike shadowed by the figure of a sweeper (we critics might think of the staff in our department offices). In *The Waves* the sweeper returns whenever the woman writer appears: "'The lady sits between the two long windows, writing. The gardeners sweep'"; "'I see the lady writing. I see the gardeners sweeping'" (17); "'the lady writing and the gardeners with their great brooms'" (192). Jane Marcus insists on the difference between Woolf and this lady writing, by emphasizing the word "lady" and aligning her with an aristocratic class to which Woolf does not belong. But given the mingling of Woolf's voice with Bernard's, it follows that the book which the charwoman comes wearily to sweep up is Woolf's as well as Bernard's. They depend equally on sweepers, on an economy of subordinations founded on sublimations. The book we read, with its introjected, sublimated savagery, belongs to us all.

6.

Is Woolf writing (in) the wake of the sublime? Is there nothing recoverable in the sublime's appealingly cosmic reach? I look up from writing and see that tonight the moon is full. It draws me out and gives me back to myself like the sunlight it reflects. I borrow from its borrowing from the excesses of a living universe. Sublime seems the right word for its influence.

Yet I tell you this in words, in an image, perhaps a metaphor. "'"Like" and "like" and "like,"'" Rhoda laments in double quotation marks (to which I must add my own), "'—but what is the thing that lies beneath the semblance of the thing?'" (163). The sublimity a feminist critic, or a woman writer, wants to recover is after all a sublimity of words and *their* excesses or borrowings. A feminine or female sublime is no less discursive than Bernard's or Woolf's, no less a quote whose source has been effaced and sublimated.

Yet then again once I acknowledge this, the quotation marks themselves take on a kind of presence, a presence signaling rather than deferring or effacing their origin in otherness. All speech in *The Waves* is in either quotes or italics. It calls attention to its writtenness. It is situated speech, printed speech, historical. The emphatic marks themselves insist on their phenomenality, as the visible marks of a history of writing bodies, the history in(to) which we read ourselves.

Here is a sublimity that claims no extension, no supersession, no heroic transgression: no transcendence except in the differing of sign from sign, of one typography from another, which now appears as a double presence, as the materiality of writing: the paradoxical presence of the written image. This is the sublime that is ours to claim. It is fork-tongued but when it marks itself as quote, as *italic*, as imported from there to here, as what he said and she said but speaking through me and in this curious shape on the page: then it can let fall its imagined burden—to speak nature.

Notes

1. In addition to those works cited below, see Furniss and Freeman.

2. "Capacious gestures" is Weiskel's phrase (6).

3. See Burke, especially 144–45 and sections xiv–xviii. Also see chapter 2 in Suleri.

4. See Doyle, "The Racial Sublime."

5. See Pocock and discussion in Murphy 5.

6. See Doyle, "The Racial Sublime."

7. Hertz introduced the idea of the "sublime turn" in his essay, "A Reading of Longinus."

8. Monk's review of the critical literature remains authoritative and extremely useful.

9. For a fuller discussion of these later developments, see Doyle, *Bordering on the Body*, especially chapters 2 and 3.

Works Cited

Barthes, Roland. *Mythologies*. Trans. Annette Lavers. New York: Hill and Wang, 1972.

Blair, Hugh. "A Critical Dissertation on Poems of Ossian." *The Poetical Works of Ossian*. Trans. James MacPherson. Boston: Crosby and Nichols, 1863. 88–180.

Burke, Edmund. *A Philosophical Enquiry into the Origin of our Ideas of the Sublime and Beautiful*. Ed. J. T. Boulton. London: Routledge and Kegan Paul, 1958.

DeGuy, Michael. "The Discourse of Exaltation: Contribution to a Re-Reading of Pseudo-Longinus." *Of the Sublime: Presence in Question*. Trans. Jeffrey Librett. Albany: SUNY P, 1993. 5–24.

Doyle, Laura. *Bordering on the Body: The Racial Matrix of Modern Fiction and Culture*. New York: Oxford UP, 1994.

———. "The Racial Sublime." In *Romanticism, Race, and Imperial Culture, 1780–1834*. Ed. Sonia Hofkosh and Alan Richardson. Bloomington: Indiana UP, 1996.

Freeman, Barbara. *The Feminine Sublime*. Berkeley: U California P, 1995.

Furniss, Tom. *Edumund Burke's Aesthetic Ideology: Language, Gender, and Political Economy in Revolution*. Cambridge: Cambridge UP, 1993.

Hertz, Neil. "A Reading of Longinus." *Critical Inquiry* 9 (1983): 579–96.

Hurd, Richard. *Letters on Chivalry and Romance*. 1762. Ed. Hoyt Trowbridge. Los Angeles: William Andrews Clark Memorial Library, 1963.

Kant, Immanuel. *Observations on the Feeling of the Beautiful and Sublime*. Trans. John T. Goldthwait. Berkeley: U of California P, 1991.

Knox, Robert. *The Races of Men: A Fragment*. Philadelphia: Lea and Blanchard, 1850.

Longinus. *On the Sublime*. Trans. Benedict Einarson. Chicago: Packard and Co., 1945.

Low, Donald A., ed. *Robert Burns: The Critical Heritage*. Boston: Routledge, 1974.

Marcus, Jane. "Britannia Rules *The Waves*." *Decolonizing Tradition: New Views of Twentieth-Century "British" Literary Canons*. Ed. Karen Lawrence. Urbana: U of Illinois P, 1991. 136–62.

McGee, Patrick. "The Politics of Modernist Form: Or, Who Rules *The Waves*." *Modern Fiction Studies* 38 (1992): 631–50.

Mitchell, W. J. T. *Iconology: Image, Text, and Ideology*. Chicago: U of Chicago P, 1987.

Mitford, William. "Inquiry into the Principles of Harmony in Language and of the Mechanism of Verse, Modern and Antient." London: T. Cadell and W. Davies, 1804.

Monk, Samuel H. *The Sublime: A Study of Critical Theories in Eighteenth-Century England*. Ann Arbor: U of Michigan P, 1960.

Morrison, Toni. *Playing in the Dark: Whiteness and the Literary Imagination*. New York: Random House, 1993.

Murphy, Michael. "Antiquary to Academic." *Anglo-Saxon Scholarship: The First Three Centuries*. Ed. Carl T. Berkhout and Milton Gatch. Boston: G. K. Hall and Co., 1982. 1–17.

Nichol, James. Editor's Introduction. *Reliques of Ancient English Poetry*. By Thomas Percy. Edinburgh: James Nisbet and Co., 1958. ix–xxii.

Ossian. *The Poetical Works of Ossian*. Trans. James MacPherson. Boston: Crosby and Nichols, 1863.

Percy, Bishop Thomas. Preface. *Northern Antiquities; or, an Historical Account of the Manners, Customs, Religion and Laws . . . of the Ancient Scandinavians. With Incidental Notices Regarding Our Saxon Ancestors*. 1770. By M. Mallet. Trans. Bishop Percy. London: Henry G. Bohn, 1847. 1–21.

———. Preface. *Reliques of Ancient English Poetry*. Ed. James Nichol. Edinburgh: James Nisbet and Co., 1958. xxxi–xciii

Pocock, J. G. A. *The Ancient Constitution and the Feudal Law*. Cambridge: Cambridge UP, 1957.

Procupius. *History of the Warres of the Emperour Justinian*. Trans. Henry Holcroft. London: Humphrey Moseley, 1653.

Saleeby, Caleb. *Parenthood and Race Culture: An Outline of Eugenics*. New York: Moffat, Yard, 1911.

Suleri, Sara. *The Rhetoric of English India*. Chicago: U of Chicago P, 1992.

Weiskel, Thomas. *The Romantic Sublime*. Baltimore: Johns Hopkins UP, 1986.

Winstanley, Gerard. *The Law of Freedom in a Platform*. Ed. Max Radin. Sutro: California State Library, 1939.

Woolf, Virginia. *The Waves*. New York: Harcourt Brace Jovanovich, 1931.

Wordsworth, William. *The Recluse. Poems*, vol. 1. Ed. John O. Hayden. New York: Penguin, 1977. 699–717.

Yaeger, Patricia. "Toward a Female Sublime." *Gender and Theory*. Ed. Linda Kauffman. New York: Basil Blackwell, 1989. 191–212.

THE POLITICS OF

MODERNIST FORM;

OR, WHO RULES *THE WAVES*?

Patrick McGee

After the recent publication of Jane Marcus' essay, "Britannia Rules *The Waves*," interpretations of Virginia Woolf's novel cannot legitimately ignore its political content. As for myself, before I had the opportunity to read the essay, I had already written briefly on the *implicit* critique of imperialism in *The Waves* (McGee 116–120) in such a way as to suggest my agreement with Marcus that the novel is about "the submerged mind of empire" (the words of J. M. Coetzee, cited by Marcus 136). Still, Marcus goes beyond my understanding of an implicit and partial critique to argue that an *explicit* critique of imperialism constitutes the center and organizing principle of the novel. Marcus has articulated a new space for reading *The Waves*—a space that should become the enabling ground for future readings of the novel. By articulating this space in the form of a political interpretation, she also makes visible the internal boundary or blank space that any interpretation hollows out of itself. This blank space allows me to pose the question of literary form that Marcus fails to address adequately with her emphasis on the transparency of social content and literary references. She does not claim, of course, that the meaning of the novel is obvious but that it becomes obvious once the text has been plugged into the specific dimensions of the historical context from which it derives. Marcus wants to reverse the critical history of *The Waves* that has tended to identify the novel as a static representation of upper-class culture and forms of identity.

Originally published in *Modern Fiction Studies*, Autumn 1992.

On the contrary, Marcus insists, "the project of cultural studies . . . now allows one to read *The Waves* as a narrative about culture making" (139). I agree with this statement. Still, by subordinating the novel's form to its context without paying sufficient attention to the process of mediation, Marcus tends to overlook the politics of literary form at the heart of *The Waves* and possibly of the modernist project itself. In order to explain this politics, I will need to interrogate some aspects of Marcus' interpretation in detail.

For example, in part at least, she hinges her claim that Woolf *intended* to produce a full-blown critique of imperialism in *The Waves* (indeed, that the novel "records a precise historical moment—the postcolonial carnivalesque" [144]) on a particular reading of the poetic interludes. Marcus notes that these interludes "take the form of a set of Hindu prayers to the sun, called Gayatri, marking its course during a single day. These (Eastern) episodes surround a (Western) narrative of the fall of British imperialism" (137). Woolf supposedly got the idea for using this metrical form found in the *Rig Veda* from her cousin Dorothea Jane Stephen's 1918 book, *Studies in Early Indian Thought*. However, the term "Gayatri" does not appear in this book, and Stephen's chapter on the *Rig Veda* is very general and does not offer any concrete indication that Woolf was imitating Indian verse. If one thumbs through the *Rig Veda* itself, it does not seem altogether clear that Woolf's interludes have any direct relation to the Sanskrit hymns. Although the interludes trace the path of the sun during the course of a day, they are not exactly invocations of the sun, like the Gayatri, nor do they conform to the expanded significance of the Gayatri as a recitation leading to the fulfillment of human desire. Woolf certainly does not imitate the Gayatri meter of twenty-four syllables, usually in triplets of eight syllables each.

I would not deny that Woolf may have had her cousin's study in mind when she wrote the interludes and may have wanted "to call up Indian philosophy and its emphasis on astronomy and the randomness of the universe" (Marcus 155). She may have wanted to create an echo of or resonance with the idea behind one of her cousin's summary statements: "In early Indian thought we have the boldest and the most consistent effort that the human mind has ever made to show that it is nothing" (cited by Marcus 155; see Stephen 172). Nevertheless, these borrowings from and echoings of European scholarship on Eastern philosophy hardly constitute a critical challenge to imperialist ideology. On the contrary, assimilating Eastern thought in this vague, imprecise manner seems to me a rather typical gesture within modernist art and literature. Marcus herself refers to Yeats's approval of echoes of Eastern thought in Woolf's novel (156), an echoing Yeats did himself on a much more grand scale. Yet, despite his nationalist alignments in Ireland, Yeats was not a profound critic of the imperialist system.

Another of Marcus' historical reductions fails to do justice to the formal complexity of *The Waves*. She reads the novel as a *roman à clef*, particularly in making its structure pivot on the relationship between the two characters, Percival and Bernard. "Bernard," we are informed, "is Desmond [MacCarthy] and Percival is J. K. Stephen, the patriarchal imperialist makers of British culture" (153). She blatantly projects the personal characteristics of these two historical figures onto the characters of Bernard and Percival in a way that completely overstates what Woolf actually puts into the novel. For the most part, I agree with her main point: "*The Waves* is about the ideology of white British colonialism and the Romantic literature that sustains it. Its parody and irony mock the complicity of the hero and the poet in the creation of a collective national subject through an elegy for imperialism" (145). Although the relation to Percival surely does link all the characters in this novel to the patriarchal-imperialist subject as the form of their collective identity, this relation is not the only defining one in the novel, nor is it the last word on the concept of the subject. The critic Desmond MacCarthy, Woolf's friend from the Bloomsbury group, may have possessed the qualities Marcus applies to Bernard: "rigid Tory politics, imperialistic hero-worship, and barely repressed homosexuality" (157). He may well have been a model for Bernard (as well as Neville). But I would insist that the Bernard in *The Waves* is not so easily pinned down as Marcus' labels would suggest. Although Bernard mourns for the death of Percival in the elegiac mode, he hardly repeats in his discourse the trivial and emotionally indifferent tone of Desmond MacCarthy's "portrait" of J. K. Stephen. In fact, MacCarthy's portrait of Woolf's cousin reads more like a parody than does Bernard's elegiac passages on Percival. (MacCarthy's conclusion suggests a more muted admiration than Percival receives in *The Waves*: "J. K. S. belongs to those dim, romantic figures, who have loomed much greater in intimacy than in performance—only he was not so lucky in his generation" [224].) More important, however, there is no indication in *The Waves* that Bernard ever actually becomes the poet he plays at being or that his sentences and perpetually unfinished stories ever amount to anything more than reverie, social chatter, and jottings in his notebook. Are the references to his biographer anything more than stereotypical forms of intellectual vanity? Again, I do think the novel implicates literature in the imperialist process but not exactly in the transparent and reflective manner upon which Marcus insists.

Another figure in the novel who is pinpointed by Marcus as an emblem of the male artist's evasion of the social responsibility of art is the "lady writing." Bernard "authorizes his role as an inheritor of civilization by summoning a recurring vision of the 'lady at a table writing, the gardeners with their brooms sweeping.' This is a vision in which English culture is represented as an aristocratic female figure in a grand country house called Elvedon, leisure for creativity provided by the security of the fixed class position of servants" (139).

After reading Marcus, I would have to revise partially my previous reading of this figure of the female writer at Elvedon as one that disrupts the patriarchal order (that is, the order of the school that the children are attending when Susan and Bernard first see the woman in the window). Now I would see this figure as more ambivalent and the site of a social contradiction. For Marcus accurately stresses that Woolf, "who urged the thirties poets to convert members of their own class to divest themselves of privilege, rather than become missionaries to the lower classes," would not have endorsed an aesthetic "which figures English culture as a lady, *not a woman*, and insists on the unalterable relationship between the gardener and the lady, the working class and the writing class" (154, my emphasis). Yet if the choice of the word "lady" is to carry such weight, it should at least be noted that Bernard uses the word "woman" or "women" to describe the "lady writing" in the window on four occasions in the text (*Waves* 124, 241, 255, and 285). These observations suggest some ambivalence in Woolf's understanding of this figure. In *Three Guineas*, Woolf attacks the patriarchal concept of "the lady" as an ideological justification of economic oppression: "It was the lady who could not earn money; therefore the lady must be killed" (133). Yet the Woolf who wrote *A Room of One's Own* could not have been blind to the fact that, under the capitalist system, the production of women's writing, like the production of men's, requires some economic privilege and that this privilege is structurally at the expense of the working classes, which would include both the gardeners and Mrs. Moffat, Bernard's housekeeper. Furthermore, Woolf respected the potential power of the working classes when she suggested in *Three Guineas* that educated women, like herself,

> are weaker than the women of the working class. If the working women of the country were to say: "If you go to war, we will refuse to make munitions or to help in the production of goods," the difficulty of war-making would be seriously increased. But if all the daughters of educated men were to down tools tomorrow, nothing essential either to the life or the war-making of the community would be embarrassed. Our class is the weakest of all the classes in the state. We have no weapon with which to enforce our will. (13)

Woolf's analysis of the social power of the working class based on its relation to the means of production simply leaves out all kinds of other factors, including lack of education and of the symbolic authority resulting therefrom, that keep working-class men and women from realizing their power in actuality. As Eric Hobsbawm observes, during the critical period before the First World War and leading up to the achievement of women's suffrage after the war, "there was little enough change in the condition of most women of the labouring classes anywhere," except for a declining birth rate in the "developing" countries alone (193).

One cannot read Woolf's mind, but to me it makes sense that she would construct the image of the woman writing with the gardeners sweeping as the figuration of the social contradiction underlying her own creative process. Bernard encounters this vision as a child and it haunts him for the rest of his life. It is not a part of the official program that he learns in school, but it has in some ways a more profound impact in that it represents a dimension of his social experience that cannot be easily assimilated and then forgotten as a conventional attitude. Woolf understood, as do more contemporary feminists like Hélène Cixous, that the political significance of women's writing, wherever it comes from, is affirmative; but her common sense about the economic conditions necessary for the production of writing would not have allowed her to ignore the social contradictions that necessarily underlie such a symbolic act. The gardeners who sweep or those like Mrs. Moffat who clean up after the upper-class men and women, and the women who write (from any class, although a woman from the upper classes will be forever inscribed as a "lady" on the mind of an upper-class Victorian boy) threaten the capitalist class system that could also be said to have created them in the first place. As the history of the twentieth century demonstrates, this threat can be contained and managed by capitalism itself. Nevertheless, I believe that Woolf inserts this figure into her text not only to vilify Bernard as a character but also to signify the social contradictions of modernist aesthetics and to take responsibility for her own social emplacement.

The whole point of my dissent from these aspects of Marcus' argument can be summed up in one final contradiction. In the last paragraph, she paraphrases a remark by Andreas Huyssen that "the mark of modernism is fear of contamination." Then she concludes:

> This is Bernard's fear (Mrs. Moffat will sweep it all up). Rhoda fears the puddle and all human beings; Neville fears the recurrence of murder; Louis fears the "great Beast stamping" in the East; Susan hates Ginny [sic] all her life

for having kissed Louis. The contamination of kisses and classes, the fear of dirt, disorder, and dying, the fear of Africa and India, is the recurring theme of the speakers' monologues. (159)

Marcus is mostly right in this summary. But she also replicates the "mark of modernism" by insisting that Woolf completely transcends the imperialist ideology that interpellates her characters and thus remains uncontaminated by the process she represents. This fear of contamination forces Marcus to argue repeatedly that all the negative aspects of aesthetic politics in *The Waves* are "historically specific to Bernard in England in the early 1930s" and in no way endorsed by Woolf (154). I believe that Woolf's novel is critical of the aesthetics of modernism, but it does not seem to me that Woolf's relation to her characters is one of complete detachment and impersonal dissociation. For one thing, the Bernard who says in the last section that he does not know if he is man or woman (*The Waves* 281) makes a rather odd figure for the fear of contamination by others. Similarly, Rhoda's fear of puddles and Neville's fear of murder (or "death among the apple trees" [*The Waves* 24]) were also Woolf's fears as she recorded them in her late autobiography, "A Sketch of the Past" (71, 78; see also *Diary* 2: 113). There would seem to be other echoes of Woolf's autobiography in Rhoda's pervasive feeling of alienation and exclusion; and while the other characters are less direct representations of Woolf's own life, I have no doubt that she distributes pieces of herself in all of them. In fact, I do not see how it is possible to separate the voice of the author from the voice of the character in this crucial moment of Bernard's final monologue, a moment that virtually roots human identity in a process of social contamination:

> And now I ask, "Who am I?" I have been talking of Bernard, Neville, Jinny, Susan, Rhoda, and Louis. Am I all of them? Am I one and distinct? I do not know. We sat here together. But now Percival is dead, and Rhoda is dead; we are divided; we are not here. Yet I cannot find any obstacle separating us. There is no division between me and them. As I talked I felt, "I am you." This difference we make so much of, this identity we so feverishly cherish, was overcome. Yes, ever since Mrs. Constable lifted her sponge and pouring warm water over me covered me with flesh I have been sensitive, percipient. Here on my brow is the blow I got when Percival fell. Here on my neck is the kiss Jinny gave Louis. My eyes fill with Susan's tears. I see far

> away, quivering like a gold thread, the pillar Rhoda saw,
> and feel the rush of the wind of her flight when she leapt.
> (*The Waves* 289)

I suspect that when Bernard says, "Who am I?," Woolf is producing a double-voiced discourse in which the content of the subject has become so unstable as to subvert the normal relationship between the reader and the author as textual functions. "Bernard" as the name of a character no longer centers Woolf's novel, if he ever did. His name is just one in a series. Insofar as his final story describes the mortality of the human subject, it foregrounds the isolation of that subject, which, as Sigmund Freud understood, seeks to master and possess death in its own way. But death, which seems to create a final and irreversible separation, is also the truest signifier of that radical alterity that inhabits the subject as its material ground, as the impossibility of any metaphysical difference that would transcend history and culture and root the authority of the subject in some version of the Absolute. The "I" who says, "I am you," is not Bernard in any conventional sense but the Other who has no Other. It could be thought of as Woolf's signature, but that signature would be one that insists on displaying the absence of any metaphysical authority. Only in that sense is difference overcome.

Mrs. Constable, the boy Bernard's nurse, is a maternal figure who grounds for a lifetime his relation to his own body. She has the function of what Ellie Ragland-Sullivan calls the m/Other, a formula expressing "the idea that the human subject first becomes aware of itself by identification with a person (object), usually [but not necessarily] the mother" (11). Shari Benstock clarifies this Lacanian *mirror stage* as one revealing "a (false) sense of mastery and wholeness, a notion of *the body as a unity*" (12). Furthermore, in her reading of Julia Kristeva, Benstock emphasizes the subject's ambivalence toward this process of separation/individuation:

> The pre-Oedipal, pre-mirror stage infant experiences itself
> as coextensive with the mother. This state of apparent
> at-oneness with the mother is thrown into crisis when the
> child misapprehends itself as separate, whole, complete,
> and in control of itself. The joy (*jouissance*) in discovering
> separation and difference is coupled with pain in the loss
> of an Imaginary identification with the mother. (30)

For Marcus, Mrs. Constable plays a crucial role in Bernard's formation as a patriarchal subject: "She is his muse, and the primal scene of writing is for him the memory of her turning over pages of a picture book and naming the objects" (157; see *Waves* 239). On the one hand, Mrs. Constable prepares the child to enter the symbolic order of names and identities; on the other, she stands for the Other that is simultaneously recognized and lost in the process of individuation, in discovering the "arrows of sensation" (*Waves* 26, 239) that construct the body as a unified ground for the patriarchal subject that it must become. "To the nurses of other newborns," Bernard "could implore them not to squeeze the sponge over that new body" (*Waves* 239). For Marcus, "Woolf is laying out a psychological trail to explain Bernard's origin as the self-appointed arbiter of British culture" (157). The passage I have quoted above, however, suggests that the developmental models used by Ragland-Sullivan, Benstock, Marcus, and, to some extent, Jacques Lacan himself may not do justice to the symbolic process Woolf is recording.

Bernard's ambivalence toward the process of individuation—the pleasure-pain he associates with it—points toward the ambivalence of the subject itself. The subject, even the patriarchal subject, is not a stable formation that is autonomous or that, *from the outside*, ever completely dominates the other (including the sexual other) who seems to stand apart from it. On the contrary, the subject is already constructed by the cultural system that makes the subject's representation of the other a form of self-representation. Bernard is the subject constituted in contradiction. His identity as a patriarchal male constantly wavers, that is, oscillates between the contradictory poles of his social being, on the waves, so to speak. He cannot stand apart from those others who have made up his life; and he cannot merge with them either. He is both in love with death and fearful of it, in love with Rhoda and Percival and fearful of what they represent in himself. Rhoda, the subject without a face who kills herself, and Percival, the imperialist subject who has no voice, represent the polar opposition inside Bernard's own identity. The others are gradations of the same process. Neville embodies not only Bernard's homosocial love of Percival but his pretentious assertion of the ideology of art without the uncertainty or self-doubt that constrains Bernard's ability to master the other with words. Jinny and Susan taken together represent the two poles of the patriarchal woman as a social construction: the woman who gives sexual pleasure (though I do not agree with Marcus that Jinny is literally a prostitute [146]) and the natural woman, or mother, who nurtures. They articulate the relation to m/Other in the composition of the patriarchal subject (Bernard) as a historical formation. Louis is the subject of the capitalist system that translates patriarchal law into an ideological defense of economic violence.

All of these characters would make up Bernard if Bernard were identical to himself. But, if anything, Bernard represents the non-identity of the subject. The ambivalence of his gender points to the ambivalence of the genre or literary form of *The Waves*. It suggests the ambivalence underlying the author-function itself in this novel. If, as Marcus argues, the interludes are Woolf's attempt to articulate the repressed of the imperialist social order as the frame of the novel, they also make a significant *return of the repressed* in the main body of Bernard's final monologue. No longer italicized, no longer safely confined to the margins, the voice of the interludes erupts from within the discourse of the imperialist subject:

> I can visit the remote verges of the desert lands where the savage sits by the campfire. Day rises; the girl lifts the watery fire-hearted jewels to her brow; the sun levels his beams straight at the sleeping house; the waves deepen their bars; they fling themselves on shore; back blows the spray; sweeping their waters they surround the boat and the sea-holly. The birds sing in chorus; deep tunnels run between the stalks of flowers; the house is whitened; the sleeper stretches; gradually all is astir. Light floods the room and drives shadow beyond shadow to where they hang in folds inscrutable. What does the central shadow hold? Something? Nothing? I do not know. (*The Waves* 291–292)

Quite simply, what is the reader to think? Has Bernard been the narrator all along? Was it Bernard who *intended* to subvert his own patriarchal and imperialist authority by framing the autobiography of his social class with a voice from Eastern culture (if we accept for a moment Marcus' reading of the interludes as imitations of the Gayatri from the *Rig Vega*)? Has the whole novel been the contradictory and sexually ambivalent internal monologue of a Western patriarchal subject? It seems to me that in *The Waves* Woolf successfully produces an implicit ideology critique that may have a special significance for contemporary feminism. She calls into question the assumption that the Western patriarchal subject is transparent as to its meaning and social effects, not to mention as to its gender. In fact, she questions the commonsense view of the gender of patriarchy. (Perhaps this is the reason why so many feminist critics, including Jane Marcus until recently, have avoided reading *The Waves*, which is frequently declared to be Woolf's masterpiece and yet, like *Finnegans Wake*, suffers from a dearth of significant criticism.)

Bernard's final monologue, when it fuses with the poetic interludes, calls into question any simple understanding of the author-function in this text, including the principle of its intentional structure, by dramatically foregrounding the undecidability of the boundary-line between the text and its context. Indeed, in the passage I have cited, there is an inscription of this undecidability. Everything up to the reference to a sleeper more or less corresponds to the material in the interludes. But who is the sleeper? This figure seems to suggest that beyond the self-conscious subject of modernist art that produces its fictional mouthpiece in Bernard (and to different degrees in the other characters) lies another subject or the subject as the Other. This "sleeper" is the unconscious subject of the discourse of the novel, the subject of those effects that exceed the overt message that the monologues of the six characters and the poetic interludes want to convey. It is possible to say that the interludes make up the dream of this sleeper which somehow constitutes the frame of the entire novel. Still, if Bernard's final monologue is *explicitly* contaminated by the voice of the interludes that are supposed to frame it, then the entire set of monologues, by virtue of the abstractness of Woolf's style, is *implicitly* contaminated by such a frame. The monologues of the characters become a dream within a dream. As Jacques Derrida stresses, "The frames are always enframed . . . by a given piece of what they contain" (*Post Card* 485n).

This instability of the frame is also an instability of the center which is suggested by the image of light driving "shadow beyond shadow to where they hang in folds inscrutable" (292). Ironically, if the infusion of light brings about an awakening of the sleeper who now stretches, it does not efface the shadows of the dream but rather foregrounds the inscrutable boundary that they constitute within the economy of the subject. "What does the central shadow hold? Something? Nothing? I do not know." The boundary constituted by the central shadow is not the site of a stable identity but of the instability of identity which is always contaminated by the unconscious processes from which it emerges. There is no strict division between the unconscious and the conscious, between the sleeper who dreams and the speaking subject who narrates. Finally, if Bernard is not identical to himself but one more member of a series without closure, then Woolf's name has to be added to the series as the frame that is also a part of what it frames. *The Waves* subverts the intentional authority of its own author-function.

According to Marcus, the figure of Britannia in the title of her essay "is meant to convey the national anxiety of the former colony about the colonizing process itself" (140). Britannia was originally a figure on a Roman coin celebrating the Roman colonization of Britain, but she was carried over the waves of historical process to become the symbol of British imperialism in the nineteenth century. In *The Waves*, as Marcus reads it, she becomes a figure for the ideological containment of the writing process itself:

> The Lady at a Table Writing serves as a "Britannia" figure
> and an allegory for Bernard. But in order to read it this way,
> one has to be open to irony in Woolf's voice, particularly
> toward Bernard, the writer figure, and be aware of and open
> to Woolf's critique of class and empire. Bernard is a parody
> of authorship; his words are a postmodern pastiche of quo-
> tation from the master texts of English literature. (140)

It seems to me that Marcus gives too much credit to Bernard
and not enough credit to the subtlety of Woolf's *unstable* irony. The
lady or woman writing is not just Bernard's projection, although she
may very well be a figure of the woman who rules *The Waves*. To
solicit the (unintended?) pun in Marcus' title, the woman who rules
The Waves is not only the emblem of British imperialism but also the
woman who rules in another sense—the last three senses given to
the verb *rule* in the *O.E.D.*: 1) to arrange or set in order; 2) to mark
(paper, etc.) with parallel straight lines drawn with a ruler or by a
machine; and 3) to form or mark out (a line) with or as with a ruler.
The woman who rules *The Waves* is the one who draws the lines that
determine its form or arrangement—who decides what is inside and
what is outside. In the case of Woolf's novel, she is also the one who
draws the lines in such a way as to call attention to the undecidability
of those limits, to the very arbitrariness of modernist form.

To say that Bernard is a parody of authorship is to grant authorship an authority that Woolf's novel calls into question by insisting on
the artificiality or constructedness of the frame that gives the author
power over the text he or she writes. This is not to say, of course,
that there is no parody in Woolf's construction not only of Bernard
but also of all the other characters in this fiction. But this parody is
only a technique, not the ruling principle. The lady/woman writing
is not simply an algebraic symbol of Bernard's patriarchal fantasies
but a signifier of the ambivalent process that *rules* Woolf's novel.
On the one hand, it displays the capture of the woman writer in the
frame—the window as the frame—of a patriarchal culture that rules
or constructs her as a "lady"; on the other, it situates the author of
the text, the one who rules *The Waves*, that is, draws the lines that
constitute its form, in a margin or on the borderline of the text she
writes. She is framed by the text she frames—she is ruled by the text
she rules. In this way, she discloses the contradiction in the ideology
of modernist form by making visible the social machinery that enables
its production. In seeking to transcend historical process, modernist
form is captured by it.

Astradur Eysteinsson describes one common view of modernism,
foregrounded in the Brecht-Lukács debate, that may have bearing
on the present discussion: "the aesthetic proclivities of modernism

seem bound to go against the very notion of narrativity, narrative progression, and storytelling in any traditional sense. One way to define modernism would be to say that it resists reality-fabrications that are recuperable as 'stories' or as situations that can readily be reformulated in sociopragmatic terms" (187). Such a statement does not mean that modernist texts have no relation to reality but that they challenge the view that reality can be captured or adequately mapped by a traditional narrative which privileges coherence and continuity between the representation and the represented. On the contrary, modernism suggests that reality is not reducible to a "seamless 'totality'" (Ernst Bloch's description of Georg Lukács's concept of reality) that can be mimetically reproduced even in a critical fiction that discloses the grounds of class struggle and social change. One of the conditions of modern literature, as Bloch suggested for German Expressionism, may be the knowledge that "authentic reality is also discontinuity" (22). Lukács generally saw European modernism as a form of decadence because it emptied art of any social content or relation to the movement of real history. On the other hand, Fredric Jameson, who does not reject Lukács's argument so much as he tries to recuperate its implicit critique of modernist form, reformulates the argument to suggest that modernism is not

> a way of avoiding social content—in any case an impossibility for beings like ourselves who are "condemned" to history and to the implacable sociability of even the most apparently private of our experiences—but rather of managing and containing it, secluding it out of sight in the very form itself, by means of specific techniques of framing and displacement which can be identified with some precision. (138)

It seems to me that Jameson describes a particular modernist strategy that is not accurately understood if we think of it as "a way of avoiding social content." Rather than suggesting that social content is secluded out of sight by modernist form, it could be argued that, on the contrary, social content is no longer contained by literary form but rather *represented* by it. In fact, Jameson's aside about beings condemned to history and the "implacable sociability" of private experience may be the central point that needs to be stressed in this context.

Although it is always dangerous to make universal judgments about literary form, it still should be said that the significance of modernist form lies in its revelation of the social and symbolic nature of private experience, which leads to the secondary recognition that history determines the formation of human subjectivity precisely through the mediation of symbolic structures. In other words, modernism, at least in some of its practices, is not a retreat from the social into the private but an insistence on the sociality of the private. However, it may be more useful to insist on the duality of modernist form as to its effects. In writers such as Ernest Hemingway and F. Scott Fitzgerald, for example, the effect of self-conscious style and form may be exactly what Jameson says: a way of avoiding content by reducing it to the objectivity of an aesthetic gaze. The form contains and decontextualizes the subject matter. In writers such as Woolf and James Joyce, on the other hand, social content is no longer safely contained by the objective boundaries of the frame; since the frame is unstable, the content becomes a social force and a ground of political contention that any reading must confront if it is to make sense out of the work.

In alienating narrativity in the traditional sense by destabilizing its frame, Woolf produces an effect in *The Waves* that resembles a kind of Brechtian epic theater, at least as Bertolt Brecht has been rewritten in contemporary critical terms by Terry Eagleton. For Brecht, acting should be "hollow or void," which leads to "a kind of Derridean 'spacing,' rendering a piece of stage business exterior to itself . . . dismantling the ideological self-identity of our routine social behavior." The dramatic gesture represents such a behavior

> in all its lack, in its suppression of material conditions and historical possibilities, and thus represents an absence which it at the same time produces. What the stage action represents is the routine action as differenced through the former's non-self-identity, which nevertheless remains self-identical—recognizable—enough to do all this representing rather than merely to "reflect" a "given" non-identity in the world. (Eagleton 167)

In Woolf's novel, of course, the place of the actor is occupied by the linguistic signifier that produces a character or social identity without ever effacing its own materiality. Marcus, therefore, correctly rejects previous readings of *The Waves* that describe it as "ahistorical" (144); but in my opinion she ought to give these errors some credit for pointing toward the very historicity that Woolf wants to represent. Woolf suppresses "material conditions and historical possibilities" in order to reveal the process of history in those conventional gestures and activities that make up the life of the subject as an intersubject, as a composite or hybrid in the symbolic order of everyday life. By oversimplifying the relationship between text and context, Marcus virtually tames Woolf's text by making it a far more naive representation than it actually is. Woolf suppresses the family romance and straightforward references to the social and historical background in order to foreground or make present the historicity of language itself: like Brechtian theater, she "deconstructs social processes into rhetoric, which is to say reveals them as social *practices*" (Eagleton 168).

Let me rewrite Eagleton's sentence about Brecht to fit Woolf: what her literary-linguistic actions in *The Waves* represent are social identities as ideological constructions which can be articulated as differential forms through the "non-self-identity" of the signifier, which nevertheless can be recognized as self-identical in a set of social positions that virtually hail or *interpellate* (in Louis Althusser's sense of the word) social beings which are not simply "reflected" or exposed as non-identities but called into identity by the process of representation itself. For example, the signifier of gender calls a woman into being as a social construction through a self-identical linguistic structure that is nevertheless rooted in the non-self-identity or arbitrariness of the material signifier. As in Lacan's notorious example of the signifiers "Men" and "Women" on the doors of unisexual lavatories, there is no escaping the self-identity of the signifier as a structure of social determination that requires every human being to line up on one side or the other of the gender line. Still, representation as the differentiation and symbolic ordering of the real (which can be thought of as an undifferentiated process without natural demarcations since, as Lacan stressed, the real has no order [11]) is only possible because the signifier is arbitrary and thus can operate as an element in a cultural system. Such an element assumes value or meaning as an effect of the system itself—the system of differences.

Perhaps Marcus' most productive observation for understanding Woolf's complex representation of the European system of cultural differences lies in her linking of Indian philosophy, with its emphasis on the randomness of the universe, with relativity theory and the new physics. In a note, she cites Woolf's diary for the evidence that Woolf had been "reading and discussing Sir James Jeans's books and listening to his lectures on the radio" while she revised *The Waves* (160). The book form of Jeans's lectures, *The Mysterious Universe*, was published in November 1930, a month before Woolf referred to it in her diary (3: 35–36). While this book could hardly have influenced Woolf's original draft of *The Waves*, it surely contains ideas that Woolf would have been familiar with and might have influenced her thinking about how to represent human identity in her novel. Consider these passages from Jeans's book:

> Light, and indeed radiation of all kinds, is both particles and waves at the same time. . . . Now it behaves like particles, now like waves; no general principle yet known can tell us what behaviour it will choose in any particular instance.

> Clearly we can only preserve our belief in the uni-
> formity of nature by making the supposition that particles
> and waves are in essence the same thing. . . . A duality
> has recently been discovered in the nature of electrons and
> protons similar to that already known to exist in the nature
> of radiation; these also appear to be particles and waves
> at the same time. (42–43)

Woolf may have taken the cue from contemporary science for the double focus of her book. On the one hand, *The Waves* is organized around a group of discrete individuals: Bernard, Neville, Louis, Susan, Jinny, and Rhoda. Each discourse or monologue has a speaker or subject who literally represents the interpellated form of social being. There can be no discourse without a subject, and there can be no subject without the subject-object relationship that solicits the other as the receptacle of a message. However, as critics have pointed out before, this relationship is not stable in *The Waves* (Minow-Pinkney 172–173). The line of demarcation that distinguishes the addresser from the addressee has been effaced so that the difference is undecidable. Just as Bernard's final monologue subverts the difference between the frame (that is, the poetic interludes) and the main body of the text, the abstraction of style in all the monologues tends to efface the conventions of character that would govern the articulation of voice throughout the novel. In effect, the characters as individual psyches are both present and absent. The reader cannot do without them as he or she tries to make sense of the novel by identifying the contents of the monologues with different characterological types. But the boundaries marked out by these conventions are constantly being transgressed by a style that has the effect of "*emptying* syntax of its function of articulation" (Minow-Pinkney 172). The characters as individual particles or elements, in other words, are subordinated to the wave-structure of the novel as a whole. The function of articulation is framed in such a way as to dramatize its dissolution into the symbolic process that could be said to constitute the historical itself. Still, the wave is not more real or more unreal than the particle or the discrete body of the individual. The wave and the particle symbolize one discontinuous process. Although irreconcilable as concepts, each is the effect of a symbolic mediation that is never reducible to, or a transparent window on, the real. In this view, history is neither identical to the real nor self-identical.

The Waves is a historical novel in this unconventional sense. It presents the European subject as a differentiated structure of relationships that are irreducible to a unitary or transcendental signifier. In a sense, Percival discloses the impossibility of that signifier by representing the presence in absence of the magisterial or imperialist subject. Percival has no voice in the novel and only exists as a fiction in the discourse of the others. He virtually gives a name to what Gayatri Spivak would call, after Derrida, the "blank part of the text" ("Can the Subaltern Speak?" 294), that internal boundary that locates what has been excluded from representation as the historical condition and limit of representation. Percival embodies those "standards of the West" that effectively solve "the Oriental problem" through the use of "violent language." After this speech in which Bernard celebrates Percival as the God of Eurocentric ideology, Rhoda chimes in with this figure of his relation to the social microcosm of the novel: "He is like a stone fallen into a pond round which minnows swarm. Like minnows, we who had been shooting this way, that way, all shot round him when he came. Like minnows, conscious of the presence of a great stone, we undulate and eddy contentedly" (*The Waves* 136).

Almost literally, Percival is a speechless monument; and if his death occupies the center of the novel, it can be said that he is really dead even before he dies because he seems to manifest the death principle at the heart of European subjectivity. In a moment expressing the utopia of class identity, when, according to Louis, "the circle in our blood, broken so often, so sharply, for we are so different, closes in a ring" —at this moment Jinny describes this social bonding as a "globe whose walls are made of Percival, of youth and beauty, and something so deep sunk within us that we shall perhaps never make this moment out of one man again" (*The Waves* 145). Woolf's novel implies, however, that the European culture that produced Jinny and the others will have no difficulty coming up with another Percival since he represents not a living presence but a symbolic position that can be occupied by almost anyone. As a god, if he did not exist, he would have to be invented. Again, just before the speech that identifies Percival with the "standards of the West," Neville comments that "Percival is going. . . . We are walled in here. But India lies outside" (*The Waves* 135). Percival is the wall or boundary that determines the form of the European subject. The voiceless unity he represents is belied by the voices of the others which are so interwoven as to suggest that the individual subject is an effect of the discourse of the Other or the symbolic process itself. The unity of the European subject and of European culture is an imaginary construction, but this construction justifies imperialist authority and power by enabling the "violent language" of imperialist rule.

Of course, the violence of imperialism is not merely linguistic, a recognition that points toward the political limit of Woolf's novel and to what destabilizes its formal unity as a critique of imperialism. *The Waves* as a cultural text is organized *like a language*. The boy

Neville says as much in the first section when he responds to the process of schooling: "Each tense . . . means differently. There is an order in this world; there are distinctions, there are differences in this world" (*The Waves* 21). The novel as a whole maps out a system of gender and class differences not through the dynamics of struggle between contradictory class positions but through the articulation of a set of relatively homogeneous subjects who constitute a class formation. There are obvious and subtle differences of gender and class among the six characters, but all of them are shaped by the imperialist ideology into which they are fitted and into which they fit. Louis may be the boy "with a colonial accent" who becomes a global capitalist (*The Waves* 52); Rhoda may resist the rules that chain her "to one spot, one hour, one chair" until she takes her own life (204); and the others may follow different social trajectories within their class as the homosexual artist (Neville), the natural and nurturing mother (Susan), the sensuous woman of high society (Jinny), the man of culture (Bernard), or the official representative of imperialism (Percival). Nevertheless, they all accept the rhetorical parameters of a world view that could be considered the other side of Joseph Conrad's representation in *Heart of Darkness*. For example, in the same monologue in which she describes Percival as the great stone, Rhoda continues by describing the cultural unity of the group:

> One, two; one, two; the heart beats in serenity, in confidence, in some trance of well-being, in some rapture of benignity; and look—the outermost parts of the earth—pale shadows on the utmost horizon, India for instance, rise into our purview. The world that had been shrivelled, rounds itself; remote provinces are fetched up out of darkness; we see muddy roads, twisted jungle, swarms of men, and the vulture that feeds on some bloated carcass as within our scope, part of our proud and splendid province, since Percival, riding alone on a flea-bitten mare advances down a solitary path, has his camp pitched among desolate trees, and sits alone, looking at the enormous mountains. (*Waves* 137)

The collective identity of all these individualized characters depends on the ethnocentric mapping of the world into areas of light and areas of darkness, the same economy of representation that operates in *Heart of Darkness,* however self-reflexive that work may be, and in most colonial fiction, including E. M. Forster's *A Passage to India*.

The "trance of well-being" that these privileged Europeans feel is founded on the construction of non-Europeans as *the Other*, captured by a world of darkness that can only be illuminated by the European gaze and the manipulation of the European will to knowledge. The world outside European civilization becomes the object of European science and commerce. (Later, Louis, who resembles Conrad's Kurtz in this instance, refers to rolling "the dark before me, spreading commerce where there was chaos in the far parts of the world" [*Waves* 168].) The ultimate extreme of this ideology is the belief that the end of Western history is the end of history itself, the subversion of light by darkness. Marcus claims that "Woolf surrounds the text of the decline and fall of the West (the transcendental self striving and struggling against death) with the text of the East, random natural recurrence." By the text of the East, of course, she means the interludes as "a Western imitation or homage to the Hindu Gayatri" (155). But this reading still would have Woolf dividing the world along ethnocentric lines in a zone of light associated with culture (the West) and a zone of darkness associated with nature (the East).

Such a view corresponds rather closely to what Louis says about history: "But listen . . . to the world moving through abysses of infinite space. It roars; the lighted strip of history is past and our Kings and Queens; we are gone; our civilisation; the Nile; and all life. Our separate drops are dissolved; we are extinct, lost in the abysses of time, in the darkness" (*Waves* 225). In this view, the "random natural recurrence" of the East and of all the non-European world is the realm of darkness from which the light of European civilization has torn itself away. History would be the exception to the rule of darkness and death, a "lighted strip." Such a description more or less corresponds with Marlow's view of the Congo as "a prehistoric earth," a "night of first ages" (*Heart of Darkness* 37), that is, the darkness that precedes history and that will presumably follow it. To the extent that the East is associated with "random natural recurrence," it is also associated with death and the absence of history. Even in Marcus' reading, therefore, Woolf cannot be said to escape the ethnocentrism of a European system of representation.

My purpose in this reading of a reading is not to make Woolf out to be an imperialist or a racist. There is no question in my mind that in *The Waves* she struggles toward a critique of the European cultural system that she knew and that her family had participated in making. Her great-grandfather, grandfather, and father were culture makers, and Woolf understood that the machine of imperialism could not operate without the conscious or unconscious cooperation of the many family members, friends, and acquaintances who made up her world. As Bernard realizes after the death of Percival, the mechanisms of imperialist culture have a life of their own: "The machine then works; I note the rhythm, the throb, but as a thing in which I have no part, since he sees it no longer. . . . About him my feeling was: he sat there in the centre. Now I go to that spot no longer. The place is empty" (*The Waves* 153). In effect, Bernard says that his identity as a hege-monized subject of imperialism has died with the death of Percival; the center is empty. Like Woolf herself in *A Room of One's Own*, he feels the "sudden splitting off of consciousness, say in walking down Whitehall, when from being the natural inheritor of that civilisation," he becomes "outside of it, alien and critical" (*Room* 101). Bernard's alienation is not permanent, however; and he later has the fantasy of receiving a telephone call requesting him "to assume command of the British empire" (*The Waves* 261). Woolf, one imagines, would never have dreamed of or desired to receive such a call. For her the center of the imperialist machine is always empty, but that does not prevent it from operating with cold-blooded efficiency. Woolf does not have to identify with or support imperialism to be implicated in it, and she does not escape implication simply by representing (even in a critical or alienated form) the ideological system that underpins the European consciousness of the more privileged classes.

In *Heart of Darkness*, Marlow comes to the realization that "All Europe contributed to the making of Kurtz" (50). Marlow has also contributed to the making of Kurtz; and Conrad's novella ends with his telling a lie that puts the final touches on the historical construction of the Eurocentric subject. Marlow is a good company man who uses his talent for decentered and impressionistic storytelling to evade the responsibility of hearing any other voice outside the circle of European men sitting on the deck of the *Nellie*. By transferring to Marlow his own storytelling powers, Conrad is also implicated in a discursive order, the stylistic force and literary power of which is rooted in the silence of the other. Conrad can say with Marlow, "Mine is the speech that cannot be silenced" (*Heart of Darkness* 38). Woolf cannot be silenced either, nor should she be. But it would be historically naive to separate Woolf the subject from the historical context that must have exercised some determination on her literary production. It is contradictory to argue that, on the one hand, *The Waves* must be read as a fiction rooted in the historical context and, on the other, that the author fully transcended that context in order to produce an objective critique of it. *The Waves* must be read not only for what it says and represents but for what it does not represent or create a subjective space for.

Gayatri Spivak has argued that "the tropological deconstruction of masculism does not exempt us from performing the lie of impe-rialism" ("Imperialism and Sexual Difference" 234). It seems to me that this "lie of imperialism" remains to be confronted in the politics of modernist form. Today it is possible to describe a political mod-ernism that would include at least the work of Woolf and Joyce and portions of other oeuvres by authors as different as Conrad, Forster, Gertrude Stein, William Faulkner, H.D., and Jean Rhys. All of these writers employ modernist style and form to frame European culture in such a way as to exhibit its historical constructedness and non-universalizability. The rule of modernist form is that no form—not even the form of realism—is natural or self-evident and, for that reason, beyond history. Nevertheless, the form that modernism rules or draws the lines of, so to speak, does not exempt it from appealing to the sources of authorization and legitimacy in the culture of imperialism itself. Even a feminist-modernist like Woolf has to be situated by a critique such as the one Spivak has tried to conduct in a dialogue with European and American feminism. Her caveat is that

> feminism within the social relations and institutions of the metropolis has something like a relationship with the fight for individualism in the upwardly class-mobile bourgeois politics of the European nineteenth century. Thus, even as we feminist critics discover the troping error of the masculinist truth-claim to universality or academic objectivity, we perform the lie of constituting a truth of global sisterhood where the mesmerizing model remains male and female sparring partners of generalizable or universalizable sexuality who are the chief protagonists in that European contest. ("Imperialism and Sexual Difference" 226)

That modernist works have exposed the limits of European culture does not necessarily mean they have articulated the space in which the voice of the other can be heard—the other whose exclusion from the discourse of modernism is one of the grounds of its authority. The lie of imperialism still survives, even in the most radical deconstructions of Western culture like *The Waves* and *Finnegans Wake*, in the belief that Western culture is able to know itself from the outside, is able to produce its own self-critique without entailing the exclusion of the others who have traditionally suffered from the construction of European subjectivities. Postmodernism, although it should never be read as a complete break with modernism, must be situated within the historical framework of postcolonial revolutions and struggles (McGee 169–171). This new historical situation enables us to recognize the limits of modernist form in its implicit belief that formal revolutions can bring about social revolutions by transforming the consciousness of the European subject.

In the postcolonial situation, form is always a matter of political strategy that must be related to a larger historical context and specific political goals. For example, African writers like Chinua Achebe, Ngugi wa Thiong'o, and Bessie Head use realism, allegory, and other

modes of literary representation to produce a literature that is par-
ticipatory in the process of decolonization. These decisions are based
not on a naive understanding of language but on a commitment to
the political effects of writing that require an author to consider the
social impact of literary form. Achebe chooses realism and rejects the
inward gaze of modernism; Ngugi writes historical fictions in English
but then shifts to allegories and parables in a native African language;
Head (in *A Question of Power*) employs what might be considered
a modernist style to examine the conflict between colonizing and
decolonizing forces in the mind of an African woman. Still, even for
these writers, there is no simple way out of the historical contradictions that are the legacy of colonialism and the continuing reality of
neocolonialism. The difference between their literary acts and the acts
of modernists is that postcolonial writers cannot *not* hear the other,
cannot fail to take into account the cultural difference that would
constitute the relation to knowledge in the postcolonial world. It is not
just feminism that runs the risk of reinscribing the lie of imperialism
but any discursive practice that tries to generalize the grounds of its
own production and value. For the moment, the only way beyond
the politics of modernist form is through the recognition of cultural
difference and the commitment to perpetual negotiation across the
borders of that difference without any appeal to universal grounds
or authority. Translation of cultural difference is both necessary and
impossible. It is therefore interminable.

Perhaps the greatest lie of imperialism is the belief that self-
criticism and self-knowledge lead to self-liberation and knowledge of
the other. In *The Waves*, Woolf succeeds in articulating a perspective
on Western culture that challenges any reductive concept of its self-
identity or universality. The value of Marcus' reading of *The Waves* is
that it foregrounds the way Woolf has circumscribed her representation of European culture with determinations of class, gender, and
race. There is no unified subject of Europe as a generalizable human
essence. The characters in the novel are abstract constructions, not
universal types. Like the waves of the sea, their lines of individuation
are the illusions of a world in historical motion where nothing is ever
the same except the difference of difference.

Works Cited

Benstock, Shari. *Textualizing the Feminine: On the Limits of Genre*. Norman: U of Oklahoma P, 1991.
Bloch, Ernst. "Discussing Expressionism." In *Aesthetics and Politics: The*

Key Texts of Classic Debate within German Marxism. New York: Verso, 1980. 16–27.

Conrad, Joseph. *Heart of Darkness.* Ed. Robert Kimbrough. 3rd ed. New York: Norton, 1988.

Derrida, Jacques. *The Post Card: From Socrates to Freud and Beyond.* Trans. Alan Bass. Chicago: U of Chicago P, 1987.

Eagleton, Terry. "Brecht and Rhetoric." *Against the Grain: Essays 1975–1985.* London: Verso, 1986. 167–172.

Eysteinsson, Astradur. *The Concept of Modernism.* Ithaca: Cornell UP, 1990.

Hobsbawm, E. J. *The Age of Empire: 1875–1914.* New York: Pantheon, 1987.

Jameson, Fredric. "Reflections on the Brecht-Lukács Debate." *The Ideologies of Theory: Essays 1971–1986. Volume 2: The Syntax of History.* Minneapolis: U of Minneapolis P, 1988. 133–147.

Jeans, Sir James. *The Mysterious Universe.* Cambridge: Cambridge UP, 1930.

Lacan, Jacques. "Le sinthome." *Ornicar?* 10 (1977): 5–12.

MacCarthy, Desmond. "J. K. Stephen." *Portraits.* London: Putnam, 1931. 248–254.

Marcus, Jane. "Britannia Rules *The Waves.*" *Decolonizing Tradition: New Views of Twentieth-Century "British" Literary Canons.* Ed. Karen Lawrence. Urbana: U of Illinois P, 1992. 136–162.

McGee, Patrick. *Telling the Other: The Question of Value in Modern and Postcolonial Writing.* Ithaca: Cornell UP, 1992.

Minow-Pinkney, Makiko. *Virginia Woolf and the Problem of the Subject.* Brighton: Harvester, 1987.

Ragland-Sullivan, Ellie. *Jacques Lacan and the Philosophy of Psychoanalysis.* Urbana: U of Illinois P, 1986.

Spivak, Gayatri Chakravorty. "Imperialism and Sexual Difference." *Oxford Literary Review* 8 (1986): 225–240.

———. "Can the Subaltern Speak?" *Marxism and the Interpretation of Culture.* Ed. Cary Nelson and Lawrence Grossberg. Urbana: U of Illinois P, 1988. 271–313.

Stephen, Dorothea Jane. *Studies in Early Indian Thought.* Cambridge: Cambridge UP, 1918.

Woolf, Virginia. *A Room of One's Own.* New York: Harcourt, 1957.

———. *The Waves.* New York: Harcourt, 1959.

———. *Three Guineas.* New York: Harcourt, 1966.

———. *The Diary of Virginia Woolf.* Ed. Anne Olivier Bell. 4 vols. New York: Harcourt, 1977–1982.

———. "A Sketch of the Past." *Moments of Being.* Ed. Jeanne Schulkind. 2nd ed. London: Hogarth, 1985. 64–159.

THE JEW IN THE BATH

IMPERILED IMAGINATION IN

WOOLF'S *THE YEARS*

Maren Linett

Many of the earliest critical discussions of Virginia Woolf suppressed her antifascist politics and polemical feminism, charging her with elitism and a fondness for the ivory tower. In an effort to counter such a limited portrait, much "second-wave" feminist discourse since the mid-1970s has, conversely, celebrated Woolf's progressive political views without spending sufficient energy interrogating their lacunae. In this chapter I hope to join current efforts toward more nuanced inquiry into Woolf's often conflicting and sometimes troubling political positions.[1] In particular, this essay offers a corrective to a lingering critical reluctance to investigate Woolf's antisemitism.[2] Such reluctance may result in part from an unexamined assumption, common in post-Holocaust conceptualizations of the early twentieth century, that those who protested fascism must also have harbored steadfast sympathy with Jews. It may also be the case that because T. S. Eliot's clear distaste for Jews and Ezra Pound's virulent antisemitism are more obviously germane to their work, Woolf's less dramatic antipathy has seemed incidental. A willingness to study Woolf's antisemitism, however, is essential for understanding her intellectual and political concerns in the 1930s. Analyzing antisemitism's role in these concerns will allow us to map rich intersections among Woolf's anxieties about Jews, her worries about social, intellectual and imaginative freedom, and, indeed, her antifascist commitments.

Originally published in *Modern Fiction Studies*, Summer 2002.

The Years, which Woolf conceived in 1932 and published in 1937, offers material for analysis of just such intersections: a scene where a greasy Jew impedes the free imaginings and lyrical conversation of the novel's most charming and enigmatic character, Sara Pargiter. The fear that autonomous imagination was imperiled was an important component of Woolf's critique of militarism and fascism. If, in spite of the evidence, we read this scene as ironized, as critical of Sara and definitively distanced from Woolf's own point of view, we miss an opportunity to understand a cluster of ideas that permeates not only this novel and its draft versions in *The Pargiters*, but also its partner-text *Three Guineas* and Woolf's political vision of the 1930s.

The scene in question takes place in the "Present Day" section of *The Years*, as Sara sits in her "sordid" flat discussing poetry with her young cousin North. Their privacy is violated by the sounds of a Jewish neighbor taking a bath in the "room opposite." This man, Abrahamson, is not the first interruption in the scene: North's Aunt Eleanor has just phoned, intruding upon the cousins' colloquy. In fact, the novel is laden with interruptions, with truncated conversations and thoughts. The text emphasizes these intrusions when North begins to recite Andrew Marvell's poem of Edenic isolation, "The Garden."

> But as he reached the end of the second verse—
>   Society is all but rude—
>   To this delicious solitude . . .
> he heard a sound. Was it in the poem or outside of it, he wondered? Inside, he thought, and was about to go on, when she raised her hand. He stopped. He heard heavy footsteps outside the door. Was someone coming in? Her eyes were on the door.
>   "The Jew," she murmured.
>   "The Jew?" he said. They listened. He could hear quite distinctly now. Somebody was turning on taps; somebody was having a bath in the room opposite.
>   "The Jew having a bath," she said.
>   "The Jew having a bath?" he repeated.
>   "And tomorrow there'll be a line of grease round the bath," she said.
>   "Damn the Jew!" he exclaimed. The thought of a line of grease from a strange man's body on the bath next door disgusted him.
>   "Go on—" said Sara: "Society is all but rude," she repeated the last lines, "to this delicious solitude."
>   "No," he said. (*Years* 339–40)

Just as Marvell's speaker discovers that innocence and quiet are precluded by "busie Companies of Men," Sara and North find their thoughts deflated when the thin walls fail to protect them from the sounds of the neighbor as he dirties the communal bathtub. The grease of the "strange man's body" invades their privacy and thwarts their communication, so that North must repeat Sara's words in an effort to understand her meaning.

When North is too disgusted to continue the poem, Sara explains that she too has felt burdened by Abrahamson's presence. She tells North that when she first saw the grease on the tub, she thought she had better find a job, even though it would mean sacrificing her autonomy. That first morning, we learn, she "rushed out in a rage," stood on a bridge, and watched the workers passing by beneath:

> And there were people passing; the strutting; the tiptoe-ing; the pasty; the ferret-eyed; the bowler-hatted, servile innumerable army of workers. And I said, "Must I join your conspiracy? Stain the hand, the unstained hand,"—he could see her hand gleam as she waved it in the half-light of the sitting-room, "—and sign on, and serve a master; all because of a Jew in my bath, all because of a Jew?" (*Years* 341)

As Sara describes to North, she felt she must enslave herself to a "master"—to find employment—because of Abrahamson's presence.

This scene raises compelling interpretive and political questions: first, how does Abrahamson's Jewishness relate either to the apparent defeat of imagination represented by the abandoned poem or to Sara's fear that she must "stain the hand" by entering the professional world? Second, in a broader sense, how and why did the figure of a Jew become entwined with the issues of imaginative autonomy and privacy that occupied Woolf during the writing of *The Years* and *Three Guineas?* Third, what does this scene reveal about Woolf's own views about Jews after 1933, when, married to a Jew for more than twenty years, she felt endangered by the rise of Nazism in Germany?

This third question seems to have become a stumbling block that keeps critics from asking the two previous questions. Faced with an unappealing and apparently gratuitous portrayal of a Jew, many critics become more concerned with defending Woolf from charges of antisemitism than with interpreting the scene's significance for the novel or understanding its relevance within Woolf's intellectual concerns in this period. Their defenses can for the most part be grouped under two rubrics: biographical and interpretive. The biographical defenses claim that Woolf overcame her antisemitism two decades earlier when she decided to marry Leonard, and so the portrayal of

Abrahamson must be ironized, demonstrating Sara's prejudice but not Woolf's. The interpretive defenses argue that Abrahamson actually plays a positive role in Sara's mental life, either by inspiring her to move toward a democratic coalition or at least by giving her the opportunity to grow past her antisemitic bias.

As I offer an interpretation of the scene that addresses the first two questions, I need also to demonstrate that these critical claims reflect desire rather than reality, that Woolf did not abandon her antisemitism when she married Leonard, and that, in fact, Sara's concerns in this scene are very much congruent with those that perplexed Woolf during the middle thirties. However, the fact that Woolf retained antisemitic prejudices throughout her marriage does not necessarily help us understand this particular Jewish figure. I simply hope first to dislodge misleading views that have clouded our critical vision, in order to explore the import of this scene clear-sightedly. For this unexpected moment in *The Years* does not merely offer a window into Woolf's personal antipathies. It offers a condensed and illustrative version of a process common in interwar British literature: it makes of a specific reaction to a Jew—in this case to a male Jewish body, whose image leaves its trace in the grease on the bathtub— an abstracted collection of meanings supple enough to support the weight of multiple social and aesthetic concerns.[3] Exploring this process of abstraction aids us in unraveling the tangled threads of Woolf's political commitments during the decade in which she wrote *The Years* and *Three Guineas*.

Many scholars allege that Woolf simply couldn't endorse Sara's views because of her marriage to Leonard. Grace Radin, for example, in her otherwise compelling discussion of *The Years* and its draft versions, dismisses this scene with a footnote, asserting that Sara's view of Abrahamson "may well have been Virginia Stephen's own attitude before she came to know Jews like Leonard Woolf and S. S. Koteliansky" (94–95); but antisemitism is far more flexible than this assertion implies. In spite of her long marriage, Woolf's diaries and letters through the thirties show that she associated aspects of Leonard's family that she disliked with their Jewishness,[4] and maintained the "snobbery" she admitted in the much-quoted 1930 letter to Ethel Smyth. In fact, even in that confession, Woolf reproduced stereotypes of grasping, quickly proliferating Jews:

> How I hated marrying a Jew—how I hated their nasal voices, and their oriental jewellery, and their noses and their wattles—what a snob I was: for they have immense vitality, and I think I like that quality best of all. They cant die—they exist on a handful of rice and a thimble of water—their flesh dries on their bones but still they pullulate, copulate, and

amass (a Mrs Pinto, fabulously wealthy came in) millions of money. (*Letters* 4:195–96)[5]

Two other letters from the early 1930s suffice to show that Woolf did not conquer her prejudices in 1912 when she married Leonard. In 1932 she wrote, again to Ethel Smyth, about a gathering with Leonard's family: "talk, talk, talk, and all save perhaps 2 hours and 10 minutes utter waste. When the 10 Jews sat around me silently at my mother in law's tears gathered behind my eyes, at the futility of life: imagine eating birthday cake with silent Jews at 11pm" (*Letters* 5: 23). The significance of this letter is not that Woolf found the gathering boring, but that after all those years she could not stop seeing the Woolfs merely as a collection of Jews rather than as her husband's particular family. The next year she wrote to Quentin Bell that she wanted to skip a party for a woman engaged to a Rothschild: "I've no clothes and can't be bothered to rush out and buy gloves, hat, and shoes, all for a Jew" (*Letters* 5: 258).The diction and cadence of the phrase "all for a Jew" recall us to Sara's refrain in *The Years*, "all because of a Jew in my bath, all because of a Jew." Given letters such as these, we certainly cannot use biographical data to insist that Woolf disavowed Sara's aversion to Abrahamson.

The second sort of defense, rather than appealing to Woolf's private sympathies, willfully reads the scene against its manifest grain. In her important study of Woolf's oeuvre, Jane Marcus reads this scene as a "sacred drama," where Sara, in solidarity with Jews and workers, decides that she must join a redemptive and democratic "conspiracy," which will "work toward a better world." Marcus links this conspiracy to the "society of outsiders" described in *Three Guineas* (64). But to "sign on" is to do quite the opposite of what Woolf's "Outsiders' Society" advocates. Marcus's positive vision of the "conspiracy" contradicts Sara's description of the procession of workers as "servile," her lament that she has to "sign on and serve a master," and her "rage" at feeling pressured to join them. It is not to achieve solidarity with Jews or workers that Sara feels this pressure but to escape from her Jewish neighbor. North understands that her words "meant that she was poor; that she must earn her living" (*Years* 342). Sara, at least at the time she is describing to North, wanted to move out of the flat where she had to share the bathroom with Abrahamson but could only do so by earning more money. And so she tried to elicit sympathy from the man at the newspaper office: "'But the Jew's in my bath,' I said—'the Jew . . . the Jew . . .'" (*Years* 342).

Since Sara is still living in this flat and sharing the bathroom with Abrahamson, *The Years* suggests that she decided against accepting the job. In "The Loudspeaker and the Human Voice," Margaret

Comstock argues that since Sara has not moved out of the flat, we can infer that she has confronted her antisemitism, and now exhibits solidarity with her working-class Jewish neighbor (273). Because the novel abandons the topic without further explanation, this reading may seem possible. However, if we look not only at this scene but also at Sara's character in the novel as a whole, we find another explanation for her continued presence in the flat. Sara is characterized by her refusal to think or act along socially prescribed lines.[6] She is describing to North a time when she felt pressured to "sign on" to the world of workers; but by remaining in the flat, she demonstrates her triumph over the mental slavery that the newspaper job would have entailed. The drafts support this interpretation as well: we see Sara—called Elvira in the early versions—decide it would be worse to write for pay and corrupt her sense of truth than to live next to Abrahamson. She wonders how she could possibly "put [the truth] into 2,000 words. No, I shall say, I had rather share my bath with Abrahamson. . . . For all I know he's a good fellow" (*Pargiters* 8: 12). Comstock is right, then, that Sara has moved past the *acute* phase of her disgust by the time she talks to North; but her conclusion that Sara stays in the flat as a gesture of solidarity is unconvincing. It seems instead that refusing to write for pay *even though* it would allow her to escape from Abrahamson only demonstrates Sara's integrity in refusing to take her place in the social hierarchy.

This returns us to the first question posed earlier: what does Jewishness have to do with the pressure Sara feels to corrupt her vision by entering the world of journalism? How is it linked to the themes, encapsulated by the interrupted Marvell poem, of solitude invaded, privacy broken, and communion destroyed? A consideration of Woolf's attitudes about her work and her society in the early 1930s helps to begin answering this question.

After Hitler took power in Germany, Woolf found that the ostensibly private decision she had made to marry Leonard had political consequences. For instance, when she was preparing for their trip to Germany in 1935, she wrote, "Oh so many dreary letters to dispatch—German Embassy today to get a letter out of Prince Bismarck, since *our* Jewishness is said to be a danger" (*Letters* 5:386; emphasis added).[7] Before her marriage Woolf's Englishness was precarious because she was a woman,[8] and now Leonard's Jewishness seemed to mark her as well, meaning danger on their European trip, and death for them both should the Nazis invade England.[9]

Demonstrating her awareness that her own word could not define her or grant her safety in Germany, Woolf wrote a letter of introduction into this very scene in *The Years:* Sara needs a letter of introduction to be admitted to the newspaper office where she goes to apply for a job. In the 1934 drafts of the scene, Elvira does not yet have a letter of introduction; she simply tells the man at the office that her grandfather went to Eton. But as Woolf revised the scene soon after her trip to Germany, the letter from Prince Bismarck seems to have worked its way in, becoming Sara's "talisman."[10]

Woolf's need for the letter of introduction points to the powerful social significance that her marriage to Leonard assumed. As public events pressed closer than ever before, her identity seemed to shift without her consent. When she referred to herself, and not just to Leonard, as Jewish, she was acknowledging the power of external events and definitions. Woolf also felt pressured by Leonard and many of their Labour Party friends and acquaintances to abandon her pacifism and "sign on" by supporting England's rearmament. Especially after 1935 Leonard's views "hardened," differing significantly from her own.[11] In 1936 she aligned herself with Aldous Huxley, a pacifist who had refused to sign a manifesto that supported sanctions against Italy.[12] As England coalesced into an antifascist militarized bloc that itself threatened free imagination, Woolf did not yield to the pressure to support military solutions; but she did decide to expand the ways in which her fiction engaged with the sociopolitical world.

Although the antifascist, feminist essay that would become *Three Guineas* was simmering in her head, she postponed it to write *The Pargiters*, at that time an "essay-novel" with essays explaining the issues each fictional chapter addressed. She wanted this novel to emphasize anonymity and "facts" instead of personality and "vision."[13] But addressing the world of facts created a new aesthetic problem, making the novel that became *The Years* extremely difficult for Woolf to write.[14] She had been wondering since 1933 how she could include "millions of ideas [in this novel] but no preaching?" (*Diary* 4: 152). She was "doubtful of the value of those figures . . . afraid of the didactic" (*Diary* 4: 144–45).

This turn away from "vision" was an important and anxiety-provoking shift in Woolf's art. Although she had never hidden from her society behind a cloak of hermetically beautiful language, as some New Critics had it, she had certainly emphasized, especially in *To the Lighthouse* (1927) and *The Waves* (1931), her characters' interior lives. These interior lives were, of course, politically inflected, and Woolf had astutely analyzed the effects of patriarchal tyranny on the psyches of both male and female characters. Now, though, she focused on social more than psychological results of oppression, refusing to allow her characters profound or even coherent meditations. As she was "breaking the mould made by The Waves" (*Diary* 4: 233), she had to "reassure herself that her studied denial of lyricism and inner life [was] not misguided" (Whittier-Ferguson 90). She needed to reassure herself because her new focus on the visible aspects of people, on the surfaces of objects, could not completely allay the loss involved in turning away from the interior life and embarking on the often painful work of her novel of "fact."

Sara's reaction to Abrahamson suggests an analogy between Sara's and Woolf's predicaments (an analogy highlighted when Woolf adds the letter of introduction). Both Woolf and Sara are pressured by the proximity of a Jewish man to turn outward, to leave aside their own visions and identities in favor of broader social concerns. Sara feels pressured to do this by writing for a newspaper, Woolf by supporting the use of force as a means of fighting fascism. Instead of abandoning her pacifism, Woolf decided to expand her inquiries (ongoing at least since *A Room of One's Own*) into the links between patriarchal and fascistic oppression, writing the political texts *The Pargiters/The Years*, and *Three Guineas*.[15] Insofar as Woolf may have felt obliged by Leonard's status and its effects on her own social identities to engage with sociopolitical realities in broader terms, we can see Sara's neighbor as a sort of metatextual scapegoat. He seems to bear responsibility not just for the threat to Sara's mental freedom, but also for political and artistic pressures on Woolf herself: to abandon her pacifism and to sacrifice her modernism of interiority and "vision."

When she chose a Jew to represent social and financial demands on Sara Pargiter, Woolf confused victims of social systems with oppressors. After all, Abrahamson is a victim of the racially inflected class system that enslaves him to a tallow factory; and Nazism, not Leonard, was to blame for threatening Woolf's safety. And yet Woolf illustrates the threat to privacy and imagination in *The Years* by repeated reference to a Jew's presence. She thus creates her own version of the characteristically irreconcilable claims current in interwar British society, where Jews were viewed as poverty-stricken, slum-dwelling victims and at the same time as rich and powerful international conspirators.[16] In Woolf's version, Jews are victims of unjust systems that define them from the outside—systems she condemns throughout *Three Guineas*—and yet their mere presence threatens the imaginative freedom of others.

The fear that imaginative autonomy might be unrecoverable animates this scene in *The Years*, all its draft versions and *Three Guineas* as well. By reading the drafts of the "Jew in the bath" scene alongside *Three Guineas*, one can see clearly the intersections between Woolf's figuration of the Jew's threatening presence and her intellectual and political concerns. Woolf assigned Sara a version of her own fear of intellectual prostitution and of her own dismay at how little force the imagination seemed to possess. The drafts demonstrate how suitable the figure of the Jew seemed to Woolf for representing these threats to the imagination; they also reveal a predecessor for Abrahamson who resembles Leonard more closely than the factory worker. By turning to earlier versions of the scene, however, I do not wish to claim that they reveal Woolf's unchanging intentions or the scene's authentic core; indeed, I want to trace both the relative consistency of her concerns over the period from 1934 until the publication of *Three Guineas* in 1938, and the changes in the ways she decided to illustrate them.

When Woolf finished *Three Guineas* in June 1938, she sighed with relief: "Anyhow thats the end of six years floundering, striving, much agony, some ecstasy: lumping the Years and 3 Gs together as one book—as indeed they are" (*Diary* 5: 148). As Woolf acknowledged, *The Years* and *Three Guineas* share many preoccupations. Among these is the worry that modernity—in particular, but not solely, the rise of fascism—would stamp out freedom of thought, encroach on the privacy of the mind.

   Three Guineas meditates on the possibility for disinterested-ness, for freedom from ties that bind the imagination: "By freedom from unreal loyalties is meant that you must rid yourself of pride of nationality in the first place; also of religious pride, college pride, school pride, family pride, sex pride and those unreal loyalties that spring from them" (80). The narrator of *Three Guineas* describes how writing professionally, as Sara Pargiter was considering, prevents this disinterestedness, and is, in fact, a sort of mental prostitution:

> "But what," she may ask, "is meant by 'selling your mind without love?'" "Briefly," we might reply, "to write at the command of another person what you do not want to write for the sake of money."

   Even though such a writer may be a victim of her poverty, her corruption nevertheless spreads to affect her whole culture, making the victim into a menace: "But when a brain seller has sold her brain, its anaemic, vicious and diseased progeny are let loose upon the world to infect and corrupt and sow the seeds of disease in others" (*Three Guineas* 93).This nervous strand within *Three Guineas* explains Sara Pargiter's predicament. Her privacy is being infringed upon and her creativity dampened by the Jew who shares her bathroom; but if she gets a job to escape him, she falls into a similar trap, still forfeiting her solitude and mental freedom. By showing the writer who needs pay "infect[ing] and corrupt[ing]" others, the above passage also suggests a parallel to Abrahamson's allegedly corrupting influence.

   Woolf wrote the "Jew in the bath" scene many times over during the summer of 1934. She began one set of drafts on 4 June and worked on it throughout the month, then began a second set on 1 July. In the July versions of the scene, Elvira goes to the newspaper office in a clear effort to escape from her lodgings. The man there asks her if she has any experience in journalism and she replies, "No . . . no training, no education, not a letter to my name, my lord duke: repeating . . . like the burden of a song, But the Jew's in my bath." This produces sympathy in the man. He sends her to another department, where they "deal with iron stains in tablecloths, how to fry fish in batter" (*Pargiters* 7: 3).[17] If Elvira wants to escape from Abrahamson, she will have to prostitute her mind by writing about insipid domestic dilemmas.

George (whose name will become North by 1936) interprets Elvira's quirky phrases for readers and wonders about her meanings and motives. This version addresses the interestedness of contemporary society, especially of literary culture, more explicitly than the published scene. Like her later incarnation, Elvira has to "stain the hand"—that is, she must write for money. Here we are in George's head:

> Elvira had gone back to the book that she had dropped. She was flicking over the pages; she was dipping, diving, she was caught within some machine: the blood royal, the unstained hand—he remembered the phrases; they meant, he supposed, that in some vague way that she felt . . . that it is better to give than to take; better to remain outside the patriarchy—that is, the hierarchy of organized society, than to accept membership; better to remain obscure, unpaid, subsisting on a meager allowance. But why better? What was the idea . . . behind such an impulse? Something that was difficult to express, some ancient prejudice or instinct to the effect that human nature degrades itself by taking? that pleasure, happiness lie in what is voluntary? in our day the traitorous are the successful; that it is they who impede progress, put a ring on the natural expanse of the mind. (*Pargiters* 7: 6)

The constraints (rings) that those who are successful within the "hierarchy" put around the mind are made literal by the ring Abrahamson puts around the bathtub. Here, in George's thoughts, is an argument similar to one that will appear in *Three Guineas*: only by remaining outside "organized society" can one protect one's autonomy. To accept membership, for example by writing for another, is slavery or prostitution of the mind.

Again we must ask, why is this mental prostitution figured by a Jew? According to the drafts, there is a link between Jews and financial interest that explains the association. "Caught by a law, she observed. Every ~~man~~ one who writes, a lecturer [who] gets himself up to instruct the people should ~~be forced~~ to add, ~~'the Jews in my bath'~~ in capital letters, The Jews in my bath. ~~She meant, he supposed, that the tract she had been skimming~~ She meant that they wrote for money, he supposed" (*Pargiters* 7: 8). All those who own culture, Elvira says, ought to be honest enough to admit that they write for money, that they are themselves "owned." Their sale of the mind is indicated by this incessant phrase, "the Jew[']s in my bath."

But this is the second version of this passage. A few pages earlier Woolf writes:

> "~~If I were Lord Chancellor,~~ she remarked, I should make it
> ~~It ought to be a law,~~ she remarked:
> ~~Every lecturer, every preacher every~~
> The Jews in my bath. . . .
> The Jews in his bath tub, she observed;
> but he doesn't have the common honesty to say so.
> She meant that the article she was skimming was written for money, he supposed. (*Pargiters* 7: 5)

Here the "he" who is not honest enough to admit his affiliations is the writer of the article Sara is skimming. In the July drafts of this scene, then, Woolf uses a Jew to represent the money interest that in *Three Guineas* prostitutes the mind of the writer. Whereas in *The Years* Abrahamson represents an abstracted invasion into Sara's private space, connected with the world of professional writing only by driving Sara toward the "servile innumerable army of workers," here Jews represent a direct involvement with money, a commercialism that shows in greater detail why it is so difficult to preserve private judgment.

In *Three Guineas* the narrator asks her interlocutor: "Do you pursue the same rather extravagant policy there—glance at three daily papers and three weekly papers if you want to know the facts about pictures, plays, music and books, because those who write about art are in the pay of an editor, who is in the pay of a board, which has a policy to pursue?" (96). Being "in the pay of" someone else was crucial already in *The Pargiters*, where Elvira suggests that the more successful one is, the more one must play into this system of intellectual harlotry: "Big wigs, all took pay; they had Jews in their baths" (*Pargiters* 7: 9). The Jew in the bath of a "big wig" represents the same kind of prostitution that is described more straightforwardly in *Three Guineas*:

So to ask the daughters of educated men who have to earn their livings by reading and writing to sign your manifesto would be of no value to the cause of disinterested culture and intellectual liberty because directly they had signed it they must be at the desk writing those books, lectures, and articles by which culture is prostituted and intellectual liberty is sold into slavery. (92)

Taken as "one book," *The Pargiters* and *Three Guineas* connect the ideas of slavery, prostitution, Jews, disease, corruption, and money interest until they describe what ails British culture.[18] George accepts Elvira's metaphor of "the Jew" and wonders too how to create an expansive, free culture: "The Jew was in all their baths as she put it. The problem, how to get rid of the line of grease, how to live in decently, expansively" (*Pargiters* 7: 10).[19] He and Elvira use the figure of the Jew to represent both an invasion into the private home and the corruption of the public world.

In the earliest versions of the scene, written in June 1934, Elvira is more overtly disgusted with the Jew and has not, as she may have in *The Years*, moved past the most acute stage of her reaction. Here it is she rather than George/North who exclaims "Oh damn the Jew!" And the "grease" of the later versions—which critics sometimes connect to his trade, and read as a sympathetic portrayal of the plight of a worker—is called instead "slime." "[H]e'll use all the hot water, but that's not what I mind. [I]ts leaving a track of slime around the edge of the bath" (*Pargiters* 6: 112). This scene does more than say that culture is prostituted by the "Jew in the bath." It denies any purpose to culture and literature at all if they are to be thus compromised: "If Abrahamson is going to have a bath, whats the good of reading The Tempest?" Furthermore, Abrahamson is the direct cause of a breakdown of communication and creativity: "Water was running. As it ran, the play, the play they were creating together, which Elvira had been making, wore thin, collapsed" (*Pargiters* 6: 113).

During the June attempts at this scene, Woolf often halts, begins again. Elvira and George hear and react to the Jewish neighbor several times. Woolf simply writes multiple versions, often not bothering to cross out the older ones. In one passage, Elvira describes to George (as Sara does in *The Years*) what it was like when, one cold morning, she first discovered the line of grease on the tub. In this version of the story, the Jew does not represent pressures on the imagination or the breakdown of communication or money interest; Elvira simply asserts that she ought to be protected from such people by her class. "The man Abrahamson had left a line of grease. ~~And I the granddaughter of a man who ought have been a bishop . . . . And I the~~

granddaughter of a bishop" (*Pargiters* 6: 11). Here the problem is a more personal and direct aversion, a fear of contamination by class and race, but not by Jewishness turned into a metaphor for social or financial pressures. This story appears closely related to what must be the original germ of the "Jew in the bath" scene: an episode narrated earlier in volume 6 of *The Pargiters*. There it is not yet the "Jew in the bath" who threatens to compromise mental privacy, but a character with whom Elvira is intimate.

In this scene, also written in June 1934, George and Elvira are eating dinner in her flat, when the telephone interrupts them.

> "I'm not here, I'm not here!" she exclaimed.
> The telephone went on ringing.
> "That's the voice of Nicholas,["] she said; ["]peremp-
> tory . . . *breaking into the privacy of the mind; violating solitude*["]. (*Pargiters* 6: 75; emphasis added)

The character of Nicholas remains in the published text as a homosexual who carries on what the other characters find a strangely intimate relationship with Sara. There, Eleanor sees immediately that Nicholas is foreign, and thinks he looks "Russian, Polish, Jewish?—she had no idea what he was, who he was" (*Years* 282). Nicholas identifies himself as a Pole shortly thereafter (*Years* 287). But here, in the early drafts, Elvira explains to George that Nicholas is "a wretched Polish Jew without a coat to his back; and a twinkle in his eyes; and he came to me, when I was alone too" (*Pargiters* 6: 76). Instead of a homosexual Polish friend, this Nicholas is Elvira's Jewish lover.

The Jewish Nicholas not only intrudes on her privacy but also has compromised his integrity in some unspecified way: "Thats Nicholas; but I say to him, you who have forfeited, who have compromised, commuted . . ." Instead of *representing* intellectual harlotry like the more impersonal "Jew in the bath," Nicholas has forfeited values that are important to Elvira. But she does not simply detest him; she is torn. She tells George, "Theres two sides to the soul, to the every situation: The moon has two faces; life is very complex. Call it simple? Call love simple?" (*Pargiters* 6: 75). Nicholas's Jewishness seems a major source of this uncertainty, not only for Elvira, but for Woolf, who suppresses (crosses out) the connection between his Jewishness and Elvira's ambivalence: "Nicholas, whom I dont love, do love, the Jew" (*Pargiters* 6: 76).

In the published novel, Sara's ambivalence remains enigmatic. North is puzzled in *The Years* by Sara's unwillingness to speak to the man she has just said she loves.

> "You love him . . . " he began. But here the telephone
> rang.
>   "There he is!" she exclaimed. "That's him! That's
> Nicholas!" She spoke with extreme irritation.
>   The telephone rang again. "I'm not here!" she said.
> The telephone rang again. "Not here! Not here! Not here!"
> [. . .] "Tell him I'm not here!" she said. (*Years* 324)

Readers, too, may be puzzled not only by Sara's irritation but by the text's anxious-sounding repetition. While *The Years* offers no explanation for this scene, the drafts suggest that Sara's anxiety may be left over from her reaction to Nicholas's earlier Jewishness.

Elvira's worry, that a Jew whom she loves but whose integrity she distrusts will violate the "privacy of [her] mind," gets transmuted and diffused when Woolf alters Nicholas's identity and creates Elvira's Jewish neighbor, as if to find another focal point for the menace. The physical intimacy between Elvira and her Jewish lover leaves its trace in *The Years* in the hairs and grease left on the tub by the "strange man's [naked] body." All the versions of this scene betray a consistent worry about the loss of mental privacy and associate this concern with Jews. But the figure changes as the drafts progress: by the published version, the bearer of the threat is no longer an intimate, who has *committed* an act of treason, but a far more distant "Jew in the bath," who *represents* it. A Jew who elicits from Sara a specific and personal aversion is developed, through Woolf's revisions, into an abstraction, a metaphor for multiple pressures, anxieties, and losses.

This metamorphosis supports the idea that Sara's feeling of oppression by her Jewish neighbor bore some resonance for Woolf herself. At the same time that she expressed solidarity by referring to herself and Leonard as Jews, Woolf appears to have felt trapped by the way Leonard's Jewishness endangered and redefined her. She was also disappointed—and perhaps felt betrayed—that he now strongly favored rearmament while she remained a pacifist. After all, it was in part England's own rearmament, the mobilization of her society into an antifascist bloc that left little room for disinterested thinking, that Woolf indicted via the figure of Abrahamson and throughout *Three Guineas*. These negative feelings were uncomfortable enough, perhaps, that Woolf revised the scene so that the threat to imagination no longer comes from Nicholas, an educated Jewish intimate of Elvira's who would have been understood as a representation of Leonard, but "the Jew in the bath," a dirty, working-class neighbor. This barely suppressed resentment may even explain why Woolf did not let Leonard read *The Pargiters* or *The Years* in draft form, as she did with her other novels.[20] Instead, she waited until *The Years* was in galley proofs—when Nicholas is no longer Jewish and Abrahamson bears the weight of the betrayal—before allowing him to see it.

Reading the scene, its drafts, and *Three Guineas* together, we find a complex set of implied arguments, anxieties, and protests. On one level, Woolf linked a Jewish figure to the forces that threaten Sara's imagination because, as a target of Nazism, he exemplified Woolf's worry that externally imposed identities were usurping the imagination's power to define the self. In *Three Guineas* Woolf acknowledges that Jews are victims of Nazism, that they are "being shut out, [. . .] being shut up, because [they] are Jews" (103). But Woolf seems to have viewed this victimization as potentially contagious. Like *Three Guineas*'s "brain-seller," Woolf's fictional Jewish victim is also a contaminant, "sow[ing] the seeds of disease" in Sara Pargiter, threatening to "infect" her with the same plight.

While Woolf openly protested fascism, we find in *The Years* scene and the *Pargiters* drafts evidence to suggest that she may have covertly blamed Leonard for the way her marriage to him intensified and multiplied the threats tyranny posed to her own safety. Since his Jewishness meant that they would both be targeted by potentially invading Nazis, it may indeed have seemed to her that victimization was contagious. To resent Leonard for his Jewishness was, of course, to allow her own social antisemitism to pervert her understanding of where exactly the menace lay.

In expressing her political and personal anxieties, Woolf caught herself in an ideological bind. While she opposed fascism and any other system—such as patriarchy—that reduced people to their social roles, and while she affirmed the sublimity of individual imagination, she failed to differentiate clearly between the victim and the source of political oppression. Even leaving aside whatever role Leonard may have played in her delineation of Nicholas and Abrahamson, the fact remains that Woolf chose a Jew to represent the threat against which the mind must be guarded. When she revised the scene from 1934 for the book's publication in 1937, she did not uncouple the figure of the Jew from this danger; she only transferred the threat from an educated Jewish lover to a working-class Jewish neighbor. By using a Jew to figure this peril to the imagination, Woolf exposed her own imagination as imperiled by a resilient antisemitism sustained alongside and even within the fervent antifascist commitments that animate *The Years*.

Notes

1. Other critics who seem engaged in such a project include Hermione Lee, John Whittier-Ferguson, Phyllis Lassner, and Natania Rosenfeld. A new collection, *Virginia Woolf and Fascism*, edited by Merry Pawlowski, offers a broad set of perspectives on Woolf's complex political views.

2. I follow many in the social sciences in not capitalizing "semitism"; while no more than a gesture, this spelling indicates a rejection of the racial category "Semite."

3. For example, Dorothy Richardson uses a Jewish character to explore Miriam Henderson's conflicted femininity and misogyny in *Pilgrimage*. James Joyce, even as he created the most complex Jew in modern literature, also turned Leopold Bloom's Jewishness into an abstraction (most notably in "Ithaca") so as to reflect and define Stephen Dedalus's need for exile and artistic detachment.

4. In *Virginia Woolf and Anti-Semitism*, Jean Moorcroft Wilson argues that some of Woolf's antisemitic comments about her mother-in-law ought to be attributed to "perfectly natural family tensions." She points out that when Woolf wrote about Leonard's brothers, whom she liked, she did not mention their Jewishness (9–10). Instead of offering evidence that Woolf was not antisemitic, Moorcroft Wilson has inadvertently offered evidence to the contrary: when she didn't like someone, Woolf focused on his or her Jewishness; when she did, she left Jewishness, evidently a negative attribute, aside.

5. I have not corrected the punctuation or spelling in Woolf's diaries and letters; she often omits apostrophes, hyphens, and periods used to mark abbreviations.

6. Radin puts it like this: the "keystone of Elvira's [Sara's] character will be her repudiation of society's bribes and rewards" (41).

7. She also writes to Margaret Llewelyn Davies: "We have got a letter from Prince Bismarck in our pockets, as people say we might be unpopular as we are Jews" (*Letters* 5: 388).

8. "[B]y law [a woman] becomes a foreigner if she marries a foreigner" (*Three Guineas* 108).

9. The threat of a Nazi invasion appeared possible at various points during Hitler's regime, but especially, of course, during the war. In May of 1940 Leonard and Virginia "discussed suicide if Hitler land[ed]" (*Diary* 5: 284).

10. "'But I had a talisman, a glowing gem, a lucent emerald'—she picked up an envelope that lay on the floor—'a letter of introduction. And I said to the flunkey in the peach-blossom trousers, Admit me, sirrah'" (*Years* 341).

11. Hermione Lee writes, "From 1935 onwards [Leonard's] position on rearmament changed and hardened—the cause of prolonged and unresolved debate between them" (668).

12. "Aldous [Huxley] refuses to sign the latest manifesto because it approves sanctions. He's a pacifist. So am I. Ought I to resign [from the Labour Party]. L[eonard] says that considering Europe is now on the verge of the greatest smash for 600 years, one must sink private differences and support the League" *(Diary* 5: 17).

13. Woolf uses the terms "fact" and "vision" about her work on *The Pargiters.* (See *Diary* 4: 151.) John Whittier-Ferguson writes: "What changes throughout the 1930s is the openness with which Woolf recognizes and exposes the sociopolitical effects of [the ego's] tyranny and the rigor with which she attempts to eradicate the marks of the ego from her own work. 'I came to the stage 2 years ago,' she writes in her memoir of Julian Bell (1937), 'of hating "personality"; desiring anonymity'" (85).

14. Her diaries through the mid-thirties keep returning to her distress, which she is sure is worse than it had been with earlier novels. "I'm worried too with my last chapters. Is it all too shrill and voluble?" (*Diary* 4: 234). "Seldom have I been more completely miserable than I was . . . reading over the last part of The Years. Such feeble twaddle. . . . [Leonard] said This always happens. But I felt, no it has never been so bad as this" (*Diary* 5: 8).

15. In this sense *Three Guineas* served as both a concession to arguments that all English people must involve themselves in fighting fascism, and a rebuttal: an argument that the best way to resist fascism was to resist all "unreal loyalties," including support of any military organizations.

16. For an analysis of self-contradictory "semitic discourse" in modern British literature and society, see Bryan Cheyette's important study, *Constructions of 'the Jew' in English Literature and Society: Racial Representations 1875–1945.*

17. Mitchell Leaska's published version of *The Pargiters* ends where Woolf gave up the idea of inserting essays between the chapters, before the "Present Day" section. I have therefore transcribed the quotations from *The Pargiters* volumes 6 and 7 from Woolf's notoriously poor handwriting as it appears in the Virginia Woolf Manuscripts of the Berg Collection. The quotations are accurate to the best of my knowledge. When Woolf omits quotation marks and apostrophes, I have usually transcribed the sentences exactly as the manuscript gives them. Where I have corrected anything for the sake of clarity, I have done so within brackets.

18. *Three Guineas* suggests that women, if they preserve poverty, mental chastity, and "freedom from unreal loyalties" (78), might be able to alleviate these problems. But their existence, Woolf argues, may

mean that culture has not been created in the first place: "Therefore let us define culture for our purposes as the disinterested pursuit of reading and writing the English language. And intellectual liberty may be defined for our purposes as the right to say or write what you think in your own words, and in your own way" (91).

19. George's musings are, in the published version, given to Eleanor, but without reference to this metaphor of grease on a tub: "When shall we be free? When shall we live adventurously, wholly, not like cripples in a cave?" (*Years* 297).

20. "We have decided to take this unusual course—that is to print it in galleys before L. sees it" (*Diary* 5: 15).

Works Cited

Cheyette, Bryan. *Constructions of 'the Jew' in English Literature and Society: Racial Representations 1875–1945*. New York: Cambridge UP, 1993.

Comstock, Margaret. "The Loudspeaker and the Human Voice: Politics and the Form of *The Years*." *Bulletin of the New York Public Library* 80 (1977): 252–75.

Lassner, Phyllis. "'The Milk of Our Mother's Kindness Has Ceased to Flow': Virginia Woolf, Stevie Smith, and the Representation of the Jew." *Between 'Race' and Culture: Representations of 'the Jew' in English and American Literature*. Ed. Bryan Cheyette. Stanford: Stanford UP, 1996.

Lee, Hermione. *Virginia Woolf*. New York: Vintage, 1999.

Marcus, Jane. *Virginia Woolf and the Languages of Patriarchy*. Bloomington: Indiana UP, 1987.

Pawlowski, Merry M. *Virginia Woolf and Fascism: Resisting the Dictators' Seduction.* New York: St. Martin's, 2001.

Radin, Grace. *Virginia Woolf's The Years: The Evolution of a Novel*. Knoxville: U of Tennessee P, 1981.

Rosenfeld, Natania. *Outsiders Together: Virginia and Leonard Woolf*. Princeton: Princeton UP, 2000.

Whittier-Ferguson, John. *Framing Pieces: Designs of the Gloss in Joyce, Woolf, and Pound*. New York: Oxford UP, 1996.

Wilson, Jean Moorcroft. *Virginia Woolf and Anti-Semitism*. London: Cecil Woolf, 1995.

Woolf, Virginia. *The Diary of Virginia Woolf*. 5 vols. Ed. Anne Olivier Bell. New York: Harcourt, 1977.

———. *The Letters of Virginia Woolf*. 6 vols. Ed. Nigel Nicolson and Joanne Trautmann. New York: Harcourt, Brace, Jovanovich, 1975–1980.

——. *The Pargiters*. The Virginia Woolf Manuscripts from the Henry W. and Albert A. Berg Collections of the New York Public Library, Reel 10. Woodbridge, CT: Research Publications International, 1993.

——. *Three Guineas*. 1938. New York: Harcourt, 1966.

——. *The Years*. 1937. New York: Harcourt, 1965.

AFTERWORD

_____

Mark Hussey

Despite prediction's inherent risk of subsequent embarrassment, it seems safe enough to say that Woolf scholarship will continue to expand into new areas and to flourish in the coming decades. I will comment briefly on what I see as five significant contexts for such scholarship: the "new" modernist studies; discoveries of new material; archival research; new editions; and ethics and the role of the humanities.

The new modernist studies, exemplified in the programs of the Modernist Studies Association's annual conference and the contents of its journal *Modernism/modernity*, indicate the likely emphases of Woolf studies for the twenty-first century. Nevertheless, scholarship on Woolf could be seen as having provided for some time a paradigm for the "new" modernist studies: It has been interested in questions of politics, empire, poetics, race, popular and mass culture, class, psychoanalysis, film, music, sexuality, photography, the urban, the pastoral, tradition, the new, intertextuality, aesthetics, kitsch, and the visual for at least the past two decades. Transnationalism, encounters with feminisms other than the Anglo-American version, and with "bad" modernisms (cf. Mao and Walkowitz) all might prove fertile frameworks for continuing scholarship on Woolf. As Anna Snaith's recent *Palgrave Advances in Virginia Woolf Studies* attests, Woolf is "a writer who matters" (Snaith 1), and yet she has seemed to matter less than some of her canonical contemporaries perhaps because of what Woolf describes in *Three Guineas* as the "aroma" of sex (62).

One inspiration for new scholarship is new material. Estate sales and attics emptied for moving house can produce serendipitous discoveries. In 2002, for example, a 1909 diary of Woolf's turned up in a drawer where it had lain since 1968 when the young woman who had agreed to type it for Leonard Woolf put it away, uncertain what to do with it following his death. The publication of this holograph diary in *Carlyle's House and Other Sketches* in 2003 (Bradshaw) cautions against assuming that the archive is complete. And although they tend to be beyond the means of most scholars, items offered for sale by auction houses also signal unfinished business to be attended to once they have found their way to accessible collections. In November 2007, Christie's of London auctioned letters from Woolf to Motier Harris Fisher and a typescript related to Woolf's late essay "Thoughts on Peace in an Air Raid," the publication of which in an American periodical Woolf and Fisher were discussing. The *Bulletin* of the Virginia Woolf Society of Great Britain, too, has regularly published newly found letters and sketches.

Scholars also continue to make discoveries that can affect our reading of Woolf's oeuvre. In 2007, as one example, Georgia Johnston located in the archive of the National Federation of Women's Institutes at the Women's Library in London the typescript of the talk Woolf gave to the Rodmell Women's Institute in 1940 about the 1910 "Dreadnought Hoax." It is in perhaps overlooked or hitherto unvisited archives that Woolf will be placed in new relationships and reframed by unfamiliar associations. Furthermore, some recently published material from the archive has yet to be adequately assimilated into the scholarly and critical response to Woolf, such as the correspondence from readers transcribed and edited by Beth Rigel Daugherty, and the *Three Guineas* correspondence edited by Anna Snaith.

Transcriptions of Woolf's urtexts undertaken in the 1970s and 1980s were published before the recent profound reorientation that has taken place in textual editing theory (see Shillingsburg). Mitchell Leaska's 1983 edition of the typescripts of *Pointz Hall*, for example, takes great liberties with transcription to present "as readable a form as possible" (Leaska 21), but the ascription of authorial intention such readability depends on has been thoroughly questioned by a body of textual editing theory that pays close attention to the social and bibliographic aspects of producing a text. While new transcriptions of Woolf's holograph and typescript materials are unlikely, it is already the case that scholars are returning when possible to the original documents to consider her creative processes. The relatively scant contact between literary and textual scholars (Groden 259) is likely to improve as more and more opportunities to work on texts in rich digital environments become available.

It is in the field of studies of creativity and the writing process that such research may prove particularly fruitful and this is likely to be aided by the development of increasingly sophisticated technologies. The project begun by the late Julia Briggs is one powerful instance of how textual editing and software development can marry to produce intriguing new avenues of approach both to Woolf's cultural and philosophical contexts and to her methods of creating her work (www.woolfonline.com). As the capabilities and attendant theory of digital texts continue to evolve, Woolf's composition and revision practices are likely to come under fresh scrutiny with results that will provide fruitful new contexts within which to read her works.

The Cambridge University Press edition of the works of Virginia Woolf will begin publication in 2009 under the general editorship of Jane Goldman and Susan Sellers. This edition is being produced specifically for an international scholarly audience, in contrast to the paperback annotated series published by Harcourt, which is intended primarily for classroom use. New editions facilitate new readings. Readers of the 2006 Harcourt edition of *Three Guineas* will for the first time since the 1938 edition have available the photographs that Woolf included in her text. Their absence from all reprints in the United States since that first edition has sometimes hampered commentators on this text. In a salient example, Jane Marcus pointed out that Susan Sontag's apparent lack of awareness of the photographs in an excerpt from her 2003 book *Regarding the Pain of Others* resulted in a distorted impression of Woolf's politics (Marcus, "In the Mail"). It is likely that new editions of Woolf's works will continue to proliferate as her copyrights lapse. Learning to distinguish among those that are the result of publishers' opportunism and those that usefully provide new and reliable texts and apparatus will be necessary in the coming decades.

Sontag's prominent use of Woolf in her meditation on the visual representation of suffering is an example of a broader concern with ethics that the most recent of the essays in this collection also display. Now is a time of "crisis" in the humanities, when even professors of English feel the need to ask "Why Teach Literature Anyway?" Yet, Woolf's presence as a public intellectual is gradually beginning to gain wider acceptance. Jessica Berman, in her chapter included in this volume, announces the urgency of a project that will interest more scholars working in modernism as Woolf becomes less an isolated feminist icon or narrative innovator and more a central philosophical presence in discussions of ethics and aesthetics: "The renewed potential for bringing together ethics and epistemology for the problem of aesthetics is crucial for the study of Woolf because so much of her writing takes up the question of ethical reality" (265).

Work remains to be done on Woolf as philosopher, particularly in the wake of Ann Banfield's *Phantom Table* (Cambridge UP, 2000); it will be fruitful to bring Woolf's work into the field animated by study of such contemporary thinkers as Giorgio Agamben and, as Berman has, Emmanuel Levinas. The large questions of race and racism have yet to find their adequate treatment: what was Woolf's engagement with the African presence in London in the 1920s and

1930s, for example? What are the meaningful relations between her private references to Jews and those that she published? More work will be done to illuminate the modernist incorporation of popular and mass culture, and Woolf will figure prominently in these studies. Scholarship on little magazines continues to evolve rapidly and will provide new insights into Woolf as an essayist engaged with her contemporaries. And in the pipeline is absorbing new work on Woolf as publisher and editor at the Hogarth Press. Woolf studies is located in numerous sites: in major journals such as *MFS*, in glancing remarks in the mainstream media, in the chatter of listservs, discussions in classrooms, and long conversations in conference center corridors; it is in new monographs and in editions of her works, and it is, above all, in the energies of scholars who bring their newest hypotheses and insights to bear on her writing.

Works Cited

Bradshaw, David, ed. Virginia Woolf. *Carlyle's House and Other Sketches*. London: Hesperus, 2003.

Daugherty, Beth, ed. "Letters from Readers to Virginia Woolf." *Woolf Studies Annual* 12 (2006): 25–212.

Groden, Michael. "Contemporary Textual and Literary Theory." In *Representing Modernist Texts: Editing as Interpretation*. Ed. George Bornstein. Ann Arbor: U of Michigan P, 1991. 259–86.

Leaska, Mitchell A. *Pointz Hall: The Earlier and Later Typescripts of Virginia Woolf's* Between the Acts. New York: University Publications, 1983.

Mao, Douglas, and Rebecca L. Walkowitz, eds. *Bad Modernisms.* Durham: Duke UP, 2006.

Marcus, Jane. "In the Mail: What Woolf Saw." *The New Yorker*, 13 June 2003. 7.

Shillingsburg, Peter. *From Gutenberg to Google: Electronic Representations of Literary Texts*. Cambridge: Cambridge UP, 2006.

Snaith, Anna, ed. *Palgrave Advances in Virginia Woolf Studies*. New York: Palgrave Macmillan, 2007.

———, ed., *"Three Guineas* Letters." *Woolf Studies Annual* 6 (2000): 17–168.

Sontag, Susan. *Regarding the Pain of Others.* New York: Farrar, Straus, and Giroux, 2003.

"Why Teach Literature Anyway?" Program arranged by the Division on the Teaching of Literature. Modern Language Association, Chicago, 28 Dec. 2007.

Woolf, Virginia. *Three Guineas*. Annotated and with an introduction by Jane Marcus. Orlando: Harcourt, 2006.

FICTION ANALYZED IN PARTICULAR CHAPTERS

Work discussed	Chapter author(s)
The Voyage Out	**Friedman**
Night and Day	**Cumings**
Jacob's Room	**Bishop**, **Clewell**
Mrs. Dalloway	**DeMeester**, **Hoffman**, **Scott**
To the Lighthouse	**Clewell**, **Emery**, **Seshagiri**, Berman, DeMeester
Orlando	**Berman**, **Lawrence**
The Waves	**Boone**, **Doyle**, **Gorsky**, **McGee**, Scott
The Years	**Linett**
Between the Acts	**Summerhayes**, **Zorn**, Scott
"Moments of Being"	**Hafley**

Note: Boldface indicates detailed discussion of work.

Woolf Essays in *Modern Fiction Studies* by Date

Church, Margaret. "Concepts of Time in Novels of Virginia Woolf and Aldous Huxley." *Modern Fiction Studies* 1.2 (1955): 19–24.

Beebe, Maurice. "Criticism of Virginia Woolf: A Selected Checklist with an Index to Studies of Separate Works." *Modern Fiction Studies* 2 (1956): 36–45.

Baldanza, Frank. "Virginia Woolf's 'Moments of Being.'" *Modern Fiction Studies* 2 (1956): 78.

———. "Clarissa Dalloway's 'Party Consciousness.'" *Modern Fiction Studies* 2 (1956): 24–30.

Doner, Dean. "Virginia Woolf: The Service of Style." *Modern Fiction Studies* 2 (1956): 1–12.

Hafley, James. "On One of Virginia Woolf's Short Stories." *Modern Fiction Studies* 2 (1956): 13–16.*

Hunting, Constance. "The Technique of Persuasion in Orlando." *Modern Fiction Studies* 2 (1956): 17–23.

Zorn, Marilyn. "The Pageant in *Between the Acts.*" *Modern Fiction Studies* 2 (1956): 31–35.*

Hungerford, Edward A. "'My Tunneling Process': The Method of Mrs. Dalloway." *Modern Fiction Studies* 3 (1957): 164–67.

Leyburn, Ellen Douglass. "Virginia Woolf's Judgment of Henry James." *Modern Fiction Studies* 5 (1959): 166–69.

Page, Alex. "A Dangerous Day: Mrs. Dalloway Discovers Her Double." *Modern Fiction Studies* 7 (1961): 115–24.

Cohn, Ruby. "Art in *To the Lighthouse.*" *Modern Fiction Studies* 8 (1962): 127–36.

Kreutz, Irving. "Mr. Bennett and Mrs. Woolf." *Modern Fiction Studies* 8 (1962): 103–15.

Summerhayes, Don. "Society, Morality, Analogy: Virginia Woolf's World *Between the Acts.*" *Modern Fiction Studies* 9.4 (Winter 1963–64): 329–37.*

Rosenberg, Stuart. "The Match in the Crocus: Obtrusive Art in Virginia Woolf's *Mrs. Dalloway.*" *Modern Fiction Studies* 13 (1967): 211–20.

Hoffmann, Charles G. "From Short Story to Novel: The Manuscript Revisions of Virginia Woolf's *Mrs. Dalloway.*" *Modern Fiction Studies* 14 (1968): 171–86.*

Payne, Michael. "The Eclipse of Order: The Ironic Structure of *The Waves.*" *Modern Fiction Studies* 15 (1969): 209–18.

Asterisks indicate essays in this volume.

Webb, Igor M. "'Things in Themselves': Virginia Woolf's *The Waves.*" *Modern Fiction Studies* 17 (1971): 570–73.

Ames, Kenneth J. "Elements of Mock-Heroic in Virginia Woolf's *Mrs. Dalloway.*" *Modern Fiction Studies* 18 (1972): 363–74.

Beker, Miroslav. "London as a Principle of Structure in *Mrs. Dalloway.*" *Modern Fiction Studies* 18 (1972): 375–85.

Chapman, R. T. "'The Lady in the Looking Glass': Modes of Perception in a Short Story by Virginia Woolf." *Modern Fiction Studies* 18 (1972): 331–37.

Cumings, Melinda Feldt. "*Night and Day*: Virginia Woolf's Visionary Synthesis of Reality." *Modern Fiction Studies* 18 (1972): 339–49.*

Fox, Stephen D. "The Fish Pond as Symbolic Center in *Between the Acts.*" *Modern Fiction Studies* 18 (1972): 467–73.

Gorsky, Susan Rubinow. "'The Central Shadow': Characterization in *The Waves.*" *Modern Fiction Studies* 18 (1972): 449–66.*

Latham, Jacqueline E. M. "The Manuscript Revisions of Virginia Woolf's *Mrs. Dalloway:* A Postscript." *Modern Fiction Studies* 18 (1972): 475–76.

Morgenstern, Barry S. "The Self-Conscious Narrator in *Jacob's Room.*" *Modern Fiction Studies* 18 (1972): 351–61.

Pratt, Annis. "Sexual Imagery in *To the Lighthouse:* A New Feminist Approach." *Modern Fiction Studies* 18 (1972): 417–31.

Samuels, Marilyn S. "The Symbolic Functions of the Sun in *Mrs. Dalloway.*" *Modern Fiction Studies* 18 (1972): 387–99.

Stewart, Jack F. "Existence and Symbol in *The Waves.*" *Modern Fiction Studies* 18 (1972): 433–47.

Weiser, Barbara. "Criticism of Virginia Woolf from 1956 to the Present: A Selected Checklist with an Index to Studies of Separate Works." *Modern Fiction Studies* 18 (1972): 477–86.

Whitehead, Lee M. "The Shawl and the Skull: Virginia Woolf's 'Magic Mountain.'" *Modern Fiction Studies* 18 (1972): 401–15.

Schaefer, Josephine O'Brien. "Sterne's *A Sentimental Journey* and Woolf's *Jacob's Room.*" *Modern Fiction Studies* 23 (1977): 189–97.

McLaughlin, Ann L. "The Same Job: The Shared Writing Aims of Katherine Mansfield and Virginia Woolf." *Modern Fiction Studies* 24 (1978): 369–82.

Pomeroy, Elizabeth W. "Garden and Wilderness: Virginia Woolf Reads the Elizabethans." *Modern Fiction Studies* 24 (1978): 497–508.

Snider, Clifton. "'A Single Self': A Jungian Interpretation of Virginia Woolf's *Orlando.*" *Modern Fiction Studies* 25 (1979): 263–68.

Boone, Joseph Allen. "The Meaning of Elvedon in *The Waves*: A Key to Bernard's Experience and Woolf's Vision." *Modern Fiction Studies* 27.4 (1981): 629–37.*

Richter, Harvena. "The Canonical Hours in *Mrs. Dalloway.*" *Modern Fiction Studies* 28.2 (1982): 236–40.

Pellan, Françoise. "Virginia Woolf's Posthumous Poem." *Modern Fiction Studies* 29.4 (1983): 695–700.

Banks, Joanne Trautmann. "Some New Woolf Letters." *Modern Fiction Studies* 30.2 (1984): 175–202.

Beattie, Thomas C. "Moments of Meaning Dearly Achieved: Virginia Woolf's Sense of an Ending." *Modern Fiction Studies* 32.4 (1986): 521–41.

Scott, Bonnie Kime. "The Word Split Its Husk: Woolf's Double Vision of Modernist Language." *Modern Fiction Studies* 34.3 (1988): 371–85.*

Abbott, Reginald. "What Miss Kilman's Petticoat Means: Virginia Woolf, Shopping, and Spectacle." *Modern Fiction Studies* 38.1 (1992): 193–216.

Bishop, Edward L. "The Subject in *Jacob's Room.*" *Modern Fiction Studies* 38.1 (1992): 147–75.*

Childers, Mary M. "Virginia Woolf on the Outside Looking Down: Reflections on the Class of Women." *Modern Fiction Studies* 38.1 (1992): 61–79.

Emery, Mary Lou. "'Robbed of Meaning': The Work at the Center of *To the Lighthouse.*" *Modern Fiction Studies* 38.1 (1992): 217–34.*

Friedman, Susan Stanford. "Virginia Woolf's Pedagogical Scenes of Reading: *The Voyage Out, The Common Reader,* and Her 'Common Readers.'" *Modern Fiction Studies* 38.1 (1992): 101–25.*

Hussey, Mark. "Refractions of Desire: The Early Fiction of Virginia and Leonard Woolf." *Modern Fiction Studies* 38.1 (1992): 127–46.

Jones, Ellen Carol. "Virginia Woolf." *Modern Fiction Studies* 38.1 (1992): 1–14.

Kirkpatrick, B. J. "Virginia Woolf: Unrecorded *Times Literary Supplement* Reviews." *Modern Fiction Studies* 38.1 (1992): 279–301.

Lawrence, Karen R. "Orlando's Voyage Out." *Modern Fiction Studies* 38.1 (1992): 253–77.*

Lokke, Kari Elise. "*Orlando* and Incandescence: Virginia Woolf's Comic Sublime." *Modern Fiction Studies* 38.1 (1992): 235–52.

McGee, Patrick. "The Politics of Modernist Form; or, Who Rules *The Waves.*" *Modern Fiction Studies* 38.3 (1992): 631–50.*

Moran, Patricia. "Virginia Woolf and the Scene of Writing." *Modern Fiction Studies* 38.1 (1992): 81–100.

Silver, Brenda R. "What's Woolf Got to Do with It? Or, The Perils of Popularity." *Modern Fiction Studies* 38.1 (1992): 21–60.*

Wang, Ban. "'I' on the Run: Crisis of Identity in *Mrs. Dalloway.*" *Modern Fiction Studies* 38.1 (1992): 177–91.

Christian, Barbara. "Layered Rhythms: Virginia Woolf and Toni Morrison." *Modern Fiction Studies* 39.3–4 (1993): 483–500.

Webb, Caroline. "Life after Death: The Allegorical Progress of *Mrs. Dalloway.*" *Modern Fiction Studies* 40.2 (1994): 279–98.

Doyle, Laura. "Sublime Barbarians in the Narrative of Empire; or, Longinus at Sea in *The Waves.*" *Modern Fiction Studies* 42.2 (1996): 323–47.*

Burns, Christy L. "Powerful Differences: Critique and Eros in Jeanette Winterson and Virginia Woolf." *Modern Fiction Studies* 44.2 (1998): 364–92.

DeMeester, Karen. "Trauma and Recovery in Virginia Woolf's *Mrs. Dalloway.*" *Modern Fiction Studies* 44.3 (1998): 649–73.*

Marshik, Celia. "Publication and 'Public Women': Prostitution and Censorship in Three Novels by Virginia Woolf." *Modern Fiction Studies* 45.4 (1999): 853–86.

Todd, Richard. "Realism Disavowed? Discourses of Memory and High Incarnations in Jackson's Dilemma." *Modern Fiction Studies* 47.3 (2001): 674–95.

Linett, Maren. "The Jew in the Bath: Imperiled Imagination in Woolf's *The Years.*" *Modern Fiction Studies* 48.2 (2002): 341–61.*

Snaith, Anna. "Of Fanciers, Footnotes, and Fascism: Virginia Woolf's *Flush.*" *Modern Fiction Studies* 48.3 (2002): 614–36.

Berman, Jessica. "Ethical Folds: Ethics, Aesthetics, Woolf." *Modern Fiction Studies* 50.1 (2004): 151–72.*

Clewell, Tammy. "Consolation Refused: Virginia Woolf, the Great War, and Modernist Mourning." *Modern Fiction Studies* 50.1 (2004): 197–223.*

Cohen, Scott. "The Empire from the Street: Virginia Woolf, Wembley, and Imperial Monuments." *Modern Fiction Studies* 50.1 (2004): 85–109.

Dalgarno, Emily. "A British *War and Peace*? Virginia Woolf Reads Tolstoy." *Modern Fiction Studies* 50.1 (2004): 129–50.

Doyle, Laura. "Virginia Woolf." *Modern Fiction Studies* 50.1 (2004): 1–7.

Dymond, Justine. "Virginia Woolf Scholarship from 1991 to 2003: A Selected Bibliography." *Modern Fiction Studies* 50.1 (2004): 241–79.

Hussey, Mark. "Mrs. Thatcher and Mrs. Woolf." *Modern Fiction Studies* 50.1 (2004): 8–30.

Johnson, Erica L. "Giving up the Ghost: National and Literary Haunting in *Orlando.*" *Modern Fiction Studies* 50.1 (2004): 110–28.

Levy, Heather. "'These Ghost Figures of Distorted Passion': Becoming Privy to Working-Class Desire in 'The Watering Place' and 'The Ladies Lavatory.'" *Modern Fiction Studies* 50.1 (2004): 31–57.

Monson, Tamlyn. "'A Trick of the Mind': Alterity, Ontology, and Representation in Virginia Woolf's *The Waves.*" *Modern Fiction Studies* 50.1 (2004): 173–96.

Seshagiri, Urmila. "Orienting Virginia Woolf: Race, Aesthetics, and Politics in *To the Lighthouse.*" *Modern Fiction Studies* 50.1 (2004): 58–84.*

Wolfe, Jesse. "The Sane Woman in the Attic: Sexuality and Self-Authorship in *Mrs. Dalloway.*" *Modern Fiction Studies* 51.1 (2005): 34–59.

Lilienfeld, Jane. "'To Have the Reader Work with the Author': The Circulation of Knowledge in Virginia Woolf's *To the Lighthouse* and Toni Morrison's *Jazz.*" *Modern Fiction Studies* 52.1 (2006): 42–65.

Pawlowski, Merry. "Virginia Woolf's Veil: The Feminist Intellectual and the Organization of Public Space." *Modern Fiction Studies* 53.4 (2007): 723–54.

Crangle, Sara. "The Time Being: On Woolf and Boredom." *Modern Fiction Studies* 54.2 (2008): 209–32.

Woolf Essays in *Modern Fiction Studies* by Author's Name

Abbott, Reginald. "What Miss Kilman's Petticoat Means: Virginia Woolf, Shopping, and Spectacle." *Modern Fiction Studies* 38.1 (1992): 193–216.

Ames, Kenneth J. "Elements of Mock-Heroic in Virginia Woolf's *Mrs. Dalloway*." *Modern Fiction Studies* 18 (1972): 363–74.

Baldanza, Frank. "Virginia Woolf's 'Moments of Being.'" *Modern Fiction Studies* 2 (1956): 78.

———. "Clarissa Dalloway's 'Party Consciousness.'" *Modern Fiction Studies* 2 (1956): 24–30.

Banks, Joanne Trautmann. "Some New Woolf Letters." *Modern Fiction Studies* 30.2 (1984): 175–202.

Beattie, Thomas C. "Moments of Meaning Dearly Achieved: Virginia Woolf's Sense of an Ending." *Modern Fiction Studies* 32.4 (1986): 521–41.

Beebe, Maurice. "Criticism of Virginia Woolf: A Selected Checklist with an Index to Studies of Separate Works." *Modern Fiction Studies* 2 (1956): 36–45.

Beker, Miroslav. "London as a Principle of Structure in *Mrs. Dalloway*." *Modern Fiction Studies* 18 (1972): 375–85.

Berman, Jessica. "Ethical Folds: Ethics, Aesthetics, Woolf." *Modern Fiction Studies* 50.1 (2004): 151–72.*

Bishop, Edward L. "The Subject in *Jacob's Room*." *Modern Fiction Studies* 38.1 (1992): 147–75.*

Boone, Joseph Allen. "The Meaning of Elvedon in *The Waves*: A Key to Bernard's Experience and Woolf's Vision." *Modern Fiction Studies* 27.4 (1981): 629–37.*

Burns, Christy L. "Powerful Differences: Critique and Eros in Jeanette Winterson and Virginia Woolf." *Modern Fiction Studies* 44.2 (1998): 364–92.

Chapman, R. T. "'The Lady in the Looking Glass': Modes of Perception in a Short Story by Virginia Woolf." *Modern Fiction Studies* 18 (1972): 331–37.

Childers, Mary M. "Virginia Woolf on the Outside Looking Down: Reflections on the Class of Women." *Modern Fiction Studies* 38.1 (1992): 61–79.

Christian, Barbara. "Layered Rhythms: Virginia Woolf and Toni Morrison." *Modern Fiction Studies* 39.3–4 (1993): 483–500.

Church, Margaret. "Concepts of Time in Novels of Virginia Woolf and Aldous Huxley." *Modern Fiction Studies* 1.2 (1955): 19–24.

Clewell, Tammy. "Consolation Refused: Virginia Woolf, the Great War, and Modernist Mourning." *Modern Fiction Studies* 50.1 (2004): 197–223.*

Cohen, Scott. "The Empire from the Street: Virginia Woolf, Wembley, and Imperial Monuments." *Modern Fiction Studies* 50.1 (2004): 85–109.

Cohn, Ruby. "Art in *To the Lighthouse*." *Modern Fiction Studies* 8 (1962): 127–36.

Crangle, Sara. "The Time Being: On Woolf and Boredom." *Modern Fiction Studies* 54.2 (2008): 209–32.

Cumings, Melinda Feldt. "*Night and Day:* Virginia Woolf's Visionary Synthesis of Reality." *Modern Fiction Studies* 18 (1972): 339–49.*

Dalgarno, Emily. "A British *War and Peace*? Virginia Woolf Reads Tolstoy." *Modern Fiction Studies* 50.1 (2004): 129–50.

DeMeester, Karen. "Trauma and Recovery in Virginia Woolf's *Mrs. Dalloway.*" *Modern Fiction Studies* 44.3 (1998): 649–73.*

Doner, Dean. "Virginia Woolf: The Service of Style." *Modern Fiction Studies* 2 (1956): 1–12.

Doyle, Laura. "Sublime Barbarians in the Narrative of Empire; or, Longinus at Sea in *The Waves.*" *Modern Fiction Studies* 42.2 (1996): 323–47.*

———. "Virginia Woolf." *Modern Fiction Studies* 50.1 (2004): 1–7.

Dymond, Justine. "Virginia Woolf Scholarship from 1991 to 2003: A Selected Bibliography." *Modern Fiction Studies* 50.1 (2004): 241–79.

Emery, Mary Lou. "'Robbed of Meaning': The Work at the Center of *To the Lighthouse.*" *Modern Fiction Studies* 38.1 (1992): 217–34.*

Fox, Stephen D. "The Fish Pond as Symbolic Center in *Between the Acts.*" *Modern Fiction Studies* 18 (1972): 467–73.

Friedman, Susan Stanford. "Virginia Woolf's Pedagogical Scenes of Reading: *The Voyage Out*, *The Common Reader*, and Her 'Common Readers.'" *Modern Fiction Studies* 38.1 (1992): 101–25.*

Gorsky, Susan. "'The Central Shadow': Characterization in *The Waves.*" *Modern Fiction Studies* 18 (1972): 449–66.*

Hafley, James. "On One of Virginia Woolf's Short Stories." *Modern Fiction Studies* 2 (1956): 13–16.*

Hoffmann, Charles G. "From Short Story to Novel: The Manuscript Revisions of Virginia Woolf's *Mrs. Dalloway.*" *Modern Fiction Studies* 14 (1968): 171–86.*

Hungerford, Edward A. "'My Tunneling Process': The Method of *Mrs. Dalloway.*" *Modern Fiction Studies* 3 (1957): 164–67.

Hunting, Constance. "The Technique of Persuasion in *Orlando.*" *Modern Fiction Studies* 2 (1956): 17–23.

Hussey, Mark. "Refractions of Desire: The Early Fiction of Virginia and Leonard Woolf." *Modern Fiction Studies* 38.1 (1992): 127–46.

———. "Mrs. Thatcher and Mrs. Woolf." *Modern Fiction Studies* 50.1 (2004): 8–30.

Johnson, Erica L. "Giving up the Ghost: National and Literary Haunting in *Orlando.*" *Modern Fiction Studies* 50.1 (2004): 110–28.

Jones, Ellen Carol. "Virginia Woolf." *Modern Fiction Studies* 38.1 (1992): 1–14.

Kirkpatrick, B. J. "Virginia Woolf: Unrecorded *Times Literary Supplement* Reviews." *Modern Fiction Studies* 38.1 (1992): 279–301.

Kreutz, Irving. "Mr. Bennett and Mrs. Woolf." *Modern Fiction Studies* 8 (1962): 103–15.

Latham, Jacqueline E. M. "The Manuscript Revisions of Virginia Woolf's *Mrs. Dalloway*: A Postscript." *Modern Fiction Studies* 18 (1972): 475–76.

Lawrence, Karen R. "Orlando's Voyage Out." *Modern Fiction Studies* 38.1 (1992): 253–77.*

Levy, Heather. "'These Ghost Figures of Distorted Passion': Becoming Privy to Working-Class Desire in 'The Watering Place' and 'The Ladies Lavatory.'" *Modern Fiction Studies* 50.1 (2004): 31–57.

Leyburn, Ellen Douglass. "Virginia Woolf's Judgment of Henry James." *Modern Fiction Studies* 5 (1959): 166–69.

Lilienfeld, Jane. "'To Have the Reader Work with the Author': The Circulation of Knowledge in Virginia Woolf's *To the Lighthouse* and Toni Morrison's *Jazz*." *Modern Fiction Studies* 52.1 (2006): 42–65.

Linett, Maren. "The Jew in the Bath: Imperiled Imagination in Woolf's *The Years*." *Modern Fiction Studies* 48.2 (2002): 341–61.*

Lokke, Kari Elise. "*Orlando* and Incandescence: Virginia Woolf's Comic Sublime." *Modern Fiction Studies* 38.1 (1992): 235–52.

Marshik, Celia. "Publication and 'Public Women': Prostitution and Censorship in Three Novels by Virginia Woolf." *Modern Fiction Studies* 45.4 (1999): 853–86.

McGee, Patrick. "The Politics of Modernist Form; or, Who Rules *The Waves*." *Modern Fiction Studies* 38.3 (1992): 631–50.*

McLaughlin, Ann L. "The Same Job: The Shared Writing Aims of Katherine Mansfield and Virginia Woolf." *Modern Fiction Studies* 24 (1978): 369–82.

Monson, Tamlyn. "'A Trick of the Mind': Alterity, Ontology, and Representation in Virginia Woolf's *The Waves*." *Modern Fiction Studies* 50.1 (2004): 173–96.

Moran, Patricia. "Virginia Woolf and the Scene of Writing." *Modern Fiction Studies* 38.1 (1992): 81–100.

Morgenstern, Barry S. "The Self-Conscious Narrator in *Jacob's Room*." *Modern Fiction Studies* 18 (1972): 351–61.

Page, Alex. "A Dangerous Day: *Mrs. Dalloway* Discovers Her Double." *Modern Fiction Studies* 7 (1961): 115–24.

Pawlowski, Merry. "Virginia Woolf's Veil: The Feminist Intellectual and the Organization of Public Space." *Modern Fiction Studies* 53.4 (2007): 723–54.

Payne, Michael. "The Eclipse of Order: The Ironic Structure of *The Waves*." *Modern Fiction Studies* 15 (1969): 209–18.

Pellan, Françoise. "Virginia Woolf's Posthumous Poem." *Modern Fiction Studies* 29.4 (1983): 695–700.

Pomeroy, Elizabeth W. "Garden and Wilderness: Virginia Woolf Reads the Elizabethans." *Modern Fiction Studies* 24 (1978): 497–508.

Pratt, Annis. "Sexual Imagery in *To the Lighthouse*: A New Feminist Approach." *Modern Fiction Studies* 18 (1972): 417–31.

Richter, Harvena. "The Canonical Hours in *Mrs. Dalloway*." *Modern Fiction Studies* 28.2 (1982): 236–40.

Rosenberg, Stuart. "The Match in the Crocus: Obtrusive Art in Virginia Woolf's *Mrs. Dalloway*." *Modern Fiction Studies* 13 (1967): 211–20.

Samuels, Marilyn S. "The Symbolic Functions of the Sun in *Mrs. Dalloway*." *Modern Fiction Studies* 18 (1972): 387–99.

Schaefer, Josephine O'Brien. "Sterne's *A Sentimental Journey* and Woolf's *Jacob's Room*." *Modern Fiction Studies* 23 (1977): 189–97.

Scott, Bonnie Kime. "The Word Split Its Husk: Woolf's Double Vision of Modernist Language." *Modern Fiction Studies* 34.3 (1988): 371–85.*

Seshagiri, Urmila. "Orienting Virginia Woolf: Race, Aesthetics, and Politics in *To the Lighthouse*." *Modern Fiction Studies* 50.1 (2004): 58–84.*

Silver, Brenda R. "What's Woolf Got to Do with It? Or, The Perils of Popularity." *Modern Fiction Studies* 38.1 (1992): 21–60.*

Snaith, Anna. "Of Fanciers, Footnotes, and Fascism: Virginia Woolf's *Flush*." *Modern Fiction Studies* 48.3 (2002): 614–36.

Snider, Clifton. "'A Single Self': A Jungian Interpretation of Virginia Woolf's *Orlando*." *Modern Fiction Studies* 25 (1979): 263–68.

Stewart, Jack F. "Existence and Symbol in *The Waves*." *Modern Fiction Studies* 18 (1972): 433–47.

Summerhayes, Don. "Society, Morality, Analogy: Virginia Woolf's World *Between the Acts*." *Modern Fiction Studies* 9.4 (Winter 1963–64): 329–37.*

Todd, Richard. "Realism Disavowed? Discourses of Memory and High Incarnations in Jackson's Dilemma." *Modern Fiction Studies* 47.3 (2001): 674–95.

Wang, Ban. "'I' on the Run: Crisis of Identity in *Mrs. Dalloway*." *Modern Fiction Studies* 38.1 (1992): 177–91.

Webb, Caroline. "Life after Death: The Allegorical Progress of *Mrs. Dalloway*." *Modern Fiction Studies* 40.2 (1994): 279–98.

Webb, Igor M. "'Things in Themselves': Virginia Woolf's *The Waves*." *Modern Fiction Studies* 17 (1971): 570–73.

Weiser, Barbara. "Criticism of Virginia Woolf from 1956 to the Present: A Selected Checklist with an Index to Studies of Separate Works." *Modern Fiction Studies* 18 (1972): 477–86.

Whitehead, Lee M. "The Shawl and the Skull: Virginia Woolf's 'Magic Mountain.'" *Modern Fiction Studies* 18 (1972): 401–15.

Wolfe, Jesse. "The Sane Woman in the Attic: Sexuality and Self-Authorship in *Mrs. Dalloway*." *Modern Fiction Studies* 51:1 (2005): 34–59.

Zorn, Marilyn. "The Pageant in *Between the Acts*." *Modern Fiction Studies* 2 (1956): 31–35.*

JESSICA BERMAN is an associate professor and chair of the English Department at the University of Maryland, Baltimore County, where she teaches courses primarily on twentieth-century fiction and theory. She also holds an affiliate appointment in Gender and Women's Studies. She is the author of *Modernist Fiction, Cosmopolitanism and the Politics of Community* (Cambridge UP, 2001, 2006) and was the coeditor with Jane Goldman of *Virginia Woolf Out of Bounds* (Pace UP, 2001), papers from the tenth annual conference on Virginia Woolf, which she organized. This essay forms part of her book in progress on the connection between ethics and politics in transnational modernism.

EDWARD L. BISHOP is a professor in the Department of English and Film Studies, University of Alberta. He has produced the Shakespeare Head critical edition of *Jacob's Room* (2004), *Virginia Woolf's* Jacob's Room: *The Holograph Draft* (Pace UP, 1998), *The Bloomsbury Group* (Dictionary of Literary Biography, Gale, 1992), *Virginia Woolf* (Macmillan, 1991), and *A Virginia Woolf Chronology* (Macmillan, 1989). As Ted Bishop he published *Riding with Rilke: Reflections on Motorcycles and Books* (Norton, 2006), named a Best Book in Canada by the *Toronto Globe and Mail*.

JOSEPH ALLEN BOONE is a professor of English at the University of Southern California. The recipient of Guggenheim, Rockefeller, ACLS, Huntington, and other fellowships, he is the author of *Tradition Counter Tradition: Love and the Form of Fiction* (Chicago, 1998) and *Libidinal Currents: Sexuality and the Shaping of Modernism* (Chicago, 2008), and the coeditor of *Engendering Men: The Question of Male Feminist Criticism* (Routledge, 1990) and *Queer Frontiers: Millennial Geographies, Genders, and Generations* (Wisconsin, 2000). He originally composed "Searching for Elvedon" as a seminar paper his first year in graduate school at the University of Wisconsin–Madison.

TAMMY CLEWELL is an associate professor of English at Kent State University. Her work has appeared in *Modern Fiction Studies*, *College Literature*, *Journal of the American Psychoanalytic Association*, and *Literature/Film Quarterly*. Her book, *Mourning, Modernism, Postmodernism*, is forthcoming from Palgrave in 2009.

MELINDA FELDT CUMINGS wrote her dissertation on Virginia Woolf at the University of Wisconsin–Madison, where she received her Ph.D. in 1973. Her eclectic career included teaching literature and composition, practicing psychotherapy, and making documentary films. She currently lives in Truth or Consequences, New Mexico.

KAREN DEMEESTER is a project manager and associate in research at the Learning Systems Institute of Florida State University. She conducts research and manages initiatives to improve teachers' use of technology to enhance student learning, to improve education in rural communities, and to explore the use of storytelling as an instructional approach. She revised the article in this collection for inclusion in *Virginia Woolf and Trauma: Embodied Texts* (Pace UP, 2007) and has a chapter entitled "Enhancing Soldiers' Resiliency to Combat Stress Injuries through Stories" in the forthcoming book *Storytelling and Instruction* (Rotterdam: Sense Publications, 2009).

LAURA DOYLE is a professor of English at the University of Massachusetts–Amherst. She is author of *Bordering on the Body: The Racial Matrix of Modern Fiction and Culture* (Oxford, 1994) and *Freedom's Empire: Race and the Rise of the Novel in Atlantic Modernity, 1640–1940* (Duke, 2008), and editor of two essay collections, *Bodies of Resistance: New Phenomenologies of Politics, Agency, and Culture* (Northwestern UP, 2001) and, with Laura Winkiel, *Geomodernisms: Race, Modernism, Modernity* (Indiana UP, 2004). Her current project is a study of the transcultural dynamics and anticolonial histories that have given rise to diverse modernisms in world literature.

MARY LOU EMERY is a professor of English at the University of Iowa. Her most recent book is *Modernism, the Visual, and Caribbean Literature*, published with Cambridge University Press (2007). Her work on intersections of British modernist, Caribbean, and postcolonial literatures began with a book on the Dominican-born writer, Jean Rhys, titled *Jean Rhys at "World's End": Novels of Colonial and Sexual Exile* (U of Texas P, 1990), and extends to current projects that include an essay on "Caribbean Modernism: Plantation to Planetary" and a longer study titled "Global Homes and the Arts of Modernism."

SUSAN STANFORD FRIEDMAN is the director of the Institute for Research in the Humanities and the Virginia Woolf Professor of English and Women's Studies at the University of Wisconsin–Madison. She is coeditor of the new Oxford University Press journal *Contemporary Women's Writing*. She is the author of *Psyche Reborn: The Emergence of H.D.* (Indiana UP, 1987), *Penelope's Web: Gender, Modernity, H.D.'s Fiction* (Cambridge UP, 1991), and *Mappings: Feminism and the Cultural Geographies of Encounter* (Princeton UP, 1998). She also edited *Analyzing Freud: Letters of H.D., Bryher, and Their Circle* (New Directions, 2002), *Joyce: The Return of the Repressed* (Cornell, 1993), and *Signets—Reading H.D.* (Wisconsin, 1991). She is currently working on books on modernism and on migration.

SUSAN RUBINOW GORSKY is currently on the faculties at the University of California, Santa Cruz, and at Cabrillo College. She formerly taught at Cleveland State University in Ohio and at the Punahou School in Honolulu, Hawaii. She is the author of *Virginia Woolf* (Twayne, 1978/1989), *An Introduction to Medical Hypnosis*, with Benjamin Gorsky (Medical Examination Publishing Company, 1981), and *Femininity to Feminism: Women and Literature in the Nineteenth Century* (Macmillan, 1992). Her articles have appeared in such journals as *Modern Drama*, *The Journal of Popular Culture*, *Modernist Studies*, *The Virginia Woolf Miscellany*, *The Journal of Women's Studies in Literature*, *Literature and Medicine,* and of course *MFS*.

JAMES HAFLEY was a professor at the Catholic University of America and then at St. John's University, where he taught until his death in 2004. During his long and productive career, he published articles on Virginia Woolf, Ford Madox Ford, D. H. Lawrence, William Faulkner, Stephen Crane, William Carlos Williams, Gerard Manley Hopkins, and others. He also published a book entitled *The Glass Roof: Virginia Woolf as Novelist* (University of California Press, 1954).

CHARLES G. HOFFMANN published numerous essays on an array of modernist authors in journals such as *PMLA, Texas Studies in Literature and Language, English Literature in Transition*, and *College English*. He was the author of books on Henry James (Bookman, 1957), Joyce Cary (University of Pittsburgh Press, 1964) and Ford Madox Ford (Twayne, 1967/1990). Professor Hoffmann taught at the University of Rhode Island from 1952 until his retirement in 1977.

MARK HUSSEY is founding editor of *Woolf Studies Annual* and author of *Virginia Woolf A to Z* and *The Singing of the Real World: The Philosophy of Virginia Woolf's Fiction*. He edited *Virginia Woolf and War* and has published many articles on Woolf. He teaches at Pace University in New York.

KAREN R. LAWRENCE became the tenth president of Sarah Lawrence College in August 2007, after serving as Dean of the School of Humanities at the University of California, Irvine. In addition to numerous scholarly articles, Professor Lawrence has written or edited five books, including *Penelope Voyages: Women and Travel in the British Literary Tradition* (Cornell UP, 1994), which includes a longer version of the essay in this collection as well as a discussion of Woolf's first novel, *The Voyage Out.* Other books include *The Odyssey of Style in* Ulysses (Princeton UP, 1981), *Transcultural Joyce* (Cambridge UP, 1998), and *Decolonizing Tradition: New Views of Twentieth-Century "British" Literary Canons* (U of Illinois P, 1992). She has just completed *Techniques for Living: Fiction and Theory in the Work of Christine Brooke-Rose.*

MAREN LINETT is an associate professor of English at Purdue University. Her first book, *Modernism, Feminism, and Jewishness,* was published by Cambridge University Press in 2007. Her work has appeared in *Modern Fiction Studies, The Journal of Modern Literature, Twentieth-Century Literature,* and the *James Joyce Quarterly.* She has edited a special issue of *Modern Fiction Studies* entitled Modernism's Jews / Jewish Modernisms (2005), and she is editor of the forthcoming *Cambridge Companion to Modernist Women Writers.*

PATRICK MCGEE is the McElveen Professor of English at Louisiana State University, Baton Rouge. He is the author of seven books, including *Joyce beyond Marx: History and Desire in* Ulysses *and* Finnegans Wake (UP of Florida, 2001), *From* Shane *to* Kill Bill: *Rethinking the Western* (Performing Arts, 2006), and the forthcoming *Theory and the Common from Marx to Badiou.*

BONNIE KIME SCOTT is a professor and the chair of Women's Studies at San Diego State University and President of the International Virginia Woolf Society. Recent books include the critical anthology, *Gender in Modernism: New Geographies, Complex Intersections* (U of Illinois P, 2007), a sequel to *The Gender of Modernism* (1990). She is completing a book on *Virginia Woolf and Modernist Uses of Nature.*

URMILA SESHAGIRI is an assistant professor of English at the University of Tennessee, where she teaches modernism, postcolonial studies, and Asian American literature. She is the author of *Race and the Modernist Imagination: The Politics of Form, 1890–1930,* which will be published by Cornell University Press in 2009. Her work has appeared in *Modern Fiction Studies, Cultural Critique, Modernism/modernity, Woolf Studies Annual,* and *The Journal of Asian American Studies.*

BRENDA R. SILVER, Mary Brinsmead Wheelock Professor at Dartmouth College, is the author of *Virginia Woolf Icon* and *Virginia Woolf's Reading Notebooks.* She has also written articles on writers such as Charlotte Brontë, E. M. Forster, and John le Carré and topics such as anger, hypertext, and mailing list culture. Her current projects include articles on popular fiction in the digital age and Virginia Woolf's virtual afterlife.

DON SUMMERHAYES (1931–2007) was a much published and honored Canadian poet, teacher, memoirist and critic. Some of his major publications were *This Old Man Reclines on the Field of Heaven: Poems 1979–1999* (Exile Editions, 2000), *Watermelon* (Coach House Press, 1992), and a deconstructive memoir entitled *Mystory* (Exile Editions, 1997). His work has been internationally anthologized, and a posthumous volume of poetry is planned. He was a professor emeritus at York University in Toronto at the time of his death.

MARILYN ZORN has published articles in *Modern Fiction Studies*, *Studies in Short Fiction*, and the *Great Lakes Review*. She taught at Central Michigan University for more than twenty years, retired in 1989, and continues to reside in Mt. Pleasant, Michigan.

INDEX

Abel, Elizabeth, 56n13, 194n9, 328
Achebe, Chinua, 397–98
Adorno, Theodor, 188
Albee, Edward. See *Who's Afraid of Virginia Woolf*
Althusser, Louis, 137–44, 147, 155, 159, 167n27, 391
antisemitism, 400–414, 422
Ariès, Philippe, 175, 193n5
Auerbach, Eric, 177, 243
Austen, Jane, 6, 65–67, 69, 78, 178

Bakhtin, M. M., 66, 141, 280
Bal, Mieke, 266, 277n1
Ballet Russes, 307, 321n8, 333, 347–48n10
Banfield, Ann, 263, 265, 277n9, 421
Barker, Pat, 214, 216n9, 217n15
Barnes, Djuna, 350n25
Barthes, Roland, 331, 366–68
Bazin, Nancy Topping, 187
Beer, Gillian, 37n25, 192
Bell, Clive, 145–46, 262–64, 313–14
Bell, Quentin, 13–16, 30–33
Bell, Vanessa Stephen, 264–65, 304, 306–7, 315
Bell, Vikki, 259
Benjamin, Walter, 147–49, 155
Bennett, Alan, 16–17
Bennett, Arnold, 142
Bennett, Susan, 148
Benstock, Shari, 384–85
Berman, Jessica, 421
Between the Acts, 52–55, 238–45, 247–53
Bhabha, Homi, 296
Bloch, Ernst, 389
Bowen, Elizabeth, 30
Brecht, Bertolt, 145–51, 388–91
Briggs, Julia, 420
Brownstein, Rachel, 79
Burke, Edmund, 357, 364
Butler, Judith, 179

Cameron, Julia Margaret, 23–24
Cameron, Norman, 203
Cannadine, David, 174
Caramagno, Thomas, 172
Cardinal, Marie, 357–58
Carlyle's House and Other Sketches, 419
Carpenter, Edward, 285–88, 291–92, 295
Caughie, Pamela, 183
Chanter, Tina, 258, 272
Chatman, Seymour, 150–51, 157–79
Cheyette, Bryan, 416n16
Cixous, Hélène, 13, 46
"Common Reader, The," 74–80
Comstock, Margaret, 404–5
Conrad, Joseph, 67, 148, 286, 302, 337, 394–97
Constantinople, Woolf's reactions to, 300–302, 320n2
Cornell, Drucilla, 257

Daiches, David, 150, 162
Daugherty, Beth Rigel, 420
De Lauretis, Teresa, 12, 152–53
Deleuze, Giles, 266–67
Derrida, Jacques, 56n9, 181, 387
DeSalvo, Louise, 72–73, 82n15, 82n16, 161
Diaghilev, Sergei. See Ballet Russes
DiBattista, Maria, 46, 57n24
Docherty, Thomas, 142–44
Dreadnought Hoax, 305–6, 420
Duckworth, George, 161
Duckworth, Gerald, 161–62
DuPlessis, Rachel Blau, 56n11, 80n3, 81n4, 82, 282, 283

Eagleton, Terry, 164n10, 390–91
Eco, Umberto, 33, 152
Eliot, T. S., 43, 46, 83n21, 214, 218n17, 239, 400
Ellis, Havelock, 285–88, 291–92

Erikson, Erik, 204
Eysteinsson, Astradur, 388

Felman, Shoshana, 78, 80n2
feminism, 2–3, 14–16, 31–33; ethics,
    257–77; gendered metaphors,
    43–55; and the Other, 280–97,
    396–98; woman as "common
    reader," 75–76. *See also
    individuals and individual works*
Fetterley, Judith, 79
Fishelov, David, 163n3
Fisher, H. A. L., 152
Forster, E. M., 394
Foucault, Michel, 151, 165n20, 366
Frank, Joseph, 200
Frankl, Victor, 206–7, 217n10
Frears, Stephen. See *Sammy and
    Rosie Get Laid*
Freedman, Ralph, 236n8, 236n10
Freud, Sigmund, 175–77, 202,
    328–29, 339–40, 346n3
Freund, Gisèle, 24
Friedman, Norman, 55n1
Froula, Christine, 64
Fry, Roger, 262–65, 306–7, 308,
    314–17, 321n7
Fussell, B. H., 53
Fussell, Paul, 176

Gilbert, Sandra, 45, 55n2, 297n7
Goldman, Jane, 264–65, 421
Grant, Duncan, 315, 316, 321,
    322n17
Graves, Robert, 186, 190, 214
Greek language and literature, 64,
    77, 82n9, 157, 159–60, 178
Griffin, Susan, 46
Gubar, Susan, 45, 55n2, 297n7
Gurney, Ivor, 184
Guth, Deborah, 213, 218n16

Handley, William, 182
Harrison, Jane, 47
Hartman, Geoffrey, 343
Haule, James, 187
Head, Bessie, 397–98
Heath, Stephen, 25
Heilbrun, Carolyn, 46
Heine, Elizabeth, 72
Henke, Suzette, 202–3, 215nn2–3
Herman, Judith, 199, 201, 211,
    215n4, 216n8

Hobsbawm, Eric, 382
Hochman, Baruch, 163
Hogarth Press, 159–62, 308, 322n9,
    422
Holtby, Winifred, 171
homosexuality: debates over Woolf's
    sexuality, 30–31; reactions to
    Bloomsbury's, 7–8, 21–22;
    regarding Septimus (character in
    Mrs. Dalloway), 202–3, 215n2;
    Woolf's relationship with Vita
    Sackville-West and, 330–34. *See
    also* Butler, Judith; Carpenter,
    Edward; *Orlando*
"How It Strikes a Contemporary," 78
Hurd, Richard, 362–63
Hussey, Mark, 265
Huxley, Aldous, 406, 416n12
Huyssen, Andreas, 297n7, 382
Hynes, Samuel, 167n28

Irigaray, Luce, 63, 258–60, 272, 340,
    348n12, 350n25

J'Accuse, 3, 33–34
Jacob's Room, 137–62; character in,
    137–44; mourning in, 173–83
Jacobus, Mary, 55n4
James, Henry, 239, 242
Jameson, Fredric, 148, 389–90
Jardine, Alice, 63
Jeans, James, 391–92
"Jessamy Brides, The," 334, 348n15.
    See also *Orlando*
Johnston, Georgia, 420
Johnston, Jill, 30
Johnston, John, 200–201
Joyce, James, 390; *A Portrait of the
    Artist as a Young Man,* 51, 82n14,
    141; *Ulysses,* 44, 46, 348n14,
    350n24, 415n3
Jung, Karl, 229, 237n12

Kant, Immanuel, 261–64, 364–65
Keynes, John Maynard, 145
Knox, Robert, 366
Kristeva, Julia, 44–45, 66, 384
Kureishi, Hanif. See *Sammy and
    Rosie Get Laid*

Lacan, Jacques, 45, 63, 154, 385,
    391
Lauter, Jane Hamovit, 187

"Leaning Tower, The," 43–44
Leaska, Mitchell, 236, 416n17, 420
le Bon, Gustave, 11–12
Lee, Hermione, 194n4, 305, 416n11
Lee, Judith, 180, 216n5
Leibniz, Gottfried, 266–67
Lenare, 25
Levenback, Karen, 194n6, 217n14
Levinas, Emmanuel, 257–61, 272,
    278nn13–14
Lewis, Wyndham, 46
Lilienfeld, Jane, 192
Longinus, 355–56, 358–60, 365–66
Lukács, György, 388–89
Lundberg, Patricia Lorimer, 79

MacCarthy, Desmond, 262, 380
MacDonald, Dwight, 2
Man Ray (Emmanuel Radnitsky), 3,
    16, 24, 27
Mao, Douglas, 419
Marcus, Jane, 56n16, 81n4, 165n14,
    404, 421; gendered modes of
    reading, 81n8; "lupine criticism,"
    55n5; and The Waves, 302–3,
    349n21, 357, 370, 378–91, 398
Marder, Herbert, 81n3, 97n9
Marvell, Andrew, 401–2
McGee, Patrick, 357, 370
Medusa, 11–13, 22–26, 31–32
Melymbrosia, 72–74
Mepham, John, 172
metaphors, gendered, 43–55
"Middlebrow," 5
Miller, J. Hillis, 56n17, 177
Minow-Pinkney, Makiko, 80n3, 81n5,
    149, 193n4, 392
Mitchell, W. J. T., 357
"Modern Fiction," 43, 44, 77–78
Moi, Toril, 55n3, 80n3, 165n14
"Moments of Being: 'Slater's Pins
    Have No Points,'" 116–21
Montagu, Lady Mary Wortley, 344,
    351n31
Montrose, Louis, 156
Moore, G. E., 262–63, 277n9
Morgenstern, Barry, 155
Morrell, Ottoline, 305
Morrison, Toni, 357
Mrs. Dalloway, 46, 48–51, 98–113,
    198–215, 274–76; ethics in,
    274–76

"Mrs. Dalloway in Bond Street," 98,
    108, 112–13

Nancy, Jean-Luc, 261, 276
Naremore, James, 47, 57n18, 191
"Narrow Bridge of Art, The," 43
Nazism, 405, 407, 414, 415n9
Ngugi wa Thiong'o, 397–98
Nicolson, Harold, 337
Nietzsche, Friedrich, 206
Night and Day, 87–97
Nussbaum, Martha, 265

Oliver, Kelly, 260–61
Olsen, Tillie, 191
Omega Workshops, 307–8, 315–16
Orlando, 267–71, 327–46;
    Orientalism in, 329–46
Orwell, George, 13

Pacteau, Francette, 340–41, 351n26
Pargiters, The, 406, 407, 409–14
Paulin, Tom. See J'Accuse
Phelan, James, 137–38, 163n2
Poems of Ossian, 361–62
postimpressionism, 306–7. See also
    Fry, Roger
posttraumatic stress disorder. See
    trauma
Pound, Ezra, 400
"Prime Minister, The," 98–103,
    114n15
"Professions for Women," 46–47

Radin, Grace, 403, 415n6
Ragland-Sullivan, Ellie, 384–85
Ramanazi, Jahan, 179
Reliques of Ancient English Poetry,
    361–62, 363
Richardson, Dorothy, 47, 415n3
Rig Veda, 379, 386, 395
Rodden, John, 13, 31
Room of One's Own, A, 5, 191,
    280–81, 301, 302, 320, 381, 396
Rosenberg, Isaac, 184
Ruotolo, Lucio, 283, 297n8

Sackville-West, Vita, 25, 308,
    322n10, 330–34, 346, 347nn6–8,
    349n20
Sammy and Rosie Get Laid, 16–33
Sappho, 65–66

Sartre, Jean-Paul, 214
Sassoon, Siegfried, 176, 214
Scarry, Elaine, 215n5
Schlack, Beverly Ann, 50, 56n12, 64, 69, 72
Scholes, Robert, 65, 66
Schweickart, Patrocinio, 81n6
Sellers, Susan, 421
sexology. See Ellis, Havelock; Carpenter, Edward
Shay, Jonathan, 199–200
shell shock. See trauma
Shell-shock, Report of the War Office on, 204
Showalter, Elaine, 45, 47, 62, 81n3, 171–72
Silverman, Kaja, 153–55
"Sketch of the Past, A," 44, 47–48, 179
Smith, Susan Bennett, 172
Snaith, Anna, 419, 420
Sontag, Susan, 421
Spilka, Mark, 171
Spivak, Garyatri, 20–21, 56n9, 393, 396–97
Squier, Susan, 334
Stein, Gertrude, 345
Stephen, Adrian, 305–6
Stephen, Dorothea Jane, 304, 379
Stephen, J. K., 380
Stephen, Julia Duckworth, 23–24, 192
Stephen, Sir Leslie, 62, 82n10; and forebears, 304
Stephen, Thoby, 47, 180, 304–5
Stephen, Virginia. See Woolf, Virginia
Stevens, Wallace, 239, 244
sublime, the, 355–75
Suleri, Sara, 357

Tal, Kalí, 203, 208–10, 216n6, 217n11
Tennyson, Alfred, Lord, 190, 200
"Thoughts on Peace in an Air Raid," 420
Three Guineas, 301, 381, 401–14, 420, 421; class structure in, 75–76; feminism/gender and, 31, 177–78, 187; imperialism in, 302, 304; outsiders in, 45, 293
Tiffin, Helen, 297n3
To the Lighthouse, 183–93, 281–97, 271–74, 300–320; ethics in, 271–

74; lighthouse as symbol, 317; mourning in, 183–93; Orientalism in, 309–20; representation of working-class women in, 283–97
Torgovnick, Marianna, 306
trauma, 198–215
Trilling, Diana, 2, 9–11, 27–30, 35n10
Turkey, in Orlando: 334–38, 342. See also Constantinople
"Two Antiquaries: Walpole and Cole," 221

van den Abbeele, George, 342
Voyage Out, The, 64–80

wa Thiong'o, Ngugi. See Ngugi wa Thiong'o
Walkowitz, Rebecca, 419
Wang, Ben, 217n12–13
Waves, The, 51–52, 122–32, 220–35, 355–75, 378–98; characterization in, 220–35; Elvedon, 123–32; imperialism in, 367–74, 378–98; lady writing, gardeners sweeping, 127–31, 374, 381
Weiskel, Thomas, 356
Welty, Eudora, 357–78
West, Rebecca, 142
Whittier-Ferguson, John, 406, 416n13
Who's Afraid of Virginia Woolf, 6–9, 11–12
Wiesel, Elie, 204
Williams, Raymond, 21, 351n30
Wilson, Jean Moorcroft, 415n4
Wilson, Robert, 141
Winter, Jay, 176
Woodward, Kathleen, 193
Woolf, Leonard, 321n8, 413–14, 415n11; and Hogarth Press, 161–62; as a Jew, 308, 402–6; publishing Virginia's diaries, 5, 419; worldview of, 158–59
Woolf, Virginia: appearance of, 22–23, 28–31; and art, 61, 306–8; in the classroom, 60–62; elitism of, 2, 5, 9–11, 19; experimentalism of, 18, 62–63, 80, 123, 161, 301, 307, 308, 334; mental health of, 14, 74, 171–72; racial attitudes of, 302–8, 368–71, 373–74, 400–414; reputation of, 1–34, 81n3; and Vita Sackville-West, 330–34;

and war, 161, 172–74, 175, 402, 406; and Leonard Woolf, 308, 402–6, 413–14, 415n11. *See also individual family members and individual works*
Wordsworth, William, 363
World War I, 172–93, 198–215
World War II, 178, 206, 208, 244, 400. *See also* Nazism
Writer's Diary, A, 5–6, 30

Yeager, Patricia, 356, 357
Years, The, 3, 400–414
Yeats, W. B., 379

Zwerdling, Alex, 18, 151, 167n28, 182, 283, 297n8, 301